To Defend and Deter:
The Legacy of the United States Cold War Missile Program

John C. Lonnquest and David F. Winkler

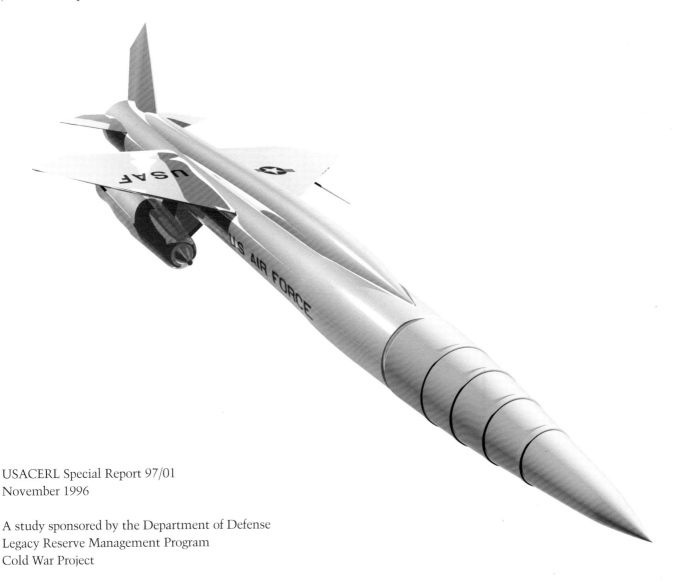

USACERL Special Report 97/01
November 1996

A study sponsored by the Department of Defense
Legacy Reserve Management Program
Cold War Project

For information on reprinting and purchasing, contact:

Hole in the Head Press
Samuel E. Stokes, Publisher
P.O. Box 807, Bodega Bay, CA 94923
sestokes@sonic.net
www.holeintheheadpress.com

1 2 3 4 5 6 7 8 9

ISBN: 978-0-9761494-5-3

Publisher: Samuel E. Stokes
Design and production: Carole Thickstun and Marlena Ormsby
Maps and 3D Illustrations: Lawrence Ormsby
Editor: Roxane Buck-Ezcurra

Printed and bound in Canada

Originally published by the U.S. Army Construction Engineering
Research Laboratories, Champaign, IL
Defense Publishing Service, Rock Island, IL

Reformatted, additonal photographs added, new illustrations and
maps by Hole in the Head Press, 2014.

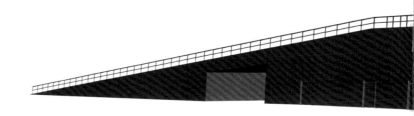

THE LEGACY COLD WAR PROJECT

One of the nine task areas within the Department of Defense Legacy Resource Management Program, the Cold War Project seeks to "inventory, protect, and conserve DoD's physical and literary property and relics" associated with the Cold War.

Under the direction of Dr. Rebecca Cameron of the Air Force History Support Office, the Cold War Project has commissioned several studies to examine the evolution of the American military during the Cold War. The first of these, *To Defend and Deter: The Legacy of the United States Cold War Missile Program*, traces the growth of the Army and Air Force missile programs. A similar study, *Navy Cold War Guided Missile Context: Resources Associated with the Navy's Guided Missile Program, 1946–1989*, examines the development of the Navy's missile program.

A second group of Cold War studies takes a wider, more topical approach. Jointly sponsored by the Cold War Project and the United States Air Force Air Combat Command, these are broad studies designed to provide historians and cultural resource managers with a national context for examining the military's Cold War era programs, structures, and artifacts. The first of the series, *Training to Fight: Training and Education During the Cold War*, examines the changes in military training brought on by the expansion of the military and the sophistication of its Cold War era weaponry. Additional, two companion pieces were published in 1997, *Developing the Weapons of War: Military RDT&E During the Cold War* and *Forging the Sword: Defense Production During the Cold War*.

FOREWORD

The Department of Defense (DoD) Legacy Resource Management Program was established under the Defense Appropriations Act of 1991 to "determine how to better integrate the conservation of irreplaceable biological, cultural, and geophysical resources with the dynamic requirements of military missions." One of Legacy's nine task areas is the Cold War Project, which seeks to "inventory, protect, and conserve [DoD's] physical and literary property and relics" associated with the Cold War.

During the early months of 1993, Dr. Rebecca Hancock Cameron, Cold War Task Area Manager for Legacy, assembled an *ad hoc* committee of approximately 20 cultural resources experts from throughout the DoD to explore the cultural resources of the Cold War. Their mission was to develop a plan for inventorying and managing these resources. A two-pronged approach, which had been agreed on before the meeting, included site-specific and national studies. The more immediate thrust was to compile site-specific documentation of the most significant Cold War installations and sites. At the time of the *ad hoc* meeting, studies were already beginning in such places as Vandenberg Air Force Base, Air Combat Command installations, and several important missile sites. Some of these sites are now listed on the National Register of Historic Places.

The second thrust was to develop a series of national theme and context studies, addressing the more prominent military themes during the Cold War era. These studies were designed to provide a tool by which installations and sites of all types and sizes could determine the significance of their Cold War cultural resources. The committee developed an initial list of theme and context topics that ranged from missiles and intelligence to hospitals and day care centers. While all of the topics were important in their own right, a decision was made to focus only on those issues that held direct relationship to primary Cold War missions.

The initial committee meeting, and the many meetings and telephone conversations that followed, helped to trim the nearly endless list of potential topics down to a short list that DoD would support as national theme and context studies. Those selected included: missiles, radars, research and development, testing and evaluation, and training—*To Defend and Deter: The Legacy of the United States Cold War Missile Program*—is the first and largest of these studies.

To Defend and Deter is the product of a 2-year effort by personnel from the Tri-Services Cultural Resources Research Center, located at the U.S. Army Construction Engineering Research Laboratories (USACERL), working in cooperation with Dr. Cameron and other members of the military history community. The goal of this effort was to develop a history and reference guide suitable for use in identifying and evaluating the historical significance of missile-related cultural resources. The authors have supplied the information necessary to locate, identify, and understand Army and Air Force guided missile facilities. This, coupled with evaluative guidelines currently being developed within DoD, will help cultural resources personnel make substantive evaluations.

Three members of the USACERL cultural resources staff served as primary contributors to this publication. Dr. John Lonnquest and David Winkler, a doctoral candidate at the American University in Washington, DC, prepared the narrative. Dr. Lonnquest, the lead historian, wrote the sections on the evolution of missile technology and the development and deployment of the long-range deterrent missile systems. He also edited the manuscript, selected the photographs, and compiled the bibliography. Mr. Winkler focused his attention on the development of the defensive missile systems, the social and economic impact of the Cold War missile program, and arms control. Mr. Winkler also prepared the histories of the missile development and deployment sites. Mr. Winkler wrote the weapon system profiles for the defensive missile systems, and Dr. Lonnquest prepared the system profiles for the long-range deterrent missile systems. Mr. James Eaton, a graduate student in architecture at the University of Illinois at Urbana-Champaign, identified and contacted all of the known missile sites within the United States and developed the state-by-state guide to the applicable missile launch facilities in the United States. All three of these gentlemen contributed energetically and selflessly throughout the project. In addition, Ms. Gloria J. Wienke of USACERL served as managing editor for the project. Her input and perseverance during the final stages of this project are greatly appreciated.

Virge Jenkins Temme
Julie L. Webster
Principal Investigators

USACERL

PREFACE

Over the course of this project the authors received help from a great many people. First and foremost, we would like to thank Dr. Rebecca Hancock Cameron, director of the DoD Legacy Cold War Project. Her guidance and constant encouragement enriched our work. We also want to acknowledge the help we received from Ms. Virge Jenkins Temme, the Cold War series coordinator at the U.S. Army Construction Engineering Research Laboratories. She helped smooth out many of the bureaucratic hurdles we encountered, critiqued our work, and ever-so-gently reminded us of our deadlines. In May 1996, Ms. Julie L. Webster became the principal investigator for this project. Over the following summer and fall, she carefully and patiently shepherded the study through completion. We gratefully acknowledge her help and good humor.

Dr. William Baldwin, of the U.S. Army Corps of Engineers Office of History, and Dr. Alfred Beck, formerly of the Air Force History Office, have been involved with this project since its inception. They reviewed our manuscript as did Dr. Raymond Puffer, formerly the chief historian at the Air Force Ballistic Missile Organization, and Dr. Dill Hunley, historian at the National Aeronautics and Space Administration. Their careful scrutiny and rigorous questioning improved our work.

During the long course of our research Dr. Martin Gordon and Ms. Lisa Wagner guided us through the Army Corps of Engineers Research Collection. Chief historian Mr. Michael Baker and Mr. Claus Martel of the Army Missile Command supplied many of the administrative and weapon system histories on the Army missile program. Dr. Jim Walker, chief historian at the Army Space and Strategic Defense Command, furnished us with information on antiballistic missile (ABM) development. Dr. David Stumpf of the University of Arizona reviewed the Titan weapon system profile, and Mr. Eric Lemmon of the Thor Association reviewed the Thor section. Ms. Nancy Stillson, librarian at the Redstone Scientific Information Center, provided us with information on early Army missile development as well as the growth of Huntsville during the 1950s and 1960s. Mr. Tony Turhollow, historian at the Army Engineer District, Los Angeles, supplied us with background information on the formation of the Corps of Engineers Ballistic Missile Construction Office.

Air Force Flight Test Center historian, Ms. Cheryl A. Gumm, helped us identify materials discussing Edwards AFB's role in missile development. Dr. Donald Baucom, historian at the Department of Defense Ballistic Missile Defense Organization, provided us with both documents and advice in our section on ABM development. At the Air Force Historical Research Agency's Archives Branch, Mr. Archie DiFante helped us track down documents, and in a number of cases, declassified them for us. Another important ally was Ms. Grace Rowe, Chief of the Records Management Branch, Office of the Secretary of the Air Force, who provided the authors with access to the Air Force Chief of Staff for Guided. Missiles (AFCGM) records at the Federal Records Center, Suitland, Maryland.

Locating the photographs and illustrations for this study was an arduous task. The authors gratefully acknowledge help they received from Mr. Bryon Nicholas at the National Air and Space Museum Archives; Mr. David Chenoweth at the Air Force History Office, Mr. Dave Menard of the USAF Museum's Research Division; Dr. Harry Waldren of the Space and Missile Systems Center History Office; Dr. Todd White at the U.S. Strategic Command; and Ms. Ramona Ruhl at the National Park Service's Rocky Mountain System

Support Office. Colonel Milton B. Halsey, Jr., USA (Ret.), the National Park Service's Nike Site Manager at the Golden Gate National Recreation Area, provided us with illustrations and photographs of various Nike sites and reviewed the air defense sections of the study. Mark Morgan, a ranger with the National Park Service, furnished us with photographs and descriptions of many of the Cold War missile sites he visited.

Archaeologist Martin D. Tagg at Holloman AFB, New Mexico, provided drawings and interpretation for Holloman AFB missile testing sites. At the Titan II Missile Museum at Green Valley, Arizona, Museum Manager Becky Roberts arranged for our researchers to tour the launch facility and discuss our project with the museum staff. At White Sands Missile Range, Public Affairs Officer Deborah S. Bingham supplied us with information on the missile range and set up interviews with Range Archaeologist Robert J. Burton and Diane H. Fulbright of the Range Commander's Council. Sam Hoyle, Museums Division Chief at Fort Bliss, helped us identify source materials and artifacts at the U.S. Army Air Defense Museum. At the Army Air Defense School Colonel Steve Moeller provided us a copy of his Master's thesis about the history of the Army's Air Defense Command, and Patricia Rhodes identified some primary source materials relating to early missile defense. Also, architect John Cullinane provided us with information on the BOMARC missile program and reviewed the BOMARC-related passages of this report.

In preparing this study the authors were fortunate to receive the advice and counsel of many people. While their assistance enhanced our work, the responsibility for any errors or omissions is solely our own.

John Lonnquest and David Winkler, November 1996.

CONTENTS

INTRODUCTION: THE COLD WAR AND THE NATION

Between 1945 and 1989 the United States and the Soviet Union were locked in an intense political, military, and economic confrontation that came to be known as the Cold War. The struggle between the two superpowers dominated international affairs, and the conflicts it spawned raged across the globe. The world was seemingly divided into two armed camps: the United States and its allies against the Soviet Union and the communist bloc.

The competition between the two superpowers was played out at many levels, but none was more visible, more consistent, or had a greater impact on the United States than the arms race. It was a race driven by fear and fueled by uncertainty; a contest depicted by both sides as a struggle for national survival. In the United States the arms race became a national obsession. Politicians promoted it, the military exploited it, and the press gave it extensive coverage. But apart from the public debate, the arms race was a battle for technological supremacy; a battle that was waged in laboratories and factories across the country and encompassed the entire spectrum of military technology from conventional arms to nuclear weaponry. As the arms race unfolded, a new class of weapons—guided missiles armed with nuclear warheads—emerged as the defining weapons technology of the Cold War.

In retrospect it is difficult to recapture the sense of fear and anxiety that, for many Americans, characterized the early years of the Cold War. From the United States' perspective the Soviet Union and its communist allies appeared to be on the offensive around the globe, occupying Eastern Europe, taking over China, waging war in Korea, conspiring with Fidel Castro in Cuba, and inciting revolution in Latin America, Africa, and Asia. These were the days of the "Red Menace," a time when school children crouched under their desks during air raid drills; worried homeowners built fallout shelters; and the government conducted an intrusive campaign to ferret out shadowy "communist sympathizers" suspected of plotting against the nation.

Defense vs. Deterrence

At the end of World War II the United States was confronted by a host of challenges, the most critical of which lay overseas. As the leader of the Western alliance, the United States took the leading role in helping Europe and Japan rebuild their shattered economies, but in doing so found itself increasingly at odds with the Soviet Union. The situation was especially tense in Europe, where the United States faced a strong military challenge from Soviet forces in Eastern Europe. Unable to match the conventional military might of the Red Army, the United States chose to protect the beleaguered nations of Europe by extending its nuclear umbrella overseas.

Between 1945 and 1949, when the United States had a monopoly on nuclear weapons, that remained a viable strategy. But the strategic balance of power changed quickly in 1949 when the Soviet Union acquired nuclear weapons. Suddenly the United States found itself vulnerable to Soviet air attack. To counteract the Soviets' new offensive capability, the United States hurriedly bolstered its air defense system by deploying additional antiaircraft artillery batteries, and also by accelerating the development of the Nike and BOMARC surface-to-air missiles. Simultaneously the nation expanded its strategic nuclear deterrent; it increased the production of nuclear weapons, built new long-range bombers, and developed long-range guided missiles.

These strategic and air defense missiles had distinctly different roles, which reflected the divergent concepts of deterrence and defense. The so-called strategic missiles, which included intercontinental ballistic missiles (ICBMs) and air-breathing strategic missiles (the predecessors of today's cruise missiles), were deterrent systems. In conjunction with the bombers of the Air Force's Strategic Air Command (SAC), the deterrent systems were intended to discourage an aggressor from attacking either the United States or its allies for fear of triggering a swift and certain nuclear retaliation. In contrast, the ground-based antiaircraft missile systems, and later antimissile systems, were purely defensive. Defense was a fallback position; a means of minimizing the destruction in the event deterrence failed.

The Evolution of Strategic Doctrine

Although deterrence was relatively simple in concept, the composition of the United States' nuclear deterrent and the conditions governing its use were hotly debated. The nation's strategic doctrine underwent numerous revisions during the Cold War. In the mid–1950s the Eisenhower administration, anxious to trim defense expenditures by reducing conventional forces, formulated a new defense policy called the "New Look." Its central tenet was the concept of massive retaliation: the United States would respond to communist aggression anywhere in the free world with atomic strikes on the Soviet Union and China.

A number of influential critics found significant flaws in the concept of massive retaliation. First, it was based on the assumption that U.S. strategic forces would survive a Soviet first strike with the ability to retaliate; second, it seemed unlikely that the United States would risk a nuclear war over disputes in Asia or the Middle East.

In 1961 the Kennedy administration implemented a new defense posture called "Flexible Response." Believing that the New Look was overly reliant on nuclear weapons, the administration designed Flexible Response on the premise that the United States needed to maintain a mixture of conventional and nuclear forces to respond to a variety of threats in a proportionate manner. Today, Flexible Response remains the cornerstone of American defense planning.

The Development of the Defensive Missile Force

The primary responsibility for defending the United States against air attack rested with the Air Force. To accomplish this mission, the Air Force developed a defense-in-depth strategy that encompassed early warning radars, fighter aircraft, and long-range antiaircraft missiles positioned to detect and engage the enemy before they entered American airspace. If the enemy penetrated this outer layer, the last line of defense was the Army's antiaircraft missile batteries that defended key urban, industrial, and military targets.

The long-range antiaircraft missile was the Air Force's BOMARC. Development began in 1946 but the first units were not deployed until 1959. BOMARC resembled a long, sleek fighter with sharply swept wings. The 45-foot missile was powered by ramjet engines and traveled at nearly four times the speed of sound. It had an effective range of 440 miles and could carry either a conventional or nuclear warhead.

During the 1960s eight BOMARC missile squadrons were deployed along the eastern seaboard and in the midwest.

The Army's contribution to the air defense network was the Nike antiaircraft missile system. Development of the initial model, the Nike Ajax, began in 1945, and the first battery was deployed in early 1954. The liquid-fuel missile was 21 feet long, had a range of 30 miles, and carried a conventional warhead. By 1958, 200 Nike batteries, each site covering 40 acres, had been built across the country.

In 1958 the Army began to deploy the more capable Nike Hercules. The new missile was 41 feet long and used both a solid-fuel motor and boosters that increased its range to 75 miles and operational ceiling to 150,000 feet."[a] The Nike Hercules was the first antiaircraft missile to be armed with a nuclear warhead. The new missiles replaced the Nike Ajax, and were eventually deployed at 137 sites.

The Development of the Strategic Missile Force

To bolster the nation's strategic nuclear deterrent, the Army Air Forces (the predecessor of the Air Force) had been working since 1946 to develop two types of strategic missiles: the winged, air-breathing missile and the futuristic ballistic missile.

The air-breathing missiles looked and performed like aircraft. They had wings to generate aerodynamic lift, used jet engines that required an external oxygen supply, and were powered and guided throughout their flight. In contrast, the ICBM was bullet-shaped, carried an internal oxygen supply, and the majority of its parabolic trajectory was outside the earth's atmosphere. It was called a ballistic missile because once the warhead reached the apogee of its flight path, it followed a ballistic trajectory to its target.

The Air Force's two air-breathing missile programs, the Snark and the Navaho, began in 1945 and 1946, respectively. The 70-foot long Snark had a top speed of nearly 600 miles per hour and could carry a 7,000-pound warhead 5,000 miles. The Navaho was a more ambitious project. It was equivalent in size and range to the Snark, but was propelled by two powerful ramjet engines that gave it a top speed of 2,150 miles per hour.

Until 1954 the Air Force favored the air-breathing missiles over ICBMs because it believed the former would be easier to build and was a convenient technological midpoint in the development of an ICBM. Both were erroneous assumptions. The Snark and Navaho programs were beset with severe guidance and control problems that were never adequately resolved. After spending hundreds of million of dollars, the Air Force canceled the Navaho program in 1958. It briefly deployed one squadron of Snark missiles in the early 1960s.

While the Air Force was spending huge amounts of money on its air-breathing missiles, the Atlas ICBM program, which began in 1946, languished in obscurity. Many Air Force officers dismissed the ICBM as "Buck Rogers" stuff. The critics charged that the ICBM was not technologically feasible; they also begrudged it the money it was diverting from the service's aircraft development programs.

Given the technology of the day, the ICBM was a radically new weapon. The Atlas stood 82 feet tall, was 10 feet in diameter, and powered by three large liquid-fuel rocket boosters. Depending on the propulsion system and payload, Atlas had a range of 5,500 to 6,750 nautical miles and a guidance system accurate enough

---

[a] *The range of the BOMARC and Nike air defense missiles was expressed in terms of statute miles.*

to land the warhead within 2 nautical miles of its target.[b] Flying at nearly 16,000 miles per hour, a flight of 6,750 miles would take just 43 minutes. Moreover, once in flight, the ICBM was virtually impossible to intercept.

After considerable foot-dragging, the Air Force accelerated the Atlas program in the spring of 1954; then progress became rapid. But Atlas was not the only ICBM program underway in the late 1950s. In 1955 the Air Force began work on a second ICBM, the large liquid-fuel Titan, as a hedge in case the Atlas failed. Three years later it started work on a third ICBM, the solid-fuel Minuteman.

In the late summer of 1957 the Soviet Union boasted it had an operational ICBM, and the following October shocked the West when it launched Sputnik. As the tiny satellite whirled around the earth, Congress demanded to know the status of the American missile program and the phrase "missile gap" entered the political lexicon. Beginning in June 1959 the Air Force, in conjunction with its European allies, deployed seven squadrons of Thor and Jupiter intermediate range ballistic missiles (IRBMs) in Europe. The IRBMs had a range of 1,500 miles and were based in Great Britain, Italy, and Turkey. Within the United States the first Atlas ICBMs went on operational alert in September 1959, followed by the first Titan squadron in April 1962, and the first ten Minuteman missiles in October 1962. The Air Force continued to deploy ICBMs throughout the decade, and by 1969 1,054 missiles stood poised in their underground silos.

The Changing Face of the U.S. Missile Force

The 1960s and 1970s saw widespread changes in the U.S. defensive missile force. Beginning in the mid-1960s the Army began to close many of its Nike installations, a move prompted in part by improved relations with the Soviet Union and also by the need to pay for America's rapidly escalating involvement in Southeast Asia.

But important technological changes were also at work. By the mid-1960s it became apparent that the Soviet Union was not going to build a large fleet of long-range bombers. Instead it focused on developing a large ICBM and submarine-launched ballistic missile (SLBM) force, and in doing so, rendered much of the U.S. air defense system obsolete. In an effort to regain the technological initiative, the Army experimented twice with developing an antiballistic missile (ABM) defense system, but the program was canceled shortly after the Anti-Ballistic Missile Treaty was signed in 1972.

The cancellation of the ABM program reflected the United States' realization that it could do little to defend itself against a Soviet ICBM attack other than to respond in kind. It was that grim logic that drove the Reagan administration to embrace the Strategic Defense Initiative during the 1980s. Despite the billions of dollars spent on the program, the end of the Cold War and the absence of a domestic consensus on the need for such a system led to its demise.

While defensive missile systems went into decline in the 1960s new and upgraded ICBMs continued to enter the inventory throughout the Cold War. Over time the missiles became progressively more powerful and more accurate, and their launch complexes better hardened to withstand a nuclear attack. By 1965 the Air Force had retired all its temperamental Atlas missiles and replaced the Titan Is with the improved Titan

[b] A nautical mile is equal to 1.15 statute miles. The ranges and accuracy requirements for the ICBMs and IRBMs cited in this study are expressed in nautical miles.

IIs. It had also deployed 800 of the new solid-fuel Minuteman missiles, each housed in an unmanned silo and ready to fire at a moment's notice.

Starting in 1966 the Air Force began upgrading the Minuteman force with the new Minuteman II. This missile had a longer range, a more accurate guidance system, and carried a more powerful warhead than its predecessor. Further improvements followed, and in 1971 the Air Force deployed its first Minuteman III. The new missiles were the first ICBMs to be fitted with multiple independently targetable reentry vehicles (MIRVs). Each missile carried three warheads, each accurate to within 800 feet.

The final installment in the Cold War ICBM program was the Peacekeeper or MX missile. Concerned over the increased size and accuracy of the Soviet ICBMs the Air Force explored nearly 40 basing schemes for its new ICBM, ranging from shuttling them over the southwest on railroad cars to basing them deep in the ocean floor. While the debate over the basing strategy raged in Congress, between 1986 and 1988 the Air Force installed 50 Peacekeepers in reconfigured Minuteman III silos. The new ICBM was a four-stage solid-fuel missile that carried ten warheads, each accurate to within 400 feet. The Air Force, however, was unable to devise a satisfactory basing strategy, and Congress canceled the Peacekeeper program after the first 50 missiles were deployed.

The Physical Legacy of the Missile Program

The Army and Air Force missile programs left an indelible imprint on the American landscape. Missile launch sites, scattered from California to Maine and from Texas to North Dakota, dotted the country. The Army built 263 Nike batteries in the continental United States and Alaska, and an enormous ABM complex in North Dakota. To house its ICBM force, the Air Force built over 1,200 launch facilities clustered in and around 22 installations in 17 states. But these launch sites represent only the tip of the iceberg; behind them lay a complex infrastructure of research laboratories, test sites, production facilities, training centers, and logistics and maintenance facilities. It was these diverse elements that furnished the United States with a powerful defensive and deterrent missile force.

Today, half a century after the Cold War missile program began, many of these facilities are still in use. Many others, however, have been closed down or abandoned as a result of advancing technology, arms limitation treaties, or the post-Cold War military drawdown. Before these missile facilities and artifacts are destroyed, it is necessary that they be examined and cataloged to enable future generations to understand and assess the legacy of the Cold War missile program.

Purpose of This Document

This study was written primarily as a research guide for Department of Defense (DoD) cultural resource managers. Its purpose is three-fold. First, it traces the evolution of the Cold War missile program to enable the readers to evaluate missile facilities and artifacts in their proper historical content. Second, through the comprehensive listing of missile facilities and launch sites, the study establishes the missile program's scope and its truly national impact on the American landscape. Third, through the combination of the historical narrative, extensive bibliography, and weapon system profiles, the study aims to provide its core DoD audience, plus state historic preservation officers (SHPOs), military facility managers, and scholars with a readable, informative guide that can serve as a solid foundation for further research.

Scope of the Study

Considering the sheer number of missiles the United States developed during the Cold War, it became apparent early in the work that this study could not address them all. Some were one-of-a-kind test models, others were more fully developed but never entered production, and still others were operational for only a limited time. To deter mine which missiles should be included in the study, the authors assessed the strategic, economic, and cultural significance of each. That led to two general guidelines. First, the study includes only missiles that entered full-scale production and were deployed at fixed launch sites within the United States. Second, the study does not consider wing-mounted tactical and intermediate-range missiles because they did not exert a decisive strategic impact and had no extensive network of fixed launch sites and support facilities.

Using these selection criteria, the authors focused on missiles with intercontinental range and air-defense missiles deployed at fixed launch sites. The missiles that met these criteria were Atlas, Titan I and II, Minuteman I, II, and III, and Peacekeeper ICBMs and the Snark, an early cruise missile. The defensive systems examined included the Nike family and BOMARC, and the Sentinel and Safeguard antiballistic missile systems.

There were, however, exceptions to the listing criteria. The Thor and Jupiter intermediate-range ballistic missiles were included because, despite being deployed exclusively abroad, they were (during the late 1950s and early 1960s) a critical component of the nation's long-range ballistic missile force.

Organizing the Report

In assembling this report the authors sought to strike a comfortable balance between historical scholarship and the more concrete requirements of the cultural resource manager. Fortunately the two disciplines proved to be complementary and the needs of one invariably strengthened the other.

The study contains three parts, each one being progressively more specific. Part I is an introductory essay that examines the evolution of the U.S. missile program and its impact on the American military and society. Part II contains profiles of the weapon systems. Part III is a state-by-state listing of missile sites and related facilities.

By design, the three parts are closely intertwined. For example, because Part I is an overview of the entire missile program, it does not include detailed descriptions of the missiles systems or the facilities. That information is contained in Part II, which is a series of illustrated technical descriptions of each major weapon system included in the study. Each profile includes a developmental history, technical specifications, a description of the launch facilities, and an operational history. Part III contains information on missile sites and facilities. The state-by-state list includes launch sides; research, development, test, and evaluation (RDT&E) facilities; and logistic support, training, and government production facilities.

Each part includes bibliographic information. The bibliography for Part I is the most extensive because it covers the entire missile program. In Part II the bibliographies that accompany the weapon system profiles address the individual weapon systems; and in Part III the bibliography includes citations for each military reservation. Appendix B lists the current status of the sites listed in Part III. Note, however, that the information in the Appendix is subject to change. It was current as of mid-1995.

Photographs

This study contains many photographs and illustrations that provide vibrant images of the people, places, and weapons systems that shaped the Cold War missile program.

PART I

A HISTORY OF THE UNITED STATES COLD WAR MISSILE PROGRAM

1

IN THE BEGINNING: THE EARLY HISTORY OF ROCKET AND GUIDED MISSILE DEVELOPMENT

The U.S. Cold War missile program left a very rich and diverse legacy of artifacts, both large and small. They range from the mighty intercontinental ballistic missiles (ICBMs) to sleek Nike surface-to-air missiles; from Nike missile bases located on the outskirts of major U.S. cities to the unmanned Minuteman ICBM silos buried under the desolate plains of North Dakota; from the laboratories at the California Institute of Technology to the huge rocket engine test stands at the Redstone Arsenal, Huntsville, Alabama.

Taken individually, these artifacts might appear as nothing more than a jumble of weapons technology and abandoned launch sitcs, all of which were once supported by a complex infrastructure of test sites and support facilities. But in a larger context, the physical legacy of the Cold War missile program mirrors the broad historic themes of the period. The growth of the U.S. missile program reflected the exigencies of the Cold War, the maturation of aerospace technology, and basic changes in the nation's strategic posture.

Early Rocketry

Although the exact origin of the rocket is unclear, the Chinese are credited with inventing rockets and were known to use them in combat, primarily as incendiary weapons, in the 13th century. The missiles were relatively crude, consisting of little more than a hollow bamboo tube stuffed with black powder and affixed to a long bamboo pole for stabilization. But these weapons had all the distinguishing characteristics of modern rockets: the black powder supplied both fuel and an oxidizer to support combustion independent of an external air supply, and they were not actively guided in flight. One simply pointed the rocket at the enemy, lit the fuse, and then watched it go.

The Mongols and Arabs soon transferred rocket technology to Europe, and by 1379 the Italians were calling them *rocchetta*, from which the term "rocket" is derived. Between the 15th and 18th centuries the French, Dutch, and Germans all developed rockets, and some were used in combat. The Europeans used rockets as direct-fire weapons. Rockets were an appealing alternative to artillery; they were easier to transport, required less training to use, and could deliver explosive shells, grapeshot, or fire-bombs.

The British started experimenting with rockets at the beginning of the 19th century. In 1807, Colonel William Congreve of the Royal Laboratory of Woolwich Arsenal began developing a series of barrage rockets weighing between 18 and 300 pounds. The most popular of Congreve's rockets was the 32-pounder, which had a cast-iron warhead, was affixed to a 15-foot wooden shaft, and had a range of 3,000 yards.

Opposite: Developed by the US Army, the Kettering "Bug" combined a rudimentary inertial guidance system with aircraft technology.

Rocket design remained relatively static during the remainder of the 19th century, The British used Congreve rockets with moderate success against American forces during the War of 1812. The rockets were ineffective in the famous bombardment of Baltimore's Fort McHenry, but the memory of the "rockets' red glare" is preserved in the U.S. national anthem. American forces, armed with spin-stabilized rockets, fought in the Mexican War, but the military's interest in the technology waned after midcentury. Rockets were little used during the American Civil War as the increased range and accuracy of rifled artillery reduced the rockets' utility as direct fire weapons, and parallel improvements in communications reduced their usefulness as signaling devices.[1]

The decline of military rocketry continued in the early 20th century with the wide-spread use of radio and rifled breech-loading artillery. However, during World War I,inventors in the United States and Great Britain took the first halting steps toward the development of guided missiles when they outfitted small aircraft with automatic guidance systems to create "flying bombs" or "aerial torpedoes."[2] Although these fragile craft proved to be of little practical value, they established the idea that the difference between a rocket and missile was a matter of guidance. Rockets are not guided in flight; missiles are.

During the early 20th century a small group of civilian scientists and inventors began exploring the feasibility of using rockets for space travel. One of the most notable was an American, Dr. Robert Goddard. In 1909 Goddard, a physicist at Clark University in Worcester, Massachusetts, began detailed studies of the physical properties of liquid- and solid-fuel rocket motors. By 1914 his work had progressed to a point where the U.S. government awarded him patents for seminal innovations in the areas of combustion chambers, propellant feed systems, and multistage rockets.[3]

In 1926 Goddard launched the world's first successful liquid-fuel rocket from a farm pasture near Auburn, Massachusetts, and in 1930 he established a research facility near Roswell, New Mexico. During the following decade, Goddard and his two assistants experimented with a wide range of rockets, the largest of which was 22 feet long, 18 inches in diameter, and weighed almost 500 pounds. In the most successful test, one of his rockets soared to a record altitude of 9,000 feet.[4]

World War II

While Goddard and his assistants were developing missiles in the arid Southwest, a very different type of missile program was taking shape in Germany. In 1929 the German Army, anxious to escape the prohibition on heavy artillery contained in the Versailles Treaty, began to secretly explore the possibility of delivering explosives with long-range rockets. In 1931 the German Army Board of Ordnance established a rocket development group and in 1937 built a test station at Peenemunde on the Baltic Coast. On this isolated stretch of coastline the Germans developed the V-2, the world's first long-range ballistic missile.[5]

While the German Army was experimenting with long-range ballistic missiles, in 1935 the Luftwaffe began developing a "flying bomb," later known as the V-1.[a] Designed for mass production from inexpensive and readily available materials, the V-1 was 25 feet long with a wingspan of 16 feet. Lift was provided by the two stubby wings bolted to the midsection of the fuselage. The noisy pulsejet engine that earned the V-1 the nickname "buzz bomb" was mounted on the top of the fuselage behind the wings.

Most V-1s were catapulted off long inclined ramps, although a few were air-launched from bombers. The missiles had a cruising speed of 340 miles per hour, a range of approximately 150 miles, and were armed with an 1,800-pound conventional warhead. The guidance system, which consisted of an onboard gyroscope autopilot and an altimeter, was inaccurate. German tests showed that at a range of 110 miles, only 31 percent of the missiles would land within 15 miles of the target.[6]

Between June 1944 and March 1945 the Germans hurled 10,500 V-1s at Great Britain. Most of the missiles never reached their targets. The British were able to destroy 60 percent of the missiles in flight and in the process exposed their fatal flaw: predictability. The V-1 was slow, and it maintained a constant course, speed, and altitude. Once located, it could readily be intercepted.[8]

The V-1 served as a powerful stimulus to the fledgling U.S. missile program. In July 1944 the Army Air Forces (AAF), working from salvaged parts, reproduced the German missile and designated the American version the JB-2.[b] Initially the AAF envisioned using large numbers of JB-2s in conjunction with its strategic bombing campaign, but testing at Eglin Field, Florida, showed the missile to be too inaccurate and expensive for that purpose. When the AAF terminated production of the JB-2 in September 1945, a consortium of manufacturers had built 1,385 of these early "cruise missiles." Although the JB-2 never saw combat, it provided the AAF with valuable experience in missile development and testing.[8]

Just as Britain was learning to defend itself against the V-1s, in September 1944 the Germans unleashed a new missile, the supersonic V-2. The world's first long-range ballistic missile, the bullet-shaped V-2 was 46 feet tall, 5 feet in diameter, and weighed 14 tons. Armed with a 1,650-pound conventional explosive warhead, the V-2 had a range of 230 miles. Powered by a single liquid-fuel rocket engine and equipped with a rudimentary internal guidance sys-

[a] The so-called "V" weapons were named by the German Ministry of Propaganda. The "V" stood for *Vergeltungswaffe* (vengeance weapon): the V-1 was the first of the series and the V-2 was the second.

Dr. Robert Goddard with one of the early liquid-fuel rockets.

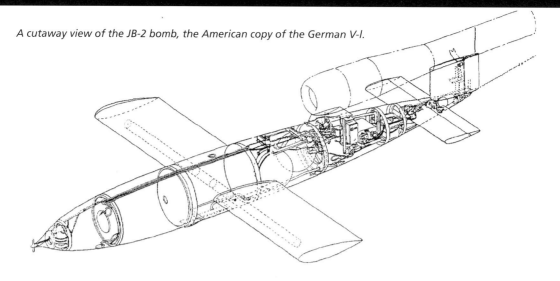

A cutaway view of the JB-2 bomb, the American copy of the German V-I.

tem, the V-2 followed a parabolic flight path that carried it 50 to 60 miles above the earths surface. After reaching the apogee of its trajectory, the V-2 plunged back to earth at several times the speed of sound, offering no warning before its deafening explosion at impact.

The V-2 was classified as a long-range ballistic missile because of its range and flight characteristics. By today's standards, the missile's 200-mile range would make it a tactical weapon, but in the mid-1940s the V-2 was considered a long-range weapon. The V-2 also had the flight characteristics of a ballistic missile. The V-2 did not use aerodynamic surfaces to produce lift; it was actively guided during the first half of its flight; and after thrust from the engines ceased, the missile followed a purely ballistic trajectory down toward its target. In other words, after the V-2 reached the apogee of its parabolic flight path, the only forces that controlled its descent were gravity and drag.

The V-2 was a technological milestone in missile development. Although its effectiveness was compromised by an inaccurate guidance system and ineffective fuse mechanism, the V-2 lent a new and more ominous meaning to the concept of air power. Once launched, the V-2 could not be stopped. It was a terror weapon in the truest sense of the word.

The Allies' reaction to the V-2 attacks was swift and predictable. First they bombed the launch sites. Next, in late 1944, the United States Army Ordnance Department launched a research program to study long-range ballistic missiles. Finally, the Army began searching for a way to intercept the V-2s in flight using antiaircraft artillery.

Independent of the stimulus that came from the German missile program, the United States was without experience in rocket development at the end of the war. In 1936 a small group of graduate students at the Guggenheim Aeronautical Laboratory (GALCIT) at the California Institute of Technology (Caltech) began experimenting with rockets. Their goal was to develop a high-altitude sounding rocket that would enable scientists to conduct experiments in the earth's upper atmosphere. Over the next two years, the

---

[b] JB stood for "Jet-Bomb." The JB–2 was one of a series of jet-bomb projects the AAF sponsored during the war.

group, led by graduate student Frank Malina, conducted numerous experiments and engine tests. By 1938 they had accumulated a substantial body of test data.[8]

In 1939 Malina's work caught the attention of the U.S. Army Air Corps, which hoped to use the rockets as supplemental power sources to help heavily-laden aircraft take off. Later that year the Army hired the GALCIT group to develop jet-assisted takeoff (JATO) apparatus, and between 1939 and 1942 the GALCIT scientists produced a series of progressively more powerful solid- and liquid-fuel JATO boosters.[10]

In the summer of 1943 Dr. Theodore von Kármán, director of the Guggenheim Aeronautical Laboratory, asked the members of the GALCIT project to evaluate several startling British intelligence reports on the German rocket program. The GALCIT group, which in 1944 began calling itself the Jet Propulsion Laboratory (JPL), considered the reports alarming and proposed initiating research to produce a long-range jet-propelled missile.

The Army Ordnance Department accepted JPL's proposal, and in January 1944 awarded the laboratory a contract to develop a missile capable of carrying a 1,000-pound warhead between 75 and 100 miles at a speed sufficient to avoid interception by fighter aircraft. Reflecting the identity of the new sponsor, the new effort was called the ORD-CIT project.[11] In December 1944 JPL fired its first 24-pound solid-fuel Private A missile from a temporary test range set up at Camp Irwin, California. The 92-inch long missile had a range of about 11 miles.

JPL continued to develop missiles after the war, and in December 1945 it launched its first liquid-fuel missile, the WAC Corporal. Powered by an Aerojet engine that generated 1,000 pounds of thrust, the missile rose to a then-record altitude of 235,000 feet.[12] In retrospect, Caltech's World War II research and development (R&D) programs made two important contributions to the postwar missile program. First, the Corporal evolved into the Army's first tactical-range surface-to-surface missile. Second, and more important, the Caltech laboratories were the training ground for many of the scientists and engineers who later played pivotal roles in the Cold War missile program.

In November 1944, in an effort parallel with JPL's, the Ordnance Department hired General Electric (GE) to study the development of long-range rockets and related equipment. The study, called the Hermes Project, had three phases: collecting and analyzing technical data on rockets and guided missiles; assembling and launching captured V-2s; and designing a family of new antiaircraft and intermediate-range surface-to-surface missiles.

In another 1944 development, the U.S. Army Ground Forces asked the Ordnance Department to explore the feasibility of developing a "direction-controlled, major caliber antiaircraft rocket torpedo." The search for a new antiaircraft weapon was prompted by the introduction of new aircraft such as the German jets and the Army's own high-flying B-29 bomber, both of which revealed the limitations of conventional antiaircraft artillery. Moreover, the Army wanted to determine if an antiaircraft missile would be a viable form of defense against the V-2.

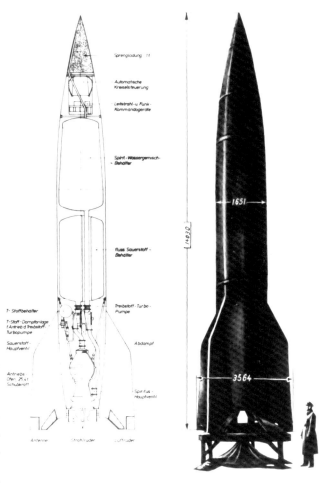

The German V–2, the world's first long-range ballistic missile.

In February 1945 the Ordnance Department contracted with Western Electric to study the feasibility of developing a surface-to-air missile capable of shooting down a bomber such as a B-29. When the Army chose Western Electric and its research affiliate, the Bell Telephone Laboratories, to design the new system, it sent aircraft manufacturers a clear message: building missiles required expertise never before used in building aircraft. The key components of the new antiaircraft missile system were radar and high-speed computers, and Western Electric and Bell Labs had ample experience in both. To compete in missile development, the airframe industry would have to develop expertise in a number of new areas, particularly solid state electronics.

The World War II-era research performed by JPL, GE, Western Electric, and Bell Labs formed a firm foundation for later missile development. Equally important, the working relationships forged between the military, the academic community, and industry served as a template for later Cold War partnerships. Finally, many of the military's premier missile-testing facilities were established during World War II. In November 1943 the Navy established a missile research and development complex at China Lake, California, and in July 1945 the Army established its White Sands Proving Ground in New Mexico. A week later, on land that would eventually become part of White Sands, another technological achievement occurred that would greatly affect the future of missile development; the detonation of the first atomic bomb.

Endnotes

1. Wernher von Braun and Frederick C. Ordway III, *History of Rocketry and Space Travel 3rd ed.* (New York: Thomas J. Crowell, 1975), pp. 22–36.

2. Kenneth I. Werrell, *The Evolution of the Cruise Missile* Press. (Maxwell AFB, Montgomery, AL: Air University, 1985), pp. 8–17.

3. During his lifetime Goddard was awarded 214 patents and made pioneering breakthroughs in the fields of liquid-fuel rocket engines, gyro-stabilization, steering, and staged engines. The scientist, however, was a secretive man and reluctant to share his findings. As a result, much of his work went unnoticed.

4. For information on Goddard see: Barton C. Hacker, "Robert H. Goddard and the Origins of Space Flight," in Carroll W. Purse, Jr. ed., *Technology in America: A History of Individuals and Ideas* (Cambridge, MA: MIT Press, 1981), pp. 228–233; G. Edward Pendray, "Pioneer Rocket Development in the United States," in Eugene M. Emme, ed., *The History of Rocket Technology* (Detroit, MI: Wayne State University Press, 1964), pp. 19–23; von Braun and Ordway, History of Rocketry and Space Travel, pp.44–56.

5. For a summary of the V-2 program see: Walter R. Dornberger, "The German V-2," in Eugene M. Emme, ed., *The History of Rocket Technology* (Detroit, MI: Wayne State University Press, 1964).

6. Kenneth P. Werrell, *The Evolution of the Cruise Press*, (Maxwell AFB, Montgomery, AL: Air University, 1985), pp. 41–43, 50, Appendix A.

7. Ibid., pp. 50, 60, 62.

8. Ibid., pp. 63–67.

9. Frank J. Malina, "The U.S. Army Air Corps Jet Propulsion Project, GALCIT project No. 1, 1939–1945: A Memoir," in R. Cargill Hall, ed., *History of Rocketry and Astronautics*, AAS History Series, Vol. 7, Part II, Vol. 2 (San Diego, CA: American Astronautical Society, 1986), reprint, pp. 2–3; R. Cargill Hall, "A Selective Chronology [of] GALCIT-JPL Developments, 1926–1950," unpublished, 1967, pp. 6–12, National Air and Space Museum (hereafter NASM), Washington DC, folder "Jet Propulsion Lab, Histories, GAL-CIT," file 05–30000–15.

10. Frank J. Malina, "The U.S. Army Air Corps Jet Propulsion Project, GALCIT," pp. 1–6; R. Cargill Hall, "A Selective Chronology [of] GALCIT-JPL Developments, 1926–1950," p. 13. Note: Malina was unable to interest any airframe manufacturers in producing the solid and liquid fuel boosters; in March 1942 he and von Kármán founded the Aerojet Engineering Corp. to manufacture them.

11. Hall, "A Selective Chronology [of] GALCIT-JPL Developments, 1926–1950," p. 25.

12. Malina, "The U.S. Army Air Corps Jet Propulsion Project, GALCIT," pp. 8–9.

2

THE IMMEDIATE POST-WAR ERA 1945–1950: OPPORTUNITIES AND CONSTRAINTS

For the U.S. missile program, the immediate post-war period was one of both tremendous opportunity and frustrating constraints. The opportunities were the product of the new technologies developed during World War II; technologies such as atomic weapons and jet aircraft that had the potential to revolutionize warfare. In contrast, the constraints were mainly a product of the immediate post-war period. Following the end of World War II the U.S. military underwent sweeping changes: the nation demobilized, defense spending plummeted, and in 1947, the National Security Act resulted in a wholesale reorganization of the military establishment.[a]

The factor that had the greatest impact on the missile program in the post-war period was the shrinking defense budget. Defense spending had peaked at $81.5 billion in 1945. In 1946 it fell to $44.7 billion, and in 1947 it further declined to $13.1 billion. The Army Air Forces' (AAF) missile program was hard-hit by the budget cutbacks. In April 1946 the AAF's comprehensive missile development program consisted of twenty-eight projects that included surface-to-surface, surface-to-air, air-to-surface, and air-to-air missiles. In December 1946 the War Department reduced the AAF's budget for missile research and development (R&D) by more than 50 percent, from $29 million to $13 million. As a result, by July 1947, the AAF was forced to cancel fourteen of its development projects.[1]

The drastic military spending cutbacks may seem paradoxical in retrospect. As the euphoria of victory subsided, the United States found itself in an international landscape changed forever by the upheavals of World War II. America's role in the international community had permanently changed: at war's end the United States was one of the world's two predominant military powers, and also the leader of the Western alliance. In that capacity the United States was confronted not only with the challenges of converting its economy back to a peacetime basis, but also with helping the war-ravaged nations of Europe and Asia rebuild their economies and stand up to challenges from an increasingly bellicose Soviet Union.

Opposite: The Snark's long-range and heavy payload made it an attractive alternative to ballistic missiles.

[a] The Act subordinated the military services under the new National Military Establishment (later to become the Department of Defense), made the Secretary of Defense the principal advisor to the President in all matters of national security, and established the Air Force as a separate service. Public Law 253, 61 Stat., Chap. 343, 80th Congress, 1st session, "The National Security Act of 1947" 26 July 1947

Relations between the United States and the Soviet Union deteriorated rapidly after the war. Soviet delays in withdrawing from northern Iran drew protests from Washington, as did the Soviet handling of occupied Eastern Europe. At the Yalta conference in February 1945 Stalin promised Roosevelt and Churchill that the Soviet Union would allow the nations of Eastern Europe to hold free and fair elections to choose their own governments. The Soviets, however, soon reneged on their promise and over the next 3 years installed a succession of satellite governments in the once-sovereign nations of Eastern Europe.

Yet despite these worsening relations, the United States did not perceive the Soviet Union to be an immediate military threat. U.S. leaders generally viewed the Soviet Union as a tired and battered nation at the end of World War II. Four years of fighting had taken the lives of 22 million of its people, and great expanses of its cities and countryside lay in ruins. Although the mighty Red Army posed a constant threat to Western Europe, the United States, then the sole possessor of the atomic bomb, was confident that it could deter Soviet aggression through the threat of nuclear retaliation.

More important, to a nation anxious to forget about the war in Europe, the Soviet Union seemed to be a distant enemy. In the late 1940s the Soviets did not have the means to strike directly at the continental United States. The Soviet Union's small fleet of long-range bombers lacked the forward air bases necessary to attack the United States, and its navy was configured primarily for coastal defense. Furthermore, American analysts predicted that the Soviets would not obtain an atomic capability until the 1950s.

The Impact of Emerging Technologies

World War II produced a revolution in weapons technology that included atomic weapons, jet aircraft, solid-state and miniaturized electronics, and long-range missiles. After the war, U.S. military planners started to assess the impact of those technologies and also began to debate which services would develop and control the new weapons. Apart from the dispute over the Air Force's self-proclaimed monopoly on delivering nuclear weapons, no issue would be more hotly contested than the struggle for control of the military's budding guided missile program.

The bitter interservice rivalry that eventually arose over long-range missile development illustrates the impact of new technology in blurring the distinction between the services' established roles and missions. Traditionally, a service's roles and missions were determined by its primary operational environment: the Army conducted combat operations on land, the Navy at sea, and the newly independent Air Force, in "all operations in the air."[2]

Although the services' areas of operation had never been completely separate, longrange missiles promised to further blur the distinctions by enabling each service to encroach on the operational environment of the others. For example, the Army could use long-range missiles to attack targets far behind the line of battle, thus undermining the Air Force's exclusive role in conducting strategic air warfare. The situation was much the same for the Navy. Each service saw long-range missiles as an opportunity to expand its scope of operations at the expense of a rival. This competition produced an inevitable succession of conflicts. Each service zealously guarded the integrity of its role because it was on that basis that missions were assigned and funding allocated.

Moreover, because neither the Army nor Navy was equipped to deliver nuclear weapons in the late 1940s, each saw missile programs as a means to acquire a nuclear capability.

Long-Range Missile Development

The jurisdictional dispute over guided missiles between the Air Force and Army began during World War II. At that time both the AAF (the Air Force's predecessor) and Army Service Forces (ASF) began developing missiles. The AAF saw missiles as an extension of aircraft technology that should be placed under its control. The ASF, which included the Army Ordnance Department, argued in response that missiles were merely an extension of artillery. In 1944, to settle the dispute, Lt. Gen. Joseph T. McNarney, the Army Deputy Chief of Staff, issued a directive assigning the AAF responsibility for missiles launched from aircraft as well as surface-to-surface missiles equipped with wings that provided aerodynamic lift. The ASF would be responsible for developing surface-launched missiles that depended exclusively on momentum for sustaining flight.[3]

Initially the McNarney Directive appeared to favor the ASF, especially considering the German missile technology the Army acquired at the end of the war. During the closing months of the war a team from the U.S. Army Ordnance Department raced into Germany just ahead of the onrushing Soviets and retrieved huge quantities of valuable technical data plus enough V-2 components to assemble 100 missiles. In an even greater coup the United States secured the services of Germany's top missile experts when Wernher von Braun, technical director of the German Army Ordnance rocket development program, surrendered to U.S. forces with approximately 120 members of his staff.[4]

Under the code name "Operation PAPERCLIP," the Ordnance Department transferred von Braun and his missile development team to Fort Bliss, Texas, to continue work on the V-2. These Germans brought to the United States extensive experience in the development and testing of airframes, liquid fuel rocket engines, and guidance systems. They also had first-hand experience in the production and deployment of a complex missile system.

Beginning in April 1946 GE personnel, working under Project Hermes, began collaborating with von Braun's team to assemble operational V-2s from the mountain of parts brought back from Germany. Over the next 5 years they launched 67 of the refurbished missiles from the White Sands Proving Ground. With this practical, hands-on training, the American engineers gained valuable insight into designing, testing, and handling large ballistic missiles.[5] The experience gained through Project Hermes was later applied to a number of successful Army missiles.

Immediately after the war both the ASF and AAF charged ahead according to their own interpretations of the McNarney Directive. In 1946, at the direction of General Henry H. (Hap) Arnold, Commanding General of the Army Air Forces, the AAF greatly expanded its missile research and development program. A key element in that program was a December 1945 study entitled "Toward New Horizons," prepared at Arnold's direction and led by Caltech's Dr. Theodore von Kármán, who was also the chairman of the AAF Scientific Advisory Group.

Von Kármán recommended that over the next 10 years the AAF engage in the "systematic and vigorous development" of new technologies including long-range guided missiles, which at that time the Air Force called "pilotless bombers."[6] The ultimate goal of the long-range missile program, von Kármán wrote, was an intercontinental missile, and he recommended that the Air Force develop two types. The first should be an air-breathing "high-altitude, pilotless, jet-propelled bomber" with a speed of Mach 2 and a range of up to 3,000 miles. These "pilotless, jet-propelled bombers" were the predecessors of today's cruise missiles. They derived aerodynamic lift from wings, required an external air supply, and were internally guided and powered throughout flight.

Von Kármán also suggested that the Air Force develop a missile of the "ultrastratospheric" type, powered by the "rocket principle" and not intended for level flight. What von Kármán envisioned was a ballistic "glide missile" with wings, which was one of the conceptual predecessors of the intercontinental ballistic missile (ICBM). The wings were intended to increase the trajectory of the missile and also provide it with additional stability during nonpowered flight.

In April 1946 the AAF missile program included eleven surface-to-surface missile-development projects, of which all but one were air-breathing; the exception was a study project by the Consolidated Vultee Aircraft Corporation (Convair) of Downey, California. Convair first became involved in the missile program in October 1945 when, in response to an AAF Technical Service Command solicitation, the aircraft manufacturer submitted a proposal to study the feasibility of building a ballistic missile capable of carrying a 5,000-pound payload up to 5,000 miles. The AAF liked Convair's approach, and in April 1946 awarded the airframe manufacturer project MX-774, a $1.4 million effort to study long-range ballistic missiles.[7]

The missile that the Convair team designed was based on the proven V-2 but included three pioneering innovations. To reduce weight, Convair abandoned the V-2's conventional fuselage composed of rings and stringers; instead the MX-774 would derive its structural rigidity from pressurized, integral fuel tanks. Second, to stabilize the missile in flight and reduce drag, Convair abandoned the carbon steering vanes, which worked much like the rudder of a boat, mounted in the engine exhaust. As an alternative it mounted the engines on gimbals, enabling them to swivel and supply directional thrust. Third, to save weight, improve post-boost flight characteristics, and reduce friction during reentry, Convair pioneered the use of a separable warhead.[8]

The Convair project, however, would soon fall victim to post-war budgetary constraints. In July 1947 Convair had been working on the MX-774 for just over a year when sweeping defense cutbacks prompted the AAF to cancel the program. The AAF decided that the program was too expensive, estimating that completing R&D would cost an additional $50 million. The AAF also forecast that the missiles would be prohibitively expensive—about $500,000 each. Rather than investing more money in the longrange ballistic missile program, the AAF' felt it would be more prudent to build air-breathing "glide type" missiles, which studies indicated would have a longer range, larger payload, and would be easier to develop.[9]

Along with fiscal constraints, interservice rivalry and bureaucratic prejudices worked against the Convair program. Maj. Gen. Donald Putt, Commander of the Air Force's Air Research and Development Command (ARDC) and later Deputy Chief of Staff, Development (DCSD), thought that the Air Force's ongoing dispute with the Army over the future of long range missiles weighed against the MX-774. Citing the McNarney Directive, throughout the late 1940s and early 1950s the Army claimed that all surface-launched ballistic missiles were merely extensions of artillery, and thus should be under its control. Putt felt that by making its missiles air-breathing and giving them wings the Air Force was consciously trying to distance itself from the Army's interpretation that missiles were extensions of artillery. "We were afraid that if we developed them [missiles] to look like rockets or a big artillery shell," Putt said, "that eventually the Department of Defense would give the mission to the Army. . . ."[10]

Despite its decision to cancel the MX-774, the AAF allowed Convair to use its remaining funds to build three small missiles to test the feasibility of the swiveling motors, guidance system, and the separable warhead. The missiles, which Convair referred to as the Hiroc (High altitude Rocket) series, or RTV-A-2, looked much like a much smaller version of the V-2. They were 32 feet high, 30 inches in diameter, and, when fully loaded, weighed slightly over 2 tons. Propulsion came from four alcohol and oxygen motors that together generated 8,000 pounds of thrust.

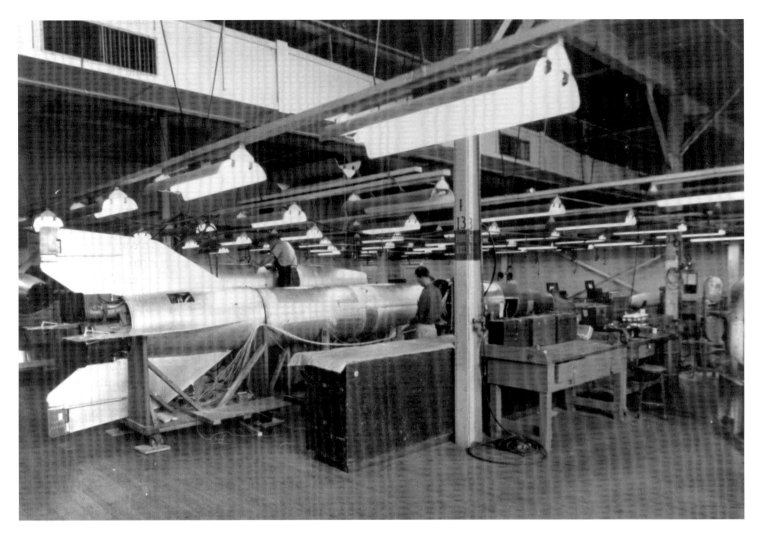

Between 1947 and 1948 Convair tested the RTV-A-2s at White Sands. Missile performance improved with every flight, and the last missile soared to an altitude of over 30 miles. Although the test results were not spectacular, they were encouraging and confirmed the desirability of using swiveling engines for flight stabilization and control.[11] Yet despite the promising results, the Air Force (it had become a separate service in September 1947) refused to allocate additional funding for the ballistic missile program. Unwilling to abandon the project and lose its lead in a potentially lucrative market, Convair decided to support the ICBM program until it could find a new government sponsor to fund it.

When it canceled the MX-774, the nation's only ICBM development program, the AAF continued to develop two strategic air-breathing missile programs: the Snark (SM-62) built by Northrop Aircraft and the Navaho (XMS-64) built by North American Aviation. From the AAF's perspective, air-breathing missiles had two distinct advantages. First, the AAP thought that air-breathing missiles could be developed quickly and easily; and second, at that time, their 5,000-mile range and 7,000-pound payload far exceeded the capabilities of ballistic missiles. The payload was the key factor; the Air Force based the payload requirement on the

Built for the MX-774 program, Convair's RTV-A-2 missiles were the forerunners of the Atlas ICBM.

23

size of its smallest atomic warhead. General Putt also noted that these missile programs benefited from the Air Force's institutional bias in favor of aircraft. "The air-breathing missiles looked like aircraft," Putt said, and psychologically that made them easier to accept than the bullet-shaped ICBMs.[12] The Air Force even reclassified its air-breathing missiles as "strategic pilotless bombers" to reinforce its claim that the missiles were an offshoot of aircraft.

Long-Range Air-Breathing Missile Development

The Snark program began in March 1946 in response to an AAF requirement for a missile capable of carrying an atomic warhead 5,000 miles at a speed of 600 miles per hour, The Snark looked much like an airplane. The swept-wing missile was 67 feet long and had a wingspan of almost 43 feet. Initially the prime contractor, Northrop Corporation, promised the Air Force that it could develop the missile within 2½ years at an average cost of $80,000 for each missile. Development of both the airframe and the guidance system proved much more difficult than Northrop expected, and the first successful flight was not launched until April 1951.[13]

To complement the Snark, the AAF began work in April 1946 on another long-range air-breathing missile, the supersonic Navaho. This new missile would have the same range and payload as the Snark, but was designed to travel at supersonic speed. In its final form the delta-wing Navaho was 70 feet long and powered by two powerful ramjet engines that gave it a cruising speed of 2,150 miles per hour. Launched vertically, the missile sat atop a 76-foot rocket booster that carried it up to its operating altitude and then fell away.

The Air Force's decision to abandon the ICBM in favor of the Snark and Navaho would have far reaching consequences. Initially, air-breathing missiles offered superior performance, but in the early 1950s, improvements in ballistic missile technology erased that early advantage. Perhaps the Air Force assumed that air-breathing missiles would be a technological midpoint in the development of the ICBM, but the assumption proved to be incorrect.[14] The Snark and Navaho programs turned out to be far more difficult than expected, and with the exception of the Navaho booster, the technology was not readily adaptable to the ICBM program.

Both the Snark and Navaho missiles were plagued with severe guidance and control problems. So many Snarks crashed during testing that the waters around Cape Canaveral, Florida, were said to be unfit for swimming because they were "Snark infested." Navaho's persistent technical problems earned it the moniker "never go-Navaho." That name proved to be prophetic: after spending $700 million the Air Force canceled the Navaho program in 1958. The Snark, on the other hand, saw brief duty. The Air Force deployed a single squadron at Presque Isle, Maine, in February 1961, then deactivated it less than 6 months later.[15]

Surface-to-Air Missiles

A debate over surface-to-air missiles eventually would mar relations between the Army and Air Force in the 1950s. The Army Ordnance Department's surface-to-air missile program began in late 1945 when it hired Western Electric to develop what later became the very successful Nike system. At the same time the Army was developing Nike, the AAF was also supporting three surface-to-air missile projects: Thumper, Wizard, and the Ground-to-Air Pilotless Aircraft (GAPA).

Thumper and Wizard were study programs. For the Thumper project General Electric envisioned a short-range "collision intercept" defense missile to counter V–2 type weapons. The Wizard project was more difficult. In that effort the AAF asked the University of Michigan to investigate the feasibility of developing a missile that could defend against incoming ICBMs.[16]

The contractor for the GAPA missile program was the Boeing Aircraft Company. The Air Force envisioned that GAPA, conceived late in World War II, would be a ramjet-powered missile launched by a solid-propellant booster capable of reaching an altitude of 60,000 feet at a range of 35 miles. Conceptually, under the provisions of the October 1944 McNarney Directive, GAPA should have been under the jurisdiction of the Army Ordnance Department. However, the AAF took considerable pains to explain that guidance for GAPA obviously would be determined by aerodynamic forces, thus placing the project within "the sphere of responsibility of the Army Air Force."[17]

GAPA showed promise. After a year of successful prototype testing from Wendover Air Force Base in Utah, the Air Force assured the President's Air Policy Commission in October 1947 that GAPA should be operational by the mid-1950s. But in 1948 budget cuts prompted the Air Materiel Command (AMC) to reduce funding for the program from $5.5 million to $3 million, hardly enough to sustain Boeing's R&D organization. The final blow to GAPA came in late 1949 when the Joint Chiefs of Staff (JCS) decided that the three services were developing too many short-range surface-to-air missiles. GAPA was canceled.[18]

The debate between the Army and Air Force over surface-to-air missiles was typical of the type of disagreements that kept appearing as the services attempted to define their respective roles and missions. Unable to wrest agreement on service functions from the JCS, Secretary of Defense James Forrestal in March 1948 held a meeting with the JCS at the naval station at Key West, Florida.

Before the Key West Conference, negotiations between the services had foundered on determining what role the Navy should have in strategic air warfare, and whether the Army or the Air Force would have responsibility for land-based air defense. After the meetings, the service chiefs agreed that the Air Force would have sole responsibility for strategic air warfare as well as the lead role in protecting the nation against air attack.[19] The Army, however, still had a role in continental air defense because it retained responsibility to "organize, train, and equip" antiaircraft artillery units. At first glance it appeared that the Army and Air Force air defense roles overlapped, but in practice the roles were quite different. Continental air defense was a huge undertaking that required a complex infrastructure of early-warning radars, fighter aircraft, and command and control facilities. In contrast, the Army's antiaircraft artillery (AAA) batteries were intended for point defense to protect targets such as a bridges, airfields, or troop concentrations.

Although the Key West Conference assigned a role for Army AAA within continental air defense, the Army refused to place its antiaircraft batteries under Air

Launched atop a rocket booster, the Navaho cruised at supersonic speed.

Force control.[20] The Army argued that if it diverted a portion of its limited antiaircraft capability to continental air defense, troops in the field would be left without an adequate air defense capability. In a sense this was true; at the time, most of the Army's AAA units were in reserve status, attached administratively to the six continental armies. The great majority of the Army's active A-4 units were deployed abroad because the Army considered a Soviet attack on U.S. forces overseas much more likely than an assault on the American mainland.

The bickering between the Army and the Air Force abated in September 1949 when a somber President Truman told the nation that the Soviet Union had developed an atomic bomb. Suddenly, continental air defense, previously a low priority, became a pressing concern. Faced with this new threat, in the fall of 1949 the Air Force began formulating an integrated air defense system, and called upon the Army and the Navy for support. In the spring of 1950 the Army deployed the 518th AAA Battalion at Hanford, Washington, to protect the atomic weapons production facilities. It was the first of many AAA units to deploy around the nation's vital military and industrial areas. In July 1950 the Army established the Anti-Aircraft Command (ARAACOM) and a month later, in a spirit of cooperation brought on by a sense of urgency, agreed to place its AAA units under operational command of the Air Force's Continental Air Command.[21]

Despite the fiscal constraints and rivalries that at times appeared to hobble the three services, between 1945 and 1950 the guided missile program made some progress. The Army's Nike program continued to make steady progress; air-breathing missile development was somewhat erratic; and the Air Force contemplated the fate of its ballistic missile program.

One notable achievement during this period was the founding or expansion of many missile development and test facilities. These facilities would later play crucial roles in the Cold War missile program. The Army's White Sands Proving Ground rapidly evolved from a few Quonset huts into a premier research, development, test, and evaluation facility used by all three services. During the late 1940s the Air Force also began building the Arnold Engineering Development Center at Tullahoma, Tennessee, which was destined to become one of the most sophisticated aerospace testing facilities in the world. At Edwards Air Force Base, California, during the same period, the Air Force began construction of a series of massive rocket engine test stands for a facility that later became known as the Rocket Propulsion Laboratory. Finally, in 1950, the Air Force established a long-range missile test range headquartered at the recently deactivated Banana River Naval Air Station on the east coast of Florida, 210 miles north of Miami. The Air Force renamed the installation Patrick Air Force Base and designated it home of the Air Force Missile Test Center. Among the facilities adjacent to the 16,000 acre base were the launch sites at Cape Canaveral.

Endnotes

1. Jacob Neufeld, *The Development of Ballistic Missiles in the United States Air Force 1945–1960*, (Washington, DC: Office of Air Force History, 1989), pp. 28–33. Richard McMullen, Interceptor Missiles in Air Defense 1944–1964, Air Defense Command (hereafter ADC) Historical Study No. 30 (February 1965), p. 7.

2. The Key West Agreement, Executive Order 9950, "Functions of the Armed Forces and the Joint Chiefs of Staff," 21 April 1948, in Richard I. Wolf, ed., *The United States Air Force: Basic Documents on Roles and Missions* (Washington, DC: Office of Air Force History, 1987), pp. 1.55–64.

3. Neufeld, *Ballistic Missiles in the United States Air Force 1945–1960*, pp. 18–19.

4. For the story of von Braun's work on the German missile program and his decision to surrender to the Americans, see Frederick I. Ordway and Mitchell R. Sharpe, *The Rocket Team* (New York, Thomas Y. Crowell, 1979).

5. Eunice H. Brown, *White Sands History: Range Beginnings and Early Missile Testing* (White Sands, NM: White Sands Proving Ground, Public Affairs Office, n.d.), pp. 65–66, 97.

6. Ltr., von Kármán to Arnold, subj: none [guide for future AAF R&D programs] 15 December 1945, in "Toward New Horizons," preface.

7. Edmund Beard, *Developing the ICBM: A Study of Bureaucratic Politics, Institute of War and Peace Studies Series* (New York: Columbia University Press, 1976), pp. 49–50; Neufeld, The Development of Ballistic Missiles, p. 45.

8. William H. Patterson, *America's First ICBM—The Atlas*, (unpublished manuscript, 1985), p. 2; G. Harry Stine, ICBM (New York: Orion Books, 1991), p. 143.

9. Memo, Richard E. Horner, Air Force Assistant Secretary for Research and Development to the Director of Guided Missiles, OSD, subj: Information on Missile Systems, undated, p. 2, in records at the Assistant Chief of Staff for Guided Missiles, Federal Records Center Suitland, MD, RG 341, Accession 61A1643, box 2, folder "AFCGM Correspondence–1957, November through December".

10. Maj. Gen. L. Donald Putt, interview by James C. Hasdorff,1–3 April 1973, Air Force Historical Research Agency, Maxwell AFB, Montgomery, AL (hereafter AFHRA), p. 150.

11. This information was drawn from the preliminary flight reports of the MX-774 launches 1, 2, and 3. The reports, prepared between October 1948 and February 1949, are available at the National Air and Space Museum, Washington, DC, Library and Archives Division, file OM–990774–02, folder, "MX-774."

12. Putt interview, p. 150.

13. Kenneth P. Werrell, *The Evolution of the Cruise Missile* (Maxwell, AL: Air University Press, 1985), pp. 82–85.

14. Maj. Gen. Donald Yates, interview by James C. Hasdorff, 10–12 June 1980, Tavernier, FL, AFHRA, p. 146. The Air Force hoped that the ramjet engines and guidance systems it developed for the air-breathing missiles would serve as the foundation for more sophisticated rocket boosters and guidance systems for longrange ballistic missiles.

15. Werrell, *The Evolution of the Cruise Missile*, pp. 92, 96, 98.

16. Richard F. McMullen, "Interceptor Missiles in Air Defense 1944–1964," Air Defense Command Historical Study No. 30, February 1965, pp. 6–7.

17. Richard F. McMullen, "Interceptor Missiles in Air Defense 1944–1964," pp. 3–5.

18. Ibid., pp. 10–14.

19. *The United States Air Force Basic Documents on Roles and Missions*, Richard I. Wolf, ed., p.151.

20. Kenneth Schaffel, *The Emerging Shield: The Air Force and the Evolution of Continental Air Defense 1945–1960* (Washington, DC: Office of Air Force History, 1990), pp. 116–7.

21. Steve Moeller, *Vigilant and Invisible: The Army's Role in Continental Air Defense, 1950–1974* (Master's thesis, Ohio State University, 1992), pp. 20,25–27; "Collins-Vandenberg Agreement, 1 August 1950," in The United States Air Force Basic Documents on Roles and Missions, pp. 219122.

3

THE BEGINNING OF REARMAMENT, 1950–1954

Upon learning that the Soviets had developed an atomic bomb, President Truman acted with characteristic dispatch. He immediately ordered the Atomic Energy Commission to launch the full-scale development of the hydrogen bomb. Soon after, he created an interdepartmental task force led by the State Department's Paul Nitze to conduct a general review of U.S. national security policy.

The study, called NSC-68, was completed in the spring of 1950. It warned that if the United States was to deter Soviet aggression, it needed to spend considerably more on national defense. Indicative of the dangers ahead, the study estimated that by 1954 the Soviets would have enough long-range bombers and atomic weapons to launch a devastating attack on the United States. To meet the Soviet threat, defense planners estimated that by fiscal year 1952 defense spending would need to rise to $40 billion; almost a 300 percent increase over the Pentagon's 1950 budget.

As if to confirm the dire warnings in NSC-68, in June 1950 North Korea launched a surprise attack on South Korea and the United States suddenly found itself embroiled in a conflict in Asia. As the military recalled reservists and mobilized to meet the challenge in Korea, a massive U.S. rearmament campaign began.

In 1950 the Army and Air Force missile programs were at different stages. The Army was making substantial progress on its Nike surface-to-air missile system and also beginning work on a 500-mile tactical-range ballistic missile."[a] While the Army was diversifying its missile program the Air Force used Secretary of Defense Louis Johnson's March 21, 1950 directive on guided missiles to claim sole responsibility for developing all long-range missiles.[1] During the early 1950s the Air Force directed most of its attention to coaxing along its slow-moving Snark and Navaho air-breathing missile programs. At the same time the Air Force's other long-range missile program, the ballistic MX-774, was in limbo. Officially canceled since 1947, the MX-774 led a curious unofficial existence, financed mainly by Convair and quietly supported by missile advocates within the Air Force.

Opposite: The father of the Air Force ICBM program, General Bernard A. Schriever.

[a] The rapid evolution of missile technology after World War II made missiles suitable for an increasingly wide range of missions. Whereas the V-2 was considered "long-range" in the mid-1940s, by the early 1950s the United States was developing three distinct classes of ballistic missiles: (1) tactical missiles with ranges under 500 miles; (2) intermediate-range missiles with ranges of approximately 1,500 miles; and (3) strategic or intercontinental-range missiles with ranges in excess of 1,500 miles.

The 1949 revelation that the Soviets had tested an atomic bomb stoked new interest in air defense, particularly the Army's Nike program, which had made great strides since its inception in 1945. The Air Force air-defense missile programs had not fared as well. The Air Force lost its first surface-to-air missile program, the ground-to-air pilotless aircraft (GAPA) project, in 1949. However, the Air Force was unwilling to allow the Army to exercise complete control over ground-based air defense, and that same year the Air Materiel Command (AMC) contracted with Boeing Aircraft and the University of Michigan's Aeronautical Research Center to develop a long-range air defense missile, which came to be known as the BOMARC (IM-99).

In October 1950 K.T. Keller, the Secretary of Defense's newly appointed Director of Guided Missiles, recommended that the Army's Nike program be accelerated. At the same time Keller also pushed to expedite the development of the Air Force's BOMARC. In November 1951 a Nike successfully intercepted a target drone in the skies over White Sands, and in 1952 Douglas Aircraft opened its first Nike production facility in Santa Monica, California. In a related development, in April 1950 the Army began to consolidate its missile development programs at the new Ordnance Guided Missile Center at the Redstone Arsenal in Huntsville, Alabama. One of the organizations transferred there was the Ordnance Research and Development Division Suboffice (Rocket) formerly based at Fort Bliss, Texas, and home to Wernher von Braun and the "Operation PAPERCLIP" team. Since 1946 the Suboffice had administered Project Hermes, and in September 1950 the Ordnance Department ordered the Guided Missile Center to make a preliminary study of a 500-mile tactical-range ballistic missile. Under the direction of von Braun, that study ultimately led to the Army's successful Redstone and Jupiter missiles.

Early ICBM Development

While the Army consolidated its missile development program at Huntsville, the Air Force allowed its ICBM program to languish. With a skepticism bred from extensive operational experience, few in the Air Staff (the planning body within the Headquarters, U.S. Air Force) believed that the ICBM could reliably and effectively attack targets at intercontinental range. Instead, the Air Force chose to invest in new bombers and, to a lesser extent, long-range air-breathing missiles.

Despite widespread hostility, a small group of ICBM advocates composed of Air Force officers and their allies in industry lobbied for the Air Force to resume its support of the ICBM program. Recent events strengthened their hand: the Soviets had developed an atomic bomb, NSC-68 recommended that the United States diversify its nuclear deterrent, and defense spending was on the rise. Even more promising, in late 1950 a study by the Rand Corporation indicated that recent advances in engines and guidance systems made the ICBM technologically feasible.[2]

This combination of events at home and abroad prompted the Air Staff to look at the ICBM program in a new light, and in January 1951 it resurrected the ICBM. Although the new study contract was essentially a continuation of the MX-774, the project was given a new name: MX-1593. Under the terms of the contract, the Air Force directed Convair to study the feasibility of developing a ballistic missile capable of carrying an 8,000-pound warhead 5,000 miles and striking within a circular error probable (CEP) of 1,500 feet.[b]

---

[b] The CEP is the radius of a circle within which half of the ordnance targeted for the center of the circle can be expected to land.

Convair completed the missile study in July 1951. The airframe manufacturer concluded that its long-range ballistic missile, which it now called Atlas, was technologically feasible, and it urged the Air Force to begin development without delay. Convair then submitted the study to the newly independent Air Research and Development Command (ARDC).[c] ARDC shared Convair's sentiments. In September 1951 Brig. Gen. John Sessums, the ARDC Deputy for Development, strongly urged the Air Staff to begin development of a long-range ballistic missile immediately, and requested additional funding to support the effort.[3]

The Air Staff did not share ARDC's enthusiasm for the ICBM. It refused to fund a full-scale development effort and ordered ARDC to limit its activities to a preliminary test program.[4] ARDC protested the Air Staff's decision, noting that the Atlas guidance system, engines, flight-control apparatus, and fuselage had already been tested successfully. It "urgently recommended" that the Air Staff establish a formal requirement for a long-range ballistic missile. With the "proper application of funds and priorities," ARDC believed Atlas could be operational by 1960. Furthermore, ARDC warned that the Soviet Union might also be developing an ICBM, and cautioned that if Atlas were delayed, "we may be running a grave risk of being subjected to an intense bombardment to which we may not be able to retaliate."[5]

The sparring between ARDC and the Air Staff continued for the next two years; ARDC wanting to plunge into an ambitious development plan with an eye toward production while the Air Staff favored a slower approach to begin with additional research. In 1953 the two sides finally reached a compromise that yielded a development plan. No definitive date was set for completing the R&D phase; instead planners estimated it would be "sometime" after 1964. The development plan provided for an operational capability in 1965, but noted that this date could be moved ahead by two or three years with additional support. [6]

ICBM Technology

As ballistic missile technology continued to improve throughout the early 1950s, the Air Staff's resistance to the ICBM program became increasingly untenable. For example, when the Air Materiel Command canceled Convair's MX-774 program in 1947, one reason given was that available engines lacked the power to deliver a warhead at intercontinental range. Yet by the early 1950s North American's XL43-NA-3 engine, developed as a booster for the Navaho missile program and capable of producing 120,000 pounds of thrust, was considered the most advanced rocket engine in the world.[7] Guidance technology was making similar strides.[8] Since the mid-1940s C. Stark Draper of the Massachusetts Institute of Technology Instrumentation Laboratory had been experimenting with radio-inertial and all-inertial guidance systems. By 1951 Draper's all-inertial systems, tested aboard long-range aircraft, were accurate to within two miles after a 3,000-mile flight.[d] There also had been substantial progress in designing a functional reentry vehicle, the protective

[c] Before 1951 R&D was controlled by the Air Materiel Command (AMC). Critics of the arrangement complained that AMC was not structured to support farreaching research programs like the ICBM, and urged that a separate R&D command be created.

[d] Radio-inertial guidance used a series of ground-based tracking radars to determine the missile's position. That information was then relayed to ground-based computers that compared the missile's position against the programmed flight path and relayed course corrections to the missile's flight control system. In contrast, the all-inertial guidance system was completely self-contained. Before launch the missile was programmed to follow a specific flight path. Using a system of gyroscopes and accelerometers, the guidance system constantly monitored the missile's position relative to its designated flight path. If the missile strayed from its programmed course, the guidance system sent course corrections to the flight control system. Unlike radio-inertial guidance, the all-inertial system was not susceptible to radio jamming.

A heat sink reentry vehicle on a Thor (SM-75) IRBM.

shroud that encased the warhead, which was considered by many experts to be the most difficult hurdle of the entire development effort.[9] In June 1952 H. Julian Allen, a scientist at the National Advisory Committee for Aeronautics, Ames Research Laboratory, pioneered the concept of the blunt-body reentry vehicle that later became a central feature of the ICBM program.

In the years that followed, the Air Force experimented with two types of reentry vehicles: heat sink and ablative. The heat sink vehicle contained a large, blunt copper core that absorbed heat to keep it away from the sensitive warhead. The ablative type was more streamlined and dissipated heat as the outer layers burned away.

During the early 1950s a revolution in thermonuclear weapons technology also hastened the birth of the ICBM. The United States began earnestly developing thermonuclear weapons in 1949, and by November 1952 successfully tested an experimental device at Eniwetok Atoll in the Marshall Islands. Further improvements followed rapidly, and by early 1953 the United States had perfected an operational thermonuclear weapon.[10] These new weapons were several orders of magnitude lighter and more powerful than the fission warheads they replaced."[e] For example, the fission bomb dropped on Hiroshima weighed approximately 10,000 pounds and had an explosive yield of 13 kilotons.[f] In contrast, by mid-1953 scientists working for the Air Force estimated that by the end of the decade the United States would be able to build a 1,500-pound thermonuclear warhead with a yield of one megaton. Only 15 percent the weight of the Hiroshima weapon, the thermonuclear weapon would be approximately 70 times more powerful.

The advent of thermonuclear weapons enabled the Atlas design team to overcome two of its most intractable problems, both related to the missile's originally specified 3,000-pound fission warhead. First, by reducing the weight of the warhead from 3,000 pounds to 1,500 pounds, they could reduce the size of the missile by half. Second, because the thermonuclear warhead was approximately 50 times more powerful than the proposed fission warhead, and also had a much larger destructive radius, the missile's CEP, a measure of error in delivery accuracy, could be expanded from 1,500 feet to several miles. Expanding the CEP made designing the guidance system much less complicated.

The Air Staff, however, failed to grasp the implications of these developments. These men, who had spent much of their careers in the cockpit, seriously questioned whether the ICBM could function as a reliable component of the nation's strategic nuclear deterrent. Other Air Force officers resisted the ICBM simply because they were unable to appreciate its tremendous potential. Many pilots were hostile to the ICBM because they feared its effect on their profession. In the early 1950s the Air Force was a tightly knit professional community dominated by pilots and centered on aircraft. Aircraft were the cornerstone of the Air Force's professional and social order, and any change threatening to disrupt that paradigm was perceived by most of the officer corps with apprehension.[11]

ICBM Advocates

Before 1953, ICBM advocates at ARDC had made little headway against their entrenched opposition. That changed in the spring of 1953 when the ICBM program gained two new advocates: Trevor Gardner and Bernard Schriever. Gardner arrived on the scene first. In February 1953 he was appointed Special Assistant to the Secretary of the Air Force for Research and Development. Gardner, 38 years old at the time, was an engineer and businessman who left his job as president of Hycon Manufacturing in Pasadena, California, to join the government.

Gardner was short and stocky, with closely cropped hair and wire-rimmed glasses. Those who liked him called him blunt, outspoken, and a gifted manager. Herbert York, the Director of the Atomic Energy Commission's Livermore Laboratories, described Gardner as "intelligent, vigorous, somewhat volatile, and

---

[e] They were called thermonuclear weapons because of the tremendous heat (nearly 100 million degrees Kelvin) required to facilitate nuclear fusion. They were also called "hydrogen bombs" because they used the hydrogen isotopes deuterium and tritium as their principal fuel. Fission weapons, such as those used at the end of World War II, generate energy by splitting the nucleus of very heavy atoms such as plutonium or uranium. In contrast, thermonuclear weapons generate energy through nuclear fusion, the process of creating heavy nuclides from lighter ones. This process makes thermonuclear weapons more powerful, because a fusion reaction generates four to five times the energy produced by fission. Thermonuclear weapons also can be made more powerful because they are not restricted by the size of the critical mass.

[f] A kiloton is equal to the explosive force of 1,000 tons of TNT; a megaton has the explosive power of 1,000,000 tons.

impatient to make changes quickly."[12] Gardner's opponents were not charitable in their descriptions-they called him "sharp, abrupt, irascible, cold, and a bastard."[13]

James Killian, President Eisenhower's respected science advisor, described Gardner as "technologically evangelical," and the new special assistant wasted little time in making his mark on the Air Force. Soon after taking office Gardner embarked on an aggressive campaign to identify and develop promising new technologies; this led him to the ICBM. Gardner became a zealous proponent of the ICBM because he believed that if the long-range missiles were developed quickly, they offered the United States a tremendous technological opportunity. He envisioned ICBMs providing the nation with a devastating and virtually unstoppable nuclear deterrent, an advantage that would catapult the United States years ahead of the Soviet Union in the arms race. Moreover, Gardner also promoted ICBMs as a way to diversify the nation's strategic nuclear deterrent, which at the time was carried exclusively by the bombers of the Air Force's Strategic Air Command (SAC).[g]

To push the ICBM program forward, however, Gardner needed an ally in the Air Force's R&D community. In March 1953 he found that ally in Brig. Gen. Bernard Schriever, the Assistant for Development Planning under the Deputy Chief of Staff for Development.

A bomber pilot and maintenance officer during World War II, the tall, soft-spoken Schriever joined the Air Staff in 1946. By 1953 he was one of the most influential members of the Air Force's then-small R&D community. Schriever was an ardent proponent of new technology, and within several months he and Gardner had joined forces to promote a stronger role for R&D within Air Force war planning. Together they formed an effective alliance. Schriever was the inside man, familiar with the Air Force's ongoing programs as well as the politics of the R&D process. Gardner made his contribution at the secretarial level. His intuitive grasp of R&D, coupled with his aggressive approach and the strong support he received from his mentor, Secretary of the Air Force Harold Talbott, made him an unusually effective advocate. Gardner also understood the practical limits of his authority, and he was not afraid to go outside of the Air Force to win support for his programs. The Atlas ICBM was a case in point.

Although both Gardner and Schriever recognized that the ICBM had tremendous potential, they were also pragmatists. They understood that their support alone was insufficient to overcome the Air Force's resistance to the missile program. Faced with widespread opposition, they realized that to accelerate the Atlas program they needed two things: a convincing justification and a cadre of influential scientists and engineers who would support their actions.

The justification Gardner and Schriever seized upon was thermonuclear weapons. In the spring of 1953 the Air Force Scientific Advisory Board (SAB) estimated that by the end of the decade the United States would develop a 1,500-pound thermonuclear warhead with yield of 1 megaton. It is important to note that thermonuclear weapons were not the single missing ingredient that made ICBMs possible; the warheads

---

[g] A 1953 study by Rand mathematician Albert Wohlstetter found that as many as 85 percent of SAC's bombers could be destroyed on the ground by a Soviet surprise attack, leaving the United States open to nuclear extortion. Fred Kaplan, *The Wizards of Armageddon* (New York: Simon and Schuster, 1983), pp. 90-102; Michael R. Beschloss, *Eisenhower, Krushchev, and the U-2 Affair* (New York: Harper and Row, 1986), p. 73.

were only one of several new technologies to be incorporated in the missile. But on a broader scale thermonuclear weapons served as a badly needed catalyst to accelerate the ICBM program. First, the new warheads furnished Gardner and Schriever with an ideal pretext to lobby for taking a fresh look at the ICBM program. Second, because thermonuclear weapons weighed far less and were tremendously more powerful than fission weapons, they made the job of developing an ICBM much less demanding and much less expensive, which in turn made the project politically feasible.

To exploit the thermonuclear technology breakthrough, Gardner and Schriever's first task was to get official confirmation of the SAB's earlier unofficial estimates. They did this through a subcommittee of the SAB's Nuclear Weapons Panel, chaired by the distinguished mathematician John von Neumann of the Institute for Advanced Study, Princeton, New Jersey. The authorization for von Neumann's study came from Air Force Vice Chief of Staff General Thomas White, who at Gardner and Schriever's urging asked the SAB to estimate the size, weight, and yield of nuclear weapons that could be developed over the coming 6 to 8 years.

Von Neumann's group completed its study in October 1953. To no one's surprise, the Nuclear Weapons Panel confirmed that in the next 6 to 8 years the United States would be able to build a thermonuclear weapon weighing 1,500 pounds and generating an explosive yield of 1 megaton. The panel also observed that the size, shape, and yield of thermonuclear weaponry made it perfectly suited for the ICBM. Equally important, the von Neumann group noted that the new weapons would have a significant impact on the current Atlas program. One of the most notable examples, the subcommittee found, was in the area of guidance accuracy. In light of the thermonuclear warheads greatly enhanced yield, von Neumann reasoned that the Atlas guidance requirements should be eased considerably.[14] He recommended expanding the CEP to a range of 3.2 to 4.5 miles, almost 16 times larger than the original 1,500-foot specification.

The Teapot Committee

The Nuclear Weapons Panel's finding enabled Gardner to convince Secretary of the Air Force Harold Talbott that the Air Force's long-range missile program needed to be evaluated "by a special group of the nation's leading scientists." With Talbott's approval Gardner began assembling his "blue ribbon" scientific advisory committee in October 1953. Officially entitled the "Strategic Missiles Evaluation Committee," everyone referred to the group by its code name: the Teapot Committee. To lead the committee, Gardner once again called on the man Time magazine called "the smartest man on earth," the brilliant and affable Dr. John von Neumann.[16]

Gardner gave the Teapot Committee a broad mandate; study the Air Force longrange missile program and make recommendations for improving it.[h] The committee began meeting in October 1953, and over the course of the next several months it made a detailed study of the Snark, Navaho, and Atlas programs.

The committee completed its succinct 10-page report in February 1954. The committee's report stated that the Atlas program was beset by a number of serious technological and managerial problems. The Committee found that many elements of Convair's design were outdated and they recommended that the entire Atlas program be reviewed in light of the recent advances in thermonuclear weapons.

Design deficiencies, however, were only the beginning of the problem. The Atlas program's most pressing need, the committee concluded, was new management. Convair's management approach, which used the technology and management techniques of the airframe industry, proved ill-suited for missile development. In its place the committee proposed creating a new "development-management" group composed of an "unusually competent group of scientists and engineers capable of making systems analyses, supervising the research phases, and completely controlling the experimental and hardware phases of the program..." The committee warned that assembling such a staff might require that the government "draft" members from industry, academia, and government. Furthermore, the committee also cautioned the Air Force that if the new group was to be effective it would have to be "relieved of excessive detailed regulation by existing government agencies."[18]

The Teapot report provided Gardner and Schriever with powerful leverage for accelerating the Atlas program, and in meetings the following month with the Air Staff and the Secretary of the Air Force they laid out the framework of a revised development plan. Their goal was to establish a preliminary ICBM capability by mid-1958, and to build 20 launch sites and 100 ICBMs by 1960. But to do that Gardner warned Secretary of the Air Force Talbott and Chief of Staff Twining that the service would have to "dramatize" the development process by simplifying standard development procedures, giving the program a high defense priority, and placing the development effort under the control of a high-ranking officer with direct access to senior Air Force officials.[19]

[h] The other members were: Hendrik Bode, Bell Telephone Labs; Louis Dunn, director of the Jet Propulsion Laboratory, California Institute of Technology; Lawrence Hyland, Bendix Aviation; George Kistiakowsky, Harvard University; Clark Millikan, president of the Guggenheim Institute, California Institute of Technology; Allen Puckett, Hughes Aircraft; and Jerry Weisner, Massachusetts Institute of Technology. U.S. Congress, House, Committee on Government Operations, Military Operations Subcommittee, Hearings on the Organization and Management of Missile Programs, 86th Cong., 1st sess., (Washington DC: GPO, 1959), p. 19.

Endnotes

1. Johnson's directive was predicated on the understanding that the services would use guided missiles in the manner and to the extent required to perform their assigned functions. In 1948 the Key West Conference established that the Air Force was responsible for strategic air warfare, and Johnson's 1950 directive reinforced that point. The directive stated that surface-launched guided missiles "which supplement, extend the capabilities of, or replace Air Force aircraft . . . will be a responsibility of the U.S. Air Force, as required by its functions." Memo, Louis A. Johnson, Secretary of Defense to the Joint Chiefs of Staff, subj: Department of Defense Guided Missiles Program, 21 March 1950, with attachment, in Richard I. Wolf, ed., *The United States Air Force Basic Document on Roles and Missions* (Washington, DC: Office of Air Force History, 1987), pp. 213–218, 210.

2. Merton E. Davies and William R. Harris, *Rand's Role in the Evolution of Balloon and Satellite Observations Systems and Related U.S. Space Technology* (Santa Monica, CA: Rand Corporation, 1988), p. 41.

3. Ltr., Brig. Gen. J.W. Sessums, ARDC Deputy for Development, to Director of Research and Development, Headquarters USAF, subj: Approval of Long-Range Rocket Missile Program ATLAS (MX-1593), 25 September 1951, Ballistic Missile Organization, History Office, Norton AFB, CA, (hereafter BMOHO) Basic Documents

4. Ltr., Brig. Gen. Donald Yates, Director, Research and Development DCSD, to Commander, ARDC, subj: Program Guidance for Long Range Strategic Rocket-Atlas (MX–1593), 11 November 1951, BMOHO, Basic Documents.

5. Ltr., ARDC to Director of Research and Development, DC&D, subj: Long Range Rocket Pilotless Program, ATLAS (MX-1593), 20 March 1952, BMOHO, Basic Documents.

6. ARDC, Development Directive No. 3082, subj: Development of the ATLAS (MX-1593) 31 July 1953, pp. 1–2, in "History of the Air Research and Development Command, 01 January 1954–30–June 1954," vol. 2, Air Force Historical Research Agency, Maxwell AFB, Montgomery, AL, file K243.01.

7. John M. Simmons, "The Navaho Lineage" *Threshold 7* (December 1987): pp. 17–19.)

8. Stark Draper, "The Evolution of Aerospace Guidance Technology and the Massachusetts Institute of Technology, 19351951," in R. Cargill Hall, ed., *History of Rocketry and Astronautics*, vol. 7, part II, vol. 2 (San Diego, CA: American Astronautical Society, 1986), pp. 244–246; Duane Roller, "Notes on Technical Aspects of Ballistic Missiles," *Air University Quarterly Review 9* (Summer 1957): pp. 39–40.

9. Edwin P. Hartmann, *Adventures in Research: A History of the Ames Research Center 1940–1965*, NASA History Series (Washington, DC: NASA, 1970), pp. 213–218.

10. Chuck Hansen, *U.S. Nuclear Weapons: the Secret History* (New York: Orion Books, 1988), pp. 50–1; Herbert F. York, *Race to Oblivion: A Participant's View of the Arms Race* (New York: Simon and Schuster, 1989), p. 39.

11. This blend of technological and professional resistance was not peculiar to the Air Force. Elting Morrison found a similar pattern in the United States Navy at the end of the 19th century. Elting E. Morrison, *Men, Machines, and Modern Times* (Cambridge, MA: M.I.T. Press, 1966), pp. 17–44.

12. York, *Race to Oblivion*, p. 84.

13. Jacob Neufeld, *The Development of Ballistic Missiles in the United States Air Force* (Washington, DC: Office of Air Force History, 1990), p. 96; Edmund Beard, Developing the ZCBM: A Study in Bureaucratic Politics, Institute of War and Peace Studies Series (New York: Columbia University Press, 1976), p. 166.

14. "Professor John von Neumann's Report on Nuclear Weapons," 21 October 1953, pp. 7–8, Air Force Historical Research Agency, Maxwell AFB, Montgomery, AL, file K168.1512–3, folder "Scientific Advisory Board, Nuclear Weapons Panel."

15. Memo, Gardner to Donald Quarles, 16 February 1954, in Neufeld, *The Development of Ballistic Missiles*, p. 252.

16. "The Cheerful Mathematician," *Time* (18 February 1957): p. 59.

17. "Recommendations of the Strategic Missiles Evaluation Committee," 10 February 1954, in Neufeld, *The Development of Ballistic Missiles*, pp. 259–60.

18. "Recommendations of the Strategic Missiles Evaluation Committee," pp. 259–61.

19. Memo, Gardner to Secretary Talbott and General Twining, subj: Intercontinental Ballistic Acceleration Plan, 11 March 1954, p. 1, Library of Congress, Washington, DC, Twining papers, Subject File 1930–1957, Box 122, folder "1957 Top Secret File (3)."

4

THE ICBM PROGRAM TAKES FLIGHT, 1954–1955

The Teapot report provided Gardner and Schriever with a powerful tool for accelerating the ICBM program, and in May 1954 Air Force Vice Chief of Staff General Thomas White ordered that the Atlas program be accelerated to the maximum extent technology would permit. White gave the ICBM program the service's top development priority and assigned. responsibility for the program to ARDC with the understanding that the research command would delegate that authority to a field office soon to be established on the West Coast.[1]

The Western Development Division

That new office was ARDC's Western Development Division (WDD), and in August 1954 Schriever became its first commanding officer. The WDD was a hybrid organization, combining the functions of a program management office with the authority of Headquarters ARDC. Reflecting the importance the Air Force now attached to the ICBM program, ARDC gave Schriever "complete control and authority over all aspects of the Atlas program . . ."[2] It was an unprecedented move, and one that gave Schriever extraordinary powers. In addition, Schriever was also given the authority to bypass Headquarters ARDC and communicate directly with major commands, the Air Staff, and the Secretary of the Air Force.[3]

Initially the WDD was housed in a former parochial school, a rambling collection of buildings on East Manchester Avenue in Inglewood, California, a suburb of Los Angeles. Schriever occupied the principal's office and used the chapel as a conference room. His staff, which called itself "the schoolhouse gang," initially consisted of officers and three enlisted men. It grew quickly. By December 1955 the WDD had grown to 166 people and in early 1955 it moved out of its temporary quarters into a new four-building complex near Los Angeles International Airport. The WDD's rapid growth continued over the next several years, and by early 1959 its military and civilian staff had grown to 1,200.[4]

But as the WDD took shape in Inglewood, Gardner was fighting a series of political skirmishes in Washington. During the fall of 1954 he and Schriever became concerned that the ICBM program's hard-won independence was being compromised by restrictive Air Force and Department of Defense budgeting procedures as well as lengthy review and approval processes. In letters to Gardner, Schriever warned that unless the troublesome requirements were lifted soon, the Atlas program would fall behind schedule.

To cut through the tangle of red tape that threatened to hold back the missile project, Gardner launched a carefully orchestrated campaign to designate the ICBM as the nation's most important research and devel-

Opposite: In June 1954 the newly established Western Development Division found temporary quarters in what was formerly St. John's Catholic School in Inglewood, California.

[a] Several of Gardner's critics charged that he wanted to wrest control of the ICBM program away from the Air Force and create a completely separate missile development agency that he would run. Col. R.E. Soper, interview by Harry C. Jordan, 29 November 1966, Air Force Historical Research Agency, Maxwell Air Force Base, Montgomery, AL, p. 5.

opment program. Gardner reasoned that if he could imbue the ICBM program with the same sense of urgency that surrounded the MANHATTAN PROJECT, he could thwart the efforts by the Air Force and DoD to exert greater control over missile development.[a] Gardner realized that to get that same type of priority would require high-level political support, and he thought the best place to get it was the White House.

Search for External Support

Initially Gardner tried to approach President Eisenhower through the Office of Defense Mobilization Science Advisory Committee (ODMSAC), a little-used organization within the Executive Office of the President. In his meetings with the advisory committee Gardner spoke forcefully of the Air Force's need to redirect its R&D programs to make better use of new and emerging technologies, and he argued that the ICBM program should be the centerpiece of that effort. The message Gardner wanted the committee to convey to President Eisenhower was clear: the White House needed to investigate the political and strategic implications of new defense technologies.[5]

The committee, however, never got to voice Gardner's concerns to the President. Instead, President Eisenhower asked the committee to study how science and technology could be used to protect the United States against the risk of a surprise attack.

In response to the President's request, the ODMSAC formed the Technological Capabilities Panel, which soon came to be known as the Killian Committee after its chairman James Killian, the president of the Massachusetts Institute of Technology. Composed of 68 of the nation's foremost scientists and engineers, the panel received several briefings over several months from Gardner and Schriever on the status of the ICBM program.

In February 1955 the Killian Committee briefed President Eisenhower and the National Security Council (NSC) on its findings. The committee had looked closely at the ICBM program and, on the whole, found that it was well run and progressing satisfactorily. But the committee shared Gardner and Schriever's concerns about the future, especially the possibility that the ICBM program could be delayed by overly restrictive development procedures. To offset that risk, the Killian Committee recommended that the NSC should break tradition, it had never previously endorsed a specific weapon system, and recognize the ICBM program as a "nationally supported program of the highest order."[6]

An unanticipated but welcomed byproduct of the Killian Report was the State Department's interest in the ICBM. The diplomats regarded the news of a possible delay in the ICBM program with grave concern, fearing that there would be serious foreign policy implications if the Soviet Union developed a long-range ballistic missile before the United States. Reflecting the State Department's concern, Under Secretary of State Herbert Hoover Jr. urged the NSC to recommend that President Eisenhower make the ICBM program the nation's top defense priority.[7]

At the same time Gardner and Schriever were feeding the State Department information on the ICBM program, other missile advocates were briefing Senator Henry Jackson (D-Washington), Chairman of the

[a] Several of Gardner's critics charged that he wanted to wrest control of the ICBM program away from the Air Force and create a completely separate missile development agency that he would run. Col. R.E. Soper, interview by Harry C. Jordan, 29 November 1966, Air Force Historical Research Agency, Maxwell Air Force Base, Montgomery, AL, p. 5.

Military Applications Subcommittee of the Joint Committee on Atomic Energy, on the hurdles facing the ICBM. Jackson was sympathetic and agreed to press President Eisenhower for more vigorous action. Consequently, in a June 1955 letter written for him by Gardner and Schriever, Jackson too urged the President to designate the ICBM program as the nation's foremost defense priority.[8]

Acting on the advice of the State Department and Congress, on July 28, 1955 President Eisenhower summoned Gardner, Schriever, and von Neumann to the White House to brief him and the NSC on the missile program. The hour-long meeting went well. The President and the NSC were receptive, and the missile advocates left the meeting with a feeling of accomplishment.[9]

In the wake of the White House briefing events moved rapidly. At the NSC meeting on August 4, 1955 Eisenhower ordered the NSC Planning Board to prepare a list of proposed changes to the ICBM program based on the Killian Committee Report and the July 28th briefing. The Planning Board submitted its proposed NSC action to the Council on August 30. Finding that "there would be the gravest repercussions on the national security and the cohesion of the free world" if the Soviets developed an ICBM before the United States, the Planning Board described the ICBM program as "one of the highest priority."

The State Department's Policy Planning Staff complained that the NSC's proposed action missed the mark. It said that designating the ICBM program as "one of the highest priority" was meaningless because 180 other projects were in the same category. The planning staff suggested that what the missile program needed instead was specific relief against its most pressing problem-the seemingly endless cycle of program reviews and budget approvals that threatened to disrupt Schriever's carefully crafted development schedule. Using information supplied by Gardner and Schriever, the State Department estimated that the ICBM program could be accelerated by a year or more by streamlining administrative procedures, and it noted that the Secretary of Defense had the authority to "short cut" the development process. "Doubtless," the Policy Planning Staff memo read, "to do so will entail certain risks of waste of funds and effort. In view of the stakes involved, it appears that these risks should be taken.[10]

The NSC ultimately recommended that the President increase his support for the ICBM program, and in September 1955 Eisenhower approved NSC Action No. 1433, which designated the ICBM program as the nation's highest R&D priority and directed the Secretary of Defense to prosecute it with maximum urgency.[11] Several days later Deputy Secretary of Defense Reuben Robertson transmitted the President's message to the Secretary of the Air Force and directed him to "recommend . . . as soon as possible such additional actions or administrative arrangements as he considers necessary . . . to implement this responsibility."[12]

This was the chance the missile advocates had been impatiently waiting for. To provide the Secretary with the requested recommendations, in mid-September Gardner asked Hyde Gillette, Deputy for Budget and Program Management in the Office of the Air Force Assistant Secretary for Financial Management, to lead a study to streamline management of the ICBM program. After a five week review, the committee released the "Air Force Plan (revised) for Simplifying Administrative Procedures for the ICBM and IRBM Programs."[b] The document soon came to be known simply as the "Gillette Procedures."

[b] The Intermediate-Range Ballistic Missile, IRBM, had a range of 5,000 miles.

The Gillette Procedures

The Gillette Procedures were a thorough, top-to-bottom restructuring of the ICBM program's management structure and procedures. The focus of the procedures was the reallocation of authority: they required the DoD to delegate, to the greatest extent possible, responsibility for the ICBM program to the Air Force, which in turn would delegate that authority to Schriever and the WDD.[13]

The Gillette Procedures enabled the WDD to exercise greater control over procurement and facilities construction, and they also established a separate budget category for the ICBM program. The Gillette Procedures also overhauled the weapons system planning process. Previously, WDD's annual development plans were reviewed by literally dozens of DoD and Air Force agencies, reviews that sometimes could take months. The Gillette Procedures swept that cumbersome system away and in its place established two powerful new committees: the Office of the Secretary of Defense Ballistic Missile Committee (OSD BMC), and the Air Force Ballistic Missile Committee (AFBMC). The OSD committee was the "single program review and approval authority" at its level, and it delegated administrative authority to the Air Force committee "to review, approve, and direct implementation of the Ballistic Missile Program." With review and approval authority centralized within these two committees, decisions that previously took weeks could be made within hours.[14]

The breadth of Schriever's newfound authority put a premium on astute program management. For that Schriever came to rely heavily on his systems engineering and technical direction (SE/TD) contractor, the Ramo-Wooldridge Corporation.[c] The young company was named after its founders, Simon Ramo and Dean Wooldridge, and had been a part of the ICBM program since the days of the Teapot Committee.

Ramo-Wooldridge's role in the ICBM program was a significant departure from the Air Force's established procedures. In the past, when developing a new aircraft or missile, the Air Force had always selected an aircraft manufacturer as the prime contractor, and then relied on it to coordinate the development process. That arrangement, however, would not work on the ICBM. Neither the Air Force nor Convair had the necessary expertise in the critical areas of electronics, propulsion, and guidance to manage the development effort. Unable to manage the project itself, and unwilling to give that responsibility to Convair, the Air Force turned to Ramo-Wooldridge.[15]

Ramo-Wooldridge's role was controversial. The firm was responsible for much of the day-to-day management and administration of the missile program. While directing the efforts of the program's many contractors, Ramo-Wooldridge was acting as the government's agent. A number of critics, including the General Accounting Office (GAO), charged the Air Force with abnegating its program-management responsibilities.[16] Convair was also vociferously opposed to the arrangement, charging that Ramo-Wooldridge was using its privileged position to steal the airframe manufacturer's trade secrets, The Air Force officers who worked with Ramo-Wooldridge, however, defended the company's role, saying that its expert advice shortened the ICBM program by several years.

[c] Ramo-Wooldridge merged with Thompson products in 1958 creating Thompson-Ramo-Wooldridge, or, as it is now called, TRW.

Concurrency

The Air Force was under intense pressure to deploy an ICBM by 1960, and to meet that goal Schriever adopted a risky new development methodology he called "concurrency."[d] Before the ICBM program, the Air Force usually developed its weapons systems sequentially, completing one component and then moving to the next. Sequential development was a conservative, slow-paced approach well suited to developing aircraft in peacetime. Prototypes were built by hand and rigorously tested. Only after the Air Force made its selection did the service think about producing the weapon in quantity and maintaining it in the field.

In contrast to the ordered cadence of sequential development, concurrency was a dizzying whirl that Schriever described as "moving ahead with everything and everybody, altogether and all at once, toward a specific goal."[17] In other words, concurrency was based on the simultaneous progress of R&D, production, base construction, training, and support activities.

Inherently it was a complex process, further complicated by the breadth of the WDD's program responsibilities. Unlike the process for developing a new aircraft that could use existing runways and repair facilities, the WDD had to develop the missile, its support structure, and the launch sites all at the same time. It was comparable, Schriever liked to say, to making General Motors also build roads, bridges, service stations, and teach driver's education.[18]

There is little question that concurrency enabled the Air Force to deploy its ICBMs more quickly than it could have using sequential development. But saving time had its price. For example, because the Atlas ICBM was developed at the same time its launch facilities were being built, changes in the airframe often required costly modifications to the silos. In short, the Air Force used concurrency to buy time: it considered developing the missile quickly was more important than how much it cost.

The many managerial innovations the Air Force incorporated into the ICBM program-an independent development organization, streamlined management, and concurrency-were soon adopted by the other services. When the Army established the Army Ballistic Missile Agency (ABMA) and the Navy created the Special Projects Office to manage the Polaris project, both used the WDD as an organizational model. The similarities did not stop there. The Army and Navy programs also operated under the Gillette Procedures, used concurrency, and in one form or another, employed systems engineering and technical direction contractors.

Endnotes

1. Memo, Gen. T.D. White, Vice Chief of Staff to Air Staff, subj: Project Atlas, 14 May 1954, in Thomas S. Snyder and others, *Space and Missile Systems Organization: A Chronology 1954–1976* (Los Angeles: Office of History, HQ Space and Missile Systems Organization, 1976), pp. 19–20.

2. Memo, Lt. Gen. Thomas S. Power, ARDC Commander to Schriever, subj: Assignment of Authority, Responsibility, and Accountability, 29 July 1954, BMO/HO, Norton AFB, CA, Basic Documents.

---

[d] Strictly speaking, concurrency was not new; it had been used before, notably on the B-29 bomber program. Schriever, however, was the first to apply concurrency on such a large scale.

3. Ltr. Lt. Gen. Donald Putt, DCS/D to Commander, ARDC, subj: Project Atlas, 21 June 1954, p. 2, Schriever papers, Office of Air Force History, Bolling AFB, Washington, DC (hereafter AFHO), file K168.7171.175, Folder, "Western Development Division;" Ethel M. DeHaven, Aerospace: *The Evolution of USAF Weapons Acquisition Policy 1945–1961*, vol. I (Andrews AFB, Landover, MD: Air Force Systems Command, 1962), p. 33.

4. Air Force Ballistic Missile Division (AFBMD) Report, "Study of Air Force Ballistic Missile Division Organizational Structure," 1959, p. 5, Air Force Historical Research Agency, Maxwell AFB, AL, file K168.7035-2.

5. David Z. Beckler, executive secretary of the ODMSAC, telephone interview by John Lonnquest, 25 February 1992.

6. Office of Defense Mobilization, "Report to the President by the Technological Capabilities Panel of the Science Advisory Committee," 14 February 1955, vol. I, p. 37, Dwight D. Eisenhower (hereafter DDE) Library, Abilene, KS, White House Office, Office of the Staff Secretary, Subject Series, Alpha Subseries, box 16.

7. Lt. Col. Vincent T. Ford, interviews by John Lonnquest, 22 February and 28 March 1992, Chevy Chase, MD; General Bernard Schriever, interview by John Lonnquest, 27 August 1993, Washington, DC.

8. Schriever interview, 27 August 1993; Ford interview, 22 February 1992; Col. R.E. Soper, interview by Harry C. Jordan, 29 November 1966, Air Force Historical Research Agency, Maxwell AFB, Montgomery, AL, pp. 3–4. See also, ltr., Senators Clinton Anderson and Henry Jackson, Joint Committee on Atomic Energy to President Eisenhower, subj: none [comments on the intercontinental ballistic missile program], pp. 3–6, DDE Library, White House Office, Office of Staff Secretary, Subject Series, Alpha Subseries, box 4, folder, "Atomic Energy, Joint Committee on (1)."

9. Ford interview, 22 February 1992; Schriever interview, 27 August 1993.

10. Memo, Robert Bowie, Director of the [State Department] Policy Planning Staff to the Acting Secretary of State [Herbert Hoover Jr.], subj: NSC agenda item for September 8, 1955: "Intercontinental Ballistic Missiles Program," 30 August 1955, in *Foreign Relations of the United States, 1955–1957*, Vol XIX, *National Security Policy* (Washington, DC: GPO, 1990), pp. 110–11.

11. Everett Gleason, "Memorandum of Discussion at the 258th Meeting of the National Security Council, Washington, September 8, 1955," in *Foreign Relations of the United States*, 1955–1957, pp. 121–122.

12. Ltr., Deputy Secretary of Defense Reuben Robertson to the Secretaries of the Army, Navy, Air Force, Joint Chiefs of Staff, and Assistant Secretary of Defense (R&D), 17 September 1955, p. 2, AFHO, Schriever papers, file 168.7171-84, folder "Memos, September 1955."

13. "Air Force Plan (revised) for Simplifying Administrative Procedures for the ICBM and IRBM Programs," (hereafter the Gillette Procedures), 10 November 1955 in Jacob Neufeld, *The Development of Ballistic Missiles in the United States Air Force 1945–1960* (Washington, DC: Office of Air Force History, 1990), pp. 276–7; Col. R.E. Soper, telephone interview by John Lonnquest, 20 August 1992.

14. Gillette Procedures, pp. 276–301.

15. Brig. Gen. Bernard Schriever, USAF, "A Study of the Development Management Organizations for the Atlas Program," BMO/HO, pp. 6–7.

16. GAO audited the ICBM program and its report was harshly critical of Ramo–Wooldridge's role. The Air Force aggressively defended the company, and the GAO withdrew most of its accusations. See, The Comptroller General of the United States, "Report on Initial Phase of Review of Administrative Management of the Ballistic Missile Program of the Department of the Air Force, Part II," January 1960, BMO/HO, Norton AFB, box F-13. The Air Force's rebuttal is incorporated in its 17 March 1960 comments, in the same box. GAO's final report, "Findings Resulting from the Initial Review of the Ballistic Missile Programs of the Department of the Air Force," B–133042, was sent to Congress on 27 December 1960.

17. Maj. Gen. Bernard Schriever, USAF, "The USAF Ballistic Missile Program," *Air University Quarterly Review* 9 (Summer 1957); pp. 5–21.

18. U.S. Congress, House, Committee on Government Operations, Military Operations Subcommittee, *Hearings, Organization and Management of Missile Programs*, 86th Cong., 1st sess., (Washington, DC: GPO, 1959), p. 14.

5

THE DEBATE OVER INTERMEDIATE-RANGE BALLISTIC MISSILES, 1955–1958

At the same time the Air Force ICBM program was taking shape on the West Coast, the Army was expanding its ballistic missile program at the Ordnance Guided Missile Center at Redstone Arsenal, Huntsville, Alabama. One of the missile center's primary missions in the early 1950s was developing tactical-range surface-to-surface missiles. Under the direction of Wernher von Braun, the Guided Missile Center in late 1950 began work on the Redstone missile, designed to deliver a 1,500-pound payload 500 miles.[1]

To complement the Redstone, the Army also wanted to develop a ballistic missile with a range of 1,000 miles, capable of engaging targets anywhere within a theater of operations. By 1953 experience gained from the Redstone program convinced von Braun and his staff that developing such a missile was within the Guided Missile Center's reach, and they petitioned the office of the Chief of Ordnance for permission to do it.[2]

Killian Report

Despite several proposals by von Braun, the Chief of Ordnance showed little interest in developing the 1,000-mile-range missile. The program likely would have remained a low-priority study had not the February 1955 Killian Report sparked the Army's interest in the missile. In its report to the President, the Killian Committee urged that the United States, in addition to the ICBM, should also develop a new class of 1,500-mile intermediate-range ballistic missiles (IRBMs) to counter a similar program thought to be underway in the Soviet Union. Anticipating that an IRBM would be easier to build than an ICBM, the committee feared that the Soviets would deploy their IRBMs before the American ICBMs were ready. Not only would that be a blow to American prestige, it would also allow the Soviets to intimidate U.S. allies in Europe and Asia.

To counter the Soviet missile program, the committee recommended that the United States develop both land- and sea-based IRBMs. Stationed at bases in Western Europe and on ships steaming just off the Soviet coast, the missiles would counter-balance the Soviet IRBMs and serve as a forceful reminder of the United States' resolve.[3]

The Army and Navy were pleased with the committee's recommendations. The IRBM program offered them a chance to expand their missile programs and diversify their nuclear delivery capabilities. The ruling also set another important precedent; it broke the Air Force's monopoly on long-range ballistic missile development.

President Eisenhower endorsed the committee's recommendations, and during the fall of 1955 the three military services debated how they would develop the new missiles. Initially the Army proposed building the land-based IRBM for the Air Force at the Redstone Arsenal, but the Air Force, doubting that the Army would relinquish control of the missile after it was completed, declined the offer. Initially the Air Force showed little enthusiasm for starting yet another missile program. Its hesitation sprang from Schriever's concern that diverting crucial resources to develop an IRBM would impede the ICBM program. But when faced with the prospect of losing the mission to the Army or Navy, the Air Force decided to build its own IRBM. At first the Western Development Division (WDD) proposed developing the IRBM as a derivative of the ICBM, but after a DoD study panel showed that approach to be impractical, the Air Force decided to design a new missile, the Thor (SM-68).[a]

By the fall of 1955 all three services were requesting permission to build and operate an IRBM, and that led to another round of interservice squabbling over roles and missions. In November 1955 Secretary of the Army Wilber Brucker made an impassioned plea to the National Security Council (NSC) that his service be allowed to deploy an IRBM, but the council did not support his cause. Later that month the Joint Chiefs of Staff were unable to decide which service would build the new missile, and as a compromise they recommended that the Air Force develop a land-based IRBM and the Army and Navy jointly develop the sea-based version.[4] In December 1955 President Eisenhower showed his support for the IRBM when he designated it as one of the nation's top-priority programs, second in importance only to the ICBM.[5]

Army and Air Force IRBM Programs

When the Army was negotiating with DoD to win a share of the IRBM program it promised to establish an independent development organization to manage the effort. On February 1, 1956 it kept that promise by activating the Army Ballistic Missile Agency (ABMA) at Redstone Arsenal. The Army created the ABMA exclusively to develop the Redstone (XSM A-14) and the new Jupiter (SM-78) IRBM. Much as the Air Force did when it established the WDD, Secretary of the Army Brucker granted the ABMA's first commander, the flamboyant Maj. Gen. John B. Medaris, wide-ranging authority. The Army gave Medaris complete control over its tactical and IRBM programs, and also allowed him to waive normal procurement regulations and communicate directly with the Army Chief of Staff.[6]

From the outset the Air Force opposed the Army's Jupiter program, and relations between the WDD and ABMA were strained. Incensed that the Army was meddling in an area that had been its exclusive preserve, the Air Force was also concerned that the Army IRBM, which depended on many of the same manufacturers and suppliers as the ICBM, would impede work on the larger missile.[7] The Air Force also was deeply suspicious of the Army's motives for entering the IRBM program. Many at the WDD feared that the Jupiter program was only the opening salvo of an all-out Army attack to seize the ICBM program and dominate the future military space program.[8]

A comparison between the Jupiter and Thor missiles reveals few major differences. The Jupiter was a single-stage, liquid-fuel missile 60 feet tall, 9 feet in diameter, and weighed 110,000 pounds. Guided by an all-inertial navigation system, Jupiter could carry a 1,500-pound payload 1,500 miles. The Thor was a bit taller and slimmer, 65 feet high and 8 feet in diameter, but weighed almost the same. It too used an all-inertial guidance system, carried the same payload, and had a 1,650-mile range. Both missiles used the same

---

[a] It should be noted that although Thor had a new airframe, it used the booster engine and guidance system from the Atlas ICBM.

power plant-a single 150,000-pound thrust Rocketdyne engine that had been developed for the Atlas program.[9]

The biggest difference between the Army and Air Force missile programs was not the missiles but the methodology used to develop them. ABMA used a modification of the Army's time-honored arsenal concept. The missile was designed and the initial test models assembled by the ABMA and Redstone Arsenal. Once the Army was satisfied with the prototypes, it awarded the production and technical management contract to the Chrysler Corporation Ballistic Missile Division in Detroit, Michigan.

The Air Force used a different development approach called the Air Force-Industry concept. Instead of developing the weapons system in-house, the Air Force relied on a team of contractors. Naturally, the Army was critical of the Air Force's methods, alleging that the contractors, not the Air Force, were running the missile program. The Air Force fired right back: it argued that the arsenal approach failed to make full use of the nation's scientific and industrial capabilities. Furthermore, it charged that the handcrafted Jupiter prototypes built at Redstone had little operational value.[10]

Less than a year into the IRBM program, Jupiter suffered two major setbacks. The first came in September 1956 when the Navy withdrew from the project to build the solid-fuel Polaris submarine-launched ballistic missile (SLBM). Two months later Jupiter suffered what many thought was a mortal blow when Secretary of Defense Charles Wilson finally gave the Air Force sole responsibility for building and operating all surface-launched missiles with a range in excess of 200 miles. In practical terms that meant the Army would never operate the missile it was building. With the Jupiter pro-

A Jupiter IRBM undergoes preflight inspection at Cape Canaveral.

A Thor IRBM is readied for a test flight at Vandenberg AFB.

gram perilously close to being canceled, Medaris took his case to Washington. In a meeting with Secretary of the Army Brucker and Deputy Secretary of Defense Reuben Robertson, Medaris pointed out that in contrast to the Redstone and Jupiter's many successful test flights, the Air Force had yet to fly a single missile. Given the uncertain nature of the Air Force's relatively new ballistic missile program, Medaris told the group that if the United States wanted to develop an IRBM quickly, Jupiter was its only chance. The Army general must have presented a convincing case, because Jupiter survived. [11]

Medaris and the ABMA greeted DoD'S decision with a huge sigh of relief. It was, however, only a partial victory. Because Jupiter's range exceeded 200 miles, the Army would not be allowed to deploy the missile; that task still would fall to the Air Force. Despite the Secretary of Defense's ruling, Medaris and the ABMA nurtured hopes that in a head-to-head competition Jupiter would prove superior to Thor, which would in turn prompt Secretary Wilson to rescind the 200-mile restriction. To that end Medaris directed the ABMA to exert every effort to get Jupiter flying as quickly as possible. He hoped that a string of early successful test flights would sway DoD'S support over to the Jupiter program.

In the race to develop an IRBM, the Army initially had a sizable advantage because it was building on the Redstone program and was able to use 28 of those missiles as Jupiter A and C test platforms. Jupiter A testing, which focused on general design criteria, the guidance system, and propulsion thrust control, began in September 1955 and continued through June 1958. The Jupiter C was an elongated Redstone with clusters of scaled-down Sergeant rockets forming the second and third stages. This configuration was designed to test reentry vehicles and procedures, and in September 1956 a Jupiter C

On April 19,1958, the second test flight of a Thor IRBM ended in a thunderous explosion on the launch pad at Cape Canaveral.

test vehicle fired from the Army Missile Range at Cape Canaveral, Florida, logged a successful flight of 3,300 miles. The following May a prototype Jupiter soared 1,150 miles out over the Atlantic, an event the Army billed as the nation's first successful IRBM launch.[12]

While the Army prepared press releases touting Jupiter's success, it also pointed out that the Thor program had fallen several months behind schedule. Thor flight testing began inauspiciously in January 1957 with four successive failures. The Army used each miscue to argue that the Air Force was not qualified to be the sole custodian of the nation's ballistic missile program. The Air Force refuted the Army's charges, noting that unlike the Jupiter, which it dismissed as an upgraded Redstone, the Thor was a completely new missile and would take longer to develop. Finally, in October 1957, a Thor IRBM staged a successful 1,100-mile test flight, an event the Thor program manager said may have saved the Air Force missile program.[13]

The competition between the Thor and Jupiter programs reached fever pitch in the summer and fall of 1957 as Secretary of Defense Wilson prepared to select one missile to put into full production. In an attempt to influence the outcome, each side sought to discredit the other, and charges and counter-charges flew about in congressional debates and in the press. General Medaris led an intense public relations campaign against the Air Force missile, and one of his officers, Col. John C. Nickerson Jr., was court-martialed for leaking secret documents to investigative reporter Drew Pearson.[14] The Air Force responded in kind: it claimed the Army's flight-test data amounted to a "mish-mash of half-truths and outright fabrications," and that Jupiter would not be operational until several years after Thor.[15]

Effect of Sputnik

This interservice bickering was still raging when the Soviet Union launched Sputnik, the world's first man-made satellite, on October 4, 1957. Suddenly the debate over which missile to deploy became irrelevant: on October 10, 1957, President Eisenhower ordered DoD to build both Jupiter and Thor. The move was intended not only to boost production, but also to provide for a generous degree of redundancy between the missile systems. Should either the Thor or Jupiter unexpectedly fail, the United States could still deploy the other.

On the surface Eisenhower's decision appeared to be a victory for the Army. But that did not prove to be the case. The Army was unable to demonstrate that Jupiter was superior to the Air Force IRBM, and also was unable to convince DoD to allow it to operate missiles with ranges in excess of 200 miles. As a result, although ABMA was allowed to build the Jupiter, it did so as a subcontractor to the Air Force.

In retrospect, it is difficult to understand what the Army hoped to gain from its long and acrimonious defense of the Jupiter program. It appears that Medaris and the ABMA were gambling that Jupiter would win the IRBM competition, thus enabling the Army to mount a new challenge to the Air Force missile program, or perhaps, make a bid to run the entire military space program. When the Army failed to secure a clear victory in the IRBM competition, however, its fortunes in long-range missile development began to wane. Although the Army missile program did score several later successes, notably the launching of the nation's first satellite on January 3, 1958, its days of developing longrange missiles were rapidly drawing to a close. In December 1959 the Army agreed to transfer Wernher von Braun and the Development Operations Division, along with many of its test and development facilities, to the newly created National Aeronautics and Space Administration (NASA).[16]

Four Thor squadrons, each comprising 15 missiles, were deployed in England. Britain's decision to accept the missiles was the subject of fierce political debate in that country, and critics charged that their island nation was being turned into an American missile base. To assuage British fears, the missiles were manned by Royal Air Force (RAF) crews, but the warheads remained under American control. The first RAF Thor squadron went on operational alert in June 1959, and by April 1960 the remaining three had been activated.[b] Three Jupiter squadrons were deployed abroad: two in Italy and one in Turkey. The squadrons in Italy went on operational alert in July and August 1960, and the squadron in Turkey became operational in November 1961. The overseas deployment, however, was short-lived. Once the Atlas and Titan ICBMs went on operational alert in 1960, the IRBMs were quickly withdrawn from service. All of the missiles in England were taken off operational alert in August 1963, and Jupiter squadrons in Italy and Turkey were deactivated at the same time.

[b] Placing the missiles on operational alert was the culmination of the deployment process. It indicated that the missiles were in place and ready to fire.

Endnotes

1. In early 1951 the Ordnance Department increased the Redstone's payload from 1,500 to 6,900 pounds to accommodate an atomic warhead. The heavier warhead shortened the range to 150 miles, but the Army accepted the change as an expedient means to achieve a limited nuclear delivery capability. John W. Bullard, *History of the Redstone Missile System* (Redstone Arsenal, Huntsville, AL: U.S. Army Missile Command, 1965), p. 35.

2. James M. Grimwood and Frances Strowd, *History of the Jupiter Missile System* (Redstone Arsenal, Huntsville, AL: U.S. Army Missile Command: 1962), pp. 3–4.

3. "The Report to the President by the Technological Capabilities Panel of the Office of Defense Mobilization Science Advisory Committee," February 14, 1955, vol. II, pp. 63–5, Dwight David Eisenhower Library, Abilene, KS, White House Office, Office of the Staff Secretary, Subject Series, Alpha Subseries, box 16.

4. Jacob Neufeld, *The Development of Ballistic Missiles in the United States Air Force 1945–1960* (Washington, DC: Office of Air Force History, 1989), p. 145.

5. Stephen E. Ambrose, *Eisenhower, vol. II, The President* (New York: Simon and Schuster, 1984), p. 283.

6. Memo, Brig. Gen. W.C. Westmoreland, Secretary of the General Staff, subj: Organization for the Prosecution of the 1500-Mile Missile Program, 27 January 1956, pp. 1–2 in "Special Powers Delegated to the Commanding General of the Army Ballistic Missile Agency, 1 February 1956–31 March 1958," U.S. Army Missile Command Historical Office, Huntsville, AL, (hereafter MICOM). See also, Helen Brents Joiner and Elizabeth C. Joliff, *The Redstone Arsenal Complex in its Second Decade, 1950–1960* (Redstone Arsenal, Huntsville, AL: U.S. Army Missile Command, 1969), pp. 60–61.

7. Schriever, Memo for Record, subj: Interaction of TBMS with ICBM, 12 December 1954, p. 1, Air Force History Office, Bolling AFB, Washington, DC, Schriever papers, file 168.7171–73, folder "Memos, 1954."

8. Memo, Brig. Gen. Ben Funk to General E.W. Rawlings, Commander, Air Materiel Command, subj: BMO Summary Analysis, 23 September 1957, p. 1, in Ethel M. DeHaven, "Air Materiel Command Participation in the Air Force Ballistic Missile Program Through December 1957," vol. III, dot. No. 106, Air Force Historical Research Agency, Maxwell AFB, Montgomery AL, file K215.18. Note: The military, especially the Air Force, hoped to use its long–range ballistic missile as the foundation of the nation's space program. In a February 1957 speech to a gathering of eager aerospace engineers, Schriever told the audience that 90 percent of the developments of the ballistic missile program could be applied to space vehicles. "From a technological standpoint," Schriever said, "it was a normal transition from these ballistic missiles into satellites, moon rockets, and going to the planets." Robert Frank Futrell, *Ideas, Concepts, Doctrine: Basic Thinking in the United States Air Force*, vol. I (Maxwell, AL: Air University Press, 1989), p. 545.

9. Grimwood and Stroud, *History of the Jupiter Missile System*, pp. 55–60; *Chronology of the Ballistic Missile Organization 1945–1990* (Norton, AFB, CA: Ballistic Missile Organization, History Office, 1990), pp. 221–23.

10. Speech by Maj. Gen. John B. Medaris, "The Army Ordnance System," 11 March 1959, pp. 1–9, MICOM, file No. 870–5e, folder "Medaris, John B, Speeches"; "When is a Decision Not a Decision," *Air Force Magazine* (October 1957): pp. 32–36.

11. "Summary of the Jupiter Chronology, February 1956 to 16 November 1959," p. 4, in "The Jupiter Story," ABMA report to Secretary of the Army Brucker, 16 December 1959, file 870–5e, MICOM; "Effect of the Wilson 26 November 1957 Memorandum on Roles and Missions and Navy Withdrawal on Jupiter," pp. 4–6, in "The Jupiter Story."

12. Grimwood and Strowd, *History of the Jupiter Missile System*, pp. 81, 155–57.

13. Col. Richard K. Jacobson, Thor program manager, interview by John Lonnquest, 24 August 1991, Washington, DC.

14. "Spy Case Dropped, Nickerson Admits Leak on Missiles," *New York Times*, 26 June 1957, pp. 1, 14; "Army Suspends Nickerson from Rank for One Year," *New York Times*, 30 June 1957, pp. 1, 17.

15. "When is a Decision Not a Decision?," pp. 35–36.

16. Joiner and Joliff, *The Redstone Complex in its Second Decade, 1950–1960*, p. 124.

6

THE AIR DEFENSE DEBATE

Of all of the interservice battles over missions and roles in the post-war period, few were so intensive as the feud between the Army and Air Force over control of groundbased antiaircraft batteries.

At the end of World War II the Army insisted on maintaining a "point defense" antiaircraft capability to protect troop concentrations and vital installations on or near the battlefield. Because the Army dedicated its antiaircraft batteries to supporting combat troops, when the Army demobilized after the war, it placed the vast majority of antiaircraft artillery (AAA) units in reserve status under the control of the six continental armies. In the immediate post-war period the Army saw defending the continental United States from enemy air attack as a secondary mission.[1]

At the March 1948 interservice Key West Conference, the Joint Chiefs of Staff agreed that the Air Force would have primary responsibility for protecting the nation against air attack. At that time the Air Force was funding the Ground-to-Air Pilotless Aircraft (GAPA) surface-to-air missile system with the intent of fielding it around America's key military, industrial, and urban centers by the mid-1950s. However, there was no sense of urgency because the Soviets did not pose an immediate threat. Intelligence revealed that the Soviets did not have the planes or the bases from which to attack the United States. Furthermore, analysts believed that the Soviets were still years away from developing the atomic bomb. With defense dollars tight, the Air Force invested its money in developing strategic bombers and long-range air-breathing missiles. Thus, GAPA missile funding was cut and a radar net to detect an air attack remained only in the planning stages. Further cuts were made to fighter forces. Almost by default the Army was being given the role of providing point air defenses for America's strategic targets during a time of elevated tensions.[2]

This time of increased tension occurred during 1948–1950, and included events ranging from the Communist takeover of China and the Berlin crisis to the Soviet detonation of an atomic bomb. These tensions prompted a reevaluation of U.S. objectives and strategic plans. This reevaluation, documented in NSC 68, recommended boosting military expenditures. This policy paper, dated April 7, 1950, warned that the Soviets would have a fission bomb stockpile of 200 by 1954. Based on this critical fact, NSC 68 "estimated that the Russians could deliver between 75 and 125 atomic bombs on targets in the United States, unless defenses are greatly increased."[3]

As NSC 68 was being prepared, the Air Force exerted pressure on the Army to deploy antiaircraft artillery units around America's strategic sites. The first AAA battery arrived at Hanford, Washington, in March 1950. Soon the Army activated and deployed additional 90mm and 120mm guns (and their associated troops) around the outskirts of areas identified as having strategic value.[4]

The outbreak of the Korean War validated NSC 68 recommendations for increased spending to include improved air defenses, and the Department of Defense (DoD) consequently initiated steps for better coordi-

Opposite: A battery of Nike Ajax missiles in 1959. Note the heavy earthen berm that surrounds the refueling area at the extreme right of the picture.

Nike Ajax surface-to-air missiles on their launchers. The launchers were hinged at the base; here they are shown at maximum elevation.

nated air defenses to include antiaircraft missiles. [5] In July 1950, the Army Anti-Aircraft Artillery Command (ARAACOM) was established to assume command of all of the gun batteries being activated and to coordinate directly with the Air Force's Continental Air Command (CONAC).[a]

Meanwhile Western Electric, Bell Telephone Laboratories, Douglas Aircraft Company, and other subcontractors continued work on developing a missile capable of knocking down high-altitude bombers. Throughout the late 1940s dozens of Nike missile prototypes soared into the heavens over White Sands.

Accelerating the Nike Ajax Program

In October 1950, Secretary of Defense Charles E. Wilson named K.T. Keller of Chrysler Corporation to the newly established position as the DoD'S Director of Guided Missiles. Keller reviewed the progress of all antiaircraft missile programs in development and quickly concluded that the Army's Nike program was furthest along. In view of the 'ongoing Korean War, Keller recommended accelerating the program to build 1,000 production models by December 31, 1952, with a production capacity of 1,000 missiles per month thereafter.

In January 1951, Secretary Wilson approved Keller's recommendations despite the need for additional testing of the system. Testing continued, and on November 27, 1951, a Nike missile succeeded in destroying a drone QB-17 bomber flying over White Sands.[6]

In April 1952, the Army impressed visiting VIPs in a demonstration of the system's viability. Yet, the Army Ordnance Department already understood that

[a] CONAC was created in December 1948 as an efficiency measure to incorporate fighters of the Tactical Air Command (TAC) with those of the Air Defense Command (ADC). Both TAC and ADC would continue to exist as subordinate commands of CONAC. This structure lasted 2 years. During the Korean War, TAC and ADC were re-elevated to major command status. From December 1950 until September 1954, the Air Force's Air Defense Command held responsibility for the nation's air defense.

AKAACOM, formed in July 1950, was redesignated as U.S. Army Air Defense Command in 1957 and Army Air Defense Command (AKADCOM) in 1961. ARADCOM lasted until 1975. Through a 1950 agreement between the Army and Air Force Chiefs of Staff, ARAACOM came under operational control of the Air Force. This arrangement changed on September 1, 1954 with the formation of the Continental Air Defense Command (CONAD) under direct control of the Joint Chiefs of Staff. With the activation of CONAD, the Joint Chiefs usurped responsibility from the Air Force for the nation's air defense. ARAACOM, along with the Air Force's Air Defense Command (later Aerospace Defense Command) and a U.S. Navy component, became subordinate commands of CONAD.

The inclusion of the Canadian Air Defense Command within the air defense structure in 1957 forced a reorganization and the formation of a combined command that became known as the North American Air Defense Command (NORAD).

"Nike I" had limitations in discerning targets within closely packed aircraft formations. However, if the warhead could be made more lethal, the problem would not matter. During the following month, the Chief of Ordnance asked Bell Telephone Laboratories to investigate the feasibility of placing a nuclear warhead on the missile.

After consulting with Sandia Laboratories and Picatinny Arsenal, New Jersey, Bell returned with two options: (1) place an XW-9 "gun-type" warhead on the current missile, dubbed "Nike Ajax," or (2) design a wider missile with a greater range to carry the XW-7 warhead. The Army selected the second option with the condition that the follow-on missile could be deployed using the same ground infrastructure being designed for the Nike Ajax missile. In December 1952, the Army approved a development plan for the follow-on missile that would eventually be known as "Nike Hercules." Consequently, development of the warhead for Nike Hercules commenced at Sandia Laboratories in Albuquerque and at Los Alamos. Eventually they produced the W-31, a warhead with variable nuclear yields. The low-yield setting produced the explosive equivalent of two kilotons of TNT, the higher yield produced an explosion 20 times more powerful. In March 1953, this program received a 1A priority designation from the Joint Chiefs of Staff.[7]

While the Army received the go-ahead to develop a follow-on missile, Nike Ajax production models were undergoing evaluation at White Sands. With consistent testing successes, the Army began training its troops to deploy with the new weapon. Training was conducted at Fort Bliss, Texas, and at the newly established Red Canyon range in New Mexico. The first battalion began arriving at Fort Meade, Maryland, late in 1953, and the first Nike Ajax battery was put into operation in April 1954. The 34-foot long missile had a range of 25 to 30 miles, carried a conventional warhead, and could engage targets at altitudes of up to 70,000 feet. Soon after, Nike Ajax batteries began replacing gun units that had been stationed in and around cities such as Boston, Los Angeles, Chicago, Detroit, New York, and San Francisco.[8]

The Air Force welcomed Nike Ajax deployment as an enhancement of the point-defense mission that the Army provided for the nation's strategic targets. Although the Air Force had always expressed concern that a lack of coordination between the services could place Air Force aircraft within range of the Army's anti-aircraft forces, interservice cooperation between ARAACOM and the Air Defense Command (ADC) had resolved many of the coordination problems.[9] Besides, the Air Force believed that two strategic concepts, deterrence and defense, if fully supported, would prevent Soviet bombers from getting close to American cities.

Air Force Air Defense

The first concept, which took precedence in Air Force as well as national strategic doctrine, was deterrence through possession of overwhelming offensive capability. For example, in the event of a Soviet invasion of Western Europe, SAC bombers would destroy the bases from which Soviet bombers could lift off. In the Eisenhower administration this strategy served as a key component of a national strategic doctrine titled "the New Look."[10]

The second strategic concept was based on the engagement of incoming enemy bombers before they reached American territory. The best way to do that, the Air Force thought, was through the area defense concept, which engaged attacking enemy bombers far from their targets. Ironically, Air Force proponents of defense had to compete for limited defense dollars with proponents of deterrence within their own service.

With SAC receiving a greater share of the available resources, the Air Defense Command struggled to build up a radar network supported by a command and control organization. To compensate for early radar limitations, ADC recruited a volunteer civilian Ground Observer Corps to look out for radar-evading low-flying planes swooping down from the Arctic.[b] ADC planners also understood that advance warning had little value unless the defending commander could quickly distribute orders to interceptor squadrons and missile batteries to destroy the intruding force.[11]

In December 1951, the Air Force awarded the Massachusetts Institute of Technology (MIT) a contract to conduct a study on air defense that eventually became known as the "Lincoln Project." By mid-1952, MIT Lincoln Laboratory scientists proposed that a computer-driven air defense network was feasible, effectively cutting down evaluation and decision-making times. In April 1953, after considering an alternative computer-driven air defense scheme proposed by the Willow Run Research Center of the University of Michigan, ARDC selected MIT's Lincoln Laboratory to proceed on the "Lincoln Transition System," which eventually became known as the Semi-Automatic Ground Environment (SAGE) system.

Under SAGE, targets being tracked by remote radars would be displayed instantaneously at central SAGE command centers, along with the targets' speed, direction, and altitude. Using that information, air defense commanders could efficiently allocate their fighters to engage the enemy aircraft. Another defensive asset the Air Force intended to incorporate into the SAGE system was a long-range surface-to-air missile.[12]

As noted previously, in the immediate post-war years the Boeing Aircraft Company developed and launched GAPA missiles from sites in Utah and New Mexico. Then in 1949, Boeing received a contract and subsequently teamed up with the University of Michigan Aeronautical Research Center to design a defensive missile dubbed BOMARC for the Boeing and Michigan Aeronautical Research Center. When guided missile director K.T. Keller directed the Army to accelerate Nike production, he also raised the priority for development of this new Air Force surface-to-air missile.

BOMARC looked very much like a manned fighter aircraft. The missile was 45 feet long, had sharply swept wings, and was powered by two ramjet engines that gave it a top speed of Mach 4 and a range of 440 miles. Beginning in September 1952, prototype BOMARCs lifted off from Patrick Air Force Base into the skies over the Atlantic Ocean. However, not until February 1955 did the BOMARC perform in a manner that could be considered successful. Testing continued. On August 15, 1958, BOMARC engineers reached another milestone when a SAGE computer in New York directed a BOMARC A missile from Cape Canaveral, Florida to intercept a drone flying over the Atlantic. By this time the Air Force's BOMARC program was seen as a direct competitor to the Nike Hercules program.[13]

While testing continued on the BOMARC, development and production of the Army's Nike Hercules missile had proceeded rapidly. On September 10, 1956, the first Nike Hercules launch against a drone occurred over White Sands. Nike Hercules backers claimed that the missile provided not only point defense but also area defense because it had a range of 75 miles. Furthermore, the Army also realized that its command and control system needed to be automated, and contracted with The Martin Company (formerly the

---

[b] As the Air Force's radar net grew in size and sophistication in the mid-1950s, the Ground Observer Corps was disbanded.

An Air Force BOMARC surface-to-air missile being removed from test equipment prior to launch at Patrick AFB, Florida, in August 1958.

Martin Aircraft Company) to build a system to coordinate Nike engagements so that two batteries would not end up shooting at the same aircraft. The product of Martin's work, the "Missile Master" system, was considered by the Air Force to be duplicative and a challenge to SAGE. Secretary of Defense Charles E. Wilson's June 1956 directive placing SAGE in control of all air defense weapons, and directing SAGE to pass information on to Missile Master, only served to keep the feud going.[14]

Ceremony marking the conversion from Nike Ajax to Nike Hercules at Fort Barry in Sausalito, California. This site has been restored and is now maintained by the National Park Service.

The solid-fuel Nike Hercules, the second generation of the Nike series.

Competition Between BOMARC and Nike Hercules

As BOMARC development showed promise, Air Force officials began to openly criticize the Army's system. The New York Times featured a representative salvo in an article headlined "Air Force Calls Army Nike Unfit To Guard Nation." This piece, dated May 21, 1956, cited an Air Staff analysis that challenged the Nike testing program and questioned the missile's ability to intercept high-speed bombers. Responding to the Air Force criticism, Defense Secretary Wilson reminded Americans in a Newsweek article that "one hard solid fact emerges above them all: no matter what the Nike is or isn't, it's the only land-based operational anti-aircraft missile that the U.S. has."[15] From the Air Force perspective, this situation had to change.

In 1958 the Army began replacing some of its Nike Ajax batteries with the improved Nike Hercules system. The solid-fuel Hercules was a significant improvement over the Ajax. The new missile was 41 feet long, had a range of over 75 miles, could carry either a conventional or a nuclear warhead, and could engage enemy aircraft at altitudes up to 150,000 feet. By late 1958, with the Hercules being deployed around America's major cities, the debate between the Army and the Air Force over air defense intensified. In a television interview in late August, Senator Stuart Symington (D-Missouri) bemoaned the fact that the government had invested upwards of $7.5 billion in the Nike system.[c] Shortly thereafter, an article titled "Air Force Seeks to Abolish Chicago Nike Installations" appeared in the Chicago Sun-Times. In the article, Air Force officials declared the new Nike missile inadequate. Similar articles comparing the merits of Nike Hercules unfavorably with BOMARC appeared throughout the country. Noting that these articles always seemed to appear in cities slated to receive Nike Hercules batteries, Army Air Defense Commander Lt. Gen. Charles E. Hart asked the Secretary of Defense to order the Air Force to stop what appeared to be a well organized campaign to discredit the Nike Hercules system. In addition, the Army began its own public relations campaign dubbed "Project Truth."[16]

In November 1958, Secretary of Defense Neil H. McElroy seemingly resolved the feud by announcing the procurement and deployment of both the Nike and BOMARC systems, which he saw as complementary. However, both programs and their congressional allies realized that under such an arrangement neither side would receive the funding necessary to meet the Soviet threat. The Air Defense Command lowered its deployment goal from 40 to 31 BOMARC

[c] Symington has served as Secretary of the Air Force during the Truman administration.

squadrons, but most senior Air Force officials realized this new goal was unrealistic because of rapidly unfolding events.

With the Soviet launch of Sputnik in October 1957, many in Congress questioned funding defenses against "obsolete" bombers. Military officials contributed to the congressional dilemma by successfully arguing for increased appropriations to fund U.S. ballistic missile systems as the best hedge against Soviet attack. Also, unexpectedly high defensive system operating expenses, such as the cost of AT&T (American Telephone and Telegraph) land line hookups between radars and SAGE centers, stunned many in Congress.

Consequently, in 1959 House and Senate committees began scrutinizing two missile systems that many saw as duplicative. After their respective hearings, the Senate and House Armed Services Committees came to opposite conclusions. The Senate Committee recommended cutting funds for Nike Hercules and the House Committee recommended cutting off BOMARC. Ultimately, Congress supported the Master Air Defense (MAD) Plan developed by the Office of the Secretary of Defense. MAD retained both missile programs, but reduced SAGE construction and cut the number of BOMARC squadrons to 18.[17]

Although it may have been premature to do so, in an effort to obtain favorable publicity, on September 1, 1959, the Air Defense Command declared the BOMARC squadron at McGuire Air Force base operationally ready. According to Air Defense Command historian Richard McMullen, the announcement strained the concept of operational readiness. As of that date, of the 46th Air Defense Squadron's 60 missiles, only one was operational. While the Air Force and Boeing engineers struggled through the fall to get a second missile operational at McGuire, efforts continued to have a second BOMARC squadron declared operational at Suffolk County, New York, by year's end.[18]

The publicity effort failed to impress Congress. During House appropriation hearings for fiscal year (FY) 1961 held in January 1960, congressmen again bitterly attacked the Air Force program. DoD officials who spoke on behalf of the missile seemingly lacked conviction as they offered their testimony in the wake of a series of failed BOMARC B tests. Still, Air Force leadership remained committed to deploying all 18 BOMARC squadrons.

Nevertheless, this commitment was not yet firm. In an unusual move, the Air Force requested that the House hold hearings to consider revisions to the FY 61 budget. On March 24, 1960, Air Force Chief of Staff General Thomas D. White surprised many of his officers by recommending that BOMARC be deployed only to eight U.S. sites and two Canadian locations, and that SAGE improvements be canceled. White urged that the money would be better spent for ICBMs. White's recommendation stunned the Air Defense Command and prompted several congressmen to question the need for continuing any further funding for BOMARC.[19] In the wake of the House hearings, retired Army Brig. Gen. Thomas R. Phillips wrote an article for the *St. Louis Post-Dispatch*, published on April 10, which concluded that the BOMARC program and companion SAGE had been the "most costly waste of funds in the history of the Defense Department."[d]

---

[d] Estimated final costs were given for BOMARC and SAGE at about $2.2 billion and $1.6 billion, respectively.

BOMARC-3

However, an obituary for BOMARC would have been premature. The missile still had friends in the Senate, including Senator Henry Jackson (D-Washington). Three days after the Phillips article was published, the Air Force finally staged its first successful BOMARC B launch. Another successful test on May 17 allowed General White to approach the Senate Appropriations subcommittee with a willingness to support a limited BOMARC deployment. The Senate restored the funding to build and equip 10 sites (including 2 in Canada), and even added $75 million for 2 additional sites in the northwest. The additional sites were deleted when the conference committee met in July, but work would continue to deploy BOMARCs at the eight U.S. sites. Some of these sites remained operational until 1972.[20]

The apparent victor in this interservice missile program showdown was the Army's Nike Hercules. Because the Army deployed Nike Hercules ahead of BOMARC, the idea of scrapping a deployed system in favor of an untested system of questioned reliability was unacceptable to many in Congress. In addition, there is little doubt that the Army decision at this time to incorporate National Guard units into the ARADCOM infrastructure also pleased many members of Congress. By 1963, phaseout of Nike Ajax had been nearly completed and ARAD-COM boasted of some 134 Nike Hercules batteries in service. However, like BOMARC, most of these batteries would be deactivated by the early 1970s.

Endnotes

1. Kenneth Schaffel, *The Emerging Shield: The Air Force and the Evolution of Continental Air Defense 1945–1960* (Washington, DC: Office of Air Force History, 1991), pp. 116–17.

2. Ibid., See also Richard F. McMullen, *Interceptor Missiles in Air Defense, 1944–1964*, ADC Historical Study 30, (1965), available on microfilm, file K410.011–30, at the Air Force History Office, Bolling Air Force Base, Washington, DC (hereafter AFHO) and in hard copy at the Air Force Historical Research Agency, Maxwell Air Force Base, Montgomery, AL (hereafter AFHRA).

3. "Summary of a report of April 7, 1950 concerning a reexamination of United States Objectives and Strategic Plans" (NSC 68), Dwight D. Eisenhower Papers, DDE Library, Abilene, KS.

4. Lt. Col. Steve Moeller, USA, "Vigilant and Invincible: The Army's Role in Continental Air Defense" (Master's thesis: Ohio State University, 19921, p. 25.

5. Ibid., pp. 11–12, 15–16; Schaffel, pp. 279–83.

6. Mary T. Cagle, *Development, Production, and Deployment of the Nike Ajax Guided Missile System: 1945–1959* (Redstone Arsenal, Huntsville, AL: Army Rocket and Guided Missile Agency, 1959), pp. 110, 125–27.

7. Mary T. Cagle, *History of the Nike Hercules Weapon System* (Redstone Arsenal, Huntsville, AL: U.S. Army Missile Command, 19731, pp. 35–37; Mark Morgan, *Nike Quick Look III* (republished as *Rings of Steel*, Hole in the Head Press), *BOMARC/AF Talos* (Ft. Worth, TX: AEROMK, 1990), p, 152.

8. Moeller, pp. 47–48; Morgan, see listings for named cities.

9. Schaffel, pp. 135–36, 188.

10. John Lewis Gaddis, *Strategies of Containment: A Critical Appraisal of Postwar American National Security Policy* (New York: Oxford University Press, 1982), pp. 148–52.

11. See Denys Volan's *The History of The Ground Observer Corps*, ADC Historical Study 36 (1968); and Richard F. McMullen's *The Birth of SAGE*, 1951–1958, ADC Historical Study 33, (1965). Both are available on microfilm at AFHO and in hard copy at AFHRA.

12. Schaffel, pp. 197–209.

13. Ibid., pp. 215–38; Morgan, pp. 157–62. See also Richard F. McMullen's *Interceptor Missiles in Air Defense*, ADC Historical Study 30 (1965).

14. Cagle, *Hercules*, p, 97; Schaffel, pp. 206–7.

15. Cagle, *Hercules*, p. 145n.

16. Ibid., *Hercules*, pp. 146–48, discusses the controversy. File 228.10 HRC 471.94 at the Center for Military History provides an indexed folder of clippings containing articles deriding the Army Nike system.

17. McMullen, *Interceptor Missiles*, pp. 70–73.

18. Ibid., pp. 83–84.

19. Ibid., pp. 86–92.

20. Ibid., pp. 91–94; Morgan, pp. 168–77.

Unloading an Atlas

7

BUILDING MISSILES, 1954–1966

The ICBM program that Trevor Gardner and Bernard Schriever set in motion in 1954 grew at an astounding rate over the next 12 years. After accelerating the Atlas program in May 1954, the Air Force launched two other ICBM programs before the end of the decade. In April 1955 the Western Development Division (WDD) began work on the Titan, a large two-stage liquid-fuel ICBM, and in February 1958 it began developing the revolutionary Minuteman—the nation's first solid-fuel ICBM. These new weapons systems not only demonstrated the growing sophistication of American missile technology, they also reflected the

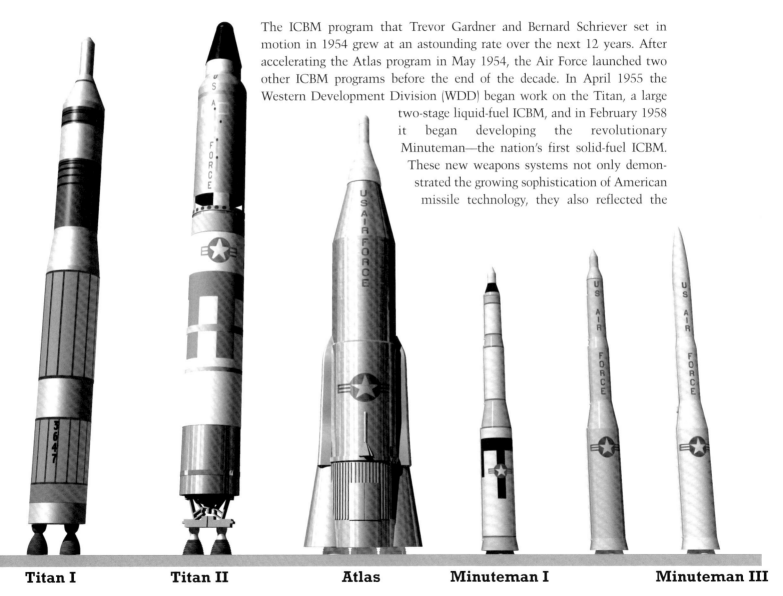

Titan I   **Titan II**   **Atlas**   **Minuteman I**   **Minuteman III**

Minuteman II

deadly seriousness of the arms race between the United States and Soviet Union.

As the United States' ICBM program grew, the military kept a wary eye on events in the Soviet Union. Throughout the 1950s American intelligence had little success collecting reliable information on the Soviet missile program, and its capabilities remained a troubling mystery.[1] In 1952, German scientists repatriated from the Soviet Union told American intelligence personnel that the Soviets were working hard to develop a long-range ballistic missile. Soon after that the Central Intelligence Agency (CIA) began monitoring Soviet ballistic missile tests from a radar station in Turkey. Using the information provided by the Germans, coupled with the CIA's observation of Soviet missile tests, the United States estimated that the Soviets would be able to field a ballistic missile with a range of 2,300 miles between 1955 and 1957.[2]

Sputnik and the Missile Gap

The Air Force and CIA were well aware that the Soviets were rushing to develop a longrange ballistic missile. However, Congress and the American public, secure in their perception of American technological supremacy, were shocked when the Soviet Union placed the world's first artificial satellite, Sputnik I, into orbit in October 1957. As Sputnik whirled overhead, Congress demanded to know why the Soviet Union, a nation widely regarded as technologically backward, could have surged ahead of the United States in missile development. Suddenly the ICBM program was thrust into the national spotlight and became the focus of a furious political debate over the effectiveness of the Eisenhower administration's defense policy. The administration's critics charged that the President's efforts to trim defense spending and balance the budget had compromised national security and created the so-called "missile gap."[3]

Those claiming that a missile gap existed argued that Sputnik, coupled with the Soviet Union's August 1957 pronouncement that it had successfully tested an ICBM, convincingly demonstrated that the Soviet missile program was years ahead of the U.S. program. These critics speculated that the Soviets would have operational IRBMs and ICBMs years before the United States, thus creating a missile gap that would tilt the strategic balance of power heavily in the Soviets' favor. That situation, the critics charged, would be catastrophic. In one missile gap scenario, appropriately called "nuclear blackmail," analysts speculated that a surprise attack by Soviet ICBMs could destroy all of SAC's bombers on the ground. Shorn of its nuclear retaliatory capability, the United States would be vulnerable to Soviet extortion.

The missile gap was front-page news across the country. The Air Force, the aircraft industry, and Congress all attempted to exploit it toward their own ends. The Air Force used the missile gap as justification for expanding its strategic arsenal; the missile manufacturers used it to bolster sales; and the Democrats seized upon it as a powerful issue for the upcoming 1960 presidential elections. In November 1958 Senator John F. Kennedy (D-Massachusetts) charged that the missile gap was caused by the Eisenhower administration placing fiscal policy ahead of national security. As a result, he said, the nation faced "a peril more deadly than any wartime danger we have ever known."[4]

President Eisenhower refused to succumb to the clamor for a radical overhaul of the ICBM program. Based on photographs taken during U-2 reconnaissance flights over the Soviet Union, which began in June 1956, the President was certain that there was no missile gap. Because the U-2 photographs were top secret, however, Eisenhower could not use them to justify his seemingly conservative missile development policy. Rather than restructure the missile-development program that had made such great strides over the pre-

ceding three years, the administration made several prudent mid-course corrections. In addition to his previously mentioned decision to build both the Thor and Jupiter IRBMs, the President also increased the number of Atlas squadrons from four to nine, blocked the cancellation of the forthcoming Titan II ICBM program, accelerated the Navy's Polaris submarine-launched ballistic missile (SLBM) program, and authorized the Air Force to develop the solid-fuel Minuteman.

The severity of the missile gap remained a subject of widespread rumor and speculation until the 1960 presidential election, and it was no coincidence that the issue disappeared soon after the Democrats took control of the White House. In reality the missile gap never existed: in August 1960 the first U.S. reconnaissance satellite revealed that the vaunted Soviet ICBM program consisted of four missiles then undergoing testing. In February 1961 Secretary of Defense McNamara created a political firestorm when, at a press briefing, he admitted that there was no missile gap. Although the administration vainly tried to put

a positive slant on McNamara's remarks, the *New York Times* observed that "'the missile gap' like the 'bomber gap' before it is now being consigned to the limbo of synthetic issues, where it always belonged."[5]

It is important to note, however, that long before Sputnik and the missile gap became a national obsession, the Air Force had been pushing its ICBM program forward at a breakneck pace. Based on the recommendations of the Teapot Committee, in May 1954 the Air Force accelerated the Atlas program and modified the design to incorporate the latest technology. The Air Force, Convair, and Ramo-Wooldridge overhauled the system specifications and in January 1955 formulated a new design and modified development schedule. From there, both figuratively and literally, the program took off.

Atlas ICBM

Nowhere was the explosive growth of the ICBM program more evident than at Convair. In March 1953 Convair had ten people assigned to the missile program, but just seven years later Convair Astronautics (the company had been acquired and made a division of General Dynamics) had 12,000 workers building Atlas missiles at its new two million square foot facility at Kearney Mesa outside San Diego.[6] Reflecting the truly national scope of the Atlas program, Convair employed 30 major subcontractors, 500 lesser contractors, and 5,000 suppliers scattered across 32 states.[7]

Standing on the launch pad the Atlas was 82 feet tall and weighed 267,000 pounds when fueled. Depending on the model and payload, the missile had a range of 6,400 to 9,400 miles. It was armed with a l-megaton thermonuclear warhead and was guided to its target by either a radio-inertial or all-inertial guidance system accurate to within 1.5 miles. Atlas was powered by two large booster engines and a smaller sustainer engine that worked together to form what Convair called a "stage-and-a-half" propulsion system. It was an innovative compromise to a difficult problem. Optimally, the Convair engineers would have equipped Atlas with a two- or three-stage propulsion system. The benefit of that arrangement would have been that as each stage burned out and the engine and fuel tanks dropped away, the missile would have become progressively smaller and lighter. The problem was that when WDD and its contractors reconfigured Atlas in 1954, they did not know if it would be possible to start a rocket engine in the vacuum of space.

Unwilling to take the risk of building a multistage missile that might later prove unworkable, Convair built the Atlas around its unique stage-and-a-half propulsion system. In this configuration, the three largest engines, the two boosters and the smaller sustainer engine, were ignited at liftoff. At the end of the first stage the two boosters fell away, but the huge first-stage fuel tanks that constituted 80 percent of the missile's mass, and any unspent fuel they contained, remained attached to the missile. To compensate for the additional weight, Convair reduced the weight of the fuselage by discarding the rigid internal framework traditionally used in missiles and aircraft. Instead, the missile derived its structural rigidity from its pressurized, integral fuel tanks.

Atlas flight testing began at Cape Canaveral in June 1957. After several spectacular failures, in November 1958, an Atlas logged a successful test flight of 6,350 miles. To provide the United States with an interim or emergency ICBM capability, in August 1959 the Air Force rushed three missiles, operated largely by con-

---

[a] The normal atmospheric pressure at sea level is 15 psi. Overpressure is an additional, transient pressure created by the shock or blast wave following a powerful explosion. Buildings collapse at 6 psi overpressure. Humans can withstand up to 30 psi overpressure, but a level over 5 psi can rupture eardrums and cause internal hemorrhaging.

Clockwise from lower left, three different Atlas launch configurations: Atlas D, Atlas E, and Atlas F.

tractor personnel and mounted on unprotected launch pads, into service at Vandenberg Air Force Base (AFB), California.

The following September, the first operational Atlas squadron equipped with six Atlas D missiles based in above-ground launchers, went on operational alert at F.E. Warren AFB, Wyoming. By the end of 1962, SAC had deployed eleven more squadrons. Each of the three missile variants, the Atlas D, E, and F series, were based in progressively more secure launchers. For example, the three Atlas D squadrons, two near F.E. Warren AFB, Wyoming and one at Offutt AFB, Nebraska, were based in above-ground launchers that provided blast protection against overpressures of only five pounds-per-square-inch (psi)."[a]

In comparison the Atlas E squadrons at Fairchild AFB, Washington; Forbes AFB, Kansas; and F.E. Warren were also deployed horizontally, but the majority of the launcher was buried underground. These launchers were designed to withstand overpressures of 25 psi. The six Atlas F squadrons based near Shilling AFB, Kansas; Lincoln AFB, Nebraska; Altus AFB, Oklahoma; Dyess AFB, Texas; Walker AFB, New Mexico; and Plattsburgh AFB, New York were the first ICBMs to be stored vertically in underground silos. Built of heavily-reinforced concrete, the huge silos were designed to protect the missiles from overpressures of up to 100 psi.

Titan ICBM

The Air Force's next ICBM, the liquid-fuel Titan I (SM-68) was an outgrowth of studies commissioned in the summer of 1954 to accelerate and reorient the Atlas program. From the outset the Air Force acknowledged that Atlas had obvious limitations, notably its untested airframe and stage-and-a-half propulsion system, but decided to ignore these shortcomings because it thought Atlas could be deployed before any other comparable system. To avoid becoming overly reliant on the untried Atlas, however, in January 1955 WDD requested permission to develop a new two-stage ICBM it called Titan. The Air Force approved the project in April 1955, and the following October WDD awarded the Titan I contract to the Glenn L. Martin Aircraft Company of Baltimore, Maryland.

An important consideration in the Air Force's decision to build a second ICBM was its desire to disperse the nation's ICBM production capability away from the East and West Coasts. The Air Force worried that Convair's facilities in Southern California were within range of Soviet bombers and Soviet submarine-launched IRBMs, and Secretary of the Air Force Harold Talbott insisted that the Titan facilities be built in the central United States.[8] Martin decided to build its plant outside Denver, Colorado, on a sprawling 4,500-acre tract that would house production and test facilities.[9]

Raised from its underground silo, a Titan I ICBM stands ready for inspection at the Operational System Test Facility at Vandenberg AFB.

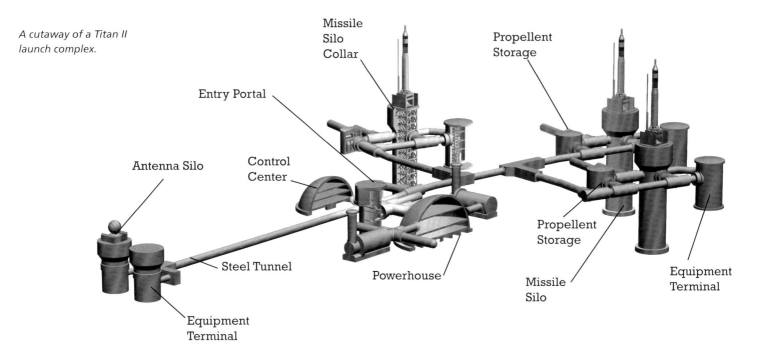

A cutaway of a Titan II launch complex.

Missile Silo Collar

Propellent Storage

Entry Portal

Antenna Silo

Control Center

Propellent Storage

Steel Tunnel

Powerhouse

Missile Silo

Equipment Terminal

Equipment Terminal

Titan I was a larger, more powerful missile than the Atlas. The Titan I was 98 feet tall and its rigid, self-supporting airframe housed a powerful two-stage propulsion system. Unlike Atlas' stage-and-a-half propulsion system, when Titan's first and second stages were exhausted the engines and fuel tanks for those sections dropped off, thereby decreasing the weight and mass of the vehicle. This made the missile more efficient, which translated into a longer range and heavier payload capacity.[10] Powered by two large liquid-fuel Aerojet engines, Titan I had a range of 6,350 miles and could carry a payload of 3,825 pounds, more than twice the capacity of Atlas. Titan I also incorporated other desirable features. From the outset the Air Force decided to base the missiles in hardened underground silos that would protect them against overpressures of up to 100 psi. The Titan's larger airframe and two-stage propulsion system also made the missile more adaptable than Atlas, in terms of both range and payload.[11]

Work on the Titan program began at the end of 1955 and construction of the Martin plant began soon thereafter. By September 1958 the Martin Company and its associate contractors had 16,000 people at work on the program. Flight tests began in early 1959, and a year later a Titan I fired from the Air Force Missile Test Center (AFMTC) at Cape Canaveral staged a successful 5,000-mile flight. While the missiles were being built, the Army Corps of Engineers was

overseeing the construction of the huge Titan I launch facilities, the largest and most expensive underground launch complexes ever built.

These three-missile launch complexes resembled futuristic underground cities. Heavily hardened to survive a nuclear attack, the missile silos, control center, powerhouse, and various other support facilities were connected by almost half a mile of steel tunnel, all buried more than 40 feet underground.

The missiles could not be launched from within their silos. After a missile was fueled, an elevator carried it to the mouth of the silo, and then it was fired.

In this 1960 photograph, work on the main tunnel of the Titan I launch complex at Vandenberg AFB nears completion. Forty feet beneath the surface, the tunnel connected the control center to the missile silos.

The Air Force activated its first Titan I squadron at Lowry AFB, Colorado, in April 1960. By 1962, the service deployed five more Titan I squadrons: another at Lowry AFB, Colorado; and one each at Mountain Home AFB, Idaho; Beale AFB, California; Larson AFB, Washington; and Ellsworth AFB, South Dakota.

Minuteman ICBM

From the underground launch control center in the right of the picture, a two-person Minuteman crew controls a flight of ten missiles, each based at a remote launch facility. The launch facilities were spaced at least 3 miles apart.

As the Atlas and Titan missile programs took shape during the late 1950s the Air Force began to realize that its first generation of liquid-fuel ICBMs was of limited use. Owing to the hazards inherent in their caustic, volatile liquid-fuel systems and vulnerability of their radio-inertial guidance systems, the early ICBMs were dangerous to operate, expensive to maintain, and difficult to deploy. The Atlas and Titan silos, for example, had to be oversized to accommodate the complicated propellant-loading system, which included storage tanks, piping, and pumps to handle the hundreds of thousands of pounds of gaseous helium, liquid oxygen, and RP-1, a highly refined form of kerosene.[12] It took fifteen minutes to pump 249,000 pounds of propellant aboard the "quick firing" Atlas F. It was dangerous work. Four Atlas silos were destroyed when propellant-loading exercises went awry. Two Titan I silos also met a similar fate.[b]

The problems inherent in liquid-fuel missiles came as no surprise to the Air Force. The WDD and Ramo-Wooldridge had considered using solid-fuel engines for Atlas in 1954, but believed that the large solid-fuel motors would be difficult to cast, would not produce sufficient thrust, and would be difficult to control.[13] The Air Force, however, remained interested in solid-fuel engines. Under the direction of Col. Edward Hall, the WDD's chief of propulsion and later Thor program manager, the Air Force funded research in solid fuels throughout the mid-1950s. By March 1957, Hall and his researchers were convinced that solid fuels could power a new generation of ICBMs.

In the summer of 1957 Hall had a major falling out with the WDD's commanding officer, General Schriever. Temporarily without a job, Hall was given a desk in an unused office and told to study solid-fuel missiles. Hall did much more than study the problem. Working alone, over the course of several months, he designed a family of solid fuel missiles of tactical, intermediate, and intercontinental range. Hall called his ICBM the Minuteman, and proposed that thousands of the relatively small, low-maintenance missiles could be based in unmanned underground silos and fired at a moment's notice.[14]

Initially WDD, which became the Air Force Ballistic Missile Division (AFBMD) on June 1, 1957, had little interest in Minuteman; it was preoccupied with other projects. The Navy, however, had been keeping close tabs on Hall's work, and it incorporated the Air Force's research into its Polaris program. Based in part on Hall's research, the Navy program improved to such an extent that in the fall of 1957 the Navy proposed developing a ground-based version of Polaris for use by the Air Force. Alarmed by the possibility of the Navy's encroachment, the AFBMD promptly began to reconsider the merits of a solid-fuel ICBM.[15]

In February 1958 Schriever flew Hall to Washington to brief the Secretary of Defense, the Secretary of the Air Force, and SAC commander General Curtis LeMay on the Minuteman concept. In comparison to the Atlas and Titan, Minuteman was a diminutive missile, 53 feet tall and weighing only 65,000 pounds. Hall's plan called for a three-stage missile capable of delivering a 1- to 5-megaton warhead at ranges between 1,500 and 6,500 miles. The missiles would be based in widely dispersed unmanned silos, hardened to withstand 200 psi overpressure. The low-maintenance missiles would need minimal ground support equipment, limited field maintenance, and a single two-person launch control facility for every ten missiles. The solid-fuel engines would give Minuteman a virtually instantaneous launch capability, and because the missiles were to be launched from inside their silos, they would be protected until the moment they took flight. Hall emphatically told his audience that solid-fuel technology was ready now, and he estimated that a force of 1,600 Minuteman missiles could be in place by 1965.[16]

Both the Air Force and DoD leadership were captivated by Hall's presentation. They agreed that the present ICBM program was "less than that achievable and desirable," and within 24 hours of Hall's briefing the Air Force authorized the AFBMD to begin limited R&D on the Minuteman. [17] In July 1958 the AFBMD began component development and selecting contractors. In September 1959 the AFBMD selected Boeing Airplane Company of Seattle, Washington, as the Minuteman assembly and test contractor. Boeing later built the missiles at a huge new plant constructed by the Army Corps of Engineers at Hill AFB, Utah.

[b]Fortunately, the accidents did not result in any fatalities because the missile crews, stationed in their underground launch control centers, were protected from the explosions by specially reinforced accessways and huge steel blast doors designed to contain the explosions.

This series of photographs, taken at Cape Canaveral in 1961, follows the flight of a Minuteman I ICBM from ignition in the silo through liftoff.

Once the Air Force selected its contractors, the Minuteman program took shape rapidly. In February 1961 the first Minuteman test flight, an "all up" test that included all three stages and the guidance system, was a complete success. The Air Force placed the first flight of 10 Minuteman missiles on operational alert in October 1962, just in time for the Cuban Missile Crisis. In the years that followed, hundreds more Minuteman missiles were deployed, and by November 1966 SAC's Minuteman I force stood at 800 missiles.

Endnotes

1. John Prados, *The Soviet Estimate: U.S. Intelligence and Soviet Strategic Forces* (Princeton, NJ: Princeton University Press, 1986), p. 58.

2. Walter McDougall,... *the Heavens and the Earth: A Political History of the Space Age* (New York: Basic Books, 1986), p. 117.

3. This was not the first time the Air Force discovered a weapons "gap." In 1955 the Air Force estimated that Soviet bomber production far exceeded that of the United States and warned that unless the situation was rectified soon, by the early 1960s the Soviets would have more bombers than the United States, thus resulting in a "bomber gap." In 1957 the bomber gap disappeared when U-2 photographs revealed that the Air Force had grossly overestimated Soviet production capability. Instead of a fleet of hundreds of jet bombers, the Soviets had built only 50 and demonstrated little inclination to build more. Prados, *The Soviet Estimate*, pp. 41-47.

4. John F. Kennedy and Alan Nevins, ed., *The Strategy of Peace* (New York: Harper & Brothers, 1960), p. 41.

5. *The New York Times*, editorial, 27 November 1961.

6. Gladwin Hill, "Factory Opened for Atlas ICBM," *New York Times*, p. 6, 12 July 1958; James R. Dempsey, former President of Convair Astronautics, interview by John Lonnquest, 26 August 1991, North Arlington, VA.

7. "Wide Industrial Base Supports Atlas," *Missiles and Rockets* (22 September 1958): p. 25.

8. U.S. Congress, House Subcommittee of the Committee on Appropriations, *Hearings, Department of Defense Appropriations for 1960*, 86th Cong., 1st sess. (Washington, DC: GPO, 1959), p. 616.

9. Alfred Rockefeller, Jr., "History of Titan 1954–1959," pp. 9-10, Ballistic Missile Organization, History Office, Norton AFB, CA, box L-l.

10. "Relationship of Atlas/Titan Program," n. d., pp. 1-2, Air Force History Office, Bolling AFB, Washington, DC, Schriever papers, folder "Mahon Briefing," file K168.7171-149.

11. Rockefeller, "History of Titan," pp. 14-15.

12. U.S. Army Corps of Engineers, Ballistic Missile Construction Office, "History of the Propellant Systems Division, August 1960-April 1962," pp. 9-10, Research Collection, Office of History, Headquarters, U.S. Army Corps of Engineers, Alexandria, VA, Military Files XVII-3-2.

13. Roy Neal, *Ace in the Hole* (Garden City, NJ: Doubleday, 1962), p. 68.

14. Col. Edward Hall, USAF (ret.), telephone interview by John Lonnquest, 31 August 1991; Col. Francis J. Hale, USAF (ret.), interview by John Lonnquest, 5 November 1991, Raleigh, NC.

15. Maj. Gen. Osmand J. Ritland, interview by Lt. Col. Lynn R. Officer, Solona Beach, CA, March 18-21, 1974.

16. Memorandum for Record, Col. Ray E. Soper, Chief, Ballistic Missile Division, Office of the Chief of Staff for Guided Missiles, subj: Secretary of Defense Review of Air Force Ballistic Missile Proposals, 10 February 1958, p. 1, in DeHaven, *Aerospace: The Evolution of USAF Acquisition Policy, 1945–1961*, dot. no. 212.

17. Ibid, p. 2.

8

ICBM DEPLOYMENT

After developing the Atlas, Titan, and Minuteman ICBMs, the Air Force's next task was determining how many to buy, where to deploy them, and what type of launch facilities to build. These decisions had to be made quickly, because building the missiles and their launch and support facilities would take several years. However, these decisions also had to be made judiciously because the Air Force realized that the decisions it made in the late 1950s and early 1960s would determine the size and shape of the nation's ICBM force for decades to come.

The size of the nation's ICBM force expanded considerably during the late 1950s and early 1960s. In late 1955 the Air Force hoped to have a force of 120 Atlas missiles in place by 1960, and in late 1956 President Eisenhower thought "that 150 well-targeted missiles might be enough" to deter a Soviet first strike.[1]

By early 1958, however, the threat of the Soviet missile program, crystallized in the furor over Sputnik and the debate over the missile gap, prompted the United States to deploy more ICBMs. In 1957 the influential Gaither Report recommended a force of 600 ICBMS, and by 1958 the Air Force proposed deploying 1,600 Minuteman missiles.[2] The commander of SAC, General Curtis LeMay, wanted even more; at one point he proposed that his command deploy 10,000 of the solid-fuel missiles. As it turned out the Minuteman proved to be so effective that a force of that size was unnecessary. In the early 1960s Secretary of Defense Robert McNamara fixed the nation's land-based ICBM force at 1,000 Minuteman missiles plus the 54 Titan IIs then under construction. The force remained that size for the next 25 years.

Site Selection

The Air Force determined where to locate the missile launch facilities based on missile range and the distance to the target.[3] For example, the Air Force originally decided to deploy the first operational Minuteman squadron at Vandenberg AFB, on the California coast northwest of Los Angeles. Shortly thereafter the Air Force discovered a flaw in the first stage of the Minuteman IA, the first production model, that reduced its range from 6,300 to 4,300 miles. The defective nozzles promised to be a major setback because, for the missiles based at Vandenberg, a range of 4,300 miles was insufficient to carry them over the North Pole and strike targets in the central Soviet Union. However, rather than delay deployment by the six months to a year needed to redesign the first stage, the Air Force neatly resolved the problem by moving the first Minuteman wing from Vandenberg to Malmstrom AFB, Montana. The move had two advantages. First, since Malmstrom was 600 miles farther north, the move put the missiles that much closer to their targets in the Soviet Union. Malstrom's 3,500-foot elevation was also a plus because it made boosting the missiles into space easier.[4]

Opposite: An Atlas E missile towers above its launch facility. The underground launch operations building, marked by the two square metal ventilators, is in the foreground.

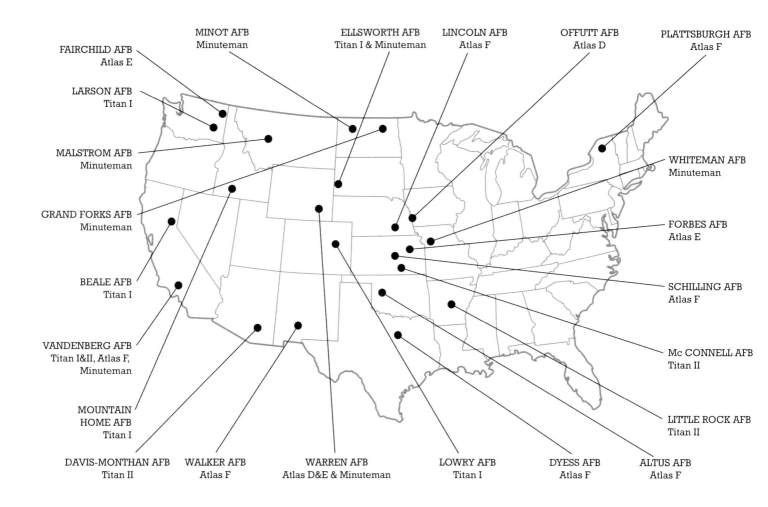

FAIRCHILD AFB
Atlas E

MINOT AFB
Minuteman

ELLSWORTH AFB
Titan I & Minuteman

LINCOLN AFB
Atlas F

OFFUTT AFB
Atlas D

PLATTSBURGH AFB
Atlas F

LARSON AFB
Titan I

MALSTROM AFB
Minuteman

WHITEMAN AFB
Minuteman

GRAND FORKS AFB
Minuteman

FORBES AFB
Atlas E

BEALE AFB
Titan I

SCHILLING AFB
Atlas F

VANDENBERG AFB
Titan I&II, Atlas F,
Minuteman

Mc CONNELL AFB
Titan II

MOUNTAIN
HOME AFB
Titan I

LITTLE ROCK AFB
Titan II

DAVIS-MONTHAN AFB
Titan II

WALKER AFB
Atlas F

WARREN AFB
Atlas D&E & Minuteman

LOWRY AFB
Titan I

DYESS AFB
Atlas F

ALTUS AFB
Atlas F

Other factors also affected ICBM site selection. Not only were the sites to be within the continental United States, at locations that would "provide the most effective coverage of enemy targets," they were also to be located far enough inland to be out of range of Soviet submarine-launched missiles. To save money, the Secretary of the Air Force ordered that wherever possible the launch facilities and support installations were to be placed on government installations, preferably positioned so they could derive support from a community of 50,000 or more people.

The launch sites themselves were to be spaced far enough apart to ensure that each constituted a separate target. At a minimum the sites were to be separated such that a 10-megaton burst would not destroy the neighboring facilities. The Air Force summarized its deployment strategy as fourfold: maximizing operational capability; minimizing the sites' vulnerability; minimizing the danger to the people of the United States and Canada; and making wise use of the taxpayers' money throughout the process.[5]

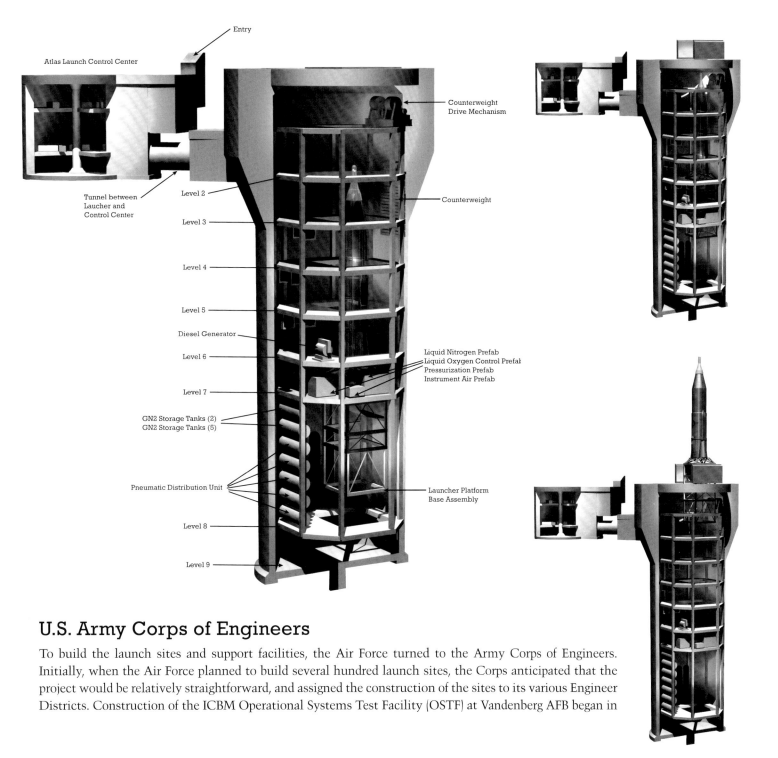

Atlas Launch Control Center

Entry

Counterweight Drive Mechanism

Tunnel between Laucher and Control Center

Level 2

Counterweight

Level 3

Level 4

Level 5

Diesel Generator

Level 6

Liquid Nitrogen Prefab
Liquid Oxygen Control Prefab
Pressurization Prefab
Instrument Air Prefab

Level 7

GN2 Storage Tanks (2)
GN2 Storage Tanks (5)

Pneumatic Distribution Unit

Launcher Platform Base Assembly

Level 8

Level 9

U.S. Army Corps of Engineers

To build the launch sites and support facilities, the Air Force turned to the Army Corps of Engineers. Initially, when the Air Force planned to build several hundred launch sites, the Corps anticipated that the project would be relatively straightforward, and assigned the construction of the sites to its various Engineer Districts. Construction of the ICBM Operational Systems Test Facility (OSTF) at Vandenberg AFB began in

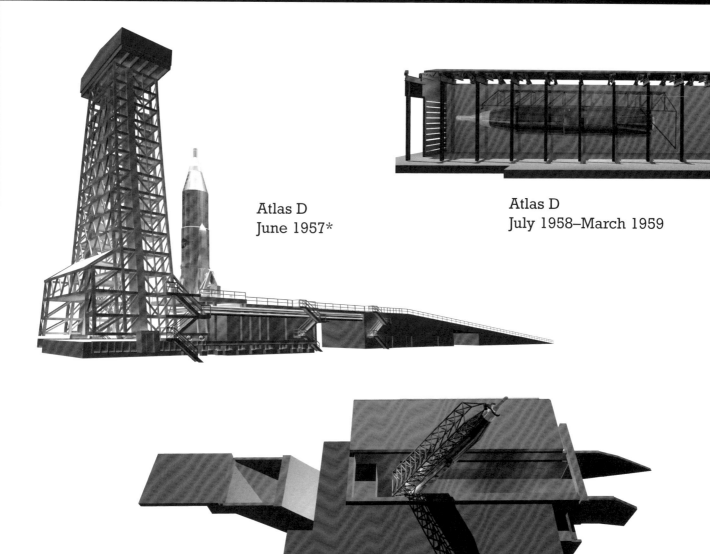

Atlas D
June 1957*

Atlas D
July 1958–March 1959

Atlas E
April 1959–December 1959

The evolution of ICBM launch facilities. The Air Force based the missiles in progressively more secure facilities, and beginning with the Titan II, the ICBMs could be launched from within their silos. Also, beginning with the Minuteman series, the missiles were based in remote, unmanned, and widely dispersed launch facilities.
*Dates refer to Contract Award Dates

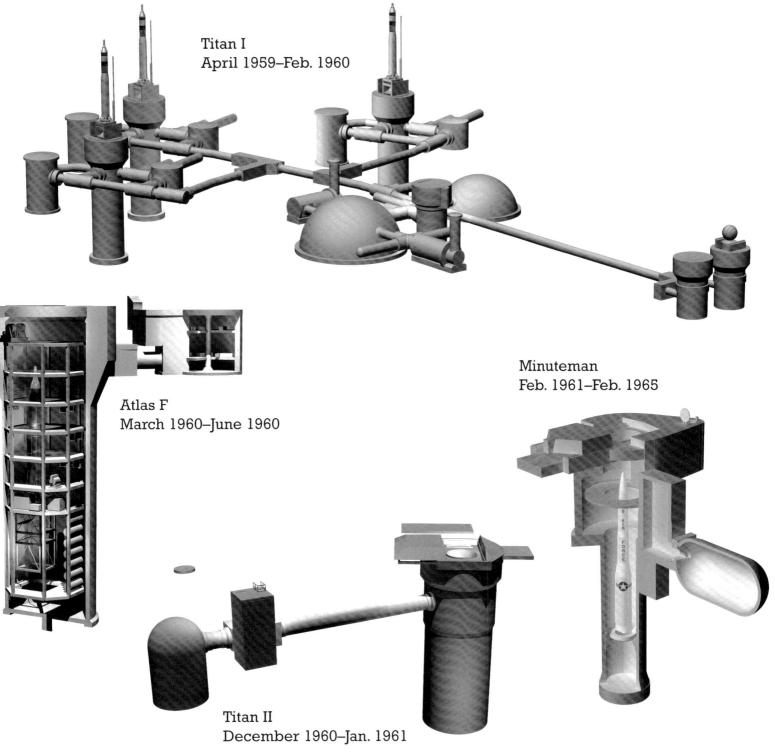

Titan I
April 1959–Feb. 1960

Atlas F
March 1960–June 1960

Minuteman
Feb. 1961–Feb. 1965

Titan II
December 1960–Jan. 1961

81

June 1957, and work on the first operational Atlas site at F.E. Warren AFB, Wyoming, began in July 1958.

The exigencies of the Cold War, however, spurred rapid growth of the ICBM program, and the scope of the Corps of Engineers' construction effort expanded with it. The Air Force increased the number of Atlas squadrons from four to twelve; built six squadrons each of the Titan Is and Titan IIs; and began planning to deploy 1,000 Minuteman missiles. To further complicate matters, whereas all of the early Atlas launchers were built at or near ground level, all subsequent launch facilities were hidden deep beneath the ground and hardened to withstand a nuclear attack. Also, President Eisenhower ordered that the entire ICBM program be accelerated. The net effect of the changes was that Army engineers had to build more launch facilities, of a progressively more difficult design, in less time.

To further complicate matters, the Air Force was developing the ICBMs using the "concept of concurrency," meaning that it was designing and testing the missiles at the same time the Army was building the launch facilities. Frequently, when the Air Force made a design change in the missile, the change forced the Corps of Engineers to alter the launch facilities. All too often that meant ripping out work and starting over. For the Army, keeping up with the frequent change orders was an expensive and nerve-wracking process. For example, as of April 1962 the Corps of Engineers had issued 2,676 contract modifications and change orders for the construction of the Atlas D, E, and F launch facilities. The cost of those changes was $96 million, a 40 percent increase over the base contract price.[6]

The expanded scope, complexity, and tighter schedule of the facility construction program soon began to tax the resources of the Corps districts, and it became apparent that a central coordinating body was necessary to oversee the entire project. In July 1959 the Chief of Engineers established a special branch, the Los Angeles Field Office (LAFO), to coordinate the nationwide effort. LAFO reported directly to the Chief of Engineers. To improve the Army's often-troubled relations with the Air Force, LAFO's offices were located within the Air Force Ballistic Missile Division's office complex near the Los Angeles airport.[7]

Although the creation of LAFO provided a greater degree of centralized coordination and control to the mammoth project, the changes were not enough. In 1960 construction was still badly snarled and Congress held hearings to investigate what the press had dubbed "the missile mess."

Work stoppages frequently delayed construction. These workers, members of the Cement and Masons Union, walked off the job because their employer would not pay travel time to the distant work sites.

Corps of Engineers Missile Construction Office

Confronted with a sea of unfavorable publicity, the Corps of Engineers moved quickly to create a new organization that would both defuse the criticism and manage the construction effort more efficiently. In August 1960 the Army established the Corps of Engineers Ballistic Missile Construction Office (CEBMCO), an independent organization under the Chief of Engineers, to supervise site construction. To further improve coordination between the Corps and the Air Force, an April 1961 agreement between the two services placed CEBMCO under the operational control of the Air Force Systems Command Ballistic Systems Division (BSD), the successor organization to the AFBMD.[8] CEBMCO remained under Air Force control until the Army disbanded the construction organization in 1967.

The goal in creating CEBMCO was to lend the construction program the uniformity of centralized control without constraining the engineers at the sites. To do that CEBMCO's commanding officer appointed weapon system directors for the Atlas F, Titan I, Titan II, and Minuteman facility construction programs. The weapon system managers monitored their programs through a network of CEBMCO area offices, one of which was located at each major site.[9] The area offices directly supervised construction. Although the Engineer Districts no longer built the launch facilities, under CEBMCO supervision they built missile test and training facilities, and also provided CEBMCO with help in real estate acquisition and administrative support.[10]

The growth of CEBMCO mirrored its expanded responsibilities. When established in August 1960 it had a staff of twenty-seven, but within six years grew to 3,000 people managing 22 projects spread over seventeen states.[11] CEBMCO's responsibilities encompassed the entire construction effort. Although CEBMCO did not design the launch facilities (which usually was the responsibility of the structures and assembly contractor), it reviewed the plans, solicited bids, evaluated the proposals, and awarded the contracts. CEBMCO then supervised construction, and after the launch facilities were completed, it stayed on the job as a member of the Air Force site activation task force, which turned the empty silos into operational missile bases.

Building the launch sites and support facilities was one of the largest military construction programs ever undertaken by the Corps. Over the course of approximately ten years, CEBMCO and its predecessor organizations built approximately 1,200 launch facilities, each consisting of multiple structures. The actual construction was performed by many of the nation's largest construction firms, including companies like Peter Kiewit and Sons, and Morrison-Knudsen. In some cases, strong local or regional firms formed partnerships to win the lucrative contracts. By 1962 construction costs totaled $2 billion, and in the years that followed CEBMCO spent several billion dollars more completing the Minuteman program.[12] By 1961 contractors had already moved 26 million cubic yards of earth and stone, poured more than 3 million cubic yards of concrete, and used 764,000 tons of steel. Another indication of the size of the program was the labor devoted to it: in early 1961, 21,300 people were laboring to build the missile facilities.

Building Launch Facilities

The construction work was exacting, frequently dangerous, and often performed under adverse conditions. In many cases, transporting construction materials to the remote building sites was difficult. Construction material for the Titan I sites at Mountain Home AFB, Idaho, for example, had to be brought in from either Seattle or Salt Lake City. Other problems arose when the building supplies reached the work site. To find adequate quantities of water, for example, CEBMCO had to drill deep wells. Harsh weather conditions were

(left) An Atlas F launch facility under construction at Walker AFB, New Mexico. In the foreground workers are installing concrete reinforcing bar in the launch control center (LCC). The silo is to the left of the LCC.

(bottom) An overhead view of an Atlas F silo under construction near Plattsburgh, New York. The launch control center is on the left. The steel crib that supported the missile and its ancillary equipment is nearing completion.

also a problem. During the summer the temperature in Idaho soared to 109°F, and in the winter it plunged to -22°F. One of the most serious problems caused by the subzero temperatures was getting concrete to cure properly; to keep construction moving, the contractors resorted to building heated enclosures around the forms.[13]

Conditions were little better building the Minuteman sites at Minot AFB, North Dakota. One hundred launch sites were spread over a sparsely populated area of 12,000 square miles. To reach the sites CEBMCO often had to build new roads or upgrade existing ones. Transporting the 6,000 workers and construction materials to the sites required a fleet of 1,100 vehicles. At times during the spring thaw the roads became impassable, and the only means of transportation was by helicopter.[14]

Construction within the silos was hazardous and demanding work. More than fifty men died in construction accidents, and many more were killed in traffic accidents around the work sites.[15] Despite generous pay in some of the more remote locations, such as Mountain Home, the contractors had difficulty finding skilled laborers. Keeping them working often was difficult too. Virtually all of the construction sites were struck with some type of labor unrest. In late 1960 a dispute over work assignments at the Atlas E sites at Forbes AFB, Kansas, between the hoisting engineers and electrical work-

(right) Workers from U. S. Steel's American Bridge Division put the finishing touches on the last of more than 100 silo liners it installed in Minuteman launch facilities around Malmstrom AFB, Montana.

ers resulted in a two-month work stoppage. To get things moving again, the Air Force asked the President of the AFL-CIO, George Meany, to intervene.[16] At other times construction was delayed by shortages of key materials, in part attributable to the 1959 nationwide steelworkers' strike.

Anti-nuclear activists occasionally disrupted construction too. At Davis Monthan AFB, Arizona, the Committee Against Ringing Tucson with Titans and the Committee for Non-Violent Action demonstrated against the construction of the Titan II sites. Most of the protests were peaceful, but on occasion CEBMCO turned trespassers over to Federal marshals for prosecution. A few protests resulted in injuries. In August 1959 a young Phi Beta Kappa from the University of Chicago was badly injured when he was run over by a truck while attempting to block access to an Atlas construction site at F.E. Warren AFB, Wyoming.

Despite the bad weather, shortages, labor problems, and protests, the missile site construction program raced forward. The launch facilities for the liquid-fuel Atlas and Titan I were the most difficult to build. The Atlas F silos, for example, were 174 feet deep and 55 feet in diameter. Construction began with an open cut excavation down to a depth of 60 feet, the level of the launch control center floor; from there the silo was mined to its final depth. During the mining operation the contractors supported the silo walls with steel beams, wire mesh lagging, and sprayed-on concrete. Within the silo workers then built a huge steel framework, equivalent in size to a fifteen-story building, to support the missile and all of its ancillary equipment. Building six Atlas F squadrons required moving 2,700,000 cubic yards of earth, pouring 565,000 cubic yards of concrete, and erecting 100,000 tons of steel.[17]

Compared to building the complex Atlas F launch facilities, construction of the Minuteman silos was much less challenging. The silos were smaller, only 80 feet high and 12 feet in diameter,

and contained neither the complicated propellant loading system nor the elevator that lifted the missile into firing position.

Most Minuteman silos were built using the same procedures. Construction crews excavated a circular cut down to a depth of 34 feet. From there, using either a clamshell bucket or a huge auger, the builders excavated a 15-foot diameter shaft down to 94 feet. After the shaft was dug, a 62-foot prefabricated steel silo liner, built of quarter-inch steel plate and ringed with concentric rings of reinforcing bar, was lowered into place. After the liner was aligned, concrete was pumped around it to form the external silo wall. When the silo was complete the underground launch equipment and support buildings were constructed, and the excavation was backfilled.

On average, a Minuteman silo, including an allowance for its associated launch control facility, required only 15 percent of the earth moving, 20 percent of the steel, and 15 percent of the concrete necessary to build an Atlas F silo. [18] Whereas the construction of twelve Atlas sites near Plattsburgh, New York, cost $44 million, building 150 Minuteman silos at Ellsworth AFB, South Dakota cost $75 million. On a unit-cost basis, an Atlas silo cost $3.6 million compared to $500,000 for a Minuteman launcher. Smaller and easier to build than the Atlas and Titan silos, the Minuteman launch facilities were installed using prefabricated components and standardized installation plans. Between 1961 and 1966 CEBMCO built 1,000 Minuteman launch facilities at the incredible rate of one every 1.8 days. [19]

Despite considerable obstacles, between 1958 and 1966 CEBMCO and the Air Force designed and built the missile launch facilities and support infrastructure that would serve as the backbone of the nation's ICBM force throughout the Cold War. These structures and facilities, which ranged from cavernous Atlas silos to huge missile assembly and checkout buildings, were often built at remote locations and under extremely difficult conditions. Yet, in the short span of eight years, ICBM launch sites spanned the nation, stretching from the dusty brown hills at Vandenberg AFB on the California coast to the cool pine forests around Plattsburgh AFB in upstate New York. In the process, this construction program left an indelible imprint on the American landscape.

Endnotes

1. For the Air Force estimates see, Ltr., General Thomas D. White, Air Force Vice Chief of Staff, to Commander ARDC, subj: Initial Operational Capability, SM-65, 29 November 1955, pp. 1–2, in Ethel M. Dehaven, *Aerospace: The Evolution of USAF Acquisition Policy, 1945–1961*, doc. # 124. For Eisenhower's view on the size of the ICBM force see General Andrew Goodpaster, memo of 16 December 1956, in David Allen Rosenberg, "The Origins of Overkill: Nuclear Weapons and American Strategy, 1945–1969," International Security 7 (Spring 1983), p. 46.

2. Eisenhower commissioned the Gaither study in the spring of 1957 to review the nation's strategic posture. The committee completed its top-secret report in late 1957. It described the Soviet Union as a belligerent and expansionist power, and estimated that if the current trends continued, the Soviets would pose a critical threat to the United States as early as 1959 or 1960. The report recommended accelerating the U.S. missile program, launching a crash development program for an anti-ballistic missile defensive system, and building a nationwide system of fallout shelters. Walter A. McDougal, . . . the Heavens and the Earth: A Political History of the Space Age (New York: Basic Books, 1985, p. 151.

The information on Minuteman comes from: Memo, AFCGM to Director of Guided Missiles, OSD, subj: ICBM Force Objectives, 21 February 1958, p. 1, in records of the Assistant Chief of Staff for Guided Missiles (hereafter AFCGM records), Federal Records Center, Suitland, MD (hereafter FRC Suitland), RG 341, Accession 61B1643, box 3, folder "AFCGM Correspondence–1958, January thru March."

3. Memo, Brig. Gen. Charles McCorkle, Assistant Chief of Staff for Guided Missiles to Director of Plans, subj: Target nominations for ICBM force, 7 January 1958, p. 1, AFCGM records, FRC Suitland, RG 341, Accession 61A1643, box 3, folder "AFCGM Correspondence–1958, January thru March."

4. Roy Neal, *Ace in the Hole* (New York: Doubleday, 1962), pp. 155-56.

5. Memo, General Curtis LeMay, Air Force Vice Chief of Staff, to Secretary of the Air Force, subj: ICBM siting, 6 June 1958, AFCGM records, FRC Suitland, RG 341, Accession 61A643, box 3, folder "AFCGM correspondence-1958, April thru June."

6. U.S. Army Corps of Engineers, Ballistic Missiles Construction Office, "History of the Operations Division," n.d. Annex C, p. 1, Research Collection, Office of History, Headquarters, Army Corps of Engineers, Alexandria, VA (hereafter Corps of Engineers Research Collection), Military Files XVIII-2-7.

7. Maj. C.D. Hargreaves, USA, "The Historical Report of the Corps of Engineers Ballistic Missile Construction Office and History of the Command Section," n.d. p. 20, Corps of Engineers Research Collection, Record Series 18, box 1.

8. General T.J. Hayes, USA, "ICBM Site Construction," *The Military Engineer* (November–December 1966); p. 399.

9. Col. T.J. Hayes, AGC speech at Bismarck, n.d., in U.S. Army Corps of Engineers Ballistic Missile Construction Office, "History of the Operations Division," Corps of Engineers Research Collection, Military Files XVIII-2-2.

10. Hargreaves, "The Historical Report of the Corps of Engineers Ballistic Missile Construction Office and History of the Command Section," p. 24.

11. Ibid., pp. 4, 28.

12. U.S. Army Corps of Engineers, Ballistic Missile Construction Office, History of the Operations Division, Annex C, p. 1.

13. U.S. Army Corps of Engineers, Ballistic Missile Construction Division, "Mountain Home Area Historical Summary February 1960-May 1962," pp. 1–3,26–27,33, 52–55,97–103, Corps of Engineers Research Collection, Military Files XVIII-25-3B.

14. U.S. Army Corps of Engineers, Ballistic Missile Construction Office, "Minuteman Missile Facilities: Minot Air Force Base," n.d., pp. 18–19, 49–65, 67–71, 110–112, Corps of Engineers Research Collection, Military Files XVIII-10-7.

15. Despite hazardous working conditions, between 1958 and 1962, CEBMCO's accident frequency rate was two-thirds below the national average. U.S. Army Ballistic Missile Construction Office, "Titan I Directorate Historical Summary Report, 1 August 1960–15 May 1962, 1962, figure 4, Corps of Engineers Research Collection, record series 18, box 1.

16. U.S. Army Corps of Engineers, Ballistic Missile Construction Office, "History of the McConnell Area U.S. Army Corps of Engineers Ballistic Missile Construction Office," nd., pp. 18–26, 51–57,66, 80–90, Corps of Engineers Research Collection, Military Files XVIII-2G-1B.

17. Hayes, "ICBM Site Construction," p. 401.

18. U.S. Army Corps of Engineers, Ballistic Missile Construction Office, "Warren Area Minuteman History," n.d., p. 9, Corps of Engineers Research Collection, Military Files XVIII-12-1.

19. For the cost of the Atlas F silos at Plattsburgh, see: U.S. Congress, Senate, Committee on Armed Services, Preparedness Investigating Subcommittee, *z, Construction of Air Force Atlas and Titan Missile Sites*, 84th Cong., 2nd sess. (Washington, DC: GPO, 1962, p. 10; Hargreaves, "The Historical Report of the Corps of Engineers Ballistic Missile Construction Office and History of the Command Section," p. 16.

9

AMERICA'S MISSILE COMMUNITIES: SOCIAL AND ECONOMIC IMPACT

The American missile program reached its zenith in the early 1960s. The Air Force briefly deployed the Snark in Maine, and operated Thor and Jupiter IRBM bases overseas. At home, three versions of the Atlas ICBM were deployed in a variety of launch configurations. The Titan I missiles were placed in the vicinity of five military bases, and construction of Titan II silos proceeded around three locations. Minuteman I was on alert status during the Cuban missile crisis. The Navy deployed Polaris.

To evaluate the improving large-rocket technology, launch activity increased at Cape Canaveral, Florida, and Vandenberg AFB, California, while engine testing and additional research continued at installations such as Redstone Arsenal, Arnold Engineering Development Center, White Sands Missile Range, and the Rocket Propulsion Laboratory at Edwards AFB, California. Much of the knowledge gained from these efforts would be incorporated into the nation's manned space program, for which President Kennedy had set the goal of placing an American on the moon by the end of the decade.

The military deployed defensive as well as deterrent missile systems. At eight locations in the United States, the Air Force deployed versions of the BOMARC A and B antiaircraft missiles while continuing tests at Eglin AFB, Florida. At the same time the Army began phasing out its Nike Ajax batteries and replacing them with the longer-range Nike Hercules positioned at almost 200 locations. New Nike Hercules batteries protected key industrial cities and strategic air bases. During the Cuban Missile Crisis, the Army also deployed Nike Hercules batteries in south Florida. At the same time the Nike Hercules was becoming operational, Army scientists and engineers at Redstone and White Sands were making enormous strides in developing a follow-on missile system capable of intercepting an ICBM in flight. In 1962 a Nike Zeus missile demonstrated that capability when it intercepted an Atlas ICBM high above the Pacific Ocean.

Just as the development and deployment of new missile systems changed America's deterrent and defensive military capabilities, it also changed America. The billions of dollars spent had an immense economic and social impact on many U.S. communities. This chapter briefly profiles these impacts, on communities adjacent to research, development, testing, and evaluation (RDT&E) facilities, and those near deployment sites.

Opposite: Held securely in a massive test stand, a Titan I first stage awaits the addition of the second stage, the final step before the Missile Compatibility Firing. The testing took place at the Martin facility outside Denver.

RDT&E Sites

Developing ballistic missiles requires massive amounts of money, facilities, and expertise. The rapid influx of industry, coupled with the setup of advanced research laboratories and testing facilities, brought wholesale change to communities near these sites. The story of White Sands, New Mexico, a small ranching community in the arid southwest, is typical of the changes that took place in other parts of the country. At White Sands, the government established whole new economic, social, educational, and research infrastructures where few previously existed.

White Sands

Since the acquisition of this territory by the United States in the wake of the Mexican-American War, there had always been a U.S. military presence in the region. To the south, the Army established a post at El Paso, Texas, in the 1840s, which evolved into the modern Fort Bliss that served as a major antiaircraft artillery training center during World War II. During that war the Army Air Forces constructed an airfield at nearby Alamogordo, New Mexico.

Nevertheless, until the Federal government filed condemnation suits to acquire the land in 1945, ranching remained the area's dominant economic activity. For example, the 105,000-acre San Augustin Ranch had been one of the dominant livestock-producing holdings in the region. This property, comprising a large portion of the present-day missile range, dated back to the late 1840s. The arrival of the missile range forced a dramatic reduction in cattle ranching as a small city suddenly began growing on the western side of the Tularosa Valley. Eventually, this city would serve as landlord to a tract larger than the combined areas of Rhode Island, Delaware, and the District of Columbia.

Over the years, the billions of dollars spent by the Army on construction, procurement, and personnel have spurred enormous growth and transformed the region's socioeconomic infrastructure. For example, in 1989 the White Sands installation employed more than 11,000 people with a combined income approaching $300 million. In addition to these dollars pouring into the local economy, some 20,000 to 30,000 White Sands retirees remain in the area, spending their pension checks at local businesses. Also in 1989, the missile range spent nearly $380 million in the local economy to procure the multitude of products and services necessary to support various range activities and projects. During 1989, according to one estimate, the value of facility property, structures, and testing equipment topped $4 billion.

Besides displacing ranchers and pumping dollars to support new service industries, the White Sands missile testing facility had other regional impacts. Las Cruces, New Mexico, located 30 miles west of the installation, was described in 1945 as a "sleepy desert hamlet." The presence of White Sands spurred its growth into a bustling city of more than 50,000. In 1989, half of the range's employees and numerous retirees lived within Las Cruces city limits. These people have contributed to the community through direct participation in organizations such as the volunteer fire department and the chamber of commerce.

The presence of White Sands has also spurred the growth of higher education. In 1945, the Ballistic Research Laboratory (BRL) at Aberdeen Proving Grounds contracted with the New Mexico College of Agriculture and Mechanical Arts (or New Mexico A&M) in Las Cruces to support surveys of the new missile range. This relationship expanded when BRL Chief Scientist Dr. Thomas Johnson wrote to his Yale classmate at New Mexico A&M, Dr. George Gardiner, seeking student support to help interpret camera data on missile flights. Willing to support BRL's request, New Mexico A&M's board of regents established a research unit that would later be known as the Physical Sciences Laboratory (PSL).

Throughout the Cold War PSL received contracts and subcontracts to support Army and Navy programs, and to cooperate with the Applied Physics Laboratory at Johns Hopkins University. As a result of this long-term relationship with Johns Hopkins, PSL grew into one of the top academic research institutions in the country, and the College of Agriculture and Mechanical Arts has grown and evolved into New Mexico State University.

Changes in the region also attracted NASA to establish a test facility near White Sands. By the mid-1960s, the White Sands Test Facility (WSTF) employed more than 1,600 people. Its primary mission was to test rocket propulsion systems. By 1991 WSTF had tested more than 325 different rocket engines by conducting over 2.2 million firings. Several private-sector high-tech firms also have located in the area.[1]

In this August 1958 photo, a missile assembly building takes shape at the Army's White Sands Proving Ground, New Mexico.

Missile Production and Testing

Complementing the RDT&E facilities was a vast array of factories that built the missiles and their all-important support equipment. For example, Convair, maker of the Atlas ICBM, built a huge new manufacturing complex on the outskirts of San Diego. Located on a 252-acre tract of land, the 28-building complex had 1.5 million square feet of floor space and housed 12,000 workers. The Martin Company built its Titan ICBM plant near Denver, and by September 1958 Martin and its subcontractors had 16,000 people at work on the missile program. At a former aircraft plant in Santa Monica, California, Douglas Aircraft employed several thousand skilled workers, first building the Nike Ajax, and later the Nike Hercules antiaircraft missile. Simultaneously, on the other side of the country, workers at Western Electric's facility in Burlington, North Carolina, assembled components for the Nike guidance systems.

The engines for the Thor and Jupiter IRBMs were built and tested at the Rocketdyne Division of North American Aviation in Neosho, Missouri, a small community nestled in the foothills of the Ozark Mountains. The 228,000 square foot manufacturing plant, and the adjacent 200-acre test facility, were built on the old Fort Crowder military reservation. The sprawling test complex contained two high-thrust engine test stands, a reinforced concrete control building equipped with banks of sensors and remote cameras, and an extensive network of earthen revetments to isolate the test stands from the propellant storage area. At the height of operations the Neosho facility employed 1,500 people.[2]

Nike Ajax missiles move down the assembly line at the Douglas Aircraft plant in Santa Monica, California. Douglas built the missiles under a subcontract with Western Electric.

Convair engineers performed Atlas captive system and subsystem testing at the Sycamore Canyon test facility. Authorized in 1954, the test stands took two years to build.

The Martin Company tested its Titan engines using a huge new test stand near Denver. Convair built its missile test stands at Sycamore Canyon, northeast of San Diego. During spectacular captive-flight tests, Convair engineers fired the engines and tried to replicate flight conditions.

Missile maintenance and testing continued long after the missiles left the factory. Within Vandenberg AFB's large missile assembly building (MAB), technicians ran exhaustive diagnostic routines to test each of the Atlas ICBMs 300,000 parts. Every strategic and defensive missile periodically had to be taken off operational alert and returned to the MAB for scheduled maintenance. This process was replicated throughout the Air Force; every base that supported a strategic missile squadron operated a similar facility. Antiaircraft missiles required similar facilities.

Deployment Sites

The construction of ICBM silos and Nike missile batteries was sometimes disruptive as workers, earth movers, and concrete trucks suddenly appeared near a family farm or within a suburban community. Often local roads, power grids, and sewage systems were upgraded to support site construction and follow-on deployment. Ultimately, local citizens had to adjust to the constant presence of their new military neighbors.

ICBM Installations

In the case of ballistic missile silos and launch control centers located in rural parts of the country, the Air Force desired to maintain a low profile for security reasons. The Air Force did not want to draw attention to these sites because they were potential targets for terrorists.

Local people expressed mixed feelings about their new neighbors. Few regretted the influx of dollars that missile deployment brought into the local community. For example, at Plattsburgh AFB in upstate New York, the installation of 12 Atlas missile silos cost the government some $37 million, with most of the money spent directly with area contractors, support services, and workers. Also, at Plattsburgh and elsewhere, Air Force public relations efforts and the public's deep sense of patriotism combined to promote a positive atmosphere. For many, there was a pride in the feeling that they were contributing to America's stand against the Soviets. In Roswell, New Mexico, the townspeople threw a parade to escort the first Atlas missile through town.[3]

While many citizens viewed the arrival of missiles with patriotic pride, others were apprehensive. In Kansas, for example, a number of civic and religious groups opposed the deployment of Atlas F ICBMs near Shilling AFB. In October 1961 alone, the city of Roswell recorded ten building permit requests for bomb shelters as some local residents realized that the nearby Atlas silos had suddenly made their town a target for the Soviet strategic rocket, forces. Occasionally, citizen opposition coalesced into direct protest. For example, at Forbes AFB, Kansas, students from nearby McPherson College picketed and vandalized an Atlas E construction site. Although protesters made their voices heard, they did not slow construction.[4]

Once its missile silos were in place, the Air Force worked to foster good community relations. Often, missile crews and their families contributed to this objective by becoming active in the surrounding communities. Malmstrom AFB, Montana, surrounded by 200 Minuteman missile silos, is a typical example of how a SAC missile base affected the nearby community. The Malmstrom Management Analysis Division's annual report for 1969 stated:

Surrounded by the apartment buildings of downtown Chicago, these Nike Hercules crewmen race to their battle stations.

The millions of disposable dollars earned by the Malmstrom employees flow into the local community through expenditures for food, housing, clothing, household appliances, transportation, and other needs which were satisfied by merchants in this area. The Malmstrom family of 23,200 people represents approximately one-third of the people who shop in the Great Falls Area.

Malmstrom's value cannot be assessed entirely in dollars and cents . . . but, the Malmstrom family also contributes many services which add much to the civic and cultural well-being of Central Montana . . . one of 18 teachers in the city (Great Falls) schools belongs to a Malmstrom family. . . more than 125 dependents of base personnel are employed by the city's hospitals . . Malmstrom personnel contributed about 61,000 dollars to welfare funds through the Consolidated Federal Campaign . . . Malmstrom personnel donated 504 pints of blood . . . Aircraft of all types flew many missions into our wilderness areas searching for and rescuing lost and or injured persons, in 1969 Malmstrom employed as many as 45 students . . . Malmstrom personnel are doing their part whenever possible to serve the community and to promote good community relations.[5]

Nike Installations

In marked contrast to the remote ICBM launch facilities, many Army Nike sites were located in America's cities and suburbs. Moreover, some sites initially located in rural areas found themselves engulfed in suburban sprawl as Americans moved away from the cities during the post-war building boom.

In selecting sites for its missile batteries the Army faced a problem: it seemed the public was in favor of air defense as long as a missile battery was not deployed next door. To accommodate local concerns and cut land acquisition costs, the Army Corps of Engineers reduced the acreage needed by placing the missiles within underground magazines. The Army located batteries on existing military lands wherever possible, but often condemnation suits had to be filed against property owners to acquire needed properties. One extreme property acquisition case involved the Army's attempt to acquire land at the end of a runway at Los Angeles International Airport. City officials battled the acquisition, claiming that the proposed missile battery would be a potential threat to flight operations. Calling the local Army representative "bull-headed" and "short-sighted," Los Angeles Mayor Norris Paulson flew to Washington, DC, to meet with legislators and armed-services officials to press for a location change. Eventually the city won and the Nike site was relocated.[6]

Once the Army obtained the land and permission to build, aesthetics became a consideration. In contrast to the temporary antiaircraft batteries the Army hastily erected in the mid-1950s, which were built around tents, wooden walkways, and dirt roads, the Nike facilities were designed with habitability and outward appearance in mind. The one-story cinderblock sloped-roof structures looked much like many of the school buildings being erected elsewhere in the community to educate children of the baby boom. Shrubbery enhanced facility appearance.[7]

As part of its public relations effort, the Army Air Defense Command sponsored "fact-finding" trips for local VIPs to observe training at Fort Bliss, Texas, and to receive air defense briefings at Ent AFB, Colorado. Under "Operation Understanding," the Army asked hundreds of community leaders for a public show of support. To alleviate the neighbors' concerns about potential danger, the Army assured the public that the missile sites were as safe as local gas stations.[8]

Over the years, tens of thousands have visited Nike batteries during open houses. Boy Scouts often stayed overnight at the on-site barracks. Missile site personnel also became involved in community activities. A sense of community "ownership" of a local battery especially prevailed when the National Guard assumed responsibility for many of the sites. Starting with the realignment of a battery in the Los Angeles area on September 14, 1958, to California's 720th Missile Battalion, Guard responsibility grew to cover almost half of the missile sites. For Hawaii's defense, the National Guard was responsible for all sites from activation to deactivation. The assumption of missile battery duty by the National Guard represented an unprecedented experiment; for the first time a key component of the nation's defense had been turned over to America's citizen soldiers. They manned the batteries around the clock.[9]

In the wake of the May 1958 Nike Ajax explosion that killed ten people at Middletown, New Jersey, and the previously mentioned Air Force campaign waged to challenge the Nike's capability, the Army sought to bolster the program's image. In 1958 the owner of San Francisco's Fairmont Hotel, who was a graduate of "Operation Understanding," proposed a novel solution. On July 23, 1959, in "Operation Grassroots," the Fairmont's ballroom was converted into a mock Nike command center while outside a Nike missile stood posed on display. The exhibit attracted thousands. Encouraged by the positive public response, the U.S. Army Air Defense Command expanded "Operation Grassroots" into a national program eventually dubbed "Nike in the Attack." Soon Americans attending state fairs and other public gatherings could watch demonstrations of the Nike antiaircraft missile system in action.[10]

Life at the Missile Sites

Different missile missions affected the composition, size, and attitudes of the crews manning the sites. Initially, SAC called on mature aviators to operate the first ICBM silos. However, as more veteran airmen left for combat in Southeast Asia, SAC began recruiting missile crews directly from commissioning sources. As a result, the typical age of a combat crewman in the 1970s was between 22 and 30 years old, with only a minority having any flying experience. During this period SAC had to procure 900 new missile combat crewmen per year to fill all shifts at the 1,054 silos then operational.

To become a "missileer," each candidate underwent extensive medical and psychological evaluation by SAC's Human Reliability Program. After certification, training consisted of a three-step process. First, the candidate attended an Air Training Command school for familiarization with the weapon system. Potential Titan crewmen were sent to train at Sheppard AFB in Texas while Minuteman candidates went to school at Chanute AFB in Illinois. Next, the candidate was assigned to the 1st Strategic Aerospace Division at Vandenberg AFB for operational training. Finally, the prospective crewman arrived at his

This 8-ton blast door guarded the entrance to the Delta One launch control center near Ellsworth AFB, South Dakota. As one of the many safeguards against an unauthorized launch, two people were required to be in the launch control center at all times.

(right) The participants in Olympic Arena were famous for their elaborate costumes. Here, members of the 90th Strategic Missile Wing, based at F.E. Warren AFB, Wyoming, celebrate after being named Best Minuteman Maintenance Team.

Displaying jubilation is Minuteman maintenance tea they had scored 1779 poin sible 1800 points in the They went on to win the assigned wing for familiarization with conditions unique to that area.

Once placed on the duty rotation schedule for a Minuteman missile wing, a two-man crew averaged five tours per month of 36 to 40 hours per tour. Travel time to and from the silo could be considerable. For example, some silos at Minot AFB in North Dakota required a trip of 150 miles. During the 36-hour shift, the two-man crew stood two twelve-hour shifts in the underground launch control center (LCC), broken up by a twelve-hour on-site rest period while another crew stood watch.[11]

While on duty the crew commander and his deputy spent much of their time conducting frequent status checks of the missiles and their support systems. Duty in a missile silo was demanding. The missile crews took pride in their work, and sometimes even expressed a sense of humor about it. The crew of Delta Flight, 66th Missile Squadron, 44th Missile Wing, Ellsworth AFB, South Dakota, painted the 8-ton blast door that guarded the entrance to the LCC to resemble a Domino's pizza box. The crew's hand-painted logo promised "World Wide Delivery in 30 Minutes or Less, or Your Next One Is Free."

SAC encountered morale problems early in the program. Graduates of the Reserve Officers' Training Corps (ROTC) and the Air Force Academy initially assigned to missile crew duty tended to leave after they fulfilled their service obligation. Although they understood the responsibility and the importance of their duties, they often resented what they perceived to be their lesser status compared to their pilot counterparts.[12]

To attract high-quality officers to missile crew duty, SAC offered the inducement of an advanced-degree program. As early as December 1961, SAC had expressed the view that a good educational program would permit missile crews to put the long hours of alert duty to profitable use. However, the

From their underground launch control center, the two-man crew of Delta Flight kept watch over the ten Minuteman II ICBMs.

The first Strategic Air Command missile competition. Nine strategic missile wings participated.

demanding maintenance requirements of the first-generation missiles left little extra time for study.[13]

With the introduction of the solid-propellant Minuteman missiles, less maintenance was required so crew sizes could be dramatically reduced. In contrast to a 12-missile Atlas F Squadron, which kept sixty men underground at all times, a 150-missile Minuteman wing could do the same job with thirty, as each two-man crew had responsibility for ten missiles. (In 1978, for the first time, women joined men on missile crew duty.) Even though fewer crew members were responsible for more missiles, these crews still had much more free time than their first-generation predecessors. Although much of the time was spent reviewing procedures in preparation for random Operational Readiness Inspections or running practice drills, the second-generation missileers had time to pursue advanced degrees while on alert duty. Also, to enhance *esprit de corps*, an annual missile crew competition was established in 1967 at Vandenberg AFB to measure crew competency. This competition eventually became known as "Olympic Arena."[14]

Nike sites were more labor-intensive than the ICBM sites because they operated both radar tracking equipment and the missile launchers. Approximately 225 men worked at the two 20-acre sites. Batteries became tight-knit communities as many missilemen lived in on-site barracks or with their families in nearby military housing. For Nike sites not located near existing military housing, the Army constructed housing for soldiers with spouses and children. Later, transferring many of the sites to the National Guard allowed the Army to reduce housing costs as guardsmen commuted to duty from home.

To keep the crews ready for the attack that never came, drills were frequently run to test readiness. Like their SAC counterparts, the Nike missilemen could also expect an annual test. In the 1950s, crews prepared for their Annual Service Practice at Fort Bliss, in which national recognition was bestowed on the best battery crew. In the early 1960s, the annual practices occurred on a short-notice basis. In both cases, crews vied for top missileer recognition.[15]

However, once on duty Nike missilemen had to battle boredom, as did their ICBM counterparts in America's prairies. Recreational activities were vigorously pursued, including team competition in many sports. One New York missile battery even built itself a miniature golf course. For entertainment, Alaska's missilemen looked forward to bingo night. Many other batteries hosted beauty contests to select a local woman to compete in the Miss Army Air Defense beauty pageant.[16]

Endnotes

1. Information extracted from a long series of articles by Tom Starkweather published in *White Sands Missile Ranger* from 1 December 1989 to 1 January 1991, and from public affairs fact sheets produced in 1994 by the White Sands public affairs office.

2. Norman L. Baker, "Thor Engine Reaches Production Test," *Missiles and Rockets* (7 July 1958), pp. 24–25.

3. "Missiles Meant Economic Boom for North Country," *Plattsburgh Press–Republican* (7 July 1964), p. 3–B; Fritz Thompson, "Atlas' Lair," *Albuquerque Journal* (27 February 1994), pp. A1, A10.

4. U.S. Army Corps of Engineers, Ballistic Missile Construction Office, "History of Corps of Engineers Activities at Forbes Air Force Base: April 1959-June 1962," Corps of Engineers Research Collection, Office of History, Headquarters Army Corps of Engineers, Alexandria, VA, Military Files.

5. "History of the 341st Strategic Missile Wing and 341st Combat Support Group: 1 April-30 June 1970," pp. 66–69. Available on microfilm, file K-WG-341-HI, at the Air Force History Office, Bolling AFB, Washington, DC (hereafter AFHO) or as paper copy at the Air Force Historical Research Agency, Maxwell AFB, Montgomery, AL (hereafter AFHRA).

6. Mary T. Cagle, *Development, Production and Deployment of Nike Ajax Guided Missile System: 1945–1959* (Redstone Arsenal, Huntsville, AL: Army Rocket and Guided Missile Agency, 1959), pp. 190–192.

7. Ibid. See also Lt. Col. Steve Moeller's "Vigilant and Invincible: The Army's Role in Continental Air Defense," (master's thesis, Ohio State University, 1992); and *Argus* (February 1, 1958) article that discusses beautification efforts at a Pittsburgh site by a local garden club.

8. *Argus* (September 1959). Argus was the monthly news magazine of the U.S. Army Air Defense Command. A nearly complete set can be found at the Military History Institute at Carlisle Barracks, Pennsylvania.

9. For a summary of this unique chapter in military history see Lt. Col. Timothy Osato's "Militia Missilemen: The Army National Guard in Air Defense 1951–1967, nd. Available at the Center for Military History Washington, DC. See also, Brig. Gen. Bruce Jacobs, "Nike Hercules is Phased Out of the Army National Guard," *The National Guardsman*: (November 1974), reprint.

10. See *Argus* (September 1959 and July 1965).

11. David A. Anderton, *Strategic Air Command: Two–thirds of the Triad* (New York: Charles Scribner's Sons, 1976), pp. 140-148 provides a detailed overview of a typical shift. For a more recent account, see Michael R. Boldrick, "Life in the Egg," *Air and Space Smithsonian*, 9 (October–November 1994): pp. 68-73.

12. "History of the 389th Strategic Missile Wing," (1963), pp. 59-63. Available on microfilm, file K-WG-389- HI, at AFHO, or as paper copy at AFHRA.

13. Second Air Force History, Jul–Dec 1962," pp. 130–133. Available on microfilm, file K432-01 v.1, at AFHO or as paper copy at AFHRA.

14. Anderton, *Strategic Air Command*. Chapter 17 discusses "Olympic Arena" 1973.

15. The missile shoots received consistent front-page coverage in Argus; see also Moeller, pp. 52–54.

16. Moeller, pp. 54–55.

Under the watchful gaze of the tracking radar, the crew at the Nike site in Grand Island, New York, play on the battery's miniature golf course.

This photograph traces the evolution of the Nike missile. From left to right: Nike Ajax, Nike Hercules, and Nike Zeus.

10

ANTIBALLISTIC MISSILE DEFENSE: NIKE ZEUS THROUGH SAFEGUARD

As the Cold War missile race unfolded, American scientists and engineers began searching for a way to protect the nation against long-range ballistic missiles. Disagreement over whether such an antiballistic missile (ABM) defense system was technologically feasible and strategically advisable spurred one of the longest and fiercest debates of the Cold War. The controversy over the Reagan administration's Strategic Defense Initiative (SDI), often called "Star Wars" by the news media, was a continuation of the political and technological debate that began with the first ABM system, the Nike Zeus (1956–1963), and continued through the development of the Nike X (1963–1967), Sentinel (1967–1969), and Safeguard (1969–1976) systems. The Safeguard system, built around the Sprint and Spartan missiles, was the only ABM system to become operational.

In contrast to the thousands of ICBM silos and the hundreds of air defense missile batteries that the United States built during the Cold War, there are few physical reminders of the enormous sums of money the nation invested in developing an ABM capability. The Army Corps of Engineers began construction of three Safeguard sites in Massachusetts, Montana, and North Dakota, but only the North Dakota site became operational. The legacy of the ABM program, however, extends far beyond those three sites. The Department of Defense sponsored billions of dollars of research, development, and testing at facilities such as Redstone Arsenal, White Sands, and Kwajalein Atoll in the Marshall Islands. Moreover, ABM and SDI research also included other government organizations, scores of research universities, and hundreds of civilian contractors.

Events Leading to Deployment

The U.S. ABM program actually had its genesis in the German V-2 missile attacks on Great Britain during World War II. Although schemes to intercept the V-2s in flight never advanced beyond theory, American scientists recognized that long-range missiles such as the V-2 would pose a potent threat in the future.[a] After

[a] After evaluating the German missile program during the closing days of the war, a team of American scientists concluded that if the war had continued into 1946, the Germans might have developed a modified V-2 capable of reaching the United States.

inspecting captured German missile plants and test facilities, in July 1945, the scientists recommended that the United States initiate a research and development effort to defend against rockets like the V-2. A May 1946 report issued by the War Department Equipment Board concluded that to defend against such a threat would require "guided interceptor missiles, dispatched in accordance with electronically computed data obtained from radar detection stations."[1]

The Army Air Forces, having reached a similar conclusion, had already begun two missile defense studies called Project Thumper and Project Wizard. Project Thumper was canceled in 1948, but Project Wizard, initially awarded to the University of Michigan, provided the theoretical foundation for development of an "anti-missile missile" capable of destroying a target traveling at speeds upwards of 4,000 miles per hour in the upper atmosphere. By the mid-1950s the Air Force had two consortia of defense contractors working on anti-missile missile development. Project Wizard survived until 1958.

The Army took a different approach toward developing an ABM. Rather than building a completely new missile system, it proposed adapting much of the same missile and guidance technology from its Nike Ajax and promising Nike Hercules antiaircraft missile systems for use in the antiballistic missile program.[b] The new missile was the Nike Zeus.

With an eye toward the future, in March 1955, the Army hired Bell Laboratories to undertake a study projecting the evolution of defensive missile technology through the early 1960s. In late 1956, the Bell scientists reported that within the next several years the development of high-capacity computers and long-range, high-rate acquisition radar would enable a defensive missile to intercept an incoming ICBM.

At the same time the Army was exploring the feasibility of developing an ABM system, it was also locked in a fierce interservice battle with the Air Force over the future of air defense. Beginning in the spring of 1956, the Air Force launched an aggressive public relations campaign charging that the Army's Nike Ajax and soon-to-be-deployed Nike Hercules were unfit to guard the nation.

In an attempt to quell the vitriolic debate, in November 1956, Secretary of Defense Charles Wilson clarified the Army and Air Force roles in providing air defense. The secretary made the Army responsible for the "point defense" of specific geographic areas, cities, and vital military and industrial installations. Under the point defense concept, the Army was authorized to develop and deploy surface-to-air missiles such as the Nike Hercules with ranges up to 100 miles. To complement the Army's capability, Wilson gave the Air Force responsibility for the much broader area defense mission.[2]

While Wilson's ruling resolved the air defense debate, it was silent on the question of which service would develop the ABM system. Both the Army and the Air Force were anxious to acquire the promising new mis-

---

[b] The Nike Ajax program began in 1945 and the first missiles were deployed in early 1954. The liquid-fuel missile had a range of 25 to 30 miles and carried a conventional warhead. The missile was guided by two different radars: The target-tracking radar that followed the incoming aircraft, and the missile-tracking radar that guided the missile to the intercept. Concerned that the Nike Ajax's limited range and conventional warhead would be incapable of blunting a massed Soviet air attack, in early 1953 the Army began developing the solid-fuel Nike Hercules. Substantially larger than its predecessor, the new missile had a range of over 75 miles. Although it used the same fire control radars and computer as the Nike Ajax, the electronics used in the Nike Hercules system were all solid-state. Nike Hercules flight testing began in 1955.

sion. The Army initially had a head start because it was using much of its existing Nike hardware for the ABM. Based on the results of the Bell Laboratories study, in early 1957 the Army awarded Western Electric, and its research and development arm, Bell Laboratories, a contract to develop the Nike Zeus antiballistic missile system.

The Air Force was anxious to block the Army's ABM program, and it launched a public relations campaign against the Army missile system. The campaign was unsuccessful. In January 1958 Secretary of Defense Neil H. McElroy assigned the Army the lead role in ABM development based on the progress it had already made in the Nike Zeus program. At the same time McElroy ordered the Air Force to continue working on the radars and command-and-control system under Project Wizard so that these technologies could be incorporated into the Army program."[3]

The Army designed the Nike Zeus system to defend population and industrial centers from a relatively light missile attack. The defensive missile system's most expensive component, and also its weakest link, were its four target-tracking and missile guidance radars.[4] Those four radars were: (1) the Zeus Acquisition Radar (ZAR)—a highly accurate, three-dimensional long-range search radar that could detect small targets at extreme range; (2) the Discrimination Radar (DR)—a high-resolution radar designed to detect incoming warheads amidst the clouds of debris resulting from a missile attack, (3) a Target- Tracking Radar (TTR)—a precise, long-range, narrow beam radar designed to follow small, high-speed targets during the final phase of descent; and (4) the Missile-Tracking Radar (MTR)—a radar designed to track and guide the outbound Zeus to its target.[5]

The Army was anxious to deploy the Nike Zeus system, but between 1959 and 1961 Congress and the White House refused to approve such a move. Instead, they authorized only enough money to sustain the research and development effort. Opponents of the Nike Zeus system, which included Hans Bethe of Cornell University and Jerome Wiesner of the Massachusetts Institute of Technology, argued convincingly against deploying the missile. They pointed out that the Nike's mechanical radars could track only a limited number of targets at once, making it relatively easy for the Soviets to "blind" the system by launching a barrage of missiles, some of which probably would have been equipped with decoy reentry vehicles.[c] Another drawback was that the Nike Zeus was not designed for low-altitude intercepts. That drawback negated an important defensive advantage because target identification, the process of sorting out the real warheads from the decoys and expended stages, is easier at low altitude due to the fact that with the exception of the reentry vehicles, most of the other hardware burns up before it enters the earth's atmosphere.

The research and development effort yielded its first major success on July 19, 1962, when a Nike Zeus missile fired from Kwajalein intercepted an Atlas ICBM launched from Vandenberg AFB. The Army scored the test as successful because the Nike's dummy nuclear warhead came within two kilometers of the incoming Atlas. In a subsequent test on December 22, 1962, the Nike Zeus passed within 22 meters of the targeted reentry vehicle.[6]

Despite a string of successful tests, Secretary of Defense McNamara did not believe the Nike Zeus system could defend against the large Soviet ICBMs that were expected to be deployed by the late 1960s. McNamara was concerned that the ABM system lacked the sophistication to discern between real and decoy warheads. Also, he believed the ABM could be overwhelmed in a saturation attack because the radars

[c] The Nike Zeus target- and missile-tracking radars worked in tandem, and each pair could only track a single target at a time. Tracking each additional target required another TTR and MTR pair.

and computers could manage only one intercept at a time. Because of these flaws, in 1963 McNamara decided against deploying the Nike Zeus. Rather than cancel the program, however, he directed a program reorganization to field a more advanced ABM system. Accordingly, DoD ordered the Army to begin developing a new missile defense system with higher speed, higher-capacity radars and computers, and a short-range interceptor missile fast enough to intercept an enemy warhead after it entered the earth's atmosphere.

In April 1964, DoD ordered the Army to begin work on a new defensive missile system called Nike X. The Nike X was to be a "layered" system. The first line of defense would be a reconfigured Nike Zeus missile, renamed Spartan, that would intercept the incoming warheads at an altitude of 70 to 100 miles. Next, the warheads that evaded the Spartan intercepts would be engaged by the new short-range Sprint missile. The 27- foot long Sprint would engage the targets at an altitude of 20 to 30 miles.

The key difference between the Nike Zeus and Nike X systems was Nike X's use of a phased-array radar pioneered under the Defense Department's Advanced Research Projects Agency (ARPA). The new radar was a technological breakthrough because, in contrast to the acquisition and tracking radars used by the Nike Ajax and Nike Hercules systems, phased-array radars could track several targets and direct multiple intercepts simultaneously. With advances in electronics and computer technology, integration of radar data on multiple targets could be swiftly translated into instructions for the Spartan and Sprint interceptors. Two types of phased-array radar would be used. The first, the perimeter acquisition radar, would be used for long-range target acquisition. The second, the missile site radar, would handle short-range target discrimination and interceptor guidance.

To test Nike X under combat conditions, however, would require resumption of atmospheric nuclear detonations in violation of the recently signed Nuclear Test Ban Treaty. In an October 1964 edition of Scientific American, Wiesner, along with former ARPA chief scientist Herbert York, argued strongly against atmospheric testing. Furthermore, they maintained that deployment of an ABM system actually increased the possibility of nuclear war: ABM deployment by one side would, they argued, encourage the other side to launch a preemptive attack if it foresaw a potential loss of ability to retaliate against a nuclear attack. This point would become a rallying cry for opponents of the ABM, and that opposition grew in proportion to public disenchantment with the United States' expanding role in Vietnam.[7]

In 1963, McNamara formed a commission to look into how the ABM could affect nuclear warfare and United States-Soviet relations. Although the commission's report shed a positive light on ABM deployment, the opposition within the scientific community strongly influenced McNamara's views. He was committed to a deterrence-based strategy that assured the destruction of the Soviet Union in response to any nuclear attack. The ABM program distracted from that commitment; it also competed for funding needed to support the U.S. effort in Vietnam. Again in 1965 and 1966, McNamara approved funding only for continuing research of the Nike X program, overriding the Joint Chiefs of Staff recommendation for deployment. In 1966, however, Congress allocated partial funding for an ABM system. Although both houses approved the funding by wide margins, a small but vocal group of opponents within each chamber argued against deployment.

ABM Deployment

Despite McNamara's sympathies with the ABM's opponents, events overseas pressured the defense secretary to consider some sort of antimissile defensive scheme. The detonation of an atomic bomb by China in 1964 meant that the United States faced a second potential nuclear threat if and when the

Chinese deployed their own ICBMs. Furthermore, intelligence reports confirmed that the Soviets were building their defensive missile system. Realizing that President Lyndon Johnson was under growing pressure to deploy an ABM system, McNamara recommended a compromise, offering to field a defensive system should the Soviets not respond to proposed negotiations intended to limit such systems. Unfortunately at the June 1967 Glassboro, New Jersey, summit between President Johnson and Premier Aleksei N. Kosygin, the Soviet leader refused to accept the American overture. Kosygin defended the Soviet ABM program on the grounds that people-killing offensive missiles were morally wrong while missile-killing defensive missiles were morally defensible.

In September 1967, McNamara announced that the United States would deploy many elements of the Nike X program in the new Sentinel antiballistic missile defense system. The key components of the Sentinel system were the huge perimeter acquisition radar (PAR), the shorter-range missile site radar (MSR), and the Sprint and Spartan missiles. The PAR was designed to acquire and track targets at ranges in excess of 1,000 miles. The MSR, which had a range of several hundred miles, provided precise, close-in targeting information. The MSR also controlled launching the missiles and guiding them to their targets.

The goal of the Sentinel system was three-fold: to protect the nation's urban and industrial areas against ICBM attack from the People's Republic of China; to provide a defensive missile shield against an accidental launch; and to allow the United States to protect its Minuteman ICBM launch facilities.[8]

The initial Sentinel deployment plan envisioned installing the Sentinel at thirteen sites in the continental United States and at one site in both Alaska and Hawaii. Because Sentinel would be deployed around major cities such as Boston, Seattle, Chicago, Detroit, and San Francisco, opponents of the ABM system could unite with scientists and peace activists from those communities to halt construction. In Seattle the

Map showing the location of the proposed Sentinel ABM sites.

ABM Committee of the Seattle Association of Scientists attacked the deployment scheme. In Chicago, five scientists formed the West Suburban Concerned Scientists Group and argued that local ABM deployment would only subject the city to extra Soviet ICBMs in the event of war.[9]

The scale of opposition became apparent when the Army began constructing the Sentinel facility at Sharpner's Pond near Boston. In the wake of a January 29, 1969, Army community relations meeting that gave opponents a forum to denounce Sentinel, Senator Edward Kennedy (D-Massachusetts) wrote a letter to the new Nixon Administration's Secretary of Defense, Melvin Laird, challenging Sentinel. Kennedy's letter touched off a heated debate within the Senate on the system's viability. The controversy in the Senate forced Laird to halt construction at the Sharpner's Pond site pending completion of an already-scheduled program review.

President Nixon also adopted a cautious position on ABM system development. He shared National Security Adviser Henry Kissinger's concern that construction of the ABM system could lead the Soviets to believe that the United States was attempting to achieve a first-strike capability that could survive a retaliatory counterstrike. Trying to avoid a move that could be construed as provocative, Nixon elected to modify the Sentinel system. Instead of trying to erect a limited nationwide ballistic missile defense, the President directed that the new ABM system be positioned to protect part of the United States' ICBM force. His goal was to ensure that a sizable portion of the nation's ICBMs survived a Soviet first strike, thus ensuring that the United States would always possess an adequate retaliatory capability. By leaving the nation's cities open to attack, Nixon hoped to assure the Soviets that the United States would never conduct a first strike. On March 14, 1969, Nixon announced the deployment of a "modified Sentinel system," which he called Safeguard.[10]

The Safeguard program initially called for twelve sites. With the exception of the site intended to protect Washington, DC, all of the facilities were to be located well away from densely populated urban areas. Despite moving the system away from urban areas where it was vehemently opposed, Safeguard still faced rigorous Congressional scrutiny. Numerous *ad hoc* groups sprang up either to support or to stop Safeguard deployment. Again, scientists Jerome Wiesner of the Massachusetts Institute of Technology and Nobel Laureate Hans Bethe played prominent roles in providing scientific arguments on behalf of the opposition. Meanwhile, former Secretary of State Dean Acheson and Paul Nitze formed the "Committee to Maintain a Prudent Defense Policy" to pressure Congress to deploy Safeguard. In the Senate, the debate over Safeguard continued through much of July 1969, with anti-ABM forces making headway against the administration's arguments that the system would provide President Nixon an additional bargaining chip in upcoming strategic negotiations with the Soviets. However, on August 6, 1969, by a scant one-vote margin, the Senate voted to deploy Safeguard at two of the twelve sites.[11]

When the Senate authorized construction of Safeguard sites in North Dakota and Montana to protect the nearby Minuteman ICBMs, U.S. negotiators found their Soviet counterparts more receptive at arms limitation talks that began in November 1969. As the talks continued, the Nixon administration hoped to provide its negotiating team additional leverage by having Congress appropriate funds for six additional sites, including one near the nation's capital. However, in 1970, the Senate Armed Services Committee extended appropriations to cover only the building of additional sites to defend ICBMs stationed near Whiteman AFB, Missouri, and F.E. Warren AFB, Wyoming. Again, when the bill went to the Senate on August 12, 1970, Safeguard proponents narrowly defeated an amendment cutting appropriations.[12]

Safeguard

After Congress appropriated the necessary funds, construction at the Safeguard site near Grand Forks, North Dakota, proceeded rapidly. In contrast, at the Montana site, located north of Malmstrom AFB, labor disputes caused serious construction delays. Construction at both Safeguard sites was well underway when President Richard Nixon and General Secretary Leonid Brezhnev signed the Anti-Ballistic Missile Treaty at the May 1972 Moscow Summit. In conjunction with the ABM treaty signing, the two national leaders signed an interim agreement to place limitations on certain strategic offensive arms.

The ABM Treaty and the interim agreement resulted from ongoing Strategic Arms Limitation Talks (SALT) begun in November 1969. Interest in the United States for arms control talks was rooted in the mid-1960s as the Soviets began to make inroads on American strategic superiority through deployment of numerous land- and sea-based offensive strategic nuclear-tipped missiles. Soviet deployment of a Galosh antiballistic missile system around Moscow also concerned American strategic planners. Conversely, the proposed American deployment of an ABM system far more capable than Galosh was a factor that motivated the Soviets to come to the negotiation table.[13]

The treaty permitted the United States to retain two ABM facilities: one protecting the nation's capital and the other guarding a single ICBM launcher area. When the ABM Treaty was signed, the Safeguard facility near Grand Forks was 85 percent complete, while the site near Malmstrom was only 10 percent done. Since the treaty allowed only one ICBM field to be protected, work at the Malmstrom site ended.[14] The government salvaged all of the usable material and then covered the foundations of the unfinished structures with topsoil. Today only the first story of the huge unfinished perimeter acquisition radar building is visible on the site.

Construction continued at Grand Forks, and the nation's first, and ultimately only, Safeguard site became operational in 1975. Realizing that this single site could do little against the hundreds of Soviet warheads that could be launched against it, the Army decided to operate the site for a single year to gain operational experience. When the Army's plan to cease operation reached Congress, appropriations for the site were cut, forcing the deactivation to occur sooner. However, a portion of the ABM installation (the perimeter acquisition radar) remained active as a tracking component for NORAD.[15]

In 1974, when Congress decided to terminate the Safeguard program, it also directed the Army to refocus its ballistic missile defense program toward developing the next generation of missile defense technology. Accordingly, in May 1974, the Army abolished the Safeguard System Organization and in its place created the Ballistic Missile Defense Organization (BMDO). Like its predecessor, BMDO was based at the Army's Redstone Arsenal, Huntsville, Alabama. Despite a reduction in funding, over the next ten years the Army studied and experimented with a wide range of missile defense technologies. Many of the new technologies stemmed directly from the Safeguard program, while others were completely new. On the whole, the Army's research focused on three areas: developing new sensors to locate and track targets, developing nonnuclear interceptors to destroy incoming reentry vehicles, and developing new defensive strategies to optimize the capabilities of the new technology.

Indicative of a decade of development, in June 1984 the BMDO's Homing Overlay Experiment demonstrated that it was possible to intercept and destroy a target outside of the earth's atmosphere using a nonnuclear interceptor. In the words of one observer, the Army tests proved it was possible to "hit a bullet with a bullet."[16]

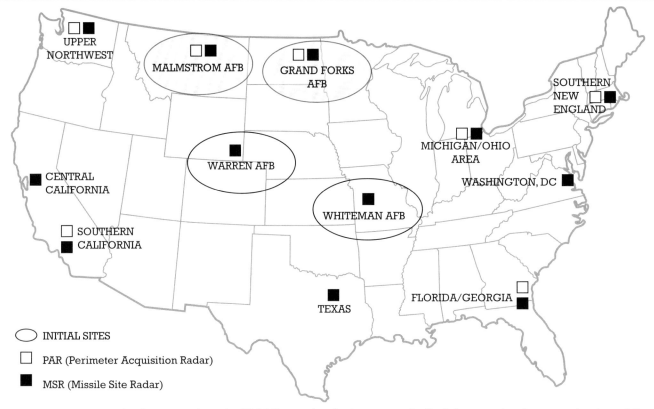

Map showing the Safeguard deployment plan in March 1969.

At the same time the BMDO was developing new missile defense technology, newly elected President Ronald Reagan was searching for a way to circumvent the grim constraints of the theory of Mutual Assured Destruction (MAD).[d] Shortly after Reagan took office, he began seeking advice on creating a workable ballistic missile defense. Acting on the advice of, among others, Dr. Edward Teller, the father of the American H-bomb, and the Joint Chiefs of Staff, in March 1983 the President told the nation of his intent to "create a nationwide defense shield against ballistic missiles that would make nuclear weapons impotent and obsolete."[17]

Reagan called his new concept the Strategic Defense Initiative (SDI), which the media promptly dubbed "Star Wars." To direct the $17 billion program, Secretary of Defense Caspar Weinberger created the Strategic Defense Initiative Organization (SDIO), a joint service, independent development organization that reported directly to him.

The Army's missile defense expertise formed the backbone of the SDIO, and in July 1985 the new Army Strategic Defense Command replaced BMDO. Working together, researchers from the SDIO, the Army, and the Air Force developed a new layered defense strategy. The new plan was based on attacking enemy missiles soon after they had been launched, in midcourse, and as they neared their targets.

[d] MAD was based on the premise that neither the United States nor the Soviet Union would unleash their nuclear arsenals because of the swift and sure retaliation that would follow. Reagan thought that MAD was inadequate because it left the United States with few options. If the Soviets ever launched a first strike, there was nothing the United States could do to protect its citizens. Once informed of the Soviet missile launch, the President's only option would be to launch a counterstrike while there was still time.

Some of the exotic technologies the SD10 planned to use included space- and ground-based lasers, space-based rocket interceptors, and a neutral particle beam weapon. The untried technology was both controversial and expensive. The Soviet Union, as well as some of the United States' European allies were harshly critical of SDI, claiming it would upset the balance of power. President Reagan, however, was unmoved by controversy and remained an ardent proponent of ballistic missile defense. With Reagan's support, SDI funding grew rapidly, increasing from $1.4 billion in fiscal year 1985 to $4.5 billion in 1989.[18]

In 1989 the collapse of the Soviet Union led to significant cutbacks in the missile defense program. With the threat of a Soviet missile attack diminishing, the United States turned its attention from developing a nationwide missile defense to concentrating on localized theater missile defense.

Endnotes

1. Donald Baucom, *The Origins of SDI, 1944–1983* (Lawrence, KS: University of Kansas Press, 1992), pp. 6–7.

2. Memo, Secretary of Defense Charles Wilson to the members of the Armed Forces Policy Council, subj: Clarification of Roles and Missions to Improve the Effectiveness of Operation of the Department of Defense, 26 November 1956, pp. 297–298, reprinted in, Richard I. Wolf, ed., *The United States Air Force Basic Documents on Roles and Missions* (Washington, DC: Office of Air Force History, 1988).

3. Baucom, *The Origins of SDI* pp. 8–15.

4. Bell Laboratories, *ABM Research and Development at Bell Laboratories: Project History* (Whippany, NJ: Bell Laboratories, 1975), p. II–1.

5. Ibid., pp. 1–4 through 1–21.

6. Erwin N. Thompson, *Pacific Ocean Engineers: History of the U.S. Army Corps of Engineers in the Pacific, 1905–1980* (Ft. Shafter, HI: U.S. Army Engineer Division, Pacific Ocean, 1980), pp. 274–275.

7. Baucom, *The Origins of SDI*, pp. 17–22. Jerome Wiesner and Herbert York, "National Security and the Nuclear-Test Ban," *Scientific American* 211 (October 1964): pp. 27, 31–33, 35.

8. Ruth Currie-McDaniel and Claus R. Martel, *The U.S. Army Strategic Defense Command: Its History and Role in the Strategic Defense Initiative*, 3rd ed., (Huntsville, AL: U.S. Army Strategic Defense Command, 1989), p. 7.

9. Baucom, pp. 25–39.

10. James H. Kitchens, *A History of the Huntsville Division, 15 October 1967–31 December 1976* (Huntsville, AL: U.S. Army Engineer Division, Huntsville, 1978), pp. 31–33.

11. Ibid., pp. 35–36. In *The Origins of SDI*, author Donald Baucom speculates that Senator Kennedy's widely publicized personal problems related to his July 1969 automobile accident at Chappaquiddick Island impaired his effectiveness as the Senate's lead ABM opponent, and that this may have made a difference in the outcome of the Safeguard vote.

12. Baucom, pp. 58–61.

13. John Newhouse, *Cold Dawn: The Story of SALT* (New York: Holt, Rinehart and Winston, 1973), pp 73, 102.

14. Kitchens, pp. 75–77, 94-95.

15. For details of ABM construction and deployment see the Spirit and Spartan weapon system profiles and site history in Parts II and III of this study.

16. Historical Office, U.S. Army Strategic Defense Command, "Defending the Homeland: Supporting the Force," n.d., p 22.

17. "Defending the Homeland," p. 23; Donald R. Baucom, "The U.S. Missile Defense Program, 1944–1994: Fifty Years of Progress," 1994, pp. 4-5. Note: Dr. Baucom is the historian at DoD'S Ballistic Defense Organization, the successor to SDIO.

18. Currie, *The U.S. Army Strategic Defense Command*, p. 65.

11

MODERNIZING THE ICBM FORCE

Deployment of Minuteman I in 1962 marked the beginning of the second generation of Air Force ICBMs. Following in its wake came the Titan II (1963), Minuteman II (19661, and Minuteman III (1971). Each missile was more capable than its predecessor: the Titan II carried a larger payload, Minuteman II had more efficient engines, and Minuteman III was the first ICBM to carry multiple warheads. For most of the Cold War era these missile systems comprised the majority of the nation's ICBM force.

As the United States modernized its ICBM force, so did the Soviet Union. Until the late 1960s, U.S. ICBMs were far superior to Soviet missiles, both in terms of quality and quantity. The original Soviet ICBM, the Sapwood (SS-6), achieved a limited operational capability in 1961. It was inaccurate and unreliable, but for the Soviets it was a start. They were committed to achieving nuclear parity with the United States, and during the 1960s deployed four new ICBMs, each more sophisticated than the previous one. The technological evolution of the Soviet Strategic Rocket Forces (SRF) followed a pattern much like the U.S. missile program. By the mid-1960s the Soviet Union had equipped its ICBMs with storable fuel and was basing them in secure, widely dispersed underground silos. In 1965 the SRF unveiled a solid-fuel intermediate-range ballistic missile (IRBM).

By the late 1960s the Soviet aerospace industry had resolved its early production and quality-control problems, and Soviet ICBM production rose steadily. By 1970 the Soviet ICBMs outnumbered American missiles 1,299 to 1,054.[1] The United States regained nuclear superiority in the early 1970s when it deployed Minuteman III ICBMs equipped with multiple independently targetable reentry vehicles (MIRVs). This new technology enabled a single missile to carry multiple warheads, each programmed to strike a different target. By the end of the decade, however, the Soviets also had MIRVs, and by the early 1980s the U.S. lead had evaporated once again. The Air Force, however, had anticipated the development of the new Soviet missiles, and beginning in the late 1970s argued that it urgently needed a new

Opposite: Titan launch

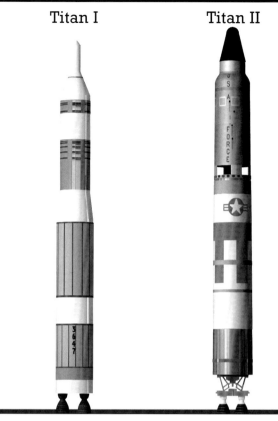

Titan I   Titan II

Titan I vs. Titan II Simplification

A I R B O R N E		
Relays	49	7
Umbilicals	32	4
Valves and Regulators	91	16
G R O U N D E Q U I P M E N T		
Periodic Checkout Functions	322	35
Launch Functions	230	23
Major Underground Structures	42	18
Underground Tunnels (in feet)	6,000	945
Power Requirements (kw) per squadron	12,000	2,700
Squadron Chassis requirements	945	414
Elevator Components per squadron	13.050	0
Ground Guidance Rack	111	36
PTSP Components per squadron	5.640	1.355
Interconnecting Cables per missile		
Total Cables	194	80
Total Wires	3,500	1,900
Total Terminations	8,100	3,840

ICBM not to regain superiority, but to assure parity. Finally, in 1986 the Air Force's Peacekeeper ICBM entered the inventory-the first new U.S. ICBM in fifteen years.

Over the course of the Cold War the evolution of missile technology, coupled with the ever-increasing Soviet nuclear threat, led to widespread changes in the U.S. ICBM force. A steady stream of innovations created missiles that could strike farther, with more power, and with greater accuracy than the first-generation ICBMs. Equally important, the later missiles (the Titan II, Minuteman II, and Minuteman III) were easier and less expensive to maintain than their predecessors. Moreover, the new ICBMs were also more survivable. To enable its missiles to "ride out" a Soviet first strike, the Air Force in the 1960s began "hardening" its missile launch and command and control facilities. It buried the facilities deeper underground and wrapped them in additional layers of reinforced concrete. These facilities were also shielded against the debilitating effects of electromagnetic pulse-a burst of electromagnetic energy generated in a nuclear explosion that can disable electronic systems, interrupt communications, and destroy computer data.

The first missile to undergo extensive modification was the Titan. Throughout the late 1950s the Air Force Ballistic Missile Division (AFBMD) searched for a way to remedy the two major weaknesses that plagued its first generation ICBMs: cryogenic (liquid oxygen) propellant and radio-inertial guidance.

Searching for a fuel alternative, in January 1959 the AFBMD learned that with minor modifications, Titan I could use a noncryogenic oxidizer (nitrogen tetroxide) and a storable fuel that was a mixture of hydrazine and unsymmetrical dimethylhydrazine. The benefits of the new propellant were threefold. First, because the fuel and oxidizer could be stored onboard, the missile could be kept in a constant state of readiness and fired within a minute or two. Second, the new propellant would markedly reduce the chances of a calamitous in-silo explosion such as the ones that had already destroyed two Titan I silos. Third, the new propellant would make it possible to launch the missile from inside its underground silo, thereby reducing its vulnerability to attack.

Several months later, the Air Force decided that, beginning in October 1962, it would equip all of its Titan missiles with all-inertial guidance systems. Shortly thereafter, the AFBMD proposed incorporating both changes (storable, noncryogenic propellant, and all-inertial guidance) into a new ICBM called Titan II.[2]

In November 1959 DoD authorized the Air Force to proceed with the Titan II (SM- 68B) program.[3] The new missile offered a host of advantages over Titan I including in-silo launch, quicker reaction time, improved reliability, reduced main-

---

[a] One spectacular accident occurred while a maintenance worker attempted to replenish a Titan II's onboard oxidizer. During the operation he punctured one of the missile's fuel tanks. The fuel, which was hypergolic, came in contact with oxidizer and burst into flame. The earth-shaking explosion that resulted destroyed the silo and flung the warhead into a nearby field.

tenance, longer range, and a heavier payload. In light of Titan II's clear superiority, in March 1960 Secretary of Defense Thomas Gates ordered the Air Force to suspend the Titan I program after completing six of the anticipated twelve squadrons. Instead he directed that the final six squadrons would be equipped with the Titan II.

The Titan II was the largest ICBM the United States ever built. Standing 108 feet tall and weighing 330,000 pounds, the missile's powerful new first- and second-stage engines increased its range to 9,000 miles. Titan II also carried a payload of 7,500 pounds, almost twice that of its predecessor, which enabled it to carry a devastating 9-megaton warhead.[4] Moreover, the Titan II's inertial navigation system freed the missile from its dependence on a central, ground-based guidance facility. Consequently, Titan II silos could be widely dispersed, with at least seven miles separating each launch facility. In addition, the Titan II launch facilities were "super hardened" to withstand overpressures of between 300 and 350 psi.

The Air Force awarded the Titan II production contract to the Martin Company, and the first captive test flights took place in December 1961 at the company's test facilities outside of Denver.[5] In February 1963 a Titan II fired from the Air Force Missile Test Center (AFMTC) at Patrick AFB, Florida, completed a 6,500-mile test flight, and afterwards the AFBMD judged the missile to be ready to deploy. By December 1963 all six Titan II squadrons, 54 missiles in all, had been turned over to SAC crews.[6] To save money, the Air Force deployed its Titan II squadrons in pairs. Two squadrons were based near Davis-Monthan AFB, Arizona; two more near McConnell AFB, Kansas; and the remaining two squadrons were placed near Little Rock AFB, Arkansas.

Initially the Air Force projected that the Titan IIs would serve into the 1970s but a steady stream of weapon system enhancements and a thorough service life extension program kept the ICBMs on operational alert well into the 1980s. By 1981 the Titan II's advancing age, coupled with a rash of accidents, led the Air Force to recommend deactivating all of its Titan IIs.[a] That process began in 1982 and was completed in 1987.[7]

In conjunction with the Titan II development program, in March 1962 the Air Force contracted with Boeing to begin planning and initial testing for the "Improved Minuteman," later designated Minuteman II (LGM-30F). The Air Force awarded Boeing the Minuteman II production contract in October 1963, and the contractor staged the first Minuteman II test flight in September 1964.

[b] The Minuteman II program proved so successful that in January 1965 the Air Force announced that it would deactivate its Atlas and Titan I squadrons by June of that year. The older missiles were too expensive to keep. Each of the older missiles cost $1 million a year to maintain; the solid-fuel Minuteman cost one tenth of that. *Chronology of the Ballistic Missile Organization 1945–1990* (Norton AFB, CA: Ballistic Missile Organization, History Office, 1990), p. 102.

The Minuteman II was a tremendous improvement over Minuteman I. Although the new ICBM was only 2 feet taller and 8,000 pounds heavier than its predecessor, a new secondstage engine extended the missile's range from 6,300 to 7,000 miles and increased the payload to enable it to carry a 1.2-megaton warhead. Minuteman II was also equipped with a new Autonetics guidance system that narrowed the circular error probable (CEP) to 1.5 miles at maximum range. The Air Force calculated that Minuteman II's greater range, larger warhead, and improved accuracy gave it eight times the "kill" capability of Minuteman I.[8]

The first Minuteman II squadron went on operational alert at Grand Forks AFB, North Dakota, in May 1966, and by April 1967 the Air Force had deployed 200 of the new missiles.[b] Throughout the late 1960s the Air Force replaced many of the older Minuteman I missiles with Minuteman IIs, and by May 1969 the Air Force's solid-fuel ICBM force stood at 1,000 missiles-500 Minuteman Is and an equal number of Minuteman IIs.

The Minuteman IIs remained on duty throughout the Cold War. In 1991 they were taken off operational alert in accordance with the provisions of the Strategic Arms Reduction Talks (START) Agreement. As a result of that accord, the United States and the former Soviet Republics (Russia, Belarus, Kazakhstan, and Ukraine) agreed to limit their longrange missile and bomber forces to 1,600 launchers, and reduce the number of warheads distributed among those delivery systems to 6,000 warheads. [9] Currently the Minuteman IIs are being removed from their silos, and the launch facilities and launch control centers are being demolished.

Soon after the Minuteman II staged its first successful test flight, the Air Force started work on Minuteman III. Although not much larger than its predecessor, the addition of a new third stage increased Minuteman III's range to 8,000 miles and significantly increased its payload. More important, Minuteman III was the first ICBM to be fitted with MIRVs. This new technology enabled a

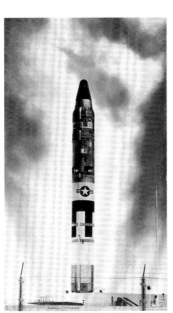

The Titan II was the first ICBM that could be "hot launched" from within its underground silo. The missile, preceded by plumes of smoke from the exhaust ducts that vent the silo, roars skyward.

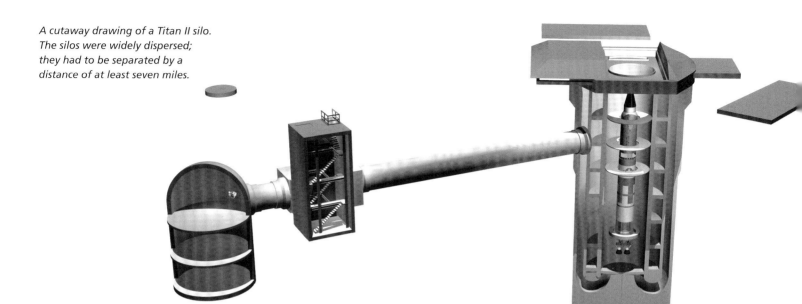

A cutaway drawing of a Titan II silo. The silos were widely dispersed; they had to be separated by a distance of at least seven miles.

single missile to carry multiple warheads, each directed at a different target. Each Minuteman III could carry either two or three warheads, and with the help of a new postboost propulsion system and improved guidance system, each of the 375-kiloton or 170-kiloton warheads was reportedly accurate to within 800 feet of its target.[10]

SAC placed its first squadron of Minuteman IIIs at Minot AFB, North Dakota, on operational alert in January 1971. To make room for the new missiles, all of which were to be placed in reconfigured Minuteman I and II silos, the Air Force retired all of its Minuteman Is and fifty of its older Minuteman IIs. By July 1975 the force modernization was complete and the nation's land-based ICBM force stood at 450 Minuteman IIs, 550 Minuteman IIIs and 54 Titan IIs. Twenty years later, 530 of those Minuteman IIIs are still on guard, and it is expected that the Air Force's Minuteman Integrated Life Extension Program will keep them operational well into the 21st century.

Soon after the first Minuteman IIIs were deployed, SAC planners began their search a third-generation ICBM that would carry the nation's strategic nuclear deterrent into the next century. In April 1972 the Air Force designated its new advanced ICBM program "Missile-X," or MX, and over the next eight years it struggled to determine what capabilities the MX should have and how it should be based.

Basing was a critical consideration. In the early 1970s SAC became increasingly concerned that the next generation of Soviet ICBMs would carry multi-megaton warheads and guidance systems accurate enough to destroy U.S. ICBMs within their hardened silos. To protect the MX from a Soviet first strike, SAC planners considered two alternatives: a mobile launch platform or a super-hardened launch facility. They concentrated on the former. Between 1972 and 1979 the Air Force evaluated almost forty different basing schemes that included trains, transport aircraft, and shuttling the missiles between hundreds of above-ground launch sites scattered over the deserts of the southwest. After seven years of study, the basing mode issue remained unresolved. In June 1979 President Carter could wait no longer; he threw his support behind the Multiple Launch Shelter scheme and authorized the Air Force to proceed with full-scale engineering development.

The Air Force, however, never found a mobile basing mode that Congress liked. As an interim measure in 1983 the Department of Defense authorized the Air Force to install 100 of the newly designated Peacekeeper (LGM-18A) missiles in reconfigured Minuteman III silos at F.E. Warren AFB, Wyoming. Congress objected to the plan and in 1985 voted to limit the deployment to 50 missiles until the Reagan administration could produce a more survivable basing plan. In 1986 the Air Force proposed basing the remaining fifty missiles on twenty-five specially configured trains, an approach it called the Peacekeeper Rail Garrison. The collapse of the Soviet Union, coupled with a shrinking defense budget, prompted President Bush to cancel the program in 1991.[11]

The fifty Peacekeepers at FE. Warren AFB were placed on operational alert between 1986 and 1988. This third-generation ICBM is a four-stage solid-fuel missile that can carry up to ten 500kiloton warheads. The Peacekeeper is 70 feet tall and weighs 195,000 pounds-2 1/2 times the weight of the Minuteman III. Fitting these larger missiles into the existing Minuteman silos was a challenge. It was possible because during the mid-1970s the Air Force envisioned that Peacekeeper would be a mobile missile, and it designed the ICBM to be "cold launched" from a sealed canister. By making certain modifications to the Minuteman silo, the Air Force was able to load the sealed Peacekeeper canister into the existing structure.

To launch the missile, high-pressure steam blows the canister out of the silo and up to an altitude of 150 to 300 feet, whereupon the first-stage engine ignites and the missile streaks off toward its target. Among the many advanced features incorporated in the Peacekeeper is an advanced inertial reference system (AIRS) that can reportedly guide the Peacekeeper's warheads to within 400 feet of their targets.[12]

Today, nearly forty years after deploying its first Atlas missile, the United States continues to rely on ICBMs to provide a vital component of its strategic nuclear deterrent. But just as the Cold War gave the ICBM program life, that conflict's much-heralded passing has had sweeping repercussions on the missile program. With a single stroke of his pen, President Bush in 1991 ordered the deactivation and eventual destruction of 450 Minuteman II missiles. Over the past twenty-five years the nation's ICBM force has been cut almost in half, shrinking from a peak of 1,054 launchers in the mid-1970s to 580 in 1995. Further reductions are pending. Under the provisions of the START I Agreement, almost all of the now-abandoned missile silos, with the exception of the Atlas and Titan I facilities, are being systematically destroyed.

The grates on the wall of the Titan II silo folded down to provide access to the missile from the encircling passageways.

Endnotes

1. Two valuable books trace the evolution of U.S. and Soviet missile forces. The most recent is John Prados, *The Soviet Estimate: U.S. Intelligence Analysis and Soviet Strategic Force* (Princeton, NJ: Princeton University Press), 1986, pp. 57–66, 183–188. See also, Desmond Ball, *Politics and Force Levels: The Strategic Missile Program of the Kennedy Administration* (Berkeley, CA: University of California Press, 1980), pp. 41–58.

2. "Titan Development Plan," Air Force Ballistic Missile Division, 30 November 1959, Ballistic Missile Organization, History Office, Norton AFB, CA, Basic Documents.

3. *Chronology of the Ballistic Missile Organization 1945–1960* (Norton AFB, CA: Ballistic Missile Organization, History Office, 1990), p. 63.

4. *Chronology of the Ballistic Missile Organization*, p. 225; *From Snark to Peacekeeper: A Pictorial History of Strategic Air Command Missiles* (Offutt AFB, NE: Office of the Historian, HQ Strategic Air Command, 1990), p. 23.

5. *Chronology of the Ballistic Missile Organization*, pp. 68, 82.

6. Ibid., pp. 88, 94.

7. With the exception of the Titan II launch complex at Green Valley, Arizona, which has been preserved as a museum, and the Titan II operation and training facility at Vandenberg AFB, all of the Titan II launch facilities have been destroyed in accordance with the arms limitation agreements.

8. "Rockets, Missiles, Spacecraft," *DMS Market Intelligence Reports* (October 1967), p. 2.

9. Treaty Between the United States and the Union of Soviet Socialist Republics on the Reduction and Limitation of Strategic Arms, 31 July 1991. U.S. Arms Control and Disarmament Agency, U.S. Department of State Dispatch Supplement.

10. "Missiles," *DMS Market Intelligence Reports* (1988).

11. *From Snark to Peacekeeper*, pp. 47–48.

12. "Missiles," *DMS Market Intelligence Reports* (1988).

A technician inspects a
Minuteman III in its silo
near Grand Forks AFB.
Note the contrast between
the Minuteman silo and
the Titan II silo picture
opposite.

Technicians at Malstrom AFB, Montana, inspect the two MIRVed warheads mounted on a Minuteman III reentry bus.

12

ARMS CONTROL AGREEMENTS: THE LEGACY FOR PRESERVATION

Throughout the 1960s and 1970s the proliferation of nuclear weaponry and sophisticated delivery systems gave soldiers and diplomats, both in Washington and Moscow, cause for concern. Both sides saw the nuclear arms race as costly and dangerous, and in the late 1960s the two superpowers opened arms limitation talks. These talks led to a series of arms control agreements that began in the early 1970s and continued through the 1994 ratification of the Strategic Arms Reduction Talks Agreement, called START I. Implementation of the START I Agreement led to significant reductions in the U.S. ICBM force and, as a result, hundreds of missiles and launch facilities have been destroyed to comply with the treaty.

SALT I

The movement toward limiting nuclear weaponry began in the mid-1960s when President Lyndon Johnson made several overtures to the Soviet Union to limit nuclear weapons. At that time the United States held a commanding four-to-one advantage in strategic nuclear weapons, and the Soviets had little interest in entering into an arms control agreement that would lock them into a position of permanent inferiority.[a] In fact, the U.S. advantage did not last long. Soviet ICBM production steadily increased throughout the 1960s and American intelligence analysts predicted that by the end of the decade the Soviet ICBM force would equal that of the United States. The Soviets would have probably continued building more ICBMs and ignoring calls for strategic arms limitations had they not been concerned that an American breakthrough in antiballistic missile (ABM) technology could negate their efforts. Consequently, on August 19, 1968, Soviet Ambassador Anatoly Dobrynin announced that the Soviets had agreed to join in strategic arms limitations talks (SALT). Because of the change in U.S. administrations, the start of the bilateral talks was postponed until November 1969. The talks, alternating between Helsinki and Vienna, lasted for the next thirty months.

[a] In 1965 the United States had 854 ICBMs, 496 SLBMs, and 630 long-range bombers compared to the Soviet Union's 224 ICBMs, 102 SLBMs, and 160 bombers.

The SALT I Interim Agreement essentially froze the number of land- and sea-based launchers then in place. By the terms of the agreement the United States could keep 1,054 ICBMs and the Soviet Union 1,618. American conservatives opposed the accord, complaining that the agreement allowed the Soviets far more ICBMs than the United States. Moreover, they also pointed out that the Soviet missiles were far larger and carried more powerful warheads than U.S. ICBMs. Proponents of the agreement were quick to note that the American missiles were far more accurate, and that the Soviet edge in ICBMs was offset by the United States' three-to-one superiority in manned bombers.

On the other end of the political spectrum, U.S. liberals criticized the agreement for not going far enough. They complained that the treaty did not limit force modernization or prohibit arming missiles with multiple independently targetable reentry vehicle (MIRV) technology, which enabled a single missile to carry multiple warheads, each programmed to strike a different target. Indeed, the critics had a valid point. With no limits on the number of warheads each side could deploy, each nation's nuclear stockpile steadily increased over the coming two decades. As the leader in MIRV technology, the United States gained a strategic advantage in the early 1970s when it began equipping each Minuteman III ICBM with three MIRV warheads. However, SALT opponent Senator Henry Jackson (D-Washington) noted that in time the Soviets also would develop MIRV technology and, because their missiles were larger, they would be able to deploy even more warheads. In addition, the SALT I Interim Agreement included no provision to prevent future deployment of mobile missile launchers.[1]

SALT II

As its name implied, the Interim Agreement was intended as a transition toward a more comprehensive accord. Work began in November 1972 to forge a permanent comprehensive agreement and to correct the perceived flaws of the first accord. At the outset, negotiators hoped to sign the SALT II accord quickly. But their original optimism soon faded.

As the Watergate scandal created distraction and discontinuity in the Executive Branch, and east-west relations soured over such issues as the fall of South Vietnam and the Angolan civil war, the negotiations virtually stalled. The introduction of new weapons systems also complicated the arms control equation, as long-range air-launched cruise missiles (ALCMs) entered the American strategic weapons inventory and the Soviet Union deployed long-range Backfire bombers.

After years of tedious, complex negotiations, President Carter and General Secretary Brezhnev signed the SALT II agreement in Vienna on June 18, 1979. The accord limited each side to 2,400 launchers, which included ICBMs, submarine-launched ballistic missiles (SLBMs), heavy bombers, and air-to-surface missiles. SALT II included provisions banning construction of additional ICBM launchers, limiting the number of warheads each missile was allowed to carry, and imposing ceilings on missile size and payload.

The U.S. Senate never ratified SALT II, however, and President Carter withdrew the agreement from consideration in the wake of the December 1979 Soviet invasion of Afghanistan. However, both President Carter and successor Ronald Reagan declared that the United States would do nothing to violate the unratified accord so long as the Soviets acted likewise.[2]

Arms Control in the Reagan Era

Although agreeing to abide by the unratified SALT II accord, the Reagan administration felt the agreement tipped the strategic balance in favor of the Soviet Union. Before engaging in new arms control negotiations, the administration embarked on a wholesale modernization of U.S. strategic forces. Although staying within the confines of SALT II, during the 1980s the United States replaced its aging Titan II ICBMs with the controversial MX and deployed the B-1B bomber and Trident SLBM. With this modernization program underway, in a speech before the National Press Club on November 18, 1981, President Reagan outlined his strategy and proposed to engage the Soviets in Strategic Arms Reduction Talks (START) aimed at substantially reducing the number of nuclear weapons deployed by the two superpowers.

Nearly ten years would pass before a strategic arms reduction accord was reached, and another three years would pass before it could be implemented. A complicating factor in these negotiations was the United States' decision to deploy long-range Pershing II missiles and ground-launched cruise missiles (GLCMs) in western Europe to counter the Soviet Union's earlier deployment of SS-20 intermediate-range missiles in western Russia. 'The crucial sticking point was determining which missiles would, and would not be covered under the agreement. From the Soviets' viewpoint, the new American nuclear-tipped weapons, capable of striking targets deep within their territory, affected the overall superpower strategic balance and thus should be included as part of any strategic arms reductions. In contrast, the Soviets argued that their SS-20 missiles could not reach U.S. cities, and therefore should not be included in the negotiations. However, despite a Soviet propaganda campaign that helped feed a huge antinuclear movement in western Europe as well as pressures at home to compromise, the Reagan administration stuck with its "zero-option" plan: the North Atlantic Treaty Organization (NATO) would remove the U.S. missiles only if all Soviet SS-20 missiles we also dismantled.

Other factors that delayed the strategic arms reduction talks were leadership changes within the Kremlin that finally stabilized with the rise of Mikhail Gorbachev, and President Reagan's Strategic Defense Initiative (SDI), unveiled in 1983. Over the next four years the arms control talks lagged as the Soviets tried to place limits on SDI as a condition for reducing their stock of offensive ballistic missiles.

In 1987, with U.S. Pershing II and cruise missiles in place, the Soviets finally yielded to Reagan's zero-option plan for eliminating intermediate- and short-range missiles from Europe. The signing of the Intermediate Nuclear Forces (INF) Treaty on December 8, 1987, removed one of the major obstacles on the way toward strategic arms reductions. But as negotiators haggled over the strategic arms balance, the geopolitical balance rapidly began to change, and in 1989 the "Iron Curtain" dividing eastern and western Europe tumbled down.

START I and II and the End of the Soviet Union

Finally, on July 31, 1991, President George Bush and President Gorbachev signed the START I treaty, which called for a gradual reduction of strategic arms over the next decade. Soon afterward, the two nations began negotiations toward a START II treaty that would provide further arms reductions. START II was signed in January 1993.

However, before START II could be ratified, START I had to be implemented. No one at the Moscow START I signing ceremony could have foreseen the events of the next month that led to the breakup of the Soviet Union. In the aftermath of the failed coup attempt of August 1991, Russian Federation President Boris

Yeltsin in effect inherited the reins of power from the beleaguered Gorbachev. In the ensuing political chaos, Soviet republics broke away from Russia to form independent states. Three of the new republics (Belarus, Kazakhstan, and Ukraine) inherited part of the Soviet Union's strategic nuclear stockpile. As a result, the three new nations had to be coaxed into the START I framework. Ukraine's divorce from the former Soviet Union, which led to numerous disputes over boundaries, economic relations, and the status of the Black Sea Fleet, was typical of the complexities of the new situation. With their new nation's potential status as the world's third-largest nuclear power, Ukrainian politicians found that they had considerable leverage in dealing with Moscow and Washington.

After extracting numerous concessions, the leaders of the three post-Soviet nuclear powers came together with Presidents Yeltsin and Clinton in Budapest on December 5, 1994, to exchange "instruments of ratification" for START I. With this exchange, START I could be implemented and START II could undergo ratification by the participating countries.[3]

The Impact of START I

START I called on the United States and the former Soviet republics to reduce their nuclear arsenals to 6,000 warheads and limit their launch platforms, including ICBMs, SLBMs, and long-range bombers, to 1,600.[4] The terms of the treaty gave both sides considerable flexibility in removing the launchers from service. Despite the upheavals in the former Soviet Union after the July 1991 signing, both sides began implementing the accord.

On September 27, 1991, President Bush appeared on national television to announce a series of steps designed to reduce Cold War-era nuclear tensions. His first step was to order the Air Force to take all of its 450 Minuteman II ICBMs off operational alert. Within 72 hours of the President's order, the missiles at Whiteman, Ellsworth, and Malmstrom Air Force Bases were taken off alert status for the first time in over twenty years.

Because Whiteman and Ellsworth Air Force Bases hosted only Minuteman II missiles, the presidential order truly marked the end of the missile era. Soon Air Force crews began stripping the missiles of their warheads and guidance systems, and later removed the missiles from their silos. Over the next three years demolition crews began the difficult task of destroying the Minuteman silos and launch control facilities. To raze the silos, contractors first demolished the headframes and then filled the empty tubes with rubble. Afterwards, the construction crews spread topsoil over the site and seeded the area. The launch control centers received a slightly different treatment. Contractors buried the accessways under yards of rubble and covered the site with a thick concrete cap.[b]

For Malmstrom Air Force Base, the missile era was not yet over. The Montana base had its 150 Minuteman II silos taken off alert status, but during 1993 and 1994, 30 of these silos were backfitted with Minuteman III missiles to join an additional 50 silos that had been built for the newer missiles in the late 1960s.

---

[b]Not all of the silos and launch control centers would be demolished. In 1993, the National Park Service selected Elllsworth Launch Control Facility D-1 and Launch Facility D-9 as representative samples for preservation and public display. Meanwhile, the Air Force has set aside Launch Control Center O-1 at Whiteman Air Force Base, Missouri, for preservation and public access.

Along with the 50 silos at Malmstrom that remained unaffected by President Bush's September 27, 1991, order, 450 Minuteman III silos at other sites remained on alert status, split evenly between Minot, Grand Forks, and F.E. Warren Air Force Bases. In addition, F.E. Warren continued to operate 50 Peacekeeper ICBMs.[5]

The Impact of START II

One of George Bush's last acts as President was to travel to Moscow to sign the START II Treaty. If implemented, this accord will reduce each nation's total number of warheads to 3,500. As with START I, both sides were given flexibility in the weapon systems they would withdraw from service. In the United States a Nuclear Posture Review was conducted by DoD during the summer of 1994 to assess America's strategic needs. Looking to provide the nation with a balanced nuclear deterrent, while maintaining a sizable strategic deterrent in case democratic reforms were to fail in the former Soviet Union, a team led by Assistant Secretary of Defense Ashton Carter and Vice Admiral William A. Owens projected a force structure for the year 2003 consisting of 450 to 500 Minuteman III ICBMs, 336 Trident D5 SLBMs, and 66 B-52H Stratofortress bombers. The planners also forecast that by the year 2000, the Peacekeeper ICBMs (with their ten warheads apiece) would be withdrawn from service and the Minutemen IIIs would be converted back to single-warhead missiles to comply with START II provisions.[6]

To support this force mix, the March 1995 Base Realignment and Closure (BRAC) Commission recommended the deactivation of the 321st Strategic Missile Wing at Grand Forks Air Force Base. Consequently, the survival of missile wings at F.E. Warren, Minot, and Malmstrom Air Force Bases seems assured through the end of the century.

Endnotes

1. *Arms Control and Disarmament Agreements: United States Arms Control and Disarmament Agency* (New Brunswick, NJ: Transaction Books, 1984), pp. xxxi-xxxv, 132–154; Donald Baucom, *The Origins of SDI, 1944–1983* (Lawrence, KS: University of Kansas Press, 1993), pp. 70–74.

2. *Arms Control and Disarmament Agreements*, pp. 239–277.

3. Thomas W. Lippman, "START I Agreement Takes Effect Monday," *The Washington Post* (4 December 1994), p. A46.

4. See Article II of the START I Treaty for a more detailed breakdown of implementation objectives and deadlines. *Treaty Between the United States and the Union of Soviet Socialist Republics on the Reduction and Limitation of strategic Offensive Arms*, 31 July 1991. U.S. Arms Control and Disarmament Agency, U.S. Department of State Dispatch Supplement.

5. Information for this section came from the "National Historic Landmark Nomination for the Minuteman Launch Facility and Launch Control Facility at Ellsworth AFB, South Dakota." The study was prepared by the National Park Service Rocky Mountain Region, Division of Partnership and Outreach, 1995.

6. Norman Polmar, "A Decreasing Strategic Force," *Naval Institute Proceedings* (January 1995) pp. 88–89.

13

CONCLUSION

The Cold War produced sweeping changes in the United States' military establishment and society at large. For more than forty years the nation prepared to fight a war that never came. In the process, the United States reversed its longstanding tradition against maintaining a large peacetime military establishment, and at the same time harnessed the nation's industrial might and scientific genius to fashion the world's most sophisticated weapons of war. High technology became the ultimate arbiter of military power, and nowhere was the impact of new technology more evident than on the nation's guided missile program. Armed with nuclear warheads, guided missiles quickly became the defining weapons technology of the Cold War.

The Cold War missile program was born of technologies invented during World War II and nurtured by the arms race. Immediately after World War II the United States rapidly demobilized, and the military curtailed its missile research and development (R&D) programs. But by 1950 the world had changed: the Soviet Union had developed atomic weapons and the United States became embroiled in the Korean conflict, which many thought to be a direct provocation by the Soviet Union and China. Confronted with those challenges, in 1950 America began to re-arm.

The 1950s were a tumultuous decade for the U.S. missile program. One persistent problem was interservice rivalry: the Army and the Air Force squabbled over which service would develop surface-to-air missiles, and all three services fought for the right to develop long-range ballistic missiles. There were also internal disputes within the services. The Air Force was notably reluctant to develop long-range ballistic missiles, and it took a considerable amount of external pressure to convince Air Force leadership to develop the ICBM.

Despite fierce interservice rivalries, the missile program grew rapidly during the 1950s and 1960s. The Army won primary responsibility for developing surface-to-air missiles, and by 1958 it had deployed-200 Nike missile batteries across the country. The Air Force's long-range BOMARC air defense missile program was slower taking shape, but by the early 1960s seven squadrons were based along the nation's eastern and northern borders. In addition, the Army also sought to establish a nationwide antiballistic missile defense system, but after fifteen years of controversy, the program was canceled in 1972 as a result of the Anti-Ballistic Missile Treaty signed with the Soviet Union.

After a bitter struggle in the mid-1950s, the Air Force won control of the IRBM program, and in 1959 began deploying the missiles overseas. After a slow start with the larger ICBM, the Air Force accelerated the Atlas program in 1954, and in 1955 it began work on a second ICBM—the Titan. Three years later it began work on a third ICBM, the revolutionary solid-fuel Minuteman.

Surviving the explosive controversy that erupted around Sputnik and the so-called missile gap, the Air Force placed its first squadron of Atlas missiles on operational alert in 1960. This deployment was followed by the first Titan squadron in April 1962 and the first flight of ten Minuteman missiles the following October. With the help of the Army Corps of Engineers Ballistic Missile Construction Office, which was responsible for building the launch complexes and related support facilities, the Air Force deployed 1,054 ICBMs by the end of the decade. Throughout the Cold War the Air Force continually modernized its ICBMs. In 1963 it unveiled the Titan II, followed by the Minuteman II in 1966, the Minuteman III in 1971, and the Peacekeeper in 1986. Over time U.S. ICBMs became progressively more powerful, more accurate, and better hardened to withstand the effects of a nuclear attack.

Prepared to accompany an Air Force press release, this artist's conceptualization sought to reassure Western farmers and ranchers that the Minuteman launch sites would be safe, unobtrusive neighbors.

Looking back over forty years, several impacts of the Cold War missile program are starkly evident. Within the military establishment, the Cold War missile program altered the services' traditional roles and missions and created the nuclear triad. Furthermore, the missile program recast the relationship between the military, the scientific community, and industry into what President Eisenhower called the military-industrial complex.

The missile technology and expertise developed through the Cold War missile program was the foundation for the U.S. civilian space program. Today the descendants of the Atlas, Thor, and Titan missiles are still boosting payloads into space. Moreover, many technologies developed for the missile program, such as computers, miniaturized electronics, inertial guidance systems, and high-performance fuels, have found widespread civilian applications.

The missile program also brought the Cold War home to many Americans. To farmers in the Great Plains, the Cold War suddenly came to life when the Air Force built Minuteman silos among their wheat fields.

The Army's Nike missile sites provided an even more striking reminder: many of these batteries were located near the most densely populated areas in the nation, and they provided graphic testimony to the severity of the conflict between the United States and Soviet Union.

There were important economic implications as well. The missile program brought sudden prosperity to sleepy towns like White Sands, New Mexico, and Huntsville, Alabama. Across the nation, tens of thousands of Americans found work building the complex missiles and huge launch facilities that would house the new weapons.

Most of these missile launch sites, built with frantic urgency and at great expense, now stand vacant. The Atlas and Titan I launch facilities were declared surplus in the mid-1960s. In most cases the Air Force hired contractors to remove all of the salvageable materials, and afterward the sites were turned over to the General Services Administration for disposal. Most of the silos were not readily adaptable for other uses, so there was little commercial interest in the properties.[a]

The Nike facilities, however, were more adaptable. Located near major cities, the Nike bases offered a collection of sturdy concrete buildings and a support infrastructure that could be put to a variety of uses. For example, the Nike battery outside Davidsonville, Maryland, is now a police training academy, and the battery near Gardner, Kansas, has been converted into the Nike Middle School.

In summary, the Cold War missile program left behind a large and diverse collection of artifacts and structures. Today, hundreds of Nike batteries and ICBM launch facilities still dot the countryside. These launch sites, however, reflect only a fraction of the massive U.S. investment in the Cold War missile program. Behind the launch facilities stood hundreds of research laboratories, test sites, production facilities, training centers, and logistics and maintenance facilities. Many of these sites are still in use, but many others have been closed down, put to other use, or simply abandoned. Before these structures and artifacts are either altered or destroyed, it is important that they be examined and cataloged to enable future generations to gain a better understanding of the historical and cultural legacy of the Cold War missile program.

[a] A couple of notable exceptions are the Atlas E launch sites; one has been converted to a private residence and another is being used as a science and technology center for a local high school.

BIBLIOGRAPHY

Introduction

The literature on the Cold War missile program is extensive and diverse. Fortunately, a significant amount of information is readily available in general reference works, chronologies, selected government studies, congressional hearings and reports, oral histories, monographs, and articles in the aviation press. In many cases a thorough review of these sources will provide the reader with all of the information needed.

For those who wish to delve deeper in the missile program, in addition to the published sources, there are large collections of missile program records stored at government archives and record centers, and to a lesser extent, in Army and Air Force history offices. Among the types of records on file are routine correspondence, detailed technical reports, program planning documents, and program summaries. Unfortunately, these repositories are scattered across the country and their collections are often poorly indexed. Also, getting access to the records is often difficult, for many of the documents are still classified.

Given these hurdles, this bibliography seeks to serve two purposes. The first is to introduce the reader to the existing literature on the Cold War missile program; and the second is to identify and briefly describe the archival collections the authors found useful in preparing this study.

Published Sources

Consulting the published sources is always a good first step for any researcher. Fortunately, much has been written on the missile program, ranging from scholarly monographs to magazine and newspaper articles. All of these sources have something to offer. For example, monographs are often valuable surveys and their detailed endnotes can serve as an introduction to the primary source materials. Articles in the aviation press provide valuable information on technical issues, and coverage in local newspapers reveals the impact of the missile program on small communities.

Record Repositories

Record repositories come in all shapes and sizes ranging from the National Archives and the Federal Record Center to small military history offices. The most valuable record collections that the authors consulted are listed in the following paragraphs.

Since the early 1950s the Air Force has played the predominant role in long-range ballistic missile development. The most complete set of Air Force records, ranging from the late 1940s to the early 1990s is housed at the Ballistic Missile Organization History Office, (BMO/HO) Norton AFB, San Bernardino, California. Over the years BMO/HO has amassed a trove of documents ranging from Atlas program summaries to Peacekeeper technical reports. Much of the material remains classified. For documents on the early years, see the Basic Document Collection, sometimes called the Rockefeller papers. Records relating to specific missile programs are filed by missile type. There is also a fairly detailed finding aid for the collection. Unfortunately, as this study was being prepared, the Air Force disbanded the BMO and turned its responsibilities over to the Air Force Materiel Command, Space and Missile Systems Center, Los Angeles. The BMO/HO archives are being sent to the Air Force Historical Research Agency, Maxwell AF'B, Montgomery, Alabama.

The Air Force Historical Research Agency (AFHRA) is the Air Force's most extensive archive, housing 60 million pages of records. The collection is open to the public, and the agency has a staff of archivists and historians available to assist readers. In preparing this study the authors drew upon AFHRA's extensive collection of unit and oral histories.

The Air Force History Office (AFHO), Bolling AFB, Washington, DC, maintains a small research collection and also houses microfilm copies of many of the documents accessioned at AFHRA through the mid-1970s. Since many microfilm reels contain both classified and unclassified documents, access to unclassified documents is difficult. Consequently, researchers might wish to consult the original documents on file at AFHRA.

The U.S. Strategic Command, Offutt AFB, Nebraska, is a joint command that replaced the Air Force Strategic Air Command (SAC) in the early 1990s. The Strategic Command History Office retains a small collection of SAC missile documents and photographs.

The Army Corps of Engineers supervised the construction of thousands of Cold War missile facilities. Many of the records pertaining to the construction program have been preserved in the Research Collection, Office of History, Headquarters, U.S. Army Corps of Engineers, Alexandria, Virginia. Of special interest are the Corps of Engineers Ballistic Missile Construction Office (CEBMCO) histories that describe the construction of the ICBM launch and control facilities. The Research Collection also houses construction histories for the antiballistic missile system. In addition, the History Office has prepared a helpful index of records of ICBM, Nike, and antiaircraft missile program records for the period 1950–1964, stored at the Washington National Records Center (WNRC), Suitland, Maryland. Access to those records is through the History Office.

Many Air Force and Department of Defense records related to the Cold War missile program are also stored at WNRC. The record center serves as interim storage facilities until the originating agency transfers the records to the National Archives. Researchers must work through the originating agency to gain access to the documents.

WNRC holds two record groups pertinent to the study of the Air Force missile program. Record Group 340, records of the Secretary of the Air Force, accession number 60A-1055, contains the correspondence of Under Secretaries James Douglas, Donald Quarles, and Trevor Gardner. It also contains the correspondence of Secretary of the Air Force Harold Talbott. For a detailed glimpse of the missile program from the Pentagon's perspective, see Record Group 341, records of Headquarters, United States Air Force, accession number 61B-1643. These papers contain the records of the Assistant Chief of Staff for Guided Missiles (AFCGM); the papers of the Guided Missiles Interdepartmental Operational Requirements Group (GMIORG); the papers of K.T. Keller, the Secretary of Defense's Director of Guided Missiles; and the records of the Gardner Committee, also known as the Defense Study Group on Guided Missiles.

For information on the Army's long-range missile program, consult the records at the Army Missile Command (MICOM) History Office, Redstone Arsenal, Huntsville, Alabama. Although the History Office has relatively few documents, it has prepared histories of Redstone Arsenal, the Army Ballistic Missile Agency, and program histories for the Nike Ajax, Nike Hercules, Redstone, and Jupiter missile systems.

The Army Center for Military History (CMH), Washington, DC, also has a collection of records dealing with the Army missile program, including several studies on the Nike Ajax and Hercules missile systems. In addition, the center holds annual histories and related records for the now-defunct U.S. Army Air Defense Command (ARADCOM) that describe the deployment of air defense missiles.

The United States Army Military History Institute (MHI), Carlisle Barracks, Pennsylvania, has an excellent library that includes a nearly complete collection of Argus, the monthly magazine of ARADCOM. *Argus* provided a barometer of social activity at Nike sites from the 1950s to 1970s. In addition, MHI is also the repository of the Army's command and unit histories.

The National Air and Space Museum (NASM), Archives Division, Washington, DC, holds a potpourri of material on the Cold War missile program. The data, which runs the gamut from technical reports to newspaper clippings, varies widely both in terms of quantity and quality. The Archives Branch also maintains an extensive collection of missile photographs.

The Still Pictures Branch, National Archives II, located in College Park, Maryland, maintains an excellent collection of missile photographs for the period 1953–1981. The most notable collections are Record Group 342 B (black and white) and RG 342 B (color). Also of interest is RG 111, Army Signal Corps photographs of missile facilities. For photographs taken after 1981, consult the Defense Still Media Records Center, Anacostia Naval Station, Washington, DC. The Prints and Photographs Division of the Library of Congress, Washington, DC, also maintains a sizable collection of missile photographs. The division also holds copies of the Historic American Engineering Records, including studies of Nike missile installations.

General Reference Works

These general works provide the reader with an overview of the missile program. They touch on the evolution of missile technology and also describe many of the important political and economic dimensions of the Cold War missile program. Jacob Neufeld's book on missile development, Kenneth Schaffel's book on the evolution of continental air defense, and Mark Morgan's volume on Nike are especially valuable.

Futrell, Robert Frank. *Ideas, Concepts, Doctrine: Basic Thinking in the United States Air Force 1907–1960*, vol. I. Maxwell AFB, AL: Air University Press, [1971] 1989.

Futrell, Robert Frank. *Ideas, Concepts, Doctrine: Basic Thinking in the United States Air Force 1961–1984*, vol. II. Maxwell AFB, AL: Air University Press, 1989.

Jane's Aircraft and *Jane's Weapons Systems*, various years.

Morgan, Mark. *Nike Quick Look III* (republished as *Rings of Steel*, Hole in the Head Press), *BOMARC/AF Talos*. Ft Worth, TX: AEROMK, 1990.

Mueller, Robert. *Air Force Bases, vol. I.* Washington, DC: Office of Air Force History, 1989.

Neufeld, Jacob. *The Development of Ballistic Missiles in the United States Air Force 1945–1960.* Washington, DC: Office of Air Force History, 1989.

Schaffel, Kenneth. *The Emerging Shield: The Air Force and the Evolution of Continental Air Defense 1945–1960.* Washington, DC: Office of Air Force History, 1990.

Wolf, Richard I., ed. *The United States Air Force Basic Documents on Roles and Missions.* Washington, DC: Office of Air Force History, 1988.

Chronologies

With most of the books and articles dealing with only a small part of the missile program, it is often difficult to align the scattered events in their proper sequence. These chronologies help, and many contain brief descriptive accounts found nowhere else. The Chronology of the Ballistic Missile Organization 1945–1990 is a superb resource. It gives detailed descriptions of the events, and also contains concise profiles of the missile systems involved.

Chronology of the Army Ballistic Missile Agency: A Record of Significant Events, Technological Progress, and Scientific Accomplishment Since Activation February 1956–December 1960. Redstone Arsenal, Huntsville, AL: Army Ballistic Missile Agency, 1961.

Chronology of the Ballistic Missile Organization 1945–1990 Norton AFB, CA: Ballistic Missile Organization, History Office, 1990.

Chronology Munition System Division: 1946–1989. Eglin AFB, FL: Munition Systems Division History Office, 1989.

Emme, Eugene M. *Aeronautics and Astronautics: An American Chronology of Science and Technology in the Exploration of Space, 1915–1960.* Washington, DC: NASA, 1961.

Follis, Beverly S. *Air Research and Development Command: A Chronology From 1945–1961.* Andrews AFB, MD: Office of History, Headquarters Air Force Systems Command, 1985.

Hall, R. Cargill. "A Selective Chronology [ofl GAL-CIT-JPL Developments, 1926–1950," unpublished, 1967. National Air and Space Museum, Archives Division, Washington DC, file 05-30000-15, folder "Jet Propulsion Lab, Histories, GALCIT."

Narducci, Henry M., ed. *SAC Missile Chronology 1939–1988*. Offutt AFB, NE: Office of the Historian, Headquarters, Strategic Air Command, 1989.

Snyder, Thomas S. *Space and Missile Systems Organization: A Chronology 1954–1976*. Los Angeles, CA: Office of History, Headquarters, Space and Missile Systems Organization, 1976.

U.S. Congress. House. Committee on Science and Astronautics, Special Investigating Subcommittee. *A Chronology of Missile and Astronautic Events.* House Report No. 67. 87th Cong., 1st sess. Washington DC: GPO, 1961. Available in Serial Set 12337.

Studies and Reports

The majority of these reports examine, often in considerable detail, the evolution of specific weapons systems or programs. The majority were written by the military, although some were written by organizations such as the General Accounting Office and the Rand Corporation.

"Air Force Plan (revised) for Simplifying Administrative Procedures for the ICBM and IRBM Programs," [the Gillette Procedures], 10 November 1955, in Jacob Neufeld, T*he Development of Ballistic Missiles in the United States Air Force 1945–1960.* Washington, DC: Office of Air Force History, 1989.

Army Ballistic Missile Agency, "The Jupiter Story," report to Secretary of the Army Brucker, 16 December 1959, Army Missile Command History Office, Redstone Arsenal, file No. 870-5e.

Augenstein, B.W. "A Revised Development Program for Ballistic Missiles of Intercontinental Range." Special Memorandum No. 21. Rand Corporation, Santa Monica, CA, 1954.

The Comptroller General of the United States, "Findings Resulting from the Initial Review of the Ballistic Missile Programs of the Department of the Air Force," report No. B-133042, 27 December 1960. Available at the General Accounting Office, Washington, DC.

The Comptroller General of the United States, "Report on Initial Phase of Review of Administrative Management of the Ballistic Missile Program of the Department of the Air Force," Part II, January 1960, Ballistic Missile Organization History Office, box F-13.

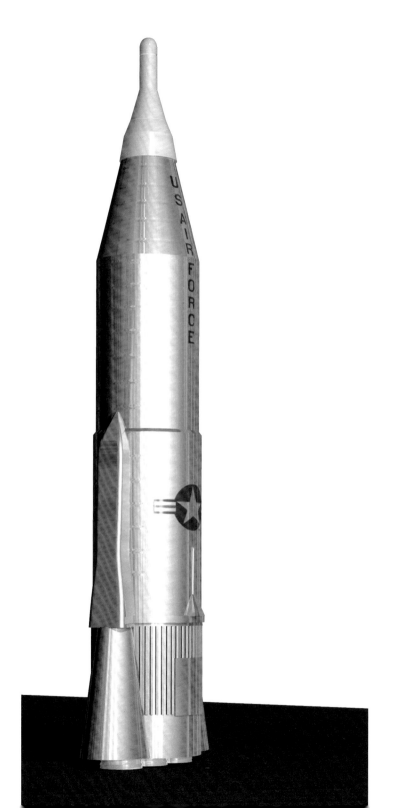

Office of Defense Mobilization, "Report to the President by the Technological Capabilities Panel of the Science Advisory Committee," 14 February 1955, vol. I, Dwight D. Eisenhower Library, Abilene, KS, (hereafter DDE), White House Office: Office of the Staff Secretary, Subject Series, Alpha Subseries, box 16.

Hatheway, Roger, Stephen van Wormer, and Allan Schilz. "Survey and Evaluation of the Nike Missile Sites in the Angeles National Forest, Los Angeles County, California." Prepared by Westec Services for the U.S. Army Corps of Engineers, Los Angeles District, 1987.

Hatheway, Roger, Stephen van Wormer, and Allan Schilz. "Survey and Evaluation of the Nike Missile Site at Fort MacArthur, White Point, Los Angeles, California." Prepared by Westec Services for the U.S. Army Corps of Engineers, Los Angeles District, 1987.

von Karman, Theodore. "Toward New Horizons: Science, the Key to Air Supremacy." A Report by the AAF Scientific Advisory Group, 1945. Reprinted by the Headquarters, Air Force Systems Command, 1992.

McMullen, Richard. *Air Defense and National Policy: 1958–1964*, ADC Historical Study No. 26, n.d. Available on microfilm at the Air Force History Office, file No. K410.011.26, or in hard copy at the Air Force Historical Research Agency.

McMullen, Richard. "Interceptor Missiles in Air Defense 1944–1964." Air Defense Command Historical Study No. 30, (1965). Available on microfilm at the Air Force History Office, file No. K410.011.30, or in hard copy at the Air Force Historical Research Agency.

McMullen, Richard. "The Birth of SAGE, 1951–1953"ADC Historical Study No. 33, (1965). Available on microfilm at the Air Force History Office, Bolling AFB, Washington, DC, or in hard copy at the Air Force Historical Research Agency, Maxwell AFB, Huntsville, AL.

Osato, Timothy, Lt. Col. USA. "Militia Missilemen: The Army National Guard in Air Defense 1951–1967." Center for Military History, Washington D.C., file No. ARADCOM- 3 Cy 1.

Osato, Timothy, Lt. Col. USA and Sherry1 Straup. "ARADCOM's Florida Defense in the Aftermath of the Cuban Missile Crisis: 1963–1968." Headquarters, U.S. Army Air Defense Command, December 1968. Available at the Center for Military History, Washington, DC.

"Professor John von Neumann's Report on Nuclear Weapons," 21 October 1953. Air Force Historical Research Agency, Maxwell AFB, file No. K168.1512-3, folder "Scientific Advisory Board, Nuclear Weapons Panel."

Rockefeller, Alfred, Jr. "History of Titan 1954–1959," n.d. Ballistic Missile Organization History Office, box L-l.

Schriever, Bernard. "A Study of the Development Management Organizations for the Atlas Program," 18 August 1954, Ballistic Missile Organization History Office, box F-2.

"Summary of a report of April 7, 1950 concerning a reexamination of United States Objectives and Strategic Plans (NSC 68)," Dwight D. Eisenhower Library, Abilene, KS.

Volan, Denys. "The History of the Ground Observer Corps." ADC Historical Study No. 36, (1968). Available on microfilm at the Office of Air Force History, or in hard copy at the Air Force Historical Research Agency.

Command and Unit Histories

Usually found in either command history offices or at military repositories such as the Air Force Historical Research Agency, the Corps of Engineers Research Collection, or the Center for Military History, these histories often hold a wealth of information. At the unit level the histories focus on the day-to-day administration and operation of the organization. In contrast, the command histories, which are usually written by trained historians, are of broader scope and more consistent quality.

Branyan, Robert L. *Taming the Mighty Missouri: A History of the Kansas City District, Corps of Engineers.* Kansas City, MO: U.S. Army Engineer District, Kansas City, 1974.

Brown, D. Clayton. *Rivers, Rockets, and Readiness: Army Engineers in the Sunbelt.* Ft. Worth, TX: U.S. Army Engineer District, Fort Worth, 1979.

Brown, D. Clayton. *The Southwestern Division: 50 Years of Service*. Dallas, TX: U.S. Army Engineer District, Southwestern, n.d.

Brown, Eunice H. *White Sands History: Range Beginnings and Early Missile Testing*. White Sands, NM: White Sands Proving Ground, Public Affairs Office, 1959.

Bucker, George E. *Sun, Sand and Water: A History of the Jacksonville District U.S. Army Corps of Engineers, 1821–1975*. Jacksonville, FL: U.S. Army Engineer District, Jacksonville, n.d.

Currie-McDaniel, Ruth and Claus R. Martel. *The U.S. Army Strategic Defense Command: Its History and Role in the Strategic Defense Initiative*, 3rd. ed. Huntsville, AL: U.S. Army Strategic Defense Command, 1989.

DeHaven, Ethel M. "Air Materiel Command Participation in the Air Force Ballistic Missile Program Through December 1957," vol. III, n.d. Air Force Historical Research Agency, file K215.18.

The Federal Engineer; Damsites to Missile Sites: A History of the Omaha District, U.S. Army Corps of Engineers. Omaha, NE: U.S. Army Engineer District, Omaha, n.d.

Ferrell, John. *Heartland Engineers*. Kansas City, MO: U.S. Army Engineer District, Kansas City, 1992.

From Snark to Peacekeeper: A Pictorial History of Strategic Air Command Missiles. Offutt AFB, NE: Office of the Historian, HQ Strategic Air Command, 1990.

Green, Sherman. *History of the Seattle District*. Seattle, WA: U.S. Army Engineer District, Seattle, n.d.

Hagwood, Joseph J. *Commitment to Excellence: A History of the Sacramento District, U.S. Army Corps of Engineers, 1929–1973*. Sacramento, CA. U.S. Army Engineer District, Sacramento, 1976.

Hargreaves, C.D. Maj., USA. "The Historical Report of the Corps of Engineers Ballistic Missile Construction Office and History of the Command Section," n.d. Research Collection, Office of History, Headquarters Army Corps of Engineers, Alexandria, VA, Military Files XVIII-1-4.

"History of the Air Research and Development Command, 01 January 1954–30 June 1954," vol. 2. Air Force Historical Research Agency, file K243.01.

"History of the 389th Missile Wing," April 1963. Available on microfilm at the Office of Air Force History, file No. K-WG-389-HI, or in hard copy at the Air Force Historical Research Agency.

"History of the 341st Strategic Missile Wing and 341st Combat Support Group: 1 April-30 June 1970." Available on microfilm at the Office of Air Force History, file No. K-WG-341-HI, or in hard copy at the Air Force Historical Research Agency.

Joiner, Helen Brents and Elizabeth C. Joliff. *History of the United States Army Missile Command: 1962–1977*. Huntsville, AL: U.S. Army Missile Command, 1979.

Joiner, Helen Brents and Elizabeth C. Joliff. *The Redstone Arsenal Complex in its Second Decade, 1950–1960*. Redstone Arsenal, AL: U.S. Army Missile Command, 1969.

Kitchens, James H. *A History of the Huntsville Division: 15 October 1967–31 December 1976*. Huntsville, AL: U.S Army Engineer Huntsville Division, 1978.

Parkman, Audrey. *Army Engineers in New England: The Military and Civil Work of the Corps of Engineers in New England*. Waltham, MA: U.S. Army Engineer District, New England, 1978.

Rice, Helen. *History of Ogden Air Materiel Area, Hill A.FB, Utah: 1934–1960*. Ogden, UT: Air Force Logistic Center, 1963.

San Bernardino Air Materiel Area, "History of the SBAMA Deactivation Task Force; November 1964-June 1967," vol. I. Air Force History Office, Washington, DC, file No. K205.1204-12.

Second Air Force History, Jul–Dec 1962. Available on microfilm at the Office of Air Force History, K432.01, vol. I, or in hard copy at the Air Force Historical Research Agency.

Snyder, Frank E. and Brian H. Guss. *The District: A History of the Philadelphia District, U.S. Army Corps of Engineers*. Philadelphia, PA: U.S. Army Engineer District, Philadelphia, 1974.

Thompson, Erwin N. *Pacific Ocean Engineers: History of the U.S. Army Corps of Engineers in the Pacific, 1905–1980*. Fort Shafter, HI: U.S. Army Engineer Division, Pacific Ocean, 1980.

Turhollow, Anthony, F. *A History of the Los Angeles District, U.S. Army Corps of Engineers: 1898–1965*. Los Angeles, CA: U.S. Army Engineer District, Los Angeles, 1975.

U.S. Army Corps of Engineers, Ballistic Missile Construction Office, "History of Atlas Missile Base Construction, Warren I," n.d. Research Collection, Office of History, Headquarters Army Corps of Engineers, Alexandria, VA (hereafter Corps of Engineers Collection), Military Files XVIII-14-3.

U.S. Army Corps of Engineers, Ballistic Missile Construction Office, "History of Atlas Missile Base Construction, Warren II," n.d. Corps of Engineers Collection, Military Files XVIII-15-3.

U.S. Army Corps of Engineers, Ballistic Missile Construction Office, "History of Atlas Missile Base Construction, Warren III," n.d. Corps of Engineers Collection, Military Files XVIII-16-18.

U.S. Army Corps of Engineers, Ballistic Missile Construction Office, "History of the Altus Area Office, 14 March 1960–28 April 1962," n.d. Corps of Engineers Research Collection, Military Files XVIII-16-3.

U.S. Army Corps of Engineers, Ballistic Missile Construction Office, "Beale Area Historical Summary: October 1959–March 1962," n.d. Corps of Engineers Research Collection, Military Files XVIII-20-3B.

U.S. Army Corps of Engineers, Ballistic Missile Construction Office, "History of the Davis-Monthan Air Force Base, Arizona, October 1960–January 1965," n.d. Corps of Engineers Research Collection, Military Files XVIII-24-1B.

U.S. Army Corps of Engineers, Ballistic Missile Construction Office, "History of the Dyess Area Office, 18 April 1960–28 April 1962," n.d. Corps of Engineers Research Collection, Military Files XVIII-16-4.

U.S. Army Corps of Engineers, Ballistic Missile Construction Office, "History of Corps of Engineers Activities at Fairchild Air Force Base, Construction of WS-107 l-A, Atlas "E" Missile Complexes, January 1959–February 1961," n.d. Corps of Engineers Research Collection, Military Files XVII-15-1.

U.S. Army Corps of Engineers, Ballistic Missile Construction Office, "History of the Corps of Engineers Activities at Forbes Air Force Base: April 1959–June 1962," n.d. Corps of Engineers Research Collection, Military Files XVIII.

U.S. Army Corps of Engineers, Ballistic Missile Construction Office, "Wing VI Grand Forks Area," n.d. Corps of Engineers Research Collection, Military Files XVIII-10-1.

U.S. Army Corps of Engineers, Ballistic Missile Construction Office, "Larson Area Historical Summary: December 1959–May 1962," n.d. Corps of Engineers Research Collection, Military Files XVII-23-3B.

U.S. Army Corps of Engineers, Ballistic Missile Construction Office, "Historical Summary Report of Major ICBM Construction, Lincoln Area," n.d. Corps of Engineers Research Collection, Military Files XVIII-17-1.

U.S. Army Corps of Engineers, Ballistic Missile Construction Office, "History of the Little Rock Area Office, 5 October 1960–31 July 1963," n.d. Corps of Engineers Research Collection, Military Files XVIII-24-3B.

U.S. Army Corps of Engineers, Ballistic Missile Construction Office, "History of the McConnell Area, U.S. Army Corps of Engineers Ballistic Missile Construction Office," Corps of Engineers Research Collection, Military Files XVIII-2G-1B.

U.S. Army Corps of Engineers, Ballistic Missile Construction Office, "History of WS-133A Minuteman Technical Facilities, Malmstrom Air Force Base," nd. Corps of Engineers Research Collection, Military Files XVIII-10-4.

U.S. Army Corps of Engineers, Ballistic Missile Construction Office, "History of Malmstrom Area During Construction of Co-located Squadron No. 20 Minuteman II ICBM Facilities," n.d. Corps of Engineers Research Collection, Military Files XVIII-10-5.

U.S. Army Corps of Engineers, Ballistic Missile Construction Office, "History of Atlas Missile Base Construction, Offutt, April 1959-July 1960," n.d. Corps of Engineers Research Collection, Military Files XVII-14-2.

U.S. Army Corps of Engineers, Ballistic Missile Construction Office, "History of the Operations Division," n.d. Annex C, Corps of Engineers Research Collection, Military Files XVIII-2-7.

U.S. Army Corps of Engineers, Ballistic Missile Construction Office, "Historical Summary, Plattsburgh Area Office: 1 August 1960-31 October 1962," n.d. Corps of Engineers Research Military Files XVIII-19-1.

U.S. Army Corps of Engineers, Ballistic Missile Construction Office, "History of the Propellant Systems Division, August 1960-April 1962," n.d. Corps of Engineers Research Collection, Military Files XVIII-3-1.

U.S Army Corps of Engineers, Ballistic Missile Construction Office, "History of the Corps of Engineers Activities at Schilling Air Force Base: March 1960-December 1961," n.d. Corps of Engineers Research Collection, Military Files XVII-20-1.

U.S. Army Corps of Engineers, Ballistic Missile Construction Office, "History of Titan I, Ellsworth Area Engineer Office, 8 December 1959-31 March 1962," n.d. Corps of Engineers Research Collection, Military Files XVII-22-1.

U.S. Army Corps of Engineers, Ballistic Missile Construction Office, "History of the Corps of Engineers Ballistic Missile Construction Office and Contract Activities at Walker Air Force Base, Roswell, New Mexico: June 1960-June 1962," n.d. Corps of Engineers Research Collection, Military Files XVIII-21-1B.

U.S. Army Corps of Engineers, Ballistic Missile Construction Office, "Lowry Area History: 29 September 1958-16 December 1961," n.d. Corps of Engineers Research Collection, Military Files XVIII-251B.

U.S. Army Corps of Engineers, Ballistic Missile Construction Office, "Minuteman Missile Facilities: Minot Air Force Base," n.d. Corps of Engineers Research Collection, Military Files XVIII-10-7.

U.S. Army Corps of Engineers, Ballistic Missile Construction Office, "Minuteman, Whiteman Area Historical Report," n.d. Corps of Engineers Research Collection, Military Files XVIII-12-3.

U.S. Army Corps of Engineers, Ballistic Missile Construction Division, "Mountain Home Area Historical Summary February 1960-May 1962," n.d. Corps of Engineers Research Collection, Military Files XVIII-25-3B.

U.S. Army Corps of Engineers, Ballistic Missile Construction Office, "Titan I Directorate Historical Summary Report, 1 August 1960-15 May 1962," n.d. Corps of Engineers Research Collection, Military Files XVIII-l.

U.S. Army Corps of Engineers, Ballistic Missile Construction Office, 'Warren Area Minuteman History," n.d. Corps of Engineers Research Collection, Military Files XVIII-12-1.

Welsh, Michael E. A Mission in the Desert: The Albuquerque District 1935–1985. Albuquerque, NM: U.S. Army Engineer District, Albuquerque, n.d.

Congressional Hearings and Reports

Congressional hearings and reports contain a wealth of information on the missile program. The coverage was especially good during the late 1950s and early 1960s as Congress struggled to come to grips with missile development and the arms race. For an initial overview of the early missile program, consult Charles Donnelly's *Report on the United States Guided Missile Program*, a concise overview that describes the missile development process and discusses the applicable technology. Another valuable overview is the 1959 House report, *Organization and Management of the Missile Programs* that summarizes and compares missile development in the Air Force, Army, and Navy. Another valuable source are the voluminous 1958 Senate hearings, *Inquiry into Satellite and Missile Programs*, which examines both the missile program and the arms race. For information on the construction of missile bases, see the 1961 House report, *Air Force Intercontinental Ballistic Base Construction Program*. Finally, for an overview of the missile program and the arms race, see the 1958 Senate Hearings, *Inquiry into Satellite and Missile Programs*.

U.S. Congress. House. Subcommittee of the Committee on Appropriations. *Hearings, Department of Defense Appropriations for 1960*, 86th Cong., 1st sess. Washington, DC: GPO, 1959. Superintendent of Documents No. (hereafter Sudoc No.) Y4.Ap6/1:D36/5/960 pts. l-5.

U.S. Congress. House. Committee on Appropriations, Subcommittee on Military Construction. *Report, Air Force Intercontinental Ballistic Missile Base Construction Program*. 87th Cong., 1st sess. Washington, DC: GPO, 1961. Sudoc No. Y4.Ap6/1:Ai7/3

U.S. Congress. House. Committee on Government Operations, Military Operations Subcommittee. Hearings, Organization and Management of Missile Programs, 86th Cong., 1st sess., Washington, DC: GPO, 1959. Sudoc No. Y4.G74/7:M69.

U.S. Congress. House. Committee on Government Operations, Military Operations Subcommittee, *Hearings. Organization and Management of Missile Programs*, 86th Cong., 2nd sess., Washington, DC: GPO, 1960. Sudoc No. Y4.G.74/7:M69/960/pts l-3.

U.S. Congress. House. Committee on Government Operations, Military Operations Subcommittee. *Report, Organization and Management of Missile Programs*. Eleventh Committee Report, House Report 1121. 86th Cong., 1st sess., Washington, DC: GPO, 1959. See serial set 12168.

U.S. Congress. Senate. Committee on Armed Services, Preparedness Investigating Subcommittee. *Hearings, Inquiry into Satellite and Missile Programs*. 85th Cong., 1st and 2nd sess. Washington, DC: GPO, 1958. Sudoc No. Y4&5/3:Sa8 pt 1 and pts 2-3.

U.S. Congress. Senate. Committee on Armed Services, Preparedness Investigating Subcommittee. *Report, The United States Guided Missiles Program*. Prepared by Charles A. Donnelly. Committee print. 86th Cong., 1st sess. Washington, DC: GPO, 1959.

Regulations and Executive Orders

The Key West Agreement, Executive Order 9950, "Functions of the Armed Forces and the Joint Chiefs of Staff," 21 April 1948, in Richard I. Wolf, ed., *The United States Air Force: Basic Documents on Roles and Missions*. Washington, DC: Office of Air Force History, 1987, pp. 155-64.

Historic American Engineering Records

"Historic American Engineering Record: Nike Missile Battery PR-79 [Foster, RI]," 1993. (HAER RI-37), Library of Congress, Washington, DC (hereafter LOC), Prints and Photographs Division.

"Historic American Engineering Record: Nike Missile Site C-84 [Barrington, IL]," 1994. (HAER IL-116), LOC, Prints and Photographs Division.

"Historic American Engineering Record: Pueblo Depot Activity," n.d. (HAER CO 51-PUEB.Vl), LOC, Prints and Photographs Division.

"Historic American Engineering Record: Redstone Arsenal," 1985. (HAER, AL 45-HUIV.V.6), LOC, Prints and Photographs Division.

"Historic American Engineering Record: Tarheel Army Missile Plant," n.d. (HAER NC l-BURL.), LOC, Prints and Photographs Division.

"Historic American Engineering Record: White Sands Missile Range V-2 Rocket Facilities," n.d. (HAER NM-lB), LOC, Prints and Photographs Division.

Oral Histories

Doolittle, James H., Lt. Gen., USAF (ret.). Interview by E.M. Emme and W.D. Putnam, 21 April 1969, no location given. National Aeronautics and Space Administration Archives, Washington, DC.

Craige, Laurence C., Lt. Gen., USAF (ret.). Interview by Maj. Paul Clark and Capt. Donald Baucom, n.d., Colorado Springs, CO. Oral History Collection, Air Force Historical Research Agency, Maxwell AFB, AL.

Douglas, James H. Interview by Hugh N. Ahmann, 13-14 June 1979, Chicago, IL. Oral History Collection, Air Force Historical Research Agency, Maxwell AFB, AL.

Putt, Donald L., Maj. Gen., USAF (ret.). Interview by James C. Hasdorff, l-3 April 1973, no location given. Oral History Collection, Air Force Historical Research Agency, Maxwell AFB, AL.

Ritland, Osmand J., Maj. Gen., USAF (ret.). Interview by Lyn R. Officer, 18-21 March 1974, no location given. Oral History Collection, Air Force Historical Research Agency, Maxwell, AL.

Soper, R.E., Col. USAF. Interview by Harry C. Jordan, 29 November 1966, Norton AFB, San Bernadino, CA. Air Force Historical Research Agency, Maxwell AFB, Montgomery AL.

Yates, Donald, Maj. Gen., USAF (ret.). Interview by James C. Hasdorff, l0-12 June 1980, Tavernier, FL. Air Force Historical Research Center, Maxwell, AL.

Interviews

Beckler, David Z., former executive secretary of the Office of Defense Mobilization, Science Advisory Committee. Interview by John Lonnquest, 12 February 1992, Washington, DC.

Dempsey, James R., former President of Convair Astronautics. Interview by John Lonnquest, 26 August 1991, North Arlington, VA.

Ford, Vincent T., Lt. Col., USAF (ret.), former executive officer to Trevor Gardner. Interviews by John Lonnquest, 22 February and 28 March 1992, Chevy Chase, MD.

Funk, Benjamin I., Maj. Gen., USAF (ret.), former commander, Special Aircraft Project Office. Telephone interview by John Lonnquest, 20 August 1991.

Glasser, Otto, Lt. Gen., USAF (ret.), former Atlas and Minuteman project director. Telephone interviews by John Lonnquest, 12, 13, 19 August 1991, 28 September 1994.

Hale, F. Joseph, Col., USAF (ret.), former Thor deputy program manager. Interviews by John Lonnquest, 4 November 1991, 27 August 1993, Raleigh, NC.

Hall, Edward, Col., USAF (ret.), former director of the Western Development Division propulsion directorate, Thor program manager, and originator of the Minuteman concept. Telephone interviews by John Lonnquest, 31 August 1991, 2 September 1991, 17 March 1995.

Jacobson, Richard K, Col., USAF (ret.), former Thor program manager. Interview by John Lonnquest, 24 August 1991, Washington, DC.

Martin, Richard, E, former Atlas engineer, Convair Astronautics. Telephone interview by John Lonnquest, 27 February 1995.

Patterson, William H, former Atlas project director, Convair Astronautics. Telephone interviews by John Lonnquest, 3 October, 22 October 1991, and 17 March 1994.

Ramo, Simon, vice president, Ramo-Wooldridge Corporation. Telephone interview by John Lonnquest, 2 October 1991.

Schriever, Bernard, General, USAF (ret.). Former commander of the Western Development Division, Air Research and Development Command, and the Air Force Systems Command. Interviews by John Lonnquest, 27 August 1991, Arlington, VA, 16 January 1992, Washington, DC; and 27 August 1993, Washington, DC.

Soper, R.E, Col. USAF (ret.). Former director of the Ballistic Missile Division, Office of the Air Force Deputy Chief of Staff for Guided Missiles. Telephone interview by John Lonnquest, 20 August 1992.

Terhune, Charles H., Lt. Gen., USAF (ret.), former vice commander, Western Development Division. Telephone interviews by John Lonnquest, 1 and 5 August 1991.

Speeches

Hayes, T.J, Col. USA. AGC speech at Bismarck, ND, n.d., contained in U.S. Army Corps of Engineers Ballistic Missile Construction Office, "History of the Operations Division," Corps of Engineers Research Collection, Military Files XVIII-18-2.

Medaris, John B., Maj. Gen. USA. Speech, no location given, "The Army Ordnance System," 11 March 1959, U.S. Army Missile Command History Office, Redstone Arsenal, Huntsville, AL, file No. 870~5e, folder, "Medaris, John B. Speeches."

Books

The Cold War missile program has been the subject of numerous books of varying quality. Some are thinly veiled promotional pieces while others are of questionable reliability There are, however, many valuable monographs that combine meticulous research and sound analysis. Among the most valuable are: Edmund Beard, *Developing the ICBM: A Study of Bureaucratic Politics*; Donald Baucom, *The Origins of SDI*; Eugene Emme *The History of Rocket Technology*; Walter McDougall *. . . the Heavens and the Earth*; John Prados, *The Soviet Estimate: U.S. Intelligence and Soviet Strategic Forces*; and Kenneth Werrell, *The Evolution of the Cruise Missile*.

Ambrose, Stephen E. *Eisenhower, vol. II, The President*. New York: Simon and Schuster, 1984.

Anderton, David A. *Strategic Air Command: Two-thirds of the Triad*. New York: Charles Scribner's Sons, 1976.

Armacost, Michael H. *The Politics of Weapons Innovation: The Thor–Jupiter Controversy*. New York: Columbia University Press, 1969.

Arms Control and Disarmament Agreements: United States Arms Control and Disarmament Agency. New Brunswick, NJ: Transaction Books, 1984.

Ball, Desmond. *Politics and Force Levels: The Strategic Missile Program of the Kennedy Administration*. Berkley, CA: University of California Press, 1980.

Baucom, Donald. *The Origins of SDI, 1944–1983*. Lawrence, KS: University of Kansas Press, 1993.

Beard, Edmund. *Developing the ICBM: A Study of Bureaucratic Politics*, Institute of War and Peace Studies Series. New York: Columbia University Press, 1976.

Bell Laboratories. *ABM Research and Development at Bell Laboratories: Project History*. Whippany, NJ: Bell Laboratories, 1975.

Bottome, Edgar M. *The Missile Gap: A Study of the Formulation of Military and Political Policy*. Rutherford, NJ: Farleigh Dickinson Press, 1971.

von Braun, Wernher and Frederick Ordway III. *History of Rockets and Space Travel*, 3rd ed. New York: Thomas Y. Crowell, 1975.

Brown, Michael E. *Flying Blind: The Politics of the U.S. Strategic Bomber Program*. Ithaca, NY: Cornell University Press, 1989.

Bullard, John W. *History of the Redstone Missile System*. Redstone Arsenal, Huntsville, AL: U.S. Army Missile Command, 1965.

Cagle, Mary T. *History of the Nike Hercules Weapon System*. Redstone Arsenal, Huntsville, AL: U.S. Army Missile Command, 1973.

Cagle, Mary T. *Development, Production and Deployment of the Nike Ajax Guided Missile System: 1945–1959*. Redstone Arsenal, Huntsville, AL: Army Rocket and Guided Missile Agency, 1959.

Chapman, John L. *Atlas: The Story of a Missile*. New York: Harper, 1960.

Cleary, Mark. *The 6555th: Missile and Space Launches Through 1970*. Patrick AFB, FL: 45th Space Wing History Office, 1991.

Cochran, Thomas B., William Arkin, and Milton Hoenig. *Nuclear Weapons Databook, vol. I, Nuclear Forces and Capabilities*. Cambridge, MA: Ballinger Publishing Company, 1988.

Davies, Merton E. and William R. Harris. *Rand's Role in the Evolution of Balloon and Satellite Observations Systems and Related U.S. Space Technology*. Santa Monica, CA: Rand Corporation, 1988.

DeHaven, Ethel M. *Aerospace: The Evolution of USAF Weapons Acquisition Policy 1945–1961*, vol. I. Andrews AFB, Landover, MD: Air Force Systems Command, 1962.

Denfield, C. Colt. *The Cold War in Alaska: A Management Plan for Cultural Resources*. Anchorage, AK U.S. Army Corps of Engineers District, Alaska, 1994.

Divine, Robert A. *The Sputnik Challenge*. New York: Oxford University Press, 1993.

Emme, Eugene, M., ed. *The History of Rocket Technology*. Detroit, MI: Wayne State University Press, 1964.

Foreign Relations of the United States, 1955–1957, Vol XIX, *National Security Policy*. Washington, DC: GPO, 1990.

Gaddis, John Lewis. *Strategies of Containment: A Critical Appraisal of Postwar American National Security Policy.* New York: Oxford University Press, 1982.

Gorn, Michael D. *Vulcan's Forge: The Making of an Air Force Command for Weapons Acquisition.* Andrews AFB, MD: Office of History, Headquarters, Air Force Systems Command, 1988.

Greene, Warren E. *The Development of the SM–68 Titan,* AFSC Historical Publication Series 62-23-l (Andrews AFB, Air Force System Command History Office, 1962) Available at AFHRA, file 243.012-7.

Grimwood, James M. and Frances Strowd. *History of the Jupiter Missile System* (U.S. Army Missile Command: Redstone Arsenal, AL, 1962).

Hansen, Chuck. *U.S. Nuclear Weapons: The Secret History.* New York: Orion Books, 1988.

Hartmann, Edwin P. *Adventures in Research: A History of the Ames Research Center 1940–1965,* NASA History Series. Washington, DC: NASA, 1970.

Hartt, Julian. *Mighty Thor: Missile in Readiness.* New York: Duell, Sloan, and Pierce, 1961.

Harwood, William B. *Raise Heaven and Earth.* New York: Simon and Schuster, 1993.

Kennedy, John F. and Alan Nevins. *The Strategy of Peace.* New York: Harper and Brothers, 1960.

Kaplan Fremone E. *The Wizards of Armageddon.* New York: Simon and Schuster, 1983.

Killian, James R. *Sputnik, Scientists, and Eisenhower.* Cambridge: MIT Press, 1977.

MacKenzie, Donald. *Inventing Accuracy: A Historical Sociology of Nuclear Missile Guidance.* Cambridge: MIT press, 1990.

McDougall, Walter. *... the Heavens and the Earth: A Political History of the Space Age.* New York: Basic Books, 1986.

Minuteman Weapon System: History and Description. Hill AFB, UT: Ogden Air Logistics Center, 1990.

Neal, Roy. *Ace in the Hole.* Gardner City, NJ: Doubleday, 1962.

Nike Hercules in Alaska. Anchorage, AK: U.S. Army Corps of Engineers District, Alaska, n.d.

Ordway, Frederick I. and Mitchell R. Sharpe. *The Rocket Team.* New York: Thomas Y. Crowell, 1979.

Patterson, Wiliam H. *America's First ICBM–the Atlas.* Unpublished manuscript, 1985.

Prados, John. *The Soviet Estimate: U.S. Intelligence and Soviet Strategic Forces.* Princeton, NJ: Princeton University Press, 1986.

Rhodes, Richard. *The Making of the Atomic Bomb.* New York: Simon and Schuster, 1986.

Schwiebert, Ernest G. *A History of Air Force Ballistic Missiles.* New York: Frederick A. Praeger, 1964.

Stine, G. Harry. *ICBM.* New York: Orion Books, 1991.

Werrell, Kenneth P. *The Evolution of the Cruise Missile.* Maxwell AFB, Montgomery, AL: Air University Press, 1985.

York, Herbert F. *Race to Oblivion: A Participant's View of the Arms Race.* New York: Simon and Schuster, 1989.

Articles

The missile program has been covered extensively in the aviation and military journals. These articles offer in-depth coverage of many of the important political and technological issues that influenced missile development. Other valuable articles, many of which were written by leading figures in missile development, are available in anthologies on rocketry.

Baker, Norman L. "Thor Engine Reaches Production Test." *Missiles and Rockets* (7 July 1958): pp. 24-5.

Boldrick, Michael R. "Life in the Egg." *Air and Space Smithsonian,* 9 (October-November 1994): pp. 68-73.

Cole, Merle T. "W-25: The Davidsonville Site and Maryland Air Defense, 1950–1974." *Maryland History Magazine* 80 (Fall 1985): pp. 240-60.

Dornberger, Walter R. "The German V-2." In Eugene M. Emme, ed., *The History of Rocket Technology.* Detroit, MI: Wayne State University Press, 1964.

Draper, Stark. "The Evolution of Aerospace Guidance Technology and the Massachusetts Institute of Technology 1935–1951," In *History of Rocketry and Astronautics* vol. 7, part II, vol. 2, Cargill R. Hall, ed. San Diego, CA: American Astronautical Society, 1986.

Ezell, William F and J.K. Mitchell. "Engine One." *Threshold* 7 (Summer 1991): pp. 52-62. (Note, the magazine is privately printed by the Rocketdyne Division, Rockwell International Corp., Canoga Park, California).

Greenwood, John T. "The Air Force Ballistic Missile and Space Program 1954–1964." *Aerospace Historian* 22 (Winter 1974): pp. 190-205.

Hacker, Barton C. "Robert H. Goddard and the Origins of Space Flight." In *Technology in America: A History of Individuals and Ideas*, Carroll W. Purse, Jr., ed. Cambridge, MA: MIT Press, 1981.

Hayes, T. J, Brig. Gen., USA. "ICBM Site Construction." *The Military Engineer* (November-December 1966): pp. 399-403.

Jacobs, Bruce, Brig. Gen., USA. "Nike Hercules is Phased Out of the Army National Guard." *The National Guardsman* (November 1974), reprint.

Lippman, Thomas W. "START I Agreement Takes Effect Monday." *The Washington Post*, (4 December 1994): p. A46.

Malevich, Steven. "Nike Deployment." *Military Engineer* (Nov.-Dec. 1955): pp. 417-20.

Malina, Frank J. "The U.S. Army Air Corps Jet Propulsion Project, GALCIT project No. 1, 1939–1945: A Memoir." In *History of Rocketry and Astronautics*, AAS History Series, vol. 7, part II, vol. 2, R. Cargill Hall, ed. San Diego, CA: American Astronautical Society, 1986, reprint.

"Missiles," *DMS Market Intelligence Reports* (1988).

Norvell, John M. "Base Construction for BOMARC." *Military Engineer* (March-April 1961): pp. 129-31.

Pendray, G. Edward. "Pioneer Rocket Development in the United States." In *The History of Rocket Technology*, Eugene M. Emme, ed. Detroit, MI: Wayne State University Press, 1964.

Perry, Robert. "Atlas, Thor, and Titan." *Technology and Culture* 4 (Fall 1963): pp. 466-77.

Pike, Iain. "Atlas: Pioneer ICBM and Space-Age Workhorse." *Flight International* 81 (January 1962): pp. 89-96.

Polmar, Norman. "A Decreasing Strategic Force." *Naval Institute Proceedings* (January 1995): pp. 88-89.

"Rockets, Missiles, Spacecraft," *DMS Market Intelligence Reports* (October 1967).

Roller, Duane. "Notes on Technical Aspects of Ballistic Missiles." *Air University Quarterly Review* 9 (Summer 1957): pp. 35-68.

Rosenberg, David Allen. "The Origins of Overkill: Nuclear Weapons and American Strategy, 1945–1969," *International Security* 7 (Spring 1983): pp. 3-71.

Schriever, Bernard, Maj. Gen., USAF. "AFBMD: Catching up with the Soviets." *Missiles and Rockets* 4 (28 July 1958): pp. 53.

Schriever, Bernard, Maj. Gen., USAF. "The Ballistic Missile Challenge as Seen by Major General Bernard A. Schriever." *Missiles and Rockets* 2 (April 1957): pp. 94-6.

Schriever, Bernard. "The Role of Management in Technological Conflict." *Air University Quarterly Review* 14 (Winter-Spring 1962-63): pp. 19-29.

Schriever, Bernard, Maj. Gen., USAF. "The USAF Ballistic Missile Program." *Air University Quarterly Review* 9 (Summer 1957): pp. 5-21.

Simmons, John M. "The Navaho Lineage." *Threshold* (December 1987): pp. 17-23.

Smith, E.D. "Missile Projects in Alaska." *The Military Engineer* 52 (March-April 1960): pp. 108-9.

"When is a Decision Not a Decision?" *Air Force Magazine* (October 1957): pp. 32-6.

"Wide Industrial Base Supports Atlas." *Missiles and Rockets* (22 September 1958): p. 25.

Wiesner, Jerome and Herbert York. "National Security and the Nuclear-Test Ban." *Scientific American* 211 (October 1964), pp. 27-36.

Newspapers

Newspapers, especially those of the small towns and military bases that were directly affected by the missile program, are often a good source of information.

"Army Suspends Nickerson From Rank for One Year." *New York Times*, 30 June 1957, pp. 1, 17.

Hill, Gladwin. "Factory Opened for Atlas ICBM." *New York Times*, 12 July 1958, p. 6.

"Missiles Meant Economic Boom for North Country." *Plattsburgh Press–Republican*, 7 July 1964, p. 3-B.

"Spy Case Dropped, Nickerson Admits Leak on Missiles." *New York Times*, 26 June 1957, pp. 1, 14.

Starkweather, Tom. A series of articles on the White Sands Proving Ground printed in the *White Sands Missile Ranger* between 1 December 1989 and 1 January 1991.

Thompson, Fritz. "Atlas' Lair." *Albuquerque Journal*, 27 February 1994, pp. A1, A10.

Theses and Dissertations

Johns, Claude Jr. "The United States Air Force Intercontinental Ballistic Missile Program, 1954–1959: Technological Change and Organizational Innovation." Ph.D. diss., University of North Carolina at Chapel Hill, 1964.

Lonnquest, John C. "The Face of Atlas: General Bernard Schriever and the Development of the Atlas Intercontinental Ballistic Missile, 1953–1960." Ph.D. diss., Duke University, 1996.

Moeller, Steve. "Vigilant and Invisible: The Army's Role in Continental Air Defense, 1950–1974." Master's thesis, Ohio State University, 1992.

Reed, George A. "U.S. Defense Policy, U.S. Air Force Doctrine and Strategic Nuclear Weapons Systems 1958–1964: The Case of the Minuteman ICBM." Ph.D. diss., Duke University, 1986.

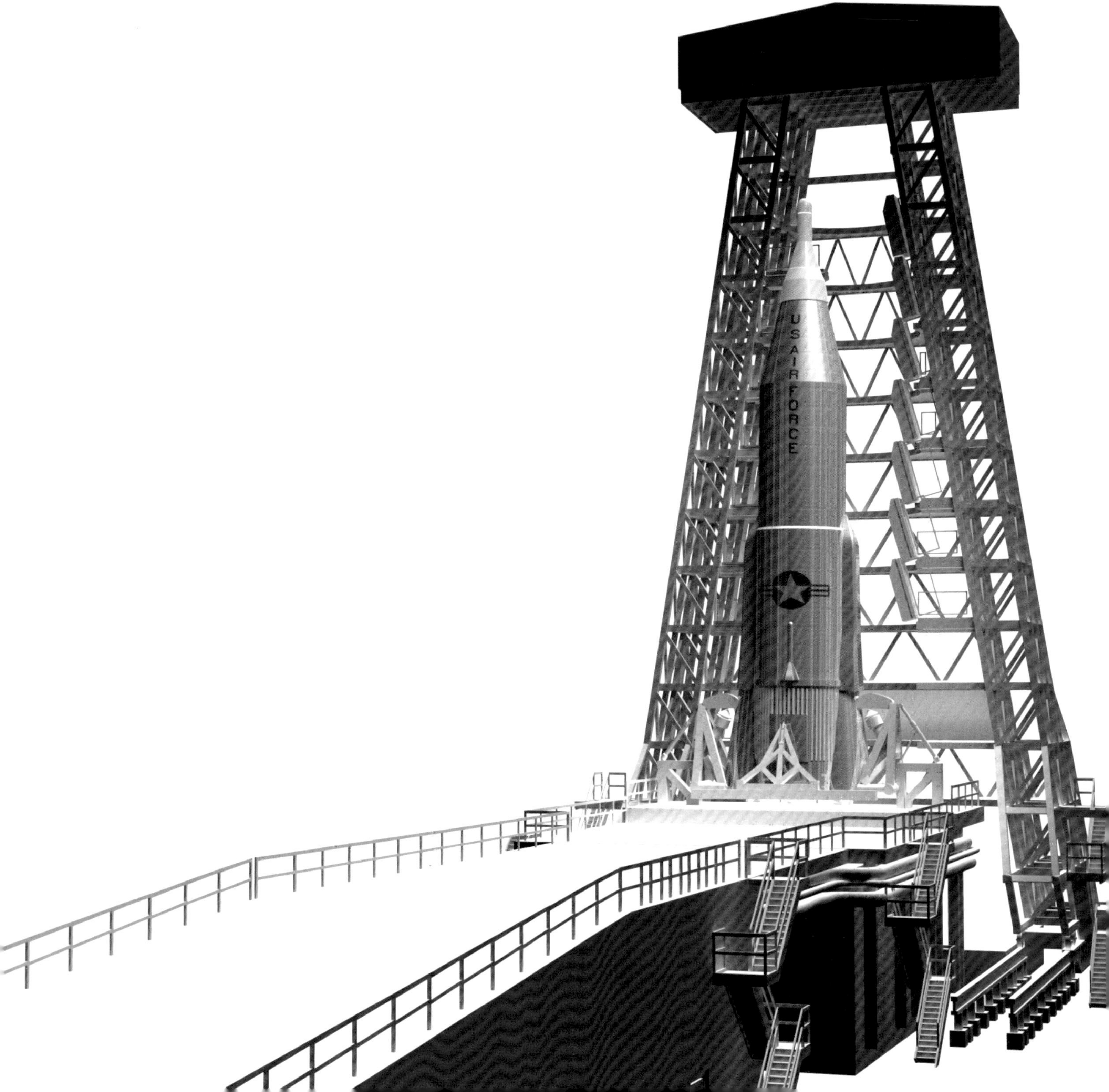
US AIR FORCE

PART II

SYSTEM PROFILES

INTRODUCTION

At the heart of the Cold War missile program were the missiles themselves. These incredibly complex weapons were capable of delivering a multi-megaton warhead half a world away, shooting down hostile aircraft, or even intercepting an incoming ICBM in flight. One must remember, however, that the missiles themselves were only a small part of the operational weapon system; something akin to a bullet in a gun. To become effective instruments of combat power, the missiles had to be based in secure launch facilities, directed to their targets by complex guidance systems, and maintained by dedicated crews and supported by an extensive logistic network.

The system profiles that follow are detailed portraits of Army and Air Force defensive and deterrent missile systems. Each profile includes the missile specifications, the contractors that built it, where it was based, and a detailed description of the launch sites it operated from. Each profile also contains a short reference section. A wide range of photographs and illustrations showing each missile and its various launch configurations complement the text.

The system profiles are grouped by weapons type, and are listed in the order in which they were developed. Also, the reader should keep in mind that the ranges cited for the long-range missiles are expressed in terms of nautical miles. The ranges given for the air-defense missiles are in statute miles.

DEFENSIVE MISSILE SYSTEMS

Nike Ajax (SAM-A-7) (MIM-3, 3A)*

Summary

In 1954, the U.S. Army deployed the world's first operational, guided, surface-to-air missile system. This system, the Nike Ajax, was conceived near the end of World War II and developed during the early years of the Cold War. With an increasing perception of a direct Soviet bomber threat to the American mainland, the Army rushed Nike Ajax into production and deployed the missile system around key urban, military, and industrial locations.

The Nike Ajax contractor, Western Electric's Bell Telephone Laboratories, teamed with numerous subcontractors to produce 350 missile batteries for domestic and overseas deployment. The primary subcontractor, Douglas Aircraft, built 13,714 missiles at its Santa Monica plant and at the Army Ordnance Missile Plant located at Charlotte, North Carolina.

By 1958, the Army deployed nearly 200 Nike Ajax batteries around the nation's cities and vital military installations. Soon thereafter, the Army began gradually deactivating the Nike Ajax batteries and replacing them with the longer-range nuclear-capable Nike Hercules. The Army Air Defense Command (ARADCOM) deactivated the last Nike Ajax batteries guarding the Norfolk, Virginia, area in late 1963.

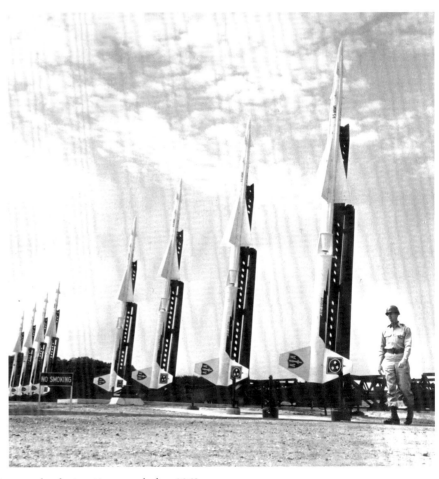

*SAM-A-7 was the designation before 1962, and MIM, 3A were the designations used after 1962.

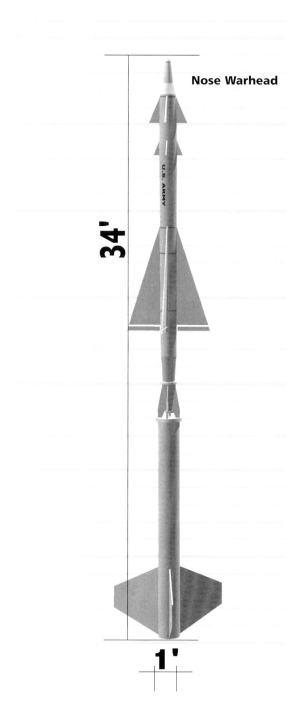

Nose Warhead

34'

U.S. ARMY

1'

NIKE AJAX

Technical Specifications

Length: 21 feet (34 feet 10 inches with booster)
Diameter: 12 inches
Wingspan: 4 feet, 6 inches
Weight: 1,000 pounds (over 2,455 pounds with booster)
Missile fuel/oxidizer: M3, a combination of JP4 jet fuel and starter fluid consisting initially of aniline/furfuryl alcohol, later dimethyl-hydrazine, and finally, red fuming nitric acid (IRFNA)
Booster fuel: Solid propellant
Range: 25 to 30 miles
Speed: Mach 2.3 (1,679 mph)
Altitude: Up to 70,000 feet
Guidance: Command by electronic computer and radar
Warhead: Three high-explosive fragmentation warheads mounted in the nose, center, and aft sections

Contractors

Airframe: Douglas Aircraft Company, Santa Monica, California
Propulsion:

> Booster: Hercules Powder Company, Radford Arsenal, Virginia
> Sustainer: Bell Aircraft Company, Buffalo, New York
> Guidance: Western Electric Company, New York, New York

System Operation

The Nike Ajax command guidance system received guidance information from a computer on the ground. Designed to engage faster and higher-flying aircraft beyond the range of conventional antiaircraft artillery, the Nike system depended on technological advances in radar and computers made during and after World War II.

A series of events preceded any missile launch. First, an Air Defense Command Post sent warning to the battery of an imminent attack. Sirens would send personnel scurrying to their assigned battle stations. At the launching area, personnel conducted last-minute prefiring checks and positioned the missiles on the launchers.

As personnel readied the missiles, the incoming aircraft was picked up on a long-range acquisition radar. For the Nike Ajax system, this radar was known as LOPAR for "Low-Power Acquisition Radar." The LOPAR search radar antenna

rotated constantly at a predetermined speed. When targets appeared on the scope, the battery commander used "electronic interrogation" to determine if the target was friend or foe.

Once the LOPAR operator designated a target as hostile, this information was transferred to a target-tracking radar (TTR). The TTR determined the target's azimuth, elevation, and range, and then automatically provided that information to a computer for use in guiding the Nike Ajax missile. Once energized, the guidance computer received a running account of the target's changing position.

Adjacent to the TTR, the missile-tracking radar (MTR) locked onto the missile selected to perform the intercept. When the hostile aircraft came within the battery's range, the battery commander launched the missile. After producing 59,000 pounds of thrust within three seconds to push the missile off the launch rail, the missile booster dropped away. Having ignited, the missile accelerated through the sound barrier. Once the missile was in the air, the MTR received continuous data on the missile's flight. In turn, by receiving updates from the TTR, the computer generated course correction information that was transmitted to guide the missile toward the target. At the predicted intercept point, the computer transmitted a burst signal that detonated the three high-explosive warheads.

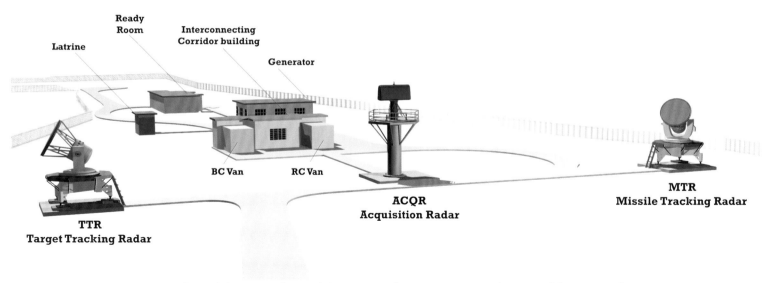

Latrine

Ready Room

Interconnecting Corridor building

Generator

BC Van

RC Van

TTR
Target Tracking Radar

ACQR
Acquisition Radar

MTR
Missile Tracking Radar

One of the major flaws of the Ajax guidance system was that it could engage only one target at a time. Also, when the system first deployed, there was no provision for coordinating fire between multiple batteries. Thus, several different batteries could engage the same target and allow other targets to pass through. To alleviate this problem, ARADCOM established command centers where incoming targets were manually plotted and engagement orders were passed to the batteries. However, the inadequacies of this voice command and control system became immediately apparent during defense exercises, which sent the Army scrambling for a new solution.

Introduced in the late 1950s the Interim Battery Data Link (IBDL) provided a "real-time" target data link between the batteries so that battery commanders could readily see what targets other batteries were actively engaging.

While IBDL was being deployed, the Army tested a successor system called "Missile Master" at Fort Meade, Maryland. After this system was proven within the Baltimore-Washington Defense Area, other major defense areas began receiving the Missile Master (AN/FSG-1) systems. Missile Master was the first truly integrating command and control system featuring automatic data communications, processing, and display equipment. By eliminating voice communications, this Martin-built system allowed an area commander to use all his batteries to engage up to 24 different targets.

Smaller defense areas with fewer batteries received another command and control system called the Battery Integration and Radar Display Equipment "BIRDIE" (AN/GSG-5).

Developmental History

In 1944, German advances in rocketry and jet aircraft, as well as the ability of bombers to fly at higher altitudes, brought to Army planners a somber realization that traditional antiaircraft artillery weaponry soon faced obsolescence. As a result of internal studies verifying the need for a "major caliber anti-aircraft rocket torpedo," the Army Chief of Ordnance issued a contract in February 1945 for Western Electric and Bell Telephone Laboratories (BTL) to determine the feasibility of such a weapon system. Army Ordnance based its selection of Western Electric/BTL on the team's experience in developing and producing gun directors and tracking radars.

Reporting back in mid-1945 that such an antiaircraft missile system was indeed feasible, Western Electric/BTL presented the parameters of a proposed system that came remarkably close to the system actually fielded eight years later. The Army selected Western Electric as the prime contractor to develop the missile system. BTL maintained control of computer and radar development and worked with the Ballistics Research Laboratory at Aberdeen Proving Ground, Maryland, in determining the optimum shape of the warhead. Picatinny Arsenal, New Jersey, received responsibility for developing the High-Explosive (HE) fragmentation device that would be placed in the warhead, while Frankford Arsenal, Pennsylvania, created the fusing device.

The Douglas Aircraft Company became a major subcontractor, responsible for aerodynamic studies on the interceptor missile. Aerojet Engineering supplied both the liquid-fueled sustainer engine and the solid-fueled booster rockets. The initial design called for eight booster rockets to be wrapped around the tail of the missile. The development schedule projected a weapon system ready for production in 1949. This schedule was not met.

The first static firing of a Nike missile occurred at White Sands Proving Ground, New Mexico, on September 17, 1946. The missile was returned to Douglas's Santa Monica plant for evaluation. A week after the first static test, the first actual launch of a missile occurred at White Sands. Several other "uncontrolled flight" launchings occurred that fall, with one missile reaching an altitude of 140,000 feet. Instead of warheads, these missiles carried onboard cameras to record instrument readings throughout the flight.

Launches at White Sands continued in 1947. Meanwhile, tracking experiments proceeded at Whippany, New Jersey, using an experimental monopulse radar.

By 1948 the missile project had fallen behind schedule. Problems with the reliability of the cluster booster configuration forced designers to adapt an Allegheny Ballistics Laboratory booster that had been developed for the Navy's antiaircraft missile program. With this single solid-fuel booster, the missile took on an elongated appearance as the missile now sat piggy-back on top of the booster. Launchings at White Sands now tested for roll stabilization and steering controls. Problems were resolved only after tedious study of telemetry records.

Technical advances continued at both White Sands and BTL. These advances sufficiently impressed the DoD Director of Guided Missiles, K.T. Keller, in October 1950 to recommend acceleration of the program. Despite the fact that system testing was still ongoing, the Army let a contract in January 1951 for Western Electric, BTL, and Douglas Aircraft to produce 1,000 Nike Ajax missiles (or the Nike I as it was then called) and sixty sets of ground equipment.

The Army's faith was justified when on November 27, 1951, a Nike successfully engaged a QB-17 drone over the skies of New Mexico. During the following April additional tests with live warheads further impressed VIPs visiting at White Sands. By July 1952, the first production-line Nike was launched. Testing continued to evaluate the missile and improve the reliability of the production models. By the following summer, the contractors were ready to turn over a complete missile battery to the Army Anti-Aircraft Command (ARAACOM). Soon soldiers were training to operate and maintain the system.

Over the next few years, hundreds of Nike Ajax missiles streaked across the southern New Mexico sky as battery crews, called "packages," trained at nearby Fort Bliss, Texas, before deploying. Later, most of these men returned to Fort Bliss to fire additional missiles during Annual Service Practices (ASPs). Beginning in 1957, many of the men who underwent initial training were National Guardsmen.

Basing Strategy

The Nike Ajax system was designed to supplement and then replace gun batteries deployed around the nation's major urban areas and vital military installations. ARAACOM's original basing strategy projected a central missile assembly point from which missiles would be taken out to prepared above-ground launch racks ringing the defended area. However, ARAACOM discarded this semimobile concept because the system needed to be ready for instantaneous action to fend off a "surprise attack." Instead, a fixed-site scheme was devised.

Due to geographical factors, the placement of Nike Ajax batteries differed at each location. In Chicago, for example, the broad expanse of Lake Michigan forced ARAACOM to erect batteries along the lakefront near the heart of the city. In planning Chicago and other area defenses, ARAACOM planners carefully examined all possible enemy aircraft approaches to ensure no gaps were left open. Initially, the planners chose fixed sites well away from the defended area and the Corps of Engineers Real Estate Offices began seeking tracts of land in rural areas. However, in late 1952, the planners determined that close-in perimeter sites would provide enhanced firepower. Staggering sites between outskirt and close-in locations gave defenders a greater defense-in-depth capability. The Corps of Engineers Real Estate Offices recognized that projected acreage requirements of 119 acres per site would not be feasible in some of the urban areas selected for missile deployment. To solve this problem, design architect Leon Chatelain, Jr., devised an underground magazine configuration that cut the land requirement down to forty acres.

The Army constructed a prototype magazine at White Sands in June 1953 and fired missiles from the magazine elevator platform to demonstrate the design's practicality. With the design proven, Chatelain, along with the architectural firm of Spector and Montgomery, began preparing drawings for nationwide distribution. On October 28, 1953, ARAACOM directed that the underground magazine design would be used in most cases.

To minimize land acquisition costs, public lands were to be used whenever possible, even at the cost of tactical considerations. Often the only public lands available were parklands. Occasionally the Army had to confront local citizens who opposed the use of parkland and were concerned with public safety. Most of the time, the Army had no choice but to acquire private property. Some private landowners, not understanding the very restrictive requirements for a Nike installation, assumed Army land demands were made either arbitrarily or capriciously. Occasionally, local opposition succeeded in getting the Army to move a planned site to a new location.

Once the land was acquired, local Corps of Engineer Districts contracted with private construction firms to execute the Chatelain plans.

Nike Ajax Deployment

The first Nike Ajax unit deployed to an above-ground site at Fort Meade, Maryland, in March 1954. Over the next four years, nearly 200 batteries were constructed around the majority of America's major northern tier and coastal cities. In June 1958, a process of conversion to the longer range Nike Hercules missile began.

Subsequently, the Nike Ajax batteries were either modified to accept the new missile or deactivated. In November 1963, Site N-63 guarding Norfolk, Virginia, was the last Nike Ajax battery to be deactivated. However, the Nike Ajax missile continued service overseas with the U.S. Army and with the military forces of America's allies for many more years.

Site Configuration

Each Nike missile battery was divided into three principle areas: the administrative area, integrated fire control area (IFC), and the launch area. The administrative area was usually collocated within the IFC or launch areas. The IFC and launch areas were separated by at least 1,000 yards, often over a mile, but were within visual sight of each other.

The administrative area included barracks, a mess hall, and a recreation/administration supply building. These buildings were typically one-story cinder block structures with flat roofs. The area also contained a large motor maintenance building with wash and grease racks and a fuel tank with a gasoline pump.

The IFC hosted the three acquisition and tracking radars as well as the battery control trailer, radar control trailer, maintenance and spares trailer, power plant, and electric cabling system.

An aerial view of the integrated fire control area, Site S-61, Vashion Island, Washington. Although this 1971 photograph shows the site configured to handle the Nike Hercules, all of the earlier Nike Ajax radars are still in place. Positioned outward from the radar dome are the Target-Ranging Radar, Target-Tracking Radar, the Missile-Tracking Radar, and at the forward edge of the installation, the low-power acquisition radar. The buildings in the foreground are barracks and support buildings.

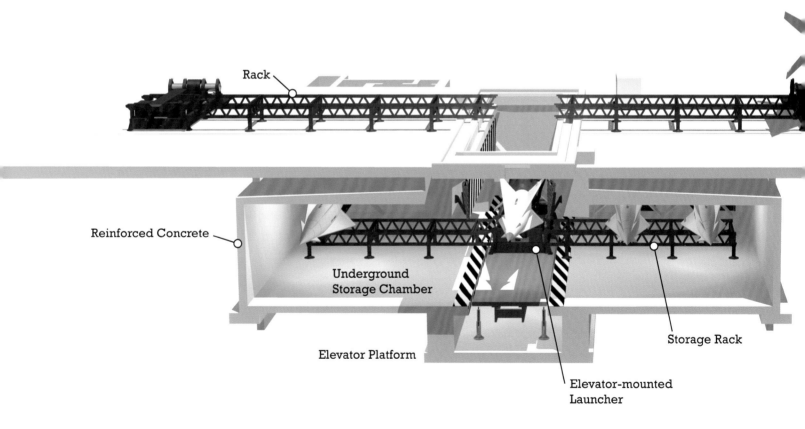

Hercules magazine and above-ground launchers

Rack

Reinforced Concrete

Underground
Storage Chamber

Elevator Platform

Elevator-mounted
Launcher

Storage Rack

The battery control trailer contained the missile guidance computer, the acquisition radar scope and controls, and the telephone switchboard. From here the battery commander identified targets and directed missile launches. The radar control trailer held controls and electronic equipment for the TTR and MTR. The maintenance and spares trailer contained test equipment and spare parts. Three 400-cycle diesel-driven generators were installed to provide electrical power to this area. The electric cabling system transmitted data within the control area and to the launch area. A collimation test mast was placed at each battery control area to provide a common reference point for adjusting the radars.

The first Nike sites featured above-ground launchers. This quickly changed as land restrictions forced the Army to construct space-saving underground magazines. Capable of hosting twelve Nike Ajax missiles, each magazine had an elevator that lifted the missile to the surface in a horizontal position. Once above ground, the missile could be pushed manually along a railing to a launcher placed parallel to the elevator. Typically, four launchers sat atop the magazine.

Near the launchers, a trailer housed the launch control officer and the controls he operated to launch missiles. In addition to the launch control trailer, the launch area contained a generator building with three diesel generators, frequency converters, and missile assembly and maintenance structures.

References

For details on missile development, see Mary T. Cagle's *Development, Production, and Development of the Nike Ajax Guided Missile System: 1945– 1959*, (Redstone Arsenal, Huntsville, AL: Army Ordnance Missile Command, 1959). Information for the technical specifications came from Mark Morgan's *Nike Quick Look III, (republished as Rings of Steel, Hole in the Head Press), BOMARC/AF Talos*, (Fort Worth, TX: AEROMK, June 1990) and Bill Gunston's *World Encyclopedia of Rockets and Missiles* (New York: Crescent Books, 1979). An excellent overview of how the Nike Ajax functioned is found at the Center for Military History in a booklet titled "Thirty-Second Antiaircraft Artillery Brigade," (HRC 471.94). Problems involved with Nike Ajax deployment are found in Steven Malevich, "Nike Deployment," *Military Engineer*, (Nov–Dec 1955).

A valuable source of information on the Nike Ajax batteries was the Historic American Engineering Records including, "Nike Missile Battery PR-79," n.d., (HAER, No. RI-37); and "Nike Missile Site C-84," 1994, (HAER No. IL-116) available at the Library of Congress, Prints and Photographs Division, Washington, DC. Other material included Roger Hatheway, Stephen Van Wormer, and Allan Schilz, "Survey and Evaluation of the Nike Missile Site at Fort MacArthur, White Point Los Angeles County, California," and "Survey and Evaluation of Nike Missile Sites in the Angeles National Forest, Los Angeles County California." Both studies were prepared for the Corps of Engineers, Los Angeles District, by Westec Services Inc. in 1987.

This 1956 photograph shows the Nike Ajax launch area belonging to the 740th AAA Missile Battalion near Fort Winfield Scott, California. Clockwise from the left are the missile assembly and electronic test building, the generator building, the large protec berm surrounding the fueling area, and the missile launchers.

Nike Hercules (SAM-N-25) (MIM-14/14A/14B)

Summary

As the Nike Ajax system underwent testing during the early 1950s, the Army became concerned that the missile was incapable of stopping a massed Soviet air attack. To enhance the missile's capabilities, the Army explored the feasibility of equipping Ajax with a nuclear warhead, but when that proved impractical, in July 1953 the service authorized development of a second generation surface-to-air missile, the Nike Hercules. As with Nike Ajax, Western Electric was the primary contractor with Bell Telephone Laboratories providing the guidance systems and Douglas Aircraft serving as the major subcontractor for the airframe.

In 1958, five years after the Army received approval to design and build the system, Nike Hercules stood ready to deploy from converted Nike Ajax batteries located in the New York, Philadelphia, and Chicago defense areas. However, as Nike Hercules batteries became operational, the bitter feud between the Army and Air Force over control of the nation's air defense missile force flared anew. The Air Force opposed Nike Hercules, claiming that the Army missile duplicated the capabilities of the soon-to-be-deployed BOMARC. Eventually, both of the competing missiles systems were deployed, but the Nike Hercules would be fielded in far greater numbers over the next six years.

During the course of the Cold War, the Army deployed 145 Nike Hercules batteries. Of that number, 35 were built exclusively for the new missile and 110 were converted Nike Ajax installations. With the exception of batteries in Alaska and Florida that stayed active until the late 1970s, by 1975 all Nike Hercules sites had been deactivated.

Technical Specifications

Length: 41 feet
Diameter: 31.5 inches
Wingspan: 6 feet, 2 inches
Weight: 10,710 pounds
Booster fuel: Solid propellant
Missile fuel: Solid propellant
Range: Over 75 miles
Speed: Mach 3.65 (2,707 mph)
Altitude: Up to 150,000 feet
Guidance: Command by electronic computer and radar
Warhead: High-Explosive fragmentation or nuclear

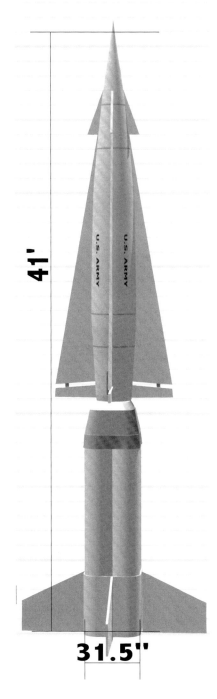

41'

31.5"

HERCULES

Contractors

Airframe: Douglas Aircraft Company Santa Monica, California

Propulsion:

Booster: Hercules Powder Company, Radford Arsenal, Virginia

Sustainer: Thiokol Chemical Corporation, Longhorn Division, Marshall, Texas

Guidance: Western Electric Company, New York

System Operation

Nike Hercules was designed to use the supporting components of the Nike Ajax system. To engage hostile targets, missilemen followed procedures similar to those used with the Nike Ajax.

Because of the increased capability of the system, there were some additions to the ground equipment. For example, a High-Powered Acquisition Radar (HIPAR) was installed to track targets at greater range. Alternate Battery Radars (ABARs) were also installed as backup units. In addition, a Target Ranging Radar was added to counter enemy radar jamming attempts.

"Missile Master" or "BIRDIE" command and control systems were installed at Army Air Defense Command Posts to ensure a coordinated defense against attacking aircraft. Despite the data automation, Missile Master was still a labor-intensive system that eventually became over-capable because the increased range of Nike Hercules reduced the number of batteries that needed to be coordinated. "Missile Mentor," a solid-state system costing one tenth of Missile Master, arrived as a replacement system in the mid-1960s.

Developmental History

In March 1952, due to limitations of the soon-to-be-deployed Nike Ajax system (including the inability to discern individual bombers within a densely-packed flying formation), the Bureau of Ordnance recommended a study of the feasibility of equipping Nike Ajax with a nuclear warhead. Two months later, the Chief of Ordnance asked Bell Telephone Laboratories (BTL) to examine the feasibility of a nuclear Nike Ajax using the current ground system. After consulting with Picatinny Arsenal and Sandia Laboratories, BTL recommended either fitting an XW-9 warhead into the Nike Ajax or building a wider missile to carry the more potent XW-7 warhead.

In August, the Chief of Ordnance approved an engineering study to investigate the latter option with the objective of fielding a weapon quickly at minimum cost. As a result of this study, in December the Deputy Chief of Plans and Research approved plans for the follow-on project.

Two months later, in February 1953, the Army asked BTL to develop detailed proposals for a Nike "B" or Hercules. A month later, Bell and Douglas Aircraft Company representatives outlined three ground guidance systems for missile designs varying in range from 25 to 50 miles. Longer range missiles would require major revisions to facilities currently being constructed for the Nike Ajax. Soon thereafter, Nike "B" received approval from the Joint Chiefs of Staff with a 1A priority.

On July 16, 1953, the Secretary of the Army formally established the Nike "B" program with the objective of obtaining a weapon that could intercept aircraft flying at 1,000 miles per hour, at an altitude of 60,000 feet, and a horizontal range of 50,000 yards.

Western Electric, BTL, and Douglas began the research and development phase and by 1955 began conducting test firings at White Sands Proving Ground,

A solid-fuel Nike Hercules missile rests on its elevator-mounted launcher. The four dark colored solid-fuel boosters are clustered together just forward of the tail.

This photograph of the integrated fire control area at Site LA-04 at Mt. Gleason, California, shows the different types of radar used by the Nike Hercules missile system. Atop the pedestal tower and covered by a protective radome was the High Power Radar (HIPAR). It had a range of approximately 350 miles. Next to it was the multi-frequency Target Ranging Radar (TRR); the Target Tracking Radar (TTR) that determined the target's speed, altitude, and direction; and the Missile Tracking Radar (MTR) that guided the outgoing missile to its target. Standing alone at the forward edge of the radar area was the T-shaped Low Power Acquisition Radar (LOPAR). Developed for the Nike Ajax program, it had a range of 150 miles.

New Mexico. To build the new missile, the Nike Hercules design team simply took the components of the Ajax missile and multiplied by four. Four solid booster rockets were strapped together to push the missile into flight. Once the booster rockets fell away, four liquid-propellant driven engines would carry the warhead to the target. Unfortunately, this design, dependent on multiple systems, hindered reliability. Of the first twenty flights, twelve had to be terminated due to malfunctions. On September 30, 1955, tragedy struck at White Sands when a liquid-fueled engine undergoing static testing exploded with such force that the protective bunker sustained damage. This explosion killed one worker and injured five others. This incident convinced designers to consider a solid propellant engine for the sustainer missile.

Testing continued. October 31, 1956, marked the first successful Nike Hercules intercept of a drone aircraft. On March 13, 1957, the first flight test using the new solid propellant sustainer engine was conducted at White Sands.

During the following summer, a test called Operation Snodgrass conducted at Eglin Air Force Base, Florida, demonstrated the ability of the missile to single out a target within a formation of aircraft. By this time, the first of several Nike Ajax sites had been converted to accept the new missile.

Meanwhile, work was well under way to improve acquisition and tracking radar capabilities that would further exploit the capabilities of the Nike Hercules. The Army pushed ahead with development of a system dubbed the "Improved Hercules" that incorporated three significant improvements. First, the Improved Hercules sites were to receive the HIPAR L-band acquisition radar to detect high-speed, non-ballistic targets. The other two improvements included improving the existing Target Tracking Radar and adding a Target Ranging Radar operating on a wide-ranging frequency band designed to foil attempts at electronic countermeasures.

The potential of the Improved Hercules was demonstrated on June 3, 1960, when a Nike Hercules missile scored a direct hit on a Corporal missile in the sky over White Sands. Beginning in June 1961, Army Air Defense Command (ARADCOM) began phasing in Improved Hercules to selected batteries.

Basing Strategy

As previously mentioned, the Nike Hercules was designed to use existing Nike Ajax facilities. With the greater range of the Nike Hercules allowing for wider area coverage, several Nike Ajax batteries could be permanently deactivated. In retrospect, air defense planners lamented the backfitting of Nike Hercules missiles into existing sites close to areas that were vulnerable to the new threat of Soviet ICBMs. In addition, sites located further away from target areas were desirable due to the nuclear warheads carried by the missile.

Fortunately, not all strategic locations faced this situation. In the late 1950s and early 1960s surface-to-air missile batteries were placed for the first time around such cities as St. Louis and Kansas City and around several Strategic Air Command (SAC) bomber bases. Unlike the older sites, these batteries were placed in locations that optimized the missiles' range and minimized the warhead damage. Nike Hercules batteries at SAC bases and in Hawaii were installed in an outdoor configuration. In Alaska, a unique above-ground shelter configuration was provided for batteries guarding Anchorage and Fairbanks.

Local Corps of Engineer Districts supervised the conversion of Nike Ajax batteries and the construction of new Nike Hercules batteries.

Nike Hercules Deployment

Nike Hercules first entered service on June 30, 1958, at batteries located near New York, Philadelphia, and Chicago. The missiles remained deployed around strategically important areas within the continental United States until 1974. The Alaskan sites were deactivated in 1978 and Florida sites stood down during the following year. Although the missile left the U.S. inventory, other nations maintained the missiles in

The launch area at Site S-61, Vashion Island, Washington. The large building near the entrance was the administration building and barracks. The building just below the launchers was the assembly and electronic test building. To the right of it, protected by a distinctive berm, was the old Nike Ajax fueling area. For the solid-fuel Nike Hercules, the fueling area was replaced by a warheading building. At the extreme right corner on the launcher area was a kennel that housed the guard dogs.

their inventories into the early 1990s and sent their soldiers to the United States to conduct live-fire exercises at Fort Bliss, Texas.

Site Configuration

As previously mentioned, converted sites received new radars and underwent modifications so the new missiles could be serviced and stored.

Because of the larger size of the Nike Hercules, an underground magazine's capacity was reduced to eight missiles. Thus, storage racks, launcher rails, and elevators underwent modification to accept the larger missiles. Two additional features that readily distinguished newly converted sites were the double fence and the kennels housing dogs that patrolled the perimeter between the two fences.

New sites, located away from populated areas did not have to be confined in acreage. Consequently, these batteries were all above ground with missile storage and maintenance facilities located behind earthen berms.

Not all sites received the complete Improved Hercules package. HIPAR radars were denied to some sites due to geographical constraints and/or to avoid duplication of radars located at adjacent sites.

References

For details on missile development, see Mary T. Cagle's *History of the Nike Hercules Weapon System*, (Huntsville, AL: U.S. Army Missile Command, 1973). The technical specifications came from Mark Morgan's *Nike Quick Look III, BOMARC/AF Talos*, (Fort Worth TX: AEROMK, 1990) and Bill Gunston's *World Encyclopedia of Rockets and Missiles*, (New York, NY: Crescent Books, 1979).

A valuable source of information on the Nike Hercules batteries was the Historic American Engineering Records including "Nike Missile Battery PR-79," n.d., (HAER No. RI-37) available at the Library of Congress, Prints and Photographs Division, Washington, DC; and Roger Hatheway, Stephen Van Wormer, and Allan Schilz of Westec Services Inc., "Survey and Evaluation of the Nike Missile Site at Fort MacArthur, White Point Los Angeles County, California" and "Survey and Evaluation of Nike Missile Sites in the Angeles National Forest, Los Angeles County, California," Prepared for the Corps of Engineers, Los Angeles District, February 1987. For information on missile batteries in Alaska, see Nike Hercules in Alaska, (Anchorage, AK: U.S. Army Corps of Engineers District, Alaska), n.d.

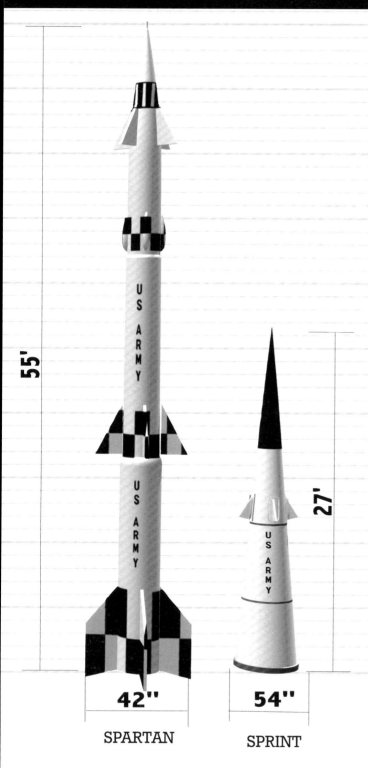

55'

42"

27'

54"

SPARTAN

SPRINT

Antiballistic Missiles (ABMs): The Safeguard System

Summary

Deployed briefly in the mid-1970s the Safeguard antiballistic missile system was the product of two decades of research, development, and testing. Army antiballistic missile development began under the Nike Zeus program (1956–1963), and continued under the Nike X (1963–1967) and Sentinel (1967–1969) programs before culminating in the Safeguard system (1969–1976). Incorporating incremental improvements in missile technology, combined with revolutionary advances in phased-array radar and advanced computers, the Safeguard system was eventually deployed at just a single site—the Stanley R. Mickelsen Safeguard Complex (SRMSC) near Grand Forks, North Dakota.

Technical Specifications

The Safeguard ARM system was composed of three main components: sophisticated radars, powerful computers, and the sleek, deadly interceptor missiles—the Sprint and the Spartan.

SPARTAN
Length: 55 feet
Diameter: 42 inches
Wingspan: 118 inches
Weight: 28,700 pounds
Fuel: Solid propellant
Maximum engagement altitude: 330 miles
Range: Approximately 465 miles
Speed: Mach 10 (7,418 mph)
Guidance: Ground-based radio directed
Warhead: Nuclear, yield 5 megatons

SPRINT
Length: 27 feet
Diameter at base: 4 feet 6 inches
Weight: 7,500 pounds
Fuel: Solid propellant
Maximum engagement altitude: 24 miles

Range: 25 miles
Guidance: Ground-based radio directed
Warhead: Nuclear, low-kiloton range yield

Contractors

Safeguard primary contractor: Western Electric Company, New York, New York
System design: Bell Laboratories, Whippany, New Jersey
Perimeter acquisition radar: General Electric, Syracuse, New York
Missile site radar: Raytheon, Boston, Massachusetts
Data processing system: Bell Laboratories, Whippany, New Jersey Western Electric New York, New York
Spartan subcontractor: McDonnell-Douglas, Santa Monica, California
Sprint subcontractor: Martin Marietta, Corporation Orlando, Florida
Guidance systems: Bell Laboratories, Whippany, New Jersey

System Operation

The Stanley R. Mickelsen Safeguard Complex consisted of four elements: the Perimeter Acquisition Radar (PAR) complex near Concrete, North Dakota; the Missile Site Radar (MSR) complex twelve miles south of

A Sprint missile being lowered into its underground silo.

A full-scale mockup of a Spartan missile.

Langdon, North Dakota; and the four Remote Sprint Launch (RSL) sites clustered within twenty miles of the MSR. The fourth element, the Ballistic Missile Defense Center (BMDC) in Colorado, was the only component of the SRMSC located outside of North Dakota. The BMDC was the highest echelon of command and control in the Safeguard system. The BMDC integrated the Safeguard within the North American Air Defense Command, and allowed the Commander of the Continental Air Defense Command (CONAD) to exercise operational command of the Safeguard system.

The defensive Sprint and Spartan missiles were technological marvels. However, the centerpieces of the Safeguard System were the tracking radars and associate computers that rapidly sorted the incoming data and provided instructions to the interceptor missiles.

The largest of Safeguard's structures, the Perimeter Acquisition Radar Building (PARB), consisted of a huge phased-array antenna mounted on a sloped surface facing due north.

The PAR was capable of identifying and tracking incoming missiles at ranges up to 2,000 miles. Unlike a conventional "moving" radar antenna, the PAR's "phased-array" antenna incorporated 6,888 elements, each sending a pulse that would bounce off an incoming target coming over the North Pole. Through comparison of the reflected signals received back from the incoming object, trajectories were computed and this information was passed to the Missile Site Radar (MSR). To operate the PAR, an Army Surveillance Battalion of about 400 personnel would be required to man a three-section watch.

The 470-acre MSR site housed the shorter-range missile control radar and nearly half of the Safeguard system's defensive Spartan and Sprint missiles.

Located in a pyramid-shaped building, the site's phased-array radar had over 20,000 elements distributed equally between its four faces. Using the radar data supplied by the PAR, the MSR located and tracked incoming missiles, computed intercept trajectories, and launched and guided the Spartan and Sprint missiles to their targets. Operating the MSR required a staff of 800 soldiers and civilians.

The Safeguard system's defensive missiles were divided between five facilities: the MSR and the four RSLs. Each RSL deployed between twelve and sixteen Sprint missiles. The sites, which were all located within a twenty-mile radius of the MSR, were under the operational control of that radar facility.

The Spartan, with a range of nearly 500 miles, was designed to intercept the incoming missiles well outside the earth's atmosphere and destroy them with a multimegaton nuclear warhead.

Anticipating that some incoming warheads could slip by the Spartan interceptions and enter the atmosphere over North America, a "layered-defense" provided for a last-ditch defense in the form of the Sprint missile. Built by Martin Marietta, the Sprint was designed to operate at hypersonic speeds within the earth's atmosphere. Sprint's skin could sustain heat greater than that produced by its own rocket motor. Like Spartan, the two-stage Sprint carried a nuclear warhead.

Developmental History

The antecedent of the Safeguard program can be traced back to March 1955 when the Army contracted with Bell Laboratories to conduct an eighteen month "Nike II" study aimed at projecting defensive missiles and supporting infrastructure requirements for the 1960s. With intelligence reporting an imminent Soviet ICBM capability, the Bell study focused on this problem and initially concluded that developing "long-range, high-data-rate acquisition radar" would be crucial. At this time, Bell also demonstrated, using analog computer simulation, that intercepting a target flying through space at 24,000 feet per second was feasible.

The results of the study were presented in October 1956 and four months later, the Army awarded Western Electric/Bell Laboratories the development contract for "Nike Zeus." Western Electric/Bell subcontracted the missile work to McDonnell-Douglas. Testing of the prototype missile began at White Sands in 1959; however; limited range considerations forced the program to use facilities at the Naval Test Range at Point Mugu, California.

As the missile work proceeded, Western Electric/Bell forged ahead on radar and supporting systems development. The process reached a point that a site needed to be selected for prototype system installation where actual ICBMs could be tracked and engaged. Already a prototype Zeus Target Track Radar (TTR) had been placed on Ascension Island downrange of Cape Canaveral. However, sensitive political considerations ruled out expanding Zeus facilities at Ascension or other islands off the west coast of Africa that were not owned by the United States. This forced planners to focus on Kwajalein in the Pacific, which already hosted a U.S. naval base. More importantly, this atoll in the Marshall Islands lay 4,800 miles downrange of Vandenberg AFB, then undergoing construction as an ICBM launch site.

This 1972 photograph shows the Perimeter Acquisition Radar (PAR) site at SRMSC under construction. To the right of unfinished radar building is the power plant. The buildings in the background include enlisted housing, a dispensary, and a community center.

As with many development programs, Nike Zeus encountered its share of catastrophic failures. Testing at White Sands proved invaluable as pieces of missiles could be recovered to determine causes for failure. Changes to the control fins corrected one of the initial problems. Meanwhile on March 29, 1961, the TTR at Ascension failed in its first attempt at tracking a Titan ICBM. Two months later, the radar recorded its first tracking success.

In addition to missile testing at White Sands, a prototype Zeus Acquisition Radar (ZAR) and another TTR were constructed and placed into operation. On December 14, 1961, these radars tracked and successfully engaged a Nike Hercules target missile with a Nike Zeus interceptor.

As the results of this demonstration were analyzed, facilities were readied at Kwajalein for the first attempt to intercept an ICBM in flight. This first attempt, on June 26, 1961, failed due to the TTR's inability to pickup the re-entry vehicle after the ICBM's propulsion section broke up. The intercepting Zeus missile also suffered a malfunction.

A partially successful intercept occurred on July 19, 1962, as a Zeus missile came within two kilometers of an incoming Atlas D ICBM. On December 12, 1962, a Zeus missile passed well within the kill radius of an incoming ICBM. On May 24, 1963, a Nike Zeus came within lethal range of an orbiting satellite. Tests continued through November 1963, showing consistent success.

Despite these successes, Defense Secretary McNamara chose not to deploy the system, but budgeted for continued research and development. McNamara's concern was that the system still lacked the sophistication to discern between real and decoy warheads and could be overwhelmed in a "saturation attack" since the radars could only manage one interception problem at a time.

The continued research and development program for a more advanced ABM program was dubbed "Nike X." Under the Nike X program, the Zeus missile evolved into the Spartan. In addition, planners identified the need for a short-range interceptor missile as well as the requirement for a radar that could track and direct the engagement of several targets simultaneously. The short-range interceptor became reality in the form of the Sprint. On March 18, 1963, Martin Marietta received the contract to develop this new missile. In 1965, the first Sprint prototype was launched at White Sands. The needed radar was already under development through a DoD Advanced Research Project Agency program called "Project Defender." Under this program, a low-power, phased-array antenna was completed in the fall of 1960 and tests showed that this nonmoving antenna, using computers, could electronically steer a radar beam in two directions. In June 1961, the Army Guided Missile Agency granted Western Electric/Bell Laboratories a contract to develop a prototype phased-array radar to be built at White Sands. Ground-breaking occurred at White Sands in March 1963.

With advances in solid-state electronics and high-speed computers, the "Zeus Multifunctional Array Radar" demonstrated the use of phased-array radars as part of an ABM defense as a breakthrough possibility. Already, Bell was studying the development of an even more powerful phased-array radar for long range tracking. This second Multifunctional Array Radar would evolve into the Perimeter Array Radar that eventually was deployed in North Dakota.

Meanwhile a smaller phased-array radar, designed to track incoming targets at close range and guide intercepting missiles, was proposed. In December 1963, the Raytheon Company received the contract to work with Bell Laboratories' people to design and build the "Missile Site Radar" (MSR).

In September 1967, Secretary of Defense Robert McNamara announced plans to deploy many elements of the Nike X program-the Perimeter Acquisition Radar (PAR), the Missile Site Radar (MSR), and the Sprint and Spartan missiles-in the new Sentinel antiballistic missile program. The initial deployment plan called for installing the Sentinel at thirteen sites in the continental United States and Alaska and Hawaii.

The plan aroused a firestorm of protest in the major cities slated to receive Sentinel installations. Not only was the Sentinel unpopular at home, but President Nixon and his National Security Advisor Henry Kissinger were also concerned that the deployment of the Sentinel system could escalate the arms race with the Soviet Union.

In March 1969, Nixon announced his intention to deploy a "modified Sentinel system" that he called Safeguard. Whereas the Sentinel system was intended to provide a limited nationwide ballistic missile defense, the President ordered that the Safeguard system be positioned to protect a portion of the United States ICBM force.

The Safeguard program initially called for twelve sites. Despite moving the installations away from the nation's major cities, the program still faced rigorous Congressional scrutiny. In August 1969, the Senate authorized the construction of only two sites; one near Malmstrom, Montana, and the other near Grand Forks, North Dakota. Only the site near Grand Forks was ever completed.

The Remote Sprint Launch Site #2 under construction in the fall of 1972. The tops of the Sprint Launchers are visible in the center of the picture. The building taking shape at the right was the Remote Launch Operations Building.

As the debate to deploy Sentinel and Safeguard continued, construction of the prototype missile facilities continued at Kwajalein. Completion of launch tubes allowed the first Spartan to be fired from Kwajalein on March 2, 1968. The MSR built on Meek Island completed its first successful track of an ICBM on December 11, 1969. On August 28, 1970, an MSR-controlled Spartan missile successfully intercepted an incoming ICBM. Four months later, this feat was repeated with an MSR-controlled Sprint missile.

Basing Strategy

The placement of facilities for what became known as the Sentinel system announced by Defense Secretary McNamara was never fully revealed to the general public. However, the deployment plan, titled "Nike X DEMOD l-67," would have placed fifteen systems within the continental United States and a system each in Alaska and Hawaii. Continental sites slated to receive Sentinel installations included Boston; New York; Washington DC; Albany, Georgia; Detroit; Chicago; Dallas; Salt Lake; Seattle; San Francisco; Los Angeles; and Whiteman, Grand Forks, Malmstrom, and Warren Air Force Bases.

Construction of the first site at Sharpner's Pond near Boston began in late 1968. However, in that era of antiwar protest, opponents of ABM packed an Army community-relations meeting in late January 1969. The appearance of an adverse public reaction led Senator Edward Kennedy to write a letter to Defense Secretary Laird questioning the viability of the system. This act touched off a heated Senate debate and led to a Presidential review of the Sentinel deployment scheme. On March 14, President Nixon announced the

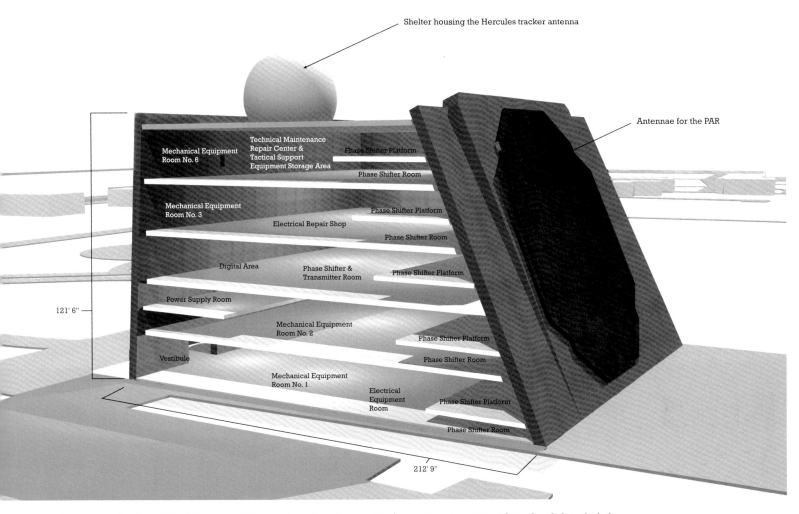

Shelter housing the Hercules tracker antenna

Antennae for the PAR

Mechanical Equipment Room No. 6

Technical Maintenance Repair Center & Tactical Support Equipment Storage Area

Phase Shifter Platform

Phase Shifter Room

Mechanical Equipment Room No. 3

Phase Shifter Platform

Electrical Repair Shop

Phase Shifter Room

Digital Area

Phase Shifter & Transmitter Room

Phase Shifter Platform

Power Supply Room

121' 6"

Mechanical Equipment Room No. 2

Phase Shifter Platform

Phase Shifter Room

Vestibule

Mechanical Equipment Room No. 1

Electrical Equipment Room

Phase Shifter Platform

Phase Shifter Room

212' 9"

deployment of a "modified Sentinel." Later that day Deputy Defense Secretary David Packard detailed the new deployment scheme to cover twelve sites. With the exception of Washington DC, the new Safeguard sites were to be located away from population centers. Instead of Boston, Detroit, Seattle, San Francisco, and Dallas, sites were to be placed in southern New England, the Michigan/Ohio area, the Northwest, central California, Southern California, and Texas. The four previously designated SAC missile bases, as well as southern Georgia, would still receive ABM defenses. New York, Chicago, Salt Lake, Hawaii, and Alaska lost out in the new scheme.

System Deployment

Phase I of ABM deployment called for immediate construction at sites near Grand Forks and Malmstrom Air Force Bases. Labor problems set back Malmstrom construction and made the base vulnerable as a bargaining chip for talks designed to limit ABM defenses. As a result of the 1972 ABM Treaty, the United States would be allowed to deploy one site away from the national command center (Washington DC) and that site would defend Grand Forks. Completed in 1974, that site was deactivated two years later.

Site Configuration

Discounting prototype facilities, the Grand Forks facility became the only location in America ever to host an ABM defense system. Unlike proposed ABM sites in Massachusetts and Montana where only traces remain of once massive construction efforts, much remains intact in North Dakota.

Aside from the Egyptian pyramids, the Safeguard PAR may be the most solidly constructed building in the world. The structure is truly one-of-a-kind as, unlike the MSR, no prototype PAR had been built. The building is 204 by 213 feet at the base and rises to over 120 feet. The structure's northern-faced antenna wall slopes away from the ground at a 25 degree angle. This antenna face wall consists of a dense reinforced concrete mesh 7 feet thick. The three other walls are also dense reinforced concrete and have a base of 8 feet, tapering to 3 feet at the top. The reinforcing bars, installed vertically, horizontally, and diagonally, are No. 11 gauge; each bar is approximately as thick as a man's wrist. The structure required 63,000 cubic yards of concrete and 8,700 tons of reinforcing steel.

The interior of this completely above-ground structure includes five full floors with a mezzanine located between the second and third floors. Entrance to the building requires passing through two blast locks or through a tunnel leading from the power plant.

The adjacent power plant was housed in a partially buried hardened concrete structure covered with earth for addition blast protection. Inside the plant, five 16-cylinder diesel engines could combine to produce 14.7 megawatts of power. Provisions for emergency operations of the plant included storage for fuel supplies and a recirculating water cooling system featuring an underground storage cavern as a heat sink.

Located some 25 miles from the PAR facility, the Missile Site Radar facility consisted of the Missile Site Control Building (MSCB) and collocated Spartan and Sprint missile launch areas. The MSCB, which housed the radar, had above-ground and below-ground sections. Above ground was a four-sided truncated pyramid; each side had a 30-foot diameter antenna mounted integrally into the 3-foot thick reinforced concrete walls. Each antenna weighed nearly 400 tons and placing the units entailed overcoming unique engineering problems.

Below the pyramid stood a two-story 231- by 231-foot structure housing the radar transmitting and receiving components, phase shifters, switching gear, and other necessary subsystems. As with the PAR, the MSCB also had an adjoining underground power plant. With six diesel generators, this plant could produce up to 17.3 megawatts of power.

As part of the Missile Site Radar facility, prefabricated launch canisters for Spartan and Sprint launches stood ready to launch the defensive missiles. Sprint launchers were also placed at four remote site locations located to the east, west, north, and south of the MSCB.

With manpower requirements at both sites consuming over 1,000 personnel, support and housing facilities were built adjoining the structures.

An aerial view of the Missile Site Radar. In the foreground are the Sprint and Spartan launch areas. Looming over them is the two-tiered Missile Site Control Building.

References

The missile technical specifications came from Jane's *All The World's Aircraft: 1971–72*, (New York: McGraw Hill, 1972) and Bill Gunston's, *Illustrated Encyclopedia of the World's Rockets and Missiles*, (New York: Crescent Books, 1979). A thorough technical overview completed for the U.S. Army Ballistic Missile Defense Systems Command is found in Bell Laboratories, *ABM Research and Development at Bell Laboratories: Project History, October 1975*, (Whippany, NJ: Bell Laboratories, 1975). Construction details came from James H. Kitchens, III, *A History of the Huntsville Division, U.S. Army Corps of Engineers*: 15 October 1967–31 December 1976, (Huntsville, AL: U.S. Army Engineer Division, Huntsville, 1978); and Erwin N. Thompson, *Pacific Ocean Engineers: A History of the U.S. Army Corps of Engineers in the Pacific, 1905–1980*, (Ft. Shafter, HI: U.S. Army Engineer Division, Pacific Ocean, 1980). Another excellent source is the Historic American Engineering Record (HAER No. ND-9) of the Stanley R. Mickelsen Safeguard Complex currently being prepared under the direction of the U.S. Army Space and Strategic Defense Command, History Office, Huntsville, Alabama. For detailed coverage of the construction of the Safeguard sites at Grand Forks, complete with superb pictures and illustrations, see the U.S. Army Corps of Engineers, Huntsville Division, "Safeguard—A Step Toward Peace," nd., in the Research Collection, Office of History, Headquarters Army Corps of Engineers, Alexandria, VA, Military Files XVIII-36. Also, Donald Baucom's, *The Origins of SDI*, 1944–1983, (Lawrence, KS: University Press of Kansas, 1992), incorporates the political debate into a finely compressed technical overview.

BOMARC (IM-99A, B)

Summary

The BOMARC program had its impetus in the immediate post-war era as the services sought to define their missions within the new political environment. The newly formed Air Force received responsibility for continental air defense. Using lessons learned from the German air defenses employed during the recently concluded war, defense planners laid out a defense strategy that used fighter interceptors against incoming attack bombers at the frontiers and Army antiaircraft batteries near the target for point defense.

Air Force planners saw a gap between the long-range fighter and point-defense systems that called for an "area-defense weapon." Integrated into the Semi-Automatic Ground Environment (SAGE) system, BOMARC A and the follow-on B model would serve as the needed area defense weapon. The Air Force phased the BOMARC A system out of operation during 1964 while the BOMARC B system stood guard until 1972. After retirement, many of the missiles saw service as target drones. The last attempted launch of a BOMARC target drone occurred at Eglin AFB, Florida, on August 29, 1985.

Technical Specifications

Length: (A) 45.25 feet; (B) 43.75 feet

Diameter: 35 inches

Wingspan: 18 feet 2 inches

Weight: (A) 15,000 pounds; (B) 16,000 pounds

Booster fuel/oxidizer: (A) JP-4 and Unsymmetrical Dimethyl Hydrazine (UDH)/Inhibited Red Fuming Nitric Acid (IRFNA) (B) solid fuel

Missile fuel: (A) 80 octane gasoline; (B) solid propellant

Range: (A) 230 miles (B) 440 miles

Top speed: Nearly Mach 4 (2,967 mph)

Cruise altitude: 60,000–70,000 feet; could climb above 80,000 feet

Propulsion: Booster (A) gimbaled rocket motor (B) M51 solid booster Main (A) Two Marquardt RJ43-3 ramjets (B) Two Marquardt RJ43-7 ramjets

Guidance: Ground radio directed until terminal phase

Terminal phase (A) DPN-34 radar (B) DPN-53 pulse-doppler radar

Warhead: Conventional: 300-pound high explosive (later expanding rod) Nuclear: W-40 (yield 7-10 kilotons)

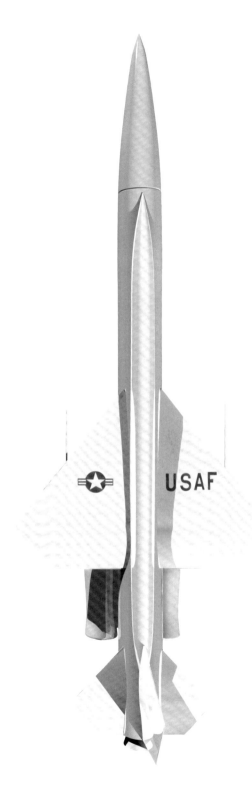

These BOMARC missiles are shown at the end of the production line at Boeing's Missile Production Center in Seattle, Washington.

AREAS

Wing	141.85 sq ft
Aileron	24.00 sq ft
Flap	Not Applicable
Horizontal Tail	48.84 sq ft
Vertical Tail	33.68 sq ft
Rudder	6.78 sq ft
Elevator	24.78 sq ft

AIR FOIL SECTIONS

Wing - Symmetrical Bi-Convex throughout
Tail - Symmetrical Bi-Convex throughout
(horizontal &. Vertical)

C.G. LOCATIONS   (distance to nose in inches)

Launching Condition (lift-off)	315.4
Boost Burnout Condition	336.5
Initial Cruise Condition	336.5
Burnout Condition	335.7

GEOMETRIC RATIO
Wing

Thickness	5%
Aspect Ratio	2.32
MAC	9.65 ft.
Incidence	0°
Dihedral	0°
Sweepback (LE)	50°

Tail (horizontal)

Thickness	5%
Aspect Ratio	2.35
Incidence	0°
Dihedral	0°
Sweepback (LE)	46°

Tail (vertical)

Thickness	5.75%
Aspect Ratio	1.34
Sweepback (LE)	31°40'

46.8'

11.3'

10.3'

14.5'

Liquid Rocket Engine

Fuel and Ramjet Engines

Guidance Equipment and Warhead

Contractors

Airframe: Boeing Pilotless Aircraft Division, Seattle, Washington

Propulsion:

Booster (A) Aerojet General Corporation, Azusa, California

(B) Thiokol Chemical Corporation, Ogden, Utah

Main (A,B) Marquardt Aircraft Company, Van Nuys, California

Guidance: Westinghouse Electric Corporation, Baltimore, Maryland

System Operation

The BOMARC system was designed to be integrated into the Air Defense Command (ADC) SAGE command system. Once a SAGE command center designated a target, a BOMARC could be in the air within two minutes of the launch order. (Later this lag time was reduced to thirty seconds.) Before launching, the missile's guidance system received preset commands for its initial flight. Launched vertically, BOMARC quickly rose to cruise altitude and received guidance from the SAGE center tracking the target. Receiving the target information from ADC's air search radar network, the SAGE center's AN/FSQ-7 system used this data to calculate the intercept geometry and command instructions that were subsequently transmitted to the missile from a ground-to-air transmitter site. Signals from the ground adjusted the missile's flight path, directed the missile when to climb or dive toward the target, and activated BOMARC's homing radar. This last event usually occurred when the missile was ten miles from its intended target. Because both A and B models used information from their own radars to compute the final intercept solution, BOMARC marked the introduction of the world's first active homing surface-to-air missile (SAM) system. The B version carried a Westinghouse DPN-53 radar, which marked the first use of a production pulse-doppler system, which gave the missile a capability

November 1958 photograph shows a BOMARC test flight taking off from Cape Canaveral, Florida.

to seek out low-altitude targets.

In addition to having advanced homing radar, the B version also had greater range because the liquid-fueled booster was replaced with a solid-fuel booster. This more compact solid-fuel booster left more room for additional liquid-fuel storage capacity Once expended, the BOMARC B jettisoned the solid booster, which helped extend the missile's range. The solid booster also allowed for safer maintenance on the ground. (See McGuire AFB, New Jersey, in the site section for an accident description involving a BOMARC IM-99A.)

Using a proximity fuse, the missile had both nuclear and conventional warhead capability. For the conventional high-explosive warhead, a detonation within 70 feet of the target was considered a kill.

Developmental History

In January 1946, the Boeing Aircraft Company won Army Air Force approval to construct and test a ground-to-air pilotless aircraft (GAPA). Initial design work on the interceptor missile concept had been ongoing during the last two years of the war. This effort paid off with the first launch of a GAPA on June 13, 1946, from an area now located just outside Hill AFB, Utah. Nicknamed "Gapa Village," the Boeing launch site witnessed 38 GAPA launchings in a two-week span that ended with a July 1 shot. The program then moved to Holloman AFB, New Mexico, with additional evaluation conducted on 73 launches completed between July 24, 1947, and May 9, 1950. The lessons learned from the project provided a wealth of technical data that would be used by Boeing engineers when that company received the contract for the IM-99 in 1949. Two months after Boeing received the IM-99 contract, an announcement was made that the University of Michigan's Aeronautical Research Center would participate in early studies of the missile program. From this combined effort came the BOMARC name representing Boeing and the Michigan Aeronautical Research Center.

On September 10, 1952, a contractor-led team launched the first XF-99 propulsion test vehicle from the Air Force Missile Test Center (AFMTC) at Patrick AFB, Florida. Unfortunately, this first test was a failure. The second test failed when the rocket booster cut out immediately after ignition. The third flight, on June 10, 1953, ended with the missile self-destructing down range. A test on August 5, 1954, ended when a wing fell off in flight.

At this point, the Air Force came under pressure to field a viable missile system or lose the program because of the Army's deployment of the Nike System and the increased threat due to the Soviet detonation of the hydrogen bomb. In February 1955, the first IM-99A using both booster and main propulsion systems successfully completed a run down the Eastern Test Range to simulate an interception of a TM-61 Matador missile. Still, by the middle of 1956,

BOMARC Deployment

Unit	Base	Model	Operational
46th ADMS	McGuire AFB, NJ	A,B	1959–1972
6th ADMS	Suffolk County AFB, NY	A	1959–1964
26th ADMS	Otis AFB, MA	A,B	1960–1972
30th ADMS	Dow AFB, ME	A	1960–1964
22nd ADMS	Langley AFB, VA	A,B	1960–1972
35th ADMS	Niagara Falls AFB, NY	B	1961–1969
37th ADMS	Kincheloe AFB, MI	B	1961–1972
74th ADMS	Duluth, MN	B	1960–1972

A map showing the locations of BOMARC operational bases in North America. The facilities at North Bay, Ontario, and La Macaza, Quebec, were operated by the Royal Canadian Air Force.

This time-lapse photograph shows a BOMARC in a Model II shelter being raised to the firing position.

the contractor-led team had launched only eight propulsion test vehicles, nine ramjet test vehicles, and five guidance test vehicles—a rather slow pace in comparison to other programs.

In 1957 and 1958, the testing pace picked up. On October 2, 1957, an operator pushed a button at an IBM test facility in Kingston, New York, and an IM-99A lifted off from Patrick AFB, Florida, and passed within lethal distance of an NAVAHO X-10 drone flying at a speed of Mach 1.6 at a height of 48,000 feet. Later that month, a BOMARC recorded a successful hit on a drone.

With full-scale production of BOMARC having commenced in 1957, the Air Research and Development Command (ARDC) announced in September 1958, that additional operational testing and evaluation had been moved to Hurlbert Field located across from Santa Rosa Island along the West Florida Gulf Coast. Site construction at this portion of Eglin AFB had begun in March 1957, and by 1958, the field hosted missile ground-testing and personnel training. Meanwhile, missile launchers were constructed on Santa Rosa Island so BOMARC missiles could be launched into what would become designated as the Eglin Gulf Test Range. Between 1958 and 1960, the A model underwent continual testing at this site, flying against QF-80, QB-47, and KD2U (Regulus II) drones. In the early 1960s testing continued with the IM-99B model with the first service test of the missile being conducted on April 13, 1960. In the following months, tests using A and B models continued to examine the capabilities of the weapon system. On March 3, 1961, an IM-99B made its first full-range flight over the Gulf to intercept a simulated target at a distance of 400 miles at a height of over 80,000 feet.

In February 1958, the ADC activated the 4751st Air Defense Missile Wing at Hurlbert Field to perform missile testing, evaluation, and training for BOMARC squadrons before and after deployment. Reduced to squadron status in 1962, the 4751st remained active at Hurlbert until 1979. Before reporting to Hurlbert, prospective crewmembers received technical training on the system at Chanute AFB, Illinois.

With the first production model coming off the assembly line in Seattle on December 30, 1957, Boeing's Pilotless Aircraft Division delivered 366 IM-99A missiles and 349 IM-99B missiles.

In 1962, the IM-99A was redesignated the CIM-10A and the IM-99B became the CIM-10B. The Ogden Air Logistic Center, Utah, handled program management and logistical support for the BOMARC system.

Basing Strategy

Back in 1952, ADC drafted its first deployment plan for the BOMARC system projecting 52 BOMARC Air Defense Missile Squadrons (ADMS). Later, ADC cut the number of planned BOMARC sites to 40 (with each site deploying 120 missiles) to accommodate the deployment of 53 Navy Talos missile squadrons. The shorter range Talos received serious consideration from ADC planners for complementing the BOMARC system. In November 1956, the Talos scheme was transferred to the Army, after Secretary of Defense Charles Wilson reaffirmed the Army's responsibility for point missile defense.

By this time, ADC had already been informed by Air Force Headquarters that deploying 120 missiles to each of the 40 launch sites would be too costly. ADC countered by recommending a reduction to 60 missiles per site. In January 1957, the Continental Air Defense Command (CONAD) backed the ADC recommendation. However, over the next two years, Air Force Headquarters would whittle down the number of planned deployment sites to 29.

Congressional debate in 1959 over the viability of the Nike versus the BOMARC system as defense against Soviet ICBMs resulted in the House cutting funds for the BOMARC and the Senate cutting funds for the Nike program. With both services facing disaster, cooperation ensued and the services presented Congress a compromise Master Air Defense Plan that reduced the number of BOMARC sites to eighteen (including two in Canada).

On March 23, 1960, Headquarters, Air Force announced that BOMARC deployment would, in effect, cease after the completion of eight United States sites and two Canadian sites.

In 1959, the Canadian Government acquired the IM-99B model for the Royal Canadian Air Force. The missiles were eventually deployed from 1962 to 1972 at bases located at North Bay, Ontario, and La Macaza, Quebec.

Site Configuration

Because of BOMARC s long range, the missile installations could be located away from the targets they were designated to defend.

Engineering and the Army Corps of Engineers. Lessons learned from construction and use of launching shelters at Cape Canaveral and Santa Rosa Island, Eglin AFB, were incorporated into the design of the first tactical base. The Cape Canaveral structure was a heavy 73- by 42-foot structure supported by 12-inch reinforced concrete walls. The shelter spread open like a clamshell standing on one end. The missile, lying horizontally facing the hinged end of the building, would be raised vertically on its erector and fired, with the thrust being deflected out the opened end of the structure. A similar structure that received much use was built at Santa Rosa; however, the Air Force opted for another design that was tested at Eglin. This design, called "Model II," was reduced in size but maintained the 12-inch reinforced concrete walls. From a distance, the above-ground adjoining launcher shelters appeared as rows of garages. Within each "garage bay," a BOMARC missile sat horizontally on an erector arm. To launch, hydraulic pressure was used to split open the roof like a drawbridge; the erector arm then raised the BOMARC to a vertical position. The arm then retracted and the missile was fired.

Although the process sounds simple, it was quite complex because each leaf of the roof structure was 60 feet long, 12 feet wide, and weighed 10 tons. The mechanical and electrical equipment for the Model II shelter was placed in a side room with 8-inch thick masonry walls.

Model II shelters were built by contractors under Corps of Engineers supervision at McGuire, Suffolk, Otis, and Dow Air Force Bases. Constant design modifications meant slight differences at each location. For example, the heat and power plant capacities were reduced at Otis and Dow and cut even further for the BOMARC B shelters. While the McGuire and Suffolk sites featured buried high- and low-pressure air, helium, and utility lines to each shelter, the next three BOMARC A sites at Otis, Dow, and Langley AFB, Virginia, installed "utilidors." Utilidors are covered concrete trenches easily accessible by pulling away concrete slabs laid across the top. McGuire and Suffolk each hosted 56 launchers, averaging $13 million while Otis and Dow, hosting only 28 launchers, averaging $7.5 million.

As improvements in missile design led to the BOMARC B, the same can be said of shelter design. With the goal of reducing construction costs, a Model III shelter featuring a pitched roof that slid down in two sections from the center was erected and evaluated at Eglin. Concurrently, a Model IV prototype was erected in Seattle. This design was adopted for Langley, Niagara Falls, Kincheloe, and Duluth.

A major cost-saving feature of the Model IV placed the mechanical and electrical equipment in a pit beneath the launcher erector. In addition, an aluminum roof parted down the middle and slid back to expose the missile. This roof feature allowed engineers to dispense with the hydraulic draw-bridge roof design of Model II. Along with a light roof, Model IV incorporated thinner precast concrete walls. Because of the thinner walls, the BOMARC B shelters were spaced further apart to prevent a chain-reaction should an accident occur within one of the shelters.

Langley AFB was the first site to receive these new shelters even though Langley deployed the BOMARC A for a year before switching to the new missile. Thus, Langley can be considered a BOMARC base in transition. Because the BOMARC B was solid-fuel propelled, there was no requirement at Niagara Falls, Kincheloe, or Duluth for fueling facilities, stainless steel pipe, helium and high pressure lines, or utilidors. With the BOMARC B having an internal cooling system, additional savings were gained by eliminating air conditioning for the Model IV shelters built at Niagara Falls, Kincheloe, and Duluth. The savings were substantial although the construction cost was between $3 and $4 million at each base.

Later, IM-99B missiles were backfitted to McGuire and Otis Air Force Bases. Rather than reconfigure the Model II shelters, which were expensive to maintain, Model IV shelters were erected on adjacent property to house the new missiles.

References

Test flight details can be found in Mark C. Cleary, "The 6555th: Missile and Space Launches Through 1970," (Patrick AFB, FL: 45th Space Wing History Office, 1991); and *Chronology Munition Systems Division: 1946–1989*, (Eglin AFB, FL: Munition Systems Division History Office, 1989). Missile history and specification data came from, "Boeing background information: BOEING BOMARC INTERCEPTOR MISSILE," (Boeing Aerospace Company Public Relations, undated); Bill Gunston, *The Illustrated Encyclopedia of the World's Rockets and Missiles*, (New York: Crescent Books, 1979), Mark Morgan, *Nike Quick Look III, BOMARC/AF Talos*, (Fort Worth: TX: AEROMK, 1990) and the United States Air Force, "Standard Missile Characteristics, IM-99A BOMARC," 8 May 1958, available at the USAF Museum, Wright-Patterson AFB, OH, Research Division, file "C1/BOMARC." An additional overview of the BOMARC program with a focus on the logistical support effort can be found in Helen Rice, *History of the Ogden Air Material Area, Hill Air Force Base, 1934–1960*, (Hill AFB, UT Air Force Logistics Command, 1963). An excellent overview of BOMARC site construction is featured in John M. Norvell, "Base Construction for BOMARC," *The Military Engineer*, (March-April 1961): pp. 129–131. For information on the various BOMARC bases, see Boeing Airplane Company, "IM-99A Bases Manual," D5-4684, n.d., courtesy of John Cullinane Associates. Construction problems associated with the first BOMARC site in New Jersey are detailed in Frank E. Snyder and Brian H. Guss, *The District: A History of the Philadelphia District U.S. Army Corps of Engineers, 1866–1971*, (Philadelphia, PA: U.S. Army Engineer District, Philadelphia, 1974).

An aerial view of the BOMARC launch complex at McGuire AFB, New Jersey. The 56 garage-like missile shelters are clustered at the right. The buildings at left house the missile assembly and maintenance buildings and propellant storage tanks.

INTERCONTINENTAL BALLISTIC MISSILES

Atlas (SM-65)

Summary

First deployed in September 1959, the Atlas (SM-65), was the nation's first operational intercontinental ballistic missile (ICBM). The missiles, however, saw only brief service and the last squadron was taken off operational alert in 1965. Despite its relatively short life span, Atlas served as the proving ground for many new missile technologies. Perhaps more importantly, its development spawned the organization, policies, and procedures that paved the way for all of the later ICBM programs.

Technical Specifications

Length: 82.5 feet
Diameter: 10 feet
Weight: 267,136 pounds (fueled) 18,104 pounds (empty)
Fuel: Rocket grade RP-1 (Kerosene)
Oxidizer: Liquid oxygen
Range: Between 6,400 and 9,000 miles
Propulsion: The Atlas propulsion system included three types of engines: two large booster engines, a sustainer engine, and two small vernier engines.
Primary booster: Atlas A, B, and C: two MA-1 engines generating a combined 357,400 pounds of thrust. Atlas D, two MA-2 engines generating 368,000 pounds of thrust. Atlas E and F, two MA-3 engines generating 389,000 pounds of thrust.
Sustainer: A single engine generating 57,000 pounds of thrust
Vernier: Two engines each generating 2,000 pounds of thrust
Guidance: Atlas A, B, C, and D models: Radio-inertial Atlas E and F models: All-inertial
Accuracy: 2 nautical miles Reentry vehicles: Atlas B and C models: Mark 2–heat Sink; Atlas D model: Mark 3–ablative; Atlas E and F models: Mark 4–ablative
Warhead: Atlas D–W49, 1.44 megaton yield Atlas E, F series–W38, 4 megaton yield

Contractors

Airframe: Convair (later a division of General Dynamics Corp.), San Diego, California
Propulsion: Rocketdyne Division, North American Aviation, Canoga Park, California
Guidance: Radio-inertial (Atlas A, B, C, and D models): The radar was built by General Electric in Syracuse, New York, and the computer by Burroughs in Paoli, Pennsylvania. All-inertial (Atlas E and F models):

American Bosch Arma, Garden City, New York
Reentry Vehicles: Mark 2 and 3: General Electric Corporation, Philadelphia, Pennsylvania
Mark 4: AVCO, Wilmington, Massachusetts

Technical Notes

The Air Force built six variations of the Atlas missile. The Atlas A, B, and C models were used exclusively for flight testing. The later Atlas D (PGM-16D/CGM-16D), the Atlas E (CGM-16E), and Atlas F (HGM-16F) models all saw service in the field.

The Atlas incorporated two novel features. The first was its "stage-and-a-half" propulsion system consisting of two large booster engines flanking a smaller sustainer engine. Unlike the later ICBMs in which the first, second, and third stages fired in sequence, all of the Atlas engines were ignited at liftoff.

Another interesting feature was the pressurized integral fuel tanks. The Convair designers adopted this technique to save weight. The huge tanks, which constituted 80 percent of the missile's mass, were built from thin sheets of stainless steel, ranging

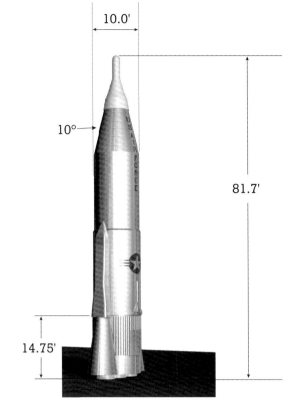

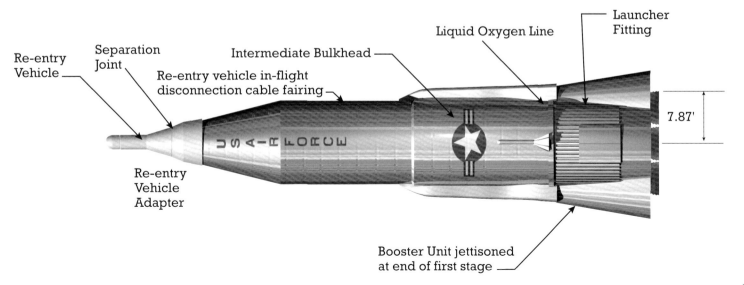

Re-entry Vehicle

Separation Joint

Re-entry vehicle in-flight disconnection cable fairing

Intermediate Bulkhead

Liquid Oxygen Line

Launcher Fitting

Re-entry Vehicle Adapter

7.87'

Booster Unit jettisoned at end of first stage

between 0.1 and 0.4 inches thick. When empty, the tanks were filled with nitrogen gas at 5 psi to maintain a positive internal pressure.

System Operation

During the launch sequence, the two boosters and the sustainer engine were ignited on the ground and the two small vernier engines mounted above the sustainer came to life 2.5 seconds after lift-off. After leaving the launch pad, the missile accelerated rapidly, gradually nosing over in a gentle arc toward the target. Once in flight, the booster engines burned for 140 seconds. After receiving a staging signal from the ground station, the booster engines and turbo-pumps were jettisoned into space. The sustainer engine continued to burn for another 130 seconds, and then it too fell silent. Final course and velocity corrections were made by the vernier engines. At the apogee of its elliptical flight path the missile reached an altitude of 763 miles and a speed of approximately 16,000 miles per hour. Elapsed time for a flight of 6,788 miles: 43 minutes.

During powered flight, the Atlas A, B, C, and D models were guided by a General Electric/Burroughs radio-inertial guidance system that received course corrections from ground-based computers. The Atlas E and F models used the American Bosch Arma all-inertial guidance system. The all-inertial system was capable of detecting deviations from the preprogrammed flight path and formulating midcourse corrections independently.

Developmental History

The Atlas traces its lineage to 1945 when the Army Air Forces (AAF) first expressed interest in developing a "strategic" missile with a range of 5,750 miles. The Consolidated Vultee Aircraft Corporation, commonly referred to as Convair, submitted a proposal to study the matter and in April 1946 the AAF awarded it the MX-774 project to evaluate long-range air-breathing and ballistic missiles.

Within a year budget cutbacks forced the AAF to cancel the air-breathing portion of the study, freeing Convair to concentrate on the ballistic missile. Convair's initial ICBM design was based on the proven V-2 airframe, but incorporated three major modifications: pressurized, integral fuel tanks to reduce weight; gimbaled engines to improve directional stability; and a separable warhead to simplify reentry.

In June 1947, further budget reductions led the AAF to cancel the remainder of the MX-774 program. Since Convair's work was well under way, the Air Force (it became a separate service in September 1947) allowed the company to use its remaining funding to build three small missiles to test the feasibility of the swiveling motors, guidance system, and the separable warhead. The tests, conducted in late 1948 and early 1949 at the White Sands Proving Grounds in New Mexico, were encouraging. The missiles, called the Hiroc (for high altitude rocket) or RTV-A-2s, confirmed the practicality of Convair's innovations. The results, however, were not enough to dissuade the Air Force from canceling the project, and without a government sponsor, the future of the ICBM appeared dim. At the last moment Convair decided to support the program itself, and over the next two years invested $3 million in it.

The Air Force renewed its support for the ICBM program in January 1951, an action prompted by the enthusiastic endorsement of the Rand Corporation and a substantial increase in research and development (R&D) funding brought on by the Korean War. The Air Force designated the new effort the MX-1593 project and directed Convair to evaluate air-breathing and ballistic missiles capable of carrying an 8,000-pound warhead 5,750 miles and striking within a circular error probable (CEP) of 1,500 feet. (A measurement of accuracy, the CEP is the radius of a circle within which half of the ordnance targeted for the center of the circle can be expected to land.)

Convair completed the missile study in July 1951, and once again the airframe manufacturer reaffirmed its support for ICBM. The design it submitted for the ICBM, which it now called Atlas, called for a mammoth weapon 160 feet tall, 12 feet in diameter, and powered by 5 or 7 large engines.

In September 1951 the Air Research and Development Command (ARDC) urged that Headquarters, USAF (often referred to as the Air Staff) immediately begin full-scale development of the ICBM. ARDC estimated that with the "proper application of funds and priorities" Atlas could be operational by 1960. The Air Staff demurred. It did not share ARDC's enthusiasm; instead it advocated a more cautious approach. It wanted to develop the major subsystems such as the engines, fuselage, guidance system, and reentry vehicle first, and then build the test vehicle.

New technology soon changed the nature of the debate. In 1952 ARDC learned that forthcoming improvements in nuclear weaponry would soon reduce the weight of the missile's warhead from 7,000 to 3,000 pounds without reducing the yield. At the same time the United States was also making major strides in developing powerful new rocket engines and precision guidance systems.

In the fall of 1952 those new technologies, coupled with the Army and Navy's attempts to wrest control of the ICBM program away from the Air Force, forced the Air Staff to act. At its request ARDC formulated a list of military characteristics for a "Strategic Ballistic Rocket System" capable of carrying a 3,000-pound atomic warhead 6,325 miles to within 1,500 feet of its target. ARDC estimated that if Atlas was accorded a 1-A development priority it would be operational by 1962.

The Air Staff refused to accord the missile program with the priority ARDC sought, and as a

In an October 1960 test flight, this Atlas D lifts-off from Cape Canaveral, Florida.

Atlas Development

Unit	Storage	Operational Dates	Launch Configuration	Missile Series
576 SMS Vandenberg AFB, California				
576A (Vertical above ground)		1959	3x1	D
576B (Horizontal above ground)		1960–1965	3x1	D
576C (Horizontal above ground)		1961–1965	1x1	E
576D (Silo)		1961–1965	1x1	F
576E (Silo)		1962–1965	1x1	F
564 SMS F.E. Warren AFB, Wyoming	ABG/H	1960–1964	3x2	D
565 SMS F.E. Warren AFB, Wyoming	ABG/H	1961–1964	3x3	D
566 SMS Offutt AFB, Nebraska	ABG/H	1961–1964	3x3	D
567 SMS Fairchild AFB, Washington	BG/H	1961–1965	1x9	E
548 SMS Forbes AFB, Kansas	BG/H	1961–1965	1x9	E
549 SMS F.E. Warren, Wyoming	BG/H	1961–1965	1x9	E
550 SMS Schilling AFB, Kansas	Silo	1962–1965	1x12	F
551 SMS Lincoln AFB, Nebraska	Silo	1962–1965	1x12	F
577 SMS Altus AFB, Oklahoma	Silo	1962–1965	1x12	F
578 SMS Dyess AFB, Texas	Silo	1962–1965	1x12	F
579 SMS Walker AFB, New Mexico	Silo	1962–1965	1x12	F
556 SMS Plattsburg AFB, New York	Silo	1962–1965	1x12	F

Note: Vandenberg AFB was a test and training facility. As an emergency measure missiles undergoing testing were placed on operational alert. SMS = Strategic Missile Squadron; ABG/H = Above ground/horizontal; BG/H = Below ground/horizontal.

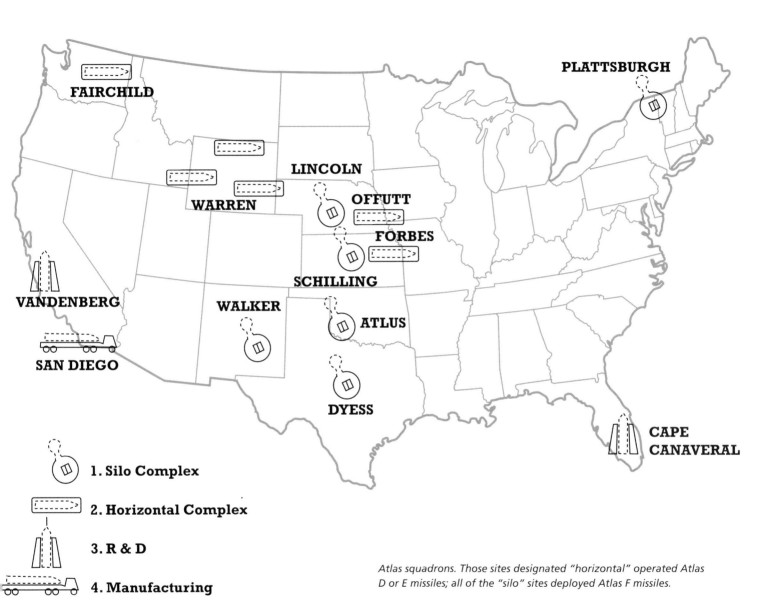

PLATTSBURGH

FAIRCHILD

LINCOLN

OFFUTT

WARREN

FORBES

VANDENBERG

SCHILLING

WALKER

ATLUS

SAN DIEGO

DYESS

CAPE CANAVERAL

1. Silo Complex

2. Horizontal Complex

3. R & D

4. Manufacturing

Atlas squadrons. Those sites designated "horizontal" operated Atlas D or E missiles; all of the "silo" sites deployed Atlas F missiles.

191

compromise, in February 1953 ARDC proposed a three-tier test plan using test vehicles powered by one, three, and five engines with the last missile serving as an operational prototype. ARDC estimated that the revised R&D program would take approximately ten years and cost $378 million.

The Air Staff approved the revised plan in October and issued ARDC a development directive to begin work. The directive, however, lacked the vigor that ARDC sought. It estimated that the R&D phase would not be completed until sometime after 1964 and also assigned Atlas a 1-B development priority.

ARDC designated the Atlas program Weapon System (WS)-107A. Although scaled down from earlier designs, the missile remained an ambitious undertaking. It was 110 feet high, 12 feet in diameter, and when fully loaded, weighed 440,000 pounds. Propulsion was to come from five engines: four first-stage engines clustered around a single sustainer engine.

At the Air Staff's insistence the Atlas program would have continued down its slow and conservative path had it not been for the February 1954 Teapot Committee report. Chaired by the renowned mathematician John von Neumann, the committee recommended a "radical reorganization" of the entire Atlas program. The committee estimated that if the government followed all of its recommendations, Atlas could be operational in six to eight years.

The Air Force accepted the Teapot Committee recommendations, and on May 14, 1954, it accelerated the Atlas program to the "maximum extent that technology would permit." It accorded Atlas a 1-A top priority status, and of equal importance, directed that it be given priority over all other Air Force programs.

During the spring and fall of 1954 the Air Force and the two most important contractors, Ramo-Wooldridge Corporation (systems engineering and technical direction) and Convair (structures and assembly), worked feverishly to revise the Atlas design based on a 1,500-pound, 1-megaton warhead. The thorough redesign cut the size of the missile almost in half: the weight decreased from 440,000 to 240,000 pounds and the number of engines was reduced from five to three.

Flight testing for the Atlas A began in June 1957. The initial test vehicle, the Atlas A, contained only the two booster engines and a dummy nosecone. Six of eight test flights blew up on the launch pad or were destroyed shortly after takeoff. Two missiles had successful flights of 600 miles.

The Atlas B series was a more sophisticated missile complete with a sustainer engine and separable nosecone. In July 1958 the first one exploded soon after launching, but the following November an Atlas B roared 6,000 miles down range.

The Atlas C was a semi-operational version that contained several advanced features. It was first launched successfully in December 1958.

The Atlas D was equipped with radio-inertial guidance. First tested in April 1959, three Atlas Ds were place on operational alert at Vandenberg AFB in late 1959.

The Atlas E was the first to use an all-inertial guidance system and the improved MA-3 propulsion system. Its first successful test flight was in February 1961.

The Atlas F had an improved fuel loading system that allowed the missile to be fueled and fired more quickly. It was also designed to be stored vertically in hardened silos. The first successful Atlas F flight was in July 1961.

Basing Strategy

The hallmark of the Atlas deployment schedule was urgency; escalating tensions with the Soviet Union sent the Air Force scrambling to deploy the missiles as rapidly as possible. Initially the Air Force planned to deploy four squadrons of ten missiles each, but in December 1957 the Department of Defense expanded the missile force to nine and later thirteen squadrons. Originally the location of the launch sites was determined exclusively by the missile's range; they had to be within 5,000 miles of their targets in the Soviet Union. Later, other factors that influenced the placement of the sites was that they be inland, out of range of Soviet submarine-launched intermediate range missiles; close to support facilities; and as a cost cutting measure, be built on government property whenever possible.

This 1960 photograph shows two Atlas D ICBMs deployed on open launch pads at Vandenberg AFB, California. This was a stopgap measure, intended to serve only until the protected, horizontal launchers were ready.

Site Configuration

The Air Force deployed Atlas models D, E, and F; each was based in a different launch configuration.

As an emergency measure, in September 1959 the Air Force deployed three Atlas Ds on open launch pads at Vandenberg AFB. Completely exposed to the elements, the three missiles were serviced by a gantry crane. One missile was on operational alert at all times.

The first full Atlas D squadrons became operational in 1960. In these so-called "soft" sites, which could only withstand overpressures of 5 pounds per square inch (psi), the missiles were stored horizontally within a 103- by 133-foot launch and service building built of reinforced concrete. The missile bay had a retractable roof. To launch the missile, the roof was pulled back, the missile raised to the vertical position, fueled, and fired.

An individual Atlas D launch site consisted of a launch and service building, a launch operations building, guidance operations building, generating plant, and communications facilities. The launch operations buildings were two-story structures built of reinforced concrete measuring 73 by 78 feet with earth mounded up to the roof lines. Constructed much like blockhouses at missile test ranges, these buildings housed the launch operations crew and were equipped with entrance tunnels, blastproof doors, and escape tunnels. The guidance operations buildings, which sent course corrections to the missile in flight, were one-story structures, 75 by 212 feet, with a full basement. The basement walls were reinforced concrete and the remaining walls were of concrete block. The power plant was a 63- by 65-foot single-story, concrete block building. It housed three large diesel generators and the pumps for the water system.

At the first Atlas D squadron at F.E. Warren AFB, six launchers were grouped together, controlled by two launch operations buildings, and clustered around a central guidance control facility. This was called the 3x2 configuration: two launch complexes of three missiles each constituted a squadron. At the two later Atlas D sites, a second at F.E. Warren AFB, and at Offutt AFB, Nebraska, the missiles were based in a 3 x 3 configuration: three launchers and one combined guidance control/launch facility constituted a launch complex, and three complexes comprised a squadron. At these later sites the combined guidance and control facility measured 107 by 121 feet with a partial basement. To reduce the risk that one powerful nuclear warhead could destroy multiple launch sites, the launch complexes were spread 20 to 30 miles apart.

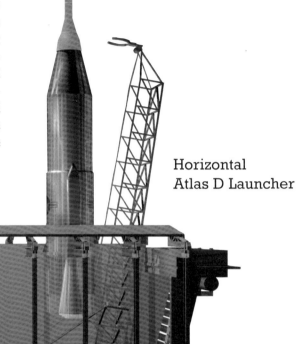

Horizontal
Atlas D Launcher

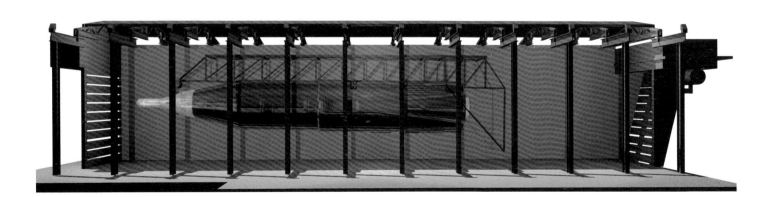

The major enhancement in the Atlas E was the new all-inertial system that obviated the need for ground control facilities. Since the missiles were no longer tied to a central guidance control facility, the launchers could be dispersed more widely Thus, the three Atlas F squadrons located at Fairchild AFB, Washington; Forbes AFB, Kansas; and F.E. Warren AFB, Wyoming; were based in a 1x9 configuration: nine independent launch sites comprised a missile squadron.

The Atlas Es were based in "semi-hard" or "coffin" facilities that protected the missile against overpressures up to 25 psi. In this arrangement the missile, its support facilities, and the launch operations building were housed in reinforced concrete structures that were buried underground; only the roofs protruded above ground level. The missile launch and service building was a 105- by 100-foot structure with a central bay in which the missile was stored horizontally. To launch a missile, the heavy roof was retracted, the missile raised to the vertical launch position, fueled, and then fired. The 54- by 90-foot launch operations building was 150 feet from the missile launch facility; the two were connected by an underground passageway. The launch operations building contained the launch control facilities, crew's living quarters, and power plant. The Atlas E launch sites were spaced approximately twenty miles apart.

The Atlas F, the most advanced of the Atlas series, were designed to be stored vertically in "hard" or "silo" sites. With the exception of a pair of massive 45 ton doors, the silos, 174 feet deep by 52 feet in diam-

Atlas E Launch sequence

eter, were completely underground. The walls of the silo were built of heavily reinforced concrete. Within the silo the missile and its support system were supported by a steel framework called the crib, which hung from the walls of the silo on four sets of huge springs.

Adjacent to the silo, and also buried underground, was the launch control center. Built of heavily reinforced concrete, it was 27 feet high, 40 feet in diameter, and contained the launch control equipment plus living arrangements for the crew. The control center was connected to the silo by a cylindrical tunnel 50 feet long and 8 feet in diameter. The tunnel provided access to the silo and served as a conduit for the launch control cabling.

In the firing sequence the missile was fueled, lifted by an elevator to the mouth of the silo, and then fired. Although the silo sites were by far the most difficult and costly sites to build, they offered protection from overpressures of up to 100 psi.

The Air Force deployed six squadrons of Atlas Fs, one each at Schilling AFB, Kansas; Lincoln AFB, Nebraska; Altus AFB, Oklahoma; Dyess AFB, Texas; Walker AFB, New Mexico; and Plattsburg AFB, New York (the only ICBMs ever based east of the Mississippi). Each squadron included twelve launch sites. Distances between the sites ranged from 20 to 30 miles.

References

Information for the Atlas technical specifications came from two reports by the Convair Division of General Dynamics: "Atlas Intercontinental Ballistic Missile," 1960, file K208-20A, Air Force Historical Research

First Level

A   Ready Room & Storage

B   Janitor's Room

C   Medical Supply Room

D   Toilet

E   Kitchen and Mess

F   Power Distribution Room

G   Hall

Second Level

H   Battery Room

J   Office

K   Communications Equipment Room

L   Launch Control Room

Equipment Key

1   Alternate Command Console
       (One Per Squadron)

2   Power Plant Remote Control Panel

3   Launch Control Console

4   TV Monitor

5   Office Equipment

6   Lighting Distribution Transformer

7   Fire Alarm Panel Exit & Emergency,
       Lighting Panel, Normal Lighting Panel,
       Lighting Distribution Panel

8   Batteries & Rack

9   Telephone Terminal Cabinet

10   Charger Bay

11   Communication Power Dist. Panel

12   PA System Cabinet

13   Communication Equip. Panel "B"

14   Main Distribution Frame

15   Miscellaneous Trunk Bay
        (Direct Lines)

16   Motor Control Center

17   Finder Connector Bay

18   Power Board

19   Miscellaneous Relay Rack

20   Selector Bay

21   X-Time Clock Bay

22   Register Bay

23   Translator Bay

24   Facility Remote Control Panel

25   Sass Bay

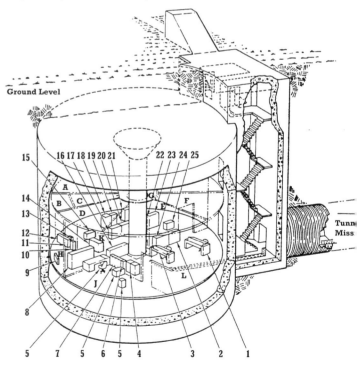

LAUNCH CONTROL CENTER

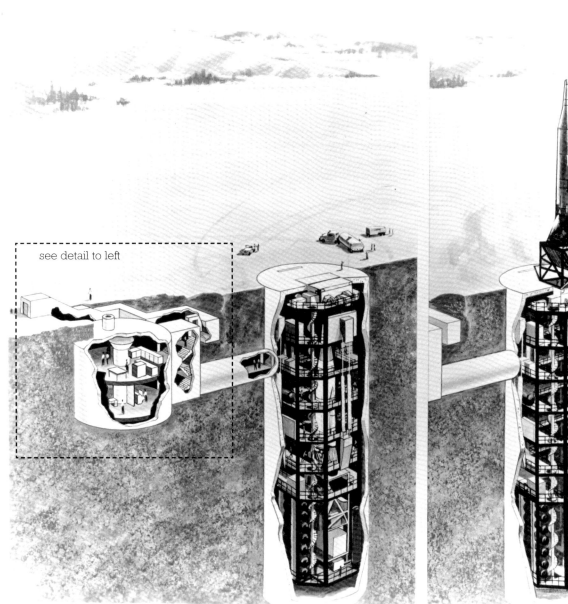

see detail to left

Performance data from a typical Atlas mission.

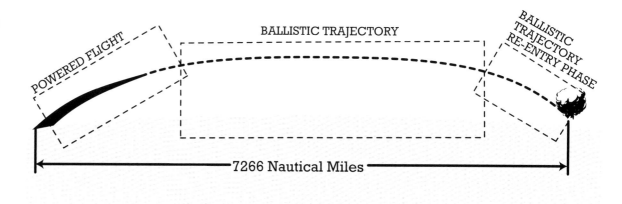

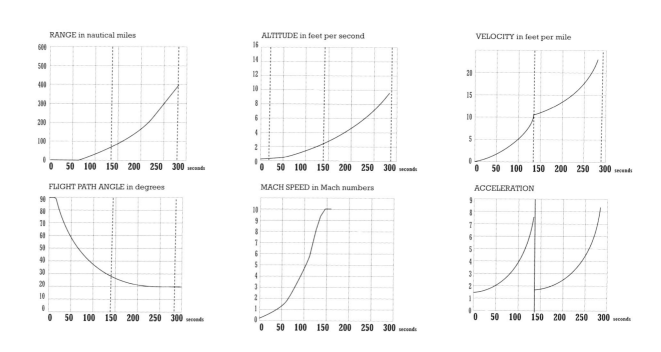

Agency, Maxwell AFB, Montgomery, AL (hereafter AFHRA) and "Standard Missile Characteristics, HGM-16F," March 1964, file OA-40105501, folder F ICBM, National Air and Space Museum Archives, Washington, DC, (hereafter NASM). Another very valuable source is the comprehensive "SM-65E Missile Weapon System General Manual," T.O. 21-SM65E-1Y, dated September 1960, in folder C1/Atlas/ops at the Research Center, USAF Museum, Wright-Patterson AFB, Dayton, OH (hereafter the Research Center). Other helpful material came from: The *Chronology of the Ballistic Missile Organization: 1945–1990* (Norton, CA: Ballistic Missile Organization History Office, 1993); Iain Pike, "Atlas: Pioneer ICBM and Space-Age Workhorse," *Flight International* 81 (January 1962), pp. 89–96; and *Jane's All the World's Aircraft 1962–1963* (London, Jane's Publishing, 1963).

Information for the development history came from several sources. A useful summary is Jacob Neufeld, *The Development of Ballistic Missiles in the United States Air Force 1945–1960* (Washington, DC: Bolling AFB, 1989). For a detailed look at the bureaucratic and technological factors that shaped the debate over Atlas, see Edmund Beard, *Developing the ICBM: A Study in Bureaucratic Politics,* Institute of War and Peace Study Series (New York: Columbia University Press, 1976).

A very useful summary of Atlas deployment is Henry Narducci, *From Snark to Peacekeeper: A Pictorial History of Strategic Air Command Missiles* (Offutt, AFB, NE: Office of the Historian, HQ, Strategic Air Command, 1990). The size of the Atlas force, and the basing strategy that guided the placement of the launch sites are discussed in the correspondence of Brig. Gen. Charles M. McCorkle, the Assistant Chief of Staff for Guided Missiles, in the records of the Air Force Chief of Staff for Guided Missiles (hereafter AFCGM records) Federal Records Center, Suitland, MD (hereafter FRC Suitland) RG 341, box 2, folder "AFCGM Correspondence–1957" and box 3, "AFCGM Correspondence- 1958." For an excellent summary of ICBM basing strategy see the memo from General Curtis LeMay, Vice Chief of Staff, to Secretary of the Air Force, subj: ICBM Siting, 6 June 1958, AFCGM records, FRC Suitland, RG 341, box 3, folder "AFCGM Correspondence–1958."

For a comparison of the different launch site configurations, see Convair's "Base Activation," n.d., in folder C1-0 at the Research Center. An exhaustively well documented survey of the Atlas F silos is General Dynamics Astronautics, "Integrating Contractor's Base Activation Project Manual, Series F Silo Bases," Report No. 600-200, n.d., in folder C1-0 at the Research Center.

For a summary of ICBM site construction, see T.J. Hayes, "ICBM Site Construction," *The Military Engineer* (November–December 1966): pp. 399–403. For detailed information on the construction and location of the Atlas launch sites, see the Corps of Engineers Ballistic Missile Construction Office (CEBMCO) site construction histories in the Research Collection, Office of History, Headquarters, U.S. Army Corps of Engineers, Alexandria, VA. Another valuable source is the pending "Historic American Engineering Record of the Atlas F Missile Site S-8," prepared by the Tri-Services Cultural Resources Research Center of the U.S. Army Construction Engineering Research Laboratories, Champaign, IL, for the Fort Worth District, Corps of Engineers.

Titan I and Titan II

Summary

The Titan I (SM-68A) program began in January 1955 and took shape in parallel with the Atlas (SM-65/HGM-25) intercontinental ballistic missile (ICBM). The Air Force's goal in launching the Titan program was twofold: one, to serve as a backup should Atlas fail; and two, to develop a large, two-stage missile with a longer range and bigger payload that also could serve as a booster for space flights. Like Atlas, Titan I's liquid cryogenic fuel was a severe drawback. Consequently, in 1959 the Air Force Ballistic Missile Division (AFBMD) began developing Titan II (SM-68B/LGM-25C). A larger missile, Titan II featured an all-inertial guidance system and a storable, noncryogenie oxidizer and fuel that were hypergolic, igniting on contact with one another.

Titan I was on operational alert only briefly, between 1962 and 1965, but the improved Titan IIs had a much longer service life and remained on operational alert between 1963 and 1987.

Technical Specifications

Length:	Titan I: 98 feet	Titan II: 108 feet
Diameter:	Titan I: First stage–10 feet	Titan II: First stage–10 feet
	Second stage–8 feet	Second stage–8 feet
Weight fueled:	Titan I: 220,000 pounds	Titan II: 330,000 pounds
Fuel:	Titan I: Rocket grade RP-1 (kerosene)	Titan II: Aerozine 50[a]
Oxidizer:	Titan I: Liquid oxygen	Titan II: Nitrogen tetroxide

Propulsion:

The Titan ICBMs were two-stage, liquid fuel missiles. The specifications for each stage are given below.

Titan I First stage: 300,000 pounds of thrust; Second stage: 80,000 pounds of thrust

Titan II First stage: 430,000 pounds of thrust; Second stage: 100,000 pounds of thrust

Range:	Titan I: 6,300 miles	Titan II: 9,000 miles
Guidance:	Titan I : Radio-inertial	Titan II : All-Inertial[b]
Reentry Vehicle:	Titan I: Mark 4, ablative	Titan II: Mark 6, ablative
Warhead:	Titan I: one W-38 warhead, 4 megaton yield	Titan II: one W-53 warhead, 9 megaton yield

Opposite: In this October 1962 photograph a Titan II ICBM slowly rises from the launch pad at Cape Canaveral,

---

[a] Aerozine 50 was composed of equal parts unsymmetrical dimethylhydrazine and hydrazine.
[b] American Bosch Arma was originally selected to build the inertial guidance system for Titan, but in 1957 the Air Force decided to use the Bosch Arma for Atlas and brought in AC Spark Plug to build the Titan system.

Contractors

Airframe: Glenn L. Martin Aircraft Company, later Martin Marietta, Denver, Colorado

Propulsion: Aerojet General Corporation, Sacramento, California

Guidance: Titan I: radio-inertial guidance. The radar was built by Bell Telephone Laboratories in Allentown, Pennsylvania, and the guidance computer by Remington Rand UNIVAC in St. Paul, Minnesota
Titan II: all-inertial guidance system. The system was built by AC Spark Plug, Milwaukee, Wisconsin

Reentry vehicles: Mark 4–AVCO, Wilmington, Massachusetts; Mark 6–General Electric, Philadelphia, Pennsylvania

Technical Notes

Titan was the United States' first true multistage ICBM. At the conclusion of the first and second stage firings, the engines and fuel tanks for those sections dropped away, thereby decreasing the weight and mass of the vehicle. That made for a more efficient missile, which resulted in increased range and a larger payload.

The most notable difference between the Titan I and Titan II was the type of oxidizer and propellant each used. Titan I used liquid oxygen as an oxidizer. It was cryogenic, meaning it had to be kept at an extremely low temperature, generally around –195°C. It had to be stored in special refrigerated tanks and pumped aboard the missile before it was fired. Liquid oxygen is extremely volatile, inflammable, and very difficult to handle, especially within the confines of an enclosed missile silo.

In contrast, Titan II used a noncryogenic oxidizer that could be stored aboard the missile. It also used a hypergolic fuel, meaning it spontaneously burst into flame when it came in contact with the oxidizer.

System Operation

Titan I

The launch sequence took approximately 15 minutes. After receiving a launch order, the crew filled the missile's tanks with 200,000 pounds of liquid oxygen and RP-1. After the missile was fueled, it rode to the surface on the silo elevator and then was fired. The flight began with the ignition of the large first-stage engine that burned for 134 seconds and propelled the missile to an altitude of 35 miles. As the first stage expired and fell away, the second stage fired; it burned for another 156 seconds, boosting the missile to an altitude of 150 miles and a velocity of 22,554 feet per second. After the second stage fell silent, two small vernier engines fired for an additional 50 seconds making final course corrections to the trajectory. After the vernier engines burned out, the reentry vehicle carrying the warhead followed a ballistic trajectory, and at the apogee of its flight soared to an altitude of 541 miles above the earths surface. Time elapsed for a 5,500 mile flight: 33 minutes.

Titan II

With the exception of the launch sequence, the Titan II followed much the same mission profile as its predecessor. The Titan II's hypergolic fuel and noncryogenic oxidizer were stored within the missile's fuel tanks,

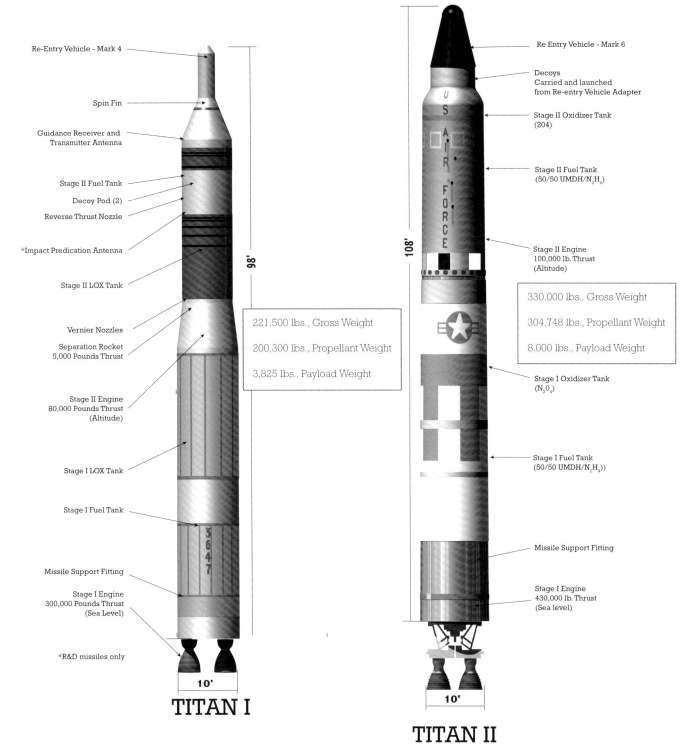

Re-Entry Vehicle - Mark 4

Spin Fin

Guidance Receiver and
Transmitter Antenna

Stage II Fuel Tank

Decoy Pod (2)

Reverse Thrust Nozzle

*Impact Predication Antenna

Stage II LOX Tank

Vernier Nozzles

Separation Rocket
5,000 Pounds Thrust

Stage II Engine
80,000 Pounds Thrust
(Altitude)

Stage I LOX Tank

Stage I Fuel Tank

Missile Support Fitting

Stage I Engine
300,000 Pounds Thrust
(Sea Level)

*R&D missiles only

98'

10'

221,500 lbs., Gross Weight

200,300 lbs., Propellant Weight

3,825 lbs., Payload Weight

TITAN I

Re Entry Vehicle - Mark 6

Decoys
Carried and launched
from Re-entry Vehicle Adapter

Stage II Oxidizer Tank
(204)

Stage II Fuel Tank
(50/50 UMDH/N$_2$H$_4$)

Stage II Engine
100,000 lb. Thrust
(Altitude)

Stage I Oxidizer Tank
(N$_2$O$_4$)

Stage I Fuel Tank
(50/50 UMDH/N$_2$H$_4$))

Missile Support Fitting

Stage I Engine
430,000 lb. Thrust
(Sea level)

108'

10'

330,000 lbs., Gross Weight

304,748 lbs., Propellant Weight

8,000 lbs., Payload Weight

TITAN II

205

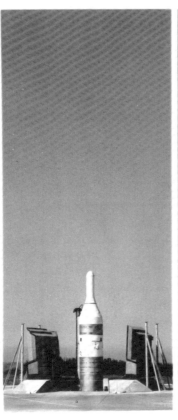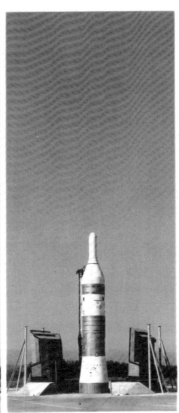

which enabled the new ICBM to be fired within a single minute after the launch sequence began. Moreover, the Titan II was intended to be launched from inside the silo-the first liquid-fuel missile to have this capability. Titan II was also equipped with an all-inertial guidance system that ended the missile's dependence on ground-based radars. The new guidance system was a significant improvement; it allowed the missiles to be based in widely dispersed, individual silos.

Developmental History

Titan I

The ICBM Scientific Advisory Committee planted the seeds of the Titan program in July 1954 when it recommended that the Air Force's Western Development Division (WDD) explore alternate missile configurations before entrusting the nation's entire ICBM program to the untested Atlas (SM-65).[c]

The following month the WDD directed its systems engineering and technical direction (SE/TD) contractor, the Ramo-Wooldridge Corporation, to institute a study of alternate ICBM configurations. Shortly thereafter the contractor hired Lockheed Aircraft Corporation and the Glenn L. Martin Aircraft Company to help with the task.

[c] The ICBM Scientific Advisory Committee was a group of prominent civilian scientists and engineers that advised the Air Force on the missile program.

When the study began, both the WDD and Ramo-Wooldridge were leery of becoming overly reliant on Atlas. Convair's design reflected an unconventional approach, and while many tests had been made, it had not been flight tested nor could it be for nearly three years.

Based on the preliminary results of its study, in October the WDD recommended that Convair go ahead with Atlas, but at the same time the development agency also suggested that the Air Force broaden its ICBM program to include a missile with a rigid, aircraft type fuselage and an alternate engine configuration. The WDD stressed that developing a second ICBM would allow the Air Force to pursue a more ambitious design and would also stimulate competition between the two ICBM programs.

In January 1955 the ICBM Scientific Advisory Committee reviewed the WDD's findings and recommended that the Air Force pursue an alternate ICBM configuration, most probably one with a two-stage propulsion system. Based on the committee's recommendation, in April 1955 Secretary of the Air Force Harold Talbott authorized the WDD to begin work on a second ICBM. His only stipulation was that the winning contractor agree to build its missile production facility in the central United States.[d]

The Air Force solicited bids for the second ICBM in May 1955 and the following October awarded the Glenn L. Martin Aircraft Company of Baltimore, Maryland a contract to develop the new Titan I (SM-68A) ICBM. Martin built its Titan production facility outside of Denver, Colorado. The Air Force accepted delivery of its first production Titan in June 1958, and began testing shortly thereafter. In April 1959 the Army Corps of Engineers began supervising the construction of the first Titan I launch facilities at Lowry AFB, Colorado. Three years later that site hosted the first Titan I squadron to be placed on operational alert.

This January 1961 photograph shows a Titan I ICBM taking off from Cape Canaveral, Florida.

Titan II

Even as the first Titan I missiles were rolling off the assembly line, the Air Force was searching for a way to modify the missile to use an oxidizer other than liquid oxygen. Searching for a way to improve the Titan I at a reasonable cost, in January 1959 the Air Force Ballistic Missile Division (AFBMD–the name was changed from WDD on June 1, 1957) found that with minor modifications Titan I could be modified to use a noncryogenic, storable propellant. That amounted to a major breakthrough, for it enabled the propellant to be stored within the missile itself, thereby permitting the Titan II to be fired in a single minute. Moreover, the new propellant made it possible to launch the missile from within the silo, simplified maintenance, and reduced the risk of accidents.

[d] Since the early 1950s it had been Air Force policy to move vital industrial facilities well inland, out of reach of Soviet submarine-launched intermediate-range ballistic missiles.

In November 1959 the Department of Defense (DoD) authorized the development of the Titan II (SM-68B/LGM-25C) and at the same time directed that the Titan I program be discontinued after six squadrons. As planned, Titan II would be a larger, more advanced missile than its predecessor. It would be equipped with an all-inertial guidance system, a storable noncryogenic oxidizer, hypergolic fuel, and have in-silo launch capability.

In June 1960 the Air Force awarded the Martin Company the Titan II contract. Developed in parallel with the Titan I program, the Titan II took shape rapidly. Captive flight tests began in December 1961, and in February 1963 a Titan II fired from the Air Force Missile Test Center (AFMTC) in Florida logged a successful 6,500-mile flight. The following October the AFBMD's site activation task force turned over the first Titan II strategic missile wing to the Strategic Air Command (SAC). By December 1963 all six Titan II squadrons were on operational alert.

Basing Strategy

In October 1957, Congress authorized the Air Force to deploy four Titan I squadrons. Later that number increased to 12 squadrons, evenly split between Titan I and Titan II. With their 6,300-mile range, the Air Force based the Titan Is between Colorado and Washington state. The Titan IIs, on the other hand, had a 9,000-mile range and could be based farther south. By locating the Titan II bases in Arizona, Kansas, and Arkansas, the Air Force achieved a wider national dispersal pattern. Other factors that affected the location of the Titan launch facilities were population density under the missile's projected flight path, and the location of existing bases to provide logistical support.

Titan Deployment

The Titan I was deployed in a 3x3 configuration, meaning a squadron of nine missiles was divided into three, three-missile launch complexes. The Titan II was deployed in a 1x9 configuration. Each squadron consisted of nine separate launch facilities, each housing a single missile.

Site Configuration

Titan I

In 1956 the Air Force decided that all of the Titan I missiles should be based in "super-hardened" silos buried deep underground. Using data from above-ground nuclear tests, the Air Force found that at a reasonable cost it could construct the launch facilities to withstand overpressures of 25 to 100 pounds per square inch (psi). Subsequently, all of the Titan I launch sites were built to withstand overpressures of 100 psi.

The Army Corps of Engineers Ballistic Missile Construction Office (CEBMCO) began building the first Titan I launch facilities at Lowry AFB, Colorado, in May 1959. Each squadron consisted of nine missiles evenly divided among three launch complexes. The missiles were grouped in clusters of three because they had to remain close to their ground-based radars and guidance computers.

The mammoth underground complexes were miniature cities, complete with their own power and water supplies. The entire complex was buried deep beneath the ground, and all the parts were linked by underground passageways. At one end of the complex were the three missile silos, each 160 feet deep and 44 feet

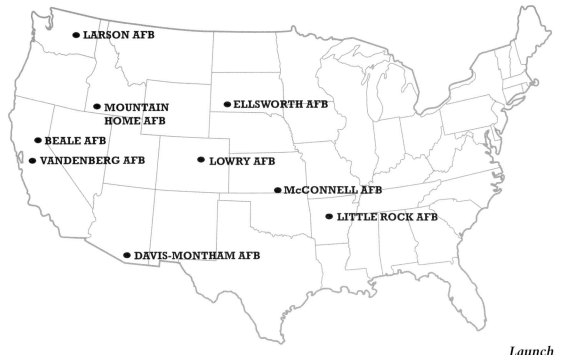

Unit	Base	Basing Mode	Operational Dates	Launch Configuration	Missile Series
724 SMS	Lowry AFB, Colorado	Silo-lift	1962–1965	3x3	I
725 SMS	Lowry AFB, Colorado	Silo-lift	1962–1965	3x3	I
569 SMS	Mt. Home AFB, Idaho	Silo-lift	1962–1965	3x3	I
851 SMS	Beale AFB, California	Silo-lift	1962–1965	3x3	I
568 SMS	Larson AFB, Washington	Silo-lift	1962–1965	3x3	I
850 SMS	Ellsworth AFB, South Dakota	Silo-lift	1962–1965	3x3	I
570 SMS	Davis-Monthan AFB, Arizona	Silo	1963–1984	1x9	II
571 SMS	Davis-Monthan AFB, Arizona	Silo	1963–1983	1x9	II
533 SMS	McConnell AFB, Kansas	Silo	1963–1985	1x9	II
532 SMS	McConnell AFB, Kansas	Silo	1963–1986	1x9	II
573 SMS	Little Rock, Arkansas	Silo	1963–1987	1x9	II
374 SMS	Little Rock, Arkansas	Silo	1963–1986	1x9	II

Notes: The two Titan I squadrons at Lowry were placed in service as the 848th and 849th Strategic Missile Squadrons. On July 1, 1961 SAC disbanded those squadrons and in their places organized the 724th and 725th SMS.

in diameter. They were built of reinforced concrete that ranged in thickness from 2 to 3 feet. Within the silo was a steel framework that housed both the missile and the elevator that carried it to the surface. The only parts of the silo that protruded above the surface were two horizontal doors, each weighing 125 tons.

Adjacent to each silo were the propellant storage and equipment terminal buildings, both of which were buried under 17 to 24 feet of earth. Several hundred feet away were the control room and power house. Both were domed structures built of reinforced concrete and buried 10 to 17 feet beneath the surface. The control room was 40 feet high, 100 feet in diameter, and housed all of the launch control equipment. The nearby power house was 60 feet high, 127 feet in diameter, and contained generators and the power distribution system. Nestled between the two buildings was the cylindrical entry portal, 72 feet deep and 38 feet in diameter, that controlled access to the underground complex.

At the base of the complex were two radar antennas that were part of the missile's ground-based guidance system. The antennas were housed in two silos, each 67 feet deep and 38 feet in diameter. The launch crews raised the antennas above ground as they readied the missile for firing. The antennas were approximately 1,300 feet from the farthest silo. More than 2,500 feet of corrugated steel tunnel, 9 feet in diameter and buried 40 feet beneath the surface, connected all the buildings within the complex.

Titan II

The Titan II silos were markedly different from the Titan I launch complexes. Most notably, the Titan II's all-inertial guidance system no longer required that the missiles remain tethered to a ground-based guidance system. Instead the Titan IIs were based separately, and each silo was at least seven miles from its closest neighbor. The Air Force deployed six squadrons of Titan II missiles. Each squadron contained nine missiles, and to save money, the squadrons were grouped in pairs, forming an operational base. All of the logistic and support functions were based at existing SAC bases, and the missiles were located nearby.

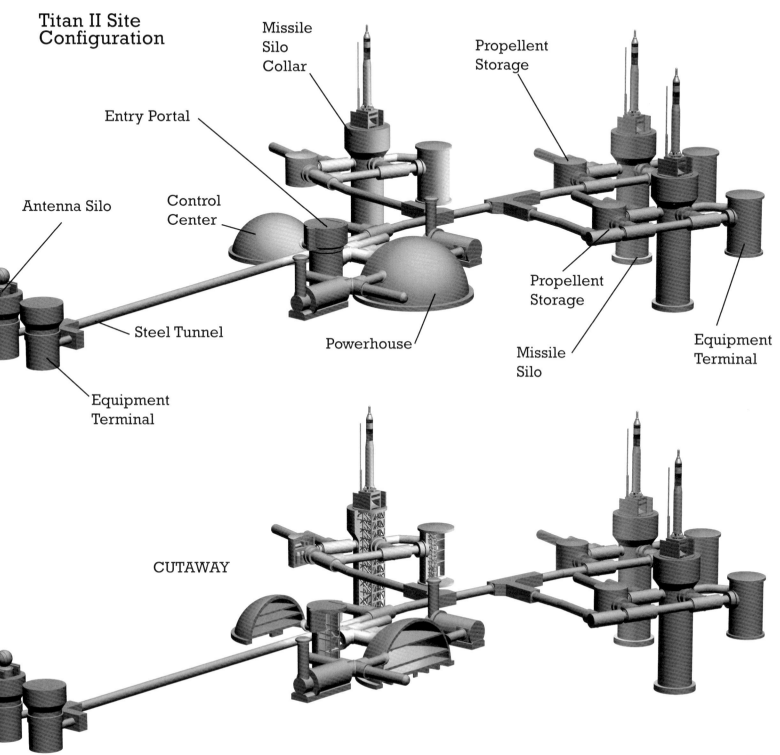

Titan II Site Configuration

Missile Silo Collar

Propellent Storage

Entry Portal

Antenna Silo

Control Center

Propellent Storage

Steel Tunnel

Powerhouse

Missile Silo

Equipment Terminal

Equipment Terminal

CUTAWAY

On the surface, the Titan II launch facilities covered an area of approximately 600 feet by 600 feet. All of the launch facilities were underground. The silo was built of heavily reinforced concrete, and was 147 feet deep and 55 feet in diameter. It was wider than a Titan I silo because the Titan II was designed to be "hot launched" from within the silo. To deflect and channel the exhaust gases, each silo was fitted with a flame deflector at the base and two exhaust ducts that ran up the length of the silo and vented to the surface. Inside the silo there were nine levels of equipment rooms and missile access spaces. The silo was covered with a steel and concrete door that weighed 740 tons and could be opened in 17 to 20 seconds.

The silo was connected to the missile control center by a 250-foot long access tunnel. Between the silo and the launch control center was the blast lock, a single level, heavily reinforced concrete structure containing three rooms. To enter the launch facility the missile crews descended through a 35 foot deep access portal that opened into the blast lock area. Each end of the blast lock was covered by a pair of large steel blast doors, each weighing 6,000 pounds, designed to protect the launch center from either a surface nuclear blast, or the explosion of the missile within the silo. The doors were designed to withstand an overpressure of 1000 psi.

The launch control center was a dome-shaped reinforced concrete structure 37 feet in diameter and containing three levels. The three floors within the launch center were suspended from the ceiling to minimize blast shock. These shock mounts were designed to permit a static floor load of 100 psi. The control center provided space for all of the launch control and communications equipment, as well as a mess and sleeping quarters for the four-person combat crew.

References

The best overview of the early days of the Titan program is Alfred Rockefeller, "History of Titan 1954–1959," in the files of the Ballistic Missile Organization, History Office, Norton AFB, California. Another excellent source is Warren E. Greene, *The Development of the SM–68 Titan,* AFSC, Historical Publications Series 62-63-1, August 1962 and available at the Titan Missile Museum Archives, Green Valley, AZ. Also see Maj. Francis X. Ruggiero, USAF, "Missileer's Heritage," report no. 2065-81, n.d., available at the Titan Missile Museum Archives. A concise summary of the events surrounding the decision to begin the Titan program is Frank Robert Futrell's, *Ideas, Concepts, Doctrine: Basic Thinking in the United States Air Force*

1907–1960, vol. I, (Maxwell AFB, Montgomery, AL: Air University Press, [1971] 1989), pp. 491–2. A colorful but less reliable source is Ernst G. Schwiebert, *A History of the U.S. Ballistic Missiles* (New York: Frederick A. Praeger, 1964). Jacob Neufeld's *The Development of Ballistic Missiles in the United States Air Force 1945–1960* (Washington, DC: Office of Air Force History, 1990) is also helpful and integrates the Titan program within the larger context of missile development.

The Titan technical specifications came from *Chronology of the Ballistic Missile Organization 1945–1990* (Norton, AFB, CA: History Office, Ballistic Missile Organization, 1990), appendices 3 and 4; "Rockets, Missiles, Spacecraft," *DMS Market Intelligence Reports* (1967); "Missiles," *DMS Market Intelligence Reports* (1987). Information on the warhead reentry vehicle combinations also came from "ICBM/IRBM/SLBM Warhead-RV Combinations," n.d., p. 1, Ballistic Missile Organization, History Office, Norton AFB, CA.

CEBMCO records in the Research Collection, Office of History, Headquarters Army Corps of Engineers, Alexandria, VA (hereafter Corps of Engineers Research Collection). For the construction of the Titan I sites see the "Beale Area Historical Summary: October 1959–March 1962," n.d., Military Files XVIII-20. For information on construction of the Titan II sites see "Titan II Facility Construction Status," (1961) in Col. R.H. Dunn, personal files, box 1, Corps of Engineers Research Collection.

Aerial view of a Titan II launch facility. The various trucks and tanks around the silo are transfer points for fuel and liquid nitrogen.

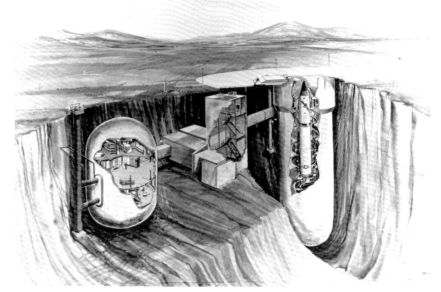

Cutaway illustration of a Titan II silo and launch control facility.

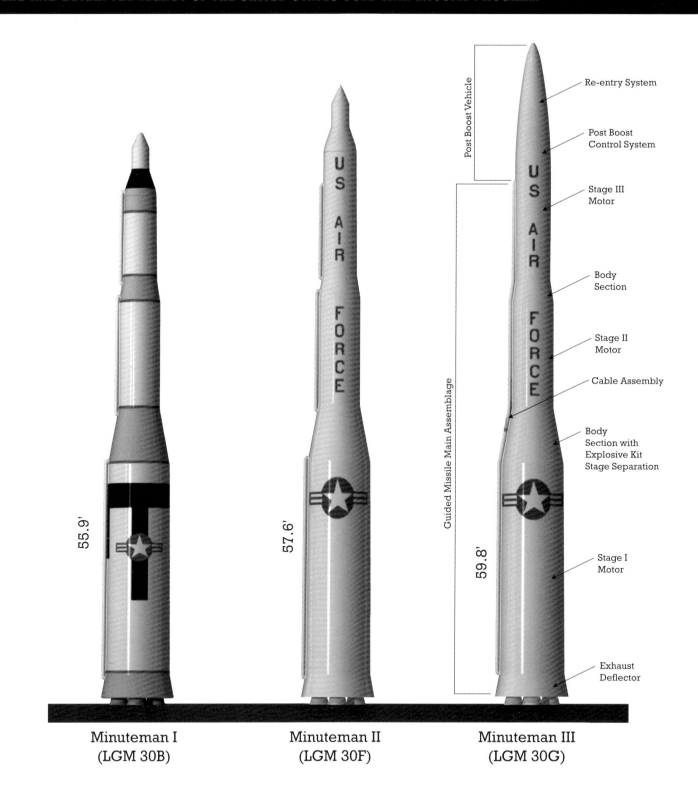

Minuteman I
(LGM 30B)

Minuteman II
(LGM 30F)

Minuteman III
(LGM 30G)

Minuteman (SM-80/LGM-30)

Summary

In the late 1950s advances in solid-fuel propellants enabled the Air Force to develop its first solid-fuel ICBM, the Minuteman I (LGM-30A/B). Formal development began in September 1958, and after an extraordinarily rapid development program, the Air Force put its first ten Minuteman ICBMs on operational alert at Malmstrom AFB, Montana, in October 1962. Deployment proceeded at an equally furious pace, and within five years 1,000 of the solid-fuel missiles stood poised in their silos. Twice the Air Force modernized the Minuteman, greatly enhancing its capabilities. It deployed the first Minuteman IIs (LGM-30F) in 1966 and the first Minuteman IIIs (LGM-3OG) in 1971. The Minuteman III was the first ICBM to be fitted with multiple independently targetable reentry vehicles (MIRVs) that enabled a single missile to carry up to three warheads, each aimed at a different target. The Minuteman force remained at 1,000 missiles for most of the Cold War. Although 450 Minuteman IIs were taken off operational alert in 1991, 500 Minuteman IIIs will remain on duty well into the twenty-first century.

Technical Specifications

Length:	53.8 feet (MM I/A)
	55.11 feet (MM I/B)
	57.7 feet (MM II)
	59.9 feet (MM III)
Weight:	65,000 pounds (MM I)
	73,000 pounds (MM II)
	78,000 pounds (MM III)
Range:	6,300 miles (MM I)
	7,021 miles (MM II)
	8,083 miles (MM III)

Propulsion:

Minuteman was a three-stage, solid-fuel missile. The specifications for each stage are given below.

Stage I: MM I, MM II, and MM III used the same 210,000-pound thrust motor

Stage II: MM I and MM II used a 60,000-pound thrust motor; MM III used a 60,300-pound thrust motor

Stage III: MM I and MM II used a 35,000-pound thrust motor; MM III used a 34,000-pound thrust motor

Guidance:	All-inertial
Accuracy:	MM I = 1.5 miles
	MM II = 1.0 miles
	MM III = 800 feet
Reentry vehicle:	MM I/A–Mark 5
	MM I/B–Mark 11
	MM II–Mark 12
	MM III–Mark 12A

Warhead:

> MM I/A: one W-59 warhead, 1 megaton yield
> MM I/B: one W-56 warhead, 1.2 megaton yield
> MM II: one W-56 warhead, 1 to 2 megaton yield
> MM III: two or three W-62 or W-78 warheads
> W-62 = 170 kiloton yield
> W-78 = 375 kiloton yield

Contractors

Airframe: Boeing Airplane Company, Seattle, Washington
Propulsion:

> Stage I: Thiokol Chemical Corporation, Brigham City, Utah
> Stage II: Aerojet Solid Propulsion Company, Sacramento, California
> Stage III: Hercules Powder Company, Magna, Utah

Guidance: Autonetics Division of Rockwell Corporation, Anaheim, California
Reentry Vehicles:

> Mark 5–AVCO, Wilmington, Massachusetts
> Mark 12–General Electric, Philadelphia, Pennsylvania
> Mark 12A–General Electric, Philadelphia, Pennsylvania

Technical Notes

Minuteman I was deployed in two variants, Minuteman I/A and I/B. Minuteman I/A was an interim weapon because a flawed first stage reduced its range by 2,000 miles. Rather than delay the entire Minuteman program while it corrected the problem, the Air Force elected to go ahead and deploy 150 Minuteman I/As.

System Operation

Upon receiving a launch order, the two-officer crew in the underground Minuteman launch control center (LCC) would check the launch instructions and then set the required war plan and launcher selector switches. Next, the officers would insert keys into the launch switches, located at opposite ends of the LCC, and simultaneously turn the keys to initiate the automatic launch sequence. Sixty seconds later the missiles roared out of their underground silos.

Unlike the large liquid-fuel ICBMs that rose slowly into the air, the Minuteman, preceded by a large smoke ring, streaked out of the silo. Three seconds after launch the missile began a gentle turn toward the target. The first stage separated after 60 seconds at an altitude of 15 miles. The second stage separated after 117 seconds, and the third stage after 181 seconds, at which time the missile had reached an altitude of 118 miles and was traveling at a velocity of 23,000 feet per second. At the apogee of its parabolic flight path the reentry vehicle reached an altitude of 710 miles above the earth's surface.

The Minuteman II and III deployed penetration aids such as small rockets and explosive charges to help camouflage the warhead during reentry, Also, the Minuteman III carried a postboost propulsion system, sometimes referred to as a fourth stage, that precisely positioned the reentry system at selected points before releasing the penetration aids and the multiple independently targetable reentry vehicles containing the warheads.

Minuteman Flight Characteristics

	Time	Altitude	Range
Stage 1 Ignition	0	0	0
Stage 2 Ignition	61 secs	100,000 ft.	18 Nautical Miles (NM)
Stage 3 Ignition	125 secs	300,000 ft.	120 Nautical Miles
Stage 3/RV Separation	186 secs	750,000 ft.	210 Nautical Miles

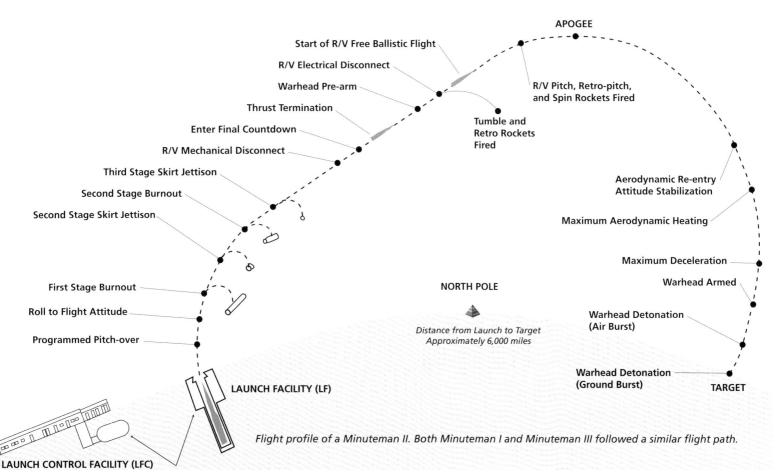

Flight profile of a Minuteman II. Both Minuteman I and Minuteman III followed a similar flight path.

APOGEE

Start of R/V Free Ballistic Flight

R/V Electrical Disconnect

Warhead Pre-arm

Thrust Termination

Enter Final Countdown

R/V Mechanical Disconnect

Third Stage Skirt Jettison

Second Stage Burnout

Second Stage Skirt Jettison

First Stage Burnout

Roll to Flight Attitude

Programmed Pitch-over

R/V Pitch, Retro-pitch, and Spin Rockets Fired

Tumble and Retro Rockets Fired

Aerodynamic Re-entry Attitude Stabilization

Maximum Aerodynamic Heating

Maximum Deceleration

Warhead Armed

Warhead Detonation (Air Burst)

Warhead Detonation (Ground Burst)

TARGET

NORTH POLE

Distance from Launch to Target Approximately 6,000 miles

LAUNCH FACILITY (LF)

LAUNCH CONTROL FACILITY (LFC)

Distance from LCF to LF Ranges from 4 to 14 miles

Developmental History

Minuteman I

The Western Development Division (WDD) was interested in solid-fuel ICBMs in 1954, but at the time found that solid-fuel motors did not produce sufficient thrust and were difficult to control. The Air Force, however, did not abandon the technology, and the WDD and the Wright-Patterson Air Development Center sponsored research in solid fuels throughout the mid-1950s.

By the spring of 1957, Air Force research indicated that a solid-fuel ICBM was possible. That fall the Air Force Ballistic Missile Division's (AFBMD–it changed its name effective June 1, 1957) Col. Edward Hall designed the revolutionary Minuteman ICBM. In marked contrast to the first generation Atlas and Titan I liquid-fuel missiles, Hall proposed building a relatively small, three-stage solid-fuel missile that would be inexpensive to build and maintain. He envisioned basing thousands of the missiles in unmanned, heavily hardened and widely dispersed silos linked electronically to a series of central launch control facilities.

The Air Force was initially cool toward the new concept, but was spurred into action when the Navy proposed modifying its Polaris submarine-launched ballistic missile (SLBM) for use as an ICBM. Anxious to defend its role in solid-fuel development, in February 1958 AFBMD sent Hall to Washington to brief the Secretary of Defense, the Secretary of the Air Force, and the Strategic Air Command's General Curtis LeMay on the Minuteman concept. They were impressed with the program, and quickly allocated the AFBMD $50 million to begin research and promised the development center another $100 million if they proved that the Minuteman was indeed feasible.

In July 1958 AFBMD began to develop the components and select the contractors. By the following September the missile development command had made sufficient progress to convince the Air Force to support full Minuteman system development, and the following month the AFBMD chose the Boeing Airplane Company as the missile assembly and test contractor. Shortly thereafter, the AFBMD awarded the guidance contract to the Autonetics Division of North American Aviation (later a Division of Rockwell International) and the reentry vehicle contract to AVCO Corporation. To develop the first-, second-, and third-stage motors AFBMD sponsored a competition between the Thiokol Chemical Corporation, the Aerojet General Corporation, and the Hercules Powder Company. The Air Force awarded the initial contracts with the understanding that the company with the most promising design would win the production contract.

In September 1959 the AFBMD successfully launched a Minuteman first stage motor directly from an underground silo, thus proving that the missile would survive the rigors of a subsurface launch. In February 1961 the AFBMD launched a Minuteman containing all three stages and operational subsystems from the Air Force Missile Test Center in Florida.[c] This was called an "all up" test. The missile performed flawlessly and after a flight of 4,600 miles its reentry vehicle landed within the designated impact zone.

Based on the success of the initial test flight, in March 1961 the Department of Defense formally accelerated the Minuteman program and gave it the same development priority as the Atlas and Titan ICBM programs. In November 1961 the AFBMD launched a complete Minuteman from a silo at the Operational Standardization and Test Facility (OSTF) at Vandenberg AFB, California. The missile recorded a successful flight of 3,000 miles.

[c] The Air Force aimed to have Minuteman operational in 1963, but Secretary of the Air Force James Douglas got the dates confused and told Congress 1962. Rather than amend his testimony Douglas ordered the AFBMD to move the schedule forward a year, and the only way to do that was abandon component testing and do a single "all up test." The Air Force was not overly optimistic that the test would be a success, and the Minuteman program manager said it was a "miracle" that the missile performed so well. Lt. Gen. Otto Glasser, first Minuteman program manager, telephone interview by John Lonnquest, 13 August 1991.

In conjunction with the Minuteman development effort, the Army Corps of Engineers Ballistic Missile Construction Office (CEBMCO) built the launch facilities. Construction of the launch facilities and launch control centers at the first Minuteman squadron at Malmstrom AFB, Montana began in March 1961 and was completed late the following September. On October 22, 1962, SAC placed its first flight of ten Minuteman missiles on operational alert.

Deployment of the Minuteman force was accomplished with amazing speed. The Minuteman launch facilities were much smaller and easier to build than the Atlas and Titan launch facilities. Using prefabricated components and standardized construction techniques, CEBMCO built 1,000 silos by 1966.

As soon as the silos were completed, AFBMD's Site Activation Task Force (SATAF) made final modifications and the sites were turned over to their SAC crews. By July 1963 150 Minuteman missiles were on operational alert; that number increased to 300 in October 1963, 450 by March 1964, and in June 1965 the 800th Minuteman I missile was turned over to its SAC crew at F.E. Warren AFB, Wyoming.

Minuteman II

Even as the Minuteman I program raced forward, the Air Force began developing the new Minuteman II. The new missile was a significant improvement over its predecessor. A new second-stage motor with a single nozzle and a secondary liquid injection for thrust vector control increased the missile's range from 6,300 to 7,000 miles. The new motors also enabled the Minuteman to carry the larger W-56 warhead with a yield of 1.2 megatons. An improved guidance system made the missile more accurate, and it could store a larger number of preprogrammed targets within its internal memory. Moreover, Minuteman II also carried penetration aids to camouflage the reentry vehicle during reentry.

The Air Force awarded Boeing the Minuteman II contract in March 1962 and the Seattle-based contractor conducted the first test flight in September 1964. In May 1966 SAC placed its first Minuteman II squadron on operational alert, and by April 1967 accepted its 200th Minuteman II. At that point the Minuteman force stood at 1,000 missiles; 800 Minuteman Is and 200 Minuteman IIs. Continuing its missile modernization effort, throughout the late 1960s the Air Force replaced many of its Minuteman Is with Minuteman IIs, and by May 1969 it had 500 Minuteman Is and an equal number of Minuteman IIs on operational alert.

This May 1962 photograph shows the Minuteman launch control center (LCC) N-I near Malmstrom AFB, Montana, nearing completion. After the LCC was complete, the construction crews backfilled the excavation and then built the launch control facility support over the top of the concrete accessway.

Minuteman III

Development of the last of the series, the Minuteman III, began in December 1964. The new missile contained an improved third-stage motor with a liquid injection altitude control system and a fixed nozzle that increased the range to over 8,000 miles and significantly increased the payload. The missile was the first ICBM to be outfitted with MIRVs that enabled a single missile to carry multiple warheads, each programmed to attack a different target. The Minuteman III could carry three warheads. A liquid-fuel postboost propulsion system maneuvered the missile before deployment of the reentry vehicles. An improved guidance system with an expanded memory also improved the system accuracy; the Minuteman III warheads are said to be accurate to within 800 feet.

In February 1968 the fourth Minuteman III test vehicle fired from Vandenberg AFB completed a successful 5,500-mile flight. In January 1971 the first squadron of Minuteman IIIs was turned over to the 91st Strategic Missile Wing at Minot AFB, North Dakota. The force modernization effort continued throughout the early 1970s and by July 1975 there were 450 Minuteman IIs and 550 Minuteman IIIs under SAC's control.

Beginning in 1966 the Air Force instituted a comprehensive long-term maintenance program to ensure that the Minuteman force remained a strong and viable deterrent for years to come. In 1966 the Air Force initiated a Minuteman ageing surveillance program and in 1976 began a long-range service life extension analysis for the propulsion system. The latter effort resulted in the remanufacturing of the Minuteman II second-stage motor and an investigation of the condition of the liner in the Minuteman III third stage. Also during the 1970s many of the Minuteman launch facilities were further hardened and the missiles were fitted with new command data buffers that facilitated faster retargeting. In 1985 the Air Force began the comprehensive Rivet MILE (Minuteman Integrated Life Extension) program destined to take the Minuteman force into the twenty-first century.

A further change in the Minuteman force occurred in January 1986 when the Air Force began removing 50 Minuteman IIIs from their silos at F.E. Warren AFB and began replacing them with the new Peacekeeper ICBM. When that process was completed, the nation's ICBM force stood at 450 Minuteman IIs and 500 Minuteman IIIs. It remained at that level until 1991 when President George Bush ordered all 450 Minuteman IIs taken off operational alert. The Air Force is now in the process of removing the missiles from their silos and destroying the launch facilities.

Basing Strategy

The Air Force initially contemplated deploying Minuteman as far south as Georgia, Texas, and Oklahoma. But when it became apparent that the early Minuteman I/A had a range of only 4,300 miles, Air Force planners decided to base the missiles in Montana and South Dakota to bring them closer to their targets in the Soviet Union. Later, after the range of the Minuteman increased, the Air Force built Minuteman launch facilities as far south as Missouri.

The AFBMD's original proposal called for deploying 1,600 Minuteman missiles. The Air Force soon reduced that to 1,200 missiles, and in December 1964 decided to limit deployment to 1,000 missiles. The Minuteman force remained at 1,000 missiles until 1986, when it was reduced to 950 to make way for the Peacekeeper ICBM.

The Air Force grouped its Minuteman force into six wings, each composed of either three or four 50-missile squadrons. Each squadron was divided into five flights, each composed of ten missiles. A flight consisted of an underground launch control center (LCC) and ten unmanned launch facilities (LFs). The LCCs were located a minimum of three miles from the nearest LF, and the individual LFs were separated by a similar distance. That degree of dispersal called for vast tracts of sparsely populated land. Minuteman Wing II, based at Ellsworth AFB, North Dakota, sprawled over 15,000 square miles, and Minuteman Wing III, based at Minot AFB, North Dakota, covered 12,000 square miles.

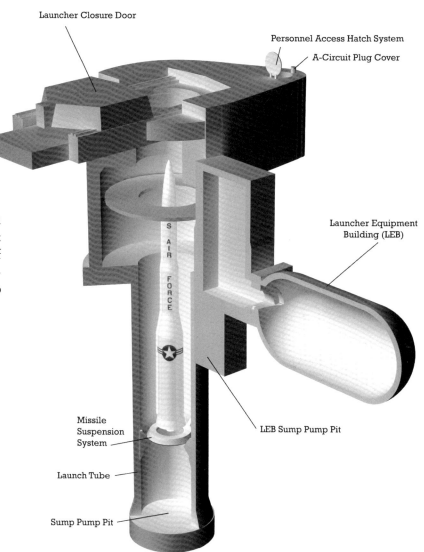

Launcher Closure Door

Personnel Access Hatch System

A-Circuit Plug Cover

Launcher Equipment Building (LEB)

LEB Sump Pump Pit

Missile Suspension System

Launch Tube

Sump Pump Pit

In keeping with the Air Force's policy of using public land and existing government facilities to support the missile program wherever possible, all of the Minuteman wings were built around existing SAC bases. The bases housed the missile maintenance facilities and the wing administrative and support buildings.

Minuteman Deployment

As of 1990, SAC had six wings of Minutemen IIs and IIIs.

Missile Deployed			
Wing	Location	MM II	MM III
Wing 1	Malmstrom AFB, Montana	150	50
Wing II	Ellsworth AFB, South Dakota	150	
Wing III	Minot AFB, North. Dakota		150
Wing IV	Whiteman AFB, Missouri	150	
Wing V	F.E. Warren AFB, Wyoming		150
Wing VI	Grand Forks AFB, North Dakota		150
	TOTAL[f]	450	500

[f]The total does not include the 50 Minuteman II silos at F.E. Warren AFB that were converted, in the mid-1980s, to accommodate the new Peacekeeper ICBM.

Site Configuration

A representative example of the many Minuteman launch control facilities (LCF) built during the 1960s is the D-1 LCF belonging to Delta Flight of the 66th Strategic Missile Squadron of the 44th Missile Wing based at Ellsworth AFB, South Dakota.[g] The facility is located on a 6-acre tract of land and is surrounded by two fences. The outer fence is a standard three-strand wire farm fence built to mark the property line and to keep animals from wandering onto the site. The inner fence is a chain link security fence topped with barbed wire that surrounds the launch control facility support building (LCFSB).

The LCFSB is the largest building on the site, providing living accommodations for the LCF crew, a security checkpoint for the Air Police detachment, and housing for the environmental support systems for the underground command center. The LCFSB is a one-story wooden frame structure measuring 33 feet wide and 128 feet long. Adjacent to it is a large garage.

Forty feet beneath the support building is the launch control center (LCC) that commands the ten missiles of Delta flight. To enter the LCC one has to first pass through the security control center manned by Air Force Security Police and then climb down a 40-foot ladder encased within a 10-foot square reinforced

[g]The National Park Service recently proposed designating this facility, as well as a nearby Minuteman missile silo, as the Minuteman National Historic Site.

concrete passageway The passageway empties into a reinforced concrete vestibule, the end of which is dominated by an 8-ton steel blast door that goes into the LCC. The door can only be opened from the inside.

The shape of the LCC resembles a huge thermos bottle lying on its side; 59 feet long and 29 feet in diameter. The LCC contains two separate structural elements: a 4-foot thick outer wall built of reinforced concrete and lined with ¼-inch steel plate. Suspended inside it is a box-like enclosure, approximately 12 feet high by 28 feet long, that houses the two-person Air Force crew and the specialized equipment to monitor and launch the missiles.

The LCC described above was of the type used at Minuteman Wings I and II at Malmstrom and Ellsworth Air Force Bases. For the remaining wings, the environmental support equipment for the LCC was moved out of the support building and down into a heavily reinforced launch control equipment building located adjacent to the LCC.

From their underground command center the two officers of Delta flight kept constant watch over ten missiles, each based in a distant launch facility. The LFs are unmanned, heavily hardened facilities that serve as a temperature- and humidity-controlled longterm storage area, service platform, and launch site for the Minuteman ICBM.

An aerial view of Minuteman launch control facility D-1. The building in the center of the photograph is the launch control facility support building.

The LF contains three elements: the launch tube, a cylindrical two-level equipment room that encircles the top of the launch tube, and an adjacent launch facility support building. The launch tube is a prefabricated cylinder made of ¼-inch steel plate, 12 feet in diameter and approximately 62 feet long. The lower 52 feet of the tube are surrounded by 14 inches of heavily reinforced concrete. The missile rests within the tube, suspended by a three-point pulley system affixed to a series of shock absorbers mounted on the silo floor.

Encircling the upper third of the launch tube is the cylindrical, two-level equipment room. Built of heavily reinforced concrete with a steel liner, the equipment room houses generators, surge arresters to protect the electronic equipment against electromagnetic pulses resulting from nuclear explosions, gas generators to open the silo's 80-ton reinforced concrete door, guidance equipment, and communications equipment to connect the LF to the LCF.

At Delta Flight's D-9 launch facility, adjacent to the launch tube is the launch facility support building. The support building is an underground structure with its roof at ground level. Measuring 16 feet wide, 25 feet long, and 11 feet deep, the support building houses heating and cooling equipment for the launch facility and generators to serve as the auxiliary power supply. The design changed over time. At the facilities built at Wings III, IV, and V, only a corner of the support building was exposed at ground level. At the Minuteman III sites, the support buildings were encased in heavily reinforced concrete cylinders buried deep beneath the ground.

References

There has been surprisingly little written about the Minuteman program. A helpful account of the program's early days is Roy Neal, *Ace in the Hole* (Garden City, NY: Doubleday, 1962). The author supplemented Neal's account with interviews, most notably with Col. Edward Hall, the father of Minuteman; General Bernard Schriever, the commander of WDD and later AFBMD; and Lt. Gen. Otto Glasser, the first Minuteman program manager. Further information came from the oral history of Maj. Gen. Osmand Ritland, who succeeded Schriever as the AFBMD commander. Ritland's oral history is available at the U.S. Air Force Historical Research Agency, Maxwell AFB, Montgomery, AL.

The Minuteman technical specifications came from Chronology of the Ballistic Missile Organization 1945–1990 (Norton AFB, CA: Ballistic Missile Organization, History Office, 1990), appendices 3 and 4; "Rockets, Missiles, Spacecraft," DMS Market Intelligence Reports (1967); and "Missiles," DMS Market Intelligence Reports (1987).

Information on the warhead and reentry vehicle combinations also came from "ICBM/IRBM/ISLBM Warhead-RV Combinations," n.d., pp. 1–2, Ballistic Missile Organization, History Office, Norton AFB, CA.

For a brief illustrated overview of the Minuteman program see *From Snark to Peacekeeper: a Pictorial History of Strategic Air Command Missiles* (Offutt AFB, NB: Office of the Historian, HQ Strategic Air Command, 1990); *Minuteman Weapon System: History and Description* (Hill AFB, UT: Ogden Air Logistic Center, 1990). The latter is helpful but often vague and cryptic. Another useful overview, complete with superb drawings and pictures is the "National Historic Landmark Nomination for the Minuteman Launch Facility and Launch Control Facility at Ellsworth AFB, South Dakota." The study was prepared by the National Park Service Rocky Mountain Region, Division of Partnership and Outreach, 1990. A more recent study is: "Minuteman Missile Sites: Ellsworth Air Force Base, South Dakota," prepared by the National Park Service, Rocky Mountain Region, in cooperation with the Department of Defense Legacy Resource Management Program, published in 1995. Both are available through the Park Service's Rocky Mountain Regional Office.

For an overview of the construction of the Minuteman ground support facilities, see General T.J. Hayes, "ICBM Site Construction," *The Military Engineer* (November- December 1966). For detailed construction information on the Minuteman launch and command facilities, see the U.S. Army Corps of Engineers Ballistic Missile Construction Office (CEBMCO) records in the Research Collection, Office of History, Headquarters, U.S. Army Corps of Engineers, Alexandria, VA. The CEBMCO "Warren Area Minuteman History," n.d., Military Files XVIII-12 is especially useful.

INTERMEDIATE-RANGE BALLISTIC MISSILES

Jupiter (SM-78/PGM-19A)

Summary

In early 1956 the Army began developing the Jupiter, an intermediate range ballistic missile with a range of 1,500 miles. The missile program was initially a joint development effort between the Army and the Navy, but after the Navy withdrew from the program in late 1956 the Army won approval to continue on its own. Although many critics complained the Army missile was of limited use, beginning in July 1960 the United States deployed three Jupiter squadrons in Italy and Turkey. The missiles, however, were operational for only a short time; the last were withdrawn from service in April 1963.

Technical Specifications

Length: 60 feet
Diameter: 8 feet, 9 inches
Weight: 108,804 pounds (fully fueled)
Fuel: Rocket grade RP-1 (kerosene)
Oxidizer: Liquid oxygen
Propulsion: A single S-3D engine generating 150,000 pounds of thrust
Range: 1,500 miles
Guidance: All-inertial
Accuracy: 1,500 meters
Reentry vehicle: Mark 3–ablative
Warhead: W-49, 1.44 megaton yield

Jupiter Deployment

Designation	Squadrons	Base	Operational
NATO I	2	Gioia Dell Colle, Italy	1960–1963
NATO II	1	Cigli AB, Turkey	1962–1963

Contractors

Airframe: Prototypes were built by the Army Ballistic Missile Agency, Redstone Arsenal, Huntsville, Alabama. Full-scale production was by the Chrysler Corporation Ballistic Missile Division, Detroit, Michigan.
Propulsion: Rocketdyne Division of North American Aviation, Canoga Park, California
Guidance: Ford Instrument Company, Long Island City, New York
Reentry vehicle: General Electric, Saratoga, New York

Technical Notes

Jupiter was originally designed for shipboard use, and adapting a liquid-fuel missile to operate in that environment posed a host of challenges. For example, the Army initially proposed building a missile over 90 feet long, while the Navy wanted a 50-foot missile. After some discussion they compromised on a missile that was 60 feet long and 105 inches in diameter.

System Operation

Immediately after the launch control officer pressed the firing button, the main engine roared into life. It burned for 157.8 seconds, boosting the missile to a speed of Mach 15.4 and an altitude of 73 miles. Two seconds after the main engine burned out and fell away, the solid-fuel vernier motor fired. The vernier burned for approximately 12 seconds until the missile reached the desired velocity, whereupon the engine shut down and detached from the reentry vehicle. Almost 10 minutes into the flight the missile, now 800 miles from its launch point and soaring at an altitude of 384 miles, reached the apogee of its elliptical flight path. From there it began its gradual descent toward the target. Total flight time from takeoff to impact: 15½ minutes.

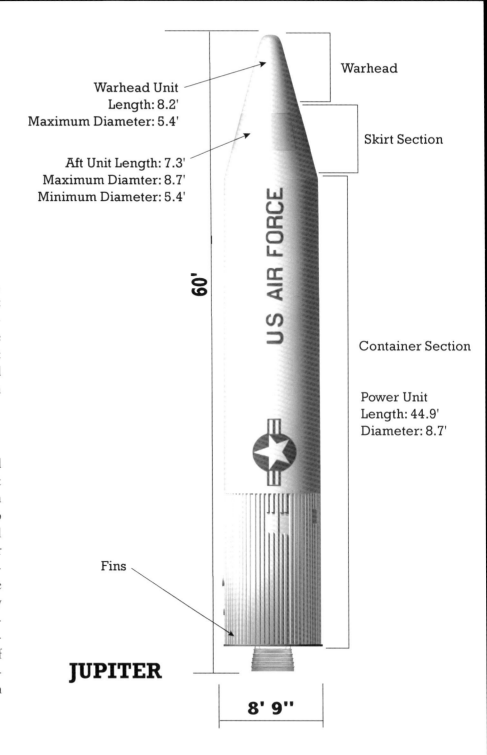

Warhead Unit
Length: 8.2'
Maximum Diameter: 5.4'

Aft Unit Length: 7.3'
Maximum Diamter: 8.7'
Minimum Diameter: 5.4'

Warhead

Skirt Section

Container Section

Power Unit
Length: 44.9'
Diameter: 8.7'

60'

US AIR FORCE

Fins

JUPITER

8' 9"

This July 1960 photograph shows two Jupiter IRBMs at launch site number 2 at Gioia del Colle Air Base, Italy. Note the "flower petal shelter" that protected the base of the missile.

Developmental History

The Jupiter was the direct descendant of the Army's Redstone, a tactical-range ballistic missile with a range of 150 miles. Under the direction of Dr. Wernher von Braun, the Redstone program began in 1951 at the Army's newly established Ordnance Guided Missile Center (OGMC) at Redstone Arsenal in Huntsville, Alabama.

As the Redstone took shape, the Ordnance Department also expressed interest in developing a ballistic missile with a range of 1,000 miles. By 1953 experience gained from the Redstone program convinced von Braun that building the longer range missile was feasible, and he petitioned the Chief of Ordnance for permission to develop it.

Initially the Army showed little interest in von Braun's proposal, and the Chief of Ordnance relegated the 1,000-mile range missile program to a low priority study project. The project would have probably languished there had it not been for the Killian Report, released in February 1955.

In its influential report to President Eisenhower, the Killian Committee urged that in addition to the intercontinental ballistic missiles (ICBM) the United States should also develop a new class of 1,500-mile intermediate-range-ballistic missile (IRBM) as a counterweight to a similar program thought to be under way in the Soviet Union. The committee recommended that the United States develop both land- and sea-based variants of the new missile. By stationing the missiles at bases in Europe, and on ships hovering off the Soviet coast, the committee envisioned that the IRBMs would counterbalance the Soviet program and reassure the United States' skittish allies.

Spurred on by the committee's recommendations, by the fall of 1955 all three services requested permission to develop IRBMs. Before development could begin, however, the military had to resolve the crucial issue of which major service would operate the new missiles. In early November the Joint Chiefs of Staff were unable to reach a consensus on the issue, forcing Secretary of Defense Charles Wilson to fashion a compromise: the Air Force would develop the ground-launched version and a joint Army/Navy team would develop the ship-launched model. Reflecting the urgency of the situation, in December 1955 President Eisenhower designated the IRBM one of the military's most pressing programs, second in importance to only the ICBM.

Because of the Army's considerable experience in missile development, the Navy agreed that Jupiter development and the initial fabrication would take place at Huntsville. To manage the new program, in February 1956 the Army established the Army Ballistic Missile Agency (ABMA) at Redstone Arsenal. Secretary of the Army William Brucker granted the ABMA's first commander, General John B. Medaris, sweeping authority to manage every facet of the IRBM development effort.

In many ways the political hurdles facing the Army program were more daunting than the technological challenges. Within a year the Jupiter program suffered two major setbacks. The first came in September 1956 when the Navy withdrew from the project in order to build the solid-fuel Polaris submarine-launched ballistic missile (SLBM). Two months later Jupiter suffered what many thought was a mortal blow when Secretary of Defense Charles Wilson finally gave the Air Force sole responsibility for building and operating all surface-launched missiles with a range in excess of 200 miles. The ruling meant that the Army would never operate the missile it was building, and it appeared that there was little reason to continue the program. Brucker and Medaris thought otherwise, and in response to their impassioned plea, the Department of Defense (DoD) allowed the Army to continue developing Jupiter as an alternative to the Air Force's troubled Thor IRBM program.

Using the proven Redstone missile as a test platform, beginning in September 1955 the Army launched 28 Jupiter A and C missiles from the Atlantic Missile Range (AMR) at Cape Canaveral, Florida. Jupiter A testing, which focused on general design criteria, the guidance system, and propulsion thrust control, began in September 1955 and continued through June 1958. The Jupiter C was an elongated Redstone with clusters of scaled-down Sergeant rockets forming the second and third stages. This configuration was designed to test reentry vehicles and procedures, and in September 1956 a Jupiter C fired from the AMR completed a successful flight of 3,300 miles. In May 1957 a prototype Jupiter soared 1,150 miles out over the Atlantic, an event the Army hailed as the United States' first successful IRBM launch.

Although the Jupiter program was living on borrowed time, Medaris and the ABMA hoped that the missile's early success, which was a marked contrast to the Air Force's Thor program, would convince the Secretary of Defense to choose the Army missile. External events, however, would soon dramatically alter the nation's IRBM program. In October 1957 the Soviet Union launched Sputnik I, the world's first artificial satellite. The event shattered American complacency and bred fresh fears over the danger posed to the United States by the Soviet missile program. Anxious to take action to blunt the Soviet advantage and reassure the American public, on October 10, 1957, President Eisenhower ordered both the Jupiter and Thor into full production.

Although the President's decision appeared to be a victory for the Army missile program, it had little lasting effect. The ABMA was never able to convince the Pentagon that Jupiter was superior to Thor, and neither was it able to reverse Secretary Wilson's November 1956 ruling barring the Army from operating

In this April 1961 photograph a Jupiter IRBM is readied for a test flight at Cape Canaveral, Florida.

long-range missiles. As a result, although the Army won the right to build Jupiter, it did so as a subcontractor to the Air Force. Much to the Army's chagrin, in early 1958 the Air Force began to assume control of the Jupiter program. In early February 1958 the Air Force opened a Jupiter program management office at the ABMA, and the following month established the Jupiter Liaison Office (JUPLO) to coordinate activities between the Army and the Strategic Air Command, the Air Materiel Command, and the Air Training Command.

While the Army and the Air Force were forging the necessary infrastructure to deploy the missile, in mid-January 1958 the Air Force activated the 864th Strategic Missile Squadron at ABMA. Although the Air Force briefly considered training its Intermediate-Range Ballistic Missiles Jupiter crews at Vandenberg AFB, California, it later decided to conduct all of its training at Huntsville. In June and September the Air Force activated two more strategic missile squadrons at the ABMA: the 865th and 866th.

At the same time the Air Force was training Jupiter crews, the State Department was searching for a host nation willing to accept the missiles. In late April 1958 DoD told the Air Force that it had tentatively planned to deploy the first three Jupiter squadrons in France. Negotiations between the two nations fell through, however, prompting the United States to explore the possibility of deploying the missiles in Italy and Turkey. In late 1958 the Italian government agreed to accept two squadrons, with the proviso the missiles be manned by Italian crews. In May 1959 the first contingent of Italian airmen arrived at Lackland AFB, Texas, for language and technical training. In late October 1959 the Turkish government also agreed to host a squadron of the American missiles, under similar terms.

The Air Force accepted delivery of its first production Jupiter in August 1958. Prior to that, Air Force missile crews received individual and crew training on Redstone missiles. Once Jupiter missiles and ground support equipment became available, the Air Force crews began Integrated Weapons System Training (IWST) on a launch emplacement set up on a large field at the Redstone Arsenal. On October 20, 1960, an Air Force crew successfully fired a Jupiter missile under simulated tactical conditions from AMR. The first three-missile Jupiter launch position in Italy went on operational alert in July 1960, and by June 20, 1961, both squadrons in Italy were fully operational. The first Jupiter squadron in Turkey did not become operational until 1962.

Basing Strategy

The United States began negotiations to deploy Jupiter missiles abroad in the spring of 1958. The discussions were complex and time consuming because deploying the missiles on foreign soil involved the delicate issues of national sovereignty, as well as more mundane matters such as training, technology transfer, maintenance, and who would foot the bill.

The United States and Italy concluded an arrangement to base Jupiters in that Mediterranean nation in March 1958 and Italian crews began training in the United States in May 1959. All of the technical details were resolved in a supplemental agreement signed the following August, and in October 1960 the Italian Air Force crews completed their training in the United States. Under the terms of the basing agreement, the missiles would be operated by Italian Air Force crews but the warheads would remain under American control.

Negotiations to deploy Jupiter missiles in Turkey took slightly longer. The two governments reached an understanding in October 1959, and in May 1960 a technical agreement cleared up the remaining questions. To hasten the deployment process, the Turkish government agreed that at the outset, the missiles would be manned by United States Air Force personnel. The United States would, however, train Turkish crews to

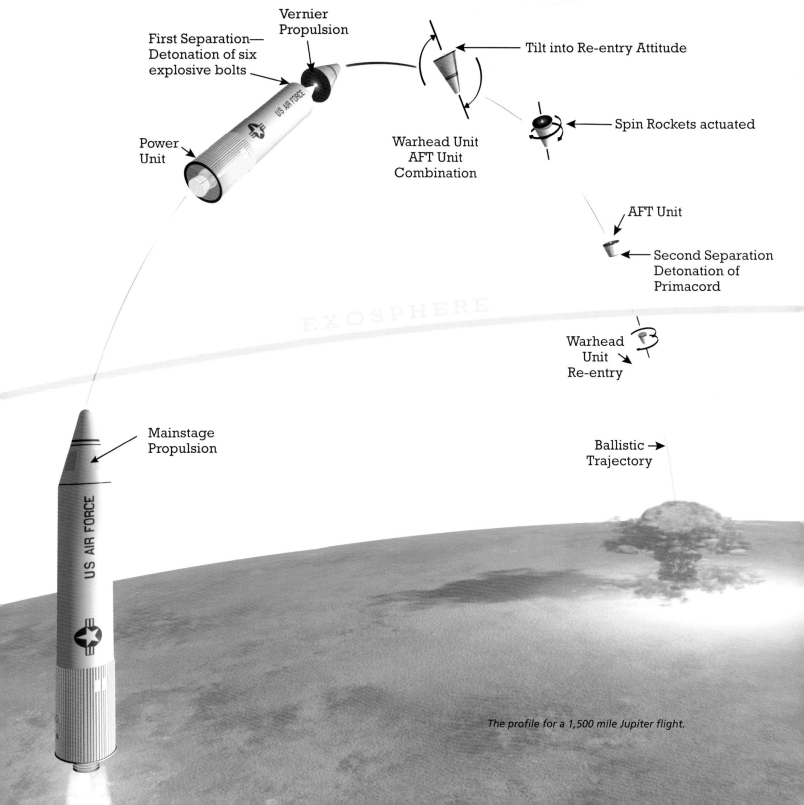

First Separation—
Detonation of six
explosive bolts

Vernier
Propulsion

Tilt into Re-entry Attitude

Power
Unit

Warhead Unit
AFT Unit
Combination

Spin Rockets actuated

AFT Unit

Second Separation
Detonation of
Primacord

EXOSPHERE

Warhead
Unit
Re-entry

Mainstage
Propulsion

Ballistic →
Trajectory

US AIR FORCE

The profile for a 1,500 mile Jupiter flight.

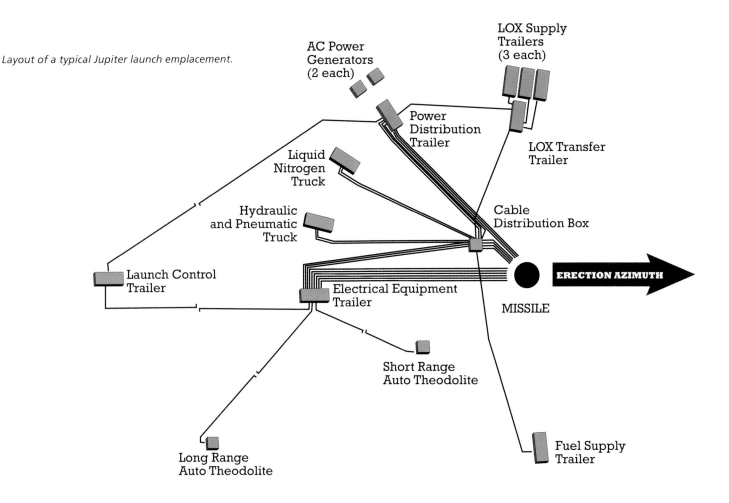

Layout of a typical Jupiter launch emplacement.

operate the missiles and would eventually relinquish control of the site to the host nation. By April 1962 the Air Force declared its Jupiter at Cigli Air Base, Turkey, operational.

Site Configuration

The Army originally planned that Jupiter would be a mobile missile; a road-transportable weapon that could be moved from one location to another in a matter of hours. The Air Force thought there was little to be gained in having a mobile IRBM and elected to deploy the missiles at fixed launch sites.

A Jupiter squadron consisted of fifteen missiles and approximately 500 officers and men. The missiles were organized into five "flights" of three missiles each. To reduce their vulnerability, the flights were located several miles apart. Each flight contained three launch emplacements, each of which was separated by a distance of several hundred years. Each flight was composed of five officers and ten airmen.

The ground support equipment for each emplacement was housed in approximately twenty vehicles. They included two generator trucks, a power distribution truck, short- and long-range theodolites, a hydraulic and pneumatic truck, and a truck carrying liquid oxygen. Another trailer carried 6,000 gallons of fuel, and three liquid oxygen trailers each carried 4,000 gallons.

The missile arrived at the emplacement on a large trailer. While it was still on the trailer, the crew attached the hinged launch pedestal to the base of the missile. Using a powerful winch, which drew a cable through a succession of "A" and "H" frames, the crew pulled the missile into its upright firing position. Once the missile was vertical, the crew attached the fuel lines and encased the bottom third of the missile in a so-called "flower petal shelter." The shelter consisted of a dozen wedge-shaped metal panels and allowed the crew to service the missile during inclement weather.

The missiles were stored in an upright position on the launch pad. The firing sequence, which consisted primarily of pumping 68,000 pounds of liquid oxygen and 30,000 pounds of RP-1 aboard, took about fifteen minutes. The three missiles that comprised each flight were controlled by an officer and two crewmen seated in a mobile launch control trailer.

Each squadron was supported by a receipt, inspection, and maintenance (RIM) area well to the rear of the emplacements. RIM teams accepted and inspected new missiles, and also provided both scheduled maintenance and emergency repair to missiles in the field. Each RIM area also housed 25-ton liquid oxygen and nitrogen generating plants. Several times a week, tanker trucks carried the gases from the plant to the individual emplacements.

References

Substantive information on the Jupiter program is difficult to find. The best account is James M. Grimwood and Frances Strowd, *History of The Jupiter Missile System* (U.S. Army Missile Command, Redstone Arsenal, Huntsville, AL, 1962). This volume contains a good summary of the Jupiter program plus missile specifications, a detailed chronology, test summary, and glossary. Another good source is an ABMA report, "The Jupiter Story," written in December 1959. The report, filled with bitter denunciations of the Air Force and the Thor program, is available at the Army Missile Command History Office, Huntsville, Alabama, file No. 870-5e. For information on the Army's activities at Redstone, see Helen Brents Joiner and Elizabeth C. Joliff, "The Redstone Complex in its Second Decade, 1950–1960" (Redstone Arsenal, AL: Army Missile Command, 1969) also available at the Missile Command in Huntsville.

For additional information on the Jupiter program, including a chronology, technical specifications, launch site configuration, and deployment locations, see *Chronology of the Ballistic Missile Organization* (Norton AFB, Ballistic Missile Organization, History Office, 1990), appendices 3 and 4; and Evert Clark, "Speed Marks Jupiter Development," *Aviation Week* (13 April 1959): pp. 54–67.

Thor (SM-75/PGM-17A)

Summary

Fearful that the Soviet Union would deploy a long-range ballistic missile before the United States, in January 1956 the Air Force began developing the Thor, a 1,500-mile intermediate- range ballistic missile (IRBM). The Thor program unfolded with amazing speed, and within 3½ years of the program's inception the first Thor squadron became operational in Great Britain. The Thor was a stop-gap measure, however, and once the first generation of ICBMs based in the United States became operational, the Thor missiles were quickly retired. The last of the missiles was withdrawn from operational alert in 1963.

Technical Specifications

Length: 65 feet
Diameter: 8 feet
Weight: 110,000 pounds (fueled)
Fuel: Rocket grade RP-1 (kerosene)
Oxidizer: Liquid oxygen
Propulsion: A single combustion chamber from a MB-1 or MB-3 engine generating 150,000 pounds of thrust. Two vernier engines, each generating 1,000 pounds of thrust.
Range: 1,500 miles
Guidance: All-inertial
Accuracy: 2 miles
Reentry vehicle: Mark 2
Warhead: W-49, 1.44 megaton yield

Opposite: Shown in the semi-upright position, this Thor IRBM was the last missile to be taken off operational alert at RAF Hemswell in May 1963.

Contractors

Airframe: Douglas Aircraft, Santa Monica, California
Propulsion: Rocketdyne Division of North American Aviation, Canoga Park, California
Guidance: AC Spark Plug Division, General Motors, Detroit, Michigan
Reentry vehicle: General Electric, Saratoga, New York

System Operation

All of the Thor missiles deployed in Great Britain were based at above-ground launch sites. The missiles were stored horizontally on transporter-erector trailers and covered by a retractable missile shelter. To fire the weapon, the crew electronically rolled back the missile shelter and then, using a powerful hydraulic launcher-erector, lifted the missile to an upright position. Once it was standing on the launch mount, the missile was fueled and fired. The entire launch sequence took about 15 minutes.

When the launch control officer pressed the firing button, the main engine ignited with a roar. It burned for almost 2½ minutes, boosting the missile to a speed of 14,400 feet per second. Ten minutes into its flight the missile reached an altitude of 280 miles, close to the apogee of its elliptical flight path. At that point the reentry vehicle separated from the fuselage and began its descent down toward the target. Total flight time from launch to impact: 18 minutes.

Developmental History

The origins of the Air Force IRBM program can be traced back to the Matador (TM-61), a subsonic, tactical-range missile. In 1951 the Air Force's Wright Air Development Center (WADC) located at Wright-Patterson Air Force Base (AFB), Ohio, became concerned that the Matador, which followed a relatively slow and predictable course toward its target, could be readily intercepted in flight. Searching for an alternative to the air-breathing missile, WADC recommended that the Air Force develop a tactical-range ballistic missile (TBM). The Tactical Air Command endorsed the concept, and Air Force Headquarters ordered the Air Research and Development Command to formulate a development plan for the TBM by June 1, 1955. The goal was to have the new missile flying by 1960.

In mid-1954 ARDC selected four contractors (the Glenn L. Martin Company, Douglas Aircraft, Lockheed Aircraft, and General Electric) to perform design studies on the TBM. As outlined in the December 1954 General Operational Requirement (GOR), the mission of the TBM was the destruction of surface targets within a range of 600 to 1,000 miles. The GOR stressed that the new missile needed to combine the merits of simplicity, mobility, and flexibility to operate in all parts of the world. Late the following year the Air Force increased the required range to between 1,200 to 1,500 miles and changed the name to Medium-Range Ballistic Missile (MRBM). Shortly thereafter, the Air Force set up the MRBM program office at WADC.

Events outside of Wright-Patterson, however, soon changed the face of the missile program. The impetus for change came from two sources. The first was the Air Force's burgeoning intercontinental ballistic missile (ICBM) program. In May 1954 the Air Force escalated the ICBM to its top research and development priority and established a powerful program office, called the Western Development Division (WDD). Located in Inglewood, California, a suburb of Los Angeles, the WDD quickly emerged as the focal point of the Air Force's long-range ballistic missile development effort.

In this September 1959 photograph Thor IRBM No. 222 lifts off launch pad 17 at Cape Canaveral, Florida.

Shown in Royal Air Force livery, two Thor missiles stand ready at an unidentified launch complex in Great Britain. The large structure in the background is the missile squadron receiving, inspection, and maintenance (RIM) building.

The second factor that changed the nature of the MRBM was the Killian Report. The report was prepared by the Killian Committee, a high-level government study group directed by President Eisenhower to determine how to use new and emerging technologies to reduce the risk of a surprise attack on the United States. In the February 1955 report the committee urged that in addition to the ICBM, the United States should also develop a new class of 1,500-mile IRBM to counter a similar program thought to be under way in the Soviet Union. Anticipating that the IRBM would be far easier to build than the ICBM, the committee feared that the Soviets would deploy their IRBMs before the American ICBMs were ready. Not only would that be a blow to American prestige, it would also allow the Soviets to intimidate U.S. allies in Europe and Japan.

To counter the Soviet missile program, the committee recommended that the United States develop both land- and sea-based IRBMs. President Eisenhower endorsed the committee's recommendations, and by the fall of 1955, all three services proposed to build and operate IRBMs. The interservice competition was keen. Unable to decide which service would develop the IRBM, in November the Joint Chiefs of Staff recommended that the Air Force develop the land-based IRBM and the Army and Navy jointly develop the sea-based version.

Initially the Air Force was reluctant to begin yet another missile program. Its hesitation sprang from the WDD's concern that diverting engineers and equipment to the IRBM would delay the ICBM program. However, with the prospect of losing the mission to the Army or Navy, the Air Force decided it had to build an IRBM of its own. At first the Air Force proposed developing the IRBM as a derivative of the ICBM, but after a Department of Defense study panel showed that approach to be impractical, the Air Force elected to develop a new missile, the Thor (SM-75).

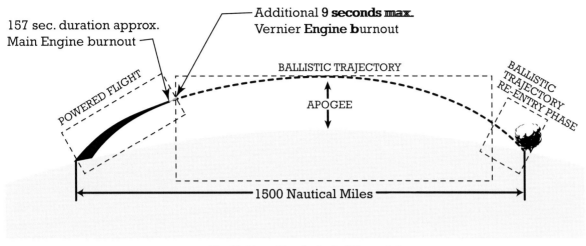

The flight profile of a typical Thor mission.

Anxious to integrate the IRBM program within the broad outlines of the ICBM program, in May 1955 the Air Force transferred responsibility for the IRBM from Wright-Patterson to the WDD. Throughout the summer and early fall, the WDD refined its development approach and solicited preliminary IRBM designs from a variety of airframe manufacturers, industrial concerns, and the Army Ordnance Department's Redstone Arsenal.

After evaluating the prospective contractors, on November 30, 1955, the WDD invited three to bid: Douglas Aircraft, Lockheed Aircraft, and North American Aviation. The WDD gave the firms a week to prepare their proposals. At the end of December the Air Force awarded a contract to build the Thor airframe and then assemble and test the missile to Douglas, the California aircraft manufacturer.

To expedite the new program the Air Force sought to use existing ICBM components wherever possible. Thor's engine was one-half of an Atlas ICBM primary booster; its guidance system and reentry vehicle also came from the Atlas program. The only components Douglas had to design and develop were the airframe and the ground support equipment.

The availability of off-the-shelf components made developing the IRBM less challenging than building the ICBM, but these advantages were offset by the Air Force's fervent desire to stage Thor's first test flight in January 1957, a mere thirteen months after it awarded Douglas the contract. Although the Air Force was ostensibly racing to beat the Russians, in reality the air service saw the Army's IRBM, the Jupiter (SM-78), as the more immediate threat. Both services were racing to be the first to develop an operational IRBM, a step each saw as crucial in winning control of the IRBM mission.

Initially the Army missile program had a substantial lead over the Thor program. The Army had already built ample missile test facilities, and its Redstone tactical-range missile provided an effective test platform for Jupiter's components. In contrast, in January 1956 the Air Force had yet to complete any of its test facilities. Progress, however, came rapidly. By March 1956, construction of the engine and captive missile test stands was under way at Edwards AFB, California, as was the construction of the Thor launch facilities at

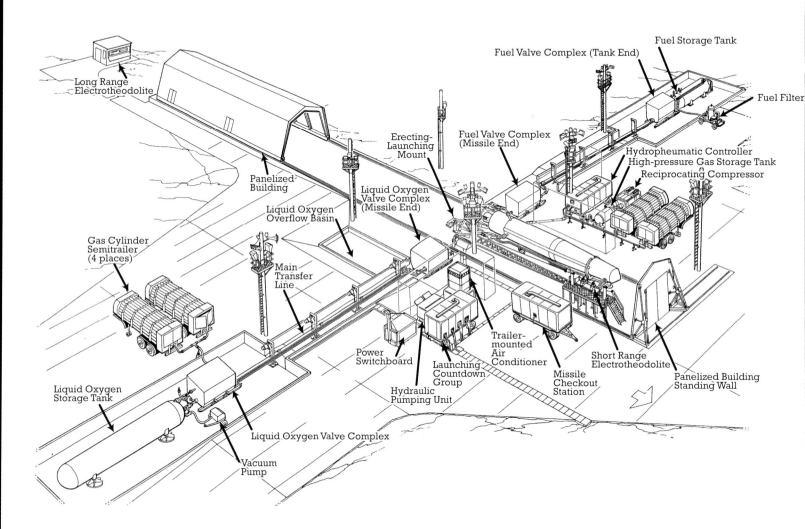

Drawing of a Thor launch emplacement showing the ground support equipment.

Cape Canaveral on Florida's east coast. Also in March 1956, Douglas and the WDD completed the airframe design, and Douglas began setting up the Thor production line at its Santa Monica, California plant.

The engine test stands at Edwards were completed in July 1956, and from then until November, Rocketdyne and Douglas engineers worked three shifts a day, seven days a week to test the engine and integrate the powerplant into the airframe. The first two Thor test vehicles were flown to Patrick AFB in the late fall of 1956. To keep pace with the Army, the Air Force was very anxious to stage a successful flight as quickly as possible, and was willing to accept a substantial risk to do so. The WDD classified Thor as a "maximum risk" program, meaning the WDD set minimum performance and reliability requirements for the initial test flights.

Thor flight testing began inauspiciously. In January 1957 the first flight ended in a cataclysmic explosion within a few feet of the launch pad. On the second test flight, conducted in late April, the missile appeared to be on its way to a perfect test flight when the Air Force range safety officer (RSO) destroyed it in mid-air. Soon afterward the Air Force found that the missile's tracking transponder had been installed backwards. As a result, although observers standing outside the blockhouse could see the missile was heading out over the ocean, on the RSO's monitor it appeared to be flying inland, and he had to destroy it. A month later a third test flight ended in a sheet of flame on the launch pad.

Despite the string of failures, the Air Force and Douglas were able to fix the problems fairly quickly, and at the end of August, a Thor staged a partially successful test flight. Finally, on September 20, the fifth test vehicle logged a successful test flight of 1,300 miles.

The successful test came not a moment too soon. In early October the Soviet Union placed the world's first artificial satellite, the famous Sputnik, into orbit. Within a week President Eisenhower ordered Thor into full production, and at the end of December the President announced that the United States would deploy four squadrons of IRBMs overseas. In early February 1958 the United States and Great Britain reached an agreement to deploy the missiles in that island nation. Under the terms of the agreement the missiles would be operated by Royal Air Force (RAF) crews, but the warheads would stay under American control.

In mid-December 1958 a Strategic Air Command (SAC) crew fired a Thor from an operational test facility at Vandenberg AFB, California, and the following April an RAF crew fired a missile from the same installation. In June 1959 the Air Force placed its first Thor squadron on operational alert, and by the following April it had activated the remaining three.

Thor Deployment

Unit	Base	Operational
77 RAE SMS	Feltwell, England	Jun 1959-Aug 1963
97 RAF SMS	Hemswell, England	Sep 1959-Aug 1963
98 RAF SMS	Driffield, England	Nov 1959-Aug 1963
144 RAE SMS	North Luffenham, England	Apr 1960-Aug 1963

Douglas Aircraft built a mockup Thor launch facility at its Santa Monica plant in 1958. With the exception of the truncated missile shelter, the support equipment shown in the photograph was all standard equipment.

Basing Strategy

United States defense planners originally envisioned deploying Thor in Europe. In June 1958 the Air Force also began making plans to place a Thor squadron in the vicinity of Fairbanks, Alaska, but the idea never went beyond the design stage.

The United States first broached the idea of placing long-range missiles in Britain in February 1955. The British were receptive to the idea, and in early 1957 the Departments of State and Defense began negotiations to establish IRBM bases in Great Britain. Although SAC wanted to keep the missiles under its control, the British were anxious that at least some of the missiles be operated by the RAF. Under the terms of the final agreement, signed in February 1958, all of the Thor missiles deployed in Great Britain would be operated by the RAF, but the warheads would remain under American control.

Site Configuration

Together the Air Force and the RAF deployed four squadrons of Thor missiles in Great Britain. A squadron consisted of fifteen missiles. Each squadron maintained five launch positions, each containing three launchers. Each launcher was separated from the adjacent facility by 200 to 300 yards. To expedite deployment, all of the Thor launch facilities were built above ground, offering protection only from the elements.

The missile at each launch position was stored horizontally, and covered by a barnlike metal shed. Mounted on rails, the 100-foot-long shed was electronically retracted before elevating the missile to an upright position. The missile shelter and launch platform were mounted on a heavily reinforced concrete strip, approximately 250 feet long and 50 feet wide.

Abutting that central strip were two large concrete aprons that contained propellant storage tanks and parking for the mobile ground support equipment. Each launch site had its own generators, mounted in large self-contained vans and protected by concrete revetments.

References

Information on the Thor program is sparse. A useful summary of the program's beginnings is Alfred Rockefeller's "History of Thor 1955–1959," K243.012-27, at the Air Force Historical Research Agency, Maxwell AFB, Montgomery, Alabama. For a less authoritative account see Julian Hartt, *The Mighty Thor* (New York: Duell, Sloan, and Pearce, 1961). Information on the political dimension of the IRBM program can be found in Michael Armacost, *The Politics of Weapons Innovation: The Thor–Jupiter Controversy* (New York: Columbia University Press, 1969).

To fill in the gaps in the existing literature, the author interviewed Col. Edward Hall, the initial Thor program manager; his executive officer Col. Francis Hale; and Hall's successor, Col. Richard Jacobson.

For technical information on the Thor IRBM see "General Manual, USAF Model SM- 75 Missile Weapon System," T.O. 21-SM75-1, 12 April 1962, courtesy of the Thor Association, Lompoc, CA. Another valuable source is United States Air Force, "Standard Missile Characteristics, XSM-75 Thor," July 1958, available at the Research Center, USAF Museum, Wright-Patterson AFB, file "C1-Thor." See also, *Chronology of the Ballistic Missile Organization* (Norton AFB, CA: Ballistic Missile Organization, History Office, 1990), appendices 3 and 4 and "Thor: A Study of a Great Weapon System," *Flight 5* (December 1958): pp. 861–72. Also useful was "Thor Booster Systems," prepared by D.I. Raines at the Missile and Space Systems Division, Douglas Aircraft Corporation, n.d., file C1-Thor, at the Research Center, USAF Museum, Dayton, OH.

After the Air Force retired the Thor IRBM, the Thor space booster was a mainstay of the Air Force's and NASA's space programs, logging over 500 successful flights. For a description of Thor's evolution from IRBM to space booster, see W.R. Arms, "Thor: the Workhorse of Space A Narrative History," MDC G3770, 31 July 1972. The author's copy was courtesy of the Thor Association, Lompoc, CA.

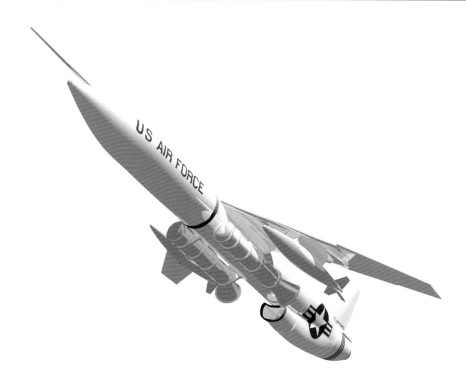

LONG-RANGE, AIR-BREATHING MISSILES

Snark (SM-62)

Summary

Built by Northrop Aircraft, the Snark was a large, winged, air-breathing missile with intercontinental range. The program began with much promise in 1946, but development proved to be far more difficult than either the contractor or the Air Force anticipated, and the first missiles did not become operational until 1960. By that time Snark's utility had been eclipsed by the Air Force's new intercontinental ballistic missiles. The Air Force withdrew its sole Snark squadron from active duty in June 1961.

Technical Specifications

Length: 67.2 feet
Wing span: 42.2 feet
Height: 15 feet
Weight: 49,000 pounds
Propulsion: A single Pratt and Whitney 557 turbojet engine generating 10,500 pounds of thrust
Boosters: Two, each generating 130,000 pounds of thrust
Cruising speed: 524 mph
Range: 5,500 miles
Guidance: Stellar-inertial
Accuracy: 1.5 miles
Warhead: Nuclear

A Snark missile shown on its mobile launcher. The white canisters attached to both sides of the fuselage are solid-fuel rocket boosters.

Launched from Cape Canaveral, Florida, this Snark missile begins its 5,000 mile test flight down the South Atlantic missile test range. Note the under-wing fuel tanks for the ramjet engines.

Contractors

Airframe: Northrop Aircraft, Hawthorne, California
Propulsion: Pratt and Whitney, New Haven, Connecticut
Guidance: Northrop Aircraft, Hawthorne, California

System Operation

The missiles were fired from inclined mobile launchers. Once the launcher was in position, the crew started the turbojet engine, then fired the twin rocket boosters. The boosters, which burned for four seconds, carried the missile off the launcher and accelerated it to cruising speed. At that point the turbojet took over and the boosters were jettisoned.

The Snark had an operational ceiling of 50,000 feet and was guided to its target by a stellar-inertial guidance system. Initially Northrop envisioned that at the end of its intercontinental flight Snark would dive directly into its target. Tests found, however, that the missile's flight controls and superstructure were not capable of executing such a high-speed maneuver. As an alternative, Northrop outfitted the missile with a detachable nosecone. When the missile was directly over the target, the warhead separated from the fuselage and hurtled down to the ground. Shortly afterward, a set of explosive charges destroyed the missile in flight.

Developmental History

In August 1945 the Army Air Forces (AAF) solicited proposals for a subsonic missile with a range of 5,000 miles. Northrop Aircraft of Hawthorne, California, submitted a proposal, and in March 1946 the AAF awarded the aircraft manufacturer a research contract to study the feasibility of designing a subsonic missile that could deliver a 5,000-pound payload at ranges between 1,500 and 5,000 miles. Company president Jack Northrop called the new missile Snark, named after a mythical creature

A Snark missile shown on its mobile launcher. The white canisters attached to both sides of the fuselage are solid-fuel rocket boosters.

author Lewis Carroll described as part snake and part shark.

The Snark almost died on the drawing board. In December 1946, budget cutbacks prompted the AAF to cancel the program, but at the last minute Jack Northrop was able to convince the AAF to save the program. To win the Air Force's support the aircraft company president guaranteed that his firm could develop the missile in 2½ years at a cost of $80,000 each, based on a production run of 5,000 units. It was a promise the company proved unable to keep.

Northrop designated its first Snark test model the N-25. The missile looked much like an airplane. It was 52 feet long and its sharply swept wings had a span of 43 feet. Powered by an Allison 533 turbojet engine,

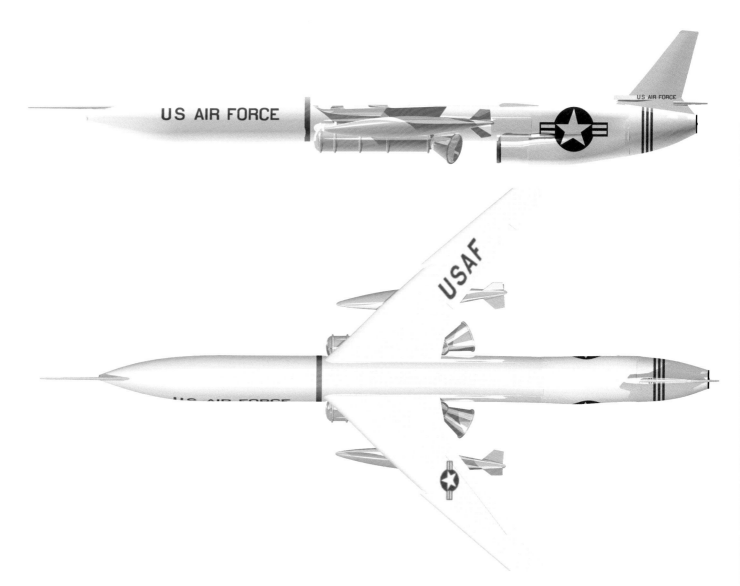

the N-25 had a launch weight of 28,000 pounds. Testing was scheduled to begin at Holloman AFB, New Mexico, in 1949, but numerous design problems delayed the first flight until April 1951.

Even before the first Snark left the ground, however, the Air Force amended the performance requirements. In June 1950 the Air Material Command ordered Northrop to provide the missile with a supersonic dash capability, and also directed the manufacturer to increase the payload to 7,000 pounds. Further complicating the development effort, the Air Force imposed more stringent guidance requirements, directing that at least half the missiles be able to strike within 1,500 feet of their targets.

To satisfy the Air Force's new requirements, Northrop redesigned the missile, calling the new weapon the N-69 or Super Snark. An enhanced version of the earlier model, the N-69 was 67 feet long, 15 feet longer than its predecessor, and also had longer wings. These changes, coupled with the new warhead, increased the launch weight from 28,000 to 49,000 pounds. To carry the additional weight, the early N-69 test models were equipped with Allison 571 engines. The final D and E models were equipped with Pratt and Whitney 557 turbojet engines.

In 1952 the Air Force ordered a reluctant Northrop to move its Snark test program from Holloman to the Air Force Atlantic Missile Range at Patrick AFB on Florida's east coast. Once in Florida, between 1953 and 1957 Northrop encountered further delays when the Air Force failed to complete vital test facilities on time.

Apart from numerous delays created by the Air Force, Northrop was running into plenty of roadblocks of its own making. In May 1955 tests demonstrated that poor handling characteristics rendered the missile unable to execute a "terminal dive" directly into its target. To compensate, Northrop modified the missile so that the warhead would be carried in a detachable nosecone. The first Snark to carry the redesigned warhead, the N-69C, logged its first test flight in late September 1955.

The Snark test program had more than its share of dramatic moments. So many missiles crashed off that Florida coast that the waters around Cape Canaveral were said to be "Snark Infested." On one test flight a missile heading out over the South Atlantic unexpectedly veered off course and disappeared into the rain forests of Brazil. The press had a field day. Noted one Miami paper, "They shot a Snark into the air, it fell to the earth they know not where."

As the miscues mounted, and the development program continued to stretch on year after year, the Strategic Air Command (SAC), the organization slated to receive the new weapon, began to question the missile's utility. As early as 1951 SAC complained about Snark's vulnerability, both on the ground and in the air. SAC planners noted that the missile would be launched from unprotected launch sites. Once in the air, they noted that the missile was slow, lacked defensive armament, and could not make evasive maneuvers.

Between 1955 and 1958 Northrop launched an extensive campaign to save its beleaguered program. In articles in the aviation press it defended the missile, pointing out that unlike bombers, Snark did not need an expensive tanker fleet for refueling, and neither did it put highly trained air crews at risk. Furthermore, Northrop argued that Snark was cost effective. About 1/10th size of a B-52, the missile cost only 1/20 as much.

Much to Northrop's consternation, advances in ballistic missile technology were rapidly encroaching on Snark's technological niche. When the Air Force initiated the Snark program in 1946, it anticipated that winged, air-breathing missiles would be able to do many things that ballistic missiles could not; namely, carry a heavy 7,000-pound fission warhead and bulky inertial guidance system. By 1954, however, improvements in ballistic missile technology offset Snark's early advantage. The advent of thermonuclear weapons shrank the size of the warhead from 7,000 to 1,500 pounds, yet increased the explosive yield 50 times. In conjunction with improvements in the warhead, American engineers also made great strides in developing large liquid-fuel rocket engines, new guidance systems, and a new series of bluntbody reentry vehicles.

The net effect was that by the late mid-1950s ICBMs promised to deliver nuclear weapons far more efficiently than Snark. In comparing the two weapon systems Air Force planners envisioned that the ICBMs, based in heavily protected underground silos, would be much harder to destroy than the Snarks in their above-ground hangars. Snark was also far more vulnerable in the air. Once in flight the ICBM would be all but invulnerable,whereas the subsonic Snark, lacking both defensive armament and the capability for evasive maneuvers, could be intercepted by conventional air defense systems.

In 1958 General Donald Irving, the commander of the Air Research and Development Command, the organization charged with overseeing the missile program, cited Snark as an outstanding example of unwarranted funding. SAC commander General Thomas Power also harbored serious reservations about the

An aerial view of the six Snark assembly and checkout buildings at Presque Isle AFB, Maine. In front of each building are two circular launch pads.

missile, arguing that Snark would add little to SAC's already potent nuclear strike force. Tired of the endless debate, Power wanted to either fix the missile or terminate the program.

Tests by SAC missile crews in the late 1950s graphically demonstrated Snark's poor reliability and accuracy. Of the first seven launches conducted by Air Force crews, only two of the missiles reached the target area and only one warhead landed within 4 miles of its aiming point. Further tests revealed that on flights of 2,100 miles, on average, Snark had a degree of accuracy of plus or minus 20 miles. Accuracy was not the missile's only shortcoming. Random mechanical failures also marred the test program. Based on the last ten test Snark launches, the Air Force estimated that the missile stood only a one-in-three chance of getting off the ground.

Basing Strategy

In March 1957 SAC's Missile Site Selection Panel recommended that the command establish its first Snark operational base at Presque Isle, Maine. Located in the northeastern corner of the state, Presque Isle was the site of an Air Force Air Defense Command (ADC) base slated for closure. Operating under the Secretary of the Air Force's orders that it use existing government property wherever possible, SAC agreed to use the installation as a Snark site, although it noted that many of the buildings were in poor condition and would require extensive renovation. The key factor in SAC's decision to base the Snark at Presque Isle, however, was the base's location. Positioned at the very northeastern corner of the nation, Presque Isle brought the Snark within range of its anticipated targets in the Soviet Union.

One of the Snark assembly and checkout buildings at Presque Isle AFB, Maine.

Snark Deployment

Despite the poor test results, and much to the dismay of its critics, the Snark program survived. The missile program endured because of the rapidly escalating tensions of the Cold War, the fierce support of the aircraft industry, and the Air Force's desire to see a tangible return on its $650 million investment. In March 1957 the Air Force selected Presque Isle, Maine to be the site of its first, and ultimately only, Snark operational base.

In January 1959 the Air Force activated the 702nd Strategic Missile Wing to man the new facility. SAC put its first Snark on alert in March 1960. Indicative of the problems inherent with Snark, and also the unforeseen difficulties in making the missile base operational, the 702nd did not become fully operational until February 1961.

The Snark, however, was obsolete well before the last of the 702nd's missiles was ready. In September 1959 the Air Force placed its first three Atlas ICBM's on alert at Vandenberg Air Force Base, and had three full Atlas squadrons scheduled to become operational the following year. With the Titan and Minuteman programs also scheduled to become operational in the early 1960s there was no compelling reason to retain Snark. In March 1961 President Kennedy ordered Snark withdrawn from service, noting that the missile was obsolete and of little military value. Subsequently the Air Force deactivated the 702nd Strategic Missile Wing at the end of June 1961. Fifteen years in the making, Snark was fully operational for a brief 6 months.

Unit	Base	Operational
702 SMW	Presque Isle AFB, Maine	1960-1961

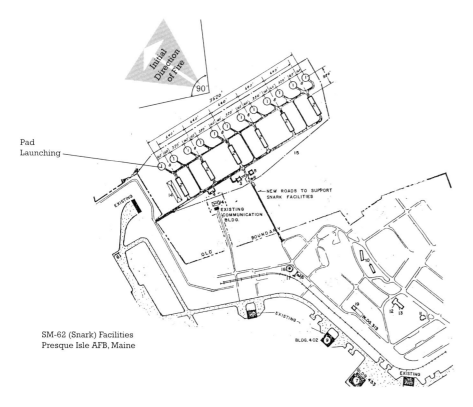

Pad
Launching

SM-62 (Snark) Facilities
Presque Isle AFB, Maine

Site Configuration

Construction of the Snark facility began in May 1956. The work was done by the J.R. Cianchete Construction Company of Pittsfield, Maine at a cost exceeding $6.8 million.

SAC built the sprawling Snark launch facility at the northeast corner of the base. Mounted on their mobile launch trailers, the missiles were stored in six large, singlestory assembly and checkout buildings. The buildings, which looked much like aircraft hangars, measured 420 feet long by 80 feet wide. They were built alongside each other, each separated by a distance of approximately 450 feet.

In front of each building were two circular launch pads, each 160 feet in diameter, made of reinforced concrete between 10 and 12 inches thick. Upon receiving a launch order, the crews drove the launchers onto the launch pads, fired their missiles, and then cleared the pad for the next launch.

Other facilities built to support the Snark launch site included a power and water pumping plant measuring 160 by 102 feet; an engine run-up facility that was 99 by 61 feet; a two-story launch and surveillance building measuring 44 by 39 feet, and a 15,000-gallon fuel tank farm with a pump house and truck filling stand.

References

For a concise history of the program through 1957 see, "Snark Program History," 29 April 1957, in the records of the Assistant Chief of Staff for Guided Missiles (AFCGM), Federal Records Center, Suitland, MD, Records of HQ USAF (RG 341), Accession 61B1643, Box 2, folder, "AFCGM Correspondence–1957, January thru October." For an excellent summary of the entire Snark program that includes both copious notes and illustrations, see Kenneth P. Werrell, *The Evolution of the Cruise Missile* (Maxwell Air Force Base, Montgomery, AL: Air University Press, 1985), pp. 82–97. See also Kenneth P. Werrell, "The Case Study of Failure," *Journal of the American Aviation Historical Society*, (Fall 1988): pp. 191–204. For a technical overview of the Snark weapon system, see the United States Air Force, "Standard Missile Characteristics SM-62A Snark," June 1960, available at the Research Center, USAF Museum, Wright-Patterson AFB, Ohio.

Information on the Snark launch facilities and base infrastructure came from two sources. For a detailed description of Snark facilities, see "Installation Plan, SM-62 (Snark) for Presque Isle, Maine," in the archives at the U.S. Strategic Command, History Office, Offutt AFB, Omaha, NE. See also, the unit histories of the 702nd Strategic Wing (SAC) (ICM-SNARK) for the periods 1 January to 31 July 1959 and 1 July to 31 July 1960, available at the Air Force Historical Research Agency, Maxwell AFB, Montgomery, AL.

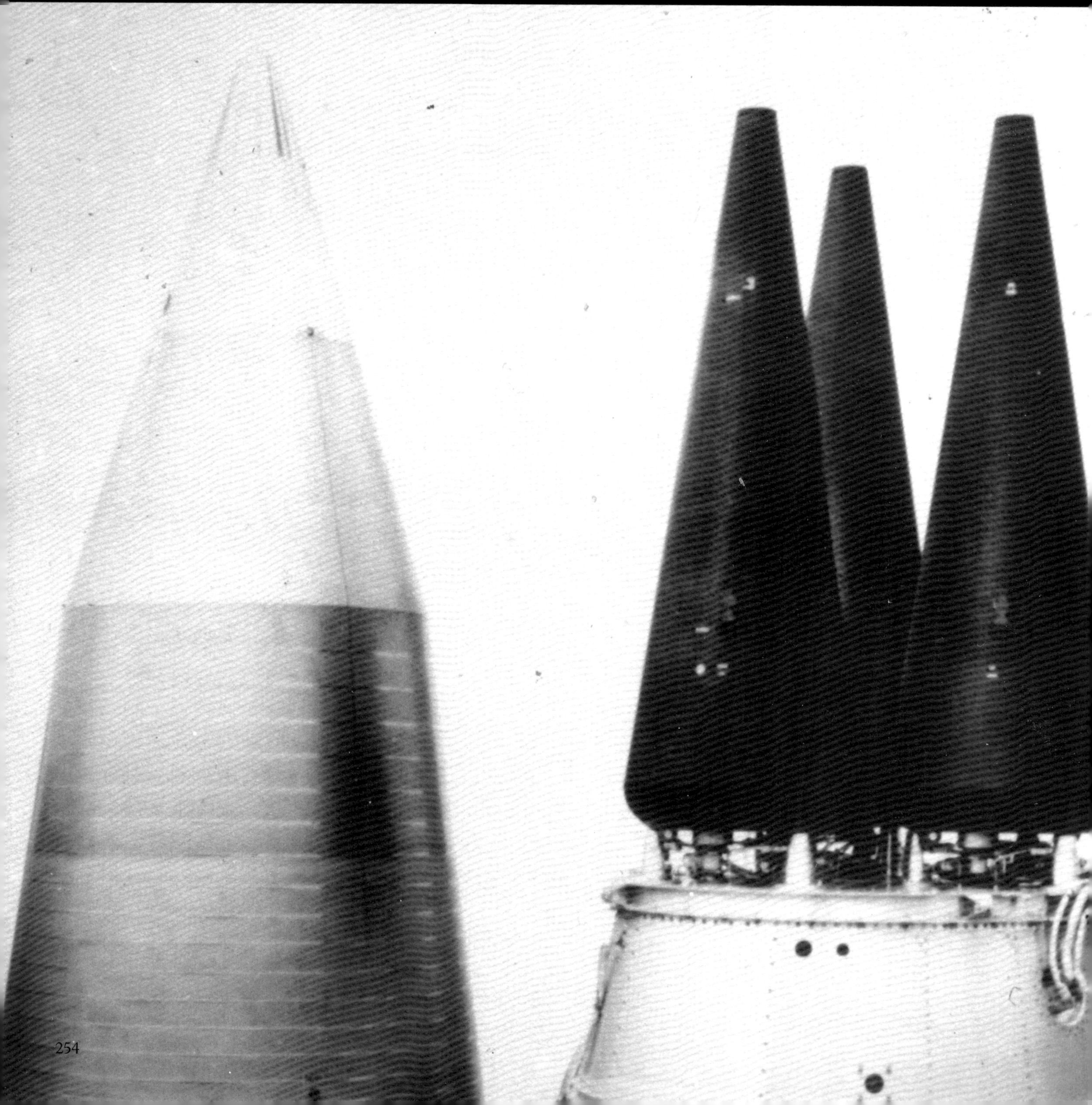

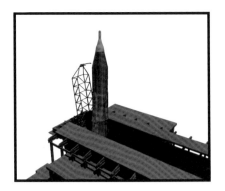

Part III

Site Overviews:
Histories of Missile
Development and Deployment
Sites in the United States

INTRODUCTION

This part provides a state-by-state listing and short histories of Army and Air Force missile research, development, testing, evaluation, government production, logistical support, training, and deployment sites within the United States and at Kwajalein Atoll in the Republic of the Marshall Islands. The listing is not comprehensive. For example, privately-owned production facilities are not listed, nor are numerous air bases and forts/posts that stored and serviced thousands of short range tactical air-to-air, surface-to-air, air-to-surface, and surface-to-surface weapons. Greater attention is given to those locations involved with defensive and deterrent systems that more directly affected the American landscape.

A Note on Sources

The site histories were prepared from secondary sources, many of which were supplied by base or wing public affairs offices, command history offices, and base environmental resource offices.

Record Repositories

The authors also consulted documents at the following repositories: The Research Collection, Office of History, Headquarters Army Corps of Engineers, Alexandria, Virginia [HQCE]; the Air Force History Office, Bolling Air Force Base (AFB), Washington, DC [AFHO]; the Archives Division, National Air and Space Museum, Washington, DC [NASM]; the Prints and Photographs Division, Library of Congress, Washington, DC [LOC]; the Center for Military History, Washington, DC [CMH]; and the United States Army Military History Institute, Carlisle Barracks, Pennsylvania [MHI]. A description of each collection accompanies the bibliography in Part I.

Reference Abbreviations

Throughout the site histories the authors used abbreviated citations for several frequently used reference works and treaties. Those citations are as follows:

Nike Quick Look

Morgan, Mark. *Nike Quick Look III, BOMARC/AF Talos.* Fort Worth, TX: AEROMK, 1990.

Air Force Bases

Mueller, Robert. *Air Force Bases: Active Air Force Bases Within the United States of America on 17 September 1982,* Volume I. Washington, DC: Office of Air Force History, 1989.

SAC Chronology

Narducci, Henry M, ed. *SAC Missile Chronology 1939–1988.* Offut AFB, NE: Office of the Historian, Headquarters, Strategic Air Command, 1990.

INF Treaty

Treaty Between the United States of America and the Union of Soviet Socialist Republics on the Elimination of their Intermediate-Range and Shorter-Range Ballistic Missiles. December 1987.

START

Arms Control and Disarmament Agreements: Treaty Between the United States of America and the Union of Soviet Socialist Republics on the Reduction and Limitation of Strategic Offensive Arms. 31 July 1991.

ALABAMA

A R M Y

Redstone Arsenal, Huntsville

In April 1941, Congress authorized funding for a second chemical warfare manufacturing and storage facility. In June, a survey team selected a site on the southwestern edge of Huntsville. A month later when the Huntsville Arsenal site was announced, the Ordnance Corps announced plans to build an assembly plant next to the chemical munitions manufacturing and storage facility. This "Redstone Ordnance Plant" would be redesignated Redstone Arsenal in 1943.

Huntsville first came into contact with missiles when the "Fred Project" was established in January 1945. The project demonstrated the "in-house" capability to produce liquid propellant. In August 1945, two JB-2 missiles[a] launched from Eglin Field in Florida validated the government's capability and the demonstration project ended.

With the end of the war, activity at the two arsenals dropped dramatically. Many facilities at Huntsville were leased for use by private sector companies. Until 1947 when Redstone was placed in standby status, work at the facility consisted of renovating and salvaging ammunition returned from overseas. On June 30, 1949, Huntsville Arsenal was deactivated. Command responsibilities were assumed by Redstone, which on June 1, 1949, had been designated as the Ordnance Rocket Center.

With the founding of the Ordnance Rocket Center, contractors were invited to submit bids to operate many of the government-owned facilities. Thiokol Corporation was one of the many aerospace industries that established themselves within the Arsenal. Thiokol's role included research, development, and production of solid propulsion systems.

Huntsville's Role in Ballistic/Guided Missile Development

In 1950, 120 German scientists led by Dr. Wernher von Braun along with American scientists and military personnel arrived

[a] "JB-2s" were American copies of the German V-1 "Buzz Bomb" (see Chapter 1).

from Fort Bliss, Texas, to begin work. Work at Redstone had initially centered on rocket-related research and development including basic and applied research on free rockets, jet-assisted takeoff engines, and solid-propellant fuels. With the arrival of the von Braun team, Redstone also became responsible for research and development of guided missiles. Their first major project was to develop a surface-to-surface missile with a 500-mile range. This missile became known as the Redstone.

The team established themselves within the confines of the former Huntsville Arsenal portion of the complex while rocket research and development continued on the southeast corner of the original Redstone tract. In September 1952, the two centers were merged to become the Ordnance Missile Laboratories.

To deploy and maintain the missiles developing at Redstone, the Army needed trained soldiers and technicians. Consequently, in 1952, the Army founded the Ordnance Guided Missile School (OGMS) at Huntsville. Eventually, the command evolved into the U.S. Army Missile and Munitions Center and School. By 1973, the school had graduated over 80,000 students.

In October 1955, divided on the issue of development of an Intermediate Range Ballistic Missile (IRBM), the Joint Chiefs of Staff recommended to Secretary of Defense Charles E. Wilson that both the Air Force and Army proceed with their respective programs. The following month, Secretary Wilson directed the Army and Navy to collaborate on IRBM Number 2, known as Jupiter. This directive gave the Army the impetus to consolidate its ongoing Jupiter program within one organization.

Consequently, on February 1, 1956, the Army Ballistic Missile Agency (ABMA) came into existence at Redstone Arsenal under the jurisdiction of the Chief of Ordnance and assumed control of the facilities of the former Guided Missile Development Division of Redstone's Ordnance Missile Laboratory. Maj. Gen. John B. Medaris became ABMA's first commander.

Throughout 1956, ABMA, working with the Navy, made steady progress on the Jupiter program. Launches at the Atlantic Missile Range were so successful that the early Jupiter test program was accelerated. In August, construction was completed at Redstone on what was then the nation's largest rocket test stand.

Unfortunately for ABMA, on November 26, 1956, Defense Secretary Wilson issued a memorandum to the Armed Forces Policy Council that gave the Air Force operational jurisdiction of long-range missiles (over 200 miles). The Jupiter program received another blow in early December when the Navy pulled out of the Jupiter program after receiving the Defense Secretary's approval to proceed with its Polaris program.

In 1957, with the future of Jupiter in doubt, von Braun's team continued to make progress while the bureaucratic battle persisted in Washington. Because of the Army's rapid progress on Jupiter development, the new Secretary of Defense Neil McElroy's decision to deploy either the Air Force's Thor or the Army's Jupiter became quite difficult. The October 4, 1957, Soviet launch of Sputnik proved to be an important factor. Although earlier ABMA offers to launch a satellite were spurred in favor of the Navy's Vanguard program, on November 8, 1957, Defense Secretary McElroy ordered ABMA to prepare a Jupiter C missile to launch a satellite. On November 25, McElroy directed that production proceed on both Jupiter and Thor missiles. Thus, in the wake of Sputnik, suddenly Maj. Gen. Medaris had the authority to take all actions necessary to get Jupiter into full-scale production.

Forced to accept this weapon into its inventory, Air Force representatives met with the Army Ballistic Missile Agency in early January 1958 to discuss operational deployment. Within a week of this meeting, the Air Force activated the 864th Strategic Missile Squadron (SMS) at Redstone Arsenal.

By midyear a substantial number of Air Force personnel had arrived in northern Alabama to attend OGMS courses on Jupiter operations. In January 1959, OGMS completed training for eight launch crews and two maintenance teams. By the end of the year, most of these graduates were in Italy; personnel of the 865th SMS later joined them in Italy. Italian Air Force personnel arrived at Huntsville in 1959 and 1960 to become trained on Jupiter operations. The Italy-based Jupiter squadrons were activated in 1961 to support the North American Treaty Organization (NATO). Personnel from the 866th SMS were eventually stationed in Turkey, manning a NATO Jupiter squadron with Turkish personnel trained at Redstone Arsenal. By 1963, these squadrons would be removed from alert status.

The successful placement of America's first satellite, Explorer I, in space on January 31, 1958, marked an apogee in the history of ABMA. However, the pace continued to be hectic. On February 28, 1958, ABMA awarded the Martin Company a contract to produce solid-fueled Pershing missiles at its Orlando, Florida, facility.[b]

A military reorganization began that eventually led to the demise of the ABMA. On March 31, the new Army Ordnance Missile Command (AOMC) stood up at Redstone Arsenal with Maj. Gen. Medaris in command. ABMA became a subordinate command of AOMC on the following day, as did the newly formed U.S. Army Guided Missile Agency (ARGMA), White Sands Proving Ground, and the Army-contracted Jet Propulsion Laboratory (JPL) at Caltech. ARGMA had management responsibilities for shorter-range surface-to-surface systems such as the Sergeant, Corporal, Littlejohn, and Honest John as well as the Nike Ajax, Nike Hercules, and Hawk surface-to-air systems. In December, President Eisenhower would transfer JPL to the newly formed National Aeronautics and Space Administration (NASA).

Over the next 2 years, ABMA provided critical support for the new space agency's Mercury program and subsequent Saturn program. On October 21, 1959, President Eisenhower ordered components of the military's space program to be transferred to NASA. Thus in July 1960, a substantial proportion of ABMA facilities was leased to NASA to become the George C. Marshall Space Flight Center. Some of these facilities later received national historic recognition for their presence during both the ABMA and NASA eras. Constructed in 1953, the Redstone Rocket Test Stand (Building 4665) is listed as a Category I property on the National Register of Historic Places. The test stand had been the first that was capable of accommodating the entire launch vehicle during static tests. Category II properties dating from the pre-NASA era include the Neutral Buoyancy Simulator (Building 47051, the Solid Rocket Motor Propulsion and Structural Test Facility (Building 4572), and the Structures and Mechanics Laboratory (Building 4619). The Mobile District of the Army Corps of Engineers supervised the construction of these various facilities. From 1950 to the time of Sputnik, the Corps had finished construction worth $42 million and had an additional $21 million under contract.

In addition to receiving $100 million worth of facilities, NASA received the services of some 4,000 former ABMA personnel led by Wernher von Braun. With the severe loss of research facilities and personnel, the Redstone Arsenal focused on tactical missile systems.[c] However, during the mid-1950s the Army assumed a mission requiring completely new types of missiles.

[b] The Pershing I and II missiles played a crucial deterrent role in Europe.

Huntsville's Role in Ballistic Missile Defense

In 1957, two years after the Army Ordnance Corps first contracted for the investigation of Ballistic Missile Defense (BMD), the first BMD program office was established at Redstone to oversee work on the Nike Zeus project being performed by Western Electric and other contractors. Reorganization in 1958 placed the program office under the Army Rocket and Guided Missile Agency, which was a subordinate command to the newly formed Army Ordnance Missile Command. Further reorganization during 1962 supplanted this command with the U.S. Army Missile Command. Under this arrangement, the Nike Zeus Project Office received administrative support from the U.S. Army Missile Command but reported directly to Army Materiel Command.

Despite the bureaucratic reorganizations, the Nike Zeus Project Office could report substantial progress, as the system capability was proven on July 19, 1962, when a Nike Zeus fired from Kwajalein Test Site came within the lethal distance necessary to knock out an incoming ICBM that had been launched from Vandenberg AFB. Although further testing validated this first feat and even proved the ability of the system to knock out orbiting satellites, Secretary of Defense Robert McNamara declined to deploy the system because it was technically incapable of countering a mass ICBM attack.

In 1963, Nike Zeus became Nike X. The Huntsville Project Office continued to fund research to develop vital components of what eventually would be dubbed the Sentinel and later Safeguard ABM systems.

With Secretary of Defense McNamara announcing in September 1967 his decision to deploy Sentinel, another reorganization placed the Huntsville Project Office under the new U.S. Sentinel Systems Command (SENSCOM). Because the Department of Defense restricted SENSCOM to functions relating to the engineering requirements needed to support Sentinel deployment, the Army set up an additional organization to support research and development (R&D) for an advanced system. This organization eventually became the U.S. Army Advanced Ballistic Missile Defense Agency (ABMDA) and reported directly to the Army's Chief of Research and Development. Although collocated in Washington with the SENSCOM System Office, ABMDA also maintained a presence in Huntsville adjacent to the SENSCOM field quarters.

To coordinate the construction of facilities for what one general called an effort comparable to the MANHATTAN PROJECT, the Army Corps of Engineers established a nationwide district based out of Huntsville to serve the needs of SENSCOM. Established on October 15, 1967, the Huntsville District's sole purpose was to construct Sentinel.

[c] Organizational Changes. With the loss of 72 percent of the Army Ballistic Missile Agency to NASA, restructuring within the Army Ordnance Missile Command became inevitable. Consequently, on August 1, 1960, the Army Rocket and Guided Missile Agency transferred to ABMA surface-to-surface missiles whose flights were preprogrammed; including Corporal, Sergeant, Honest John, and Littlejohn. Logistical support for these systems was retained by ARGMA Eventually, ARGMA and ABMA folded into AOMC in 1961 in anticipation of a planned Armywide reorganization in 1962. Logistical functions for both organizations had been assumed in mid-1961 by the newly formed Army Ordnance Missile Support Agency (AOMSA).

When ABMA and ARGMA were abolished on December 11, 1961, two deputy commanding generals were established: one to oversee ballistic missile programs and the other to manage guided missile projects. Included as ballistic missiles were Pershing, Redstone-Corporal, Sergeant, small rockets, Honest John, and Littlejohn. Guided missiles included Nike Zeus, Mauler-Redeye, Hawk-NATO Hawk, Anti-tank and Field Artillery Weapon Systems, Nike Ajax/Hercules plus target missiles.

The expected reorganization came in May 1962. The new U.S. Army Missile Command (MICOM) replaced AOMC and became subordinate to the newly formed Army Materiel Command (AMC). AOMSA came under MICOM and was redesignated as the Army Missile Support Command (AMSC).

Throughout MICOM's 15-year existence, the command program managed many of the missile systems deployed by U.S. forces in Vietnam. Laser work done at Huntsville contributed to the introduction of "Smart" bombs in that conflict. Not all missiles were managed by MICOM. For example, the Nike Zeus Program Manager reported directly to AMC although he was administratively supported by MICOM.

With the American drawdown in Vietnam in the early 1970s, MICOM was forced to cutback its work force. In the mid-1970s the Army's procurement process underwent several studies. On January 23, 1976, AMC became the U.S. Army Materiel Development and Readiness Command (DARCOM), with a smaller headquarters manning, as many operational functions were transferred to field commands. The U.S. Army Missile Command was abolished on January 31,1977. MICOM's functions were absorbed by two new organizations: the U.S. Army Research and Development Command (MIRADCOM) and the U.S. Army Missile Readiness Command (MIRCOM). These organization names reflected their new functions. However, in July 1979, the U.S. Army Missile Command was reestablished and the two spinoff organizations were recombined.

When President Nixon reoriented BMD to guard strategic forces, Sentinel became Safeguard and SENSCOM became SAFS-COM. Work at a Sentinel site outside of Boston ceased, and efforts were redirected to sites north of Grand Forks AFB, North Dakota, and Malmstrom AFB, Montana. Due to the 1972 ABM Treaty, only the Grand Forks site would reach operational status.

With this sole site coming on line during 1974, another reorganization took place, which merged SAFSCOM Systems Office and ABMDA to form the Ballistic Missile Defense Organization (BMDO). With the merger, the ABMDA office in Washington disbanded and its Huntsville component became the Ballistic Missile Defense Advanced Technology Center (BMDATC), while Huntsville's SAFSCOM organization was retitled the Ballistic Missile Defense Systems Command (BMDSCOM). These two components would be merged in 1985 during another reorganization.

During this post-Vietnam era, BMD took a back seat to a growing debate on whether to deploy new strategic missile systems to counter a growing Soviet threat. While debate raged on this sensitive issue, the Army obtained stable funding to continue BMD research. One of the potential systems that evolved from this research was a Low Altitude Defense (LOAD) that eventually became dubbed Sentry. Using a missile similar to the Sprint and downscaled site defense technology, Sentry ideally would have been deployed to defend a proposed MX missile "dense pack" configuration of missiles in clusters.

Sentry was never deployed. A Presidential Commission established by President Ronald Reagan in January 1983 recommended placing MX missiles in Minuteman silos and deploying a small ICBM, which subsequently was dubbed "Midgetman." The report rejected deployment of Sentry. However, the role of BMDO would still undergo a radical change after President Reagan announced his Strategic Defense Initiative (SDI) to the American people on the evening of March 23, 1983. To better posture its BMD component, the Army reorganized the command in 1985 with the new title of U.S. Army Strategic Defense Command (USASDC). Although the Headquarters of USASDC would be in Washington, the bulk of the organization remained in Huntsville.

*References: For pre-missile era material see Michael E. Baker, Kaylene Hughes, Redstone Arsenal Complex Chronology, Part I: The Pre-Missile Era, (Huntsville, AL: U.S. Army Missile Command, 1991). A broad overview and discussion of historical-*ly significant sites is found in "Historic American Engineering Record: Redstone Arsenal," (HAER ALA 45HUVI.V.6), 1985, [LOC]. Huntsville's role in missile defense is detailed in James H. Kitchens, A History of the Huntsville Division: 15 October 1967–31 December 1976, (Huntsville, AL: U.S. Army Engineer, Huntsville Division, 1978). A 15-year span of MICOM is covered in Helen Brents Joiner and Elizabeth C. Joliff, History of the United States Army Missile Command: 1962–1977, (Redstone Arsenal, Huntsville, AL: U.S. Army Missile Command, 1979). For details on more recent Huntsville activities see Ruth Currie-McDaniel and Claus R. Martel, The U.S. Army Strategic Defense Command: Its History and Role in the Strategic Defense Initiative, 3rd ed. (Huntsville, AL: Historical Office, U.S. Strategic Defense Command, 1989). Virgil S. Davis touches on the Corps of Engineers role at Redstone in A History of the Mobile District: 1815 to 1971, (Mobile, AL: U.S. Army Engineer District, n.d.), [HQCE].*

ALASKA

A R M Y

Anchorage Defense Area

In August 1955, the United States Army, Alaska (USARAL) announced plans to build Nike missile installations in the vicinities of Fairbanks and Anchorage to replace the gun emplacements then defending those regions. The Corps of Engineers Alaska District surveyed potential sites, acquired the needed land, and in March 1957, issued invitations to bid on the project. Patti-McDonald and M.B. Contracting Company earned the contract. This primary contracting team would eventually receive about $10 million for its work. With other contractors installing support facilities, the cost per site approached $5 million, nearly five times the average cost of sites built in the lower 48 states.

Three sites were located around Anchorage to defend the city, Fort Richardson, and Elmendorf AFB. The Army activated Site Bay, located 20 miles northwest of Anchorage, in March 1959. Site Point, located 10 miles southwest of Anchorage, was activated a month later. Situated at Fort Richardson near Anchorage, the Command Post hosted the regional air defense command and control facility.

The most challenging part of the construction project was placing a missile battery at Site Summit located on Mount Gordon Lyon. To install the launcher and control radars, a tremendous amount of blasting had to be completed to provide for access roads and level sites. Fog, high winds, and winter snows slowed work at Summit Site, delaying activation until May 1959.

Unique design features to accommodate the climate included above-ground magazines and heated radar towers. The design of the magazines represented a radical departure from those built in the lower 48 states. A typical battery featured two concrete box-shaped structures with exterior concrete aprons. Two doors opened facing the apron to allow missiles to roll on carriages to the launching rails. Before installation, a prototype of this system was constructed and tested at White Sands Missile Range. Also unlike previously constructed sites, weather conditions dictated that housing be located at the battery control. Berthing, dining, post exchange, barber shop, dispensary, and tactical radar facilities were all located under one roof within the "battery control building."

Living at these sites were men of the 4th Missile Battalion, 43rd Artillery (redesignated 1st Missile Battalion, 43rd Artillery in 1972). This Regular Army unit endured some incredibly harsh conditions. The coldest night occurred in February 1969 when the temperature dipped down to -45°F. Not only did these batteries face harsh weather, they endured the great earthquake of March 27, 1964. One of the batteries of Site Point was damaged beyond repair.

With the exception of the earthquake-damaged battery at Site Point, these batteries remained on duty until 1979.

Fairbanks Defense Area

Sites Peter (15 miles East of Eielson AFB), Mike (10 miles southeast of Eielson AFB), Jig (5 miles south of Eielson AFB), Tare (20 miles south of Nemana), and Love (10 miles northwest of Fairbanks) were installed to replace guns defending the Fairbanks area, which included Fort Wainwright and Eielson AFB. Land for the first four sites was acquired in late 1956. Peter Kiewit Sons' Company received the contract to build the facilities, for which the government paid $12.7 million. Smaller contracts further increased the final cost. Property for Site Love was obtained in 1958. B-E-C-K Constructors won the bid to build this last Alaskan Nike installation. As with the Anchorage sites, the Corps of Engineers, Alaska District, oversaw the construction.

The 2nd Missile Battalion, 562nd Artillery, manned these sites. Life during the long, dark winters was tedious. One former missileman recalled that the Bingo game was a weekly highlight. During the long summers, the region provided many outdoor recreational activities for those who were not "pulling duty."

On December 16, 1959, Site Peter gained notoriety as the first battery to conduct a live on-site Nike Hercules missile shoot. Unfortunately, the missile self-destructed after climbing 3,000 yards, disappointing the VIPs and reporters who had been invited to watch. The next day, the 2nd/562nd succeeded in putting a "bird" in the air. Fourteen missiles roared from that launch site that winter as each of Alaska's batteries launched two missiles for their annual service practice. The firings showed how the system worked under launch conditions; problems with the target tracking and acquisition radars that had been noted elsewhere were readily apparent in Alaska. As a result, in 1962 and 1963, Alaskan sites received new high-powered acquisition radar (HIPAR).

Unlike firings that were forced to cease near Anchorage, live firings would continue at Site Peter through the late 1960s. The firings attracted much local coverage and public interest.

The sites around Fairbanks were inactivated in 1970–1971.

References: The Nike Hercules in Alaska, *(Alaska: U.S. Army Engineer District, n.d.), provides an excellent overview of Nike Hercules in the 49th state [HQCE]. Lyman L.Woodman,* The Alaska District United States Army Corps of Engineers, 1946–1974, *(Elmendorf AFB, AK: U.S. Army Engineer District, 1976) pp. 44–45 [HQCE], provides some construction details. A description of the facilities is provided in E.D. Smith, "Missile Projects In Alaska,"* The Military Engineer *(March–April 1960): pp 108–9, [HQCE]. See also C. Colt Dentield,* The Cold War in Alaska: A Management Plan for Cultural Resources, *(Alaska: U.S. Army Engineer District, 1994).*

ARIZONA

A I R   F O R C E

Davis-Monthan Air Force Base

The Army established operations at Davis-Monthan in 1940, and during the war, the base supported bomber training operations. In the post-war period, Davis-Monthan fell under the command of the newly formed Strategic Air Command (SAC).

On April 20, 1960, the Fifteenth Air Force announced selection of the base to support a Titan II missile wing. As with Titan II base construction at Little Rock and McConnell AFBs, the Corps of Engineers Ballistic Missile Construction Office implemented a "three phase" concept in an attempt to alleviate "concurrency" problems that had plagued earlier Atlas and Titan I construction projects.

Three companies (Jones, Teer, and Winkelman) combined to bid $27.7 million and received the contract for the first phase of construction, which included the access road, pit and shaft excavations, and blast lock door installation. Groundbreaking was on December 9, 1960. With first phase operations moving forward, second phase operations began on July 13, 1961, as Fluor Corporation and its subcontractors began installing the supporting electrical, fueling, and other auxiliary equipment. Fluor had won the contract by submitting a low bid of $35.6 million. The sites were prepared for the final phase by mid-December 1962. The Martin Company handled phase III missile installation and check-outs.

As with previous projects, hazards faced the workers who built the huge underground structures. During the first two phases, five workers died in construction accidents and many more were injured.

Labor strife also disrupted construction. Between 1962 and 1964, 20 work stoppages occurred, resulting in 1,758 lost man-days of work. Yet, given that over one million man-days of labor were expended during the course of the project, the days lost to work stoppage were minimal.

Charges of waste and inefficiency brought three staff investigators from the Senate Preparedness Subcommittee, chaired by Senator John Stennis, to Davis-Monthan during the first week of August 1962. The subcommittee would later conclude that the

cost-overruns experienced at Davis-Monthan were comparable to those experienced at the other two Titan II bases due to design alterations during construction and inexperience with this type of project.

The January 1, 1962, activation of the 390th Strategic Missile Wing (SMW) marked the first standing up of a Titan II missile wing. Its two component squadrons were the 570th and the 571st Strategic Missile Squadrons. Launcher locations for the 570th SMS were at Oracle, Three Points, Rillito (4 silos), and Oracle Junction (3 silos). The 571st SMS silos were located at Benson (2 silos), Mescal, Pantano, Continental (2 silos), Palo Alto, and Three Points. On March 31, 1963, site 570-2 (Three Points) was turned over to SAC for operational use. Additional silos joined the SAC inventory until November 30, when the 18th and final Titan II went on alert. The 390th SMW became the first operational Titan II missile wing in the Air Force.

With a requirement to keep all 18 missiles on alert status around the clock, maintenance personnel often put in 80 to 90-hour work weeks. Eventually, response times to act on maintenance problems were loosened to allow crews to react during normal working hours. Maintenance did ease at the end of 1964, as the Davis-Monthan silos became the first to receive "Project Green Jug" treatment entailing the installation of dehumidifier equipment that eased corrosion problems within the silos. Additional modifications would be made to increase missile reliability, survivability, and reaction time. Also toward the end of 1964, the 390th SMW underwent the first operational readiness inspection for a Titan II unit.

On January 25, 1965, Vice President Hubert H. Humphrey toured complex 571-l. One month later, the 390th SMW performed the first operational launch test of one of its Titan IIs at Vandenberg AFB, California. Many more successful tests followed. Competing in SAC's first ever missile competition called "Project Curtain Raiser" in 1967, the 390th SMW garnered the first "best crew" trophy. Since 1967, the Wing earned many additional accolades at these competitions which became known as "Olympic Arena."

In October 1981, President Reagan announced that as part of the strategic modernization program, Titan II systems were to be retired by October 1, 1987. Deactivation began at Davis-Monthan on October 1, 1982. During the operation, titled "Rivet Cap," the missiles were removed and shipped to Norton AFB, California for refurbishment and storage. Explosive demolition began at the headworks of missile complex 570-7 on November 30, 1983. During the following May, the last Titan II at Davis-Monthan came off alert status. Two months later, SAC deactivated the 390th Strategic Missile Wing.

After removal from service, 17 silos had reusable equipment removed by Air Force personnel, and contractors retrieved salvageable metals before destroying the silos with explosives and filling them in. Access to the vacated control centers was blocked off. Some of the properties were then sold; other sites are retained by the Bureau of Land Management.

Local aviation enthusiasts associated with the Pima Air Museum won Defense Department approval in 1984 to set aside one silo for permanent display. The silo at Green Valley was retained by the Air Force and leased to local government for use as the "Titan Missile Museum." With a training Titan II missile in place, the silo is maintained by a dedicated organization comprised of volunteers from nearby retirement communities. The site was placed on the National Register of Historic Places as the only surviving sample of a Titan II installation. In addition to the launch complex and missile, the museum obtained auxiliary support equipment for display.

Besides preserving the Green Valley site, Davis-Monthan's relationship with missiles did not end with the removal of the Titans. The base served as a training facility for the BGM-109G Ground Launched Cruise Missile (GLCM) during the 1970s and 1980s. At the time of the signing of the December 1987 Intermediate Nuclear Forces (INF) Treaty, the training facility hosted 2 training missiles and 27 training launch canisters.

Eventually, after the closure of Norton AFB, the Titans returned to Davis-Monthan for storage.

References: The staff at the Titan Museum has assembled a vast quantity of materials relating to 390th and 308th SMW (Little Rock AFB, Arkansas) operations. Complete sets of technical manuals, hand-written engineering notes covering site construction and original "as built" blue-prints, and follow-on modifications for both the Tucson and Little Rock sites, are in storage as are site deactivation plans. Titan Museum references used include Barry J. Anderson, A Brief History of the 390th Strategic Missile Wing, (1971), and Gary P. Myers, The Story of Davis-Monthan AFB, (1982). While Anderson provides the bulk of the wing history material, Myers documented much of the site construction activities, Further information on this construction period came from "CEBMCO History of Davis-Monthan AFB, Arizona: October 1960–January 1964," (n.d.1, pp. VII.3, IV.9, IV.17, [HQCE]. Discussion on later cruise missile activities is covered in INF Treaty.

A R M Y

Yuma Proving Ground

Modern Army presence in the area dates back to World War II when the region hosted an Army Corps of Engineers testing facility for bridging equipment.

In 1952, the Yuma Test Station was activated under Sixth Army Command to conduct tests on military equipment in a desert environment. In 1962, the Army Materiel Command assumed control of the facility, and in 1963 the facility became known as the Yuma Proving Ground. In 1974, the facility was designated a Department of Defense Major Range and Test Facility. Today Yuma Proving Ground occupies 1,300 square miles within southwestern Arizona. Although not a major missile testing facility, Yuma's Kofa and Cibola test ranges have been used to evaluate the effectiveness of short-range tactical missiles such as Tow or Hellfire antitank missiles under desert conditions.

Reference: Yuma Proving Grounds Public Affairs Office.

ARKANSAS

A I R   F O R C E

Eaker Air Force Base

Formerly Blytheville AFB, this World War II vintage installation came under SAC operation control in 1958. B-52s arrived in 1960. Eventually B-52G bombers assigned here were modified to carry Air-Launched Cruise Missiles (ALCMs), which required the construction of storage and assembly facilities during the 1970s.

References: Air Force Bases, pp. 35–38; START Annex C.

Little Rock Air Force Base

On June 22, 1960, the Air Force announced plans to establish 18 Titan II launch sites at a 5-year-old SAC bomber base located at Little Rock. Once a bombardment wing, the 308th was resurrected on April 1, 1962, with a new mission of manning the 18 Titan II silos under construction around Little Rock AFB, Arkansas. Components of the 308th Strategic Missile Wing consisted of the 373rd and 374th Strategic Missile Squadrons.

The Corps of Engineers, Little Rock District, conducted site selection. Silos for the 373rd SMS were located at Mount Vernon, Rosebud, Heber Springs, Albion, Center Hill, Antioch, Velvet Ridge, Judsonia, and Hamlet. Silos for the 374th SMS were located at Mount Vernon, Blackwell, Plummerville, St. Vincent, Springfield (2), Republican, Southside, Guy, and Quitman. The Corps of Engineers Ballistic Missile Construction Office (CEBMCO) based in Los Angeles managed the overall construction.

As with Titan II sites at Davis-Monthan and McConnell AFBs, CEBMCO implemented a three-phase process in an attempt to stem the problems associated with "concurrency." Phase I at each site lasted approximately 8 months and included excavation and much of the reinforced concrete construction. Four companies based in Conway, Arkansas, won the bid to construct Phase I of the $80 million construction program. Groundbreaking at the first excavation site was held on January 9, 1961. In excavating the silos, the contractors under Army Corps of Engineer supervision, pioneered a new technique of perforating the silo's circumference to the full depth before chargehole drilling and shooting.

Phase II construction lasted approximately 39 weeks at each site and involved installing the mechanical, electrical, water, and other support systems needed to bring the silo to life.

During Phases I and II, there were 13 work stoppages having minimal impact on delaying the project. Four workers died on separate occasions due to work-related accidents.

Phase III involved the actual readying of the silos for activation. After arriving from the Martin-Marietta facility outside of Denver, the first Titan II ICBM was installed at launch site 373-4 located in White County near Albion on February 28, 1963.

For the next 2 months, the Site Activation Task Force prepared this site and the other silos for activation. Starting with the 373-4 launcher on May 16, 1963, Titan II silos entered alert status for the 308th SMW until December 31 when all 18 silos were declared on

alert status. With Titan IIs at Davis-Monthan AFB, Arizona, and McConnell AFB, Kansas, already on alert, Titan II activations around Little Rock completed the Titan II deployment program.

Crews from the 308th SMW held the distinction of being the first and last combat-ready missile crews to fire Titan IIs from Vandenberg AFB, California. Including the October 2, 1964, and June 27, 1976, launchings, Little Rock crews participated in 14 separate Vandenberg missile launchings.

On two occasions, tragedy marred the 308th SMW. On August 8, 1965, at launch site 373-4, 53 contractor workers died in a flash fire while installing modifications to the launch silo. The cause of the accident was believed to be a rupture in a high-pressure line, which spewed hydraulic fluid on the floor. Ignited by sparks from a nearby welder, the resulting fire consumed most of the oxygen in the space, suffocating the workers.

The second event, although it produced only one fatality, became more infamous because of the way the disaster occurred and the incredible damage inflicted on launcher 374-7 near Damascus. An unfortunate sequence of events began on September 18, 1980, with an incorrect maintenance procedure to add pressure to the second stage oxidizing tank. During an incorrect application of a 9-pound wrench socket to the pressure cap, the maintenance man accidentally dropped the socket, which fell onto the first stage and punctured the first stage fuel tank.

The fuel, unsymmetrical dimethylhydrazine, is hypergolic, meaning contact with the oxidizing agent creates instant ignition. Eventually, the crew evacuated the launch control center as military and civilian response teams arrived to tackle the hazardous situation. Early in the morning of September 19, a two-man investigation team entered the silo. Because their vapor detectors indicated an explosive atmosphere, the two were ordered to evacuate.

At about 0300 hours, a tremendous explosion rocked the area. The initial explosion catapulted the 740-ton closure door away from the silo and ejected the second stage and its warhead out of the silo. Once clear of the silo, the second stage exploded. Twenty-one personnel in the immediate vicinity of the blast were injured. One member of the two-man silo reconnaissance team who had just emerged from the portal sustained injuries that proved fatal.

At daybreak, the Air Force retrieved the warhead and brought it within the confines of Little Rock AFB. During the recovery the Missile Wing Commander received strong support from other military units as well as Federal, state, and local officials. Arkansas's young governor, Bill Clinton, played an important role in overseeing the proper deployment of state emergency resources.

With the missile silo destroyed, launch complex 374-7 became the first Titan II silo to be deactivated. In October 1981, President Reagan announced that all Titan II sites would be deactivated by October 1, 1987, as part of a strategic modernization program. The deactivation of the rest of the 308th SMW silos began on April 24, 1985. The wing completed deactivation on August 18, 1987.

Interestingly, the wing received some of its greatest accolades in the wake of the Damascus disaster. Perhaps realizing the public confidence had suffered a blow, wing personnel made a stronger effort to reach out to local communities. This effort won Air Force recognition in 1983, when the wing became the first missile wing ever to win the General Bruce K. Holloway humanitarian service trophy for the year 1982. The unit also earned the Omaha trophy for 1982, recognizing it as the best in SAC.

After inactivation, the Air Force removed reusable equipment and the contractor extracted metals and other salvageable components. The silos were then destroyed with explosives and filled in. An outdoor display was set up at Little Rock AFB to exhibit a reentry vehicle from a Titan II and explain the history of the 308th SMW.

References: With the Titan II Missile Museum already established at the time of 308th SMW deactivation, the Wing generously donated vast quantities of unit records, declassified maintenance/technical publications, and site "as built" and modification prints. Boxes of Public Affairs newspaper clippings about the base are in storage at the Green Valley, Arizona museum. The Titan II museum also holds unit memorabilia such as unit silver, plaques, and trophies, and intends to display these artifacts upon completion of a display hall. Sources found at Green Valley for this entry included a History of the 308th Strategic Missile Wing, (n.d.), pp. 10–17; and "The Damascus Missile Disaster" press briefing. U.S. Army Corps of Engineers Ballistic Missile Construction Office, "History of the Little Rock Area Office, 5 October 1960–31 July 1963," pp. 7–9, 117–121, [HQCE] detailed construction highlights.

CALIFORNIA

A I R   F O R C E

Ballistic Missile Organization and Predecessor Units

On July 1, 1954, the Air Research Development Command established the Western Development Division (WDD). Under the command of Brig. Gen. Bernard A. Schriever, the new organization settled in a former school building located at 409 East Manchester Road in Inglewood and began its mission of developing the Atlas ICBM. By early 1955 WDD had outgrown its temporary quarters and moved into a four-building complex fronting Arbor Vitae Street near the Los Angeles Airport.

WDD's responsibility rapidly increased, as Schriever's command assumed control of developing the Titan I ICBM and the Intermediate Range Ballistic Missile (IRBM) program. To assist in the systems engineering and the technical direction of the various missile projects, WDD contracted the Ramo-Wooldridge Corporation. This unique government/private-sector relationship would serve the Air Force well through the next three decades. This relationship was altered somewhat at the end of 1957 as Ramo-Wooldridge merged with the production-capable Thompson Products Company. To avoid possible conflicts of interest, an independent subsidiary, Space Technology Laboratories (STL), was created to continue the systems engineering function.

Redesignated as the Air Force Ballistic Missile Division (AFBMD) on June 1, 1957, the command faced a slowdown in missile development due to military budget-cuts when the Soviets launched Sputnik. With ballistic missile development again receiving top funding priority, Inglewood continued to expand. By 1958, more than 4,600 military and civilian personnel were working in 14 buildings. Included in this tally were some 2,930 STL employees and 1,120 members of AFBMD. The Air Materiel Command assigned 400 people to the complex to support logistical and procurement demands and the Strategic Air Command kept 160 people on hand to plan for training crews to deploy the new weapons. In addition to deploying the first generation of ICBM's, the workers at Inglewood started work on a Titan I follow-on missile and a revolutionary solid-fueled weapon to be called Minuteman I. In addition, AFBMD received responsibility for development of satellites and related space systems.

Because of differences in the applicable technologies and relative maturities between the ballistic missile and space systems programs, Brig. Gen. Schriever, now commanding ARDC, arranged for a divorce. On April 1, 1961, the Ballistic Systems Division (BSD) and the Space Systems Division (SSD) were formed under command of the newly organized Air Force Systems Command (AFSC).

Both organizations initially shared space at Inglewood complex now called the Los Angeles Air Force Station (AFS). However, within a year, BSD would be permanently reestablished at Norton AFB located 60 miles to the east.

The 1960s proved to be a most hectic time for BSD as Atlas, Titan, and Minuteman I missiles were fielded in hundreds of silos spread across the country. Working closely with the Corps of Engineers Ballistic Missile Construction Office,[a] BSD readied missile facilities and missiles for acceptance by the Strategic Air Command. While deployment accelerated, BSD developed follow-on Minuteman II and III missiles.

On July 1, 1967, BSD and SSD were combined to become the Space and Missile Systems Organization (SAMSO). While the headquarters of this new command was established at Los Angeles AFS, the Minuteman offices remained at Norton.

With a treaty limiting additional ICBM deployments, the United States became concerned in the late 1970s with the survivability of its deterrent force. Exploring new basing schemes and missile systems increased the SAMSO's workload and on October 1, 1979, SAMSO was split into Headquarters, Ballistic Missile Organization (BMO) and Headquarters, Space Division.

BMO assumed responsibility for all ICBM programs under development such as the Peacekeeper MX and small ICBM. In 1989, Air Force Systems Command redesignated the Norton-based command as Ballistic Systems Division. In 1990, the previous name was restored; however, the organization become subordinate to the Space Systems Division at Los Angeles AFS.

References: "Air Force Ballistic Missile Program," (K146.01-106A), [AFHO]; Chronology of the Ballistic Missile Organization: 1945–1990, (Norton AFB, CA: Ballistic Missile Organization History Office, 1990), pp. 1–11.

Beale Air Force Base

Originally a World War II Army bombing and gunnery range named for the founder of the U.S. Army Camel Corps, this base was declared surplus in 1947. However, the Air Force eventually reclaimed the facility, and in 1956, SAC took charge of this northern California installation.

On January 30, 1959, the Air Force announced plans to conduct surveys in the vicinity of Beale to determine the feasibility for missile bases. Site investigations, topographic explorations, and surveys were performed by the Corps of Engineers Sacramento District. On September 17, Col. Paul Calton, Commander of Beale's 4126th Strategic Wing, announced that the base would be the fifth Titan I missile installation.

Three complexes with three weapons each (3 x 3) were located 25 miles southwest, 37 miles west, and 71 miles northwest of Beale near the respective communities of Lincoln, Live Oak, and Chico. The Corps of Engineers also oversaw the construction at Beale AFB of mechanical, pneudraulics, cryogenic, propulsion, and liquid oxygen shops to support the nine deployed and one spare missile assigned.

---

a The Corps of Engineers Ballistic Missile Construction Office (CEBMCO) was formed on August 2, 1960 to support the Air Force-managed ICBM program.

CEBMCO had its genesis in 1956 as a Project Office within the Los Angeles District. The Project Office's fist major effort was the construction of testing and training facilities at the recently established Vandenberg AFB.

In 1959 the Project Office was upgraded to a Field Office and collocated with AFBMD. However, contracting responsibilities for the various ICBM bases were kept at the district level. Thus, for example, the Omaha District had contracting responsibility for Atlas launchers under construction in Lincoln. There was also a duplication/lack of coordination between several of the Air Force organizations. This arrangement was deemed inadequate, especially after congressional hearings highlighted inefficiencies and the Office of the Corps of Engineers responded by consolidating program management to one location. CEBMCO functions included construction surveillance, contract administration, construction progress reporting, and close liaison with the Air Force. Supporting functions included fiscal and procurement management.

After the newly formed Ballistic Missiles Division moved to Norton AFB, CEBMCO also relocated to the San Bernardino complex, arriving in June 1963. With the completion of the last 50 silos at Malmstrom AFB in 1967, CEBMCO's mission was completed and the organization deactivated.

Bids were opened on January 12, 1960, in the Empire Room of Sacramento's Hotel Senator. Peter Kiewit Sons' Company won the contract to build the silos after submitting a low bid of approximately $30.2 million. Before the job was completed, some 400 modifications to the original plans boosted construction costs to over $40 million.

Construction began on January 22, 1960. More than 600,000 cubic yards of rock and earth had to be excavated and reused as backfill. By the time the project was completed, each of the three complexes had received 32,000 cubic yards of concrete, 90 miles of cables, 300 tons of piping, and 1,800 separate supply items. Supervision of the construction initially fell on the Sacramento District; however, this responsibility was shifted on November 1, 1960, to CEBMCO.

There were six wild-cat work stoppages; only one caused an appreciable delay. In the wake of earlier labor strife at other missile sites, the Federal Government established Missile Site Relations Committees for each project. At Beale this mechanism contributed to successful management-labor relations and allowed construction to forge ahead. In addition to good labor relations, the Beale project enjoyed a good safety record. There was only one accident-related fatality.

The Air Force activated the 851st Strategic Missile Squadron (Titan I) on April 1, 1961. The first missile was moved to the 4A complex at Lincoln on February 28, 1962, where workers encountered some difficulty placing the missile in the silo. Follow-on missile installations went smoothly and the last missile was lowered into Chico complex 4C on April 20, 1962.

With missiles in place, assigned crews participated in what was called the "activation exercise procedure" in which they worked with contractors to obtain hands-on experience in maintaining the Titan I.

On May 24, 1962, during a contractor checkout, a terrific blast rocked launcher 1 at complex 4C at Chico, destroying a Titan I and causing heavy damage to the silo. After the investigation, the Air Force concluded that the two separate explosions occurred because of a blocked vent and blocked valve. On June 6, trouble again struck as a flash fire at another silo killed a worker. Subsequently, Peter Kiewit Sons' Company received a contract signed on July 30, 1962, for an initial amount of $1,250,000 to repair the silo damaged in the May blast.

In September 1962, the 851st SMS became the last Titan I Squadron to achieve alert status. After damages were repaired, the Chico complex became operational on March 9, 1963.

Two months after the squadron became fully operational, SAC subjected the unit to an Operational Readiness Inspection (ORI). The 851st SMS became the first Titan I unit to pass.

On May 16, 1964, Defense Secretary McNamara directed the accelerated phaseout of the Atlas and Titan I ICBMs. On January 4, 1965, the first Beale Titan I was taken off alert status. Within 3 months, the 851st Strategic Missile Squadron would be deactivated.

Beale AFB also hosted another type of missile during this timeframe. On August 25, 1961, the first Hound Dog missile arrived and soon thereafter was mated to a B-52.

References: For background information see Air Force Bases, *pp. 25–27 and* SAC Chronology, *pp. 32, 35-36, 39, 40, 47. For construction details see U.S. Army Corps of Engineers Ballistic Missile Construction Office, "Beale Area Historical Summary: October 1959-March 1962," pp. 15, 19, 85–87, and Joseph J. Hagwood,* Commitment to Excellence, A History of the Sacramento District U.S. Army Corps of Engineers: 1929–1973, *(Sacramento, CA: U.S. Army Engineer District, 19761, pp. 88–92, [HQCE]; Site activation information was obtained from "History of the 4126th Strategic Wing, Heavy: 1 February–30 April 1962," (K-WG-4126-HI), pp. 42–49, [AFHO].*

Edwards Air Force Base

Edwards AFB is home to the Air Force Flight Test Center. In addition to its role in military flight testing and providing a landing strip and facilities for NASA's Space Shuttle program, Edwards has also hosted activities that have contributed to the nation's missile programs. Rocketry goes back to pre-World War II days when the California Institute of Technology Guggenheim Aeronautics Laboratory used sites at the location then known as Muroc Army Air Field to test primitive engine designs. In the 1990s this tradition is carried on by Phillips Laboratory.

Phillips Laboratory

In 1947, the Power Plant Laboratory of the Air Materiel Command, headquartered at Wright Field, Ohio, selected the

Luehman Ridge at Muroc to be the site of the new Experimental Rocket Engine Test Station. In April 1947 Aerojet Engineering Corporation received the contract for the initial set of test stands and the Corps of Engineers received responsibility for design and construction of nontechnical facilities. Construction costs between November 1949 and December 31, 1952, would amount to $5 million. Construction of the technical facilities began in February 1950. As work proceeded, the facility came under the command of the newly formed Air Research and Development Command (ARDC).

Test Stand l-5 received its baptism by fire on February 26, 1952, testing a BOMARC engine from Aerojet Engineering Corporation. Within a week, Test Stand l-3 withstood the blast from a Navaho missile engine.

With the establishment of the Western Development Division (WDD) at Inglewood, California, under Brig. Gen. Bernard A. Schriever in July 1954, the Engine Test Station played an important role in the Air Force's Atlas ICBM program. The first Atlas engine test-firing occurred in November 1954. The G.A. Fuller Construction Company received a contract in 1955 for another test stand, and in 1956, the ALCO Company completed construction on a Missile Assembly Building.

With the addition of more testing facilities, "captive testing" of Atlas, Thor, and other missile propulsion systems continued through the 1950s. The tests were mostly successful. However, an Atlas missile explosion on March 27, 1959, destroyed Test Stand 1-A.

At the time of the Atlas mishap, experiments using small 2.75-inch thick rockets were demonstrating the feasibility of launching missiles from underground silos. The testing expanded to launch one-third scale and then full-scale tethered Minuteman missiles from underground silos. On September 15, 1959, the first of eight full-scale tethered launches used a Minuteman ICBM with a partially charged first stage and dummy second and third stages. With the missile attached to a 2,000-foot nylon cable, the feasibility of silo launching was demonstrated. The successful testing significantly contributed to decisions about how and where to deploy Minuteman missiles.

Also in 1959, the Wright Air Development Center transferred responsibility for rocket propulsion development to the Air Force Flight Test Center (AFFTC). Four years later, the test stands and associated facilities at Edwards were designated the Rocket Propulsion Laboratory (RPL). Rocket boosters for missiles, space-craft, and military satellites continued to be tested through the end of the Cold War and beyond. In 1987, RPL was redesignated the Astronautics Laboratory. On December 13, 1990, the Astronautics Laboratory was merged into a larger research organization. This new organization, Phillips Laboratory, combined the assets of four Air Force research facilities. Although headquartered at Kirtland AFB, New Mexico, Phillips maintains an active presence at Edwards at former Astronautics Laboratory facilities.

References: Early testing at Muroc is detailed in records, photographs, and oral interviews maintained at the Caltech and JPL Archives. During the 1960s RPL submitted annual history reports to the AFFTC historian. These reports are maintained at the AFFTC history office. Later annual reports should be maintained at RPL. Maxwell AFB is a repository for both AFFTC and RPL/AL/PL annual history reports. The Phillips Lab historian is located at Kirtland Air Force Base, NM.

McClellan Air Force Base

Sacramento Air Materiel Area

Having a reputation built on the program management and maintenance of fighter aircraft, the Sacramento Air Materiel Area (SMAMA) also had logistical support responsibilities for the SM-64 Navaho missile until June 1957. At that time, an Air Materiel Command directive removed Sacramento from direct support of missile programs.

However, Sacramento's location in relation to Vandenberg AFB and Lockheed facilities in the San Francisco area ideally suited this command to become the major focal point for space logistics. For example, in May 1959, SMAMA became the prime support manager for the Air Force Discoverer satellite program. Follow-on programs included the Agena space vehicle and the SAMOS and MIDAS satellite systems. SMAMA provided indirect support for ICBM programs by maintaining the tanks for holding the corrosive fuels and oxidizers needed for liquid-fueled rocket engines and by establishing a branch facility at Vandenberg AFB to work on telemetry and guidance components prior to missile launches.

References: Bonnie A. Olson, Fenton L. Williams, "SMAMA Mission and Management: 1 July 1960–30 June 1961," (K205.10–27) pp. 1–2, 7, [AFHO]; Helen Rice, History of the Ogden Air Materiel Area, Hill Air Force Base, Utah: 1934–1960, (Hill AFB, UT: Air Force Logistics Command History Office,

March 1963), pp. 197–199, [AFHO]; Maurice A. Miller, ed., McClellan Air Force Base, 1936–1982: A Pictorial History, (Sacramento Air Logistics Center, CA: Office of History, 1982), pp. 92–93, [AFHO].

Norton Air Force Base

San Bernardino Air Materiel Area

In addition to serving as home to the Ballistic Missile Organization, Norton AFB hosted the San Bernardino Air Materiel Area (SBAMA).

Under the command of Air Materiel Command and later Air Force Logistics Command, SBAMA, to quote an organizational history, "carried a heavy responsibility in the defense of the Free World."

The claim can be made with some justice, for in the late 1950s, the Air Force charged SBAMA with the responsibility of providing over-all logistical support to Atlas and Titan I ballistic missile bases. As the nation's primary ballistic missile logistic center, SBAMA had worldwide supply, maintenance, and procurement responsibilities not only for deployment sites within the United States, but also for Thor sites based in England.

Perhaps one of the greatest challenges this organization faced occurred in the mid-1960s, when the Air Force Logistics Command established a central management office at SBAMA for the deactivation of America's first generation of missile bases. SBAMA oversaw four phases, which included (1) removal/transportation and storage of missiles, (2) preservation of complexes, (3) screening and reutilization, and (4) disposition of the installed equipment and properties.

In an effort to cut deactivation costs, the Air Force worked with the Defense Supply Agency (DSA) and General Services Administration (GSA) to screen the sites for reusable items. For example, some 270 diesel generators that had once supplied electrical power for the missile complexes were designated for use in Vietnam. To extract reusable items at no cost to the government, the Air Force used, for the first time, a service/ salvage contract. This arrangement called for the contractor to extract, at no cost to the government, those items designated for reuse. In turn, the contractor could salvage the remaining items and sell them.

Little compensation could be obtained for the millions of dollars spent for excavation and poured concrete. Other Federal agencies showed little interest in the sites, although some sites eventually were obtained by various state universities. GSA even ran an advertisement in The Wall Street Journal in April 1965 to stimulate interest within the private sector for site reutilization. Eventually, the sites were disposed of at a tiny fraction of the cost of construction.

With the deactivation of the first generation of missiles, SBAMA remained active in logistically supporting the Titan II until that system was removed from service in the 1980s. As the big ICBMs were retired, many of them came to San Bernardino for storage. With the closing of Norton AFB, many of these missiles were forwarded to Davis-Monthan AFB, Arizona.

References: "History of the San Bernardino Air Materiel Area: 1 July 1961–30 June 1962," Vol.I, (K205.12-381, pp. 6–9, [AFHO]; "History of the SBAMA Deactivation Task Force: November 1964–June 1967," Vol. I, (K205.1204-12), [AFHO]; Frederick Taylor, "Calling Dr. Strangelove: Pentagon Hunts Users for Surplus Missiles," Wall Street Journal, (4 January 1967).

Vandenberg Air Force Base

With ICBM development receiving the highest national priority during the mid-1950s, the Air Force needed a location to test these missiles under operational conditions. Such conditions were difficult to simulate at Patrick AFB and Cape Canaveral, Florida, where missile testing had been taking place. After a nationwide search that included the evaluation of 200 different locations, in 1956 the Air Force settled on Camp Cooke, an Army facility located on the California coast 120 miles northwest of Los Angeles. Cooke was relatively far away from populated areas; enjoyed favorable climate that allowed year-round operations; had access to the ocean, which could be used as a range; and was located close to the southern California aerospace industry. Here the Air Force could build and test the missiles and launching facilities that would form the backbone of United States strategic deterrence.

In 1957, the Army transferred the northern and southern sections of the base to the Air Force and Navy, respectively. The Navy subsequently established the Naval Missile Facility at Point Arguello and the Pacific Missile Range, and maintained control of the 20,000 acre tract until 1964. At that time the Air Force assumed control of this property and the range became known as the Western Test Range. Meanwhile, much had happened on the 65,000 acres that had been renamed Vandenberg AFB on October

4, 1958, to honor the deceased former Air Force Chief of Staff.

The Air Research Development Command took control of the facility in early 1957. With Air Force control established, Headquarters U.S. Air Force, in April 1957, activated the 1st Missile Division. Later dubbed "One Strad," this organization would play important roles in training missile launch crews, supporting test launches, and performing required missile maintenance.

Throughout the duration of the Cold War, prototype launch pads, control facilities, and silos for every generation of American ICBMs were built and tested at Vandenberg AFB. The Los Angeles District of the Army Corps of Engineers played an integral part in constructing these complex facilities and their supporting administrative and housing facilities. Groundbreaking began in May 1957 for the first of these facilities and during the next 3 years the Air Force expended over $200 million on new construction and to upgrade existing facilities. Examples of support facilities include huge sheet metal covered missile assembly buildings, liquid oxygen generation plants, and instrumentation facilities.

On July 1, 1957, the 704th Strategic Missile Wing was activated to oversee activities of specific missile training squadrons scheduled to be activated in the coming months. One of these squadrons, the 392nd Missile Training Squadron assumed the duties of training prospective missilemen on the Great Britain-bound Thor IRBM. The first launch facilities completed included seven launch pads and three blockhouses for the conduct of Thor IRBM testing. These complexes would later become known as SLC-1, SLC-2, and SLC-10. On December 16, 1958, a crew from the First Missile Division successfully launched a Thor IRBM, inaugurating the intermediate-range ballistic missile portion of the Pacific Missile Range. The following April, a Royal Air Force crew duplicated the feat.

In January 1958, ARDC transferred the base to the Strategic Air Command (SAC). With facilities under construction for America's first ICBM, on April 1, 1958, Headquarters SAC activated the 576th Strategic Missile Squadron.

The first Atlas launcher to be completed (576A-1) was accepted from the contractor by the 1st Missile Division on October 16, 1958. The first Atlas D missile arrived the following February. Initially, the squadron's Atlas D missiles were deployed at complexes 576A and 576B. Complex 576A consisted of three above-ground gantries; 576B had three above-ground coffin launchers of a type that would be constructed at other sites. Each complex had one launch control center.

The 576th SMS launched its first Atlas D on September 9, 1959. Immediately following the launch, SAC's Commander in Chief, General Thomas S. Power declared Vandenberg's Atlas missile operational. A month later, the squadron's Atlas missiles were placed on an alert status. The activation had more psychological value than military value as the reliability of the Atlas D missile was highly questionable. Improved versions were already undergoing production along with launch facilities to support them. As the above-ground sites became operational, construction continued on a buried coffin launcher to hold an Atlas E missile (designated launch site 576C) and work began on two Atlas F silo lift launchers (576D and 576E). By 1962, 11 prototype Atlas complexes had been constructed at Vandenberg AFB.

On July 31, 1958, construction began on the Operational System Test Facility for the Titan I missile. This facility would serve as the prototype of the hardened Titan I launch control facility. By the fall of 1960, four Titan I lift silos had been completed with three training silos (395 A-1,-2, and -3) grouped at one complex and a fourth located in a separate area. In December 1960, an explosion ripped through this silo during a simulated launch, resulting in massive damage. By early 1961, four silos were completed or undergoing completion for the follow-on Titan II system.

With the deactivation of first generation ICBMs in 1965, Vandenberg's Atlas and Titan I sites were deactivated with major equipment being salvaged. The last Titan II site remained in service until 1977.

Vandenberg also played an important role in the Minuteman program. In 1961 construction began on six Minuteman silos and a launch control facility. By 1965, fourteen silos for Minuteman I and II missiles dotted the base's Casmalia hills south of Point Sal. Later, seven of these silos were modified to fire Minuteman III missiles. Three of these complexes underwent further modification in the 1980s to launch Peacekeeper MX ICBMs. Activated in 1960, the 394th Strategic Missile Squadron handled training and operations at these sites.

In April 1967, Vandenberg hosted a SAC-sponsored missile combat competition called "Operation Curtain Raiser" with crews from Titan II and Minuteman Wings participating. Eventually dubbed "Olympic Arena," this event grew to be an annual event with teams competing for the Blanchard Perpetual

Trophy and other honors such as the Best Combat Crew, Best Targeting Team, Best Communications Team, Best Munitions Maintenance Team Award, and Best Missile Handling Team. These annual events enhanced professionalism and *esprit de corps* among America's missilemen and provided training opportunities since annual events often were planned to coincide with test launchings that often used the visiting crews to perform the task.

In addition to being used to evaluate the capabilities of operational ICBMs and serving as a launch location for many of America's military satellites, Vandenberg played an important role in America's antiballistic missile efforts. In 1962, an Army Nike Zeus missile launched from Kwajalein Island successfully intercepted an Atlas D ICBM launched from Vandenberg. Many additional launched targets gave the Army opportunities to perfect its interceptor missiles and tracking capabilities.

By 1968, Vandenberg's 98,000 acres covered an area double that of the nation's capital, and supported a population of over 28,000. Some 1,076 buildings, 1,983 housing units, 797 trailer spaces, and a massive utility infrastructure supported the base mission.

In 1981, Space Launch Complex (SLC) 10/Thor, considered the best surviving example of 1950s launch technology, was placed on the National Register of Historic Places. The complex includes the launch pad, blockhouse, support buildings, roll-away shelter and an SM-75 Thor missile. In 1988, the Missile Heritage Foundation opened a museum at SLC-10 dedicated to preserving the history of the Air Force ICBM programs.

References: SAC Chronology, pp. 13, 17-18, 20, 23. Details on early activities can be found in Carl Berger, 1st Missile Division, 1957-1960, (Vandenberg AFB, CA: History Office, 1960); Ray A. Hanner, The 576th Strategic Missile Squadron (Atlas-ICBM), 1958-1961, (Vandenberg AFB, CA: History Office, 1961), and The First Strategic Aerospace Division, 1962-1963, (Vandenberg AFB, CA: History Office, 1964). The Los Angeles District's contribution is discussed in Anthony F. Turhollow, A History of the Los Angeles District, U.S. Army Corps of Engineers: 1898-1965, (Los Angeles, CA: U.S. Army Engineer District, 1975), pp. 301-304, [HQCE]. David A. Anderton discusses crew training at Vandenberg and has a chapter describing Olympic Arena 1973 in Strategic Air Command: Two-thirds of the Triad, (New York: Charles Scribner's Sons, 1976), pp. 150-156.

A R M Y

Salton Sea Test Base

Located in the California desert east of San Diego, this site provided ideal conditions for low-attitude Nike Ajax test firings, which were conducted in the 1950s.

Reference: Mary Cagle, Nike Ajax Historical Monograph: Development, Production and Deployment of the Nike Ajax Guided Missile System 1945–1959, (Huntsville, AL: Army Ordnance Missile Command, 1959), p. 172.

Los Angeles Defense Area

By the late 1950s Los Angeles was ringed by 16 Nike sites:

(LA-04) Mt. Gleason/Palmdale
(LA-09) Mt. Disappointment/Barley Flats
(LA-14) South El Monte
(LA-29) Brea/Puente Hill
(LA-32) Garden Grove/Stanton
(LA-40) Long Beach Airport/Lakewood
(LA-43) Fort MacArthur/White Point
(LA-55) Point Vicente
(LA-57) Redondo Beach/Torrance
(LA-70) Hyperion/Playa del Rey
(LA-73) Playa del Rey/LAX
(LA-78) Malibu
(LA-88) Chatsworth/Oat Mountain
(LA-94) Los Pinetos/Newhall
(LA-96) Van Nuys/Sepulveda
(LA-98) Magic Mountain/Laug/Saugus.

Headquarters sites were located at Signal Hill/Long Beach, Fort MacArthur, and at the Birmingham Army Hospital. As indicated by the number of sites, Los Angeles, with its aerospace industries, received extensive air defenses.

By July 1952, with the Nike missile system still under development, siting teams had already tentatively selected between fifty and sixty primary and alternate sites for missile deployment. At the time, gun batteries of the Western Army Antiaircraft Command ringed Los Angeles. (This organization became the 6th AA Region in 1955.) Throughout 1953, the Corps of Engineers Los Angeles District obtained the needed properties for the batteries. Where possible, the missiles were to be located on military property. For example, one of the first batteries was located on an old coastal fortification at Fort MacArthur. At non-DOD sites, the Corps often had to overcome the resistance of private property owners and city officials reluctant to give up park land. (The struggle for a missile site location near Los Angeles International Airport was discussed in Chapter 9, America's Missile Communities: Social and Economic Impact.)

While the quest for permanent sites proceeded, a temporary Nike Ajax site was located in Fountain Valley at the former Santa Ana Army Air Base during 1956 and 1957. Meanwhile, the Los Angeles District contracted for the construction of permanent facilities. Site LA-88 at Chatsworth became the first permanent operational battery in the nation in 1954. LA-04, located on the top of Mt. Gleason, was noted as one of the most remote and highest Nike bases in the nation. The support buildings at this base and the other mountain sites had Swiss-style roofs to accommodate the heavy snows. In addition to snow, soldiers manning the mountain sites also had to worry about fire. For example, in 1959, men of Battery B, 1st Missile Battalion, 56th Artillery, engaged in a 24-hour-a-day, 7-day vigil to preserve Nike control radars atop Mt. Disappointment from the flames of an inferno that had consumed much of Angeles National Forrest. Seven years later, a similar feat had to be performed by Battery A, 4th Missile Battalion, 65th Artillery, as flames encroached on LA-94 at Los Pinetos.

In the fall of 1958, the Army turned over the batteries at Long Beach and Fort MacArthur to the 720th AA4 Missile Battalion of the California Army National Guard. The Los Angeles Defense Area became a national leader for using Guard units to operate the sites. Eventually, National Guard units assumed responsibilities for manning other sites.

By the early 1960s LA-04, LA-29, LA-32, LA-43, LA-55 LA-78 LA-88 LA-94, and LA-96 were all converted to operate the Hercules missile. Command and control for the batteries was coordinated from a "Missile Master" facility dedicated in 1961 at Fort MacArthur.

The excellent Southern California climate promoted scores of recreational activities for the missilemen. Because of the proximity of these batteries to Hollywood, the missilemen often received visits from movie stars and other celebrities posing for photographs. Batteries often hosted open houses and demonstrations for the not-so-famous. During the late 1950s several of the batteries

held beauty contests for the regional "Miss Armed Forces Day" pageant.

In 1968, the Army deactivated LA-94 at Los Pinetos/Newhall. LA-29 at Brea/Puenta Hill closed 3 years later. In 1974, the remaining seven Nike Hercules sites were removed from service.

References: Nike Quick Look, *pp. 77–82; Mary T. Cagle,* Historical Monograph: Development, Production and Deployment of the Nike Ajax Guided Missile System 1945–1959, *(Huntsville, AL: Army Ordnance Missile Command, 1959), pp. 190–192, discussed the land acquisition controversy; Anthony F. Turhollow,* A History of the Los Angeles District, U.S. Army Corps of Engineers: 1898–1965, *(Los Angeles, CA: U.S. Army Engineer District, 1975), p. 300, briefly details the Corps role in site construction [HQCE]. Roger Hatheway and Stephen Van Wormer, "Historical Cultural Resources Survey and Evaluation of the Nike Missile Site at Fort MacArthur, White Point, Los Angeles County, California," and "Historical Cultural Resources Survey and Evaluation of the Nike Missile Sites in the Angeles National Forest," prepared by WESTEC Services Inc. for U.S. Army Corps of Engineers, Los Angeles District, February 1987, detailed these particular batteries and provided an overview of Nike operations in the Los Angeles region. The significance of the Guard takeover of Los Angeles sites is detailed in Bruce Jacobs, "Nike Hercules Air Defense is Phased Out of the Army National Guard,"* The National Guardsman, *(November 1974) and a 1968 ARADCOM study by Timothy Osato titled "Militia Missilemen: The Army National Guard in Air Defense 1951–1967," [CMI].* Argus *articles frequently detail VIP visits and activities at the sites [MHI].*

San Francisco Defense Area

By the late 1950s a dozen Nike sites ringed the bay area:

(SF-08)	San Pablo Ridge
(SF-59)	Fort Funston/Mt. San Bruno
(SF-09)	San Pablo Ridge/Berkeley (double site)
(SF-87)	Fort Cronkhite/Sausalito
(SF-25)	Rocky Ridge
(SF-88)	Fort Barry/Sausalito
(SF-31)	Lake Chabot/Castro Valley
(SF-89)	Fort Winfield Scott
(SF-37)	Coyote Hills/Newark
(SF-91)	Angel Island

(SF-51)   Milagra/Pacifica

(SF-93)   San Rafael

In addition, during 1955 and 1956, temporary Nike Ajax sites were placed at Benicia and Parks AFB. Headquarters facilities were located at the Presidio, Fort Winfield Scott, and Fort Baker.

Responsibility for the acquisition of land and the installation of Nike batteries plus support facilities in the San Francisco region fell to the Corps of Engineers San Francisco District. The missiles often replaced gun batteries that had been quickly constructed around the Golden Gate vicinity in the early 1950s. Fort Baker became the home of the Western Army Antiaircraft Command in July 1951. By 1958, this organization evolved into the 6th Region, U.S. Army Air Defense Command. Since the Corps took advantage of abandoned coastal fortifications to site the missiles, before construction commenced on underground magazines, many of the old forts received temporary above-ground launchers.

San Francisco's defenders included both Regular Army and National Guard units. Site SF-88 received the first Nike Hercules Battery in 1959. Other sites that were upgraded to host the new missile included sites SF-31, SF-51, SF-87, and SF-93. Target designation functions were handled from a "Missile Master" facility located at Mill Valley AFS. With the deactivation of Nike Ajax sites, a "Missile Mentor" system took over the command and control duties.

Sites SF-87 at Fort Cronkhite/Sausalito and SF-93 at San Rafael were deactivated in 1971. Three years later, the U.S. Army Air Defense Command deactivated the remaining three missile batteries at SF-31, SF-51, and SF-88.

When the Army abandoned the launch area of SF-88 at Fort Barry in 1974, the National Park Service assumed custody of the site, incorporating it into the Golden Gate National Recreation Area. Through the efforts of various volunteer groups, as of 1995, this is the only Nike site in the country that has been preserved and is open for public viewing.

References: Nike Quick Look, *pp. 120–123; Joseph J. Hagwood, Jr.,* Engineers at the Golden Gate, *(San Francisco, CA: U.S. Army Engineer District, 1980), pp. 270–272, [HQCE]; and "Nike Missile Site SFSSL, Fort Barry, Self-Guided Tour," prepared by the Golden Gate National Recreation Area, National Park Service, n.d.*

Travis Air Force Base Defense Area

Before becoming a Military Airlift Command base, Travis hosted SAC bombers and thus required air defense at sites, which were located at Elmira (T-101, Dixon/Lambie (T-33), Potrero Hills (T-53), and Fairfield/Cement Hills (T-86). Regular Army units manned the sites ringing the air base. Elmira (T-10) and Fairfield/Cement Hills (T-86) received modifications to accept the Nike Hercules missile. The former site remained active until 1974 while the latter closed in 1971. Headquarters facilities were located at Travis AFB.

During the late 1960s and early 1970s the Travis battalion assumed responsibility for the remaining active batteries guarding the entire San Francisco region.

The Corps of Engineers San Francisco District commenced work in 1959 on a BOMARC installation at Travis. However, on March 25, 1960, the Air Force announced a $300 million cutback in the program and work ceased at the site.

Reference: Nike Quick Look, *pp. 131–132.*

Jet Propulsion Laboratory

In 1936, the California Institute of Technology (Caltech) founded the Guggenheim Aeronautical Laboratory, which became the nation's first center devoted to the research and development of rocket and propulsion systems. Before and during the early war years, the laboratory developed jet-assisted takeoff (JATO) units for the Army. In November 1943, Laboratory Director Dr. Theodore von Kármán submitted a proposal to Army Ordnance for a long-range surface-to-surface missile. This effort eventually became known as Project ORDCIT and resulted in the development of Private "A" and Corporal missiles. In 1943, Caltech reorganized the research operation into the Jet Propulsion Laboratory (JPL). JPL worked under contract for the Army Ordnance Department to advance missile research. Caltech scientists also worked with Army personnel to participate in testing at locations such as Camp Irwin, California; Fort Bliss, Texas; and White Sands, New Mexico. Working with manufacturers on projects such as the Corporal, JPL was responsible for airframe design. JPL also built the rocket motor and other parts and telemetry equipment. The laboratory also served as the prime contractor for the Army Sergeant surface-to-surface missile programs during the 1950s. On

March 31, 1958, JPL became a contracted component of the Huntsville-based Army Ordnance Missile Command. However, JPL's days working for the Department of Defense were limited, for on October 21, 1959, President Eisenhower decided to transfer Army rocket research activities to the National Air and Space Administration (NASA). From the 1960s until the present, JPL has served as a major research contractor for NASA.

References: SAC Chronology, pp. 2–3; Helen Brents Joiner and Elizabeth C. Joliff, History of the United States Army Missile Command: 1962–1977, (Redstone Arsenal, Huntsville, AL: U.S. Army Missile Command, 1979), pp. 1–4. Both Caltech and JPL have archival holdings documenting institutional contributions to missile programs.

COLORADO

A I R   F O R C E

Ent Air Force Base

Although no missiles were ever stationed at this former base located in Colorado Springs, it played a key role in the nation's air defense. During the 1950s and 1960s the base hosted the Continental Air Defense Command (CONAD) and successor North American Air Defense Command (NORAD) as well as the component Army Air Defense Command (ARADCOM).

Cheyenne Mountain

Because of the vulnerability of Ent AFB to nuclear attack, planning began in 1956 for a secure command post. The Corps of Engineers Omaha District oversaw the massive effort to dig out caverns within Cheyenne Mountain located near Fort Carson. On May 2, 1961, Utah Construction won the bid for the excavation work of the granite mountain. In February 1963, another bid opening placed interior construction work in the hands of Continental Consolidated Corporation. By February 1966, the "rock" was completed and the North American Air Defense Command began to shift operations from Ent AFB.

The underground city would be manned at all times by approximately 425 Americans and Canadians monitoring a wide array of distant sensors warning of possible attack.

Reference: The Federal Engineer, Damsites to Missile Sites: A History of the Omaha District U.S. Army Corps of Engineers, (Omaha, NE: U.S. Army Engineer District, 1984), pp. 199–213, provides details on this massive construction project, [HQCE].

F.E. Warren Air Force Base (Wyoming)

Missile launchers associated with Wyoming's F.E. Warren AFB are placed throughout northeastern Colorado. In 1960 and 1961, Atlas E missiles were delivered to prepared sites located in the vicinity of Grover, Briggsdale, Nunn, Greeley, and Fort Collins. Placed horizontally in "coffin" shelters, these missiles of the 549th (later 566th) Strategic Missile Squadron remained on alert status until March 1965.

By this time about four dozen Minuteman I-B silos had been placed in scattered locations throughout this region. These silos came under the jurisdiction of the 319th, 320th, and 321st Strategic Missile Squadrons.

Reference: See F.E. Warren Air Force Base under Wyoming.

Lowry Air Force Base

Founded in the 1930s as a branch of the Air Corps Technical Training School, Lowry continued to train airmen and serve the nation in various other capacities for over 60 years. Lowry was unique in that it remained an Air Training Command base during the timespan when 18 Titan I missile silos, situated in 6 complexes, ringed the area.

On June 7, 1951, Lowry's 3415th Technical Training Wing formed a Guided Missiles Department. It taught courses in guidance, control, and propulsion for such systems as Matador, Falcon, Rascal, Snark, and Navaho. By 1962, the Department of Missile Training was providing the Air Force with over 1,000 trained missile specialists per year.

On March 13, 1958, the Air Force Ballistic Committee approved the selection of Lowry to be the first Titan I ICBM base. No doubt the close proximity of the Martin Company Titan missile production plant influenced the site selection. Construction of launchers and support facilities began on May 1, 1959. Deployment of the missiles entailed a 3 x 3 configuration, meaning that each of the three complexes had three silos grouped in close proximity to a manned launch control facility,

The Omaha District of the Army Corps of Engineers contracted a joint venture led by Morrison-Knudsen of Boise, Idaho, to construct the silos. A 144-day steel strike in 1959 caused delays and forced Morrison-Knudsen to resort to winter concreting. Despite this problem and others caused by constant design modifications, Morrison-Knudsen completed the project on time with the lowest construction costs of any ICBM base in the country at the time. Fairly smooth management-labor relations contributed to the success.

The project also maintained the best safety record in the missile construction program up until that time. Use of a safety net was credited with saving many lives. Three workers did die during the project, although one of these deaths was the result of a motor vehicle accident that occurred off site.

As construction proceeded, the activation of the 848th SMS on February 1, 1960, marked the first stand-up of a Titan I Squadron. Construction on all nine silos at the three launch complexes for the former 84th, redesignated the 724th, was completed by August 4, 1961. On April 18,1962, Headquarters SAC declared the 724th SMS operational, and 2 days later the first Titan Is went on alert status. A month later, the sister 725th SMS (initially designated the 849th SMS) declared it had placed all nine of its Titan Is on alert status, which marked a SAC first. Both the 724th and 725th Strategic Missile Squadrons formed components of the Lowry-headquartered 451st Strategic Missile Wing.

On November 19, 1964, Defense Secretary McNamara announced the phase-out of remaining first-generation Atlas and Titan I missiles by the end of June 1965. This objective was met; on June 25, 1965, the 724th SMS and 725th SMS were inactivated. SAC removed the last missile from Lowry on April 14, 1965.

Although the strategic missiles were gone, missile training remained a vital component of Lowry's mission. In 1972, the 3415th Technical School became the USAF School of Applied Aerospace Sciences with missile training continuing within the Department of Aerospace Munitions Training. In 1978, this department would be redesignated the 3460th Training Group.

In 1980, Lowry Technical Training Center acquired a B-52D from Davis-Monthan AFB, Arizona, and stabilized another B-52 on base for use in training crews to load Air Launched Cruise Missiles (ALCMs) and Short Range Air Missiles (SRAMs). Although Chanute AFB, Illinois, served as the primary training center for the Peacekeeper ICBM, Lowry supported training for this strategic missile by providing maintenance and repair training for the Peacekeepers' reentry vehicle at a state-of-the-art facility opened in 1985.

Lowry AFB was deactivated in 1994 as a result of a Base Realignment and Closure Act.

References: Air Force Bases, *pp. 331–337;* The Federal Engineer, Damsites to Missile Sites: A History of the Omaha Dist*rict U.S. Army Corps of Engineers, (Omaha NE: U.S. Army Engineer District, 1984), p. 192, [HQCE]; Michael H. Levy, Patrick M. Scanlan,* Pursuit of Excellence: A History of Lowry AFB, *1937–1987, (Lowry Air Force Base, CO: History Office, 1987), pp. 33, 35–36, 43, 49, 59–61, [AFHO];* SAC Chronology, *pp. 17, 22, 31, 32, 34, 35, 45;* U.S. Army Corps of Engineers Ballistic Missile Construction Office, *"Lowry Area History: 29 September 1958–16 December 1961," pp. 1-3, 62-63, 74–78,[HQCE].*

Peterson Air Force Base

In 1993 the Peterson-based Air Force Space Command inherited responsibilities for the missile wings that formerly had been under the jurisdiction of the Strategic Air Command.

A R M Y

Pueblo Depot Activity

Constructed during World War II, this facility was built to serve as an ammunition and material storage and shipping center. During the late 1950s Pueblo became a major Army missile repair and maintenance facility. The facility operated at nearly full capacity during the Vietnam era.

Although the Army eliminated most of the facility's missile maintenance responsibilities in 1975, Pueblo continued to support the Pershing missile system. At the time of the signing of the Treaty between the United States of America and the Union of Soviet Socialist Republics on the Elimination of the Intermediate-Range and Shorter-Range Missiles (INF Treaty) on December 8, 1987, 111 Pershing II missiles and 169 Pershing IA missiles were stored at this facility. Eventually these Pershing missiles were destroyed at this facility and at Longhorn Army Ammunition Plant in Texas to comply with the INF Treaty to eliminate intermediate-range missiles from the United States and former Soviet arsenals.

Pueblo's primary mission in the 1990s became the storage of chemical munitions.

References: INF Treaty; *"Historic American Engineering Record Pueblo Depot Activity," (HAER COLO 51-PUEB.V 1), [LOC].*

CONNECTICUT

A R M Y

Bridgeport Defense Area

Designations and locations of the Nike sites defending the Bridgeport area are: (BR-04) Ansonia, (BR-15) Westhaven, (BR-17) Milford, (BR-65) Fairfield, (BR-73) Westport, and (BR-94) Shelton. Headquarters facilities were located in Bridgeport.

Regular Army units manned these sites after initial activation during 1956 and 1957 with the Guard assuming duties in the waning years. Only site BR-04 was converted from Nike Ajax to Hercules. This battery would become integrated into the New England Defense Area before being deactivated in 1971.

The missilemen received recognition on April 19, 1958, when Bridgeport Mayor Samuel Tedesco declared "Nike Day" in his city. Festivities honoring the men of the 741st AAA missile battalion included a parade and ball. In addition, the missile sites were dedicated to local citizens who died in earlier wars.

References: Nike Quick Look, *pp. 31–33;* Argus, *(1 June 1958), p. 8.*

Hartford Defense Area

The designations and locations of Nike sites guarding the state capital region are as follows: (HA-08) East Windsor, (HA-25) Manchester, (HA-36) Portland, (HA-48) Cromwell, (HA-67) Plainville, and (HA-85) Avon/Simsbury.

Operational in 1956, these sites were first manned by Regular Army and later by Guard Units. Units from the Bridgeport Defense Area assisted in operating the Plainville site. Sites HA-48 and HA-08 were converted to fire the Nike Hercules missile and remained operational until 1968 and 1971, respectively.

Reference: Nike Quick Look, *pp. 65–67.*

FLORIDA

A I R   F O R C E

Patrick Air Force Base/Cape Canaveral Air Force Station

In October 1946, the Armed Forces Joint Research and Development Board created a committee to select an over-water test range for long-range missiles. The Committee on Long Range Proving Grounds initially selected California's El Centro Marine Corps Base but abandoned the site after a breakdown in talks with the Mexican Government regarding sovereignty rights for needed tracking stations. Next, the committee looked at the recently deactivated Banana River Naval Air Station located on Florida's east coast. Featuring a climate allowing year-round operations, isolation, government-owned property, an existing infrastructure associated with a naval air station, and islands downrange that would allow for tracking facilities, the area near Cape Canaveral became the committee's final selection for what would become America's spaceport.

In May 1949, President Truman authorized the establishment of a joint long-range proving ground at the eastern Florida site and a month later the Banana River Naval Air Station was reactivated. In August 1950, the facility became Patrick AFB, home to the Air Force Missile Test Center (AFMTC).

Initial responsibility for construction at the Cape and Patrick AFB fell to the Jacksonville District of the Corps of Engineers. Tasked in May 1950 with building the pad for the first missile launch at the Cape, the District succeeded in having the facility ready in time for the July 24 lift-off of a V-2 with a WAC Corporal upper stage (missile test number Bumper No. 8).

Throughout the 1950s the Jacksonville District supervised the construction of missile service gantries, control bunkers, assembly and research buildings, and other support structures. These facilities supported research, development, testing, and evaluation for such air-breathing weapons as Matador, Snark, Mace, and BOMARC.[a] In addition, the Corps built a deep-water port to allow the delivery of large components.

The Matador, first launched from the Cape on June 20, 1951, became the first Cape-tested weapon to enter the Air Force operational inventory. From 1951 to 1962, 286 Matadors lifted off into the Atlantic sky from Complexes 1–3. Another air-breathing missile to undergo extensive testing at AFTMC was the Snark. From August 29, 1951, to December 5, 1960, 97 Snarks were tested. As a follow-on to the Matador, the Martin Company produced the Mace, which underwent testing at the Cape between 1959 and 1962. Testing for the BOMARC area defense weapon began at the Cape and later continued at Eglin AFB, Florida. One AFMTC-tested long-range missile that never deployed, the Navaho, pioneered inertial guidance and large rocket engine technology that would find its way into IRBMs and ICBMs.

On August 30, 1953, the Army's Redstone became the first ballistic missile to lift off from the Cape. Two years later, the Army began testing to support development of its Jupiter IRBM. In May 1957, a Jupiter prototype launched from the Cape recorded a flight of 1,050 miles. Meanwhile, the Air Force began testing its Thor IRBM at the Florida facility in January 1957. The first successful Thor launch occurred the following October.

Cape Canaveral played a critical role in ICBM development. Atlas models A through F underwent constant testing in the late 1950s as did the Titan I. Later, the Air Force also tested its Titan II and Minuteman ICBMs at the Cape. In addition, the Navy constructed and used Cape facilities to test its sea-launched ballistic missiles. Of course Cape Canaveral became best known for its role in America's manned space program.

Because of the growth of the space program, on May 1, 1963, the Corps of Engineers created a new Canaveral District to supervise Cape construction. Eight years later, this District was disestablished with functions being assumed by a newly created Florida office of the Mobile District.

References: Mark C. Cleary, The 6555th: Missile and Space Launches Through 1970, *(Patrick AFB, FL: 45th Space Wing History Office, 1991) and George E. Buker,* Sun, Sand and Water: History of the Jacksonville District, U.S. Army Corps of Engineers, 1821–1975, *(Jacksonville, FL: U.S. Army Engineer District, n.d.1, pp. 193–202 [HQCE].*

Eglin Air Force Base

Established as a bombing and gunnery base in the 1930s, Eglin Field became an important armaments testing facility for the Army Air Force during World War II.

During the war, two projects at Eglin involved the German V-1 "buzz bomb." In January 1944, Eglin became an important contributor to "Operation Crossbow," which called for the destruction of German missile launching facilities. Thousands worked around the clock for twelve days to construct a duplicate German V-1 facility. Subsequent bombing runs against this copycat facility taught Army Air Forces tacticians which attack angles and weapons would prove most effective against the German launchers. Tactics learned at Eglin were effectively implemented as the Germans began launching cruise missiles against Great Britain.

Assistant Secretary of War for Air, Robert A. Lovett, returned from Britain just after commencement of the first V-1 attacks and determined that the United States should have a program similar to the German missile effort. With possession of an unexploded V-1 in the summer of 1944, American manufacturers quickly duplicated the jet-bomb and Eglin received its first "JB-2" for testing in the fall of 1944. With successful results, the missile was ordered into production and the Proving Ground formed a launching squadron to deploy the weapon against Japan. This unit was in place in the Philippines ready to launch American buzz bombs against Japan when the atomic bombings negated their mission.

With the sudden end of the war, the Army Air Force had several hundred JB-2s in its arsenal. On January 26, 1946, Army Air Forces created the First Experimental Guided Missiles Group to develop and test missiles at Eglin Field. In the immediate post-war years, this organization launched and evaluated the JB-2 and performed extensive work with drone aircraft.

The Climatic Laboratory Building, which could simulate climatic conditions from around the world, received its first customers in May 1947, as several aircraft entered the hangar for testing. In the following decades this facility would be used, modified, and expanded to test the reliability of numerous aircraft and missile systems.

On December 1, 1957, Eglin AFB became home to the newly established Air Proving Ground Center. At this time, the Air Research Development Command was proceeding with plans to move additional testing and evaluation of the BOMARC surface-

---

[a] Snark and BOMARC are discussed in Part I. Mace and Matador were built by the Martin Company as intermediate-range cruise missiles for overseas deployment. The two missiles resembled swept-wing fighter planes without cockpits.

to-air missile from Canaveral Air Force Station to Eglin's Hurlbert Field located across from Santa Rosa Island along the West Florida Gulf Coast. Preliminary planning for this move had started back in October 1955. Site construction at Hurlbert had been in progress since March 1957 and by 1958 the field hosted missile ground testing and personnel training facilities. Meanwhile, launchers were constructed so that BOMARCs could be fired into what became known as the Eglin Gulf Test Range. The first BOMARC launch from Santa Rosa Island occurred on January 15 1959. From 1959 through 1960, the BOMARC A underwent continual testing at this site, flying against various drone aircraft. In the early 1960s testing continued with the BOMARC B model. Designated the IM-99B, this missile underwent its inaugural service test on April 13, 1960. On March 3, 1961, an IM-99B demonstrated the ability to intercept a target at a range of over 400 miles at an altitude of over 80,000 feet. The test program for BOMARC A and B concluded in August 1963 after nearly 150 launches. BOMARC B launchings continued into the 1970s as each Air Defense Missile Squadron took turns conducting missile shoots.

As the home of the Air Force Proving Ground Center, other major missile and guided munitions programs underwent evaluation at Eglin. In 1960, Eglin-based B-52s launched prototype Hound Dog missiles and Quail decoy missiles. As America became actively engaged in Vietnam, technological advances on guided munitions were validated at Eglin.

Eglin's responsibilities were increased as on August 1, 1968, the Air Proving Ground Center was redesignated the Armament Development and Test Center. In addition to research, development, test, and evaluation functions, Eglin acquired procurement functions from the Aeronautical Systems Division located at Wright-Patterson APB, Ohio.

In October 1979, the Armament Development and Test Center was redesignated as the Armament Division of the Air Force Systems Command. In 1989 another name change designed to clarify organizational purpose occurred as the Armament Division became the Munitions Division.

References: Chronological Syllabus of the Armament Division-Part Two, The War Years: 1942–45, *(Eglin AFB, FL: Armament Division History Office, 1982), pp. 31–33, 44–45, 74–77;* Chronology Munition Systems Division: 1946–1989, *(Eglin AFB, FL: Munition Systems Division History Office, 1989), pp. 5, 8, 13, 28, 31, 35–46, 65, 102, 140;* SAC Chronology, *pp. 2, 22–23, 27;* Nike Quick Look, *p. 161.*

Tyndall Air Force Base

Home of the Air Warfare Center, doctrines for the use of tactical air-to-air missiles were developed at Tyndall. In 1958, Tyndall became the host for the biennial air-to-air weapons meet that was nicknamed William Tell. By 1986, the meet had grown from a airto-air rocketry meet into an inclusive competition involving aircrews, maintenance teams, and weapons loading specialists.

A R M Y

Homestead-Miami Defense Area

In 1958, an objectives plan of the North American Air Defense Command called for the deployment of 41 Hawk batteries along the Gulf Coast by fiscal year 1961 with Florida receiving twelve of these batteries. Despite the undetected arrival of a defecting Cuban B-26 at Daytona Beach in January 1959, the vulnerability of America's southern frontier was not apparent until the Cuban missile crisis. As part of America's posturing against the Soviet Union over the issue of missiles in Cuba, a rapid buildup of forces occurred in Florida. Part of this buildup included antiaircraft missile batteries.

Command of the arriving missile units was assumed by the Headquarters and Headquarters Battery, 13th Artillery Group, formerly of Fort Meade, Maryland, which arrived at Homestead AFB on October 30, 1962. By November 8, this command unit moved 4 miles north to a location at Princeton.

Two missile battalions arrived and quickly deployed their batteries. The 8th Battalion, 15th Artillery arrived from Fort Lewis, Washington, and set up Hawk missiles at Patrick, MacDill, and Homestead AFBs. Longer-range Hercules missiles of the 2nd Battalion, 52nd Artillery based at Fort Bliss, Texas, arrived on November 1, and within two weeks the battalion's three batteries had achieved operational status defending skies around Homestead. These missiles came equipped with high-explosive warheads.

Temporary locations included Hercules batteries at (HM-01) Opa Locka and (HM-66) eight miles southwest of Florida City, and Nike batteries at (HM-65) Florida City, (HM-05) Goulds, (HM-60) 4 miles southwest of Florida City, and (HM-80) at Miami.

With the crisis diffused, the temporary batteries remained and on April 1, 1963, these units were permanently assigned to the U.S. Army Air Defense Command (ARADCOM).

Once it became evident that the missile deployment would be long-term, the batteries were repositioned and permanent structures were built. The above-ground Nike Hercules batteries were: (HM-03) two miles northwest of Carol City, (HM-40) in North Key Largo, (HM-66) eight miles southwest of Florida City, (HM-69) twelve miles west southwest of Florida City, and (HM-95) southwest Miami. A typical Nike battery had three launchers.

Five other batteries used Hawk missiles. The designations and locations of these were: (HM-12) Miami/Old Cutler Road, (HM-39) Miami/North Canal Drive, (HM-59) six miles south of Florida City, (HM-60) four miles southwest of Florida City (relocated to site HM-59), and (HM-84) seven miles north-northwest of Homestead AFB. A Hawk site normally had six launchers with three missiles per launcher.

Headquarters facilities were located at Homestead AFB and at Naranja. Missile defense coordination was handled from Richmond Air Force Station, which hosted a "Missile Master" site. Eventually, the Army replaced Missile Master with the less costly "Birdie" system. The initial cost of the southern Florida construction program eventually topped $17 million.

The southern Florida environment posed unique challenges to these ARADCOM units as soldiers had to deal with heat and humidity, coral and glades, plus snakes and mosquitoes. The Southern Florida location also subjected these units to an inordinate number of VIP visits, especially during the winter months.

No doubt several VIP visits occurred in the wake of Hurricane Betsy. Prior to the September 1965 arrival of Betsy, the ARADCOM units had gained experience from such storms as Flora in 1963. Thus radars, vans, and other equipment were tied down and emergency plans were put into action. Despite the precautions, the storm became the greatest natural disaster to affect ARADCOM facilities as sites in the Homestead-Miami region suffered extensive damage. Sites near the coast only 5.7 feet above sea level, Battery B of the 8th Battalion, 15th Artillery at (HM-39), had concrete block walls knocked down, and radar and equipment vans ripped from their pads. Men from this Hawk unit hid for cover in the administration building and nearly drowned when flood waters came to within two feet of the ceiling. Costs associated with this storm included $500,000 to repair damage to the Homestead-Miami communications system as the storm had knocked out all but one of seventy-seven telephone circuits. Despite the damage, the missile units quickly were restored to operational status.

From Hurricane Betsy and the 1966 hurricanes Alma and Inez, the units learned the importance of having the sites released from an alert status when Hurricane.

Warning Condition IV was declared so that vulnerable equipment could be removed and stored.

Missile batteries in southern Florida continued on active duty until 1979, well beyond the 1975 demise of ARADCOM.

Key West Defense Area

As with the Homestead-Miami Defense Area, the Cuban missile crisis provided the impetus for setting up antiaircraft missile batteries, installed to provide point defense for the Naval Air Station and the air approaches to Southern Florida. Manned by the 6th Battalion, 65th Artillery (later redesignated 1st Battalion, 65th Artillery), these Hawk batteries were ready for action on October 29, 1962. With the incorporation of this battalion into ARADCOM on April 1, 1963, construction on permanent facilities began at sites at Boca Chica Key (KW-10), Sugarloaf Key (KW-15), Geiger Key (KW-24), Fleming Key (KW-80), and at the Key West International Airport (KW-65). Naval Air Station, Key West hosted the command and control "Missile Master" facility. Headquarters facilities were also located at Key West.

Cordial relations between the Navy and the Army Air Defense units eased the difficulties of the Hawk batteries as they shifted from temporary to permanent quarters. Use of Navy storage space and transportation allowed for the safe evacuation of equipment and personnel before hurricanes struck the area. These batteries remained active until 1979.

References: Timothy Osato, Sherryl Straup, "ALADCOM's Florida Defenses in the Aftermath of the Cuban Missile Crisis: 1963–1968," (Headquarters, U.S. Army Air Defense Command, 31 December 1968), pp. 2–8, 81–86, which can be found at the

Center for Military History, provides a detailed account of the struggles encountered by these units. Additional coverage of the initial deployment and hurricane damage is provided in several articles in issues of Argus located at the Military History Institute at the Army War College.

GEORGIA

A I R   F O R C E

Robins Air Force Base/Warner Air Materiel Area

The base was established as a major east coast depot in 1941. Under the command of Headquarters, Air Materiel Command during the 1950s, Robins managed the TM-61 Matador missile program. The Matador eventually deployed overseas as a medium-range tactical cruise missile.

Reference: 'Warner Air Materiel Area History, July–December 1957," (K205.14–27), Exhibit 13, [AFHO].

A R M Y

Robins Defense Area

Two above-ground Nike Hercules sites designated R-28 and R-88 were located in Jeffersonville and Byron, respectively. Manned by Regular Army units, these two batteries stood guard over Robins AFB from November 1960 until March 1966. Headquarters facilities were located at Robins.

Reference: Nike Quick Look, pp. 116–117.

Turner Defense Area

When Turner became a SAC base in 1959, the U.S. Army Air Defense Command was tasked to provide air defense. Located at Willingham/Sylvester (TU-28) and Armenia/Sasser (TU-79), the two Nike Hercules batteries were manned by Regular Army units. These above-ground sites remained active from November 1960 until March 1966. Headquarters facilities were located at Turner. Turner AFB became Naval Air Station, Albany in 1967.

Reference: Nike Quick Look, pp. 132–133.

HAWAII

A R M Y

Oahu Defense Area

In 1956, plans were made to convert the Hawaii Army National Guard's 298th Infantry Regimental Combat Team into an Antiaircraft Artillery Group. As training began for this newly designated gun unit, plans again changed. The 298th Antiaircraft Artillery Group became the first National Guard unit in the United States to be equipped with the Nike Hercules.

Originally, the U.S. Army Pacific planned to build eight batteries at six sites around the island. Eventually this plan was scaled back. Oahu received six batteries: (OA-17) Kahuku in the northeast, (OA-32) Bellows Field in the southeast, (OA-63) Barber's Point in the southwest, and (OA-84) Dillingham in the northwest. Barber's Point and Bellows Field each hosted two batteries. The antiaircraft command post was at Wahiawa and Headquarters facilities were located at Fort Ruger. Responsibility for construction of these Nike Hercules sites went to the Corps of Engineers Honolulu District. The selection of the Bellows site caused a confrontation with the new state's governor. However, the Army prevailed over Governor William F. Quinn's objections to placing two batteries along the best swimming beaches on the windward side of Oahu. Unlike many of the stateside sites that housed missiles in underground magazines, these sites were simply open-air launchers mounted on concrete pads surrounded by earthen berms. Construction contracts were awarded in 1960.

Under the Command of U.S. Army Pacific, these Nike Hercules sites hold the distinction of being completely manned by the National Guard units from activation through deactivation. On March 4, 1961, the Guard received the first battery at Bellows from the Corps of Engineers. Hawaiian Guardsmen had already distinguished themselves during training at Fort Bliss, Texas. At a December 1959 firing practice at McGregor Range, Hawaii's first missilemen contingent succeeded in besting all previous range records.

Hawaiian missilemen had an advantage over their continental counterparts as Annual Service Practices were conducted locally at the Dillingham battery site located adjacent to the Kahuku Guided Missile Range.

The sites were deactivated in 1970.

References: Nike Quick Look, *pp. 102–103; Bruce Jacobs, "Nike Hercules Air Defense is Phased Out of the Army National Guard," The National Guardsman, (November 1974), detailed the significance of the Hawaiian Guard effort. Erwin N. Thompson, Pacific Ocean Engineers: History of the U.S. Army Corps of Engineers in the Pacific, 1905–1980, (Fort Shafter, HI: U.S. Army Engineer Pacific Division, 1980), pp. 282–283, provided the details regarding site construction [HQCE].*

IDAHO

A I R   F O R C E

Fairchild Air Force Base

An Atlas E launcher attached to the 567th Strategic Missile Squadron was located in the vicinity of Rockford, Idaho during the early 1960s.

Reference: See Fairchild AFB entry under Washington.

A R M Y

Mountain Home Air Force Base

This World War II-era base located in the Snake River Valley of southwestern Idaho came under Strategic Air Command jurisdiction between May 1, 1953, and January 1, 1966. During SAC's reign, Mountain Home hosted three Titan I missile complexes at Bruneau, Oreana, and near Boise.

On February 5, 1960, Colonel Paul H. Symbol of the Walla Walla Corps of Engineers District opened bids in the House of Representatives chamber of the Idaho State Capitol Building at Boise. Of the six bidders, the joint venture of Kaiser-Raymond-Macco-Puget Sound came in with a low winning bid of approximately $28.9 million. Notice to proceed was granted on February 9th.

As the contractors proceeded with site construction, contract oversight was switched in October 1960 from the Walla Walla District to the Titan I Directorate of the Corps of Engineers

Ballistic Missile Construction Office (CEBMCO) in Los Angeles as part of a national centralization of missile construction oversight.

The remoteness of the three sites proved challenging to the contractors in recruiting a steady labor force. A shortage of certain skilled craftsmen in the Mountain Home area forced the contractors to authorize overtime and additional benefits to those laborers who were available. There were no strikes. Nine unauthorized walkouts costing 908 man-days of labor over minor issues were insubstantial in contrast to other missile site construction projects. During construction, three workers died; two due to injuries sustained in falls.

Shipping materials from cities such as Seattle and Salt Lake City also drove up costs. An added difficulty was the weather. Temperatures during construction ranged from a high of 109°F to a low of -22°F. The severe winter temperatures forced costly measures to protect concrete placement operations. During the summer, wind-driven silt and sands interfered with progress. High well-water temperatures (up to 128 degrees) and mineralization required that special water treatment and cooling systems be used before the water could be used in the construction process. To get at the water, wells varied in depth from 950 to 3,030 feet.

By May 30, 1962, there were 246 modifications to the prime construction contract. Modifications proved to be the biggest cause for added costs and delays. Some of these modifications required expensive reconstruction and contributed to the final construction tally for the project, which topped $51 million.

Yet despite the problems, the joint venture contractor team completed work before the April 1, 1962 deadline. The activation of the 569th Strategic Missile Squadron on June 1, 1961, marked the last such activation of a Titan I squadron within the Strategic Air Command. This squadron would have a relatively short existence. On May 16, 1964, Defense Secretary McNamara directed an accelerated phaseout of Titan I and Atlas ICBMs. As a result, the 569th would join with two Titan I squadrons at Lowry, to be the last Titan I squadrons to undergo inactivation in June 1965.

References: SAC Chronology, pp. 30, 48; "Mt. Home Area Historical Summary: February 1960–May 1962," pp. 1–3,26–27, 33,52–55,97–103, [HQCE].

Mountain Home Air Force Base

In 1982, White Sands Missile Range built a complex for the launching of Pershing II missiles to impact at White Sands. No launches were ever conducted from this site.

Reference: Tom Starkweather, "Range larger than 2 states," The Missile Ranger, 1 June 1990, p. 9.

ILLINOIS

A I R   F O R C E

Chanute Air Force Base

Closed in 1993, this Air Force Base had a history dating back to World War I. During the Cold War, Air Training Command (ATC) operated the base, which provided technical training support for several missile programs. Some milestones include:

- completion of maintenance training facilities for Thor IRBMs on November 26, 1958.
- acceptance of the BOMARC surface-to-air missile erector in November 1960 for training use.
- becoming ATC's primary weapons technical training center in the 1960s and 1970s for such systems as air-launched Hound Dog and Short-Range Attack Missiles.
- serving as the Minuteman and Peacekeeper training facility.

References: Air Force Bases, pp. 77–85; "Chanute Technical Training Center: History January–June 1959," (K281.46–41), [AFHO].

A R M Y

Chicago-Gary Defense Area

Site designations and locations of Chicago missile batteries are as follows:

(C-03)	Montrose/Belmont
(C-40)	Chicago's Burnham Park
(C-41)	Chicago's Jackson Park
(C-44)	Hegewisch/Wolf Lake
(C-49/50R)	Homewood
(C-51)	Worth/Palos Heights/La Grange
(C-54)	Orland Park
(C-61)	Argonne National Laboratories
(C-70)	Naperville
(C-72)	Addison
(C-80)	Arlington Heights
(C-84)	Palatine
(C-92)	Mundelein
(C-93)	Northfield/Elokie
(C-94)	Libertyville
(C-98)	Fort Sheridan

Two batteries each shared locations at (C-44) and (C-80).

The Chicago defenses were coordinated from a "Missile Master" (later Missile Minder site) situated at Arlington Heights. Site (C-98) Fort Sheridan hosted the headquarters of the Fifth Army Air Defense Command. Other regional command facilities were located at the Museum of Science and Industry, site (C-51) Orland Park, and site (C-80) Arlington Heights.

The above summary excludes the four Gary sites (see Indiana). Chicago Nike site design and construction was handled by the Chicago District of the Corps of Engineers. Batteries that underwent conversion from Nike Ajax to Nike Hercules included C-03, C-41, C-49/50R, C-61, C-72, and C-93. The June 30, 1958, reactivation of C-03 marked the first Hercules battery to become operational within Army Air Defense Command. As elsewhere, Regular Army and Guard units shared manning responsibilities.

The air defense of Chicago become a focal point for inter-service rivalry between the Army and Air Force. A few months after the deployment of Chicago's first Nike Hercules battery, a derogatory Air Force analysis of Chicago's Nike defenses was leaked to the press. The report recommended replacing the 21 Nike sites in the Chicago area with 3 BOMARC bases to be located at Duluth, Minnesota; Kinross, Michigan; and Madison, Wisconsin.

Later, in the fall of 1958, the Strategic Air Command conducted a mock attack against Chicago. With the debate in Congress continuing in May 1959 over the merits of Nike Hercules versus BOMARC, "authoritative sources" at the Pentagon leaked that "raw data" from the mock attack indicated that the Nike Hercules was only 8 percent effective against the Air Force bomber attack.

In the end, Chicago benefitted from deployment of both systems. BOMARC bases were built at Duluth and Kinross; Nike Hercules bases remained in operation at C49/50, C-72, and C-93 as well as at sites C-46 and C-47 in northern Indiana, until 1974.

References: Nike Quick Look, *pp. 36–42. Thomas B. Ross, "Air Force Seeks to Abolish Chicago Nike Installations," Chicago Sun Times, (1 September 1958), pp. 1, 5; "Poor Rating for Hercules-'Raid' Results Told," The Milwaukee Journal, (27 May 1959). A detailed discussion of Chicago Nike defense is also provided in "Historic American Engineering Record Nike Missile Site C-84," (HAER No. IL–116, 1994), [LOC].*

St. Louis Defense Area

Three sites guarded St. Louis on the east side of the Mississippi River. The designations and locations of these sites were SL-10 at Marine, SL-40 at Hecker, and SL-90 at Alton/Pere Marquette.

Along with a Missouri site, these Nike Hercules installations, active from 1960 until 1968, were manned by Regular Army units. The Chicago District of the Corps of Engineers oversaw design and construction of these sites. Command and control was handled from a "Birdie" facility located in Belleville. Headquarters facilities were located at Scott AFB.

Reference: Nike Quick Look, *pp. 117–118.*

INDIANA

A R M Y

Chicago-Gary Defense Area

Site designations and locations of the Indiana component of the Chicago-Gary Defense Area are as follows: (C-45) Gary Municipal Airport, (C-46) Munster, (C-47) Hobart/Wheeler, and (C-48) South Gary.

Activated in the mid-1950s these batteries were part of the extensive network of Nike sites defending the Chicago area and were constructed under supervision of the Chicago District of the Corps of Engineers. Sites C-46 and C-47 underwent conversion from Ajax to Hercules during 1960 and 1961 and remained in operation until 1974.

Reference: Nike Quick Look, *pp. 36–42.*

Cincinnati-Dayton Defense Area

Site CD-63 located southeast of Dillsboro contributed to the defense of the upper Ohio River Valley. This battery remained active from March 1960 to March 1970. For more information on the Cincinnati-Dayton Defense Area, see entry under Ohio.

Reference: Nike Quick Look, *p. 44.*

IOWA

A I R   F O R C E

Offutt Air Force Base, Nebraska

Located on the Iowa side of the Missouri River at a place called Missouri Valley, three Atlas D launchers of the 566th (redesignated 549th) Strategic Missile Squadron contributed to America's deterrent forces from 1960 to 1964.

Reference: See Offutt Air Force Base entry under Nebraska.

A R M Y

Offutt Air Defense Area

A Regular Army-manned Nike Hercules site at Council Bluffs contributed to the defense of Omaha; Headquarters, Strategic Air Command at Offutt AFB; and Atlas missile sites placed within the region. This battery, designated OF-10, remained active from 1960 until 1966.

Reference: Nike Quick Look, *p. 104.*

KANSAS

A I R   F O R C E

Forbes Air Force Base

In October 1958, Topeka received news that Forbes AFB would support Atlas E missile sites to be constructed in the surrounding area. The Corps of Engineers Kansas City District managed construction of the nine "coffins" where the missiles would be stored horizontally. Although Forbes was slated to have three sites with three missiles at each site, in February 1959, the Air Force directed that each missile be placed at an individual launch site, These sites were situated at or near Valley Falls, Dover, Waverly, Osage City, Delia, Wamego, Overbrook, Holton, and Bushong. Construction officially began on June 9, 1959, when Kansas Governor George Docking drove a silver nail into a construction form.

Site construction was split between two firms, with one firm responsible for work at three sites and the other for work at the other six. There were difficulties encountered due to some 519 modifications made during construction. One modification concerned the propellant loading system. Prefabricated in Pittsburgh by Blaw-Knox Manufacturing for Atlas E sites at Vandenberg AFB, California; Warren AFB, Wyoming; Fairchild AFB, Washington; and Forbes AFB, the system components were to arrive on skids bolted together. Unfortunately the skids often arrived late and testing revealed system defects that took time to correct.

Labor-management problems caused occasional setbacks in construction. During the project there were 22 work stoppages, most of which were quickly resolved. However, in October and November 1960, a long work stoppage occurred due to a work assignment dispute between the hoisting engineers and the electrical workers. The problem was resolved after the National Labor Relations Board issued a restraining order.

There were 25 lost-time accidents during construction, including two fatalities that were electricity-related. One minor disturbance occurred at one of the sites when student pickets from McPherson College arrived to protest the deployment of ICBMs.

Despite the labor problems and student pickets, the project continued on schedule. On July 1, 1960, the 548th Strategic Missile Squadron stood up. Nearly 6 months later, on January 24, 1961, the first Atlas missile arrived at Forbes. By October, all nine sites had their Atlas E missiles. The Forbes sites were completed 3 weeks ahead of schedule.

On October 16, 1961, Air Force Ballistic Missile Activation Chief, Maj. Gen. Gerrity turned over operational control of the sites to Second Air Force Commander Lt. Gen. John D. Ryan. In the ensuing press conference the two generals urged Kansans to become interested in constructing fallout shelters as an insurance policy that could enhance deterrence.

As a result of Secretary of Defense Robert McNamara's May 1964 directive accelerating the decommissioning of Atlas and

Titan I missile bases, the 548th Strategic Missile Squadron was deactivated on March 25, 1965.

References: John Ferrell, Heartland Engineers, A History, (Kansas City, MO: U.S. Army District, 1992), pp. 122–127, [HQCE]; Robert L. Branyan, Taming the Mighty Missouri: A History of the Kansas City District Corps of Engineers, 1907–1971, (Kansas City, MO: U.S. Army District, 1974), pp. 111–114, [HQCE]; U.S. Army Corps of Engineers Ballistic Missile Construction Office, "History of Corps of Engineers Activities at Forbes AFB: 18 April 1959–28 April 1962," pp. 3–3, 5–1, 4–10 through 4–12, 6–11, and 7–1 through 7–3, [HQCE].

McConnell Air Force Base

Located southeast of Wichita, this base has a diverse history, starting with the construction of a Boeing plant during World War II. SAC assumed jurisdiction of the base for 5 years commencing on July 1, 1958, and reassumed command on July 1, 1972. Besides hosting bombers, McConnell spent a quarter century supporting 18 Titan II missile silos of the 381st Strategic Missile Wing that were planted in the surrounding region.

As with Titan II projects at Davis-Monthan, Arizona, and Little Rock, Arkansas, the construction at McConnell used a three-phase approach designed to cut down additional expenses caused by "concurrency." Using this approach, 18 silos were constructed, forming a rough horseshoe around Wichita with the open end pointing slightly to the west of north. Launcher locations for the 532nd Strategic Missile Squadron included Wellington (2), Conway Springs, Viola, Norwich, Rago, Murdock, Kingman, and Mount Vernon. The 533rd Strategic Missile Squadron would have responsibility for silos at Potwin, El Dorado, Leon (3), Smileyville, Rock, Winfield, and Oxford. Additional support facilities were constructed on base.

On December 10, 1960, the Corps of Engineers notified the joint venture of Fuller-Webb-Hardeman that its bid of nearly $30.8 million had earned them the contract for Phase I. The Corps of Engineers Ballistic Missile Construction Office (CEBMCO) considered the performance of the contractors in their site excavation work to be above average. Despite weather problems and some major modifications, the joint venture completed their phase 6 days before the original deadline of February 15, 1962.

On June 26, 1961, CEBMCO notified the joint venture of

Martin K. Eby, Incorporated and Associates that their bid of nearly $37.6 million had earned their selection as the contractor team for Phase II portion, which entailed installation of mechanical, electrical, water, and other systems at the semi-completed sites. Work began on Phase HA on December 4, 1961, and finished twelve months later.

Phase III involved systems contractor Martin Company and the Site Activation Task Force (SATAF) who completed the final preparations needed before turning the silos over to Strategic Air Command.

Through all three phrases a noteworthy safety program kept fatalities to just one over a timespan in which over nine million man-hours were worked. At the peak of the program, approximately 2,200 workers were on the job. Timing helped in the recruitment of experienced workers who had recently finished work at Atlas sites at Schilling and Forbes AFBs. A proactive missile site labor relations committee stemmed management-labor difficulties.

The Air Force accepted the final silo on January 31, 1963. With the arrival of the Titan II missiles from the Martin plant near Denver, the 381st Strategic Missile Wing focused on bringing the weapons to alert status.

On August 24, 1978, an accident involving an oxidizer leak at launch complex 533-7 killed two Air Force personnel, caused the temporary evacuation of local communities, and damaged the site.

A more positive event occurred during the following month as First Lieutenant Patricia E. Dougherty became the first female officer to perform SAC Titan II alert.

On October 2, 1981, Deputy Secretary of Defense Frank P. Carlucci ordered the inactivation of the Titan II weapon system. For McConnell, the end began on July 2, 1984, when Launch Complex 533-8 was removed from alert status. This silo would be placed in caretaker status on August 31st. The deactivation process received a setback on November 2, 1984, when fire broke out at Launch Complex 532-7 after liquid fuel had been unloaded from a deactivated Titan II. As a result of the ensuing investigation, Headquarters Strategic Air Command and the Ogden Air Logistics Center determined that the accident could have been prevented if different procedures were followed. With implementation of these procedures, Titan II deactivation continued.

On August 8, 1986, the 381st Strategic Missile Wing became the second Titan II wing to be deactivated.

References: John Ferrell, Heartland Engineers, A History, (Kansas City, MO: U.S. Army Engineer District, 1992), pp. 122–127, [HQCE]; SAC Chronology, pp. 66, 77, 78, 83; "History McConnell Area U.S. Army Corps of Engineers Ballistic Missile Construction Office: 6 October 1960-30 September 1963," pp. 18–26, 51–57, 66, 80–90, [HQCE].

Schilling Air Force Base

Originally there were to be nine silos located around Schilling; however, the number increased to a dozen individual sites located at or near Bennington, Abilene, Chapman, Charton, McPherson, Mitchell, Kanopolis, Wilson, Beverly, Tescott, Glasco, and Minneapolis.

A joint venture of Utah-Manhattan-Sundt earned the nine-silo contract with a bid of $17.2 million. This group also received a $6.2 million contract to build the three additional lift-launcher silos.

As with Atlas construction projects at other sites, major design changes doubled the final cost of the project. Part of the cause of the cost-overrun was attributed to the contractor team's failure to anticipate the government's demands for rigid standards and exacting performance. In addition, high water tables at some of the excavation sites raised pumping costs.

During construction, safety was a continual problem. On several occasions the Corps Engineer warned the contractor that his safety program was faltering. Five fatalities and numerous injuries marred the construction effort.

An analysis of the project written after project completion blamed inexperience within the regional Corps of Engineers District Office for many of the construction problems. With the decision to consolidate ballistic missile construction within the Los Angeles-based CEBMCO, management was streamlined. CEBMCO took charge of project management in October 1960.

The activation of the 550th Strategic Missile Squadron along with a sister squadron at Lincoln, Nebraska, on April 1, 1961, marked the first standing up of Atlas F units.

In June 1962, the first operational sites for the Atlas F ICBMs were accepted by SAC and in September the squadron was declared operational. In the following month during the Cuban missile crisis, the 550th received orders to maintain all twelve missiles on alert status.

In the wake of Defense Secretary McNamara's May 1964 directive accelerating the deactivation of the first generation ICBMs, SAC inactivated the squadron in June 1965.

With the closing of Schilling AFB, responsibility for the sites passed to F.E. Warren AFB, Wyoming, in July 1967. The sites were disposed of in March 1971.

To defend its Atlas F missile lift-launchers, Schilling was slated to receive two Nike Hercules batteries. However, with construction well under way, the Defense Department decided to cancel the project. A headquarters unit posted at Schilling was operational for two months in the spring of 1960.

References: John Ferrell, Heartland Engineers, A History, *(Kansas City, MO: U.S. Army Engineer District, 1992), pp. 122–127, [HQCE]; SAC Chronology, pp. 30, 35, 44, 48; Air Force Bases, p. 180; "History of the Corps of Engineers Activities at Schilling Air Force Base: March 1960–December 1961," pp. 12-A-1, 12-A-3, 26-1, 26-2, chapter 24, [HQCE].*

A R M Y

Kansas City Defense Area

The two Kansas sites, KC-60 and KC-80, were located 2 miles south of Gardner and at Fort Leavenworth. Along with two sites in Missouri, these Nike Hercules sites defended this important industrial/transportation center. They were operational from 1960 to 1969.

The groundbreaking ceremony at Fort Leavenworth was highly publicized, with Kansas Governor George Docking participating in the festivities. The Corps of Engineers Kansas City District oversaw construction of the sites. The initial projected cost of construction of the four sites around Kansas City was placed at $6 million. However, modifications made during construction escalated this figure. Command and control was coordinated from a "Birdie" site at Olathe Naval Air Station. At Olathe, an Air Force SAGE blockhouse received sensor inputs from around the country and designated defensive systems (such as Birdie) to handle a threat. Headquarters facilities were also located at Olathe.

References: Robert L. Branyan, Taming the Mighty Missouri: A History of the Kansas City District Corps of Engineers, 1907–1971, *(Kansas City, MO: U.S. Army Engineer District, 1974), p.111, [HQCE]; Argus, (1 September 1958), p. 1, [MHI].*

KWAJALEIN ATOLL, MARSHALL ISLANDS

Kwajalein Atoll, Marshall Islands

Located 2,100 miles southwest of Hawaii, the Kwajalein Atoll of some 100 tiny islands makes up part of the Marshall Islands. After the American capture of the atoll during World War II, the Navy made Kwajalein a base. During the 1950s, there was much activity here as atomic testing was conducted at nearby Bikini and Enewetak Atolls. By 1959, activity had slackened, allowing the Navy to place the base on the surplus list.

However, that year two major programs were initiated that would affect activity on the atoll. The U.S. Army Rocket and Missile Agency advanced plans to use the atoll as a test base for the Nike Zeus system. Concurrently, the Advanced Research Projects Agency selected the Roi-Namur Islands as a center to study missile reentry characteristics. The Honolulu Engineering District had responsibility for constructing facilities to support both of these projects.

On June 30, 1959, the Honolulu Engineering District awarded a $3.26 million contract to a team composed of the Pacific Construction Company, Reed and Martin, and the H.B. Zachry Company for the construction of radar facilities for the Zeus installation. The team was commonly called PMZ. As installation requirements expanded, additions were made to the initial contract. By 1962, the Army had paid some $56 million to the consortium. In November 1960, PMZ also won the bid to build the facility at Roi-Namur for what was dubbed Project PRESS (Pacific Range Electromagnetic Signature Studies).

At both projects, engineers were challenged by the tropical climate, which caused severe corrosion and logistical problems inherent in construction at such remote locations. For example, in 1960, two barges carrying components for Project PRESS were lost at sea.

To provide targets for the Zeus missiles, launch facilities were to be constructed on Johnston Island. However, work on this project ceased in July 1960 when the Secretary of Defense announced a decision to use only Vandenberg AFB, California as a target launch site.

On Kwajalein, nearly all of the test facilities were completed by the end of 1962. Because of the groundwater problem, a mound to host launch silos was constructed on the northwest end of the island.

Facilities to support the Nike Zeus program were also constructed on Roi-Namur. Part of these facilities included launch pads for a rocket named Speedball that would be used to calibrate Kwajalein's radars prior to Zeus launchings.

In December 1961, the first Nike Zeus was launched from Kwajalein. In 1962, a historic launch was made in which the outgoing Zeus came within lethal range of an incoming Atlas rocket. In May 1963, the Zeus demonstrated its ability to intercept an object in orbit.

At this time, radar limitations forced the program to evolve into the Nike X program. Nike X employed a modified Zeus missile for long-range intercepts and used the Sprint for point defense. The new accompanying test radars required additional construction and, again PMZ received the contract. Meek Island, located 19 miles north of Kwajalein, was chosen to host many of the new facilities. For safety, natives from nearby islands had to be relocated. Overcrowding at the relocation site of Ebeye remained a source of tension for many years.

In July 1964, the Navy transferred Kwajalein to Army control and the facility became known as the Kwajalein Test Site. At Meek Island, construction centered around a control building that housed a phased-array radar. Completed in the fall of 1967, this facility served as a prototype of the type of structure envisioned for the Sentinel antiballistic missile (ABM) system. The modified Nike Zeus, renamed Spartan, was first successfully launched from Kwajalein's Mt. Olympus in the spring of 1968. Unfortunately, the construction of sister launch cells on Meek Island ran into extreme seepage problems, delaying activation until 1970.

Renamed in April 1968, as the Kwajalein Missile Range, the atoll base came under the jurisdiction of the Sentinel Systems Command. In March 1968, Sentinel Systems Command became Safeguard Systems Command.

Meanwhile, in 1968, Project PRESS had become a joint-service activity and was reorganized as the Kwajalein Field Measurements Program. In 1969, the Roi-Namur facility was dedicated as the Kiernan Reentry Measurements Site.

With the Meek Island facility operational, several test launch-ings of Spartan and Sprint missiles occurred in the early 1970s. Additional launchers were built on nearby Illeginni Island to conduct remote missile launches controlled by Meek Island.

In 1974, Kwajalein Missile Range came under the control of the newly formed Ballistic Missile Defense Systems Command. Construction work during this period included upgrading support structures and installing additional highly sophisticated tracking devices.

In 1981, Meek Island became host to a new facility as a huge launch tower arrived from Cape Kennedy. This tower became an important component in the Homing Overlay Experiment, an ambitious project designed to launch platforms into stationary orbit where they would be capable of discerning incoming nuclear warheads from decoys. Once the warheads were identified, these platforms would fire interceptors to destroy some of the threatening projectiles. The experiment was designed as a first step for a ballistic missile defense.

References: Erwin N. Thompson, Pacific Ocean Engineers: History of the U.S. Army Corps of Engineers in the Pacific, 1905–1980, *(Fort Shafter, HI: U.S. Army Engineer Pacific Division, n.d.), pp. 196, 265–280, 282–283, 361–364, [HQCE]. See also Benjamin M. Elson, "Kwajalein Range Plays a Unique Role,"* Aviation Week and Space Technology, *(16 June 1980), pp. 223–228.*

LOUISIANA

A I R   F O R C E

Barksdale Air Force Base

Established a decade before World War II, Barksdale spent most of its history since that war hosting SAC bombers and reconnaissance aircraft. In 1972 and 1973 storage igloos and missile assembly buildings were constructed to support the eventual deployment of Air Launched Cruise Missiles (ALCMs) for the base's B-52 wing.

Reference: Air Force Bases, *pp. 15–24.*

A R M Y

Barksdale Defense Area

Two Nike Hercules sites, BD-10 at Bellevue and BD-50 northeast of Stonewall, were installed to provide protection to Shreveport and Barksdale APB, which hosted Strategic Air Command bombers. U.S. Army Air Defense Command operated the sites with Regular Army units from 1960 until 1966. Battalion Headquarters was located at the Louisiana Army Ammunition Plant located north of Doyline.

Reference: Nike Quick Look, *pp. 25–26.*

MAINE

A I R   F O R C E

Dow Air Force Base

Located at Bangor, Maine, this World War II era Air Force base underwent reconstruction in the early 1950s to support the heavy bombers of the Strategic Air Command. In the late 1950s the Air Force Defense Command selected Dow to host the 30th Air Defense Missile Squadron (ADMS).

The Corps of Engineers managed construction of this facility located northeast of the SAC base. Upon completion in early 1959, the Corps turned over the base to the Air Force. Activated on June 1, 1959, the 30th ADMS maintained 28 BOMARC A missiles on alert for over 4 years. The squadron was deactivated on December 15, 1964.

References: Aubrey Parkman, Army Engineers in New England, *(Waltham, MA: U.S. Army Engineer New England Division, 1978), p. 153, [HQCE];* Nike Quick Look, *p. 172.*

Loring Air Force Base

The Corps of Engineers started construction of this bomber base at Limestone, Maine in 1947. The Strategic Air Command assumed command in 1953. In 1972, B-52s with the 42nd Bombardment Wing became the first bombers within SAC to be equipped with the short-range attack missile.

References: Air Force Bases, pp. 331–338; SAC Chronology, p. 59.

Presque Isle Air Force Base

In 1941, the Army Corps of Engineers Boston District constructed an airstrip at this northern Maine location, which became a major embarkation point for American aircraft ferrying to Europe. During the early Cold War, the base was converted to host SAC fighter aircraft that escorted bombers flying out of Dow, Pease, Westover, and Loring AFBs.

On March 21, 1957, the Air Force selected Presque Isle to be the first Snark missile base. On January 1, 1959, Headquarters, Strategic Air Command activated the 702nd Strategic Missile Wing, placing it under the operational control of the Eighth Air Force.

The Corps of Engineers New England Division managed the construction of 6 missile assembly and maintenance buildings as well as 12 launch pads on which the mobile launchers could be placed.

On May 27, 1959, the first Snark missile arrived at Presque Isle and on March 18, 1960, the 702nd SMW placed a Snark missile on alert status. On February 28, 1961, SAC declared the 702nd SMW to be fully operational. However, a month later, President Kennedy ordered the Snark missile to be phased out as it "was obsolete and of marginal military value." On June 25, 1961, the Snark missile and the 702nd SMW were deactivated.

References: SAC Chronology, pp. 13, 21–22, 25, 29, 30; Aubrey Parkman, Army Engineers in New England, (Waltham, MA: U.S. Army Engineer New England Division, 1978), pp. 134, 147, 154, [HQCE].

A R M Y

Loring Air Force Base Defense Area

Four Nike Ajax sites were placed around Loring AFB: (L-13) Caswell, (L-31) Limestone, (L-58) Caribou, and (L-85) Conner. Headquarters facilities were located at Loring.

The New England Division of the Army Corps of Engineers managed the construction of these sites. Manned by Regular

Army units, these sites provided defense for Loring AFB and the northeastern approaches to the United States. In 1960, sites L-13 and L-58 underwent conversion from Ajax to Hercules missiles. These sites remained operational until 1966.

The missilemen of Loring obtained some notoriety in November 1958 during Annual Service Practice at Fort Bliss, Texas. These men, members of the 3rd Missile Battalion, 61st Artillery, launched 12 Nike Ajax missiles and recorded twelve kills—a US. Army Air Defense Command first.

References: Nike Quick Look, *pp. 76–77;* Argus, *(1 January 1960), p. 1, [MHI].*

MARYLAND

A I R   F O R C E

Andrews Air Force Base

This World War II vintage installation located southeast of Washington DC hosted commands directing Air Force research and development efforts during the Cold War.

Prior to 1951, Air Force research and development was under the control of its Air Materiel Command headquartered at Wright-Patterson AFB in Dayton, Ohio. In 1949, a special committee of the Air Force Scientific Advisory Board recommended that research and development functions be split away from the Air Materiel Command. In 1951, the recommendation was implemented with the establishment of the Air Research and Development Command (ARDC) subordinate to Headquarters, United States Air Force. On June 25, 1951, Headquarters, ARDC became operational within the Sun Building located in Baltimore.

With research and development efforts accelerating as ICBMs became reality, ARDC established a new headquarters at Andrews AFB in January 1958. As a result of an Air Force reorganization in 1961, the organization Command (AFSC). A feature of the reorganization gave AFSC procurement responsibilities that formerly were held by the Air Materiel Command. AFSC was responsible for the research, development, testing, production, and procurement of aerospace systems for the Air Force inventory.

In 1992, AFSC merged with the Air Force Logistics Command

to form the Air Force Materiel Command with headquarters at Wright-Patterson AFB, Ohio.

References: "Air Force Ballistic Missile Program," (K146.01-106A), [AFHO]; Beverly Sanford Follis, Chronology: Air Research and Development Command (1945–1961), *(Andrews AFB, MD: Office of History, Headquarters Air Force Systems Command, 1985). For a general overview of the ARDC/AFSC role in long-range ballistic missile development see Ethel M. DeHaven,* Aerospace: The Evolution of USAF Weapons Acquisition Policy, 1945–1961, *(Andrews AFB, MD: Air Force Systems Command, 1962), (K243.012), [AFHO]*

A R M Y

Aberdeen Proving Ground

Congress authorized the establishment of Aberdeen Proving Ground on August 6, 1917. Shortly thereafter, Aberdeen served as a backdrop for some early American rocketry In September 1918, Dr. Robert Goddard, then a professor at Clark University, showed the Army Signal Corps some rockets he had developed for military use. These rockets subsequently were fired at Aberdeen Proving Ground on November 7, 1918. However, with the Armistice signed 4 days later, military interest in Goddard's rockets waned.

Still Aberdeen played an important role in the development of future rocket programs because during the interwar period the proving ground became the Army's center for ballistic research. The center hosted the first continuous flow supersonic wind tunnel for testing early missile and rocket airframes. The Nike I program used this facility in the post-war period.

By World War II, the Aberdeen-based Ballistic Research Laboratory (BRL) was on the technical cutting edge of the study of trajectories, using newly developed computers to increase the speed and accuracy of problem solving, and high speed cameras for better flight evaluation.

Initially, BRL detailed personnel to White Sands, New Mexico, who returned with raw data for evaluation. Eventually, BRL's detachment to White Sands became permanent and was transferred to that command.

A 1985 HABS/HAER survey (Historic American Building Survey/Historic American Engineering Record) recommended several Aberdeen facilities be considered for historic preservation.

Nominated sites that worked with missile research included the Ballistics Research Lab building 328 (Category I) and the H.R. Kent Supersonic Wind Tunnel and Laboratory housed in building 120 (Category II).

References: Tom Starkweather, "Handshake at Amador Hotel bar started PSL," White Sands Missile Ranger, (15 December 1989), p.20; Owen J. Remington, "The Army's Role in Space," Army Digest, (November 1969), p. 9, [NASM]; "Historic American Engineering Record, Aberdeen Proving Ground," (HAER MD 13 ABER 1), 1985, [LOC].

Washington-Baltimore Defense Area

Numerous Nike installations were built in Maryland to defend Baltimore and the nation's capital:

(BA-03)	Phoenix Swinton
(BA-18)	Edgewood
(BA-30/31)	west of Chestertown
(BA-43)	Jacobsville
(BA-79)	Granite (BA-09) Fork
(W-35)	Croom/Marlboro
(W-36)	Brandywine/Naylor
(W-44)	Mattawoman/Waldorf
(W-45)	Accokeek

Maryland Sites:

(BA-92)	Cronhardt
(W-13)	Fort Meade
(W-25)	Davidsonville
(W-26)	Skidmore Bay Bridge
(W-92)	Rockville
(W-93)	Derwood
(W-94)	Gaithersburg

Baltimore Area Headquarters facilities were located at Towson, Fort Smallwood, Edgewood Arsenal, and Owens Mills. Headquarters facilities on the Maryland side of Washington's defenses were located at Fort Meade and Suitland. During the 1950s Fort Meade also hosted the Headquarters, 2nd Region, Army Air Defense Command.

As indicated by the numerous sites, the capital region was well defended. On March 20, 1954, Fort Meade activated the nation's first battery. After permanent batteries were installed at other sites, this temporary above-ground site was removed, but not until after an embarrassing and potentially dangerous incident. On April 14, 1955, shortly after midday, a Nike Ajax was accidently launched westward. A soldier standing nearby received slight burns. After traveling about three miles, the missile disintegrated and pieces rained down on the newly-opened Baltimore-Washington Parkway. There was no traffic passing at the time of the crash and State Police quickly secured the site as a missile handling team from Fort Meade arrived to neutralize hazardous materials and remove the missile parts for inspection. As a result of the ensuing investigation, missile handling procedures in non-combat situations were revised.

Fort Meade also hosted air tracking radars as well as the nation's first "Missile Master" command and control facility. In 1966, Missile Master was replaced by the "Missile Mentor" system, which used solid-state electronics and required fewer people to operate it. Single gender operations ended at this Fort Meade facility in the late 1950s as women were posted within the complex.

Initially operated by Regular Army soldiers of the U.S. Army Air Defense Command, the sites eventually became the responsibility of a combination of Regular Army and National Guard Units. With the increased range of Nike Hercules, many of the sites became repetitive. Sites converted to accept Hercules missiles included BA-3, BA-18, BA-30/31, BA-79, W-25, W-26, W-44, and W-92. All but W-44 remained active until 1974. Site W-26 was the first Nike Hercules site to be turned over to the National Guard.

Some of the batteries achieved notoriety due to accomplishments and location. During the early 1960s batteries from the Rockville and Davidsonville sites consistently won top honors during the Short Notice Annual Practice (SNAP) exercises conducted at Fort Bliss, Texas. Davidsonville received special attention because of its proximity to Washington. In the aftermath of the New Jersey Nike Ajax tragedy in May 1958, a committee to review safety procedures arrived at Davidsonville to study all aspects of missile handling. (See the account of this accident in the New Jersey section, New York Defense Area.) Davidsonville replaced Virginia's (W-64) Lorton site to become the "national site" in 1963, subjecting the facility to visits from many VIPs.

VIPs were not the only people visiting the missile sites. The various batteries often welcomed tour groups such as Boy Scouts.

Typical of close community relations was Chestertown inviting the Executive Officer of the nearby battery to present merit badges at a Cub Scout meeting.

References: Nike Quick Look, pp. 22–25, pp. 134–139. For an excellent overview of a typical Nike site see Merle T. Cole, "W-25: The Davidsonville Site and Maryland Air Defense, 1950–1974," Maryland Historical Magazine, *Vol. 80 No. 3, (Fall 1985);* Argus, *(1 August 1965), p. 3, and (1 January 1959), p. 1, 7, [MHI]. For additional Washington sites see Virginia.*

MASSACHUSETTS

A I R   F O R C E

Hanscom Air Force Base

In September 1945, the Cambridge Field Station was established under the jurisdiction of the Army Air Force's New Jersey-based Watson Laboratories. Fearing the loss of a talented pool of scientists, engineers, and technical staffs at Harvard and the Massachusetts Institute of Technology (MIT) who had performed invaluable research in radar and electronics, the Army Air Forces established the station at 224 Albany Street in Cambridge. By the end of 1945, the station employed 230 civilians and within six months this number nearly tripled.

Two years later the station came under control of the Air Materiel Command. In 1949, the facility became known as the Air Force Cambridge Research Laboratories. In 1951, the Air Force Cambridge Research Center established itself adjacent to Hanscom Air Field at Bedford. Now under the command of the newly formed Air Research and Development Command (ARDC), the center took on responsibility for a project administered by MIT. "Project Lincoln" was the code name for an Air Force-contracted laboratory designed to resolve air defense problems. In 1952, MIT named its research complex, also located at Hanscom Field, the Lincoln Laboratory. At this time, MIT hosted a cadre of scientists in what became known as the Lincoln Summer Study Group. Recommendations of this group regarding air defense profoundly affected systems acquisitions over the next decade. One such system developed locally was the Lincoln Transition System. The eventual outcome of the Lincoln Transition System was the

Semi-Automatic Ground Environment (SAGE) system that used computers to decipher electronic data so that commanders could effectively employ defensive forces such as BOMARC missiles. As testing began at prototype radars erected for the SAGE system at Cape Cod, Lincoln Laboratory worked to develop complementary electronic systems for the Distant Early Warning System Line and the Ballistic Missile Early Warning System.

In 1960 the Air Force Cambridge Research Center was redesignated as the Air Force Cambridge Research Laboratories. Another name change took place in 1976, as the facility became the Air Force Geophysics a mission to understand the interaction Experiments designed to better understand over 2,000 balloon, 1,000 sounding rocket, sions. Laboratory. This organization continued in of Air Force systems in a space environment. upper-atmospheric effects took place in 150 satellite, and several space shuttle missions.

In 1990, the Geophysics Laboratory became part of the Phillips Laboratory organization.

References: E. Michael Del Papa, A Historical Chronology of the Electronic Systems Division: 1947–1980, *(Hanscom AFB, MA: Electronic Systems Center History Office, 1981); "Air Force Ballistic Missile Program," (K146.01-106A), [AFHO]; Bob Duffner, John Brownlee,* Phillips Laboratory Historical Overview, *(Kirtland AFB, NM: Phillips Laboratory History Office, 1993). See also New Mexico, Kirtland AFB; and California, Edwards AFB.*

Otis Air Force Base

Otis AFB became a major Air Defense Command installation as the 26th Air Defense Missile Squadron was activated on March 1, 1959.

The Corps of Engineers New England Division managed construction of this facility and turned it over to the Air Force in early 1960. Augmenting the Nike missiles and Air Force intercepter aircraft protecting southern New England, this base, housing 28 BOMARC A missiles, became operational in June 1960. The Corps immediately began work to build new facilities to handle the follow-on B model. This construction was completed in February 1962, and by September the B model was operational. The BOMARC facility remained in operation until April 30, 1972.

References: Aubrey Parkman, Army Engineers in New England, *(Waltham, MA: U.S. Army Engineer New England Division,*

1978), P. 153, [HQCE]; Nike Quick Look, *p. 171.*

A R M Y

Boston Defense Area

The site designations and locations of Nike batteries guarding the Boston area are as follows:

(B-03)	1.3 miles northeast of Reading
(B-05)	northwest of Danvers
(B-15)	Beverly
(B-17)	Nahant
(B-36)	Fort Duvall/Hull
(B-37)	Squantum/Quincy
(B-38)	Cohasset/Hingham
(B-55)	Blue Hills/Milton
(B-63)	west of Needham
(B-73)	1.6 miles west of South Lincoln
(B-84)	Burlington
(B-85)	west of Bedford.

Headquarters facilities were located at Chelsea, Winthrop, Quincy, Natick, and Fort Devens. Radar sections were stationed at Long Island and Fort Devens.

The Corps of Engineers New England Division based at Waltham managed construction of these facilities and the Nike defenses elsewhere in New England. While some sites had to be newly acquired, the Division used Department of Defense property whenever possible. For example, B-36 used World War II gun casements as a foundation for the missile control radars.

Boston's Nike Batteries were manned initially by Regular Army troops. In 1959, National Guard units assumed control of B-03, B-15, B-55, and B-63. In 1964, the Army turned sites B-36 and B-73 over to the Guard. After the phase-out of the Nike Ajax system, sites B-05, B-36, and B-73 remained supplied with Hercules missiles. By 1964, these three sites were merged with the remaining sites in Providence and Bridgeport to form the New England Defense Area.

The Corps of Engineers New England Division contracted Kirkland Construction Company to construct the "bomb-proof fallout-proof" Missile Master command and control facility located at Fort Heath in Winthrop. This unit, manned by up to 500 personnel, coordinated the Nike batteries throughout the Northeast.

References: Aubrey Parkman, Army Engineers in New England,
294

(Waltham, MA: U.S. Army Engineer New England Division, 1978), pp.150–153, [HQCE]; Nike Quick Look, *pp. 27–31.*

Providence Defense Area

Site PR-19 at Rehobeth and PR-29 at Swansea contributed to the air defense of Providence. These Nike Ajax sites were active from 1956 to 1959.

Reference: See Rhode Island for more details.

Sharper's Pond Sentinel ABM Site

On November 3, 1967, the Department of Defense publicly revealed the first ten locations slated to receive the Sentinel ABM system. Heading the list, Boston would host the first site. Throughout 1968, representatives from the Huntsville District and the local Army Corps of Engineers District teamed with members of the Army Air Defense Command (ARADCOM) to survey potential sites around Boston.

On August 16, 1968, DOD solicited Congress for acquisition of land near Sharpner's Pond for the huge Perimeter Acquisition Radar (PAR) facility and for a plot on a nearby National Guard facility for the Missile Site Radar (MSR). With Congressional approval granted in September, the Army implemented a three-phase construction plan.

Learning from difficulties encountered with ICBM silo construction, Corps of Engineers and Department of Labor representatives met with local labor leaders to develop dispute-handling mechanisms. The Corps also incorporated a special road damage clause into the construction contracts to assuage local government officials concerned about highway maintenance.

By submitting a low bid of just over $767,000, George Brox Inc. of Dracut, Massachusetts, won the Phase I contract to construct the site access road, clear the site, and perform some excavation work. Once the Corps gave notice to proceed on September 24, Brox quickly commenced work. Phase II began on January 22, 1969, when Morrison-Knudsen Inc. of Boise, Idaho, was awarded a $2.2 million contract for preliminary construction work.

Initially, local reaction to the construction was subdued. However, with the upcoming national election, Sentinel sites became topics for debate, especially at the locations designated to receive them. With Sentinel construction actually under way near Boston, Ballistic Missile Defense opponents had a focal point to rally against. On January 29, 1969, the Corps hosted a public relations meeting at Reading High School. Despite a blizzard, over 1,000 people attended, including many local and out-of-state BMD opponents. The meeting received wide attention in the media as Huntsville Division's Maj. Gen. Robert P. Young repeatedly was subjected to catcalls and hostile anti-BMD arguments.

The meeting sparked additional opposition efforts and the successful recruitment of Senator Edward Kennedy into the BMD opposition. The Senator's January 31st letter to Defense Secretary Melvin Laird criticizing Sentinel ignited a congressional debate. On February 6, facing the threat of congressional cutoff of appropriations, Secretary Laird directed a program review. At a press conference on March 14, President Nixon announced the results of the review, which recommended a reorientation of BMD to protect ICBM bases. This new network became known as Safeguard.

The announcement of Safeguard spelled the death-knell for the Sharpner's Pond site. With the announcement of the February 6th review, the Huntsville Division directed George Brox Inc. to limit operations to maintenance work. After the March 14 announcement, the Morrison-Knudsen contract was terminated and the Brox contract frozen. Eventually, the site became a state park centered around the water-filled PAR excavation.

Reference: James H. Kitchens, A History of the Huntsville Division: 15 October 1967–31 December 1976, (Huntsville, AL: U.S. Army Engineer Huntsville Division, 1978), pp. 23–38, [HQCE].

MICHIGAN

A I R   F O R C E

Kincheloe Air Force Base

The Air Force Air Defense Command activated the 37th Air Defense Missile Squadron on March 1, 1960. The launch site for the twenty-eight BOMARC B missiles was located at the former Race Army Air Field located northwest of Kincheloe AFB. Because the facility deployed the easier-to-maintain BOMARC B model, the Army Corps of Engineers constructed less expensive and less sophisticated Mark IV shelters. Alert status for this northern Michigan base commenced in June 1961. The unit was deactivated on October 30, 1972.

Reference: Nike Quick Look, p. 174

K.I. Sawyer Air Force Base

In the mid-1950s the Air Defense Command acquired K.I. Sawyer County Airport as a host facility for a Semi-Automatic Ground Environment (SAGE) blockhouse and fighter intercepter squadrons. Although air defense remained an important mission for this base throughout the remainder of the Cold War, the Strategic Air Command assumed operational command of the base in 1964 and deployed a B-52 bomber wing to this northern Michigan location. Eventually, the B-52Hs assigned underwent modification (ALCMs).

References: Air Force Bases, pp. 295–297; START.

Wurtsmith Air Force Base

This air base, with roots back in the 1920s, became a SAC base in 1960. With the modification of its B-52Gs to carry ALCMs, Wurtsmith constructed missile storage and assembly facilities.

References: Air Force Bases, pp. 611–615; START Annex C.

A R M Y

Detroit Defense Area

Built during the mid-1950s, Detroit Defense Area Nike batteries are located at:

(D-06)	Utica	(D-57)	Carleton
(D-14)	Selfridge AFB	(D-58)	Carleton/Newport
(D-16)	Selfridge APB	(D-61)	Wayne County Airport
(D-17)	Algonic/Marine City	(D-69)	River Rouge Park
(D-23)	Detroit City Airport	(D-86)	Franklin /Bingham
(D-26)	Fort Wayne/Detroit	(D-87)	Commence/Union Lake
(D-51)	NAS Grosse Isle	(D-97)	Auburn Heights.
(D-54)	Riverview/Wyandotte		

Missile defense coordination was controlled by Missile Master (replaced by Missile Mentor) collocated with sites at Selfridge APB. Headquarters facilities were posted at Selfridge as well as the Detroit Artillery Armory.

Site (D-58) Carleton hosted two launcher sites that were controlled by separate tracking radar sites. Between 1958 and 1961, the Army converted sites (D-06, D-16, D-26, D-58, D-61, and D-87) from Nike Ajax to Nike Hercules. The Michigan Army National Guard assumed manning responsibilities Sites D-06, D-58, and D-87 Hercules batteries remained active until 1974.

Reference: Nike Quick Look, *pp. 49–54.*

MINNESOTA

A I R   F O R C E

Duluth Air Force Base

The Air Force Air Defense Command activated the 74th Air Defense Missile Squadron on April 1, 1960 at this northern Minnesota installation. Because it was one of the last three BOMARC sites built, Duluth never deployed the liquid-fueled BOMARC A missile. Instead, engineers designed the installation to accommodate the solid-fueled B version. Thus, this base featured a Model IV type launcher shelter.

Operations began at this site with the BOMARC B missile in August 1961. The squadron was deactivated on April 30, 1972. In addition to hosting this BOMARC site, Duluth AFB hosted Air Defense Command interceptor squadrons as well as a SAGE site.

Reference: Nike Quick Look, *p. 176.*

A R M Y

Minneapolis-St. Paul Defense Area

In operation from 1959 until 1971, the following four Nike Hercules batteries guarded the approaches to the Twin Cities: (MS-20) Roberts, (MS-40) Farmington, (MS-70) Bonifacius, and (MS-90) Bethel/Isanti.

The Chicago District of the Corps of Engineers oversaw construction of these sites. The four batteries were manned by Regular Army units. The Birdie command and control facility, located at Snelling Air Force Station, provided target designation information to the batteries. Headquarters facilities were also located at Snelling.

Reference: Nike Quick Look, *pp. 86–87.*

MISSOURI

A I R   F O R C E

Whiteman Air Force Base Originally a World War II glider base, SAC converted the facility for strategic bomber use in the 1950s. With the phase-out of B-47s in the early 1960s the future of Whiteman AFB was threatened with the loss of its bomber wing. However, in April 1961 test borings made in the area around Whiteman indicated that the terrain was geologically compatible to support Minuteman missile silos.

On June 14, 1961, the U.S. Government announced that Whiteman would serve as a support base for the fourth Minuteman strategic missile wing. After the announcement, there were second thoughts about the choice as original plans called for launchers to be spread into the Lake of the Ozarks region. Due to the terrain inaccessibility and the high water table, these plans were scrapped. Consequently, when the final approval came on January 17, 1962, the launchers were placed in the vicinity of Whiteman, making this the smallest Minuteman base with regard to area.

In February 1962, the Los Angeles-based Corps of Engineers Ballistic Missile Construction Office established a resident office at Whiteman. Meanwhile, the Real Estate Division of the Corps of Engineers Kansas City District set up an office in Sedalia to acquire the needed land.

The Morrison-Hardernan-Perini-Leavell consortium submitted a low bid of $60.6 million and was awarded the contract on March 20, 1962.

Although construction commenced on April 2, official groundbreaking ceremonies occurred on April 14, 1962, with several congressmen and Governor John Dalton joining military officials at the event. The enormity of the ensuing construction effort encompassed not only installing 150 silos and 15 launch control complexes but also constructing/reconstructing numerous roads and bridges throughout rural western Missouri. The "Hardened Intersite Cable System," measuring some 1,777 miles, connected the launch control centers and required land rights-of-entry from more than 6,000 landowners.

During construction, management-labor relations were described as "excellent." With the exception of ironworkers, the local region supplied the project's manpower needs. There were five work stoppages, of which three involved union jurisdiction disputes. The Federal Mediation and Conciliation Service resolved one dispute while the others were handled at lower levels. In addition, there were only eleven "time-lost" injuries; no fatalities.

Activated on February 1, 1963, the 351st SMW traced its lineage to the 351st Bombardment Group, a unit that had seen extensive action throughout World War II. As the wing organized, construction accelerated. On June 10, 1963, the Army Corps of Engineers and civilian construction contractors turned the first flight of silos over to the Air Force Site Activation Task Force (SATAF). Over the next five months SATAF received responsibility for making final installations on the rest of the silos in preparation for final turnover to SAC. The keys to the final flight of silos were turned over to SATAF and the integration contractor (Boeing) on November 26, 1963.

The first Minuteman I missile arrived from the Boeing plant at Hill AFB, Utah, on January 14, 1964. Soon the holes dotting the Missouri landscape were filled with ICBMs. By June 29, 1964, the last flight of missiles went on alert status, making the 351st a fully operational strategic missile wing.

Beginning on May 7, 1966, and throughout the rest of 1966 and into 1967, the Air Force replaced the Minuteman I "B's" with Minuteman IIs. The completed transition in October 1967 gave the 351st SMW the distinction of being the first wing to complete the Force Modernization Program. One of the retired Minuteman Is eventually found its way to a Bicentennial Peace Park located on base.

During April 1967, SAC sponsored the first missile combat competition at Vandenberg AFB in California. The 351st Strategic Missile Wing came home with the Blanchard Perpetual Trophy for recognition as the best missile wing within SAC. The Whiteman-based unit went on to receive many more such honors at these annual competitions that became known as Olympic Arena.

In October 1967, the 510th Strategic Missile Squadron received responsibilities for the Emergency Rocket Communications System (ERCS), which was mounted on Minuteman F missiles. Successful testing of this replacement for the Blue Scout Jr. rockets stationed in Nebraska had been completed at Vandenberg during the previous year. The ERCS mission involved the trans-

mission of emergency action messages to United States nuclear forces in the event of an attack. The squadron maintained this mission until 1991.

During the 1970s Whiteman's missiles were involved in the integrated improvement program, which included hardening silos and installing command data buffers to facilitate quick missile retargeting. The completion of this program at Whiteman in January 1980, marked the end of the Air Force's last major Minuteman modification program. However, throughout the 1980s improvements to enhance missile accuracy, security, and survivability were made at the numerous launch complexes.

On November 12, 1984, four antinuclear demonstrators trespassed onto Launch Facility N-05 and caused $25,000 worth of damage. Arrested by SAC security police and brought before a U.S. District Court in Kansas City, the four demonstrators were tried, convicted, and ordered to serve sentences ranging from 8 to 18 years.

A SAC first occurred on March 25, 1986, when the first all-female crew manned one of the launch control centers. In 1988, for the first time, an all-female crew from Whiteman, along with a mixed-gender crew from Malmstrom AFB, Wyoming, competed in the Olympic Arena competition.

The September 28, 1991 order from President Bush to take Minuteman II missiles off alert status ended Whiteman's role as an active ICBM base. Subsequently, the Air Force removed Whiteman's 150 Minuteman II missiles from service. The vacated silos are scheduled to be imploded and graded over.

References: U.S. Army Corps of Engineers Ballistic Missile Construction Office, "Minuteman, Whiteman Area Historical Report," pp. I 1–5, II 1–8, VIII 4, [HQCE]; Roger D. Hooker and Richard E. Rice, Whiteman Air Force Base 50th Anniversary History (Whiteman AFB, MO: Whiteman AFB History Office, 1992); SAC Chronology, pp. 50, 52, 68, 77, 78, 82, 91.

A R M Y

Kansas City Defense Area

Site KC-10 was located two miles southeast of Lawson while site KC-30 operated five miles northeast of Pleasant Hill. These two Nike Hercules batteries, dubbed Lawson and Lone Jack, guarded the eastern approaches to Kansas City. The Corps of Engineers

Kansas City District commenced work on these sites in late spring 1958. They were active from November 1959 until February 1969.

Reference: See Kansas for additional details.

St. Louis Defense Area

Site SL-60, located five miles south of Pacific, was the lone Nike Hercules battery defending St. Louis on the Missouri side of the Mississippi. Corps of Engineers oversaw the design and construction. May 1960 until December 1968.

Reference: See Illinois for additional sites.

MONTANA

A I R   F O R C E

Malmstrom Air Force Base

Founded during World War II as a training and logistics hub, the base's mission changed on February 1, 1954, with the arrival of the 407th Strategic Fighter Wing, and the base command shifted to the Strategic Air Command (SAC). With the rapid development of the three-stage, solid-fuel Minuteman I missile in the late 1950s SAC began searching for sites to deploy this revolutionary weapon. Because Malmstrom's location placed most strategic targets in the Soviet Union within range of Minuteman, the base was a logical choice.

On December 23, 1959, the Air Force Ballistic Missile Committee approved the selection of Malmstrom AFB to host the first Minuteman ICBM base.

Although the newly formed Corps of Engineers Ballistic Missile Construction Office handled the design and supervised construction of the planned fifteen control sites and 150 silos, the initial ground work required advance engineering, site feasibility studies, surveys, soil and foundation investigations, determination of utility sources, and finally land acquisition. These tasks fell on the Seattle District of the Corps of Engineers. The land acquisition, involving some 5,200 tracts scattered across an area of 20,000 square miles of north-central Montana, amounted to the largest for any single project undertaken by the Corps. At its peak, the

Corps employed up to 80 people at its real estate office to deal with the approximately 1,378 owners of the desired parcels. Modifications in silo design required the District to renegotiate easements with the landowners on 12 different occasions over the 4-year span of the project.

In less than three percent of the cases, the government acquired the land through condemnation. Once construction commenced, tempers were tested as fences were cut, trenches were left open in cattle pastures, crops were destroyed, and water and power supplies were interrupted. Yet despite these problems, most of the local population understood the importance of the project to national security and they cooperated.

A joint venture of the George A. Fuller Company and the Del E. Webb Corporation won the construction contract with a bid of $61.7 million. The Fixed Price Incentive Contract was unique, featuring provisions for a target cost, target profit, and a formula for determining the final price and final profit. With cost overruns projected due to expected design modifications and unanticipated surprises, the Corps of Engineers Ballistic Missile Construction Office imposed a system in which excessive costs would be split, with the contractor picking up 25 percent of the tab. Using this formula, the final project cost would come to $79,284,385.

The March 16, 1961, groundbreaking ceremonies featured an interesting arrangement as key state and local politicians, and military, contractor, and labor leaders gathered on stage at the base theater. At the prescribed moment, eight of these officials threw switches, setting off explosive charges out on the plains. Each official received his switch as a memento.

As predicted, design changes occasionally slowed progress as did unanticipated high water tables, which required additional pumping capacity at the excavation sites. An electrician's strike from November 1 through 12, 1961, and spring storms in 1962 also hindered progress. Still, on December 15, contractors completed work on the 10th silo, turning the silo over to the Air Force for finishing and missile installation. During construction, six workers were killed.

On July 15, 1961, a former B-47 Bomber Group, the 341st, came back to life as a Strategic Missile Wing. A year later, in late July 1962, the first Minuteman I arrived at Malmstrom and was placed at Alpha-9 launch facility.

The timely arrival of additional missiles no doubt played a critical role in the nation's defense, as the Soviets attempted to

298

establish Intermediate Range Ballistic Missile (IRBM) bases on the island of Cuba during the fall of 1962. On October 15, 1962, U-2 photos revealed the presence of these sites. One week later President Kennedy addressed the nation and announced the establishment of a naval quarantine around Cuba. On October 24, SAC accepted control of the first flight of silos and placed them on alert status two days later. On October 28, Premier Khrushchev agreed to halt construction activity and return the IRBMs to the Soviet Union. Later, when asked if he had felt that nuclear war may have been imminent, the President responded, "I had confidence in the final outcome of our diplomacy . . . Of course, Mr. Khrushchev knew we had an ace in the hole in our improved strategic forces." (It should be noted that the strategic imbalance of the two sides would have still been lopsided favoring the United States had the Minuteman flight not come on line.)

The 10th SMS accepted its final flight on February 28, 1963. Two months later, the 12th SMS became 100 percent combat ready. In July, the 490th SMS became fully operational, giving the 341st SMW responsibility for 150 silos.

Home of the oldest Minuteman strategic missile squadron, Malmstrom also became home to the youngest, when in August 1964, the Air Force announced plans to build an additional fifty silos on the Montana prairie to house Minuteman II missiles. On February 23, 1965, Morrison Knudsen Company and Associates won the bid to build the additional silos. Construction started two weeks later. Manpower peaked in September 1965, with 1,593 men working on the sites. During construction, there were seven work stoppages, which cost 8,808 man-days lost. Overall, the project managers could boast of a good safety record as there were twelve lost time incidents and only 1 fatality.

As construction of these new silos proceeded through 1966, the 564th SMS stood up on April 1, 1966. Just over a year later America's 1,000th Minuteman missile would be in place and on alert at Malmstrom. This milestone marked the completion of Minuteman deployment by the United States.

While new Minuteman IIs deployed with the 564th, upgrading of the Minuteman I models had been ongoing with the wing starting a transition from "A" to "B" models in August 1964. By June 1969, all Minuteman, both "A" and "B" models, were replaced by Minuteman II models. In 1975, the 564th SMS switched from the Minuteman II to the Minuteman III model.

In addition to improving the missiles, many improvements were undertaken over the years to upgrade reliability and survivability. In the early 1970s, flood control dike projects alleviated drainage problems within the silos that were caused by the spring thaw. In November 1975, the wing began an integrated improvement program that included a command data buffer and an improved launch control system. In 1985, the 341st SMW became the lead unit in the Minuteman Integrated Life Extension program (Rivet Mile).

While serving as a deterrent force, the 341st SMW won numerous honors. The unit won its first Blanchard Trophy in SAC's annual Olympic Arena missile competition in 1976 and again captured this most coveted prize in 1986, 1990, and 1991. The unit has won additional accolades over the years.

In 1987, Malmstrom hosted a prototype of a small ICBM mobile launcher. Testing conducted at Malmstrom evaluated this platform's capability to support the Midgetman missile

On September 28, 1991, President Bush ordered all Minuteman IIs off alert status. This order affected three-quarters of the 200 ICBMs stationed at Malmstrom. From 1992 to 1994, the Air Force removed 150 Minuteman II missiles from their silos to comply with the pending START I Treaty. Fifty of the vacated silos received Minuteman III missiles, joining the fifty Minuteman III missiles already on alert status.

References: Land acquisition is detailed in Sherman Green, History of the Seattle District: 1896–1968, (Seattle, WA: U.S. Army Engineer District, 1969), pp. 5-5, 5-6, 5-7, [HQCE]; U.S. Army Ballistic Missile Construction Office "History of WS133A Minuteman Technical Facilities, Malmstrom Air Force Base," pp. 11-1, 11-2, 14-10, 19-3, 19-4, [HQCE]; U.S. Army Ballistic Missile Construction Office "History of Malmstrom Area During Construction of Co-located Squadron No. 20 Minuteman II ICBM Facilities," pp. 8-1, 8-2, 9-1, 9-2, Appendix II-6c, [HQCE]; SAC Chronology, p. 24; "History of 341st Strategic Missile Wing and 341st Combat Support Group: 1 April–31 June 1970," (K-WG-341-HI), pp. 55, 66–69, [AFHO]; "Chronology of Malmstrom AFB and 341st Missile Wing through 1994" courtesy Wing Historian.

A R M Y

Malmstrom Air Force Base Safeguard Site

In late 1968, the Department of Defense added Malmstrom AFB to the already growing list of locations to receive a Sentinel Ballistic Missile Defense (BMD) system. With President Nixon's March 14, 1969 announcement reorienting BMD to protect U.S. strategic forces, suddenly the proposed Sentinel sites at Malmstrom and Grand Forks, North Dakota, became a construction priority for what would become known as the Safeguard System.

With Congressional debate and votes throughout the summer of 1969 threatening to cancel the whole BMD program, little activity occurred out in Montana. However, once funding seemed assured, the Army publicly announced the pending deployment of a Safeguard System to sites near Shelby and Conrad.

In this politically conservative region, the news of the pending deployment provoked a quiet elation tempered by a concern over the impact of heavy construction within the region.

The Perimeter Acquisition Radar (PAR) would be situated about fifty miles due north of Great Falls and the Missile Site Radar (MSR) was to be placed north-northwest of Great Falls, some seven miles southeast of Conrad.

Unlike the Grand Forks site, budgetary constraints forced the Army to proceed at a slower pace at Malmstrom. Consequently, Phase I called for excavation and foundation work to proceed in 1970 and Phase II provided for completing the PAR and MSR structures during 1971.

As with the selected sites north of Grand Forks, the Huntsville Division of the Army Corps of Engineers tackled transportation and water supply problems before heavy construction could proceed. Improvements to regional secondary roads were made, and access roads leading to the future PAR and MSR sites were constructed throughout the spring and summer of 1970. With rainfall averaging only 8 to 16 inches per year, tapping groundwater supplies was out of the question. Fortunately, arrangements were made with the Department of the Interior to tap Tiber Reservoir using a 26-mile long pipeline connecting the various installations. In October, Red Samm Mining Venture, Venture Construction Inc., and Shoreline Construction Company received nearly $3.2 million to install the water supply system.

As with Grand Forks, the Corps' Omaha District conducted a detailed Community Impact Study, which focused on how the project would affect schools, medical facilities, and other community services. After visiting the construction site area in July 1970, Governor Forrest Anderson teamed up with North Dakota Governor William Guy to testify about citizen concerns before the Senate Subcommittee on Military Construction.

However, Governor Anderson's concerns became moot, as labor problems delayed the influx of workers into the region. Local labor agreements in force in the Great Falls area had generous overtime and mileage compensation rates. Local contractors had few objections to these provisions, because overtime rarely occurred on local projects and local workers had short commutes. However, potential contractors for Safeguard found it difficult to pay these costs and keep the project on budget. Although the two contractors awarded the Phase I excavation contract bowed to local union demands, the potential additional labor costs on Phase II threatened to put the project way over budget.

The Watson Construction Company of Minneapolis, Minnesota, received a contract to excavate the MSR building and adjacent power plant and lay out the first floor slab for these structures. The team of H.C. Smith Construction Company and Amelco Corporation shared a contract to do similar work at the PAR site. The contractors completed Phase I requirements on time despite the harsh winter conditions on the northern plains.

However, the timely completion of Phase I became meaningless when the government had difficulty acquiring an acceptable bid for Phase II. Two bids were opened on March 25, 1971; on April 14, 1971, Under Secretary of the Army Thaddeus R. Beal rejected the lowest bid as being "unreasonable in price." The ensuing effort to come to terms with the contractors and unions would stall work on the project during prime construction season. Because local unions insisted on maintaining benefits that could have ended up adding $45 million more to the cost of the project, obtaining a general project agreement proved to be a most difficult endeavor. To stem inflationary pressures, President Nixon had issued Executive Order 11588 that restricted labor contracts to allow inflation only up to six percent and set up a watchdog committee to review potential settlement packages. On July 29, 1971, this committee concluded a review and rejected packages that had been negotiated between the two potential contractors and nine of the local unions.

Frustrated at the local level, the Army turned to national labor organizations. An agreement was signed on October 19th, and although above the six percent guideline established by President Nixon's Executive Order, the package won approval of his watchdog committee on the following day.

By mid-February 1972, only four unions had indicated their willingness to subscribe to the contracts that had been negotiated on their behalf by their national leaders. Yet hoping that the local unions would quickly fall in line, the Corps gave Peter Kiewit Sons' Company and Associates (PKS&A) the go-ahead to start Phase II construction with a target completion date of late 1974. As spring arrived on the northern plains, additional contracts were let for the Remote Launcher Sites and the nontechnical support structures.

By the end of May, the project was about 10 percent complete and the contractor had mobilized the resources needed to launch full-scale construction. However, the project would not make much further headway. On May 26, 1972, President Nixon and General Secretary Brezhnev signed the ABM Treaty that limited both sides to one site to protect strategic forces and one site to protect the National Command Authority. With the Grand Forks complex 85 percent complete, the Secretary of Defense suspended construction at Malmstrom. The status of the site remained in limbo until October, when the Senate finally ratified both the SALT I and ABM pacts.

Terminating a project of such magnitude proved to be nearly as complex as the formulation. Some 56 contracts had to be reviewed and closed out. Hundreds of claims from suppliers had to be settled. Finally, on September 11, 1973, the Huntsville Division let two contracts to perform restoration work at the Malmstrom sites. William Clairmont, Inc. of Bismarck, North Dakota, received the contract to remove the MSR, and PKS&A was assigned to demolish the PAR site. Salvageable material was removed, and by July 1974, most of the facilities were buried under tons of earth covered with prairie grass. After the demolition, only the first level of the unfinished PAR building remained visible on the open prairie as a reminder of the massive effort that once took place.

Reference: James H. Kitchens, A History of the Huntsville Division: 15 October 1967–31 December 1976, (Huntsville, AL: U.S. Army Engineer Huntsville Division, 1978), pp. 23, 34–35, 58–64, 72–78, 95–100, [HQCE].

NEBRASKA

A I R   F O R C E

F.E. Warren Air Force Base

An Atlas E launcher of the 549th (redesignated as 566th) Strategic Missile Squadron was operational in the early 1960s at Kimball. The presence of ICBMs in western Nebraska rapidly expanded as nearly 100 Minuteman silos were constructed for the 90th Strategic Missile Wing during 1963 and 1964. These silos came under the direct jurisdiction of the 319th, 320th, and 321st Strategic Missile Squadrons.

Reference See F.E. Warren Air Force Base under Wyoming.

Lincoln Air Force Base

This World War II era training base was deactivated after the war. However, the Air Force returned in 1952, and by mid-decade, Lincoln serviced B-47 bombers and support aircraft for the Strategic Air Command. As a SAC base, Lincoln was selected to host Atlas ICBMs.

Operational sites at both Lincoln and Schilling AFB, Kansas, were originally slated to receive horizontal launchers. Site selection for three complexes of three missiles each (3 x 3) was completed in the fall of 1958. In early 1959, a decision to deploy missiles to nine separate sites required additional site surveys. As these surveys proceeded, Bechtel and Convair contractors achieved design advances on vertical launchers.

On November 27, 1959, Headquarters, United States Air Force determined that Lincoln and Schilling would receive the silo-lift configuration. During the subsequent bidding process, the number of silos to be built was increased to 12. These launchers were sited at Elmwood, Avoca, Eagle, Nebraska City, Palmyra, Tecumseh, Courtland, Beatrice, Wilber, York, Seward, and David City.

On April 12, 1960, Western Contracting Corporation earned the contract with a bid of $17.4 million for nine sites. A month later the contract price increased another $6.6 million to cover construction costs of three additional sites. Construction began on April 29, 1960.

Difficulties were encountered almost immediately. On June 13, at a site near Beatrice, builders had to combat sandy soils, which kept caving in. Two weeks later, miners briefly walked off four sites over the issue of work conditions. High water tables challenged engineers to battle a constant flooding problem. However, using the "cut and cover" method, progress was achieved on installing the twelve separate silos.

With the project one-third complete in October 1960, the Omaha District turned responsibility for construction over to the Corps of Engineers Ballistic Missile Construction Office (CEBMCO). Construction reached a peak later that month as some 1,900 workers worked "around the clock" on a 7-day schedule at twelve separate sites.

In February 1961, the President of Western Contracting testified before Congress to express his frustration with all of the change orders, yet continued expectations of meeting scheduled deadlines. He stated he expected to lose $12 million on the project. As a result of the hearings, finger-pointing began to affix blame for cost overruns at the several ongoing construction projects.

Construction at Lincoln proved costly in more ways than money. Seven men died during the building process in separate incidents, usually due to falls or being struck by objects. The final death occurred during the late summer of 1961, when a guard was hit by a tornado that lashed through the Palmyra site.

Besides developing a reputation for high fatalities, the Lincoln project also gained notoriety for labor unrest. By late April 1961, the Defense Department reported that Lincoln had suffered 33 strikes causing 1,743 man-days lost. During the following month politicians expressed rage against the work stoppages. As a result of such pressure, on May 26, the administration developed a plan that incorporated a no-strike/no lockout pledge and implemented an 11-man Missile Sites Labor Commission to settle all disputes.

In June 1962, the Strategic Air Command accepted the first silos at Lincoln for operational deployment of the Atlas F missile. On May 16, 1964, Secretary of Defense McNamara directed the accelerated phaseout of Atlas and Titan I ICBMs. Later that year, the 551st Strategic Missile Squadron received the last Operational Readiness Inspection (ORI) for such a unit. The Lincoln Atlas F missiles were deactivated on April 12, 1965, completing the phaseout of this weapon system.

References: "CEBMCO Historical Summary Report of Major ICBM Construction Lincoln Area," Chronology section, [HQCE]; SAC Chronology, pp. 35, 44, 45, 47.

Offutt Air Force Base

Offutt became the headquarters of the Strategic Air Command on November 9, 1946. The new SAC headquarters building and command control facility opened late in 1956 and was subsequently expanded in 1964. In August 1960, the newly created Joint Strategic Target Planning Staff collocated with SAC. On November 1, 1975, National Emergency Airborne Command Post E-4 aircraft arrived on station.

At one time, during the early 1960s some of the missile forces that SAC commanded were located nearby at Arlington, Mead, and Missouri Valley, Iowa.

Throughout 1958, the Corps of Engineers Omaha District repeatedly received new construction schedules, design changes, and basing modes from the Air Force Ballistic Missile Division. Finally, the district received bidding documents in January 1959. The documents contained 359 sheets of drawings and 680 sheets of specifications. The project was advertised on February 6, 1959, and bids were opened in the following month.

Malan Construction Company of New York City won the contract with a bid of almost $12.9 million to build three missile complexes in the vicinity of Omaha. Notice to proceed was issued on April 6.

Unfortunately, because Malan subcontracted the work to forty-six contractors for this complex project, the company created a coordination nightmare. Consulting firms were brought in to assist Malan, and eventually the contractors found themselves setting up 10-hour shifts, seven days a week. Despite the effort, the project was completed on July 28, 1960, four months late. Thereafter the Corps of Engineers required primary contractors to complete at least fifteen percent of the work themselves.

Other factors besides poor contractor management contributed to the project's failure to meet the intended deadline. There were 72 modifications and difficulties with the weather. Deterioration of access roads to the sites, especially those in Iowa, caused numerous delays in getting equipment and workers to the site. Labor strife was credited for setting progress back at least a month as some twenty work stoppages cost the project 1,645 man-days of work. A nationwide steel strike in 1959 also affected deliveries of important components. As with other Atlas sites, installation and testing of the propellant loading system proved a great challenge.

There were no construction-related fatalities during this project.

The local media gave the project mostly favorable coverage, highlighting visits by VIPs. However, not everyone was pleased with the ongoing construction. On June 24, 1959, peace activists converged at site "A" and picketed at the entrance for about 4 weeks. Some were arrested on occasion for scaling the fence or blocking traffic.

In November 1960, a pair of investigators from the House Appropriations Committee visited the Omaha District to look into the project's problems. One investigator questioned if political influence had been a factor in the award of the contract and asked about accusations of fraud in Malan's operations. The pair passed on Air Force accusations that the Corps of Engineers was "losing its shirt" when negotiating contract modifications. No doubt problems at Offutt contributed to the Army's decision to centralize its construction effort at a location close to the Air Force Ballistic Missile Division in Los Angeles.

In April and May 1961, the three complexes became the last Atlas D missiles to go on alert. On July 1, 1961, SAC redesignated the 566th SMS as the 549th SMS.

These Atlas Ds would be the last to be removed from alert status. The last Atlas D left Offutt on October 22, 1964.

References: U.S. Army Ballistic Missile Construction Office "History of Atlas Missile Base Construction, Offutt April 1959–July 1960," chapters 1, 4, 8, 9, [HQCE]; The Federal Engineer, Damsites to Missile Sites: A History of the Omaha District U.S. Army Corps of Engineers, (Omaha, NE, U.S. Army Engineer District, 1984), p. 191, [HQCE]; Air Force Bases, pp. 453–458; SAC Chronology, p. 45.

Emergency Rocket Communication System: Wisner, Scribner, West Point Air Force Stations

On July 11, 1963, the Air Force accepted and declared operational the launch sites at Wisner, West Point, and Tekamah for the Emergency Rocket Communication System (ERCS). SAC established ERCS as a backup method to launch a counterstrike in the event a Soviet attack destroyed other communication systems. A trailer containing a Blue Scout Jr. missile and a manned trailer hosting the launch controls were placed at each of the three sites. Once launched into orbit, the ERCS satellite could initiate a "go" signal to launch any remaining ICBMs. On December 1, 1967,

these sites were deactivated. The ERCS would be operated from Whiteman AFB using a modified Minuteman II booster.

References: SAC Chronology, pp. 41, 51, 53; David Hendee, "Tekamah Girls Knew of Missile, but Mission a Mystery," Omaha World Herald, (20 February 1994), p. B4

A R M Y

Lincoln Defense Area

Site LI-01 located at Ceresco Davey and site LI-50 at Crete were two above-ground Nike Hercules batteries operated by one Regular Army battalion that also operated sites in the Offutt Defense Area. The missiles provided defense for SAC bombers and Atlas missiles stationed at and around Lincoln AFB between 1960 and 1966.

Reference: Nike Quick Look, pp. 75-76.

Offutt Defense Area

Along with site OF-10 in Council Bluffs, Iowa, site OF-60 at Cedar Creek provided a Nike Hercules defense for Omaha's Offutt AFB, which was the Headquarters of the Strategic Air Command. Offutt also hosted SAC bombers, and Atlas missiles were deployed around the area in the early 1960s. The U.S. Army Air Defense Command operated the site from 1960 to 1966.

Reference: Nike Quick Look, p. 104.

Omaha District U.S. Army Corps of Engineers

Until the Corps of Engineers Ballistic Missile Construction Office (CEBMCO) was established in 1960, each Corps District had responsibilities for overseeing ICBM facility construction within its territorial jurisdiction. Territorial jurisdiction for the Omaha District included sites at F.E. Warren AFB, Wyoming; Lincoln AFB; Lowry AFB, Colorado; Offutt AFB; and Ellsworth AFB, South Dakota. Because of the Omaha District's experience gained through initiating Atlas construction at F.E. Warren and Titan I construction at Lowry and Omaha, it also supported other districts in missile site building endeavors.

After CEBMCO assumed overall control of the construction

effort, the Omaha District provided real estate acquisition and administrative support for CEBMCO's Minuteman projects at F.E. Warren; Ellsworth; Minot AFB, North Dakota; and Grand Forks AFB, North Dakota.

The Omaha District was also responsible for building Nike Hercules surface-to-air missile sites at Lincoln and Offutt.

In the 1960s and 1970s the Omaha District assisted the newly created Huntsville District in coordinating construction of antiballistic missile facilities. The Omaha District staffed field offices, conducted site explorations, and provided logistical support for the two Safeguard sites in Montana and North Dakota. The Omaha District conducted a planning survey in 1969 and 1970 to evaluate the impact of the project on local communities. The North Dakota site would be completed in 1974 to be operational for a short period in 1975–1976.

References: The Federal Engineer, Damsites to Missile Sites: A History of the Omaha District U.S. Army' Corps of Engineers, *(Omaha, NE: U.S. Army Engineer District, 1984), pp. 218–220, [HQCE]; James H. Kitchens,* A History of the Huntsville Division: 15 October 1967–31 December 1976, *(Huntsville, AL: U.S. Army Engineer Huntsville Division, 1978), pp. 45–46, [HQCE].*

NEW JERSEY

A I R   F O R C E

McGuire Air Force Base

McGuire AFB began in 1937 as a single dirt-strip runway, which was assigned to support the nearby Army post at Fort Dix. Airfield activities rapidly expanded during World War II. During this time, the base became involved with its first guided missile activity when the Second Army Air Force Electronic Experimental Unit set up shop at the Fort Dix Army Airfield in the summer of 1943. Supported by the 414th Service Squadron, the unit did missile-related research at Fort Dix until April 1944.

By 1954, air transport had assumed a major role in the base mission. However, because of McGuire's strategic location, the Air Defense Command selected the base to deploy its first BOMARC missile squadron, the 46th Air Defense Missile Squadron. It was located in the New Jersey Pine Barrens on a tract located 11 miles

east of McGuire AFB in Ocean County just east of county highway 539. The Philadelphia District of the Corps of Engineers supervised construction of the 56 Model II shelters and ancillary buildings. Construction began in January 1958 and took nearly two years to complete. The site was declared operationally ready on September 1, 1959. However, according to the Air Defense Command historian, this operational readiness declaration severely strained the concept of the term. As late as December, the facility hosted only one ready missile.

On June 7, 1960, disaster struck at missile shelter 204. A defective helium vessel ruptured, causing an explosion and a fire. During the 30-minute fire, the IM-99A BOMARC missile and nuclear warhead burned causing the loss of approximately 1.0 to 1.5 kilograms of plutonium. Part of the loss may have been due to the water run-off from the fire fighting effort.

Shortly after the explosion, the State Police station near Fort Dix received a call from an Air Force sergeant who stated, "an atomic warhead has exploded." The State Police quickly notified area civil defense forces and closed off area roads. Troops at Fort Dix on maneuvers were recalled to post. Shortly thereafter, a wire service sent out the following bulletin:

State Police reported an atomic warhead of a BOMARC exploded today near here sending heavy radiation throughout the area.

While overseas reports in British newspapers of "200 square miles of terror" and "mothers fleeing with their children" may have exaggerated the initial panic, there is little doubt that the vagueness of the bulletin caused considerable concern as military personnel at Fort Dix and McGuire AFB answered hundreds of calls from citizens inquiring about radiation danger. A few hours later, Air Force officials declared that "there was no radiation danger to the public."

Immediately, the Air Force took steps to contain the contamination to the area within the immediate vicinity of the shelter. Decontamination teams from Wright–Patterson and Griffiss AFBs arrived to handle the radioactive hazard. Eventually, concrete and asphalt was applied to seal the contaminated area.

The bursting helium bottle that caused the disaster was located between the missile's two fuel cells. Thereafter, the pressure within the bottles was reduced from 4,500 psi to 3,000 psi. The Air Force then placed cumbersome top-off tanks within each of the shelters. Just prior to missile launch, the helium bottle again would be charged to the 4,300 psi limit.

Damage control extended well beyond the site as the Air Force combated the negative publicity by emphasizing the minimal nature of the radioactive discharge. Unfortunately for the Air Force, the incident gave critics an opportunity to rehash the recent cutbacks in the program and the developmental problems of this weapon system.

By October 1962, the BOMARC As were replaced with the B variant. Rather than reconfigure the Model II shelters to accept the new missile, the Air Force directed that Model IV shelters be constructed on adjacent property. The New York District of the Corps of Engineers supervised the construction of these new launcher shelters.

Upon deactivation in 1972, the site was closed to access. Several environmental studies have been completed to evaluate any potential dangers of plutonium residue to the local ecosystem.

References: Nike Quick Look, *p.175; Frank E. Snyder and Brian H. Guss,* The District: A History of the Philadelphia District U.S. Army Corps of Engineers, 1866–1971, *(Philadelphia, PA: U.S. Army Engineer District, 1974), pp. 151–153, [HQCE]; Leonard Katz, Edward Kosner, "BOMARC Fire," New York Post, (8 June 1960); George Barrett, "Jersey Atom Missile Fire Stirs Brief Radiation Fear," New York Times, (8 June 1960); Philip Dodd, "Helium Bottle Burst Blamed in BOMARC Fire," Chicago Tribune, (24 June 1960); Richard McMullen, "Interceptor Missiles in Air Defense, Study No. 30, 1965), pp. 83–85, 95–96, [AFHO].*

A R M Y

Fort Monmouth

Many communications techniques essential for missile guidance were developed by Army Signal Corps scientists based at this central New Jersey installation. For example, Signal Corps Electronics Laboratory provided radar tracking beacons for the post-war Corporal missile program. A detachment from this command assigned to White Sands, New Mexico, in the late 1940s eventually became the U.S. Army Signal Missile Support Agency.

The Signal Corps made another key contribution as the development of synthetic materials for electronic communications led to experiments with gallium phosphide to create materials with high heat resistance. The Army Ballistic Missile Agency later used these materials to protect reentry vehicles.

Reference: Owen J. Remington, "The Army's Role in Space," Army Digest, (November 1969), pp. 10–12, [NASM].

New York Defense Area

Nike missile battery designations and locations in the New York Defense Area are:

(NY-53)	Leonardo/Belford
(NY-54)	Holmdel/Hazlet
(NY-56)	Fort Hancock/Sandy Hook
(NY-58/60)	South Amboy
(NY-65)	South Plainfield
(NY-73)	Summit/Watchung
(NY-80)	Livingston (double site)
(NY-88)	Mountain View/Wayne
(NY-93/94)	Ramsey/Darlington
	Mahwah/Franklin Lakes (double site).

During the 1960s Headquarters facilities were located at Fort Hancock.

Combined with the sites on the other side of the Hudson River, the Jersey sites contributed to an extensive air defense net around the nation's largest city. The New Jersey Army National Guard assumed responsibility from the Regular Army for many of these sites.

NY-54, NY-56, NY-58/60, NY-65, NY-80, and NY-93/94 replaced their Nike Ajax missiles with the longer range Hercules model. Beginning on June 6, 1960, command and control for target designation of these regional missile batteries was handled at a Missile Master facility constructed at Atlantic Highlands near Sandy Hook. Prior to Missile Master, defenses were manually coordinated from Fort Wadsworth on Staten Island.

On May 22, 1958, disaster struck NY-53, which was maintained by Battery B of the 526th AA4 Missile Battalion. On this sunny day, 14 Nike Ajax missiles were located above ground: 7 in Section A, 4 in Section B, and 3 in Section C. In Section A, an ordnance unit teamed up with battery personnel to install mechanisms. To install the devices, two of the three warheads built into each missile had to be removed to facilitate access. Judging by the size of the crater left in front of the missile that was undergoing modification, the investigating board concluded that the two warheads had been removed and were sitting on the ground when the third warhead detonated. A *Time* magazine article described the incident:

Suddenly the missile blew with a roar and a sky-searing pillow of orange flame from burning kerosene and nitric acid fuels . . . Explosion and flame touched off seven more Nikes squatting on adjacent pads, blew or burned ten men to death, showered a three mile radius with fragments. . .

In addition to destroying the other six above-ground missiles at Section A, a flying red-hot pellet apparently ignited the booster of the nearest missile sitting on its pad in Section B. This missile blasted into the side of a nearby hill. Fortunately, the Nike Ajax failed to detonate, sparing the Battery additional damage.

The subsequent investigation determined that the "point of initiation of the explosion was probably a PETN relay cap." Realizing this condition could exist in other missiles that had recently received the new arming device, the Army initiated "Operation Fix-it." By August 30, 1958, 5,971 Nike Ajax missiles had completed inspection. The new arming device was found to have been incorrectly installed on 605 of these missiles and another 309 were found to contain ruptured or damaged relay caps.

Locally, Army officials attended a special town meeting called by the Mayor of Middletown to explain what happened. Army lawyers arrived to settle claims from local residents that would total nearly $12,000. Claims ranged from repair of broken fire hoses to costs associated with fixing broken windows.

However, "fixing" the damage done to the public perception of the Army's Air Defense program would prove to be more complicated. The explosion undermined an extensive public relations campaign that had been fostered by the Army Air Defense Command to instill public confidence in these sites. In the wake of the disaster, newspaper and magazine editors mocked Army claims that a Nike installation was no more dangerous a neighbor than a gas station. *Time* concluded:

Last week the gas station blew up . . . Meanwhile the Army had little to say about a development yet to come: along with two dozen other missile installations ringing New York City, B Battery is scheduled to replace its TNT Nike Ajaxes after this year with the atomic Nike Hercules. In the wake of Leonardo's explosive afternoon, it was going to be hard to convince the neighbors in New Jersey—or around the Nikes guarding 22 other U.S. industrial com-

plexes—that living alongside atomic warheads was still like living beside a gas station.

Nike Hercules batteries NY-54 and NY 58/60 remained active until 1968 and NY-56, NY-65, and NY-93/94 held on for 3 more years. Site NY-80 at Livingston became the sole survivor, being deactivated in April 1974.

References: Nike Quick Look, pp. 87–95; Mary T. Cagle, Development, Production, and Deployment of the Nike Ajax Guided Missile System: 1945–1959, (Redstone Arsenal, Huntsville, AL: Army Ordnance Missile Command, 1959), pp. 194–200; Time, 71 (2 June 1958).

Philadelphia Defense Area

Nike batteries built in the mid-1950s to defend the eastern approaches to Philadelphia were: (PH-25) Lumberton, (PH-32) Marlton, (PH-41) Berlin/Clementon, (PH-49) Pittman, and (PH-58) Swedesboro. Headquarters facilities were located at Fort Dix and Fort Mott.

The Philadelphia District of the Army Corps of Engineers oversaw the construction of these sites. Initially, Regular Army troops manned the batteries, then many were shifted to the National Guard. Sites PH-25, PH-41, and PH-58 were upgraded to launch Nike Hercules missiles and remained active until 1974.

Reference: Nike Quick Look, pp. 105–109.

Picatinny Arsenal, Dover

Dating from the late 19th century, Picatinny Arsenal continued to contribute to the national defense in the Cold War period. In addition to research and development in such fields as pyrotechnics, plastics, and explosives, the arsenal also helped design rockets and missile warheads.

An important Korean War contribution was the development of a bazooka rocket capable of penetrating the armor of a T-34 tank. The Army set up a pilot production plant at Picatinny for this weapon. Also in the early 1950s a Naval Air Rocket Test Station was established at the former Lake Denmark Powder Depot.

Warheads were developed at Picatinny for the following tactical missiles: Nike Hercules, Hawk, Corporal, Honest John, Littlejohn, Sergeant, Patriot, and Lance.

Reference: "Historic American Engineering Record of the

National Park Service Historic Properties Report: Picatinny Arsenal, Dover, New Jersey,"(March, 1985) pp. 42–43, [LOC].

NEW MEXICO

A I R   F O R C E

Holloman Air Force Base

Personnel first arrived at Alamogordo Army Air Field on April 10, 1942, and soon the base became an important training facility for B-17 and later for B-29 aircrews. Slated for closure during the immediate post-war budget cutback, the airbase received a reprieve, as the Army decided to consolidate missile testing operations within the valley. On February 27, 1947, the base came under the jurisdiction of the Air Materiel Command and missile testing programs forged ahead. After 38 launchings in Utah (see Hill Air Force Base), the first launch of a Boeing Ground-to-Air Pilotless Aircraft (GAPA) lifted into the New Mexico sky on July 23, 1947.

On January 13, 1948, the Air Force renamed the base to honor Colonel George V. Holloman, a missile pioneer who died in a plane crash in March 1946. Holloman AFB was redesignated Holloman Air Development Center on October 10, 1952. Five years later the facility took on the title of Air Force Missile Development Center (AFMDC).

Besides GAPA, tactical missiles such as the JB-2 Loon, Snark, Mace, Matador, Falcon, Firebee, Quail, and Rascal were assembled and tested at Holloman or launched from the adjacent White Sands Proving Ground. A high-speed test track was built in increments, eventually increasing in length to 50,000 feet. Initially only 3,550 feet long, the track experienced its inaugural run on June 23, 1950. On April 16, 1951, a Snark research vehicle made a successful sled run on the track. The track has since been designated a category II historic property.

In addition to the high-speed test track, some of the facilities supporting missile development on base included the Inertial Guidance Test Facility and the Radar Target Scatter Test Facility.

The AFMDC was phased out in 1970 with many functions transferred to Eglin AFB. Testing on various missiles continued to the present as evidenced by continued use of the high-speed test track, but many of the buildings once associated with missile development have been converted for other uses, torn down, or allowed to deteriorate.

References: Records from AFMDC have been transferred to AFHRC, Maxwell AFB. Documents relating to Holloman may also be located with the History Office at Patrick AFB, Florida, as that command often had detachments at Holloman. The base does hold some records/blueprints from the missile era. The Space Center in Alamogordo also maintains some documents from the base and has oral interviews with people involved in missile activities. George F. Meeter, The Holloman Story, (New Mexico: University of New Mexico, 1967) provides eyewitness accounts of "Space Age" research at the facility.

Kirtland Air Force Base

Phillips Laboratory

Encompassing a large military reservation around the city of Albuquerque, Kirtland AFB is home to over 140 tenant organizations, the largest being the Department of Energy's Sandia Corporation. The Sandia facilities, combined with Defense Department special weapons research facilities, make Kirtland one of the most significant research and development assets in the nation.

During the Cold War, Kirtland's role in missile development has been supportive. There has been much research, development, testing, and evaluation (RDT&E) conducted here on missile components. In addition to on-base testing, Kirtland has become an important data repository for missile testing conducted elsewhere.

Named for General Samuel C. Phillips, the Phillips Laboratory came into existence on December 11, 1990. In the 1950s, General Phillips conducted engineering work involving the Falcon and BOMARC programs at Wright-Patterson AFB, Ohio. He played a key role in arranging for Thor IRBM basing in Great Britain and then took charge of the Minuteman Program during the critical period of testing and deployment from 1959 to 1963. After a stint with NASA to manage the Apollo program, Phillips assumed command of the Space and Missile Systems Organization (SAMSO) from 1969 to 1972. His final tour of duty placed him in command of the Air Force Systems Command.

The components of Phillips Laboratory based at Kirtland date back to 1952 with the establishment of the Air Force Special Weapons Center (AFSWC). Charged with developing and testing nuclear and other special weapons, the laboratory also tested components of the weapon delivery systems that carried these weapons. In 1963, the AFSWC Research and Development Directorate formed the Air Force Weapons Laboratory (AFWL) at Kirtland to conduct tests including evaluating the effects of nuclear weapons and various climatic conditions on weapon components. Missiles that received AFWL treatment included the Titan, Minuteman, and Peacekeeper intercontinental ballistic missiles (ICBMs) as well as the Spartan antiballistic missile (ABM).

On October 1, 1982, AFSWC and AFWL joined with the Rocket Propulsion Lab (renamed Astronautics Lab in 1987) at Edwards AFB, California, and the Geophysics Lab (formally AF Cambridge Research Lab) in Massachusetts to become subordinate labs to the Air Force Technology Center. Headquartered at Kirtland, this organization was Phillips Laboratory's immediate predecessor.

Among the AFWL facilities that supported missile component testing are:

- The AFWL/Los Alamos Electronic Pulse Calibration and Simulation (ALECS) facility, which has supported electromagnetic pulse (EMP) testing of various weapons and communications systems. Examples of missiles tested include Minuteman and the Navy's Poseidon.

- The Pulserad 1590 pulsed power machine, which was used from 1968 to 1976 to produce X-ray studies of the hardness levels of intercontinental and antiballistic missile guidance computers.

- The Shiva Star, which is an extensive modification of the Shiva I power source. Began in 1971, the Shiva I used cylindrical plasma liner implosions to produce intense X-rays that simulate space conditions that could affect satellites, boosters, and reentry vehicles. Modified in 1982, the Shiva Star allowed AFWL to perform research work in plasma physics, power pulse physics, and fusion technology that has earned the Air Force national recognition.

References: Phillips Laboratory has a history office that could assist with specific inquiries. Bob Duffner and John Brownlee provided "Phillips Laboratory Historical Overview," (Phillips Laboratory History Office Pamphlet Series, No. 1, 1993); and Air Force Weapons Laboratory; The Silver Anniversary, (Kirtland AFB, NM: Air Force Weapons Laboratory, 1988).

Walker Air Force Base

Built in World War II, the base became a SAC bomber base in the post-war era. For a few short years it hosted another type of strategic weapon—the Atlas missile.

With the decision to construct Atlas lift-silos around Roswell reached in January 1960, the Corps of Engineers Albuquerque District commissioned soil samples that verified that the region could geologically sustain the underground complexes. The Albuquerque District then acquired the twelve sites surrounding Roswell and on May 16, 1960, advertised for bids to convert the Bechtel Corporation blueprints into reality.

On June 15, 1960, a joint venture consisting of Macco Corporation, Raymond International, Inc., The Kaiser Co., and Puget Sound Bridge and Dry Dock Co. was announced as the winning bid. Work started a week later. In November 1960, as construction continued, the Albuquerque District transferred responsibility for construction to the Corps of Engineers Ballistic Missile Construction Office (CEBMCO) based in Los Angeles.

The last site was completed on January 6, 1962, fifty-seven days behind schedule. As at other sites, constant design changes resulting from the "concurrency" concept as well as some labor-management problems added days to the construction schedule.

During the project there were six walkouts, which led to a total of 2,512 man-days lost. Several accidents resulted in fatalities. Seventy-four disabling injuries contributed to 51,086 man-days lost on the job.

Reportedly, the first Atlas missile to arrive in Roswell received a welcoming parade. New Mexico's Governor Mecham gave the keynote speech at a Site 10 ceremony held on October 31, 1961, in which CEBMCO turned the site over to the Air Force. Although Cheves County residents took patriotic pride in the news of the missile squadron's arrival, Roswell residents submitted 10 permit requests for bomb shelters in October 1961 as construction went ahead. The 579th SMS received its first missile on January 24, 1962. In April 1962, a completed liquid oxygen plant built at Walker AFB was turned over to the Air Force. The squadron completed missile installation approximately 1 month before the Cuban Missile Crisis.

Roswell's sites developed a notorious reputation due to three missile explosions. On June 1, 1963, launch complex 579-l was destroyed during a propellant loading exercise. On February 13, 1964, an explosion occurred during another propellant loading exercise, destroying launch complex 579-5. Again, a month later, on March 9, 1964, silo 579-2 fell victim to another explosion that occurred during a propellant loading exercise. Fortunately, these missiles were not mated with their warheads at the time of the incidents. The only injury reported was that of a crewman running into barbed wire as he fled a site.

The accidents at Walker and at other Atlas and Titan I sites accelerated the decision to deactivate these systems. After the Air Force removed the missiles in 1965, the dozen sites reverted back to private ownership. Within a year of the deactivation of the 597th SMS, the Air Force announced that the base would be closed. This occurred on June 30, 1967.

It should be noted that in 1960, two above-ground Army Nike Hercules sites were constructed, but the missiles never came. Two months after activation in April 1960, the Headquarters unit deactivated.

References: U.S. Army Ballistic Missile Construction Office, "History of the Corps of Engineers Ballistic Missile Construction Office and Contract Activities at Walker AFB, Roswell New Mexico: June 1960–June 1962", pp, 1–2, 1–3, 2–1, 2–7, 4–1, 4–2, 2–40, [HQCE]; Fritz Thompson, "Atlas Lair," Albuquerque Journal, (27 February 1994), pp. 1, 10; R. Bruce Harley, A History of Walker Air Force Base, 1941–1967, (March AFB, CA: History Office, 1967), pp. 6–7, [AFHO]; Michael E. Welsh, Mission in the Desert, Albuquerque District 1935–1985, (Albuquerque, NM: U.S. Army Engineer District, n.d.), p. 101, [HQCE]; SAC Chronology, pp. 40, 43; Congress, Senate, Committee on Armed Services, "Series of Explosions of Air Force F Intercontinental Ballistic Missiles," (88th Congress, 2nd session, 8 July 1964). For an excellent overview of this project's regional impact see Terry Isaacs, "Silos and Shelters in the Pecos Valley: The Atlas ICBM in Chaves County, New Mexico, 1960–1965," New Mexico Historical Review, (October 1993).

A R M Y

Fort Bliss Hueco Range, McGregor Range, Orogrande Range, and Red Canyon Range

Reference: See entry under Fort Bliss, Texas.

White Sands Missile Range

In the fall of 1944, with advances in American missile development, the Army's Ordnance Department and California Institute of Technology's Jet Propulsion Laboratory needed a land range where missiles could be launched and recovered for further study. Ideally, the site needed to be within the continental United States covering uninhabited terrain with extensive level regions. Surrounding hills were required for observation. Constant clear skies were needed to facilitate uninterrupted testing. The War Department also wanted the site to be located near an existing Army post so that support would be available.

An Army site survey team arrived in New Mexico's Tularosa Basin in the fall of 1944. Although the potential range was not as large as the initial specifications called for, the basin met all the other criteria and was selected to become the "White Sands Proving Ground." An important factor regarding the cantonment site selection within the Tularosa Basin was the availability of well water. The site recommendation from the Army's Chief of Ordnance was approved by the Secretary of War on February 20, 1945.

Original site plans were formulated in Washington during April and May 1945, and construction began on June 25. Initially, the Army planned to use the range not more than five to six weeks during 1945 to launch only ten to fifteen long-distance projectiles. Because the facility was considered temporary, old Civilian Conservation Corps structures were transferred from Sandia base near Albuquerque. A missile assembly building, and 16-by-16-foot Dallas type hutments were built to house incoming troops.

Armed Forces Circular Number 268, dated July 13, 1945, announced that the White Sands Proving Ground had been officially activated on July 9, 1945.

Construction of launch facilities commenced on July 10, 1945, at a location approximately six and half miles east of the Headquarters site. A blockhouse designed to withstand the impact of a rocket falling freely from an altitude of one hundred miles remains and is still used.

The Navy accepted a Chief of Ordnance's offer to participate at White Sands and a Navy cantonment area was built adjacent to the Army cantonment area. On the range, the Navy built a block-house and launch site two miles east of the Army launch facility.

By this time, it was clear the military's missile effort in the Tularosa Basin would last longer than 5 to 6 weeks. On April 11, 1945, U.S. Army troops captured the German V-2 production facil-ity in the Harz Mountains. In violation of Allied agreements regarding the disposition of Axis weapons, the Ordnance Department managed to extract enough components from the facility to assemble 100 V-2s. In August 1945, with 300 freight cars en route loaded with V-2 component parts, activity at White Sands was assured.

Important participants in that near-term activity would be many of the German scientists and engineers who had designed those V-2 components. Volunteering to come to America under what would be eventually known as "Operation PAPERCLIP," a team led by Dr. Wernher von Braun, assembled at Fort Bliss, Texas, in early 1946 to assist with the various missile projects ongoing at White Sands. While the Germans were in transit, American sci-entists and engineers forged ahead.

At 1000 hours, September 26, 1945, a Tiny Tim rocket became the first projectile launched at the Proving Ground. The test deter-mined the suitability of the Navy-developed Tiny Tim to serve as a booster to the WAC Corporal missile that was being designed by Army Ordnance/Caltech ORDCIT project.

After additional test launchings of Tiny Tim/partial WAC Corporal variants, the first full WAC Corporal-A lifted off on October 11, 1945; another was launched the next day. Both rock-ets attained an altitude of 235,000 feet. Additional launchings of WAC-As continued through December 3, 1946.

Eventually, the missile evolved into the Corporal E, a projectile weighing 10,000 pounds with a planned range of seventy-five miles. Confidence in this missile increased as testing proceeded from 1947 through 1951 and allowed the Army to add this new weapon to its arsenal.

Although White Sands played an important role in fielding the American-designed and -built Corporal, the missile range actually received most of its notoriety because of the firing of V-2 rockets and the presence of German scientists. Unlike the Corporal pro-gram, the V-2 program was geared toward developing flying laboratories. Participants in various experimental flights included

the Naval Research Laboratory, Army Ground Forces, Air Materiel Command, Army Signal Corps, Applied Physics Laboratory of Johns Hopkins, Harvard, Princeton, University of Michigan, and Caltech.

Before large missile launch operations could commence, rocket engine test facilities were needed to evaluate various designs. The original test stand, built in 1946 under the supervision of German Operation PAPERCLIP scientists, was capable of withstanding units producing 100,000 pounds of thrust. The stand had an outrigging that could accommodate smaller rockets with thrusts of up to 20,000 pounds.

The first V-2 test firing occurred on March 15, 1946. The first liftoff occurred a month later on April 16th, and proved erratic-the flight was terminated 19 seconds after launch. As the program pro-gressed into 1952, there were additional failures. Perhaps the most notable fouled flight occurred on May 29, 1947, when a modified V-2 veered in the opposite direction and landed near Juarez, Mexico.

Yet the V-2 program gave American scientists and engineers valuable experience in handling larger rockets and much knowl-edge about the upper atmosphere. Biological experiments involving test animals laid the groundwork for future manned flight. "Bumper" flights, in which a WAC Corporal would be launched from the nose cone of a V-2 at a specific altitude, gave Americans experience with rocket staging. Lessons learned from the 67 V-2 firings at White Sands found applications in future mis-sile programs.

While making important contributions at White Sands, the German "Paperclippers" frankly were underutilized. This situa-tion was rectified in 1950, with the establishment of the Army Ordnance Center at Huntsville, Alabama. There, von Braun and his team designed the rocket that carried America's first satellite into space.

As missile testing activities at White Sands expanded, so did the base's infrastructure. By April 30, 1949, the technical and support-ing facilities were valued at nearly $15 million.

By 1954, additional test stands included another 100,000-pound thrust capable facility, as well as a 300,000-pound facility and a 500,000-pound facility. Protective measures to guard the testing engineers at these facilities were extensive. Still, there was danger involved as demonstrated on September 30, 1955, when a test of a Nike Hercules proto-type liquid propulsion system triggered a devastating explosion that caved in the wall of the reinforced concrete control room, killing one and injuring five.

Extensive laboratories were constructed to support preflight testing of various missile components. For example, specially designed chambers allowed for the creation of environments ranging from severe heat to subfreezing temperatures. Throughout the Cold War, these laboratories received extensive modernizations, as emerging technologies provided new testing capabilities.

Originally, individuals from the Ballistics Research Laboratory (BRL) at the Aberdeen Proving Ground came to White Sands to monitor flights and then went to Maryland to analyze test data. However, BRL quickly determined that a permanent "annex" was needed at White Sands, and in the late 1940s, approximately 40 BRL employees found themselves relocated to the southwest and having responsibilities for developing and operating the range instrumentation and reducing the data. In 1952, the "BRL-White Sands Annex" became part of an organization known as the Flight Demonstration Laboratory (FDL). FDL eventually evolved into what became known in 1966 as National Range Operations.

Working with BRL and its successor organizations, the Army Signal Corps played an important role in providing range communication and data transmission systems as well as radar, electronic, pictorial, meteorological, and signal maintenance support to the range. Over the years the Corps has accumulated maintenance responsibilities for 1,500 precisely surveyed instrumentation sites that made White Sands the most sophisticated and heavily instrumented geographical testing area in the world.

Additional Army missile projects that underwent research and testing at White Sands in the early years included Hermes, Loki, Nike, Honest John, Lacrosse, and Hawk. The Navy also took advantage of the range to launch numerous prototypes for its evolving missile program.

Based out of nearby Holloman AFB, the Air Force used White Sand facilities to evaluate Convair's MX-774 project, Northrop's MX-775 project (Snark), as well as numerous short-range tactical missiles.

Throughout the decades, the three military services as well as other government agencies and private contractors have used the range's facilities for testing and evaluating numerous projects. For example, White Sands has played important roles in the development and testing of systems for ballistic missile defense. Between 1945 and 1990, the range had tested over 1,000 weapon and space systems. Physical assets at White Sands in 1990 were then estimated to be worth $4 billion.

Seeking a location to test an Apollo propulsion system in the early 1960s NASA received DOD approval to build what was initially called the Propulsion System Development Facility. With sites to the north of U.S. 70 in the western Tularosa Basin, the facility's primary mission was (and still is) to develop, qualify, and test the limits of spacecraft propulsion systems. Renamed White Sands Test Facility (WSTF) in 1965, the facility had by 1991 tested more than 325 rocket engines by conducting over 2.2 million firings. Some of this work supported military projects such as the ABM program and Navy solid rocket exhaust studies.

In 1995, White Sands remained an Army-operated range. As part of the Army's Test and Evaluation Command under the Army Materiel Command, the range provides test facilities for organizations within and outside of the Department of Defense.

White Sands hosts several missile- and nonmissile-related historic properties. Missile-related historic properties include the Army blockhouse and V-2 gantry crane at Launch Complex 33 (Category I); the 100,000-pound and 500,000-pound rocket test stands (Category II); the Navy blockhouse, launch towers, and USS Desert Ship at Launch Complex 35; the V-2 Assembly Building 1538; and the Propulsion Unit Calibration Stand Blockhouse.

References: The Public Affairs Office provided a copy of Eunice H. Brown, James A. Robertson, John W. Kroehnke, and E. L. Cross, White Sands: Range Beginnings and Early Missile Testing *(White Sands, NM: Public Affairs Office, 1959). This volume, along with Frederick I. Ordway and Mitchell R. Sharpe,* The Rocket Team, *(New York: Thomas Y. Crowell, 1979), provided much material on the earlier years. A series of articles by Tom Starkweather, featured in the* White Sands Missile Ranger, *from 1 December 1989 to 25 January 1991 provided useful information on supporting units. "Range Commanders Council Organization and Policy Document," (U.S. Army White Sands Missile Range, NM: Secretariat Range Commanders Council, March 1994) provided information about the coordination role of that organization for all U.S. weapons ranges. The "Historic American Engineering Record" report prepared in 1985 (HAER NM,7-ALMOG. V.1), [LOC] provided a good historical overview and documented the historic properties.*

NEW YORK

A I R   F O R C E

Griffiss Air Force Base

Rome Laboratories

During 1950 and 1951, the Air Force transferred the Watson Laboratory from Eatontown, New Jersey, to Griffiss AFB. This Air Research and Development Command facility subsequently became known as the Rome Air Development Center.

As the Rome Air Development Center, the facility tested large ground electronic systems including radars and command control links needed to support the deployment of defensive and deterrent missile systems.

The base also became host to a SAC B-52 Wing, which arrived in 1960. When the Wing's B-52G aircraft underwent modification to carry Air Launched Cruise Missiles (ALCMs), ground storage and assembly buildings were constructed to provide support for this strategic weapon system. On January 11, 1981, the first two ALCMs came to the 416th Bombardment Wing for environmental and maintenance training of the troops. In April, operational models of these weapons began to arrive at Griffiss. Five months later, President Reagan called for the deployment of 3,000 ALCMs from SAC bombers.

The first training mission with B-52G-mounted ALCMs occurred on September 13, 1981. A year later, a Griffiss-based bomber conducted the first ALCM operational test launch. In December 1982, the first squadron of B-52G bombers to be equipped with nuclear-tipped ALCMs was declared combat ready.

Griffiss AFB is slated for closure under a Base Realignment and Closure Act.

References: See Leland R. Jones, Administrative and Technical Chronology of Rome Air Development Center, Griffiss AFB, New York: Feb 1942–June 1975, (Griffiss AFB, NY: Rome Air Development Center, 1976); Air Force Bases, pp. 205–210; "Air Force Ballistic Missile Program," (K146.01-106A), [AFHO]; SAC Chronology, pp. 69, 71–72; Beverly Sanford Follis, Chronology: Air Research and Development Command, 1945–1961, (Andrews AFB, MD: History Office, Headquarters Air Force Systems Command, 1985).

Niagara Falls Air Force Base

On June 1, 1960, the Air Defense Command activated the 35th Air Defense Missile Squadron. Located at Niagara Falls International Airport, this BOMARC unit augmented the Army Nike point missile defenses and Air Force and Air Guard tactical fighters to provide defense for the region. As one of the last three BOMARC facilities constructed, the base received the improved solid-fueled BOMARC B missile and thus negated the requirement for fueling and other support structures required at bases built earlier. The launch structures at Niagara Falls were of the Model IV design.

The 35th Air Defense Missile squadron went on alert in December 1961 and remained in operation until December 31, 1969.

Because Niagara had received 46 BOMARC B missiles (in contrast with 28 BOMARC Bs placed at each of the 5 other sites), during the mid-1960s "excess" Niagara missiles were removed to Eglin AFB for operational training launches.

Reference: Nike Quick Look, p. 193.

Plattsburgh Air Force Base

Plattsburgh has hosted military activities throughout much of the nation's history. An Army Barracks during World War II, the Air Force reclaimed the land in the early 1950s to host an Air Force Base for the Strategic Air Command. After extensive construction, the base received its first B-47 bombers in 1956. During the 1960s the base hosted the 556th Strategic Missile Squadron (Atlas F).

Initial plans called for three complexes with three Atlas F missiles per complex. Later, a fourth complex was added to the plans. Eventually "lift-launch" silos were placed at Champlain; Alburg, VT, Swanton, VT, Millsboro; Lewis; Au Sable Forks; Riverview; Redford; Dannemora; Brainardsville; Ellenburg Depot; and Moeers.

Construction began in June 1960, when groundbreaking occurred at a site near Champlain. Throughout the next year, hundreds of workers dug the twelve 174-foot-deep, 54-foot-wide holes into the solid rock. In addition to the three launchers, each complex had an underground launch control facility.

The Air Force conducted "missile briefings" to educate area leaders and residents on safety measures, environmental impact, and the need for the missile program. As with other construction sites around the nation, Plattsburgh suffered its share of fatalities. Seven men died in accidents and many more were injured.

Despite the dangerous work, management-labor relations were amicable. As of March 1962 only 98 man-days had been lost due to work stoppages and that did not delay construction. The first missile arrived in April 1962, and the silos were declared operational in December. As a result of Defense Secretary McNamara's 1964 directive to decommission Atlas and Titan I missile squadrons, the Atlas F missiles were removed and the 556th Strategic Missile Squadron was deactivated on June 25, 1965.

References: U.S. Army Corps of Engineers Ballistic Missile Construction Office "Historical Summary, Plattsburgh Area Office: 1 Aug 1960–31 Oct 1962," pp. IV 1-4, 59, V 1–3, VI 17–27, [HQCE]; Plattsburgh Air Force Base 25 Years, (Plattsburgh AFB, NY: History Office, 1981), pp. 12–14, [AFHO].

Suffolk County Air Force Base

The 6th Air Defense Missile Squadron augmented the New York Air Defense network with a complex that housed 56 BOMARC A missiles in what were called Model II shelters. The squadron became operational in December 1959. Rather than build Model IV shelters to accommodate the improved BOMARC B missile, the Air Force kept the squadron operational for only 5 years.

Eventually the Suffolk County Police Department Police Academy assumed title to the property for a Police Academy.

Reference: Nike Quick Look, p. 169.

A R M Y

Niagara Falls-Buffalo Defense Area

Site designations and locations of Nike sites in western New York are:

(BU-09)	Ransom Creek/Millersport
(NF-03)	Model City
(BU-18)	Lancaster/Milgrove
(NF-16)	Sanborn/Cambria
(BU-34/35)	Orchard Park
(NF-41)	Grand Island, originally designated NF-74/75.
(BU-52)	Hamburg

Buffalo and Niagara Falls were separate Defense Areas until their merger in December 1961. Sites BU-18, NF-16, and NF-41 were converted to operate Nike Hercules. Sites BU-34/35, BU-52,

NF-03, NF-16, and NF-74/75 were double sites hosting 24 launchers. Before consolidation, the Niagara Falls Defense Area was commanded from historic Fort Niagara. Command and control was handled from a "BIRDIE" site collocated with Air Force tracking radars at Lockport Air Force Station. National Guard Units operated these batteries.

Reference: Nike Quick Look, pp. 95–98.

New York Defense Area

Nike defenses were placed during the mid-1950s Both Regular Army and Army to defend the nation's most populous city. Site designations and locations of Nike batteries defending New York include:

(NY-03/04)	Orangeburg/Mt. Nebo (double site)
(NY-24)	Amityville/Farmingdale
(NY-09)	Kensico/White Plains
(NY-25)	Rocky Point/Brookhaven
(NY-15)	Fort Slocum
(NY-20)	Lloyd Harbor/Huntington
(NY29/30)	Lido Beach (double site)
(NY-49)	Fort Tilden
(NY-23)	Hicksville/Oyster Bay
(NY-99)	Spring Valley/Ramapo

Headquarters facilities were located at Tappan, Fort Totten, Fort Wadsworth, and Roslyn.

Combined with the sites located in New Jersey, the New York sites composed one of the largest defensive nets in the nation. Sites NY-03/04, NY-24, NY-25, and NY-49 received upgrades to accept Nike Hercules. Beginning in June 1960, command and control was coordinated by a "Missile Master" facility located at Atlantic Highlands, New Jersey. Earlier, New York's air defenses had been manually coordinated from Fort Wadsworth on Staten Island.

Perhaps to even a greater extent than elsewhere, New York site locations in proximity to major population centers made good public relations vital, especially in the wake of a highly publicized disaster at a New Jersey Nike site in 1958. During the following year a Nike missile exhibit participated in 40 major public events ranging from the State Fair to Boy Scout Camporees. Nike sites also were occasionally opened to the public.

As in several other states, during the 1960s the National Guard assumed a greater role in operating the sites.

References: Robert C. Toth, "Electronic Nike Control Guards Area," New York Herald Tribune, (7 June 1960); Argus, (1 September 1959, p. 9, [MHI]; Nike Quick Look, pp. 87–95.

NORTH CAROLINA

INDUSTRIAL

Charlotte Army Ordnance Missile Plant

This facility produced the Nike Ajax and Nike Hercules surface-to-air missiles for the Ordnance Department. Douglas Aircraft Company operated the plant for the Army. The facility assumed Nike Ajax production in 1955 to allow Douglas to use its Santa Monica facility for the production of the follow-on Hercules missile. Eventually the Charlotte plant also produced the longer-range Hercules. In 1962, the new U.S. Army Missile Command (MICOM) assumed responsibility for the plant. The plant employed over 2,000 people.

In 1967, with the completion of Nike Hercules production, the plant was declared excess.

Reference: Elizabeth C. Joliff, History of the United States Missile Command: 1962–1977, (Redstone Arsenal, Huntsville, AL: Headquarters, U.S. Army Missile Command, July 1979), pp. 18, 23.

Tar Heel Army Ordnance Plant, Burlington

In 1958, the Army Chief of Ordnance received jurisdiction from the General Services Administration for production facilities at Burlington, some dating from before World War II. Army ownership did not dramatically change on-site activity as the facility had been leased by Western Electric since 1946. During the 1950s Western Electric began to use the facility to produce electronic equipment for antiair and antiballistic missile systems.

With Army reorganization, the plant came under the jurisdiction of the Army Missile Command in 1962 and the plant was designated the Tar Heel Missile Plant a year later. In the 1980s the facility was still being leased by Western Electric to manufacture and refurbish missile components.

Reference: Historic American Engineering Record Tarheel Army Missile Plant, (HAER NC 1-BURL.), [LOC].

NORTH DAKOTA

AIR FORCE

Grand Forks Air Force Base

Established on August 20, 1956, Grand Forks AFB formed part of the nation's air defense network, hosting a Semi-Automatic Ground Environment (SAGE) center. The base's primary mission changed dramatically on July 1, 1963, when Aerospace Defense Command (ADC) transferred the base to the Strategic Air Command (SAC) in anticipation of the arrival of the 321st Strategic Missile Wing.

The search for a location to place "Wing VI" began in January 1961. Based on military and engineering recommendations, the Department of Defense selected a 6,500 square mile region around Grand Forks in February 1963.

A year later, the Air Force announced that Grand Forks AFB would be first to deploy the Minuteman II missile. On February 28, 1963, it was announced that Morrison-Knudsen and Associates, which had submitted a bid of just over $128 million, would serve as the primary contractor. During the following month, construction began on the first flight of missile silos. Excavations presented relatively few problems. Flooding during the winter and spring of 1964 and 1965 proved to be an exception. Many flooded components, such as diesel generators, had to be returned to the factory for rehabilitation.

Labor-management relations were exemplary. There were only two work stoppages. A Missile Site Labor Relations Committee met twice monthly to act on existing or potential problems. Seven fatalities were associated with this project.

On November 1, 1964, the 321st SMW was activated. As personnel began to report to the 321st, the wing trained for the day when the Minuteman II missile would be placed on alert status.

In March 1965, wing Headquarters found a permanent home in building 306. The 75 foot high blockhouse formerly served as a SAGE Direction Center for the ADC. Later that year, the "LE-4" missile procedures trainer was installed within the Headquarters building.

As the Headquarters staff settled into their new home, construction continued on 150 underground silos and fifteen launch control facilities, spread out over territory comparable in size to the state of New Jersey. During 1965, the wing's three missile squadrons were activated and crew training and certification began at Vandenberg AFB, California.

In August 1965, the base received its first Minuteman II missile, shipped by train from assembly plant 77 at Hill AFB, Utah. During the following March, the base received the first Minuteman II to be shipped via aircraft, an Air Force first.

On April 25, 1966, the 447th Strategic Missile Squadron and its 50 Minuteman II missiles were declared operational. Additional flights came on line throughout 1966. On December 7, 1966, the 321st Strategic Missile Wing, with its component 446th, 447th, and 448th Strategic Missile Squadrons, became fully operational.

As the first base to deploy Minuteman II missiles, Grand Forks AFB hosted "Project Long Life II," a unique reliability test in which modified Minuteman missiles were fueled to travel a few hundred yards. The first launch from a Grand Forks silo occurred on October 19, 1966 and was declared unsuccessful. Nine days later, a second attempt also failed. A third attempt under "Project Giant Boost" occurred in August 1968 and again proved unsuccessful.

Crews from the 321st SMW competed in SAC's first Missile Combat Competition held at Vandenberg AFB from April 2 through April 7, 1967. Later that month, members from the wing launched its first Minuteman II from Vandenberg. Despite the wing's relative youth, it quickly established a reputation for excellence by winning numerous honors during its first few years. For example, in 1969, the unit received numerous significant honors, including the Air Force Outstanding Unit Award, and SAC Outstanding Missile Wing Award. Throughout the next two decades, the unit would score additional triumphs at Olympic Arena missile competitions and receive numerous "best" accolades.

From December 1971 to March 1973, the wing converted to Minuteman III missiles. These missiles represented a significant technological advancement, having multiple independently targetable reentry vehicles (MIRVs). Coordinating the missile changeover required complex planning and execution. In 1972 alone, 250 separate nuclear weapon convoys motored over the roads of North Dakota.

Modifications continued that enhanced readiness and improved survivability. For instance, about mid-August 1975, "Wing Six Integrated Program" (WSIP) was implemented. WSIP included a silo upgrade that improved the missile suspension system to withstand greater blast-shock and provided the 321st with a remote targeting capability. The wing underwent continual readiness inspections and participated in numerous training exercises on base and at Vandenberg. Training improved with the expansion of on-base simulator facilities. For example, in 1970, wing crews conducted tests using "Modified Operational Missiles" which enabled them to exercise all aspects of a missile launch except igniting the engine.

Often nature threatened wing readiness. The organizational history referred to "the Great Blizzard of '66," "the storm of '75 that caused $10,000 in damages," and "one of the harshest winters [1977] which 'hampered maintenance efforts' and had 'ice storms snapping power lines'." When the heavy snows melted, floods occasionally resulted. A quick thaw in April 1979 created one of the most devastating floods within the Red River valley basin during this century. In addition to protecting the silos from flood waters, wing personnel volunteered to join the mostly successful two-week struggle to keep Grand Forks and East Grand Forks dry. This effort was repeated in April 1989.

With the restructuring of the Air Force in the early 1990s the wing first came under Air Combat Command and then Air Force Space Command jurisdiction. In March 1995, the Base Realignment and Closure (BRA0 Commission selected the 321st Strategic Missile Wing for deactivation.

References: "CEBMCO Wing VI Grand Forks Area," pp. 2, 16–17, 45–48, 53–62, 71–77, [HQCE]; "321st Missile Wing History" (1993) provided by the wing historian; SAC Chronology, pp. 50, 51, 53, 56.

Minot Air Force Base

Built in the mid-1950s to host a Semi-Automatic Ground Environmental (SAGE) complex and Air Defense Command fighter aircraft, Minot became a Strategic Air Command base on July 1, 1962, pending the imminent activation of Minuteman I-B missile launchers.

The Corps of Engineers Ballistic Missile Construction Office (CEBMCO) oversaw the construction of the 150 silos and ten launch complexes spread over a 12,000-square mile area. The prime contractor was the Peter Kiewit Sons' Company, which received the contract on December 22, 1961, with a bid of $67.8 million. At the peak of construction, Kiewit brought in 6,000 men with 1,100 vehicles and 115 cranes to ensure on-time completion of the contract. Relations between management and this work force were amicable as there were only two work stoppages that cost fifty-eight man-days lost.

To manage the project, CEMBCO used a "critical path" method, which is essentially a daily charting of progress geared to project future needs. However, despite improved management techniques, CEMBCO and the contractors faced challenges from the severe weather and logistics support for the remote locations. Recordbreaking spring rains turned roads and work sites into quagmires, making excavation and transport dangerous. Severe winter cold with temperatures as low as -35°F tested worker endurance. In the autumn, dust storms made travel hazardous.

Despite these challenges, Peter Kiewit Sons' Company used accelerated construction procedures and completed the project 51 days ahead of schedule. Two workers died in construction-related incidents and there were thirty-six disabling injuries. Four private citizens died in various traffic accidents with project construction vehicles. With construction under way, the Air Force activated the 455th Strategic Missile Wing and component 740th Strategic Missile Squadron on November 1, 1962. During the following two months, the 741st and 742nd Strategic Missile Squadrons administratively came into existence.

To preserve the continuity of units with distinguished histories, on June 25, 1968, the 455th Strategic Missile Wing was redesignated as the 91st Strategic Missile Wing. The 91st had organizational roots dating from World War II and had gained recent fame as a B-52 wing operating over Vietnam.

The first Minuteman III missile to arrive in the field was accept-ed by the 91st Strategic Missile Wing on April 14, 1970. The following August, the first Minuteman IIIs were placed on alert status. By December 1971, the switchover to the new missile was completed.

In addition to Minuteman ICBMs, Minot AFB hosted another type of strategic missile. Assigned B-52H bombers were modified to carry Air Launched Cruise Missiles (ALCMs).

References: Air Force Bases, *pp. 417–421; Construction details are found in* "CEBMCO Minuteman Missile Facilities: Minot Air Force Base," *pp. 18–19, 49–65, 67–71, 110–112; and* The Federal Engineer, Damsites to Missile Sites: A History of the Omaha District, U.S. Army Corps of Engineers, *(Omaha, NE: U.S. Army Engineer District, 1984), pp. 193–194, [HQCE]. Milestones at Minot were recorded in the* SAC Chronology, *pp. 56, 57, 60. Details on Combat Crew duty at Minot are described in David A. Anderton,* Strategic Air Command: Two Thirds of the Triad, *(New York: Charles Scribners Sons, 1976), pp. 140–149.*

A R M Y

Grand Forks Safeguard ABM Installation

On November 3, 1967, the Department of Defense revealed that Grand Forks AFB was one of ten initial locations to host a Sentinel ABM site. With President Nixon's March 14, 1969, announcement reorienting ballistic missile defense (BMD) to protect strategic forces, construction at a site outside of Boston ceased and constructing a "Safeguard" installation at Grand Forks became a top priority.

However, construction was stalled throughout mid-1969, as Congress debated the merits of BMD. Finally, after the Senate defeated amendments to kill Safeguard deployment, the Army proceeded under the assumption that appropriations would be forthcoming.

Survey teams selected sites in flat wheatlands close to the Canada-Minnesota border, north-northwest of Grand Forks. Twenty-five miles separated the 279-acre Perimeter Acquisition Radar (PAR) and the 433-acre Missile Site Radar (MSR) sites. Four remote launch sites of 36 to 45 acres each were to be situated in a circle with a twenty mile radius surrounding the MSR.

Projections called for the availability of 1,000 gallons of water per minute, which threatened to disrupt the regional ecology. To solve the problem, the Corps proposed drawing water from an aquifer located 46 miles from the MSR site and 36 miles from the PAR site. On March 9, 1970, assured that the Corps proposal would not disrupt area groundwater supplies, North Dakota issued a conditional water permit to the Army. Consequently, Zurn Engineers of Upland, California, won a $3.8 million contract to construct a system that would include ten spaced wells, three booster stations, fifty-eight miles of pipe, and on-site reservoirs.

Other environmental impact studies indicated that the facility's diesel power plants would violate State and Federal Clean Air standards. Eventually, the Army contracted Cooper-Bessemer to design and construct pollution suppression devices for their diesel generators.

A Community Impact Team from the Omaha District gauged the effect of construction and deployment on the local population and infrastructure. The study showed local communities would need to expand educational facilities and police and fire protection. Because the Army could not legally provide financial support to these communities to resolve these problems, local legislators sought and received relief from the Federal Government.

Transportation of construction materials provided an additional challenge. The Corps arranged for the Great Northern Railroad to put in a siding at Hensel and for the North Dakota Road Department to improve the light roads leading to the construction sites.

Labor relations were handled through the previously established Grand Forks Missile Sites Labor Committee and with the North Dakota Chapter of the Associated General Contractors of America, Labor Committee. After several meetings, a final "Project Agreement" emerged that would provide workers a fixed wage and fringe benefit schedule over the three-year construction period. Addressing travel, subsistence, health, safety, and grievance handling concerns, the Project Agreement provided a foundation for good labor relations during construction.

One difficulty potential contractors faced was meeting new Department of Defense guidelines regarding the hiring of minorities. Safeguard became a DOD pilot program to enforce compliance with the Title VII of 1964 Civil Rights Act and Executive Orders 10925, 11114, and 11246. Contractors were expected to make a "good faith" effort to employ minorities to fill what was unofficially understood to be 6 to 10 percent of the work force.

Potential contractors complained. Meeting the "good faith" goal in a state with a two percent minority population consisting mostly of Native Americans seemed quite unreasonable. However, the joint group of contractors that won the contract did provide an Equal Employment Opportunity (EEO) Affirmative Action Program that met the objectives of the Contracts Compliance Office of the Defense Contract Administration Services. The demographic problem made the "good faith" effort unattainable. When affirmative action goals were changed to rate progress based on percentage of overall hours that minorities worked, the contractors generally met the 6 to 10 percent requirement. Preparing a bid package was a major logistical undertaking. It consisted of 2,626,200 pages of architectural drawings and 4,340,000 pages of specifications.

On March 26, 1970, bids received were opened and the low bid of $137.8 million was subsequently accepted from the team of Morrison-Knudsen Inc., Peter Kiewit Sons' Company, Fischbach and Moore, Inc., and C.H. Leavell & Co.

Groundbreaking occurred at the PAR and MSR sites on April 6. Excavation proceeded rapidly, and the foundation holes for the PAR and MSR were in place by mid-May.

Work was temporarily halted at the MSR site near Nekoma on "International ABM Day." Consisting of a series of demonstrations held across the country on May 15, 1970, International ABM Day activity in North Dakota included a march on the Nekoma site organized by the "North Dakota Clergy and Laymen Concerned" and the "North Dakota Citizens for a Sane Nuclear Policy." Because Governor William Guy would not allocate resources to protect Federal property, the Army and the four-company consortium, Morrison-Knudsen and Associates, established a nonprovoking strategy consisting of removing all mobile equipment, roping off the excavation and setting up a stage and sanitary accommodations for the protesters away from the construction. By mid-day on the 15th, some 500 protesters arrived at what became known as the "Nekoma Festival of Life and Love." Late in the afternoon, several hundred demonstrators marched toward the excavation as kazoo players played "The Battle Hymn of the Republic." Upon arrival, the protesters descended into the hole and performed some symbolic activities such as planting seedlings. Overall, the Army's passive strategy worked, as the day went without violence or arrests and only minimal vandalism. A reporter from *Newsweek* labeled the protest a "flop."

However, the "flop," along with some minor labor work stoppages and redesign changes, set back a delicate time schedule, which required that the first two levels of the MSR and PAR be roofed over so interior work could proceed throughout the winter. Herculean efforts, including the imposition of 10-hour, 6-day shifts and continuing work as temperatures dipped below zero, allowed interior work to commence over the winter.

As exterior work restarted with the arrival of spring, the contractor faced material transport problems due to load restrictions placed on local roads by the state road department, and some minor labor strife. A shortage of skilled labor was resolved by hiring Canadians, and by late summer, the distinctive shapes laid out on the PAR and MSR facility blueprints became reality as both structures were "topped-out."

Progress was also made in constructing the Spartan and Sprint missile launchers. In addition, Chris Berg Inc. received contracts for the nontechnical support facilities for the personnel who eventually would man the site.

During the spring of 1972, Western Electric Company installed the pieces for the Missile Site Radar and Perimeter Acquisition Radar. To mount the big "Eye" on the PAR building, 245,828 individual pieces had to be assembled.

On May 26, 1972, President Nixon and General Secretary Brezhnev signed the ABM Treaty, which limited each nation to one site to protect strategic forces and one site to protect the "National Command Authority." With work about 85 percent complete at Grand Forks, the United States chose to finish construction at the North Dakota site and cease work at the sister site in Montana.

On August 21, 1972, the Corps turned over the PAR to the Safeguard Systems Command (SAFSCOM) Site Activation Team. The transfer of the MSR occurred on January 3, 1973. Work on the four remote launch sites fell behind schedule, with the last being completed on November 5, 1972. Testing of the PAR commenced during the summer of 1973.

On September 3, 1974, the SAFSCOM Site Activation Team was relieved by the U.S. Army Safeguard Command. Named the "Stanley R. Mickelson Complex," the North Dakota ABM site received its complement of nuclear-tipped Spartan and Sprint Missiles during the following spring. The site was declared operational on April 1, 1975. Due to Congressional action, the Army operated the site for less than a year. With the exception of the

PAR, the complex was abandoned in February 1976. In October 1977, the PAR came under operational control of the Air Force, which operated it thereafter as part of its early warning system.

References: James H. Kitchens, A History of the Huntsville Division: 15 October 1967–31 December 1976, *(Huntsville, AL: U.S. Army Engineer Huntsville Division, 1978) pp. 23, 34–58, 64–72, 78–94, 106–112, [HQCE]; Ruth Currie-McDaniel and Claus R. Martel,* The U.S. Army Strategic Defense Command: Its History and Role in the Strategic Defense Initiative 3rd ed., *(Huntsville, AL: Historical Office, U.S. Army Strategic Defense Command, 1989), pp. 7–16.*

OHIO

A I R   F O R C E

Newark Air Force Station, Aerospace Guidance and Meteorology Center

This facility came into existence in the early Cold War era as a heavy press plant to prefabricate large wing sections. However, with a change in national priorities to produce ICBMs, the plant never became operational.

After sitting idle for several years, the facility was selected to consolidate laboratories then located at Dayton Air Force Depot and Wright-Patterson AFB. Geologic testing confirmed that the facility could serve for calibration of inertial guidance systems for advanced missiles and aircraft program. Actual repair operations began in late 1962 with the arrival of inertial guidance systems for Atlas and Minuteman missiles. The organization was originally designated the 2802nd Inertial Guidance Group.

Over the years, the Center received numerous Air Force Logistics Command awards for the high quality of its work.

Reference: George W. Bradley, From Missile Base to Gold Watch: A History of the Aerospace Guidance and Meteorology Center and Newark AFS, *(Ohio: Newark AFS, 1982), [AFHO].*

Wright-Patterson Air Force Base

Air Materiel Command/Air Force Logistics Command

This installation hosted several organizations that contributed in various ways to the advancement of missile development and support.

In March 1946, the Air Technical Service Command at Wright-Patterson was redesignated as the Air Materiel Command (AMC). Besides handling the burden of disposing of tons of surplus equipment, such as war-weary aircraft, and maintaining logistical support for the newly forming United States Air Force, AMC became a major research and development organization during the post-war era. By 1947, AMC supported more than 2,000 research projects including several surface-to-surface, air-to-surface, surface-to-air, and air-to-air missiles. Among the missiles developed at Wright Patterson were the SM-62 Snark, and XMS-64 Navaho. One program, Convair's MX-774B ICBM, showed much promise. However, in 1948, funding constraints forced the Air Force to cancel the program.

Many of the other missile programs met a similar fate and this caused concern. Because AMC had the primary mission of supporting aircraft and weapons already in the inventory, much of the research and development dollars went towards applied research to improve already existing systems. Basic research to develop technologies for new weapons took a back seat. In 1949, a special committee of the Air Force Scientific Advisory Board, under the chairmanship of Dr. Louis N. Ridenour, recommended that research and development activities be separated within a new command. This proposal became reality with the establishment of the Air Research and Development Command (ARDC) in 1951. Although ARDC would be headquartered in Maryland, it would maintain a significant presence at Wright-Patterson.

Although AMC shed its research and development mission, it remained active in the ICBM program. The increased sophistication of missiles and aircraft forced AMC to reevaluate how it procured and supported weapon systems. Previous weapons development, acquisition, and maintenance had been separate activities with little coordination between the functional areas. That approach proved to be cumbersome for the ICBM. Instead ARDC used a weapon systems management approach, in which a project office guided a program through development, procurement, production, and logistics support. When a weapon system was under development, ARDC was designated the executive agency and AMC played a supporting role. For example, to support the Atlas ICBM project, AMC established a project office collocated with ARDC's Ballistic Missile Division in Inglewood, California. After completing development and placing the system into production, AMC became the executive agent for the weapon system.

The effectiveness of this teamwork arrangement came under question in the late 1950s as the Air Force hastened to develop and deploy ICBMs. As a result of several conferences addressing the overall organizational efficiency, changes were made. In 1961, Secretary of Defense Robert McNamara approved a plan to redesignate AMC as the Air Force Logistics Command (AFLC) and the ARDC as the Air Force Systems Command (AFSC). The significance of the change involved placing weapons system management in the hands of the Maryland-based AFSC.

The Ohio-based AFLC continued to play an important role in providing logistical support for missiles as they entered the inventory. In 1992, AFLC and AFSC were rejoined to form the Air Force Materiel Command. Headquartered at Wright-Patterson, this new command held responsibility for developing, maintaining, and modifying Air Force systems from "cradle to grave."

Research Activities at Wright-Patterson

In 1944, engineers from the Air Technical Services (ATS) Power Plant Laboratory reproduced a German V-1 pulse jet engine from salvaged parts. Within 89 days of arrival of the parts, these engineers launched a V-1 from Eglin Field in Florida. Soon ATS engineers built and tested 13 copies of the German missile that was designated the "JB-2."

In 1946, the laboratories at Wright-Patterson were transferred to the Air Materiel Command. In 1951, they were transferred again, this time to the newly established Air Research and Development Command.

The ARDC organization at Wright-Patterson was designated the Wright Air Development Center (WADC). WADC assumed control of all Air Force research and development, and conducted laboratory research in materials, aerodynamics, propulsion, and airborne guidance and navigation systems. During this time, WADC engineers worked on such missile programs as the Martin B-61A Matador, Boeing XF-99 BOMARC, Hughes XF-98 Falcon, and North American XMS-64 Navaho.

Throughout the 1950s the role of WADC evolved. In 1959, the organization was redesignated as the Wright Air Development Division (WADD). With the 1961 Air Force reorganization, WADD obtained procurement functions and subsequently became the Aeronautical Systems Division (ASD) of the newly established Air Force Systems Command. Management functions would shift over the next three decades; however, Wright-Patterson's laboratories would continue to provide invaluable support in the development of more advanced weapons systems.

References: "Air Force Ballistic Missile Program," (K146.01-106A), [AFHO]; Lois E. Walker, and Selby E. Wickam, From Huffman Prairie to the Moon: The History of Wright-Patterson Air Force Base, (Wright-Patterson AFB, OH: 2750th Air Base Wing Office of History, n.d.), pp. 358, 386. In addition, Wright-Patterson is home to the Air Force Museum with a vast collection of missile artifacts and a research library.

ARMY

Cincinnati-Dayton Defense Area

Site designations and locations of Nike Hercules sites in southern Ohio are: (CD-27) southeast of Wilmington, (CD-46) Felicity, and (CD-78) northwest of Oxford.

The Corps of Engineers Huntington District had responsibility for construction of these sites. Along with a site in Dillsboro, Indiana, these Nike Hercules sites became operational in 1960 to defend the industrial centers of the upper Ohio River Valley. A "BIRDIE" site collocated at C-27 hosted missile command and control functions for the region. The sites remained active until 1970–1971.

References: Leland R. Johnson, An Illustrated History of the Huntington District: U.S. Army Corps of Engineers 1754–1974, (Huntington, WV: U.S. Army Engineer District, 1977), pp. 194–195, [HQCE]; Nike Quick Look, p. 44.

Cleveland Defense Area

Site designations and locations of Nike Ajax sites built during the mid-1950s in northern Ohio are:

(CL-02)	Bratenahl	(CL-48)	Garfield Heights
(CL-11)	Painesville	(CL-59)	Palma/Midpark Station
(CL-13)	Willowick	(CL-67)	Lakefront Airport
(CL-34)	Warrensville	(CL-69)	Lordstown

Headquarters facilities were located at the Shaker Heights Armory and in Cleveland.

The Corps of Engineers Pittsburgh District, a component of the Ohio River Division, had responsibility for construction of these sites defending the Cleveland region. Sites CL-02, CL-11 and CL-69 were converted to fire Nike Hercules missiles. In 1968, the Cleveland Defense Area merged with Detroit's. In June 1971, the three remaining Nike Hercules batteries were deactivated.

References: An Eyewitness History of the Pittsburgh District, (Pittsburgh, PA: U.S. Army Engineer District, n.d,) p. 195, [HQCE]; Nike Quick Look, pp. 45–48.

OKLAHOMA

AIR FORCE

Altus Air Force Base

This World War II era base was reactivated by the Air Force in 1952 as a Tactical Air Command facility. In 1953 the base was transferred to SAC to host bombers and support aircraft. In late 1959, Hound Dog and Quail missiles were installed on B-52s assigned to Altus. In addition to these air-to-surface missiles, Altus was destined to host the Atlas F ICBM.

Near the end of January 1960, Senator Kerr, Senator Monroney, and Representative Toby Morris made the first public announcement regarding the installation of an Atlas F missile facility at Altus. In April, the Corps of Engineers, Tulsa District awarded the basic construction contract to Morrison-Knudsen and Hardeman and Associates. The two firms had submitted a combined bid of just over $20.9 million.

The twelve launcher locations were at or near Lonewolf; Hobart (2); Snyder; Cache; Mantiou; Frederick; Creta; Hollis; Russell; Willow; and Fargo, Texas. To acquire the needed 12,879 acres, in October, the Real Estate Division of the Tulsa District filed condemnation suits against 477 landowners in the 6 counties surrounding Altus.

As at other Atlas construction sites, Tulsa District Engineers were befuddled with the concurrency problem where improvements in the missile required constant modifications to the ongoing launcher construction. However, the Tulsa District managed to keep the project on schedule by using a "Red Ball" system that prioritized Atlas paperwork.

Problems elsewhere forced the Army to centralize construction management. Therefore in November 1960, the responsibility of construction was transferred to the newly formed Corps of Engineers Ballistic Missile Construction Office (CEBMCO). Consequently, approximately 175 Tulsa District employees found themselves working for the Los Angeles-based organization.

There were several "growing pains" associated with this project. Coordination between the Corps of Engineers, contractor, Site Activation Task Force (SATAF), and integrating consultants from Convair Astronautics (later General Dynamics Astronautics) was difficult at times. The Corps blamed the integrating consultants for lacking experience in heavy construction.

Natural difficulties were encountered as some sites had water tables that were higher than expected and at one site workers dug into underground cavities. Labor-management relations were harmonious. Only eight short work stoppages occurred, causing minimal delays. There were three project-related fatalities. In addition, two major on-site fires set back construction. As with other first generation missile projects, the installation and testing of the propellant loading system proved difficult as contaminants hindered the system's operation.

In August 1962, the first Atlas F was placed on alert status. In October, all twelve missiles were put on alert status as a result of the Cuban missile crisis.

On May 14, 1964, during a propellant loading exercise, an explosion caused the destruction of launch complex 577-6. Two days later, Defense Secretary McNamara ordered the accelerated phaseout of Atlas and Titan I ICBMs. As a result, the 577th Strategic Missile Squadron was deactivated on March 25, 1965.

References: U.S. Army Ballistic Missile Construction Office, "History of the Altus Area Office, 14 March 1960–28 April 1962," pp. 1–5, 69–73, 136–151; William A. Settle, Jr., The Dawning, A New Day for the Southwest: A History of the Tulsa District Corps of Engineers, 1939–1972, (Tulsa, OK: U.S. Army Engineer District, 1975), pp. 80–83, [HQCE]; SAC Chronology, pp. 36, 37, 44, 47.

Tinker Air Force Base

Oklahoma City Air Materiel Area/Logistics Center
During the 1950s this Air Materiel Command facility was responsible for program management of several missile systems. For example, Oklahoma City oversaw support of the BOMARC surface-to-air system. This responsibility changed with an Air Materiel Command realignment initiated on June 4, 1957, whereby BOMARC left Oklahoma City for Ogden, Utah. In return, the Oklahoma City Air Materiel Area (OCAMA) picked up responsibility for guided air-launched missiles such as the GAM-63 Rascal and GAM-72 Green Quail. In 1961, OCAMA became the logistics manager for the GAM-77 "Hound Dog" air-launched missile.

Responsibility for long-range air-launched munitions would continue. For example, in October 1974, the Oklahoma City "Air Logistics Center" became the systems manager for the Air-Launched Cruise Missile (ALCM). By the 1980s this Air Force Logistics Command facility managed support for the Short Range Air Missile (SRAM) SRAM II, ALCM, Ground-Launched Cruise Missile (GLCM) and Harpoon missiles.

References: Helen Rice, History of Ogden Air Materiel Area, Hill Air Force Base, Utah: 1934–1960, (Hill AFB, UT: Air Force Logistics Center, March 1963), p. 197, 202, [AFHO]; Tinker Air Force Base—A Pictorial History, (Tinker AFB, OK: Oklahoma City Air Logistics Center Office of History, 1982), pp. 108, 146, 148, [AFHO].

A R M Y

Fort Sill

In 1950, the Army's antiaircraft and field artillery branches merged to allow cross training for artillery officers. However, as surface-to-air and surface-to-surface missiles entered the inventory, the complexity of these new weapons again called for specialized training. Therefore, the Army decided to transfer the surface-to-surface missile training activities from Fort Bliss in Texas to the Army's Artillery Center at Fort Sill. Even before the Center was officially redesignated as "The Artillery and Guided Missile Center" in 1955, Fort Sill took on the mission of training soldiers on the use of newly developed short-range surface-to-surface rockets such as the Corporal. On June 22, 1954, the first troop-fired Honest John missile was launched. With the redesignation effected, in 1956, two Corporal battalions and ten training courses came to Fort Sill from Fort Bliss, Texas.

To accommodate the move, the Tulsa District of the Corps of Engineers acquired additional lands, which were transferred in

January 1957 to the Artillery and Missile Center.

As classroom instruction commenced, the Corps of Engineers Tulsa District oversaw construction of assembly, maintenance, storage, and other support facilities, including a large facility for Redstone missile maintenance. In 1958, two Redstone missile battalions were stationed at Fort Sill.

Fort Sill also hosted training facilities for the follow-on Pershing missiles. As of December 8, 1987, there were 78 Pershing II training missile stages and thirty-nine launchers at the base.

References: Details of the transfer of the missile training mission are found in History of the US Army Artillery and Missile School 1945–1957, *(Fort Sill, OK: Artillery and Missile School, 1958), pp. 67–73, [CMH]. Construction activities were detailed in William A. Settle, Jr.,* The Dawning, A New Day for the Southwest: A History of the Tulsa District Corps of Engineers, 1939–1971, *(Tulsa, OK: U.S. Army Engineer District, 1975), pp. 80–81, [HQCE]. The status of Fort Sill in 1987 was discussed in* INF Treaty.

OREGON

A I R   F O R C E

Camp Adair

In the late 1950s this site was selected to host a BOMARC air defense missile squadron. The Army Corps of Engineers Seattle District conducted the land acquisition, physical feasibility study, ground survey, foundation and material exploration, and facility design work. This facility neared completion in 1960, when the Air Force decided to limit the BOMARC program to eight bases.

Reference: Sherman Green, History of the Seattle District: 1896–1968, *(Seattle, WA: U.S. Army Engineer District, 1969), p. 5–3, [HQCE].*

PENNSYLVANIA

A I R   F O R C E

Olmsted Air Force Base

Middletown Air Materiel Area (AMA)

Under the command of Headquarters, Air Materiel Command (HQ AMC) during the 1950s, this command became involved in missile logistic support when it received responsibility for the SM-73 Bull Goose missile in the mid-1950s. On June 28, 1957, HQ AMC designated Middletown AMA as the logistics support manager for the Falcon and the Sidewinder air-to-air missile programs. With this realignment, management of the Bull Goose was transferred to Ogden AMA.

Olmsted AFB was closed in the 1960s and many of the personnel stationed at this facility were transferred to Ogden.

References: Lloyd S. Spancake, Howard G. Clark, and Earl J. Heydinger, "History of Middletown Air Materiel Area Olmsted Air Force Base, Pennsylvania: 1 January 1957–30 June 1957," Vol.1, (K205.04-25), pp. 1, 12–13, [AFHO]; Helen Rice, History of Ogden Air Materiel Area, Hill Air Force Base, Utah: 1934–1960, *(Hill AFB, UT: Air Force Logistics Center, March 1963), pp. 197, 200, [AFHO].*

A R M Y

Philadelphia Defense Area

In the early 1950s, a dozen gun batteries positioned 6 to 7 miles from the center of the city protected the "City of Brotherly Love." In the mid-1950s the Philadelphia District of the Corps of Engineers supervised the construction of a circle of twelve Nike Ajax sites averaging twenty-five miles from center city. Sites on the Pennsylvania side of the Delaware River included:

(PH-07)   Richboro
(PH-15)   Newportville/Krowden
(PH-67)   Chester/Media
(PH-75)   Edgemont/Delaware City
(PH-82)   Valley Forge/Paoli
(PH-91)   Worchester/Kenter Square
(PH-99)   Warrington/Eureka

Headquarters facilities were located at Swarthmore.

Sites PH-75 and PH-99 were upgraded to launch Nike Hercules missiles. Following this modernization, the remaining Nike Ajax sites were deactivated from 1961 to 1963. Site PH-75 was deactivated in 1968; PH-99 stayed on duty until 1971. These batteries were manned by both Regular Army and Pennsylvania Army

National Guard units. Command and control functions were hosted by a "Missile Master" facility based at Pedricktown, New Jersey.

The contributions of Philadelphia's defenders were recognized on April 24, 1963, as Mayor H.J. Tate presided over a ceremony declaring that spring day in Philadelphia as "ARADCOM Day."

References: Nike Quick Look, *pp. 105–109; Frank E. Snyder, Brian H. Guss,* The District:A History of the Philadelphia District U.S. Army Corps of Engineers 1866–1971, *(Philadelphia, PA: U.S. Army Engineer District, 1974), pp. 150–153, [HQCE];* Argus, *(1 May 1963), p. 1, [MHI].*

Pittsburgh Defense Area

Nike sites around Pittsburgh included:

(PI-02) Rural Ridge
(PI-03) Dorseyville/Indianola
(PI-25) Murrysville/Monroe
(PI-36) Irwin
(PI-37) Cowansburg/Herminie
(PI-42) Elizabeth
(PI-43) Elrama/east of Finleyville
(PI-52) Finleyville
(PI-62) Bridgeville/Hickman
(PI-71) Coraopolis/Beacon
(PI-92) Bryant/North Park
(PI-93) Westville

In April 1952, a column of soldiers and heavy equipment passed through McKeesport towards Pittsburgh to set up a ring of twelve hastily sited gun positions to defend the "Steel City." As in other locales, the troops that manned the guns lived in tents. With the introduction of Nike Ajax, many of these troops, who became dubbed "Buck Rogers boys," were able to move into permanent quarters that were built near the launch sites.

The Corps of Engineers Pittsburgh District, a component of the Ohio River Division, had responsibility for the construction of these sites. In July 1954 the Corps awarded the first construction contract. Pittsburgh's rugged terrain proved challenging to engineers as launchers and control radar sites had to be built apart yet within sight of each other. Construction costs ranged from $600,000 to $700,000 at each site. In 1956, four additional sites

were added to Pittsburgh's defenses.

At first, three active Army battalions manned the ring around "Steel City." With the introduction of Nike Hercules at sites PI-03, PI-36, PI-37, PI-43, PI-71, and PI-93, manning responsibilities would eventually be supplied by one active duty unit (3rd Missile Battalion, 1st Artillery) and one Pennsylvania Army National Guard battalion (The Duquesne Greys-2nd Missile Battalion, 176th Artillery). Operations at five of these Nike Hercules sites lasted until 1974.

Command and control was handled by a Missile Master/Missile Mentor facility collocated with Air Force radars posted at a military reservation near Oakdale. The Missile Master became operational in 1960.

In 1958 and beyond, Pittsburgh possibly could lay claim to having the prettiest sites in the nation as the Regional Commander worked with a "National Civic Improvement Committee of Women" to have volunteers from the National Farm and Garden Association landscape the batteries with varieties of trees, shrubs, and flowers.

References: Leland R. Johnson and Jacque S. Minnotte, An Eyewitness History of the Pittsburgh District, United States Army Corps of Engineers, *(Pittsburgh, PA: U.S. Army Engineer District, 1989), pp.193–94, [HQCE]; Leland R. Johnson,* The Headwaters District: A History of the Pittsburgh District, *(Pittsburgh, PA: U.S. Army Engineer District, n.d.), pp. 226–27, [HQCE];* Argus, *(1 February 1958), p. 7, [MHI];* Nike Quick Look, *pp. 109–13.*

RHODE ISLAND

A R M Y

Providence Defense Area

Site designation and locations of the five Nike batteries guarding Providence are as follows: (PR-38) Bristol, (PR-58) North Kingston, (PR-69) Coventry, (PR-79) Foster, and (PR-99) North Smithfield.

Two additional sites in Massachusetts contributed to the defense of Rhode Island's capital city. The five batteries became operational between 1956 and 1958. From 1959 through 1960, sites PR-38 and PR-99 were upgraded to launch Nike Hercules missiles. Site PR-79 at Foster was preserved, to be used as a State Police facility. Command and Control was handled from a BIRDIE/Missile Mentor facility located in PR-69 Coventry. This facility assumed the target designation role for all batteries in New England after the four New England defense areas were consolidated in the late 1960s.

Site PR-99 at North Smithfield stayed in operation until 1971 while PR-38 at Bristol held on until 1974.

References: "Historic American Engineering Record, Nike Battery PR-79," (HAER NO. RI-371, pp. 23–25, [LOC]; Nike Quick Look, pp. 115–116.

SOUTH DAKOTA

A I R   F O R C E

Ellsworth Air Force Base

Originally named the Rapid City Army Air Base, this World War II-era installation served as a bomber base then and throughout the Cold War. As a Strategic Air Command installation, Ellsworth hosted two generations of ICBMs and provides an outstanding case study for understanding the difficulties and costs associated with constructing a first-generation missile complex and how the experience was applied to constructing a second-generation complex.

The contractors for the Titan I project, Leavell-Scott & Associates, represented a consortium of eight partners. On December 8, 1959, this consortium was awarded the contract to build the three missile complexes of three missiles each at New Underwood, Hermosa, and Sturgis. Army Corps of Engineers oversight initially came from the Omaha Engineer District. Ten months into the project, this responsibility was transferred to the Corps of Engineers Ballistic Missile Construction Office based out of Los Angeles.

The initial estimate of the contract was $47.2 million. By March 1962, this number had grown to $64 million, an increase of 31 percent as a result of 265 modifications to the original contract. Frequently, changes required demolishing previous work.

Finding skilled labor proved to be a challenge. Eventually, many workers had to be brought to the area and the project suffered high worker turn-over rates. Labor management relations were amica-

ble. At the peak of construction, some 2,500 workers worked at the three launch complexes. There were 15 short work stoppages, most lasting less than a day. A strike at General Electric in October 1960, delayed receipt of terminals that also set back the completion date.

As at other first-generation missile sites, the installation of the propellant loading system proved to be an expensive undertaking. Excessive groundwater at complex 1C required $500,000 in additional costs to control seepage.

Difficulties between the site engineer and the Site Activation Task Force (SATAF) arose upon site completion. Because the SATAF refused to assume responsibility for the site until practically every item was in full working order, contractors often spent months maintaining equipment long after it had been installed.

With construction under way, the Air Force activated the 850th Strategic Missile Squadron on December 1, 1960. About the same time, work began on installations for the second-generation missile. On August 21, 1961, construction began on the Minuteman IB facilities. The contract to build the 150 silos and associated launch control facilities was executed by Peter Kiewit Sons' Company of Omaha, Nebraska, using designs developed by Parsons-Stavens, Architect Engineer, in Los Angeles.

Activation of the 44th Strategic Missile Wing on January 1, 1962, marked the initiation of SAC's first Minuteman "IB" wing. Seven months later, the activation of the 66th Strategic Missile Squadron marked the beginning of SAC's first Minuteman IB squadron.

As men trained for their new duties, progress continued on the silos being constructed on the South Dakota prairie. The work force peaked in September 1962 as the Peter Kiewit work force reached 2,915 workers. While these men worked out on the prairie, construction proceeded at Ellsworth AFB on converting a hanger for a missile support facility. In April 1963, the first missile was emplaced into a prepared silo. Two months later, SAC accepted the first flight of 10 Minuteman IB ICBMs and in July, some of these missiles were placed on alert status.

The final cost of Minuteman construction around Ellsworth came to just over $75.7 million. This figure for 150 silos is remarkable when contrasted to the $64 million cost of nine Titan I silos. Fewer modifications, simpler design, and improved management all contributed to lower construction costs. During construction there were 62 lost time injuries, including two fatalities. Overall, labor-management relations on this project were good: a total of 244 man-days were lost due to work stoppages. Weather conditions ranging from severe cold to heavy rains also hindered construction.

On May 16, 1964, Secretary of Defense McNamara directed an accelerated phaseout of Titan I and Atlas ICBMs. Consequently, the Titan Is of the 850th Strategic Missile Squadron were removed from alert status on January 4, 1965. The Air Force subsequently deactivated the squadron on March 25th.

Meanwhile, Ellsworth was slated to host a unique series of operational tests. Approved by the Secretary of Defense in November 1964, "Project Long Life" called for the short-range operational base launch of three modified Minuteman IB ICBMs to provide a realistic test for this system. Each missile would contain enough propellant for a 7-second flight and have inert upper stages and reentry vehicles. The first launch occurred on March 1, 1965, and successfully demonstrated the ability of a SAC missile crew to launch an ICBM.

Conversion from Minuteman IB to Minuteman II was completed at Ellsworth in 1973. With these new missiles in place, Ellsworth was selected to host "Giant Pace Test 74-1," the first Simulated Electronic Launch-Minuteman (SELM) exercise. During this test, 11 SELM-configured Minuteman II ICBMs underwent successful simulated launch on command from both underground launch-control centers and the Airborne Launch Control System.

Throughout its history, the 44th Strategic Missile Wing has competed strongly in Olympic Arena competition, frequently claiming top honors at the Vandenberg-hosted competition.

President Bush's order of September 28, 1991 to remove Minuteman II missiles from alert status profoundly affected Ellsworth. To comply with the pending START I treaty, the Air Force immediately began removing missiles from their silos. Missile removal continued through 1994 when the Air Force began imploding and grading the vacated silos.

References: U.S. Army Ballistic Missile Construction Office "History of Titan I Ellsworth Area Engineer Office 8 December 1959–31 March 1962," pp. I–II, Chapter 4, [HQCE]; U.S. Army Ballistic Missile Construction Office "History of Minuteman Construction Wing II Ellsworth Area Engineer Office 1 August 1961–31 August 1963," pp. 11–12, 118–124, 128–129, 192–194, *[HQCE]; SAC Chronology, pp. 32, 33, 35, 40–41, 44, 45, 46, 47, 55, 60.*

A R M Y

Ellsworth Air Force Base Defense Area

Four Nike Ajax batteries were positioned around Ellsworth AFB in 1957: E-01 was north, E-20 was east-northeast, E-40 was south-southeast, and E-70 was west-southwest. Headquarters facilities were located at Ellsworth. In 1958, batteries E-20, E-40, and E-70 were removed from service and E-01 was converted to fire Nike Hercules missiles. This battery remained in service until 1961.

TENNESSEE

A I R   F O R C E

Arnold Air Force Base/Arnold Engineering Development Center

After surveying the German missile development facilities in December 1945, Dr. Theodore von Kármán, Director of the Army Air Force Scientific Advisory Board, advised General H.H. Arnold that the United States needed to build research and development facilities comparable to what he had seen in Europe to include "...wind tunnel facilities to attain speeds up to three times the velocity of sound, with large enough test sections to accommodate models of reasonable size, including jet propulsion units, and one ultrasonic wind tunnel for the exploration of the upper frontier of the supersonic speed range." The availability of land, water, and power made the central Tennessee site ideally suited for the new installation.

Construction of the center at Tullahoma, Tennessee, began in 1950. On June 25, 1951, President Truman attended a dedication ceremony naming the center for the recently deceased Arnold. As test facilities were activated, the center became an important component of the newly formed Air Research Development Command. The first tests at the engine test facility were conducted in 1953. Since that time the facility grew into the world's most comprehensive aerospace ground-test center.

Large wind tunnel facilities allowed hypersonic high altitude aerodynamic tests on full-scale components. For example, in December 1982, the first full-scale test firing of the Peacekeeper missile 60,000-pound thrust second-stage solid rocket motor was conducted under a simulated altitude of 70,000 feet.

References: Chronology of the Arnold Engineering Development Center, 10 Aug 1944–30 June 1970 *(Arnold AEDC, TN: History Office, n.d.), [AFHO]; "Air Force Ballistic Missile Program," (K146.01-106A), [AFHO];* SAC Chronology, p. 72.

TEXAS

A I R   F O R C E

Altus Air Force Base

The 577th Strategic Missile Squadron at Altus AFB, Oklahoma, had an Atlas F launcher located at Fargo, Texas.

Reference: See Altus AFB narrative under Oklahoma.

Carswell Air Force Base

Established during World War II, this facility always supported bomber operations. Eventually, its B-52H wing also received the capability to launch Air-Launch Cruise Missiles (ALCM).

References: Air Force Bases, pp. 63–66; START.

Dyess Air Force Base

Originally Abilene Army Air Field, this World War II vintage fighter pilot training facility was turned over to the City of Abilene at the end of the war. After an eight year absence, the military returned in 1953 when SAC assumed command of the newly dedicated Abilene AFB. Redesignated Dyess AFB in 1956, the facility hosted SAC bombers and supporting aircraft.

Initial responsibility for constructing the twelve Atlas F silos fell on the Corps of Engineers Fort Worth District. The Fort Worth District also received responsibility for the nationwide procurement of the Atlas F's propellant loading system. With the formation of the Corps of Engineers Ballistic Missile Construction Office (CEBMCO) in 1960, the Fort Worth District was relieved of

silo construction oversight.

On May 26, 1960, six bids were opened at Abilene, Texas. The low bid of $20 million had been submitted by a joint venture composed of H.B. Zachry Company, and Brown and Root Inc. Construction commenced on June 7, 1960. The locations of the twelve liftlaunchers were Abilene, Albany, Clyde, Denton County, Oplin, Lawn, Bradshaw, Winters, Shep, Nolan, Anson, and Corinth.

Construction at Dyess proved to be an exception in that the project was completed on time. There were no work stoppages due to labor unrest. There were 3 fatalities and 33 disabling injuries associated with this project.

As construction continued, the Air Force activated the 578th Strategic Missile Squadron on July 1, 1961. Becoming operational in 1962, the 578th and its twelve missiles were all placed on alert status during the Cuban missile crisis.

From May 28 through June 2, 1963, the 578th Strategic Missile Squadron underwent the first Operational Readiness Inspection (ORI) for an Atlas F missile unit.

On May 16, 1964, Defense Secretary McNamara directed the accelerated phaseout of Atlas and Titan I ICBMs. On December 1, 1964, the first Atlas F missile at Dyess was removed from alert status ahead of schedule to preclude costly maintenance expenditures. The squadron was deactivated on March 25, 1965.

References: "History of The Dyess Area Office, 18 April 1960–28 April 1962," pp. 2, 15–17, 68–69, 94–96 ,[HQCE]; D. Clayton Brown, The Southwestern Division: 50 Years of Service, *(Dallas, TX: U.S Army Engineer Southwestern Division, n.d.), pp. 77–79, [HQCE];* SAC Chronology, pp. 7, 40, 44, 45, 47.

San Antonio Air Materiel Area/Logistics Center-Kelly Air Force Base

San Antonio Air Materiel Area held responsibility for the Air Force Nuclear Ordnance program. As such it served as the prime depot for reentry vehicles and warheads.

Reference: A Pictorial History of Kelly Air Force Base, *(San Antonio Air Logistics Center, TX: Office of History, n.d.), [AFHO].*

Sheppard Air Force Base

Established just before World War II as a technical training center, in February 1958 this Air Training Command facility began providing operational and maintenance crew training for the Atlas and Titan ICBM programs. The Atlas/Titan I training facility was dedicated in November 1959. During the early 1960s Titan II training facilities were installed. Titan II missile crews trained at these facilities for the next two decades.

References: Air Force Bases, *pp. 537–544; "History Sheppard AFB Texas: 1 Jul 61–31 Dec 61," (K288.60-35), [AFHO]; William A. Settle Jr.,* The Dawning, A New Day for the Southwest, A History of the Tulsa District Corps of Engineers, 1939–1971, *(Tulsa, OK: U.S. Army Engineer District, 1975), pp. 80–81, [AFHO].*

A R M Y

Bergstrom Defense Area

Headquartered at Bergstrom AFB, Army units defended this Strategic Air Command Base and the Austin region from two Nike Hercules sites: BG-40 located southeast of Elroy and BG-80, which was west-northwest of Austin. The Nike Hercules batteries were active from 1960 to 1966. Headquarters facilities were at Bergstrom.

Reference: Nike Quick Look, *p. 26.*

Dallas-Fort Worth Defense Area

Site designations and locations of Nike Hercules sites guarding Dallas-Fort Worth were: (DF-01) north of Denton, (DF-20) northeast of Terrell, (DF-50) southeast of Alvarado, and (DF-70) Fort Wolters. Headquarters facilities were located at Duncanville Air Force Station.

Responsibility for constructing these four sites, installed to defend Dallas with its defense production facilities, fell on the Corps of Engineers Fort Worth District. Each site required about thirty acres. At Alvarado, the Fort Worth District was forced to bring condemnation suits to acquire the land. Construction began in 1958. Total acquisition and construction costs for each site came to $1.5 million.

These Nike Hercules sites were manned by Regular Army and National Guard units and operated from 1960 to 1968. Missile defense was coordinated from a "BIRDIE" site collocated with Air Force tracking radars at Duncanville Air Force Station.

References: D. Clayton Brown, Rivers, Rockets and Readiness:

Army Engineers in the Sunbelt, *(Fort Worth, TX: U.S Army Engineer District, 1979), p. 47, [HQCE];* Nike Quick Look, *pp. 48–49.*

Dyess Defense Area

On November 19, 1959, the Army conducted groundbreaking ceremonies at Dyess AFB for the battalion headquarters of the 5th Missile Battalion, 517th Artillery of the U.S. Army Air Defense Command. Installed to defend the SAC bombers and Atlas F missile silos stationed at and around Dyess AFB, the two Nike Hercules sites were controlled by a "BIRDIE" system installed at Sweetwater Air Force Station. Site DY-10, located at Fort Phantom Hill and site DY-50, located southwest of Abilene, remained operational from 1960 until 1966.

Reference: Nike Quick Look, *p. 54.*

Fort Bliss

Founded after the Mexican War, the "Military Post in El Paso" left a colorful history as infantry and cavalry units maintained peace on the American frontier. However, during World War II, the post shifted from the nation's premier cavalry training organization to become the nation's antiaircraft artillery center. In 1944, the Army Anti-Aircraft Artillery School moved from North Carolina to take advantage of the large land holdings and favorable climate. The post also became involved in early missile testing.

Research and Development

In 1944, the Army Ordnance Department contracted with the California Institute of Technology Jet Propulsion Laboratory (JPL) to develop a long-range missile. Under the aegis of the Ordnance-California Institute of Technology (ORDCIT) project, JPL scientists came to Fort Bliss in early 1945 to test the Private-F missile. At Fort Bliss's Hueco Range (located 28 miles north/northwest of the main post) 17 rounds were fired from April 1 through 13, 1945. These tests indicated that much work needed to be done on wing and tail construction to allow for stable flight.

Meanwhile in Germany, German scientists began development on nearly 140 different missile programs. With the conclusion of the war, much of this expertise fell into American hands. The U.S. Army's "Operation PAPERCLIP" brought hundreds of German scientists into U.S. service, including the V-2 team headed by Wernher von Braun. After arriving at Fort Bliss in January 1946, the von Braun team set up shop in former hospital buildings. By March 1946, some thirty-nine German scientists based at Fort Bliss were working on projects at the newly opened White Sands Proving Grounds across the border in New Mexico.

Before the arrival of the von Braun team, the 1st Anti-Aircraft Guided Missile Battalion was formed on October 11, 1945. This unit provided support for the research effort and would eventually grow to battalion size. As research and missile fabrication occurred at Fort Bliss, facilities were prepared at White Sands for engine and flight testing. Missiles assembled at Fort Bliss and fired at White Sands during this period include the V-2, Hermes II, Corporal, and WAC Corporal missiles. After 4 years at Fort Bliss, the von Braun team moved to Huntsville, Alabama. However, while the missile development mission became the focus of the Redstone Arsenal in Huntsville and testing and evaluation became a responsibility of White Sands, Fort Bliss retained the training and deployment mission for the newly emerging missile systems.

Training at Fort Bliss

In July 1946, the 1st Missile Battalion came under the command of the newly activated Anti-Aircraft Artillery and Guided Missile Center headquartered at Fort Bliss. Since that time the organization evolved to become the U.S. Army Air Defense Artillery Center and School. Throughout this period, the command has trained new missile units and evaluated the competence of active and Army National Guard units.

With the formation of the Army Anti-Aircraft Command (ARAACOM) in 1950, activity at Fort Bliss increased as Nike Ajax batteries had to be trained and deployed around the nation. Packages of 14 officers and 123 enlisted men who formed the nucleus of a Nike battalion received job-specific training from instructors attached to the two training battalions. Once the individual elements of the future Nike battalion completed classroom training, the package came together for integrated system training. The 5-week team training period culminated with a missile shoot at the Red Canyon Range.

Red Canyon Guided Missile Range

Located approximately 165 miles north of El Paso near Carrizoza, New Mexico, Red Canyon range was established at the north end

of the White Sands Proving Ground in October 1953 to launch Nike Ajax missiles under combat conditions. Only three permanent structures were erected to support the operation. In 1958, soldiers built a chapel from scrap wood and missile pieces.

With the opening of McGregor Range, initial training was switched to the new facility while Red Canyon continued to serve as the annual practice facility for Nike Ajax crews posted around the nation. The site also served as a launch point for the surface-to-surface Honest John missile. The last annual service practices were conducted in 1959, and by 1961 the temporary camp was but a memory.

McGregor Guided Missile Range

Because of the distance to the Red Canyon Range and the longer range of the Nike Hercules being developed, the Army sought a suitable range in the vicinity of the newly designated Army Antiaircraft and Artillery and Guided Missile Center at Fort Bliss, Texas. The Red Canyon Range continued to be used by active Nike Ajax battalions for annual service practice until 1959.

The site chosen covered a 20- by 45-mile area situated to the southeast and parallel to U.S. Highway 54. Land acquisition was completed after a long period of negotiations with area ranchers, and on July 13, 1956, McGregor Range Headquarters and Service Battery were activated; facility construction began in September. Facilities included headquarters, barracks, missile assembly and storage facilities, and support structures. A range control building was constructed on Davis Dome, a volcanic rock formation overlooking the southern Tularosa basin.

The 495th Guided Missile Battalion (SAM) fired the first Nike Ajax missiles on the range in the spring of 1957. Throughout the next decade, packages completing training at Fort Bliss took their turn conducting live-fire exercises at the range. These units returned to McGregor for their annual service practice. In the early 1960s, these exercises were known as Short Notice Annual Practices (SNAP).

Launch site "one" consisted of an actual Nike Ajax magazine, elevator, and launchers. Additional sites consisted of simple concrete pads to support a missile launcher. Range modifications were made to support Nike Hercules, Hawk, Patriot, and other missiles such as the European-built Roland. Other countries have contracted to use the range for training. Japan conducted the last firing of a Nike Hercules in December 1992 at McGregor Range before retiring its Nike inventory. Just northwest of the McGregor Base Camp was a Pershing Missile Launch Complex. With the elimination of Pershings required by the Intermediate-Range Nuclear Forces (INF) treaty, the site was abandoned.

Besides preparing Nike Ajax battalions for deployment, the 1st Guided Missile Brigade also supported research, development, testing, and evaluation of surface-to-surface missiles as well as training the units that would field them. In the early 1950s, these units deployed with Corporal and Honest John missiles.

The Corporal missile was fired from the Orogrande Range, located between McGregor Range to the southeast and White Sands Proving Ground to the northwest. Both training and annual service firings of the missile were conducted at this location until the mid-1950s when surface-to-surface missile activities were transferred to Fort Sill, Oklahoma.

Fort Bliss also supported the deployment of the antiballistic missile (ABM) system. Training silos remain that were built to support handling practice of Sprint and Spartan missiles.

References: Photographic records of missile-related base facilities and testing are held by the Fort Bliss Public Affairs Office, the Air Artillery Museum, and the Fort Bliss Museum. Video Services maintains some historic footage of the early years. Blueprints and base maps are maintained by the Master Planning Branch of the Engineering Services Division. Environmental Services maintains blueprints of many structures that have been removed.

Documents are scattered within the several commands on post. Many historical records have been transferred to the National Archives and Center for Military History. Argus, (1 May 1958), p. 2, [MHI] describes Red Canyon.

Longhorn Army Ammunition Plant

This World War II era facility in Marshall, both produced and destroyed missiles. Reactivated in 1952 during the Korean War, Longhorn took on an expanded mission that included loading, assembling, and packing rocket motors and pyrotechnic ammunition.

The Thiokol Corporation, which operated a facility at Redstone Arsenal, received the contract to rehabilitate a World War II era liquid fuel facility into a solid fuel rocket motor plant. Production on the original Nike-Hercules program for sustainer motors began

at this plant in 1956. Thiokol also produced propellants and motors for the Falcon, Lacrosse, Honest John, and Sergeant missiles.

As production increased, so did capacity. In 1959 a Main Rocket Motor Assembly Building (45E) was constructed along with a Static Test Building (25T). With this added capacity, this facility produced both the first and second stages of the Pershing IA missile.

With the signing of the INF Treaty on December 8, 1987, Longhorn took on a new mission. Along with Pueblo Depot, Colorado, this facility was used to destroy Pershing IA and II missiles to comply with the treaty. After a static burn, the missiles were crushed.

Reference: "Historic American Engineering Record Longhorn Army Ammunition Plant," (HAER TEX 102-MARSH.V 2),[LOC].

Red River Army Depot

Located 18 miles west of Texarkana, this World War II vintage depot became a major Army guided missile assembly and maintenance facility beginning in the late 1950s. In 1959, Red River became an assembly facility for Hawk antiaircraft missiles. In the mid-1960s Red River became the prime depot for maintenance support for the Chaparral missile.

Reference: "Historic American Engineering Record Red River Army Depot," (HAER TEX 19-Tex 2), 1985, [LOC].

UTAH

A I R   F O R C E

Ground-to-Air Pilotless Aircraft (GAPA) Launch Site

Boeing Airplane Company launched 38 two-stage GAPA solid-rocket-propelled test vehicles from this site located three miles east and seven miles north of Knolls during a period covering June 13, 1946, through July 1, 1947.

A GAPA 600 series test vehicle, serial number 10, achieved stable supersonic flight on August 6, 1946. The program was subsequently transferred to Holloman AFB in New Mexico leaving a concrete launch pad (approximately 100 by 100 feet) and a 40-by-40 foot blockhouse. The 40-foot steel tower associated with the site has been removed. In 1980, the site was nominated for placement on the National Register.

Reference: R. Gilbert Moore, "National Register of Historic Places Inventory-Nomination Form for GAPA Launch Site and Block House," submitted February 1980.

Hill Air Force Base

Established just before World War II as the Ogden Air Depot, Hill AFB has provided program management and logistical support for many Air Force missile programs.

Ogden Air Materiel Area (OAMA)
Ogden Air Logistics Center (ALC)

Based at Hill AFB, this component of the Air Materiel Command and its successor Air Force Logistics Command played crucial program management roles for several missile systems. Ogden's significant role was made possible by an April 1, 1955, transfer of the adjacent Army Ogden Arsenal to Air Force jurisdiction. The acquisition of some 631 additional buildings and nearly 3,500 additional acres positioned Ogden as the central point for Air Force air munitions.

Even before this "merger," Ogden had been involved with emerging missile weaponry. In September 1952, Ogden began supporting the SM-62 Snark program and later became the prime maintenance depot for this long-range missile. On May 5, 1954, the Air Materiel Command assigned Ogden to be the prime maintenance depot for the GAM-67 "Crossbow" air-to-ground missile designed to knock out enemy radars. Budget cuts led to the demise of this weapon and Ogden's responsibility for it ceased in April 1957.

With its increased capacity following the acquisition of the arsenal, Ogden became the prime maintenance manager for the MB-1 Genie nuclear defense rocket, which aircraft into enemy bomber formations, the Genie's nuclear warhead made near misses fatal.

By the close of 1956, Ogden's air munitions mission included assigned ammunition and explosive materiel surveillance, safety, and disposal functions. In addition, Odgen conducted and supervised the training of other commands having responsibility to store, handle, transport, escort, inspect, renovate, and dispose of Air Force ammunition (excluding nuclear), including biological and chemical munitions in consonance with USAF operational and logistical concepts.

On June 4, 1957, Air Materiel Command reorganized program management responsibilities for its subordinate commands. Ogden then took over the SM-64 Navaho missile from the Sacramento Air Materiel Area. However, this responsibility quickly ended when the Air Force canceled the program on June 12. Ogden also became responsible for the Bull Goose decoy missile from Middletown Air Materiel Area and transferred program management on the GAM-72 Quail to the Oklahoma City Air Materiel Area. Ogden had picked up the "Green Quail" decoy missile program back in March 1956. Ogden held on to the Goose until the program's cancellation in December 1958.

The reorganization transferred from Oklahoma City Air Materiel Area a very high profile program: the IM-99 BOMARC. Ogden was assigned in 1956 as the prime maintenance and supply depot for Marquardt Aircraft Company products that were to be locally manufactured. The selection of Ogden as BOMARC manager was logical, therefore, as this air defense missile used Marquardt-produced ramjets.

Located on the outskirts of Ogden, the ramjet plant was dedicated on June 3, 1957. Two months later, construction began at a site 15 miles west of Ogden at Little Mountain on the Air Force-Marquardt Jet Laboratory. Dedicated on October 5, 1959, the $14 million Air Force-owned facility initially employed 175 Marquardt personnel to test RJ-43 engines at simulated altitudes in excess of 100,000 feet. This facility was used long after final BOMARC production. In 1970, Little Mountain was selected to house highly specialized Minuteman testing equipment, including a 15 million electron volt Xray machine, a cutting machine for solid propellants, and nuclear environment simulators. Additional evaluation facilities at Little Mountain were built in the 1980s to test the "small" ICBM and new Peacekeeper missiles.

With the Boeing-produced BOMARC entering the Air Defense Command inventory, Ogden began receiving missiles for maintenance work. To support BOMARC, Ogden dedicated 26 buildings along with scores of special testing structures. Building 1915 in zone 19 in the west area received an extensive refit to accommodate ramjet overhaul work.

One program unaffected by the Air Materiel Command (AMC)

reorganization was Ogden's management of the SM-62 Snark program. Ogden's support for this system increased on July 1, 1960, when the command received full executive management responsibility for the Snark. Although the program was canceled a year later, the invaluable experience prepared Ogden to take charge of a longer-term program.

On January 6, 1959, the Air Force named Ogden as the single assembly and recycling point for the SM-80 Minuteman ICBM program. Events leading to this milestone began with the decision of the Thiokol Chemical Company to construct a solid-propellant rocket plant 27 miles west of Brigham City. With this facility operational in late 1957, Thiokol had positioned itself to produce first-stage rocket motors for the new ICBM. When the contract came, construction of Air Force Plant 78 at the Thiokol complex gave Thiokol the capacity to mass produce the rocket motors. Meanwhile another solid-propellant producer expanded facilities at Bacchus located west of Salt Lake City. The Hercules Powder Company started work on a new solid-propellant plant in March 1958. By mid-year, both Thiokol and Hercules had research and development contracts for the Minuteman. In October 1958, the Air Force selected Boeing Airplane Company to be the prime contractor to integrate and assemble the systems developed by such subcontractors as Thiokol and Hercules.

With Utah's growing aerospace industrial base and OOAMA's experience, Ogden's commander successfully petitioned in April 1958 to have his installation designated as the logistic support facility for the new ICBM.

Having acquired responsibility for Minuteman, OOAMA set up the SM-80 Weapon System Management Division, which moved to Building 1245 in the west area in January 1960. This location placed the management division close to Boeing's Minuteman assembly facility at Air Force Plant 77. Construction of this plant began in September 1960. Nine missile assembly buildings were constructed and some 40 buildings were dedicated for rocket motor storage and support. Here Boeing assembled all of the components into missiles ready for launch site deployment.

One of the more unusual experiments at Ogden during 1960 was the mobile Minuteman project. The project swung into high gear in June 1960, as Hill AFB became home base for "Operation Big Star," a series of tests to determine the feasibility of deploying Minuteman ICBMs on railroad car launchers. A modified test train traveled across western and central states to test how communication, control, and human factors could affect such an operation. In August, after the return of the fourth test train, the Air Force declared that the tests had been satisfactorily completed. Anticipating a possible go-ahead with the project, the Air Force activated the 4062 Strategic Missile Wing on December 1, 1960. However, a year later, Defense Secretary McNamara canceled the program.

As the missile production plant neared completion, in 1961 construction began on a series of facilities for disassembly, overhaul, and reassembly work. The new maintenance complex included a Missile Engineering Surveillance Facility, otherwise known as the Aging Laboratory designed to duplicate silo environmental conditions. A Radiographic Inspection Laboratory x-rayed motors to determine if there were cracks in the solid-fuel propellant. In addition, the maintenance facilities housed clean rooms for missile guidance systems calibration and modification work.

The first production Minuteman rolled off the assembly line at Air Force Plant 77 on April 12, 1962. By March 1964, 500 Minuteman missiles had been built; the last Minuteman I came off the assembly line in May 1965. Boeing continued production with Minuteman II and, in 1968, began building the Minuteman III.

Minuteman was just one of several missile systems that kept Ogden personnel busy in the 1960s. A second strategic missile program designated the WS-138A or GAM-87 and called the Skybolt came to Ogden in July 1959. The 1,000-mile range Skybolt was designed as an air-launched ballistic missile to replace the GAM-63 Rascal air-to-surface missile and serve as a follow-on to the 500-mile range GAM-77 Hound Dog missile. In the ongoing service rivalry for the strategic mission, Skybolt served as an Air Force trump card. Chief of Staff Thomas D. White claimed that the missile gave bombers a flexibility that outmatched missiles launched from submarines. The importance of the program increased again when, in June 1960, the United States agreed to provide the missile to Great Britain. Unfortunately, test failures unfavorably impressed new Defense Secretary Robert McNamara and the program was canceled in December 1961. As compensation for its lost investment in the system, the British eventually received Polaris submarine-launched missiles.

The mid-1960s closures of depots at Rome, New York, San Bernardino, California; Middletown, Pennsylvania; and Mobile, Alabama ensured growth at Ogden, as 5,000 positions came to the Utah facility.

In 1966, a $12.5 million Minuteman Engineering and Test Facility was dedicated at Hill AFB, which consisted of a launch control facility and a silo. Another facility of this type was built at Ogden in the late 1970s.

In 1968, Ogden became the manager for the air-to-ground Maverick missile. More significantly, in 1973 the center took charge of source and repair responsibility for the strategic Air-Launched Cruise Missile.

In 1974, the command was redesignated the Ogden Air Logistics Center (ALC).

In the 1970s, additional missile management responsibilities were transferred to Ogden for the Peacekeeper MX and for such short-range missiles as the Sidewinder and Short-Range Attack Missile. By 1980, Ogden ALC served as the logistics system program manager for the soon-to-be decommissioned Titan II fleet as well as Minuteman II and III, Peacekeeper, and the proposed Midgetman ICBM. As Titan II program manager, Ogden ALC oversaw Project Rivet Cap–the deactivation of the three Titan II missile wings. With deactivation, Ogden's involvement with the Titan II program ended on September 30, 1987. As Peacekeeper entered the inventory during the late 1980s, Ogden ALC oversaw numerous modernization programs to improve the reliability and survivability of the deployed Minuteman forces. One such program initiated in 1985 was the Minuteman Integrated Life Extension (Project Rivet MILE), which upgraded missile silos and launch control facilities.

Ogden also continued to have responsibility for BOMARC drones and the remaining BOMARC B missiles not reconfigured for target duties. In 1985, the Air Force directed Ogden to dispose of the remaining 48 BOMARC airframes.

References: SAC Chronology, pp. 26–27; a comprehensive overview that details missile research and development is Helen Rice's History of Ogden Air Materiel Area Hill Air Force Base, Utah: 1934–1960, (Hill AFB, UT: Air Force Logistic Center History Office, March 1963), pp. 183–230, [AFHO]; updated versions and a detailed Ogden Chronology are maintained at the Air Force History Library at Bolling AFB, Washington, DC. This material was rewritten to form the basis of Helen Rice, Kenneth Patchin, Susan Weathers, Scott Fristknecht, and David Kendziora, History of Hill AFB (Hill AFB, UT: Ogden Air Logistics Center History Office, 1981); Portrait in Partnership, (Hill AFB, UT: Ogden Air Logistics Center History Office, 1980) provided an anniversary sketch of Ogden's activities. See also, History of Hill Air Force Base, (Hill AFB, UT: Ogden Air Logistics Center History Office, 1988), pp. 306–318, [AFHO].

Wendover Air Force Base/Utah Test and Training Range

The Army activated Wendover Army Air Field in northwestern Utah on March 1, 1942, as a research and development facility for guided missiles and pilotless aircraft as well as a training facility for heavy bomber crews. The 509th Composite Group, which flew the famed B-29 "Enola Gay," trained to carry the first atomic bomb.

The Army Air Force initially tested the JB-2 (Loon) at this location in 1945 and 1946. The program then moved to New Mexico. In the 1950s Wendover AFB served as an impact point for the Air Force Matador surface-to-surface missile. In 1958 the base came under Ogden Air Materiel Area command.

Due to Wendover's remote location, a Minuteman Missile motor testing complex was constructed there in the early 1960s to support the Minuteman program based at the Ogden Air Materiel Area. The extensive complex cost $7.5 million dollars to build.

Most of the base property was transferred from Ogden Air Logistics Center to the city of Wendover in 1973. However, a radar site was retained to support range operations for the Hill-Wendover-Dugway Range complex. Air Force Systems Command assumed range control in January 1979 and designated the facility as the Utah Test and Training Range.

The northwestern Utah range encompassed 1.7 million acres of restricted land area, and the airspace covered an additional 5.3 million acres. The range has been used for testing and evaluation of air-launched cruise missiles, air-to-surface missiles, and ground-launched cruise missiles.

References: Tom Starkweather, "Range larger than 2 states," White Sands Missile Ranger, (1 June 1990); Portrait in Partnership, (Hill AFB, UT: Ogden Air Logistics Center History Office, 1980);

History of Hill Air Force Base, *(Hill AFB, UT: Ogden Air Logistics Center History Office, 1988), [AFHO].*

A R M Y

Green River

Green River was a research and development launch site to test developmental booster systems. From this site, Pershing missiles were launched that impacted at White Sands Missile Range. The first successful Green River launch of an Air Force Athena rocket occurred on July 8, 1964. This launch tested reentry vehicles. Pershings were also fired from sites near Gilson Butte and Blanding. Two launchers existed at the time of the signing of the INF Treaty in December 1987.

References: INF Treaty; *Tom Starkweather, "Range larger than 2 states,"* White Sands Missile Ranger, *(1 June 1990).*

VERMONT

A I R   F O R C E

Plattsburgh Air Force Base

Two Atlas F lift-launchers for the 556th Strategic Missile Squadron (Atlas F) based at Plattsburgh AFB were located at Alburg and Swanton.

Reference: See Plattsburgh Air Force Base under New York.

VIRGINIA

A I R   F O R C E

Langley Air Force Base

Manned by the 22nd Air Defense Missile Squadron, this BOMARC missile site complimented Nike missile sites and air interceptor squadrons for defense of the region's vital military and naval installations.

As the fifth construction site for BOMARC, Langley represented a hybrid design between earlier and later base configurations.

When construction was completed and missiles installed, the site went on alert status in September 1960, with BOMARC A missiles requiring extensive support facilities such as pipelines and air conditioning. Thirteen months later, these necessities were dispensed with as the site received the improved B variant of BOMARC.

The base remained on alert until 1972.

References: Nike Quick Look, *p. 170; John M. Norvell, "Base Construction for Bomarc,"* Military Engineer, *(March–April 1961), pp. 129–131, [HQCE].*

A R M Y

Norfolk Defense Area

Site designations and locations of Nike missile batteries built in the mid-1950s defending the tidewater region are:

(N-02)	Fox Hill
(N-20)	Ocean View (temporary site)
(N-25/later N-29)	Fort Story
(N-36/later N-49)	Kempsville
(N-52/later N-59)	Deep Creek/Portsmouth
(N-63/later N-69)	Nansemond/Suffolk
(N-75)	Smithfield/Carrolton
(N-85/later N-97)	Denbigh/Patrick Henry
(N-93/later N-99)	Hampton/Spiegelville

Headquarters facilities were located at Fort Monroe, Ballantine School in Norfolk, Reedsville/South Norfolk, Graddock Branch/Portsmouth, and Newport News.

The world's largest naval complex received an extensive air defense network. Sites N-25, N-52, and N-85 were modernized to fire the Nike Hercules missile. Site N-63 held the distinction of being the last to operate Nike Ajax, being deactivated in November 1964. Command and control was operated from a "BIRDIE" site located at the Hampton Roads Army Terminal.

Both Regular Army and Virginia Army National Guard Units contributed to the manning of the sites. In 1958, men of the 4th Missile Battalion, 51st Artillery formed an integrated choral group that performed at local hospitals and other venues over the next few years.

Sites at (N-52) Deep Creek/Portsmouth and (N-85)

Denbigh/Patrick Henry remained active until April 1974.

References: Argus, *(1 January 1959), p.8, [MHI]; Nike Quick Look, pp. 98–102.*

Washington Defense Area

Site designations and locations of the Virginia sites defending the nation's capital were: (W-64) Lorton (double site), (W-74) Fairfax/Pohick, and (W-83) Herndon/Dranesville. Headquarters sites were at Fort Myer and Vienna.

Lorton was the prototype underground missile battery with installation completed in September 1954. During the 1950s and early 1960s, the Lorton site served as the National Site so the battery was subjected to frequent VIP visits. Foreign dignitaries and military officials, politicians, school groups, and boy scouts often toured the missile site. The sites were manned initially by Regular Army units with Virginia Army National Guard units assuming responsibilities in later years.

Lorton became the lone operational site in the Virginia part of the Washington Defense Area after 1963. This Nike Hercules battery remained active until 1974.

Reference: Argus, *(1 April 1958), p.7, [MHI]. For more on the network defending Washington, see Maryland.*

WASHINGTON

A I R   F O R C E

Fairchild Air Force Base

Established during World War II as a supply and maintenance depot, Fairchild became a SAC bomber base in the post-war era.

On July 14, 1958, the Corps of Engineers Northern Pacific Division directed its Seattle District to begin survey and mapping operations for the first Atlas E site to be located in the vicinity of Spokane. The design contractor, Bechtel Corporation, provided the Seattle District with the initial plans, design analysis, and outline specifications in December. Originally, the Air Force wanted three sites with three missiles at each (3 x 3); however, in early 1959, the Air Force opted to disperse the missiles to individual sites as a

defensive safety measure. Launchers were located at Deer Park, Newman Lake, Sprague, Davenport, Wilbur, Egypt, Reardon, Lamona, and Rockford, Idaho.

The work to build the nine sites was split between three major contractors and dozens of smaller firms. Work started at Site A on May 12, 1959, and completion at Site I occurred on February 10, 1961. Auxiliary support facilities for each site were built concurrent with the launchers. At Fairchild, support facilities, including a liquid oxygen plant, were completed by January 1961.

Several problems hindered construction. Three major contractors working together on a single site caused coordination problems. The 116-day national steel strike that commenced on July 15, 1959, caused delays up to 5 months for delivery of key components such as blast doors. Some 459 modifications to the ongoing construction added delays and added another $6.6 million to the project costs.

Working relations between the contractors and the unions were cordial. Nine work stoppages were quickly resolved and the impact on construction was minor. One worker was killed during construction.

Activation of the 567th Strategic Missile Squadron on April 1, 1960, marked the first time SAC activated an E series Atlas unit. On December 3, 1960, the first Atlas E missile arrived at the 567th SMS. Construction continued and SAC accepted the first Series E Atlas complex on July 29, 1961. Operational readiness training, which previously had been conducted only at Vandenberg AFB, California, began at Fairchild during the following month. On September 28, 1961, Headquarters SAC declared the squadron operational and during the following month, the 567th placed the first Atlas E missile on alert status. The bulk of the Fairchild force was on alert status in November.

The 567th SMS underwent the first formal Operational Readiness Inspection for a SAC Atlas E missile squadron in April 1963, and became the first SAC missile squadron to pass.

As a result of Defense Secretary McNamara's May 1964 directive accelerating the phaseout of Atlas and Titan I ICBMs, the first Fairchild Series E Atlas missiles came off line in January 1965. On March 31, the last missile came off alert status, which marked the completion of Atlas E phaseout. The squadron was deactivated within 3 months.

The departure of Atlas ICBMs did not completely close out Fairchild's involvement with strategic missiles. B-52H bombers assigned to the base underwent modification to carry Air-

Launched Cruise Missiles (ALCMs). Missile assembly and storage facilities were constructed for this purpose.

References: Air Force Bases, pp. 171–177; construction details can be found in U.S. Army Ballistic Missile Construction Office "History of Corps of Engineers Activities at Fairchild AFB, Construction of WS-107 1-A, Atlas "E" Missile Complexes, January 1959–February 1961," pp. I-1, II-4, 6, 14, 21–25, III-11–15, 29, [HQCE]; and Sherman Green, History of the Seattle District, (Seattle, WA: U.S. Army Engineer District, 1969), pp. 5-3, 4, [HQCE]. Highlights of missile activities at Fairchild are found in SAC Chronology, pp. 24, 31, 32, 40, 46, 47, 48. START Annex C discusses ALCMs.

Larson Air Force Base

Responsibility for this project initially fell on the Walla Walla District of the Corps of Engineers, which set up an area office in October 1959. Nine Titan I silos split between three sites (3 x 3) at Odessa, Warden, and Quincy would be built along with support facilities at Larson AFB. In October 1960, the construction oversight responsibilities were passed on to the Corps of Engineers Ballistic Missile Construction Office (CEBMCO).

On November 18, 1959, the Walla Walla District opened bid packages. Of the eight bid packages, the lowest submitted ($31.6 million) had been assembled by a joint venture of contractors composed of MacDonald Construction Company, The Scott Company, Paul Hardeman Company, G.H. Leavell Company, F.E. Young Construction Company, and Morrison-Knudsen Company, Incorporated. Subsequent contracts for such components as the propellant loading system (PLS) were let by the Omaha District office.

The contractor broke ground on December 1, 1959. A cut and fill method was used to install the missile silos and launcher control facilities. Water seepage proved to be a challenge at these northwestern locations. By August 1961, one site had pumps removing 175,000 gallons a day. Improved drainage around the complexes eased the problem.

Although no workers died while working at Larson, the frequency of lost-time accidents doubled that of the national average. In hindsight, the rush to get the project completed caused workers and supervisors to forsake prudent measures. With the assump-

tion of the project by CEBMCO, a full-time safety engineer took charge and the accident rate began to decline. Toward the end of the project, it had dropped well below that of comparable CEBMCO projects.

On September 28, 1962, SAC placed the 568th Strategic Missile Squadron on operational status in time for the Cuban missile crisis. The Titan Is remained on alert for just over 2 years. In May 1964 Secretary of Defense Robert McNamara directed that the phase-out of the Atlas and Titan I missiles be accelerated, and in January 1965 the missiles of the 568th squadron were taken off operational alert. The squadron was deactivated 2 months later on March 25th.

References: U.S. Army Ballistic Missile Construction Office "Larson Area Historical Summary: December 1959–May 1962," pp. 2-1, 3-1, 16-8, 16-9, 17-1, 17-2, [HQCE]; SAC Chronology, pp. 37, 44, 46.

Paine Field

This site was selected to receive a BOMARC air defense missile installation. The Army Corps of Engineers Seattle District handled site acquisition, conducted feasibility studies and ground surveys, and designed the needed facilities. The Air Force decided to halt work on the nearly completed site in 1960 after a decision to dramatically scale back the BOMARC program.

Reference: Sherman Green, History of the Seattle District: 1896-1968, (Seattle, WA: U.S. Army Engineer District, 1969), p. 5-3, [HQCE].

A R M Y

Fairchild Defense Area

Four sites initially protected the Spokane region and the Strategic Air Command Base at Fairchild. Nike Ajax Batteries were built and activated at (F-07) Spokane, (F-37) Cheney, and (F-45) Medical Lake in 1957; the fourth battery at (F-87) Deep Creek was built and activated in 1958. Medical Lake was converted to Hercules missiles in 1960 and 1961. Headquarters facilities were located at Fairchild.

The Seattle District of the Corps of Engineers had land acquisition, design, and construction supervision responsibilities. The

Army deactivated the Nike Ajax batteries in 1960. The two Nike Hercules batteries remained activated until 1966.

References: Nike Quick Look, *pp.58–59; Sherman Green,* History of the Seattle District: 1896–1968, *(Seattle, WA: U.S. Army Engineer District, 1969), p. 5-3, [HQCE].*

Hanford Defense Area

Nike missiles replaced and augmented gun batteries that had been previously installed to defend this nuclear industrial complex. Four Nike Ajax sites were constructed and activated in 1955 at (H-06) Saddle Mountain, (H-12) Othello, (H-52) Rattlesnake Mountain, and (H-83) Priest Rapids. Headquarters facilities were located at Camp Hanford. The latter three sites were deactivated in December 1958 as only Saddle Mountain was converted to the new Nike Hercules. Upon deactivation of this Hercules battery in 1960, the equipment was forwarded to the Norfork site at Deep Creek/Portsmouth.

Reference: Nike Quick Look, *pp. 64–65.*

Seattle Defense Area

Home of Boeing Aircraft Company and military installations, Seattle was ringed with defenses manned by both Regular Army and Washington National Guard units. Land acquisition, design, and construction supervision was handled by the Seattle District of the Corps of Engineers. The first missile sites were activated in 1956, and by 1959 the number had grown to 10. Batteries S-13 and S-32/S-33 built at Redmond and Lake Youngs were double sites. Other batteries designations and locations were:

(S-03)   Kenmore
(S-20)   Cougar Mt./Issaquah
(S-20)   Cougar Mt./Issaquah
(S-61)   Vashon Island
(S-62)   Ollala
(S-81)   Poulsbo
(S-82)   Winslow/Bainbridge Island
(S-92)   Kingston

Headquarters facilities were located at McChord AFB, Fort Lawton, Redmond, Phantom Lake, O'Brien, and Kent. A radar section was posted at Fort Worden.

Army units manning the Nike Ajax batteries earned a reputa-

tion as tops in the nation as in 1956, 1957, and 1958 Seattle-based batteries earned the Army Air Defense Command (ARADCOM) Commander's Trophy as a result of high scores achieved at Annual Service Practices at McGregor Range.

The Army National Guard took over some of the sites 9 months after the initial Army National Guard takeover in California. Gun batteries were part of the defense net until 1960.

Nike Ajax sites were phased out from 1960 to 1963. Sites at (S-13) Redmond, (S-61) Vashon Island, and (S-92) Kingston were upgraded to launch Hike Hercules missiles and survived until 1974. A "Missile Master" command and control complex was built at Fort Lawton. With the deactivation of the Nike Ajax batteries, a less complicated "BIRDIE" system took over the missile defense coordination duties.

References: Nike Quick Look, *pp. 125–129; Sherman Green,* History of the Seattle District: 1896–1968, *(Seattle, WA: U.S. Army Engineer District, 1969), p. 5-3, [HQCE]. Celebratory articles on the 28th and 433rd AAA Groups can be found in* Argus *(February 1958), p.1, [MHI].*

WISCONSIN

A R M Y

Milwaukee Defense Area

Site designations and locations of Nike missile batteries surrounding Milwaukee are:

(M-02)	Milwaukee/Brown Deer
(M-20)	Milwaukee/Harbor Drive
(M-42)	Cudahy
(M-54)	Hales Corners/Paynesville
(M-64)	Muskegon/Prospect
(M-74)	Waukesha
(M-86)	Lannon
(M-96)	Milwaukee/Silver Spring

Headquarters facilities were located in Milwaukee. The Chicago District of the Corps of Engineers oversaw land acquisition, design, and construction of these sites. Regular Army and National Guard units operated these sites defending southern Wisconsin and the northern approaches to Chicago. Sites M-02, M-20, and M-74 were converted from Nike Ajax to Nike Hercules. This Defense Area was merged with Chicago-Gary in 1968.

The three Nike Hercules batteries remained operational until 1971.

Reference: Nike Quick Look, *pp. 83–85.*

WYOMING

A I R   F O R C E

F.E. Warren Air Force Base

On November 21, 1957, the Department of Defense announced that F.E. Warren would become the nation's first ICBM base. Shortly thereafter, the base shifted to the Strategic Air Command from the Air Training Command.

Originally, the project design for the above-ground Atlas D ICBM launch and control facilities at "Site A" was to be completed by mid-May 1958 and construction finished in November 1959. However, design revisions forced addendums on the bid packages delaying the bid opening to July 15, 1958. To meet a previously set June 30th bid award deadline, the package was advertised without the critical Propellant Loading Skids, instrumentation, controls, expansion, anchorage and structural support, and site power facilities.

Despite these gaps, construction began at a location 23 miles northwest of Cheyenne for the facilities of the recently activated 706th Strategic Missile Wing. The Omaha District of the Army Corps of Engineers oversaw the construction at "Site A," which eventually consisted of two above-ground complexes with three launchers each. Because the Atlas D was radio-controlled from the ground, the launchers had to be clustered close to the radio transmitters.

The prime contractor, the George A. Fuller Company, worked through the fierce winter of 1958–1959 to get the job completed in 190 days. The project was not without problems, and many of these problems would later plague the construction efforts at other ICBM sites.

Inexperience, time pressure, remote locations, and constant modifications required to adjust the facility to support an evolving missile design hampered the construction effort. At Site A, also known as "Warren I," 35 modifications were made to the guidance facility and 117 to the launchers before Fuller completed the contract.

There were four work-stoppages over issues such as pay, hours, and the presence of non-union workers. There were no fatalities at this project; moreover, the number of disabling injuries was just below the average for all Corps of Engineers projects and about six times better than the national average.

On September 15, 1959, the first Atlas D missile to deploy away from Vandenberg AFB, California, went to the 564th Strategic Missile Squadron stationed at Warren I. A month later, F.E. Warren became the recipient of the first air transported Atlas missile.

With General Power (the Commander in Chief of SAC) present, the first Atlas D complex was turned over to the 564th SMS and declared operational on August 9, 1960.

As work proceeded at Warren I, the Corps contracted for yet another complex. In February 1959, bids were opened for "Warren

II," a complex that would have three sites with three Atlas D launchers at each. The Blount Company won the bid to build "annexes B, C, and D" to be scattered to the northeast, southeast, and southwest of Cheyenne. Slow material deliveries, modifications, and eleven different work stoppages hindered the construction of these complexes. Slated for completion in February, Warren II was finally ready in the summer of 1960. The 565th Strategic Missile Squadron, activated on December 1, 1959, operated the nine launchers. On a positive note, the safety record at Warren II exceeded that at Warren I.

The Martin K. Elby Construction Company of Wichita, Kansas, submitted the low bid to construct Warren III, which would host the Atlas E missile. Because the Atlas E contained inertial guidance, the launch sites need not be concentrated. Nine Atlas Es would be scattered over a go-square-mile area at single "coffin" launch sites. The term "coffin" was used because the missile laid on its side underground with the coffin roof at ground level. This configuration offered limited protection for the launcher. Work began on December 7, 1959. Coffin launchers in Wyoming were at Chugwater, Lagrange, and Pine Bluffs. One Atlas E launcher was located in Nebraska and five launchers were placed in Colorado at Grover, Briggsdale, Nunn, Greely, and Fort Collins.

As with Warren I and II, problems plagued construction. Delivery of steel was erratic in the wake of the national steel strike. Because of sites located in three states, the contractors had to recruit labor from many different locals. Consequently, work stoppages occurred at some individual sites while labor harmony prevailed at others. There were nine disabling injuries.

Again, Propellant Loading System (PLS) skids proved to be a challenge. In fairness to the contractor, Blaw-Knox, the Corps of Engineers admitted that compressed times for design and fabrication of this system and the attempts to use "off-the-shelf" components such as valves led to problems. Because of the rush to deploy, a prototype PLS for test and evaluation was not built.

Construction difficulties encountered at Warren and other ICBM sites would lead to an inter-service dispute over construction management. Eventually, the Corps of Engineers Ballistic Missile Construction Office (CEBMCO) was formed to oversee construction.

On October 1, 1960, the 549th Strategic Missile Squadron became the last Atlas E SMS to be activated. The 549th SMS was redesignated 566th SMS on July 1, 1961. On that same date the parent 706th Strategic Missile Wing stood down. Command responsibilities at Warren were assumed by the recently activated 389th Strategic Missile Wing.

In May 1964, as the Atlas D missiles were being phased out, the 389th Strategic Missile Wing received SAC's last operational readiness inspection for this system. In September, SAC deactivated the 564th SMS. During the following March, the 566th SMS would also be deactivated, completing the phaseout of the Atlas E at Warren.

The departure of the Atlas squadrons did not mark the end of F.E. Warren's role in the ICBM program. On October 15, 1962, Morrison-Knudsen and Associates won the contract to construct 200 Minuteman silos over an 8,300-square-mile area of Wyoming, Nebraska, and Colorado, located north and east of the base. Morrison-Knudsen subcontracted the task of excavating the silos to the Meridith Drilling Company of Denver. Meridith used an innovative technique of equipping cranes with 6-, 10-, and 15-foot diameter augers. These "biggest post-hole diggers on earth" allowed the crews to average drilling out one silo per day between November 1962 to June 1963. The first site, A-6, reached completion on October 2, 1963.

Besides the innovative drilling technique, the project was blessed with milder than normal weather conditions, which allowed for accelerated progress during the winter months. But access to the 200 sites proved to be a challenge. Thirty-eight miles of offsite roads had to be constructed. The Corps of Engineers Omaha Office handled numerous complaints from local owners claiming property damages. The presence of a Missile Site Labor Committee helped alleviate labor problems. The four work stoppages caused minimal impact to the construction effort. During construction, five fatalities occurred.

While construction proceeded, on July 1, 1963, the Air Force activated the 90th Strategic Missile Wing. Over the next year, the four component strategic missile squadrons activated with the 400th SMS became the last Minuteman I "B" unit to stand up on July 1, 1964.

In November 1972, SAC initiated the Minuteman Integrated Improvement Program. The program entailed silo hardening and upgrading command data buffers, which allowed for quicker missile retargeting. In addition to receiving upgraded silos and launcher control facilities, Warren also received new missiles. With conversion to the Minuteman III model, Warren's last Minuteman I model went off alert status in September 1974. On November 22, 1982, in a decision statement for Congress, President Ronald Reagan stated his plan to deploy the MX missile dubbed "Peacekeeper" to superhardened silos located at F.E. Warren. The Vice Commander-in-Chief of SAC, Lieutenant General George Miller, explained that location, geography, and geology were key factors for selecting the base.

The initial plan was to deploy 100 Peacekeepers in silos of the 400th and 319th Strategic Missile Squadrons. In July 1984, construction began for Peacekeeper support facilities at Warren. From 1986 through 1988, 50 Peacekeepers would be backfitted into silos formally occupied by Minuteman IIIs of the 400th Strategic Missile Squadron. Boeing Aerospace Company served as the primary contractor for reconfiguring the silos to accept the new missile. Unlike Minuteman, which was placed in the silo with a special transporter erector, Peacekeeper had to be assembled stage-by-stage within the silo.

References: U.S. Army Ballistic Missile Construction Office "History of Atlas Missile Base Construction, Warren I/II/III,"[HQCE]; The Federal Engineer, Damsites to Missile Sites: A History of the Omaha District U.S. Army Corps of Engineers (Omaha, NE: U.S. Army Engineer District, 1984), p. 189–191, 194, [HQCE]; SAC Chronology, *pp. 18–19, 23–24, 30, 36, 44–47, 61, 71, 72, 90, 93; on Peacekeeper see* History of Hill Air Force Base, *(Hill AFB, UT: Ogden Air Logistic Center History Office, 1988), pp. 313, 315, [AFHO].*

APPENDICES

APPENDIX A
A CHRONOLOGY OF THE UNITED STATES MISSILE PROGRAM DURING THE COLD WAR, 1945-1989

January 1945	At the request of the Army Ordnance Department, Bell Telephone Laboratories begins work on an antiaircraft missile that later becomes Nike.
January 1946	Wernher von Braun and 127 German missile experts are brought to the United States under Operation PAPERCLIP.
April 1946	Convair awarded the MX-774 project, predecessor to the Atlas intercontinental ballistic missile (ICBM).
October 1946	First Nike test flights.
July 1947	MX-774 project canceled.
September 1947	National Security Act creates the Department of Defense and makes the Air Force a separate service.
March 1948	At the Key West Conference, the services argue over roles and missions. The Air Force is given primary responsibility for continental air defense.
April 1948	The Soviets begin their blockade of West Berlin; it lasts for 321 days.
April 1949	North Atlantic Treaty Organization (NATO) established.
June 1949	The Army transfers von Braun and the Ordnance Research and Development Division SubOffice (Rocket) from Fort Bliss, Texas, to Redstone Arsenal, Huntsville, Alabama. The move to Redstone is completed in 1950.
August 1949	The Soviet Union explodes an atomic bomb. This provides impetus for the United States to develop a hydrogen bomb, the Army to build antiaircraft emplacements around strategic locations, and leads to a reappraisal of United States national security policy.
March 1950	The Joint Chiefs of Staff give the Air Force sole responsibility for developing long-range "strategic" missiles.
October 1950	The People's Republic of China established.
April 1950	NSC 68 identifies the Soviet Union as a serious military threat and prompts the United States to launch a massive rearmament program.
June 1950	Korean War begins.
July 1950	Army forms Anti-Aircraft Command (ARAACOM).
January 1951	The Air Force awards Convair the MX-1593 project that later evolves into the Atlas ICBM.
November 1951	Nike I (Ajax) intercepts target drone.
May 1952	The Army orders Bell Laboratories to investigate the feasibility of arming the Nike I, Ajax, with an atomic warhead.
November 1952	The United States explodes its first experimental hydrogen bomb.
February 1953	Bell Laboratories begins work on Nike B (Hercules).
June 1953	Armistice ends the Korean War.
August 1953	The Soviet Union detonates an operational hydrogen bomb.
October 1953	The Air Force Nuclear Weapons Panel completes its report.
February 1954	The Teapot Committee submits its recommendations.
February 1954	The United States detonates an operational hydrogen bomb.
March 1954	Based on the recommendations of the Teapot Committee, the Air Force accelerates the Atlas program.
March 1954	First Nike Ajax battalion deployed at Fort Meade, Maryland.
May 1954	The Air Force makes Atlas its highest research and development (R&D) priority.

July 1954	The Air Force establishes the Western Development Division near Los Angeles, California and names Brig. Gen. Bernard Schriever its first commanding officer.
July 1954	President Eisenhower asks James Killian to lead a study to determine if the nation is vulnerable to a surprise attack.
February 1955	Killian Report completed.
May 1955	The Air Force begins developing the Titan ICBM.
July 1955	At the Aviation Day celebration in Moscow, the Soviets fly the same 10 Bison bombers over the reviewing stand 6 times, duping the American observers into exaggerating the capabilities of the Soviet Air Force. Immediately the United States becomes concerned over the so-called "bomber gap."
September 1955	President Eisenhower designates the ICBM program the nation's top R&D priority.
September 1955	The Air Force selects the Glenn L. Martin Company to build Titan.
November 1955	Gillette Procedures implemented.
November 1955	The Secretary of Defense authorizes the Air Force and the Army to develop the Thor and Jupiter inter-mediate-range ballistic missiles (IRBMs).
December 1955	The Air Force selects the Douglas Aircraft Company to build the Thor IRBM.
January 1956	The Department of Defense gives the IRBM the same development priority as the ICBM.
February 1956	The Army Ballistic Missile Agency established at the Redstone Arsenal, Huntsville, Alabama.
June 1956	First U-2 reconnaissance flights over the Soviet Union.
November 1956	Secretary of Defense gives the Air Force responsibili-ty for all missiles with a range over 200 miles.
December 1956	The Navy begins work on the Polaris submarine-launched ballistic missile (SLBM) program.
August 1957	The Soviet Union announces its first successful ICBM test flight.
October 1957	The Soviet Union launches Sputnik, the world's first man-made satellite.
November 1957	The Soviet Union launches Sputnik II.
December 1957	The Gaither report credits the Soviet Union with a substantial lead in long-range ballistic missiles and gives rise to the so-called "missile gap."
January 1958	An Army Redstone missile carries the first U.S. satel-lite into orbit.
June 1958	The first Nike Hercules batteries are deployed around New York, Chicago, and Philadelphia.
February 1959	The Air Force begins limited R&D on the solid fuel Minuteman ICBM.
June 1959	The first Thor IRBMs are deployed in Great Britain.
September 1959	The Department of Defense determines that the Air Force will have responsibility for all military space oper-ations, with the exception of Navy's Polaris program.
September 1959	The Air Force selects the Boeing Airplane Company as the Minuteman assembly and test contractor.
October 1959	First BOMARC antiaircraft missile squadron activat-ed at McGuire Air Force Base (AFB), New Jersey.
October 1959	The Air Force begins developing Titan II.
December 1959	The first Atlas ICBMs are placed on operational alert at Vandenberg AFB, California.
May 1960	The Soviets shoot down a U.S. U-2 reconnaissance aircraft deep within Soviet airspace.
June 1960	The Army Air Defense Command's (ARADCOM) air defense network includes 88 Nike Hercules and 174 Nike Ajax batteries.
July 1960	The first Polaris submarine becomes operational.
August 1960	The Army Corps of Engineers Ballistic Missile Construction Office (CEBMCO) established.
December 1960	The first Jupiter IRBM launch emplacement at Gioia Dell Colle Air Base, Italy, becomes operational.
February 1961	The first Jupiter launch emplacement at Cigli Air Base, Turkey, placed on operational alert.
May 1962	First Titan I squadron becomes operational at Lowry AFB, Colorado.
July 1962	A Nike Zeus missile fired from the Kwajalein Test Site, Marshall Islands, intercepts an ICBM fired from Vandenberg AFB, California.

October 1962	First 10 Minuteman missiles are placed on operational alert at Malmstrom AFB, Montana.
October 1962	The United States detects Soviet IRBMs in Cuba and establishes an air and naval blockade of the island. After the Soviets remove the missiles, the blockade is lifted on November 21, 1962.
March 1963	First Titan II squadron becomes operational at Davis-Monthan AFB, Arizona.
October 1963	The Air Force begins developing the Minuteman II.
December 1963	All Thor missiles in Great Britain deactivated. The Jupiter IRBMs based in Italy and Turkey were withdrawn at the same time.
October 1964	The People's Republic of China explodes an atomic bomb.
March 1965	First U.S. combat troops sent to South Vietnam.
June 1965	The last Atlas ICBMs are taken off operational alert.
June 1965	Replacement of Titan I by Titan II completed.
April 1966	The First Minuteman II squadron becomes operational.
September 1967	The United States begins construction of the Sentinel Antiballistic Missile (ABM) system; the first site is outside of Boston.
March 1969	Nixon administration curtails the ABM program. The new Safeguard program will shield the ICBM sites at Grand Forks AFB, North Dakota, and Malmstrom AFB, Montana.
December 1970	The first Minuteman III squadron becomes operational at Minot AFB, North Dakota.
April 1972	The Air Force begins development of the MX missile, later renamed the Peacekeeper.
May 1972	The ABM treaty limits the number of ABM sites that could be built. Consequently, the site at Malmstrom is abandoned and work at the Grand Forks site continues.
October 1972	The last three BOMARC antiaircraft missile squadrons are deactivated.
April 1975	The United States evacuates its embassy in Saigon as North Vietnamese forces encircle the city.
October 1975	The Army activates the Safeguard site at Grand Forks, North Dakota.
February 1976	The Army begins to deactivate the Safeguard site at Grand Forks.
June 1979	SALT II agreement to limit long-range missiles and bombers signed by President Carter and General Secretary Brezhnev. It was never ratified by Congress.
July 1979	The Army deactivates its last Nike Hercules batteries.
December 1986	Soviet Union invades Afghanistan.
December 1986	First Peacekeeper squadron becomes operational at F.E. Warren AFB, Wyoming.
August 1987	The Air Force deactivates the last Titan II missile squadron.
December 1987	The United States and Soviet Union sign the Intermediate Nuclear Forces (INF) treaty, eliminating all intermediate-range nuclear missiles.
February 1989	Soviet Union withdraws its forces from Afghanistan.
November 1989	Berlin Wall falls.
July 1991	In signing the START treaty (START I) the United States and the Soviet Union agree to reduce their respective nuclear arsenals to 6,000 warheads.
September 1991	Indicative of decreasing tensions, President Bush orders the Air Force to remove all of its Minuteman IIs from operational alert.
December 1991	Gorbachev resigns as Soviet President and dissolves the Soviet Union.
January 1993	In signing START II, the United States and Soviet Union further reduce their nuclear stockpiles to 3,500 warheads each. The treaty remains to be implemented.
December 1993	The Air Force begins destroying Minuteman II silos to comply with the provisions of START I.

Appendix B
An Inventory of Intercontinental Ballistic Missile Launch Facilities and Air Defense Missile Sites in the United States

In this appendix, the missile sites are listed by the state in which they are located. The vast majority of the installations were combat ready launch facilities. The exceptions are the specially configured Atlas, Titan, Minuteman, and Peacekeeper test and training launchers at Vandenberg AFB that are also included in this appendix. A summary of missile launch sites, grouped by type, is included at the end of this appendix.

The following missile types are listed alphabetically within each state.

Atlas D	Minuteman I	Nike	Sprint and Spartan	
Atlas E	Minuteman II	Peacekeeper	Titan I	
Atlas F	Minuteman III	Snark	Titan II	Bomarc

To search for a missile site, locate the state in question. Then search for the desired missile type, defense area or installation, site location, or site name. Each site listing contains information concerning a particular site, or in the case of the later ICBM systems, a group of related sites. When a listing contains information concerning a group of related sites, an explanation of the grouping is given in the "Note" field of the listing. Examples of listings and their interpretations follow.

When searching for ICBM launch facilities, remember that in most cases the installation name indicates where the strategic missile wing was headquartered, not where the silos were. For that information look under the heading "Site Location."

An example of a Nike missile site located in Alaska:

Site Name: Summit
Missile Type: Nike 2AK/8L-H
Defense Area: Anchorage
Site Location: Anchorage (25 mi. NE)/Chugach Mountains
Branch: Army
Dates of Active Service: May 1959 to May 1979
Control Site Condition/Owner: Intact; Army ownership, best preserved Alaskan site
Launch Site Condition/Owner: Intact; Army ownership, best preserved Alaskan site

This listing would be interpreted as follows. The site is located 25 miles northeast of Anchorage. The name of the site is Summit and it was within the Anchorage Defense Area. The "Missile type" information (2AK/8L-H) means the site contained two Nike Ajax magazines (A), located above ground (K), with eight launchers (8L) being converted to Nike Hercules (H). A key containing the abbreviations associated with the Nike sites is provided on each page containing Nike site information. The branch of service involved was the Army and the dates of active service are taken from unit activation and deactivation records. In the Nike system, the control site and launch site were considered separate individual sites when dealing with the properties. The Summit control and launch sites happen to have the same owner and condition; however, this is not always the case. Many listings will have "FDS" following either the control site or launch site heading, which means that the site has gone through the "Formerly-Used Defense Site" program and has been transferred from DoD control to another party This party could be a private owner, a municipality, or the state. No other information was available concerning the site.

Nike Missile Type Key
Missile Storage: C=Ajax only, original design; B=Ajax or Hercules, some modifications were required for the elevator to handle the Hercules launcher; D=Either, increased access room in the magazine
Missile/Launcher: A=Ajax; AA=Double Ajax launchers; AG=Above Ground; H=Hercules; L=Launcher; K=Unofficial designation for Alaskan above ground launchers; U=Universal launcher; UA=1/2 Universal and 112 Ajax launchers; UU=Double Universal launchers
Note: *Launchers converted to Hercules are given in parenthesis; e.g. (8L-H)*

An example of a Bomarc site located in Virginia:

Site Name: Langley AFB
Missile Type: Bomarc B (56)
Installation: Langley AFB
Site Location: 5 mi. W. of Langley AFB
Squadron: 22nd ADMS
Branch: Air Force
Dates of Active Service: Sep 1, 1958 to Oct 31, 1972
Current: Site has been disposed of to the School Board of the city of Newport News and the Dept. of Education of the Peninsula Tidewater Regional Academy of Criminal Justice.

The Bomarc listing is interpreted in much the same way as the Nike listing, with a few exceptions. The "Missile Type" field contains a number in parentheses that indicates 56 missiles were deployed at the site. The "Squadron" assigned to the site has been added. The Bomarc system combined launch and control at a single site. Information concerning launch condition, control condition, and current owner is in the "Current" field.

An example of a Titan I site in Maine:

Site Name: Presque Isle AFB
Missile Type: Snark
Installation: Presque Isle AFB
Note: This is the only Snark site to be activated.
Site Location: Presque Isle AFB, Presque Isle, ME
Squadron: 702nd SMW
Branch: Air Force
Dates of Active Service: Jan 1,1959 to Jun 25, 1961
Current: Site has been disposed of to the City of Presque Isle. The site is now undergoing consideration for eligibility for the National Register.

The Snark was deployed at only one location.

An example of an Atlas F missile site in Texas:

Site Name: 1
Missile Type: Atlas F
Installation: Dyess AFB

Site Location: Abilene
Squadron: 578th SMS
Branch: Air Force
Dates of Active Service: Jul 1, 1961 to Mar 25, 1965
Current: Private ownership, materials salvaged before sold but structure remains intact.

Information for the Atlas missile sites is interpreted in much the same manner as the previous examples with the exception that each Atlas site contained one missile unless otherwise noted. All salvageable materials generally were removed by the Air Force prior to selling a site to private owners.

An example of a Titan I site in California:

Site Name: 2 (launchers 851-B-1,2,3)
Missile Type: Titan I
Installation: Beale AFB
Site Location: Live Oak
Squadron: 85 1st
Branch: Air Force
Dates of Active Service: Feb 1, 1961 to Mar 25, 1965

Information for the Titan missile sites is interpreted in much the same way as the previous examples with the exception that each Titan I site contained three missile silos. Titan II sites were single-silo facilities. As with the Atlas sites, the Air Force generally salvaged material before selling a site to a private owner.

An example of a Minuteman II missile site in Montana:

Site Name: A02-A11
Missile Type: Minuteman II
Installation: Malmstrom AFB
Note: The information listed is for launch sites A02-A11.
Site Location: Near Malmstrom AFB, Great Falls, MT
Squadron: 10th SMS
Branch: Air Force
Dates of Active Service: Dec 1, 1961 to present
Current: All sites are scheduled to undergo conversion to Minuteman III.
Conversion: 341st Strategic Missile Wing was converted to Minuteman II on

May 30, 1969 and then converted to Minuteman III on July 8, 1975.

Information within the "Site Name" field for each Minuteman missile site has been grouped according to the launch sites that were controlled by a single control site. The site in this example is for launch sites A02-A11 and would have been controlled by site AO1. This site is in "Caretaker Status," which means that it has been turned over to the Air Combat Command. The site remains in use as a Minuteman III site. The "Conversion" field lists information regarding conversion to another missile type. Because all Minuteman I sites have been converted to Minuteman II or Minuteman III sites, no sites are listed under the original Minuteman I designation.

An example of the Peacekeeper missile sites in Wyoming:

Site Name: Pl-Tll
Missile Type: Peacekeeper
Installation: F. E. Warren AFB
Note: The information listed is for missile alert facilities P1, Q1, R1, S1, T1, and launch sites P2-P11, Q2-Q11, R2-R11, S2-S11, and T2-T11.
Site Location: North of F.E. Warren AFB, Cheyenne, WY
Squadron: 400th SMS
Branch: Air Force
Dates of Active Service: Jul 1, 1964 to present
Current: All sites are currently active.
Conversion: 90th Strategic Missile Wing (400th Strategic Missile Squadron only) converted to Peacekeeper on Dec 30, 1988.

The only Peacekeeper missile sites activated are at F.E. Warren AFB. The 50 missiles deployed are all included in this listing.

An example of the antiballistic missile (ABM) site in North Dakota:

Site Name: Stanley R. Mickelsen Safeguard Complex
Missile Type: Sprint and Spartan
Installation: Missile Site Radar
Site Location: 102 miles northwest of Grand Forks; 12 miles south of Langdon
Branch: Army
Dates of Active Service: 1975–1976
Current: Held in caretaker status by the U.S. Army Space and Strategic Defense Command. The missile launchers are currently being removed.

The Stanley R. Mickelsen Safeguard Complex was the only unit of the Safeguard system ever to become operational. The complex consisted of six elements: the missile site radar (MSR) complex, the four remote Sprint launch (RSL) sites, and the perimeter acquisition radar (PAR). Only the MSR and RSLs are included in this list. Information on the PAR can be found in the Safeguard weapon system profile in Part II.

ALASKA

Nike

Site Name: Bay
Missile Type: Nike 2AK/8L-H
Defense Area: Anchorage
Site Location: Anchorage (25 mi. NE)
Branch: Army
Dates of Active Service: Mar 1959 to May 1979
Control Site Condition/Owner: Intact; State correctional facility
Launch Site Condition/Owner: Intact; Launch remains, no use known

Site Name: Point
Missile Type: Nike 4AK/16L-H
Defense Area: Anchorage
Site Location: Anchorage (10 mi. SW)
Branch: Army
Dates of Active Service: Apr 1959 to May 1971
Control Site Condition/Owner: Obliterated; FDS; foundations only remain
Launch Site Condition/Owner: Intact; Site now a city park, Kincaid Park 4 launchers standing, 1 used as a ski hut

Site Name: Summit
Missile Type: Nike 2AK/8L-H
Defense Area: Anchorage
Site Location: Anchorage (25 mi. NE)/Chugach Mountains
Branch: Army
Dates of Active Service: May 1959 to May 1979
Control Site Condition/Owner: Intact; Army ownership, best preserved Alaskan site
Launch Site Condition/Owner: Intact; Army ownership, best preserved Alaskan site

Site Name: Jig
Missile Type: Nike 2AK/8L-H
Defense Area: Fairbanks
Site Location: Eielson AFB (5 mi. S)
Branch: Army
Dates of Active Service: Mar 1959 to May 1970
Control Site Condition/Owner: Obliterated; Private ownership, demolished
Launch Site Condition/Owner: Partially Intact; Private ownership, 1 launcher used to store dynamite

Site Name: Love
Missile Type: Nike 2AK/8L-H
Defense Area: Fairbanks
Site Location: Fairbanks (10 mi. NW)
Branch: Army
Dates of Active Service: Mar 1959 to May 1971
Control Site Condition/Owner: Obliterated; State of Alaska control; demolished
Launch Site Condition/Owner: Obliterated; State of Alaska control; demolished

Site Name: Mike
Missile Type: Nike 2AK/8L-H
Defense Area: Fairbanks
Site Location: Eielson AFB (10 mi. SE)
Branch: Army
Dates of Active Service: Mar 1959 to May 1970
Control Site Condition/Owner: Obliterated; Army ownership, demolished
Launch Site Condition/Owner: Obliterated; Army ownership, demolished

Site Name: Peter
Missile Type: Nike 2AK/8L-H
Defense Area: Fairbanks
Site Location: Eielson AFB (15 mi. E)
Branch: Army
Dates of Active Service: Mar 1959 to May 1971
Control Site Condition/Owner: Obliterated; Army terrorism training site
Launch Site Condition/Owner: Obliterated; Army terrorism training site

Site Name: Tare
Missile Type: Nike 2AK/8L-H
Defense Area: Fairbanks
Site Location: Newman (20 mi. S)
Branch: Army
Dates of Active Service: Mar 1959 to May 1971
Control Site Condition/Owner: Obliterated; Corps of Engineers control, demolished
Launch Site Condition/Owner: Partially Intact; Launch remains; serves as administration facility for Chena River Lakes Recreation Area

ARIZONA

Titan

Site Name: 7
Missile Type: Titan II
Installation: Davis-Monthan AFB
Site Location: Amado
Squadron: 571st
Branch: Air Force
Dates of Active Service: May 1, 1962 to Dec 2,1983
Current: Private ownership, site imploded before sold.

Site Name: 2
Missile Type: Titan II
Installation: Davis-Monthan AFB
Site Location: Benson
Squadron: 571st SMS
Branch: Air Force
Dates of Active Service: May 1, 1962 to Dec 2, 1983
Current: Private ownership, site imploded before sold.

Site Name: 3
Missile Type: Titan II
Installation: Davis-Monthan AFB
Site Location: Benson
Squadron: 571st
Branch: Air Force
Dates of Active Service: May 1, 1962 to Dec 2, 1983
Current: Private ownership, site imploded before sold.

Site Name: 6
Missile Type: Titan II
Installation: Davis-Monthan AFB
Site Location: Continental
Squadron: 571st
Branch: Air Force
Dates of Active Service: May 1, 1962 to Dec 2, 1983
Current: Private ownership, site imploded before sold.

Site Name: 8
Missile Type: Titan II
Installation: Davis-Monthan AFB
Site Location: Green Valley
Squadron: 571st
Branch: Air Force
Dates of Active Service: May 1, 1962 to Dec 2, 1983

Current: The site is currently the Titan Missile Museum. The site has been restored and public tours are provided on a daily basis. It is the only ICBM site open to the public.

Site Name: 4
Missile Type: Titan II
Installation: Davis-Monthan AFB
Site Location: Mescal
Squadron: 571st
Branch: Air Force
Dates of Active Service: May 1, 1962 to Dec 2, 1983
Current: Private ownership, site imploded before sold.

Site Name: 1
Missile Type: Titan II
Installation: Davis-Monthan AFB
Site Location: Oracle
Squadron: 570th SMS
Branch: Air Force
Dates of Active Service: Jan 1, 1962 to Jul 31, 1984
Current: Private ownership, site was imploded before sold.

Site Name: 16
Missile Type: Titan II
Installation: Davis-Monthan APB
Site Location: Oracle Junction
Squadron: 571st
Branch: Air Force
Dates of Active Service: May 1, 1962 to Dec 2, 1983
Current: Private ownership, the site was imploded before sold.

Site Name: 17
Missile Type: Titan II
Installation: Davis-Monthan AFB
Site Location: Oracle Junction
Squadron: 571st
Branch: Air Force
Dates of Active Service: May 1, 1962 to Dec 2, 1983
Current: Private ownership, the site was imploded before sold.

Site Name: 18
Missile Type: Titan II
Installation: Davis-Monthan AFB
Site Location: Oracle Junction
Squadron: 571st
Branch: Air Force
Dates of Active Service: May 1, 1962 to Dec 2, 1983
Current: Private ownership, the site was imploded before sold.

Site Name: 9
Missile Type: Titan II
Installation: Davis-Monthan AFB
Site Location: Palo Alto
Squadron: 571st
Branch: Air Force
Dates of Active Service: May 1, 1962 to Dec 2, 1983
Current: Private ownership, site was imploded before sold.

Site Name: 5
Missile Type: Titan II
Installation: Davis-Monthan AFB
Site Location: Pantano
Squadron: 571st
Branch: Air Force
Dates of Active Service: May 1, 1962 to Dec 2, 1983
Current: Private ownership, site imploded before sold.

Site Name: 12
Missile Type: Titan II
Installation: Davis-Monthan AFB
Site Location: Rillito
Squadron: 571st
Branch: Air Force
Dates of Active Service: May 1, 1962 to Dec 2, 1983
Current: The site has not been imploded and is currently in excess to be sold by the GSA.

Site Name: 13
Missile Type: Titan II
Installation: Davis-Monthan AFB
Site Location: Rillito

Squadron: 571st
Branch: Air Force
Dates of Active Service: May 1, 1962 to Dec 2, 1983
Current: Private ownership, the site was imploded before sold.

Site Name: 14
Missile Type: Titan II
Installation: Davis-Monthan AFB
Site Location: Rillito
Squadron: 571st
Branch: Air Force
Dates of Active Service: May 1, 1962 to Dec 2, 1983
Current: Private ownership, the site was imploded before sold.

Site Name: 15
Missile Type: Titan II
Installation: Davis-Monthan AFB
Site Location: Rillito
Squadron: 571st
Branch: Air Force
Dates of Active Service: May 1, 1962 to Dec 2, 1983
Current: Private ownership, the site was imploded before sold.

Site Name: 10
Missile Type: Titan II
Installation: Davis-Monthan AFB
Site Location: Three Points
Squadron: 571st
Branch: Air Force
Dates of Active Service: May 1, 1962 to Dec 2, 1983
Current: Private ownership, site was imploded before sold.

Site Name: 11
Missile Type: Titan II
Installation: Davis-Monthan AFB
Site Location: Three Points
Squadron: 571st
Branch: Air Force
Dates of Active Service: May 1, 1962 to Dec 2,

1983

Current: The site has not been imploded and is currently in excess to be sold by the GSA.

ARKANSAS

Titan

Site Name: 4
Missile Type: Titan II
Installation: Little Rock AFB
Site Location: Albion
Squadron: 373rd SMS
Branch: Air Force
Dates of Active Service: Apr 1, 1962 to Aug 13, 1987
Current: Private ownership, site was imploded before sold.

Site Name: 6
Missile Type: Titan II
Installation: Little Rock AFB
Site Location: Antioch
Squadron: 373rd SMS
Branch: Air Force
Dates of Active Service: Apr 1, 1962 to Aug 18, 1987
Current: Site has been imploded and remains under DoD control.

Site Name: 10
Missile Type: Titan II
Installation: Little Rock AFB
Site Location: Blackwell
Squadron: 374th SMS
Branch: Air Force
Dates of Active Service: Sep 1, 1962 to Aug 15, 1986
Current: Private ownership, site was imploded before sold.

Site Name: 5
Missile Type: Titan II
Installation: Little Rock AFB
Site Location: Center Hill
Squadron: 373rd SMS
Branch: Air Force
Dates of Active Service: Apr 1, 1962 to Aug 18, 1987

Current: Private ownership, site was imploded before sold.

Site Name: 17
Missile Type: Titan II
Installation: Little Rock AFB
Site Location: Guy
Squadron: 374th SMS
Branch: Air Force
Dates of Active Service: Sep 1, 1962 to Aug 15, 1986
Current: Site has been imploded and remains under DoD control.

Site Name: 9
Missile Type: Titan II
Installation: Little Rock AFB
Site Location: Hamlet
Squadron: 373rd SMS
Branch: Air Force
Dates of Active Service: Apr 1, 1962 to Aug 18, 1987
Current: Site has been imploded and remains under DoD control.

Site Name: 3
Missile Type: Titan II
Installation: Little Rock AFB
Site Location: Heber Springs
Squadron: 373rd SMS
Branch: Air Force
Dates of Active Service: Apr 1, 1962 to Aug 18, 1987
Current: Site has been imploded and remains under DoD control.

Site Name: 8
Missile Type: Titan II
Installation: Little Rock AFB
Site Location: Judsonia
Squadron: 373rd SMS
Branch: Air Force
Dates of Active Service: Apr 1, 1962 to Aug 18, 1987
Current: Site has been imploded and remains under DoD control.

Site Name: 1
Missile Type: Titan II

Installation: Little Rock AFB
Site Location: Mount Vernon
Squadron: 373rd SMS
Branch: Air Force
Dates of Active Service: April 1, 1962 to Aug 18, 1987
Current: The site has been imploded and remains under DoD control.

Site Name: 11
Missile Type: Titan II
Installation: Little Rock AFB
Site Location: Plummerville
Squadron: 374th SMS
Branch: Air Force
Dates of Active Service: Sep 1, 1962 to Aug 15, 1986
Current: Site has been imploded and remains under DoD control.

Site Name: 18
Missile Type: Titan II
Installation: Little Rock AFB
Site Location: Quitman
Squadron: 374th SMS
Branch: Air Force
Dates of Active Service: Sep 1, 1962 to Aug 15, 1986
Current: Site has been imploded and remains under DoD control.

Site Name: 15
Missile Type: Titan II
Installation: Little Rock AFB
Site Location: Republican
Squadron: 374th SMS
Branch: Air Force
Dates of Active Service: Sep 1, 1962 to Aug 15, 1986
Current: Site has been imploded and remains under DoD control.

Site Name: 2
Missile Type: Titan II
Installation: Little Rock AFB
Site Location: Rose Bud
Squadron: 373rd SMS
Branch: Air Force
Dates of Active Service: Apr 1, 1962 to Aug 18,

1987
Current: Site has been imploded and remains under DoD control.

Site Name: 12
Missile Type: Titan II
Installation: Little Rock AFB
Site Location: Saint Vincent
Squadron: 374th SMS
Branch: Air Force
Dates of Active Service: Sep 1, 1962 to Aug 15, 1986
Current: Private ownership, site was imploded before sold.

Site Name: 16
Missile Type: Titan II
Installation: Little Rock AFB
Site Location: Southside
Squadron: 374th SMS
Branch: Air Force
Dates of Active Service: Sep 1, 1962 to Aug 15, 1986
Current: Site has been imploded and remains under DoD control.

Site Name: 13
Missile Type: Titan II
Installation: Little Rock AFB
Site Location: Springfield
Squadron: 374th SMS
Branch: Air Force
Dates of Active Service: Sep 1,1962 to Aug 15, 1986
Current: Site has been imploded and remains under DoD control.

Site Name: 14
Missile Type: Titan II
Installation: Little Rock AFB
Site Location: Springfield
Squadron: 374th SMS
Branch: Air Force
Dates of Active Service: Sep 1, 1962 to Aug 15, 1986
Current: Site has been imploded and remains under DoD control.

Site Name: 7
Missile Type: Titan II
Installation: Little Rock AFB
Site Location: Velvet Ridge
Squadron: 373rd SMS
Branch: Air Force
Dates of Active Service: Apr 1, 1962 to Aug 18, 1987
Current: Site has been imploded and remains under DoD control.

CALIFORNIA

Minuteman

Site Name: LF-02 (394 A-1)
Missile Type: Minuteman I, converted to Minuteman II in 1967 and later to Minuteman III; converted to Peacekeeper in 1985.
Installation: Vandenberg AFB
Branch: Air Force
Dates of Active Service: A test and training facility, operational between Nov 21, 1961 to present
Current: Active

Site Name: LF-03 (394-A2)
Missile Type: Minuteman I
Installation: Vandenberg AFB
Branch: Air Force
Dates of Active Service: A test and training facility, operational between Nov 21, 1961 to present
Current: Active

Site Name: LF-04 (394-A3)
Missile Type: Minuteman I, converted to Minuteman II in 1968 and Minuteman III in 1974
Installation: Vandenberg AFB
Branch: Air Force
Dates of Active Service: A test and training facility, operational between Nov 21, 1961 to present
Current: Active

Site Name: LF-05 (394-A4)

Missile Type: Minuteman I, converted to Minuteman II in 1965 and later to Minuteman III; converted to Peacekeeper in 1985
Installation: Vandenberg AFB
Branch: Air Force
Dates of Active Service: A test and training facility, operational between Nov 1, 1961 to present
Current: Active

Site Name: LF-06 (394-A5)
Missile Type: Minuteman I, converted to Minuteman III in October 1986
Installation: Vandenberg AFB
Branch: Air Force
Dates of Active Service: A test and training facility, operational between Dec 28, 1961 to present
Current: Active

Site Name: LF-07 (394-A6)
Missile Type: Minuteman I, II
Installation: Vandenberg AFB
Branch: Air Force
Dates of Active Service: A test and training facility, operational between Apr 3, 1962 to present
Current: Currently in process of being decommissioned and stripped

Site Name: LF-08 (394-A7)
Missile Type: Minuteman I; converted to Peacekeeper in March 1985
Installation: Vandenberg AFB
Branch: Air Force
Dates of Active Service: A test and training facility, operational between Mar 18, 1963 to present
Current: Active

Site Name: LF-09 (394-A7)
Missile Type: Minuteman I, III
Installation: Vandenberg AFB
Branch: Air Force
Dates of Active Service: A test and training facility, operational between Jan 15, 1964 to present
Current: Active

Site Name: LF-21
Missile Type: Minuteman I, III
Installation: Vandenberg AFB
Branch: Air Force
Dates of Active Service: A test and training facility, operational between Aug 1964 to present
Current: Although still slated as active, the site is no longer being used and has been partially stripped

Site Name: FL-10
Missile Type: Minuteman II, III
Installation: Vandenberg AFB
Branch: Air Force
Dates of Active Service: A test and training facility, operational between Nov 1964 to present
Current: Active

Site Name: LF-23
Missile Type: Minuteman II
Installation: Vandenberg AFB
Branch: Air Force
Dates of Active Service: A test and training facility, it was accepted on Oct 2, 1965, and staged its last launch Aug 26, 1966
Current: Decommissioned and stripped

Site Name: LF-24
Missile Type: Minuteman II
Installation: Vandenberg AFB
Branch: Air Force
Dates of Active Service: A test and training facility, it was accepted on Jan 5, 1965, and staged its last launch May 18, 1971
Current: Decommissioned and stripped

Site Name: LF-25
Missile Type: Minuteman II
Installation: Vandenberg AFB
Branch: Air Force
Dates of Active Service: A test and training facility, it was accepted on Jan 2, 1965, and staged its last launch Mar 4, 1976
Current: Decommissioned and stripped

Site Name: LF-26
Missile Type: Minuteman II, III

Installation: Vandenberg AFB
Branch: Air Force
Dates of Active Service: A test and training facility, it was accepted on Feb 2, 1965 to present
Current: Active

Atlas

Site Name: 576-A-1
Missile Type: Orig. Atlas D
Installation: Vandenberg
Site Location: Vandenberg
Branch: Air Force
Dates of Active Service: Oct 26, 1962 to Nov 4, 1963 then used for space program from May 25, 1965 to Sep 8, 1974
Current: Decommissioned/Stripped

Site Name: 576-A-2
Missile Type: Orig. Atlas D
Installation: Vandenberg
Site Location: Vandenberg
Branch: Air Force
Dates of Active Service: Oct 26, 1962 to Aug 5, 1965 then used for space program from Apr 6, 1968 to Sep 8, 1974 (Site of the first Vandenberg ICBM launch)
Current: Decommissioned/Stripped

Site Name: 576-A-3
Missile Type: Atlas D
Installation: Vandenberg AFB
Site Location: Vandenberg
Branch: Air Force
Dates of Active Service: Jan 26, 1960 to Present (The site was converted to commercial use, but the conversion date is unknown)
Current: In commercial use

Site Name: 576-B-1
Missile Type: Atlas D
Installation: Vandenberg AFB
Site Location: Vandenberg
Branch: Air Force
Dates of Active Service: Jul 22, 1960 to Jun 10, 1966
Current: Decommissioned/Stripped

Site Name: 576-B-2
Missile Type: Atlas D
Installation: Vandenberg AFB
Site Location: Vandenberg
Branch: Air Force
Dates of Active Service: Jun 19, 1959 to Nov 7, 1967
Current: Decommissioned/Stripped

Site Name: 576-B-3
Missile Type: Atlas D
Installation: Vandenberg AFB
Site Location: Vandenberg
Branch: Air Force
Dates of Active Service: Sep 12, 1960 to Jan 21, 1965 then used for space program from May 27, 1965 to Oct 11, 1967
Current: Decommissioned/Stripped

Site Name: 576-C
Missile Type: Atlas E
Installation: Vandenberg AFB
Site Location: Vandenberg
Branch: Air Force
Dates of Active Service: Jul 3, 1963 to Sep 25, 1963
Current: Decommissioned/Stripped

Site Name: 576-D
Missile Type: Atlas F
Installation: Vandenberg AFB
Site Location: Vandenberg
Branch: Air Force
Dates of Active Service: Mar 15, 1963 to Aug 31, 1964
Current: Decommissioned/Stripped

Site Name: 576-E
Missile Type: Atlas F
Installation: Vandenberg AFB
Site Location: Vandenberg
Branch: Air Force
Dates of Active Service: Aug 1, 1962 to Dec 22, 1964
Current: Decommissioned/Stripped

Nike

Site Name: LA-29
Missile Type: Nike 1B, 2C/18H, 30A/12L-UA, (7L-H)
Defense Area: Los Angeles
Site Location: Brea/Puente Hill
Branch: Army
Dates of Active Service: 1958 to June 1971
Control Site Condition/Owner: Private ownership
Launch Site Condition/Owner: Private ownership

Site Name: LA-88
Missile Type: Nike 1B, 2C/18H, 30A/11L-U
Defense Area: Los Angeles
Site Location: Chatsworth/Oat Mountain
Branch: Army
Dates of Active Service: 1957 to Mar 1974
Control Site Condition/Owner: Partially Intact; Relay site
Launch Site Condition/Owner: Intact; California Conservation Corps Camp

Site Name: LA-43
Missile Type: Nike 2B/12H, 20A/8L-UA
Defense Area: Los Angeles
Site Location: Fort MacArthur (upper)
Branch: Army
Dates of Active Service: 1956 to Mar 1974
Control Site Condition/Owner: Intact; City of LA; Angeles Gate Park
Launch Site Condition/Owner: Intact; City of LA; White Point Park

Site Name: LA-32
Missile Type: Nike 1B1C/12H, 20A/8L-U
Defense Area: Los Angeles
Site Location: Garden Grove/Stanton
Branch: Army
Dates of Active Service: 1956 to Mar 1974
Control Site Condition/Owner: Obliterated; Private ownership; Industrial park
Launch Site Condition/Owner: Partially Intact; CAArNG, 458th MASH

Site Name: LA-70
Missile Type: Nike 1B, 2C/30A/12L-A

Defense Area: Los Angeles
Site Location: Hyperion/Playa del Rey
Branch: Army
Dates of Active Service: 1956 to 1963
Control Site Condition/Owner: Obliterated; FDS; vacant
Launch Site Condition/Owner: Intact; City of LA Department of Airports; Jet Pets Animal Services

Site Name: LA-40
Missile Type: Nike 1B, 2C/30A/12L-A
Defense Area: Los Angeles
Site Location: Long Beach Airport
Branch: Army
Dates of Active Service: 1956 to 1963
Control Site Condition/Owner: Obliterated; Hotel and commercial development
Launch Site Condition/Owner: Obliterated; Kilroy Airport Center

Site Name: LA-94
Missile Type: Nike 1B, 2C/18H-30A/12L-UA
Defense Area: Los Angeles
Site Location: Los Pinetos/Newhall
Branch: Army
Dates of Active Service: 1955 to Nov 1968
Control Site Condition/Owner: Intact; LA County Fire Camp #9 and GTE cellular relay station
Launch Site Condition/Owner: Partially Intact; US Forest Service

Site Name: LA-78
Missile Type: Nike 1B, 2C/18H, 30A/12L-U
Defense Area: Los Angeles
Site Location: Malibu
Branch: Army
Dates of Active Service: 1963 to Mar 1974
Control Site Condition/Owner: Partially Intact; LA County Fire Department; Fire Camp #8
Launch Site Condition/Owner: Partially Intact; Microwave/Communication Facility

Site Name: LA-98
Missile Type: Nike 1B, 2C/30A/12L-A
Defense Area: Los Angeles
Site Location: Magic Mountain/Lang Saugus
Branch: Army

Dates of Active Service: 1955 to Dec 1968
Control Site Condition/Owner: Microwave relay
Launch Site Condition/Owner: Private owner; construction use

Site Name: LA-09
Missile Type: Nike 1B, 2C/30A/12L-A
Defense Area: Los Angeles
Site Location: Mount Disappointment Berkeley
Branch: Army
Dates of Active Service: Dec 1956 to 1961
Control Site Condition/Owner: Intact; LA County Probation Department work camp
Launch Site Condition/Owner: Obliterated; LA Sheriff's Department Air Station

Site Name: LA-04
Missile Type: Nike 1B, 2C/30A/12L-A
Defense Area: Los Angeles
Site Location: Mount Gleason/Palmdale
Branch: Army
Dates of Active Service: 1956 to Apr 1974
Control Site Condition/Owner: Intact; State of California prison camp
Launch Site Condition/Owner: Obliterated; State of California

Site Name: LA-73
Missile Type: Nike 1B, 2C/30A/12L-A
Defense Area: Los Angeles
Site Location: Playa del Rey/Lax
Branch: Army
Dates of Active Service: 1956 to 1963
Control Site Condition/Owner: Obliterated; Apartments; commercial use

Site Name: LA-55
Missile Type: Nike 2B/12H, 20A/8L-U
Defense Area: Los Angeles
Site Location: Point Vincente
Branch: Army
Dates of Active Service: 1956 to Mar 1974
Control Site Condition/Owner: Obliterated; City of Rancho Palos Verdes; Del Cero Park
Launch Site Condition/Owner: Intact; City Hall Park

Site Name: LA-57
Missile Type: Nike 1B, 2C/30A/12L-A
Defense Area: Los Angeles
Site Location: Redondo Beach/Torrance
Branch: Army
Dates of Active Service: 1956 to 1963
Control Site Condition/Owner: Obliterated;
City of Redondo Beach; Hopkins Wilderness
Park
Launch Site Condition/Owner: Partially Intact;
City of Torrance; Torrance Airport Civil Air
Patrol

Site Name: LA-14
Missile Type: Nike 2B/20A/8L-A
Defense Area: Los Angeles
Site Location: South El Monte
Branch: Army
Dates of Active Service: 1956 to 1961
Control Site Condition/Owner: Obliterated;
City of LA Police/fire training site
Launch Site Condition/Owner: Obliterated;
USAR Center
Launch Site Condition/Owner: Intact; City of
LA Department of Airports; Jet Pets Animal
Services

Site Name: LA-96
Missile Type: Nike
1B,2C/18H, 30A/12L-U, (8L-H)
Defense Area: Los Angeles
Site Location: Van Nuys/Sepulveda
Branch: Army
Dates of Active Service: 1957 to Sep 1974
Control Site Condition/Owner: Partially Intact;
City of LA, San Vincente Mountain Park
Launch Site Condition/Owner: Intact;
CAArNG, 261st Combat Communication
Squadron

Site Name: SF-91
Missile Type: Nike 1B, 2C/30A/12L-A
Defense Area: San Francisco
Site Location: Angel Island
Branch: Army
Dates of Active Service: 1955 to 1961
Control Site Condition/Owner: Partially Intact;
Abandoned
Launch Site Condition/Owner: Partially Intact;

NPS-GGNRA, Angel Island State Park

Site Name: SF-31
Missile Type: Nike 2B/12H, 20A/8L-U
Defense Area: San Francisco
Site Location: Lake Chabot/Castro Valley
Branch: Army
Dates of Active Service: 1956 to Mar 1974
Control Site Condition/Owner: Intact;
Communications facility
Launch Site Condition/Owner: Partially Intact;
East Bay Regional Park District, Lake Chabot
Park; Department of Public Safety, service
yard

Site Name: SF-37
Missile Type: Nike 1B, 2C/30A/12L-A
Defense Area: San Francisco
Site Location: Coyote Hills/Newark
Branch: Army
Dates of Active Service: 1955 to Mar 1963
Control Site Condition/Owner: Partially Intact;
East Bay Regional Park District, Coyote Hills
Regional Park Alameda County Sheriff's
Department; radio transmitter
Launch Site Condition/Owner: Obliterated;
Coyote Hills Regional Park

Site Name: SF-88
Missile Type: Nike 2B/12H, 20A/8L-U
Defense Area: San Francisco
Site Location: Fort Barry/Sausalito
Branch: Army
Dates of Active Service: Mar 1958 to Mar 1974
Control Site Condition/Owner: Partially Intact;
NPS-GGNRA; campsite, YMCA facility
Launch Site Condition/Owner: Intact; National
Park Service Restored Nike Site, open for
tours

Site Name: SF-87
Missile Type: Nike 2B/12H, 20A/8L-U
Defense Area: San Francisco
Site Location: Fort Cronkhite/Sausalito
Branch: Army
Dates of Active Service: 1955 to June 1971
Control Site Condition/Owner: Partially Intact;
Golden Gate National Recreation Area
Launch Site Condition/Owner: Intact; Marine

Mammal Center

Site Name: SF-59
Missile Type: Nike 1B, 2C/30A/12L-A
Defense Area: San Francisco
Site Location: Fort Funston/Mount San Bruno
Branch: Army
Dates of Active Service: 1956 to Mar 1963
Control Site Condition/Owner: FDS
Launch Site Condition/Owner: Partially Intact;
Park Picnic Area, launcher now a parking lot

Site Name: SF-89
Missile Type: Nike 1B, 2C/30A/12L-A
Defense Area: San Francisco
Site Location: Fort Winfield Scott
Branch: Army
Dates of Active Service: 1955 to Mar 1963
Control Site Condition/Owner:
Television/communications facility
Launch Site Condition/Owner: Intact;
Salvageyard

Site Name: SF-51
Missile Type: Nike 2B/12H, 20A/8L-U
Defense Area: San Francisco
Site Location: Milagra/Pacifica
Branch: Army
Dates of Active Service: 1956 to Mar 1974
Control Site Condition/Owner: National Park
Service; Sweeny Ridge Skyline Preserve
Launch Site Condition/Owner: Obliterated;
Milagra Ridge County Park

Site Name: SF-25
Missile Type: Nike 1B, 2C/30A/12L-A
Defense Area: San Francisco
Site Location: Rock Ridge
Branch: Army
Dates of Active Service: 1956 to Jul 1959
Control Site Condition/Owner: Partially Intact;
Las Trampas Regional Park and microwave
communications facility
Launch Site Condition/Owner: Intact; TRA-
COR Aerospace, Expendable Technology
Center; Las Trampas Regional Park Office

Site Name: SF-08
Missile Type: Nike 1B, 2C/30A/12L-A

Defense Area: San Francisco
Site Location: San Pablo Ridge
Branch: Army
Dates of Active Service: 1956 to Mar 1963
Control Site Condition/Owner: Obliterated; Wildcat Canyon Regional Park
Launch Site Condition/Owner: Obliterated; Wildcat Canyon Regional Park

Site Name: SF-09
Missile Type: Nike 1B,2C/30A/12L-A
Defense Area: San Francisco
Site Location: San Pablo Ridge/Berkeley
Branch: Army
Dates of Active Service: 1955 to Jun 1963
Control Site Condition/Owner: Obliterated; Wildcat Canyon Regional Park
Launch Site Condition/Owner: Obliterated; Wildcat Canyon Regional Park

Site Name: SF-93
Missile Type: Nike 3B/18H, 30A/12L-U
Defense Area: San Francisco
Site Location: San Raphael
Branch: Army
Dates of Active Service: 1957 to June 1971
Control Site Condition/Owner: Partially Intact; Harry P. Barbier Memorial Park
Launch Site Condition/Owner: Partially Intact; Martin County Waste Water Treatment Plant

Site Name: T-33
Missile Type: Nike AG/12A/12L-A
Defense Area: Travis AFB
Site Location: Dixon/Lambie
Branch: Army
Dates of Active Service: 1957 to Jan 1959
Control Site Condition/Owner: Intact; State of California Department of Health Services
Launch Site Condition/Owner: Obliterated; Private ownership

Site Name: T-10
Missile Type: Nike 3B/18H, 30A/12L-U
Defense Area: Travis AFB
Site Location: Elmira
Branch: Army
Dates of Active Service: 1958 to Mar 1974
Control Site Condition/Owner: Intact; Housing

Launch Site Condition/Owner: Intact; Private ownership

Site Name: T-86
Missile Type: Nike 1B, 2C/30A/12L-UA, (L-U)
Defense Area: Travis AFB
Site Location: Fairfield/Cement Hills
Branch: Army
Dates of Active Service: 1958 to June 1971
Control Site Condition/Owner: Private ownership
Launch Site Condition/Owner: Intact; Solano County Detention Center and Animal Shelter

Site Name: T-53
Missile Type: Nike 1B, 2C/30A/12L-A
Defense Area: Travis AFB
Site Location: Potrero Hills
Branch: Army
Dates of Active Service: 1958 to Jan 1959
Control Site Condition/Owner: Intact; Explosives Technology
Launch Site Condition/Owner: Intact; Explosives Technology

Titan

Site Name: 3 (launchers 851-C-1, 2, 3)
Missile Type: Titan I
Installation: Beale AFB
Site Location: Chico
Squadron: 851st
Branch: Air Force
Dates of Active Service: Feb 1, 1961 to Mar 25, 1965
Current: Private ownership, materials salvaged before sold but structure remains intact.

Site Name: 1 (launchers 851-A-1, 2, 3)
Missile Type: Titan I
Installation: Beale AFB
Site Location: Lincoln
Squadron: 851st
Branch: Air Force
Dates of Active Service: Feb 1, 1961 to Mar 25, 1965
Current: Private ownership, materials salvaged before sold but structure remains intact.

Site Name: 2 (launchers 851-B-1, 2, 3)
Missile Type: Titan I
Installation: Beale AFB
Site Location: Live Oak
Squadron: 851st
Branch: Air Force
Dates of Active Service: Feb 1, 1961 to Mar 25, 1965
Current: Private ownership, materials salvaged before sold but structure remains intact.

Site Name: 395-A-LE-1
Missile Type: Titan I
Installation: Vandenberg AFB
Site Location: Vandenberg
Branch: Air Force
Dates of Active Service: A test and training facility; operational between Sep 23, 1961 to Dec 8, 1964
Current: Decommissioned/Stripped

Site Name: 395-A-LE-2
Missile Type: Titan I
Installation: Vandenberg AFB
Site Location: Vandenberg
Branch: Air Force
Dates of Active Service: A test and training facility; operational between Mar 30, 1963 to Mar 20, 1965
Current: Decommissioned/Stripped

Site Name: 395A-LE-3
Missile Type: Titan I
Installation: Vandenberg AFB
Site Location: Vandenberg
Branch: Air Force
Dates of Active Service: A test and training facility; operational between Jan 20, 1962 to Jan 14, 1965
Current: Decommissioned/Stripped

Site Name: 395-B
Missile Type: Titan II
Installation: Vandenberg AFB
Site Location: Vandenberg
Branch: Air Force
Dates of Active Service: A test and training facility; operational between Feb 17, 1964 to May 20, 1969
Current: Decommissioned/Stripped

Site Name: 395-C
Missile Type: Titan II
Installation: Vandenberg AFB
Site Location: Vandenberg
Branch: Air Force
Dates of Active Service: A test and training facility; operational between Feb 16, 1963 to Jun 27, 1976 (Site of the first Vandenberg Titan II launch)
Current: Decommissioned/Stripped

Site Name: 395-D
Missile Type: Titan II
Installation: Vandenberg AFB
Site Location: Vandenberg
Branch: Air Force
Dates of Active Service: A test and training facility; operational between May 13, 1963 to Apr 5, 1966
Current: Decommissioned/Stripped

COLORADO

Atlas

Site Name: A
Missile Type: Atlas E
Installation: F. E. Warren AFB
Site Location: Fort Collins
Squadron: 566th SMS
Branch: Air Force
Dates of Active Service:
Current: Private ownership, materials salvaged before sold but structure remains intact.

Site Name: D
Missile Type: Atlas E
Installation: F. E. Warren AFB
Site Location: Greeley
Squadron: 566th SMS
Branch: Air Force
Dates of Active Service:
Current: Private ownership, materials salvaged before sold but structure remains intact.

Site Name: G

Missile Type: Atlas E
Installation: F. E. Warren AFB
Site Location: Grover
Squadron: 566th SMS
Branch: Air Force
Dates of Active Service:
Current: Private ownership, materials salvaged before sold but structure remains intact.

Site Name: L
Missile Type: Atlas E
Installation: F. E. Warren AFB
Site Location: Briggsdale
Squadron: 566th SMS
Branch: Air Force
Dates of Active Service:
Current: Private ownership, materials salvaged before sold but structure remains intact.

Site Name: M
Missile Type: Atlas E
Installation: F. E. Warren AFB
Site Location: Nunn
Squadron: 566th SMS
Branch: Air Force
Dates of Active Service:
Current: Sold to the University of Colorado, site was not salvaged. The best preserved of the F.E. Warren sites.

Minuteman

Site Name: J1-J11
Missile Type: Minuteman III
Installation: F. E. Warren AFB
Note: The information listed is for missile alert facility, J1, and launch sites J2 - J11. J flight straddles the border between Colorado and Nebraska. For this site listing, all the launch facilities have been assigned to Colorado.
Site Location: Southeast of F. E. Warren AFB, Cheyenne, WY
Squadron: 320th SMS
Branch: Air Force
Dates of Active Service: Jan 8, 1964 to present
Current: All sites are currently active.
Conversion: 90th Strategic Missile Wing converted to Minuteman III on Jan 26, 1975.

Site Name: L1-011
Missile Type: Minuteman III
Installation: F. E. Warren AFB
Note: The information listed is for missile alert facilities L1, M1, N1, O1, and launch sites L2 - L11, M2-MU, N2-N11, and O2 - O11. Although F. E. Warren AFB is located in Wyoming, portions of these sites are located in Nebraska and Colorado.
Site Location: Southeast of F. E. Warren AFB, Cheyenne, WY
Squadron: 321st SMS
Branch: Air Force
Dates of Active Service: Apr 8, 1964 to present
Current: All sites are currently active.
Conversion: 90th Strategic Missile Wing converted to Minuteman III on Jan 26, 1975.

Titan

Site Name: 1
Missile Type: Titan I (launchers 724-A-1,2,3)
Installation: Lowry AFB
Site Location: Bennett
Squadron: 724th SMS
Branch: Air Force
Dates of Active Service: Feb 1, 1960 to Jun 25, 1965
Current: Private ownership, materials salvaged before sold but structure remains intact.

Site Name: 5 (launchers 725-B-1,2,3)
Missile Type: Titan I
Installation: Lowry AFB
Site Location: Bennett
Squadron: 725th SMS
Branch: Air Force
Dates of Active Service: Aug 1, 1960 to Jun 25, 1965
Current: Private ownership, materials salvaged before sold but structure remains intact.

Site Name: 4 (launchers 725-A-1,2,3)
Missile Type: Titan I
Installation: Lowry AFB
Site Location: Deertail
Squadron: 725th SMS
Branch: Air Force
Dates of Active Service: Aug 1, 1960 to Jun 25, 1965

Current: Private ownership, materials salvaged before sold but structure remains intact.

Site Name: 2 (launchers 724-B-1,2,3)
Missile Type: Titan I
Installation: Lowry AFB
Site Location: Denver
Squadron: 724th SMS
Branch: Air Force
Dates of Active Service: Feb 1, 1960 to Jun 25, 1965
Current: Private ownership, materials salvaged before sold but structure remains intact.

Site Name: 3 (launchers 724-C-1,2,3)
Missile Type: Titan I
Installation: Lowry AFB
Site Location: Denver
Squadron: 724th SMS
Branch: Air Force
Dates of Active Service: Feb 1, 1960 to Jun 25, 1965
Current: Private ownership, materials salvaged before sold but structure remains intact.

Site Name: 6 (launchers 725-C-1,2,3)
Missile Type: Titan I
Installation: Lowry AFB
Site Location: Elizabeth
Squadron: 725th SMS
Branch: Air Force
Dates of Active Service: Aug 1, 1960 to Jun 25, 1965
Current: Private ownership, materials salvaged before sold but structure remains intact.

CONNECTICUT

Nike

Site Name: BR-04
Missile Type: Nike 3B/18H, 30A/12L-U
Defense Area: Bridgeport
Site Location: Ansonia
Branch: Army
Dates of Active Service: 1957 to June 1971
Control Site Condition/Owner: USFS
Launch Site Condition/Owner: Private ownership

Site Name: BR-65
Missile Type: Nike 1B, 2C/30A/12L-A
Defense Area: Bridgeport
Site Location: Fairfield
Branch: Army
Dates of Active Service: 1956 to Mar 1961
Control Site Condition/Owner: Town of Fairfield, Fire Training and Canine Center
Launch Site Condition/Owner: South Pine Creek Park

Site Name: BR-17
Missile Type: Nike 1B, 2C/30A/12L-A
Defense Area: Bridgeport
Site Location: Milford
Branch: Army
Dates of Active Service: 1956 to 1963
Control Site Condition/Owner: Town of Milford, board of education
Launch Site Condition/Owner: Private ownership

Site Name: BR-94
Missile Type: Nike 2B, 1C
Defense Area: Bridgeport
Site Location: Shelton
Branch: Army
Dates of Active Service: 1957 to Mar 1961
Control Site Condition/Owner: US Government ownership, storage and maintenance support facility for Fort Devens
Launch Site Condition/Owner: Park, Town of Shelton

Site Name: BR-15
Missile Type: Nike 1B, 2C/30A/12L-A
Defense Area: Bridgeport
Site Location: West Haven
Branch: Army
Dates of Active Service: 1956 to Sep 1971
Control Site Condition/Owner: CTANG; Communications site
Launch Site Condition/Owner: Town of Westhaven, Parks and Recreation Department

Site Name: BR-73
Missile Type: Nike 1B, 2C/30A/12L-A
Defense Area: Bridgeport
Site Location: Westport
Branch: Army
Dates of Active Service: 1956 to 1963
Control Site Condition/Owner: Town of Westport, Westport/Weston Health District; Bayberry Special Education Center
Launch Site Condition/Owner: Firefighting Training Center

Site Name: HA-85
Missile Type: Nike 1B, 2C/30A/12L-A
Defense Area: Hartford
Site Location: Avon/Simsbury
Branch: Army
Dates of Active Service: 1956 to 1963
Control Site Condition/Owner: Talcott Mountain Service Center
Launch Site Condition/Owner: Condominiums

Site Name: HA-48
Missile Type: Nike 1B, 2C/18H, 30A/12L-U, (7L-H)
Defense Area: Hartford
Site Location: Cromwell
Branch: Army
Dates of Active Service: 1956 to Nov 1968
Control Site Condition/Owner: Church and elderly housing
Launch Site Condition/Owner: USAR Center; Transportation Company

Site Name: HA-08
Missile Type: Nike 1B, 2C/18H, 30A/10L-U
Defense Area: Hartford
Site Location: East Windsor
Branch: Army
Dates of Active Service: 1956 to June 1971
Control Site Condition/Owner: US Government ownership
Launch Site Condition/Owner: USAR Center

Site Name: HA-25
Missile Type: Nike 1B, 2C/30A/12L-A
Defense Area: Hartford
Site Location: Manchester
Branch: Army

Dates of Active Service: 1956 to Jan 1961
Control Site Condition/Owner: Town of Manchester, Recreation Center
Launch Site Condition/Owner: Electric Lighting Company

Site Name: HA-67
Missile Type: Nike 1B, 2C/30A/12L-A
Defense Area: Hartford
Site Location: Plainville
Branch: Army
Dates of Active Service: 1956 to Mar 1961
Control Site Condition/Owner: Obliterated; Residential
Launch Site Condition/Owner: Industrial

Site Name: HA-36
Missile Type: Nike 1B, 2C/30A/12L-A
Defense Area: Hartford
Site Location: Portland
Branch: Army
Dates of Active Service: 1956 to 1963
Control Site Condition/Owner: Meskomasic State Forest
Launch Site Condition/Owner: FDS; Abandoned

GEORGIA

Nike

Site Name: R-88
Missile Type: Nike 3AG/12H/12L-H
Defense Area: Robbins
Site Location: Byron
Branch: Army
Dates of Active Service: Nov 1960 to Mar 1966
Control Site Condition/Owner: FDS
Launch Site Condition/Owner: FDS

Site Name: R-28
Missile Type: Nike 3AG/12H/12L-H
Defense Area: Robbins
Site Location: Jeffersonville
Branch: Army
Dates of Active Service: Nov 1960 to Mar 1966
Control Site Condition/Owner: FDS

Launch Site Condition/Owner: FDS

Site Name: TU-79
Missile Type: Nike 3AG/12H
Defense Area: Turner
Site Location: Armenia/Sasse
Branch: Army
Dates of Active Service: Nov 1960 to Mar 1966
Launch Site Condition/Owner: Private ownership

Site Name: TU-28
Missile Type: Nike 3AG/12H/12L-H
Defense Area: Turner
Site Location: Willingsham/Sylvester
Branch: Army
Dates of Active Service: Nov 1960 to Mar 1966
Launch Site Condition/Owner: Private ownership

HAWAII

Nike

Site Name: OA-32
Missile Type: Nike 24H/16L-H
Defense Area: Oahu
Site Location: Bellows/Waimanalo (dual site)
Branch: Army
Dates of Active Service: Mar 1961 to Mar 1970
Control Site Condition/Owner: US Army; abandoned
Launch Site Condition/Owner: Bellows AFS; 15th ABW Det. USMC amphibious training area, PACAF communications facility

Site Name: OA-63
Missile Type: Nike 24H/16L-H
Defense Area: Oahu
Site Location: Ewa/Makakilo (dual site)
Branch: Army
Dates of Active Service: Jan 1961 to Mar 1970
Control Site Condition/Owner: US Army; abandoned
Launch Site Condition/Owner: US Army; abandoned
Site Name: OA-17
Missile Type: Nike 12H/12L-H
Defense Area: Oahu

Site Location: Kauka/Kahuku
Branch: Army
Dates of Active Service: Jan 1961 to Mar 1970
Control Site Condition/Owner: US Army; range control facility
Launch Site Condition/Owner: US Army; Kahuku Army Training Area

Site Name: OA-84
Missile Type: Nike 12H/8L-H
Defense Area: Oahu
Site Location: Waialua/Dillingham
Branch: Army
Dates of Active Service: Jan 1961 to Mar 1970
Control Site Condition/Owner: USAF Training Site
Launch Site Condition/Owner: Dillingham Airport; abandoned

IDAHO

Atlas

Site Name: 3
Missile Type: Atlas E
Installation: Fairchild AFB
Site Location: Rockford
Squadron: 567th SMS
Branch: Air Force
Dates of Active Service: Apr 1, 1960 to Jun 25, 1965
Current: Private ownership, materials salvaged before sold but structure remains intact.

Titan

Site Name: 3 (launchers 569-C-1,2,3)
Missile Type: Titan I
Installation: Mountain Home AFB
Site Location: Boise
Squadron: 569th SMS
Branch: Air Force
Dates of Active Service: Jun 1, 1961 to Jun 25, 1965
Current: A portion of the site is under private ownership and is currently not being used. Over two hundred acres of the site remain under the control of the GSA.

Site Name: 1 (launchers 569-A-1,2,3)
Missile Type: Titan I
Installation: Mountain Home AFB
Site Location: Bruneau
Squadron: 569th SMS
Branch: Air Force
Dates of Active Service: Jun 1, 1961 to Jun 25, 1965
Current: Private ownership, the site is currently being used as a hazardous waste storage facility, All of the aboveground structures were demolished but the underground facilities are being used.

Site Name: 2 (launchers 569-B-1,2,3)
Missile Type: Titan I
Installation: Mountain Home AFB
Site Location: Oreana
Squadron: 569th SMS
Branch: Air Force
Dates of Active Service: Jun 1, 1961 to Jun 25, 1965
Current: Private ownership, the site is currently being used as a hazardous waste storage facility. All aboveground structures were demolished but the underground facilities are being utilized.

ILLINOIS

Nike

Site Name: C-72
Missile Type: Nike 1B, 2C/18H, 30A/10L-U
Defense Area: Chicago-Gary
Site Location: Addison
Branch: Army
Dates of Active Service: 1957 to Apr 1974
Control Site Condition/Owner: FDS
Launch Site Condition/Owner: FDS

Site Name: C-98
Missile Type: Nike 1B, 2C/30A/12L-A
Defense Area: Chicago-Gary
Site Location: Fort Sheridan
Branch: Army
Dates of Active Service: Jul 1954 to 1963
Control Site Condition/Owner: FDS

Launch Site Condition/Owner: FDS

Site Name: C-80
Missile Type: Nike 2B, 4C/60A/24L-AA
Defense Area: Chicago-Gary
Site Location: Arlington Heights (dual site)
Branch: Army
Dates of Active Service: 1950 to Aug 1974
Control Site Condition/Owner: FDS
Launch Site Condition/Owner: FDS

Site Name: C-44
Missile Type: Nike 2B, 4C/60A/24L-AA
Defense Area: Chicago-Gary
Site Location: Hegewisch/Wolf Lake (dual site)
Branch: Army
Dates of Active Service: 1955 to Mar 1963
Control Site Condition/Owner: FDS
Launch Site Condition/Owner: FDS

Site Name: C-40
Missile Type: Nike 1B,2C/30A/12L-A
Defense Area: Chicago-Gary
Site Location: Burnham Park
Branch: Army
Dates of Active Service: 1955 to Aug 1963
Control Site Condition/Owner: FDS
Launch Site Condition/Owner: FDS

Site Name: C-49/50
Missile Type: Nike 1B, 2C/18H, 30A/11L-U
Defense Area: Chicago-Gary
Site Location: Homewood
Branch: Army
Dates of Active Service: 1957 to Apr 1974
Control Site Condition/Owner: FDS
Launch Site Condition/Owner: FDS

Site Name: C-41
Missile Type: Nike 1B, 2C/18H, 30A/12L-U
Defense Area: Chicago-Gary
Site Location: Jackson Park
Branch: Army
Dates of Active Service: 1955 to Jun 1971
Control Site Condition/Owner: FDS
Launch Site Condition/Owner: FDS

Site Name: C-61
Missile Type: Nike 2B/12H, 20A/SL-U

Defense Area: Chicago-Gary
Site Location: Lemont
Branch: Army
Dates of Active Service: 1955 to Nov 1968
Control Site Condition/Owner: FDS
Launch Site Condition/Owner: FDS

Site Name: C-92
Missile Type: Nike IB, 2C/30A/12L-A
Defense Area: Chicago-Gary
Site Location: Mundelein
Branch: Army
Dates of Active Service: 1956 to 1963
Control Site Condition/Owner: Obliterated; Glenview Naval Air Station
Launch Site Condition/Owner: Obliterated; Glenview Naval Air Station

Site Name: C-94
Missile Type: Nike 1B, 2C/30A/12L-A
Defense Area: Chicago-Gary
Site Location: Libertyville
Branch: Army
Dates of Active Service: 1955 to 1963
Control Site Condition/Owner: FDS
Launch Site Condition/Owner: FDS

Site Name: C-70
Missile Type: Nike 1B, 2C/30A/12L-A
Defense Area: Chicago-Gary
Site Location: Naperville
Branch: Army
Dates of Active Service: 1956 to Mar 1963
Control Site Condition/Owner: FDS
Launch Site Condition/Owner: FDS

Site Name: C-03
Missile Type: Nike 3B, 2C/18H, 20A/20L-UA, (12L-H)
Defense Area: Chicago-Gary
Site Location: Montrose/Belmont
Branch: Army
Dates of Active Service: Oct 1955 to June 1965
Control Site Condition/Owner: FDS
Launch Site Condition/Owner: FDS

Site Name: C-93
Missile Type: Nike 2B/12H, 20A/SL-U
Defense Area: Chicago-Gary

Site Location: Northfield/Skokie
Branch: Army
Dates of Active Service: 1955 to Apr 1974
Control Site Condition/Owner: FDS
Launch Site Condition/Owner: FDS

Site Name: C-54
Missile Type: Nike 1B, 2C/30A/12L-A
Defense Area: Chicago-Gary
Site Location: Orland Park
Branch: Army
Dates of Active Service: 1955 to 1961
Control Site Condition/Owner: FDS
Launch Site Condition/Owner: FDS

Site Name: C-84
Missile Type: Nike 1B, 2C/30A/12L-A
Defense Area: Chicago-Gary
Site Location: Palatine
Branch: Army
Dates of Active Service: 1956 to 1963
Control Site Condition/Owner: FDS
Launch Site Condition/Owner: FDS

Site Name: C-51
Missile Type: Nike 2B, 1C/30A/12L-A
Defense Area: Chicago-Gary
Site Location: Worth/Pales
Branch: Army
Dates of Active Service: 1956 to Mar 1963
Control Site Condition/Owner: FDS
Launch Site Condition/Owner: FDS

Site Name: SL-90
Missile Type: Nike 3D/18H/12L-U
Defense Area: Saint Louis
Site Location: Alton/Pere Marquette
Branch: Army
Dates of Active Service: May 1960 to Dec 1968
Control Site Condition/Owner: Intact;
Abandoned; Pere Marquette State Park
Launch Site Condition/Owner: Abandoned;
Pere Marquette State Park

Site Name: SL-40
Missile Type: Nike 3D/18H/12L-U
Defense Area: Saint Louis
Site Location: Hecker
Branch: Army

Dates of Active Service: May 1960 to Dec 1968
Control Site Condition/Owner: Beck VoTech
School
Launch Site Condition/Owner: FDS

Site Name: SL-10
Missile Type: Nike 3D/18W/12L-U
Defense Area: Saint Louis
Site Location: Marine
Branch: Army
Dates of Active Service: May 1960 to Dec 1968
Control Site Condition/Owner: Private owner-
ship, abandoned
Launch Site Condition/Owner: Private owner-
ship, abandoned

INDIANA

Nike

Site Name: C-32
Missile Type: Nike 3B/12H, 20A/12L-U
Defense Area: Chicago-Gary
Site Location: Porter/Chester
Branch: Army
Dates of Active Service: 1957 to Apr 1974
Control Site Condition/Owner: Intact; HQ
Indiana Dunes National Lake Shore
Launch Site Condition/Owner: Intact; Private
ownership

Site Name: CD-63
Missile Type: Nike 3D/18H/12L-U
Defense Area: Cincinnati-Dayton
Site Location: Dillsboro (SE)
Branch: Army
Dates of Active Service: Mar 1960 to Mar 1970
Control Site Condition/Owner: FDS
Launch Site Condition/Owner: Intact; Private
ownership, home

Site Name: C-45
Missile Type: Nike 2B/20A/8L-A
Defense Area: Chicago-Gary
Site Location: Gary Municipal Airport
Branch: Army

Dates of Active Service: 1957 to June
1960
Control Site Condition/Owner: Partially Intact;
Thought to remain under DoD control
Launch Site Condition/Owner: Obliterated;
Lake County, vacant, former Civil Defense
site

Site Name: C-47
Missile Type: Nike 1B, 1C/12H, 20A/12L-U,
(8L-H)
Defense Area: Chicago-Gary
Site Location: Hobart/Wheeler
Branch: Army
Dates of Active Service: 1956 to Mar 1974
Control Site Condition/Owner: Private owner-
ship
Launch Site Condition/Owner: Portage
Township School Corporation

Site Name: C-46
Missile Type: Nike 1B, 1C/12H, 20A/12L-U,
(8L-H)
Defense Area: Chicago-Gary
Site Location: Munster
Branch: Army
Dates of Active Service: 1957 to Sep 1974
Control Site Condition/Owner: Unknown
Launch Site Condition/Owner: Partially Intact;
Private ownership

Site Name: C-48
Missile Type: Nike 2B/20A/8L-A
Defense Area: Chicago-Gary
Site Location: South Gary
Branch: Army
Dates of Active Service: 1957 to June 1960
Control Site Condition/Owner: FDS
Launch Site Condition/Owner: FDS

IOWA

Atlas

Site Name: 3 (launchers 549-C-1,2,3)
Missile Type: Atlas D
Installation: Offutt AFB
Site Location: Missouri Valley
Squadron: 549th SMS
Branch: Air Force
Dates of Active Service: Aug 15, 1959 to Dec 15, 1964
Current: Private ownership, materials salvaged before sold but structure remains intact.

Nike

Site Name: OF-10
Missile Type: Nike 3AG/12W12L-H
Defense Area: Offutt AFB
Site Location: Council Bluffs
Branch: Army
Dates of Active Service: 1960 to 1966
Control Site Condition/Owner: National Weather Service Facility
Launch Site Condition/Owner: Private ownership.

KANSAS

Atlas

Site Name: 5
Missile Type: Atlas E
Installation: Forbes AFB
Site Location: Council Grove
Squadron: 548th SMS
Branch: Air Force
Dates of Active Service: July 1, 1960 to Mar 25, 1965
Current: Private ownership, materials salvaged before sold but structure remains intact.

Site Name: 6
Missile Type: Atlas E
Installation: Forbes AFB
Site Location: Eskridge
Squadron: 548th SMS
Branch: Air Force
Dates of Active Service: July 1, 1960 to Mar 25, 1965
Current: Private ownership; renovated into residence, materials salvaged before sold but structure remains intact.

Site Name: 9
Missile Type: Atlas E
Installation: Forbes AFB
Site Location: Holton
Squadron: 548th SMS
Branch: Air Force
Dates of Active Service: July 1, 1960 to Mar 25, 1965
Current: Site is now a Junior/Senior High School, nothing remains of missile site.

Site Name: 2
Missile Type: Atlas E
Installation: Forbes AFB
Site Location: Lawrence
Squadron: 548th SMS
Branch: Air Force
Dates of Active Service: July 1, 1960 to Mar 25, 1965
Current: Private ownership: materials salvaged before sold; status of structure unknown

Site Name: 4
Missile Type: Atlas E
Installation: Forbes AFB
Site Location: Osage City
Squadron: 548th SMS
Branch: Air Force
Dates of Active Service: July 1, 1960 to Mar 25, 1965
Current: Private ownership, materials salvaged before sold but structure remains intact.

Site Name: 8
Missile Type: Atlas E
Installation: Forbes AFB
Site Location: Saint Marys
Squadron: 548th SMS
Branch: Air Force
Dates of Active Service: July 1, 1960 to Mar 25, 1965
Current: Private ownership, materials salvaged before sold but structure remains intact.

Site Name: 1
Missile Type: Atlas E
Installation: Forbes AFB
Site Location: Valley Falls
Squadron: 548th SMS
Branch: Air Force
Dates of Active Service: July 1, 1960 to Mar 25, 1965
Current: Private ownership, materials salvaged before sold but structure remains intact.

Site Name: 7
Missile Type: Atlas E
Installation: Forbes AFB
Site Location: Wamego
Squadron: 548th SMS
Branch: Air Force
Dates of Active Service: July 1, 1960 to Mar 25, 1965
Current: Private ownership, the site was originally sold to Kansas State University and was not salvaged. It is the best preserved of all Forbes sites.

Site Name: 3
Missile Type: Atlas E
Installation: Forbes AFB
Site Location: Waverly
Squadron: 548th SMS
Branch: Air Force
Dates of Active Service: July 1, 1960 to Mar 25, 1965
Current: Private ownership, materials salvaged before sold but structure remains intact.

Site Name: 2
Missile Type: Atlas F
Installation: Schilling AFB
Site Location: Abilene
Squadron: 550th SMS
Branch: Air Force
Dates of Active Service: Apr 1, 1961 to Jun 25, 1965
Current: Private ownership, materials salvaged before sold but structure remains intact.

Site Name: 1
Missile Type: Atlas F
Installation: Schilling AFB
Site Location: Bennington
Squadron: 550th SMS
Branch: Air Force
Dates of Active Service: Apr 1, 1961 to Jun 25, 1965
Current: Private ownership, materials salvaged before sold but structure remains.

Site Name: 9
Missile Type: Atlas F
Installation: Schilling AFB
Site Location: Beverly
Squadron: 550th SMS
Branch: Air Force
Dates of Active Service: Apr 1, 1961 to Jun 25, 1965
Current: Private ownership, materials salvaged before sold but structure remains intact.

Site Name: 4
Missile Type: Atlas F
Installation: Schilling AFB
Site Location: Carlton
Squadron: 550th SMS
Branch: Air Force
Dates of Active Service: Apr 1, 1961 to Jun 25, 1965
Current: Private ownership, materials salvaged before sold but structure remains intact.

Site Name: 3
Missile Type: Atlas F
Installation: Schilling AFB
Site Location: Chapman
Squadron: 550th SMS
Branch: Air Force
Dates of Active Service: Apr 1, 1961 to Jun 25, 1965
Current: Private ownership, materials salvaged before sold but structure remains intact.

Site Name: 11
Missile Type: Atlas F
Installation: Schilling APB
Site Location: Glasco
Squadron: 550th SMS

Branch: Air Force
Dates of Active Service: Apr 1, 1961 to Jun 25, 1965
Current: Private ownership, materials salvaged before sold but structure remains intact.

Site Name: 7
Missile Type: Atlas F
Installation: Schilling APB
Site Location: Kanopolis
Squadron: 550th SMS
Branch: Air Force
Dates of Active Service: Apr 1, 1961 to Jun 25, 1965
Current: Private ownership, materials salvaged before sold but structure remains intact.

Site Name: 5
Missile Type: Atlas F
Installation: Schilling AFB
Site Location: McPherson
Squadron: 550th SMS
Branch: Air Force
Dates of Active Service: Apr 1, 1961 to Jun 25, 1965
Current: Private ownership, materials salvaged before sold but structure remains intact.

Site Name: 12
Missile Type: Atlas F
Installation: Schilling AFB
Site Location: Minneapolis
Squadron: 550th SMS
Branch: Air Force
Dates of Active Service: Apr 1, 1961 to Jun 25, 1965
Current: Private ownership, materials salvaged before sold but structure remains intact.

Site Name: 6
Missile Type: Atlas F
Installation: Schilling AFB
Site Location: Mitchell
Squadron: 550th SMS
Branch: Air Force
Dates of Active Service: Apr 1, 1961 to Jun 25, 1965
Current: Private ownership, materials salvaged before sold but structure remains intact.

Site Name: 10
Missile Type: Atlas F
Installation: Schilling AFB
Site Location: Tescott
Squadron: 550th SMS
Branch: Air Force
Dates of Active Service: Apr 1, 1961 to Jun 25, 1965
Current: Private ownership, materials salvaged before sold but structure remains intact.

Site Name: 8
Missile Type: Atlas F
Installation: Schilling AFB
Site Location: Wilson
Squadron: 550th SMS
Branch: Air Force
Dates of Active Service: Apr 1, 1961 to Jun 25, 1965
Current: Private ownership, materials salvaged before sold but structure remains intact.

Nike

Site Name: KC-60
Missile Type: Nike 3D/18H/12L-U
Defense Area: Kansas City
Site Location: Gardner (2 mi. S)
Branch: Army
Dates of Active Service: Nov 1959 to Feb 1969
Control Site Condition/Owner: Gardner Unified School
Launch Site Condition/Owner: FDS

Site Name: KC-80
Missile Type: Nike 3D/18H/12L-U
Defense Area: Kansas City
Site Location: Fort Leavenworth
Branch: Army
Dates of Active Service: Nov 1959 to Feb 1969
Control Site Condition/Owner: DoD; private ownership
Launch Site Condition/Owner: unknown

Site Name: SC-01
Missile Type: Nike 3AG
Defense Area: Schilling
Site Location: Bennington (5 mi SSE)
Branch: Army
Dates of Active Service: Apr 1960 to Jun 1960

Control Site Condition/Owner: Site was never operational. Private ownership, current condition unknown.
Launch Site Condition/Owner: Site was never operational. Private ownership, current condition unknown.

Site Name: SC-50
Missile Type: Nike
Defense Area: Schilling
Site Location: Smolan (5 mi SSW)
Branch: Army
Dates of Active Service: Apr 1960 to Jun 1960
Control Site Condition/Owner: Site was never operational. Private ownership, current condition unknown.
Launch Site Condition/Owner: Site was never operational. Private ownership, current condition unknown.

Titan

Site Name: 12
Missile Type: Titan II
Installation: McConnell AFB
Site Location: Conway Springs
Squadron: 532nd SMS
Branch: Air Force
Dates of Active Service: Mar 1, 1962 to Aug 8, 1986
Current: The site has been imploded and is currently in excess to be sold by the GSA.

Site Name: 2
Missile Type: Titan II
Installation: McConnell AFB
Site Location: El Dorado
Squadron: 533rd SMS
Branch: Air Force
Dates of Active Service: Aug 1, 1962 to Nov 1, 1985
Current: The site has been imploded and is currently in excess to be sold by the GSA.

Site Name: 17
Missile Type: Titan II
Installation: McConnell AFB
Site Location: Kingman
Squadron: 532nd SMS

Branch: Air Force
Dates of Active Service: Mar 1, 1962 to Aug 8, 1986
Current: The site has been imploded and is currently in excess to be sold by the GSA.

Site Name: 3
Missile Type: Titan II
Installation: McConnell AFB
Site Location: Leon
Squadron: 533rd SMS
Branch: Air Force
Dates of Active Service: Aug 1, 1962 to Nov 1, 1985
Current: Private ownership, the site was imploded before sold.

Site Name: 4
Missile Type: Titan II
Installation: McConnell AFB
Site Location: Leon
Squadron: 533rd SMS
Branch: Air Force
Dates of Active Service: Aug 1, 1962 to Nov 1, 1985
Current: Private ownership, the site was imploded before sold.

Site Name: 5
Missile Type: Titan II
Installation: McConnell AFB
Site Location: Leon
Squadron: 533rd SMS
Branch: Air Force
Dates of Active Service: Aug 1, 1962 to Nov 1, 1985
Current: Private ownership, the site was imploded before sold.

Site Name: 18
Missile Type: Titan II
Installation: McConnell APB
Site Location: Mount Vernon
Squadron: 532nd SMS
Branch: Air Force
Dates of Active Service: Mar 1, 1962 to Aug 8, 1986
Current: The site has been imploded and is currently in excess to be sold by the GSA.

Site Name: 16
Missile Type: Titan II
Installation: McConnell AFB
Site Location: Murdock
Squadron: 532nd SMS
Branch: Air Force
Dates of Active Service: Mar 1, 1962 to Aug 8, 1986
Current: Private ownership, site was imploded before sold.

Site Name: 14
Missile Type: Titan II
Installation: McConnell AFB
Site Location: Norwich
Squadron: 532nd SMS
Branch: Air Force
Dates of Active Service: Mar 1, 1962 to Aug 8, 1986
Current: Private ownership, site was imploded before sold.

Site Name: 9
Missile Type: Titan II
Installation: McConnell AFB
Site Location: Oxford
Squadron: 533rd SMS
Branch: Air Force
Dates of Active Service: Aug 1, 1962 to Nov 1, 1985
Current: Private ownership, site was imploded before sold.

Site Name: 1
Missile Type: Titan II
Installation: McConnell AFB
Site Location: Potwin
Squadron: 533rd SMS
Branch: Air Force
Dates of Active Service: Aug 1, 1962 to Nov 1, 1985
Current: Private ownership, the site was imploded before sold.

Site Name: 15
Missile Type: Titan II
Installation: McConnell APB
Site Location: Rago
Squadron: 532nd SMS

Branch: Air Force
Dates of Active Service: Mar 1, 1962 to Aug 8, 1986
Current: The site has been imploded and is currently in excess to be sold by the GSA.

Site Name: 7
Missile Type: Titan II
Installation: McConnell AFB
Site Location: Rock
Squadron: 533rd SMS
Branch: Air Force
Dates of Active Service: Aug 1, 1962 to Nov 1, 1985
Current: Private ownership, the site was imploded before sold.

Site Name: 6
Missile Type: Titan II
Installation: McConnell AFB
Site Location: Smileyville
Squadron: 533rd SMS
Branch: Air Force
Dates of Active Service: Aug 1, 1962 to Nov 1, 1985
Current: Private ownership, the site was imploded before sold.

Site Name: 13
Missile Type: Titan II
Installation: McConnell AFB
Site Location: Viola
Squadron: 532nd SMS
Branch: Air Force
Dates of Active Service: Mar 1, 1962 to Aug 8, 1986
Current: Private ownership, site was imploded before sold.

Site Name: 10
Missile Type: Titan II
Installation: McConnell AFB
Site Location: Wellington
Squadron: 532nd SMS
Branch: Air Force
Dates of Active Service: Mar 1, 1962 to Aug 8, 1986
Current: Private ownership, site was imploded before sold.

Site Name: 11
Missile Type: Titan II
Installation: McConnell AFB
Site Location: Wellington
Squadron: 532nd SMS
Branch: Air Force
Dates of Active Service: Mar 1, 1962 to Aug 8, 1986
Current: Private ownership, site was imploded before sold.

Site Name: 8
Missile Type: Titan II
Installation: McConnell AFB
Site Location: Winfield
Squadron: 533rd SMS
Branch: Air Force
Dates of Active Service: Aug 1, 1962 to Nov 1, 1985
Current: The site has been imploded and is currently in excess to be sold by the GSA.

LOUISIANA

Nike

Site Name: BD-10
Missile Type: Nike 3AG/12H/12L-H
Defense Area: Barksdale
Site Location: Bellevue
Branch: Army
Dates of Active Service: Nov 1960 to Mar 1966
Control Site Condition/Owner: Intact; Criminal Justice Institute, and Bossier Parish School Board
Launch Site Condition/Owner: Intact; Louisiana Wildlife and Fisheries Department; Bossier Parish SWAT field training site

Site Name: BD-50
Missile Type: Nike 3AG/12H/12L-H
Defense Area: Barksdale
Site Location: Stonewall (4 mi. NE)
Branch: Army
Dates of Active Service: Nov 1960 to Mar 1966
Control Site Condition/Owner: Partially Intact; LSU School of Medicine
Launch Site Condition/Owner: FDS

MAINE

Bomarc

Site Name: Dow AFB
Missile Type: Bomarc A (14)
Installation: Dow AFB
Site Location: N.E. of former base
Squadron: 30th ADMS
Branch: Air Force
Dates of Active Service: Jun 1, 1959 to Dec 15, 1964
Current: Currently Bomarc Industrial Park

Nike

Site Name: L-58
Missile Type: Nike 1B, 2C/18H, 30A/12L-AU
Defense Area: Loring AFB
Site Location: Caribou
Branch: Army
Dates of Active Service: Sep 1957 to Jun 1966
Control Site Condition/Owner: FDS
Launch Site Condition/Owner: FDS

Site Name: L-13
Missile Type: Nike 2C, 1B/18H, 30A/10L-U
Defense Area: Loring AFB
Site Location: Caswell
Branch: Army
Dates of Active Service: Sep 1957 to Jun 1966
Control Site Condition/Owner: FDS
Launch Site Condition/Owner: FDS

Site Name: L-85
Missile Type: Nike 1B, 2C/30A/12L-A
Defense Area: Loring AFB
Site Location: Conner
Branch: Army
Dates of Active Service: Sep 1957 to Jun 1966
Control Site Condition/Owner: FDS
Launch Site Condition/Owner: FDS

Site Name: L-31
Missile Type: Nike 1B, 2C/30A/12L-A
Defense Area: Loring AFB
Site Location: Limestone
Branch: Army
Dates of Active Service: Sep 1957 to Sep 1958

Control Site Condition/Owner: FDS
Launch Site Condition/Owner: FDS

Snark

Site Name: Presque Isle AFB
Missile Type: Snark
Installation: Presque Isle AFB
Note: This is the only Snark site to be activated.
Site Location: Presque Isle AFB, Presque Isle, ME
Squadron: 702nd SMW
Branch: Air Force
Dates of Active Service: Jan 1, 1959 to Jun 25, 1961
Current: Site has been disposed of to the City of Presque Isle. The site is now undergoing consideration for eligibility for the National Register.

MARYLAND

Nike

Site Name: W-45
Missile Type: Nike 2B/20A/8L-A
Defense Area: Washington-Baltimore
Site Location: Accokeek
Branch: Army
Dates of Active Service: 1955 to Dec 1961
Control Site Condition/Owner: FDS
Launch Site Condition/Owner: FDS

Site Name: W-36
Missile Type: Nike 1B, 2C/30A/12L-A
Defense Area: Washington-Baltimore
Site Location: Brandywine/Naylor
Branch: Army
Dates of Active Service: 1957 to Dec 1961
Control Site Condition/Owner: FDS
Launch Site Condition/Owner: FDS

Site Name: BA-30/31
Missile Type: Nike 2B, 4C/18H,30A/23L-UA, (12L-H)
Defense Area: Washington-Baltimore
Site Location: Chestertown (9 mi. W)

Branch: Army
Dates of Active Service: 1954 to Apr 1974
Control Site Condition/Owner: FDS
Launch Site Condition/Owner: FDS

Site Name: BA-92
Missile Type: Nike 1B, 2C/30A
Defense Area: Washington-Baltimore
Site Location: Cronhardt
Branch: Army
Dates of Active Service: 1955 to Sep 1963
Control Site Condition/Owner: FDS
Launch Site Condition/Owner: FDS

Site Name: W-35
Missile Type: Nike 2B/20A/8L-A
Defense Area: Washington-Baltimore
Site Location: Croom/Marlboro
Branch: Army
Dates of Active Service: 1955 to Mar 1963
Control Site Condition/Owner: FDS
Launch Site Condition/Owner: FDS

Site Name: W-25
Missile Type: Nike 2B/12H, 20A/BL-U
Defense Area: Washington-Baltimore
Site Location: Davidsonville
Branch: Army
Dates of Active Service: June 1955 to Apr 1974
Control Site Condition/Owner: FDS
Launch Site Condition/Owner: Intact; Police training

Site Name: W-93
Missile Type: Nike 1B, 2C/30A/12L-A
Defense Area: Washington-Baltimore
Site Location: DERWOOD
Branch: Army
Dates of Active Service: 1955 to Aug 1960
Control Site Condition/Owner: FDS
Launch Site Condition/Owner: FDS

Site Name: BA-18
Missile Type: Nike 2B, 4C/18H, 30A/23L-UA, (12L-H)
Defense Area: Washington-Baltimore
Site Location: Edgewood Arsenal
Branch: Army
Dates of Active Service: 1954 to Apr 1974

Control Site Condition/Owner: Partially Intact; Maryland Army National Guard
Launch Site Condition/Owner: Partially Intact; Maryland Army National Guard

Site Name: BA-09
Missile Type: Nike 1B, 2C/30A/12L-A
Defense Area: Washington-Baltimore
Site Location: Fork
Branch: Army
Dates of Active Service: Nov 1955 to Dec 1962
Control Site Condition/Owner: FDS
Launch Site Condition/Owner: FDS Missile Sites in Maryland

Site Name: W-94
Missile Type: Nike 1B, 2C/30A/12L-A
Defense Area: Washington-Baltimore
Site Location: Gaithersburg
Branch: Army
Dates of Active Service: 1955 to Mar 1963
Control Site Condition/Owner: FDS
Launch Site Condition/Owner: FDS

Site Name: BA-79
Missile Type: Nike 2B,4C/24H,20A/24L-UA, (16L-H)
Defense Area: Washington-Baltimore
Site Location: Granite
Branch: Army
Dates of Active Service: Dec 1954 to Mar 1963
Control Site Condition/Owner: FDS
Launch Site Condition/Owner: FDS

Site Name: BA-43
Missile Type: Nike 1B, 2C/30A/12L-A
Defense Area: Washington-Baltimore
Site Location: Jacobsville
Branch: Army
Dates of Active Service: 1954 to Apr 1974
Control Site Condition/Owner: FDS
Launch Site Condition/Owner: FDS

Site Name: W-44
Missile Type: Nike 2B/12H, 20A/8L-UA
Defense Area: Washington-Baltimore
Site Location: Mattawoman/Waldorf
Branch: Army
Dates of Active Service: 1955 to Jun 1971

Control Site Condition/Owner: FDS
Launch Site Condition/Owner: FDS

Site Name: BA-03
Missile Type: Nike 1B, 2C/18H, 30A/12L-UA, (8L-H)
Defense Area: Washington-Baltimore
Site Location: Phoenix/Sweet Air
Branch: Army
Dates of Active Service: Nov 1955 to Apr 1974
Control Site Condition/Owner: FDS
Launch Site Condition/Owner: FDS

Site Name: W-92
Missile Type: Nike 1B, 2C/MH, 30A/12L-U
Defense Area: Washington-Baltimore
Site Location: Rockville
Branch: Army
Dates of Active Service: 1954 to Apr 1974
Control Site Condition/Owner: FDS
Launch Site Condition/Owner: FDS

Site Name: W-26
Missile Type: Nike 1B, 2C/18H, 30A/12L-U, (8L-H)
Defense Area: Washington-Baltimore
Site Location: Skidmore/Bay Bridge
Branch: Army
Dates of Active Service: 1955 to Nov 1968
Control Site Condition/Owner: FDS
Launch Site Condition/Owner: FDS

MASSACHUSETTS

Bomarc

Site Name: Otis AFB
Missile Type: Bomarc A and B (56)
Installation: Otis AFB
Site Location: Otis AFB (immediately N. of base)
Squadron: 26th ADMS
Branch: Air Force
Dates of Active Service: Mar 1, 1959 to Apr 30, 1972
Current: Currently used by Massachusetts Army National Guard as heavy equipment training and storage area.

Nike

Site Name: BO-85
Missile Type: Nike 1B, 2C/30A/12L-A
Defense Area: Boston
Site Location: Bedford
Branch: Army
Dates of Active Service: Nov 1956 to Dec 1961
Control Site Condition/Owner: Partially Intact; Private ownership; housing
Launch Site Condition/Owner: Partially Intact; Northeastern University

Site Name: BO-15
Missile Type: Nike 1B, 2C/30A/12L-A
Defense Area: Boston
Site Location: Beverly
Branch: Army
Dates of Active Service: Feb 1957 to Mar 1963
Control Site Condition/Owner: FDS
Launch Site Condition/Owner: FDS

Site Name: BO-84
Missile Type: Nike 2B/20A/8L-A
Defense Area: Boston
Site Location: Burlington
Branch: Army
Dates of Active Service: Jan 1956 to Aug 1963
Control Site Condition/Owner: FDS
Launch Site Condition/Owner: FDS

Site Name: BO-55
Missile Type: Nike 1B, 2C/30A/12L-A
Defense Area: Boston
Site Location: Blue Hills/Milton
Branch: Army
Dates of Active Service: Jun 1955 to Mar 1963
Control Site Condition/Owner: FDS
Launch Site Condition/Owner: FDS

Site Name: BO-38
Missile Type: Nike 1B, 2C/30A/12L-A
Defense Area: Boston
Site Location: Cohasset/Hingham
Branch: Army
Dates of Active Service: Nov 1956 to Dec 1961
Control Site Condition/Owner: FDS
Launch Site Condition/Owner: FDS

Site Name: BO-05
Missile Type: Nike 1B, 2C/18H,30A/12L-UA, (7L-H)
Defense Area: Boston
Site Location: Danvers
Branch: Army
Dates of Active Service: Nov 1956 to Apr 1974
Control Site Condition/Owner: FDS
Launch Site Condition/Owner: FDS

Site Name: BO-36
Missile Type: Nike 2B/12H, 20A/SL-U
Defense Area: Boston
Site Location: Fort Duvall/Hull
Branch: Army
Dates of Active Service: Jan 1956 to Apr 1974
Control Site Condition/Owner: Obliterated; Private ownership; housing
Launch Site Condition/Owner: Park; ownership by Commonwealth of Massachusetts

Site Name: BO-63
Missile Type: Nike 1B, 2C/30A/12L-A
Defense Area: Boston
Site Location: Needham
Branch: Army
Dates of Active Service: Jun 1955 to Mar 1963
Control Site Condition/Owner: FDS
Launch Site Condition/Owner: FDS

Site Name: BO-37
Missile Type: Nike 2B/20A
Defense Area: Boston
Site Location: Squantum/Quincy
Branch: Army
Dates of Active Service: Jan 1956 to Dec 1961
Control Site Condition/Owner: FDS
Launch Site Condition/Owner: FDS

Site Name: BO-03
Missile Type: Nike 1B, 2C/30A/12L-A
Defense Area: Boston
Site Location: Reading
Branch: Army
Dates of Active Service: June 1955 to Mar 1963
Control Site Condition/Owner: FDS
Launch Site Condition/Owner: FDS

Site Name: BO-73
Missile Type: Nike 2B/12H, 20A/8L-U
Defense Area: Boston
Site Location: South Lincoln
Branch: Army
Dates of Active Service: Jan 1956 to
Apr 1974
Control Site Condition/Owner: FDS
Launch Site Condition/Owner: FDS

Site Name: PR-19
Missile Type: Nike 1B, 2C/30A/12L-A
Defense Area: Providence
Site Location: Rehoboth
Branch: Army
Dates of Active Service: 1956 to Jun 1971
Control Site Condition/Owner:
MAArNG/USAR Center
Launch Site Condition/Owner: Town of
Rehobeth

Site Name: PR-29
Missile Type: Nike 1B, 2C/30A/12L-A
Defense Area: Providence
Site Location: Swansea
Branch: Army
Dates of Active Service: 1956 to Jun 1959
Control Site Condition/Owner: Private owner-
ship
Launch Site Condition/Owner: Private owner-
ship; motor company

MICHIGAN

Bomarc

Site Name: Kincheloe AFB
Missile Type: Bomarc B (28)
Installation: Kincheloe AFB
Site Location: Former Race AAF
Squadron: 37th ADMS
Branch: Air Force
Dates of Active Service: Mar 1, 1960 to act 30,
1972
Current: Site went through FDS.

Nike

Site Name: D-17
Missile Type: Nike 1B, 2C/30A/12L-A
Defense Area: Detroit
Site Location: Algonac Marine City
Branch: Army
Dates of Active Service: 1957 to Feb 1963
Control Site Condition/Owner: Private owner-
ship
Launch Site Condition/Owner: Private owner-
ship

Site Name: D-97
Missile Type: Nike 1B, 2C/30A/12L-A
Defense Area: Detroit
Site Location: Auburn Heights
Branch: Army
Dates of Active Service: 1955 to Feb
1963
Control Site Condition/Owner: Obliterated;
Oakland Community College
Launch Site Condition/Owner: Obliterated;
Oakland Community College

Site Name: D-26
Missile Type: Nike 2B, 2C/12H, 20A/16L-UA,
(BL-H)
Defense Area: Detroit
Site Location: Belle Isle
Branch: Army
Dates of Active Service: 1955 to Nov 1968
Control Site Condition/Owner: Obliterated;
City of Detroit
Launch Site Condition/Owner: Obliterated;
City of Detroit

Site Name: D-57/58
Missile Type: Nike Carlton: 3B/20A/12L-A
Newport: 3B/18H, 30A/12L-UA
Defense Area: Detroit
Site Location: Carleton/Newport (shared dou-
ble launch, separate control sites)
Branch: Army
Dates of Active Service: 1955 to Apr 1974
Control Site Condition/Owner: FDS
Launch Site Condition/Owner: FDS

Site Name: D-87

Missile Type: Nike 1B,2C/18H,30A/12L-U,
(10L-H)
Defense Area: Detroit
Site Location: Commerce/Union Lake
Branch: Army
Dates of Active Service: 1955 to Apr 1974
Control Site Condition/Owner: FDS
Launch Site Condition/Owner: FDS

Site Name: D-23
Missile Type: Nike 2B/20A/8L-A
Defense Area: Detroit
Site Location: Detroit City Airport
Branch: Army
Dates of Active Service: 1955 to Dec 1960
Control Site Condition/Owner: Obliterated;
City of Detroit
Launch Site Condition/Owner: Obliterated;
City of Detroit

Site Name: D-86
Missile Type: Nike 1B, 2C/30A/12L-A
Defense Area: Detroit
Site Location: Franklin/Bingham
Branch: Army
Dates of Active Service: 1957 to Feb 1963
Control Site Condition/Owner: Partially Intact;
State of Michigan
Launch Site Condition/Owner: Obliterated;
State of Michigan

Site Name: D-51
Missile Type: Nike 1B, 2C/20A/8L-A
Defense Area: Detroit
Site Location: Gross Isle
Branch: Army
Dates of Active Service: 1955 to Feb 1963
Control Site Condition/Owner: FDS
Launch Site Condition/Owner: FDS

Site Name: D-69
Missile Type: Nike 2B/20A/8L-A
Defense Area: Detroit
Site Location: River Rouge Park
Branch: Army
Dates of Active Service: 1956 to Feb 1963
Control Site Condition/Owner: Partially Intact;
City of Detroit
Launch Site Condition/Owner: Obliterated;

City of Detroit

Site Name: D-54
Missile Type: Nike 4B, 2C/30A/24L-M
Defense Area: Detroit
Site Location: Riverview/Wyandotte (dual site)
Branch: Army
Dates of Active Service: 1955 to Feb 1963
Control Site Condition/Owner: FDS
Launch Site Condition/Owner: FDS

Site Name: D-61
Missile Type: Nike 1B, 2C/18H, 30A/12L-UA
Defense Area: Detroit
Site Location: Romulus/Dearborn
Branch: Army
Dates of Active Service: 1957 to Jun 1971
Control Site Condition/Owner: FDS
Launch Site Condition/Owner: FDS

Site Name: D-14
Missile Type: Nike 2B/20A/8L-A
Defense Area: Detroit
Site Location: Selfridge AFB
Branch: Army
Dates of Active Service: 1955 to Feb 1963
Control Site Condition/Owner: Partially Intact;
  Army Engineering Support Buildings
Launch Site Condition/Owner: Obliterated;
  Army Tank Automotive Command

Site Name: D-16
Missile Type: Nike 2B/12H, 20A/8L-U
Defense Area: Detroit
Site Location: Selfridge AFB
Branch: Army
Dates of Active Service: 1955 to Jun 1971
Control Site Condition/Owner: Partially Intact;
  Army Engineering Support Buildings
Launch Site Condition/Owner: Obliterated;
  Army Tank Automotive Command

Site Name: D-06
Missile Type: Nike 2B/12H, 20A/8L-U
Defense Area: Detroit
Site Location: Utica
Branch: Army
Dates of Active Service: 1955 to Apr 1974
Control Site Condition/Owner: FDS

Launch Site Condition/Owner: FDS

MINNESOTA

Bomarc

Site Name: Duluth AB
Missile Type: Bomarc B
Installation: Duluth AB
Site Location: Knife River
Squadron: 74th ADMS
Branch: Air Force
Dates of Active Service: Apr 1, 1960 to Oct 30, 1972
Current: Currently under private ownership by a wood products and marble manufacturer.

Nike

Site Name: MS-90
Missile Type: Nike 3D/I8H/12L-U
Defense Area: Minneapolis-Saint Paul
Site Location: Bethel/Insanti
Branch: Army
Dates of Active Service: 1959 to Jun 1971
Control Site Condition/Owner: Insanti County Sheriff's Department
Launch Site Condition/Owner: Private ownership

Site Name: MS-40
Missile Type: Nike 3D/18H/12L-U
Defense Area: Minneapolis-Saint Paul
Site Location: Farmington
Branch: Army
Dates of Active Service: Oct 1959 to Jun 1971
Control Site Condition/Owner: USAR Center
Launch Site Condition/Owner: FDS

Site Name: MS-20
Missile Type: Nike 3D/18H/12L-U
Defense Area: Minneapolis-Saint Paul
Site Location: Roberts
Branch: Army
Dates of Active Service: Oct 1959 to Jun 1971
Control Site Condition/Owner: Bureau of Outdoor Recreation to Saint Croix County

Launch Site Condition/Owner: Bureau of Outdoor Recreation to Saint Croix County

Site Name: MS-70
Missile Type: Nike 3D/18H/12L-U
Defense Area: Minneapolis-Saint Paul
Site Location: Saint Bonifacius
Branch: Army
Dates of Active Service: Oct 1959 to Jun 1971
Control Site Condition/Owner: Private ownership
Launch Site Condition/Owner: FDS

MISSOURI

Minuteman

Site Name: A01 launch control facility and launch sites A02-A11
Missile Type: Minuteman II
Installation: Whiteman AFB
Note: The information listed is for A01 launch control facility and A02-A11 launch sites. The dates shown are from unit activation to when last site was placed under caretaker.
Site Location: Near Whiteman AFB, Knob Noster, MO
Squadron: 508th SMS
Branch: Air Force
Dates of Active Service: May 1, 1963 to Jan 21, 1994
Current: All sites are currently undergoing the deactivation process. No implosions have taken place.
Conversion: 351st Strategic Missile Wing converted to Minuteman II on Oct 3, 1967

Site Name: B01 launch control facility and launch sites B02-B11
Missile Type: Minuteman II
Installation: Whiteman AFB
Note: The information listed is for B0I launch control facility and B02-Bll launch sites. The dates shown are from unit activation to when last site was placed under caretaker.
Site Location: Near Whiteman AFB, Knob Noster, MO
Squadron: 508th SMS

Branch: Air Force
Dates of Active Service: May 1, 1963 to Apr 13, 1994
Current: All sites are currently undergoing the deactivation process. No implosions have taken place.
Conversion: 351st Strategic Missile Wing converted to Minuteman II on Oct 3, 1967.

Site Name: C01 launch control facility and launch sites C02-C11
Missile Type: Minuteman II
Installation: Whiteman AFB
Note: The information listed is for C01 launch control facility and C12-C11 launch sites. The dates shown are from unit activation to when last site was placed under caretaker.
Site Location: Near Whiteman AFB, Knob Noster, MO
Squadron: 508th SMS
Branch: Air Force
Dates of Active Service: May 1, 1963 to May 25, 1994
Current: All sites are currently undergoing the deactivation process. No implosions have taken place.
Conversion: 351st Strategic Missile Wing converted to Minuteman II on Oct 3, 1967.

Site Name: D01 launch control facility and launch sites D02-D11
Missile Type: Minuteman II
Installation: Whiteman AFB
Note: The information listed is for D01 launch control facility and D02-D11 launch sites. The dates shown are from unit activation to when last site was placed under caretaker.
Site Location: Near Whiteman AFB, Knob Noster, MO
Squadron: 508th SMS
Branch: Air Force
Dates of Active Service: May 1, 1963 to Sep 2, 1994
Current: All sites are currently undergoing the deactivation process. No implosions have taken place.
Conversion: 351st Strategic Missile Wing converted to Minuteman II on Oct 3, 1967.

Site Name: E01 launch control facility and launch sites E02-E11
Missile Type: Minuteman II
Installation: Whiteman AFB
Note: The information listed is for E01 launch control facility and E02-E11 launch sites. The dates shown are from unit activation to when last site was placed under caretaker.
Site Location: Near Whiteman AFB, Knob Noster, MO
Squadron: 508th SMS
Branch: Air Force
Dates of Active Service: May 1, 1963 to Aug 31, 1994
Current: All sites are currently undergoing the deactivation process. No implosions have taken place.
Conversion: 351st Strategic Missile Wing converted to Minuteman II on Oct 3, 1967.

Site Name: F01 launch control facility and launch sites F02-F11
Missile Type: Minuteman II
Installation: Whiteman AFB
Note: The information listed is for F01 launch control facility and F02-F11 launch sites. The dates shown are from unit activation to when last site was placed under caretaker.
Site Location: Near Whiteman AFB, Knob Noster, MO
Squadron: 510th SMS
Branch: Air Force
Dates of Active Service: Jun 1, 1963 to Apr 12, 1993
Current: All sites are currently undergoing the deactivation process. No implosions have taken place.
Conversion: 351st Strategic Missile Wing converted to Minuteman II on Oct 3, 1967.

Site Name: G01 launch control facility and launch sites G02-G11
Missile Type: Minuteman II
Installation: Whiteman AFB
Note: The information listed is for G01 launch control facility and G02-G11 launch sites. The dates shown are from unit activation to when last site was placed under caretaker.
Site Location: Near Whiteman AFB, Knob

Noster, MO
Squadron: 509th SMS
Branch: Air Force
Dates of Active Service: Jun 1, 1963 to present
Current: All sites are currently undergoing the deactivation process. No implosions have taken place. Only the control site G01 has been placed under caretaker (Jul 13, 93). Missiles have not been removed from launch sites, but reentry vehicles have been removed.
Conversion: 351st Strategic Missile Wing converted to Minuteman II on Oct 3, 1967.

Site Name: H01 launch control facility and launch sites H02-H11
Missile Type: Minuteman II
Installation: Whiteman AFB
Note: The information listed is for H01 launch control facility and H02-H11 launch sites. The dates shown are from unit activation to when last site was placed under caretaker.
Site Location: Near Whiteman AFB, Knob Noster, MO
Squadron: 509th SMS
Branch: Air Force
Dates of Active Service: Jun 1, 1963 to present
Current: All sites are currently undergoing the deactivation process. No implosions have taken place. Only the control facility H01 has been placed under caretaker (Mar 3, 94). Missile has been removed from launch site H05, but all others remain. All reentry vehicles have been removed.
Conversion: 351st Strategic Missile Wing converted to Minuteman II on Oct 3, 1967.

Site Name: I01 launch control facility and launch sites I02-I11
Missile Type: Minuteman II
Installation: Whiteman AFB
Note: The information listed is for I01 control facility and I02-I11 launch sites. The dates shown are from unit activation to when last site was placed under caretaker.
Site Location: Near Whiteman AFB, Knob Noster, MO
Squadron: 510th SMS
Branch: Air Force

Dates of Active Service: Jun 1, 1963 to Jan 26, 1993

Current: All sites are currently undergoing the deactivation process. Launch sites I02, I04, and I08 have been imploded. All other sites remain intact.

Conversion: 351st Strategic Missile Wing converted to Minuteman II on Oct 3, 1967.

Site Name: J01 launch control facility and launch sites 502-511

Missile Type: Minuteman II

Installation: Whiteman AFB

Note: The information listed is for J01 launch control facility and J02 -J11 launch sites. The dates shown are from unit activation to when last site was placed under caretaker.

Site Location: Near Whiteman AFB, Knob Noster, MO

Squadron: 509th SMS

Branch: Air Force

Dates of Active Service: Jun 1, 1963 to present

Current: All sites are currently undergoing the deactivation process. No implosions have taken place. Missiles have not been removed from launch sites, but reentry vehicles have been removed.

Conversion: 351st Strategic Missile Wing converted to Minuteman II on Oct 3, 1967.

Site Name: K01 launch control facility and launch sites K02-K11

Missile Type: Minuteman II

Installation: Whiteman AFB

Note: The information listed is for KOl launch control facility and K02-K11 launch sites. The dates shown are from unit activation to when last site was placed under caretaker.

Site Location: Near Whiteman AFB, Knob Noster, MO

Squadron: 509th SMS

Branch: Air Force

Dates of Active Service: Jun 1, 1963 to present

Current: All sites are currently undergoing the deactivation process. No implosions have taken place. Missiles have not been removed from launch sites, but reentry vehicles have been removed.

Conversion: 351st Strategic Missile Wing converted to Minuteman II on Oct 3, 1967.

Site Name: L01 launch control facility and launch sites LO2-L11

Missile Type: Minuteman II

Installation: Whiteman AFB

Note: The information listed is for L01 launch control facility and L12-L11 launch sites. The dates shown are from unit activation to when last site was placed under caretaker.

Site Location: Near Whiteman AFB, Knob Noster, MO

Squadron: 509th SMS

Branch: Air Force

Dates of Active Service: Jun 1, 1963 to present

Current: All sites are currently undergoing the deactivation process. No implosions have taken place. Only the control facility L01 has been placed under caretaker (Sep 21, 93). Missiles have not been removed from launch sites, but reentry vehicles have been removed.

Conversion: 351st Strategic Missile Wing converted to Minuteman II on Oct 3, 1967.

Site Name: M01 launch control facility and launch sites M02-Ml1

Missile Type: Minuteman II

Installation: Whiteman AFB

Note: The information listed is for M01 launch control facility and M02-M11 launch sites. The dates shown are from unit activation to when last site was placed under caretaker.

Site Location: Near Whiteman AFB, Knob Noster, MO

Squadron: 510th SMS

Branch: Air Force

Dates of Active Service: Jun 1, 1963 to Jun 17, 1993

Current: All sites are currently undergoing the deactivation process. No implosions have taken place.

Conversion: 351st Strategic Missile Wing converted to Minuteman II on Oct 3, 1967.

Site Name: N01 launch control facility and launch sites N02-N11

Missile Type: Minuteman II

Installation: Whiteman AFB

Note: The information listed is for N01 launch control facility and N02-N11 launch sites. The dates shown are from unit activation to when last site was placed under caretaker.

Site Location: Near W'hiteman AFB, Knob Noster, MO

Squadron: 510th SMS

Branch: Air Force

Dates of Active Service: Jun 1, 1963 to Oct 26, 1993

Current: All sites are currently undergoing the deactivation process. No implosions have taken place.

Conversion: 351st Strategic Missile Wing converted to Minuteman II on Oct 3, 1967.

Site Name: 001 launch control facility and launch sites 002-011

Missile Type: Minuteman II

Installation: Whiteman AFB

Note: The information listed is for 001 launch control facility and 002-011 launch sites. The dates shown are from unit activation to when last site was placed under caretaker.

Site Location: Near Whiteman AFB, Knob Noster, MO

Squadron: 510th SMS

Branch: Air Force

Dates of Active Service: Jun 1, 1963 to Oct 8, 1993

Current: All sites are currently undergoing the deactivation process. No implosions have taken place.

Conversion: 351st Strategic Missile Wing converted to Minuteman II on Oct 3, 1967.

Nike

Site Name: KC-10

Missile Type: Nike 3D/18W12L-U

Defense Area: Kansas City

Site Location: Lawson

Branch: Army

Dates of Active Service: Nov 1959 to Feb 1964

Control Site Condition/Owner: Lawson Schools

Launch Site Condition/Owner: Lawson Schools

Site Name: KC-30
Missile Type: Nike 3D/18W12L-U
Defense Area: Kansas City
Site Location: Pleasant Hill
Branch: Army
Dates of Active Service: Nov 1959 to Feb 1969
Control Site Condition/Owner: Private ownership; development company
Launch Site Condition/Owner: Department of Defense

Site Name: SL-60
Missile Type: Nike 3D/18W12L-U
Defense Area: Saint Louis
Site Location: Pacific (5 mi. S)
Branch: Army
Dates of Active Service: May 1960 to Dec 1968
Control Site Condition/Owner: Private ownership
Launch Site Condition/Owner: Nike School

MONTANA

Minuteman

Site Name: A02-A11
Missile Type: Minuteman II
Installation: Malmstrom AFB
Note: The information listed is for launch sites A02-A11.
Site Location: Near Malmstrom AFB, Great Falls, MT
Squadron: 10th SMS
Branch: Air Force
Dates of Active Service: Dec 1, 1961 to present
Current: All sites are scheduled to undergo conversion to Minuteman III.
Conversion: 341st Strategic Missile Wing was converted to Minuteman II on May 30, 1969 and then converted to Minuteman III on July 8, 1975.

Site Name: B02-B11
Missile Type: Minuteman II
Installation: Malmstrom AFB
Note: The information listed is for launch sites B02-Bll.

Site Location: Near Malmstrom AFB, Great Falls, MT
Squadron: 10th SMS
Branch: Air Force
Dates of Active Service: Dec 1, 1961 to present
Current: All sites are scheduled to undergo conversion to Minuteman III.
Conversion: 341st Strategic Missile Wing was converted to Minuteman II on May 30, 1969 and then converted to Minuteman III on July 8, 1975.

Site Name: C02-C11
Missile Type: Minuteman II
Installation: Malmstrom AFB
Note: The information listed is for launch sites C02-C1.
Site Location: Near Malmstrom AFB, Great Falls, MT
Squadron: 10th SMS
Branch: Air Force
Dates of Active Service: Dec 1, 1961 to present
Current: All sites are scheduled to undergo conversion to Minuteman III.
Conversion: 341st Strategic Missile Wing was converted to Minuteman II on May 30, 1969 and then converted to Minuteman III on July 8, 1975.

Site Name: D02-D11
Missile Type: Minuteman II
Installation: Malmstrom AFB **Note:** The information listed is for launch sites D02-D11.
Site Location: Near Malmstrom AFB, Great Falls, MT
Squadron: 10th SMS
Branch: Air Force
Dates of Active Service: Dec 1, 1961 to present
Current: All sites are scheduled to undergo conversion to Minuteman III.
Conversion: 341st Strategic Missile Wing was converted to Minuteman II on May 30, 1969 and then converted to Minuteman III on July 8, 1975.

Site Name: E02-E11
Missile Type: Minuteman II
Installation: Malmstrom AFB
Note: The information listed is for launch sites

E02-E11.
Site Location: Near Malmstrom AFB, Great Falls, MT
Squadron: 10th SMS
Branch: Air Force
Dates of Active Service: Dec 1, 1961 to present
Current: All sites are scheduled to undergo conversion to Minuteman III.
Conversion: 341st Strategic Missile Wing was converted to Minuteman II on May 30, 1969 and then converted to Minuteman III on July 8, 1975.

Site Name: F02-F11
Missile Type: Minuteman II
Installation: Malmstrom AFB
Note: The information listed is for launch sites F02-F11.
Site Location: Near Malmstrom AFB, Great Falls, MT
Squadron: 12th SMS
Branch: Air Force
Dates of Active Service: May 1, 1962 to present
Current: All sites are scheduled to undergo conversion to Minuteman III.
Conversion: 341st Strategic Missile Wing was converted to Minuteman II on May 30, 1969 and then converted to Minuteman III on July 8, 1975.

Site Name: G02-G11
Missile Type: Minuteman II
Installation: Malmstrom AFB
Note: The information listed is for launch sites G02-G11.
Site Location: Near Malmstrom AFB, Great Falls, MT
Squadron: 12th SMS
Branch: Air Force
Dates of Active Service: May 1, 1962 to present
Current: All sites are scheduled to undergo conversion to Minuteman III.
Conversion: 341st Strategic Missile Wing was converted to Minuteman II on May 30, 1969 and then converted to Minuteman III on July 8, 1975.

Site Name: H02-H11
Missile Type: Minuteman III

Installation: Malmstrom AFB
Note: The information listed is for launch sites H02-H11.
Site Location: Near Malmstrom AFB, Great Falls, MT
Squadron: 12th SMS
Branch: Air Force
Dates of Active Service: May 1, 1962 to present
Current: All sites have been converted to Minuteman III and are active.
Conversion: 341st Strategic Missile Wing was converted to Minuteman II on May 30, 1969 and then converted to Minuteman III on July 8, 1975.

Site Name: I02-I11
Missile Type: Minuteman III
Installation: Malmstrom AFB
Note: The information listed is for launch sites I02-I11.
Site Location: Near Malmstrom AFB, Great Falls, MT
Squadron: 12th SMS
Branch: Air Force
Dates of Active Service: May 1, 1962 to present
Current: With the exception of site 110, all sites have been converted to Minuteman III and are active.
Conversion: 341st Strategic Missile Wing was converted to Minuteman II on May 30, 1969 and then converted to Minuteman III on July 8, 1975.

Site Name: J02-J11
Missile Type: Minuteman III
Installation: Malmstrom AFB
Note: The information listed is for launch sites J02-J11.
Site Location: Near Malmstrom AFB, Great Falls, MT
Squadron: 12th SMS
Branch: Air Force
Dates of Active Service: May 1, 1962 to present
Current: All sites have been converted to Minuteman III and are active.
Conversion: 341st Strategic Missile Wing was converted to Minuteman II on May 30, 1969 and then converted to Minuteman III on July 8, 1975.

Site Name: K02-K11
Missile Type: Minuteman II
Installation: Malmstrom AFB
Note: The information listed is for launch sites K02-K11.
Site Location: Near Malmstrom AFB, Great Falls, MT
Squadron: 490th SMS
Branch: Air Force
Dates of Active Service: May 1, 1962 to present
Current: All sites are scheduled to undergo conversion to Minuteman III.
Conversion: 341st Strategic Missile Wing was converted to Minuteman II on May 30, 1969 and then converted to Minuteman III on July 8, 1975.

Site Name: L02-L11
Missile Type: Minuteman II
Installation: Malmstrom AFB
Note: The information listed is for launch sites L02-L11.
Site Location: Near Malmstrom AFB, Great Falls, MT
Squadron: 490th SMS
Branch: Air Force
Dates of Active Service: May 1, 1962 to present
Current: All sites are scheduled to undergo conversion to Minuteman III.
Conversion: 341st Strategic Missile Wing was converted to Minuteman II on May 30, 1969 and then converted to Minuteman III on July 8, 1975. Missile Sites in Montana

Site Name: M02-M11
Missile Type: Minuteman II
Installation: Malmstrom AFB
Note: The information listed is for launch sites M02-M11.
Site Location: Near Malmstrom AFB, Great Falls, MT
Squadron: 490th SMS
Branch: Air Force
Dates of Active Service: May 1, 1962 to present
Current: All sites are scheduled to undergo conversion to Minuteman III.
Conversion: 341st Strategic Missile Wing was converted to Minuteman II on May 30, 1969 and then converted to Minuteman III on July

8, 1975.

Site Name: N02-N11
Missile Type: Minuteman II
Installation: Malmstrom AFB
Note: The information listed is for launch sites N02-N11.
Site Location: Near Malmstrom AFB, Great Falls, MT
Squadron: 490th SMS
Branch: Air Force
Dates of Active Service: May 1, 1962 to present
Current: All sites are scheduled to undergo conversion to Minuteman III.
Conversion: 341st Strategic Missile Wing was converted to Minuteman II on May 30, 1969 and then converted to Minuteman III on July 8, 1975.

Site Name: O02-O11
Missile Type: Minuteman II
Installation: Malmstrom AFB
Note: The information listed is for launch sites O02-O11.
Site Location: Near Malmstrom AFB, Great Falls, MT
Squadron: 490th SMS
Branch: Air Force
Dates of Active Service: May 1, 1962 to present
Current: All sites are scheduled to undergo conversion to Minuteman III.
Conversion: 341st Strategic Missile Wing was converted to Minuteman II on May 30, 1969 and then converted to Minuteman III on July 8, 1975.

Site Name: PO2-P11
Missile Type: Minuteman III
Installation: Malmstrom AFB
Note: The information listed is for launch sites PO2-P11.
Site Location: Near Malmstrom AFB, Great Falls, MT
Squadron: 564th SMS
Branch: Air Force
Dates of Active Service: Apr 1, 1966 to present
Current: All sites have been converted to Minuteman III and are active.
Conversion: 341st Strategic Missile Wing was

converted to Minuteman II on May 30, 1969 and then converted to Minuteman III on July 8, 1975.

Site Name: Q02-Q11
Missile Type: Minuteman III
Installation: Malmstrom AFB
Note: The information listed is for launch sites Q02-Q11.
Site Location: Near Malmstrom AFB, Great Falls, MT
Squadron: 564th SMS
Branch: Air Force
Dates of Active Service: Apr 1, 1966 to present
Current: All sites have been converted to Minuteman III and are active.
Conversion: 341st Strategic Missile Wing was converted to Minuteman II on May 30, 1969 and then converted to Minuteman III on July 8, 1975.

Site Name: R02-R11
Missile Type: Minuteman III
Installation: Malmstrom AFB
Note: The information listed is for launch sites R02-R11.
Site Location: Near Malmstrom AFB, Great Falls, MT
Squadron: 564th SMS
Branch: Air Force
Dates of Active Service: Apr 1, 1966 to present
Current: All sites have been converted to Minuteman III and are active.
Conversion: 341st Strategic Missile Wing was converted to Minuteman II on May 30, 1969 and then converted to Minuteman III on July 8, 1975.

Site Name: SO2-S11
Missile Type: Minuteman III
Installation: Malmstrom AFB
Note: The information listed is for launch sites SO2-S11.
Site Location: Near Malmstrom AFB, Great Falls, MT
Squadron: 564th SMS
Branch: Air Force
Dates of Active Service: Apr 1, 1966 to present
Current: All sites have been converted to

Minuteman III and are active.
Conversion: 341st Strategic Missile Wing was converted to Minuteman II on May 30, 1969 and then converted to Minuteman III on July 8, 1975.

Site Name: T02-T11
Missile Type: Minuteman III
Installation: Malmstrom AFB
Note: The information listed is for launch sites T02-T11.
Site Location: Near Malmstrom AFB, Great Falls, MT
Squadron: 564th SMS
Branch: Air Force
Dates of Active Service: Apr 1, 1966 to present
Current: All sites have been converted to Minuteman III and are active.
Conversion: 341st Strategic Missile Wing was converted to Minuteman II on May 30, 1969 and then converted to Minuteman III on July 8, 1975.

NEBRASKA

Atlas

Site Name: 2 (launchers 549-B-1,2,3)
Missile Type: Atlas D
Installation: Offutt AFB
Site Location: Arlington
Squadron: 549th SMS
Branch: Air Force
Dates of Active Service: Aug 15, 1959 to Dec 15, 1964
Current: Private ownership, materials salvaged before sold but structure remains intact.

Site Name: 1 (launchers 549-A-1,2,3)
Missile Type: Atlas D
Installation: Offutt AFB
Site Location: Mead
Squadron: 549th SMS
Branch: Air Force
Dates of Active Service: Aug 15, 1959 to Dec 15, 1964
Current: Private ownership, materials salvaged

before sold but structure remains intact.

Site Name: K
Missile Type: Atlas E
Installation: F.E. Warren AFB
Site Location: Kimball
Squadron: 566th SMS
Branch: Air Force
Dates of Active Service: Apr 1, 1961 to Jun 25, 1964
Current: Private ownership, materials salvaged before sold but structure remains intact.

Site Name: 2
Missile Type: Atlas F
Installation: Lincoln AFB
Site Location: Avoca
Squadron: 551st SMS
Branch: Air Force
Dates of Active Service: Apr 1, 1961 to Jun 25, 1965
Current: Private ownership, materials salvaged before sold but structure remains intact.

Site Name: 8
Missile Type: Atlas F
Installation: Lincoln AFB
Site Location: Beatrice
Squadron: 551st SMS
Branch: Air Force
Dates of Active Service: Apr 1, 1961 to Jun 25, 1965
Current: Private ownership, materials salvaged before sold but structure remains intact.

Site Name: 7
Missile Type: Atlas F
Installation: Lincoln AFB
Site Location: Courtland
Squadron: 551st SMS
Branch: Air Force
Dates of Active Service: Apr 1, 1961 to Jun 25, 1965
Current: Private ownership, materials salvaged before sold but structure remains intact.

Site Name: 12
Missile Type: Atlas F
Installation: Lincoln AFB

Site Location: David City
Squadron: 551st SMS
Branch: Air Force
Dates of Active Service: Apr 1, 1961 to Jun 25, 1965
Current: Private ownership, materials salvaged before sold but structure remains intact.

Site Name: 3
Missile Type: Atlas F
Installation: Lincoln AFB
Site Location: Eagle
Squadron: 55lst SMS
Branch: Air Force
Dates of Active Service: Apr 1, 1961 to Jun 25, 1965
Current: Private ownership, materials salvaged before sold but structure remains intact.

Site Name: 1
Missile Type: Atlas F
Installation: Lincoln AFB
Site Location: Elmwood
Squadron: 551st SMS
Branch: Air Force
Dates of Active Service: Apr 1, 1961 to Jun 25, 1965
Current: Private ownership, materials salvaged before sold but structure remains intact.

Site Name: 4
Missile Type: Atlas F
Installation: Lincoln AFB
Site Location: Nebraska City
Squadron: 551st SMS
Branch: Air Force
Dates of Active Service: Apr 1, 1961 to Jun 25, 1965
Current: Private ownership, materials salvaged before sold but structure remains intact.

Site Name: 5
Missile Type: Atlas F
Installation: Lincoln AFB
Site Location: Palmyra
Squadron: 551st SMS
Branch: Air Force
Dates of Active Service:: April, 1961 to Jun 25, 1965

Current: Private ownership, materials salvaged before sold but structure remains intact.
Site Name: 11
Missile Type: Atlas F
Installation: Lincoln AFB
Site Location: Seward
Squadron: 551st SMS
Branch: Air Force
Dates of Active Service: Apr 1, 1961 to Jun 25, 1965
Current: Private ownership, materials salvaged before sold but structure remains intact.

Site Name: 6
Missile Type: Atlas F
Installation: Lincoln AFB
Site Location: Tecumseh
Squadron: 551st SMS
Branch: Air Force
Dates of Active Service: Apr 1, 1961 to Jun 25, 1965
Current: Private ownership, materials salvaged before sold but structure remains intact.

Site Name: 9
Missile Type: Atlas F
Installation: Lincoln AFB
Site Location: Wilber
Squadron: 551st SMS
Branch: Air Force
Dates of Active Service: Apr 1, 1961 to Jun 25, 1965
Current: Private ownership, materials salvaged before sold but structure remains intact.

Site Name: 10
Missile Type: Atlas F
Installation: Lincoln AFB
Site Location: York
Squadron: 551st SMS
Branch: Air Force
Dates of Active Service: Apr 1, 1961 to Jun 25, 1965
Current: Private ownership, materials salvaged before sold but structure remains intact.

Minuteman

Site Name: B1-E11
Missile Type: Minuteman III
Installation: F. E. Warren AFB
Note: The information listed is for missile alert facilities B1, C1, D1, E1, and launch sites B2-B11, C2-C11, D2-D11, and E2-E11. Both D and E flights straddle the border between Nebraska and Wyoming. For tracking purposes, all of the flights' missiles have been assigned to Nebraska.
Site Location: East of F. E. Warren AFB, Cheyenne, WY
Squadron: 319th SMS
Branch: Air Force
Dates of Active Service: Oct 1, 1963 to present
Current: All sites are currently active.
Conversion: 90th Strategic Missile Wing converted to Minuteman III on Jan 26, 1975.

Site Name: F1-111
Missile Type: Minuteman III
Installation: F. E. Warren AFB
Note: The information listed is for missile alert facilities F1, G1, H1, 11, and launch sites F2-F11, G2-G11, H2-H11, and 12-111.
Site Location: East of F. E. Warren AFB, Cheyenne, WY
Squadron: 320th SMS
Branch: Air Force
Dates of Active Service: Jan 8, 1964 to present
Current: All sites are currently active.
Conversion: 90th Strategic Missile Wing converted to Minuteman III on Jan 26, 1975.

Site Name: K1-K11
Missile Type: Minuteman III
Installation: F. E. Warren AFB
Note: The information listed is for missile alert facility K1, and launch sites K2-K11.
Site Location: East of F. E. Warren AFB, Cheyenne, WY
Squadron: 321st SMS
Branch: Air Force
Dates of Active Service: Apr 8, 1964 to present
Current: All sites are currently active.
Conversion: 90th Strategic Missile Wing converted to Minuteman III on Jan 26, 1975.

Nike

Site Name: OF-60
Missile Type: Nike 3AG/12H/12L-H
Defense Area: Offitt
Site Location: Cedar Creek
Branch: Army
Dates of Active Service: 1960 to 1966
Control Site Condition/Owner: FDS
Launch Site Condition/Owner: FDS

Site Name: L1-01
Missile Type: Nike 3AG/12H/12L-H
Defense Area: Lincoln
Site Location: Ceresco/Davey
Branch: Army
Dates of Active Service: 1960 to Jun 1966
Control Site Condition/Owner: High School
Launch Site Condition/Owner: Abandoned

Site Name: L1-50
Missile Type: Nike 3AG/12H/12L-H
Defense Area: Lincoln
Site Location: Crete
Branch: Army
Dates of Active Service: 1960 to Jun 1966
Control Site Condition/Owner: Housing
Development
Launch Site Condition/Owner: Private owner-
ship

NEW JERSEY

Bomarc

Site Name: McGuire AFB
Missile Type: Bomarc A and B (84)
Installation: McGuire AFB
Site Location: Fort Dix Reservation
Squadron: 46th ADMS
Branch: Air Force
Dates of Active Service: Jan 1, 1959 to Oct 31,
1972
Current: Currently site is sealed off by the Air
Force and is undergoing testing and investi-
gation.

Nike

Site Name: NY-80
Missile Type: Nike 2B, 4C/18H, 30A/23L-UA,
(12L-H)
Defense Area: New York
Site Location: Livingston (dual site)
Branch: Army
Dates of Active Service: 1955 to Apr 1974
Control Site Condition/Owner: Intact; Essex
County Park District
Launch Site Condition/Owner: Partially Intact;
General Services Administration

Site Name: NY-54
Missile Type: Nike 2B/12H, 20A/8L-U
Defense Area: New York
Site Location: Homdel/Hazlet
Branch: Army
Dates of Active Service: 1955 to Nov 1968
Control Site Condition/Owner: FDS
Launch Site Condition/Owner: FDS

Site Name: NY-88
Missile Type: Nike 1B, 2C/30A/12L-A
Defense Area: New York
Site Location: Mountain View/Wayne
Branch: Army
Dates of Active Service: 1955 to 1963
Control Site Condition/Owner: FDS
Launch Site Condition/Owner: FDS

Site Name: NY-53
Missile Type: 2C/30A/12L-A
Defense Area: New York
Site Location: Leonardo/Belford
Branch: Army
Dates of Active Service: 1957 to 1963
Control Site Condition/Owner: FDS
Launch Site Condition/Owner: FDS

Site Name: NY-93/94
Missile Type: Nike 4B, 2C/18H, 30A/24L-UA,
(12L-H)
Defense Area: New York
Site Location: Ramsey/DarlingtonMahwah
Branch: Army
Dates of Active Service: 1955 to Jun 1971
Control Site Condition/Owner: FDS

Launch Site Condition/Owner: FDS

Site Name: NY-56
Missile Type: Nike 4B/24H, 40A/16L-UU
Defense Area: New York
Site Location: Sandy Hook
Branch: Army
Dates of Active Service: 1960 to Jun 1971
Control Site Condition/Owner: Gateway
National Recreation Area
Launch Site Condition/Owner: Gateway
National Recreation Area

Site Name: NY-58/60
Missile Type: Nike 2B/12H, 20A/8L-U
Defense Area: New York
Site Location: South Amboy
Branch: Army
Dates of Active Service: 1955 to Nov 1968
Control Site Condition/Owner: FDS
Launch Site Condition/Owner: FDS

Site Name: NY-65
Missile Type: Nike 2B/12H, 20A/8L-U
Defense Area: New York
Site Location: South Plainfield
Branch: Army
Dates of Active Service: 1955 to Jun 1971
Control Site Condition/Owner: FDS
Launch Site Condition/Owner: FDS
Missile Sites in New Jersey

Site Name: NY-73
Missile Type: Nike 1B, 2C/30A/12L-A
Defense Area: New York
Site Location: Summit/Watchung
Branch: Army
Dates of Active Service: 1958 to Apr 1963
Control Site Condition/Owner: FDS
Launch Site Condition/Owner: Union County
Department of Parks and Recreation

Site Name: PH-41
Missile Type: Nike 2B, 4C/18H, 60A/23L-UA
Defense Area: Philadelphia
Site Location: Berlin/Clementon
Branch: Army
Dates of Active Service: 1956 to Apr 1974
Control Site Condition/Owner: US

Government; abandoned
Launch Site Condition/Owner: US
Government; abandoned

Site Name: PH-25
Missile Type: Nike 2B, 4C/24H, 60A/22L-UA, (14L-H)
Defense Area: Philadelphia
Site Location: Lumberton
Branch: Army
Dates of Active Service: 1958 to Apr 1974
Control Site Condition/Owner: Township of Lumberton and private owner
Launch Site Condition/Owner: Township of Lumberton

Site Name: PH-32
Missile Type: Nike 2B/30A/8L-A
Defense Area: Philadelphia
Site Location: Marlton
Branch: Army
Dates of Active Service: 1956 to 1963
Control Site Condition/Owner: Obliterated; Private ownership, future housing planned
Launch Site Condition/Owner: Partially Intact; Evesham Board of Education

Site Name: PH-49
Missile Type: Nike 1B, 2C/30A/12L-A
Defense Area: Philadelphia
Site Location: Pitman
Branch: Army
Dates of Active Service: 1956 to 1963
Control Site Condition/Owner: Intact; Bethel Church
Launch Site Condition/Owner: Private ownership

Site Name: PH-58
Missile Type: Nike 1B, 2C/18H, 30A/12L-UA, (7L-H)
Defense Area: Philadelphia
Site Location: Swedesboro
Branch: Army
Dates of Active Service: 1957 to Apr 1974
Control Site Condition/Owner: General Services Administration
Launch Site Condition/Owner: General Services Administration

NEW MEXICO

Atlas

Site Name: 2
Missile Type: Atlas F
Installation: Walker AFB
Site Location: Elkins
Squadron: 579th SMS
Branch: Air Force
Dates of Active Service: 1962 through 1965
Current: Private ownership, materials salvaged before sold but structure remains intact.

Site Name: 3
Missile Type: Atlas F
Installation: Walker AFB
Site Location: Elkins
Squadron: 579th SMS
Branch: Air Force
Dates of Active Service: 1962 through 1965
Current: Private ownership, materials salvaged before sold but structure remains intact.

Site Name: 6
Missile Type: Atlas F
Installation: Walker AFB
Site Location: Hagerman
Squadron: 579th SMS
Branch: Air Force
Dates of Active Service: 1962 through 1965
Current: Private ownership, materials salvaged before sold but structure remains intact. One of the few, if not the only, Atlas F silo that is free of ground water.

Site Name: 7
Missile Type: Atlas F
Installation: Walker AFB
Site Location: Hagerman
Squadron: 579th SMS
Branch: Air Force
Dates of Active Service: 1962 through 1965
Current: Private ownership, materials salvaged before sold but structure remains intact.

Site Name: 8
Missile Type: Atlas F
Installation: Walker AFB
Site Location: Lake Arthur

Squadron: 579th SMS
Branch: Air Force
Dates of Active Service: 1962 through 1965
Current: Private ownership, materials salvaged before sold but structure remains intact.

Site Name: 9
Missile Type: Atlas F
Installation: Walker AFB
Site Location: Picacho
Squadron: 579th SMS
Branch: Air Force
Dates of Active Service: 1962 through 1965
Current: Private ownership, materials salvaged before sold but structure remains intact.

Site Name: 1
Missile Type: Atlas F
Installation: Walker AFB
Site Location: Roswell
Squadron: 579th SMS
Branch: Air Force
Dates of Active Service: 1962 through 1965
Current: Private ownership, materials salvaged before sold but structure remains intact.

Site Name: 4
Missile Type: Atlas F
Installation: Walker AFB
Site Location: Roswell
Squadron: 579th SMS
Branch: Air Force
Dates of Active Service: 1962 through 1965
Current: Private ownership, materials salvaged before sold but structure remains intact.

Site Name: 5
Missile Type: Atlas F
Installation: Walker AFB
Site Location: Roswell
Squadron: 579th SMS
Branch: Air Force
Dates of Active Service: 1962 through 1965
Current: Private ownership, materials salvaged before sold but structure remains intact.

Site Name: 10
Missile Type: Atlas F
Installation: Walker AFB
Site Location: Roswell

Squadron: 579th SMS
Branch: Air Force
Dates of Active Service: 1962 through 1965
Current: Private ownership, materials salvaged before sold but structure remains intact.

Site Name: 11
Missile Type: Atlas F
Installation: Walker AFB
Site Location: Roswell
Squadron: 579th SMS
Branch: Air Force
Dates of Active Service: 1962 through 1965
Current: Private ownership, materials salvaged before sold but structure remains intact.

Site Name: 12
Missile Type: Atlas F
Installation: Walker AFB
Site Location: Roswell
Squadron: 579th SMS
Branch: Air Force
Dates of Active Service: 1962 through 1965
Current: Private ownership, materials salvaged before sold but structure remains intact.

Nike

Site Name: W-50
Missile Type: Nike 3AG (never operational)
Defense Area: Walker
Site Location: Hagerman
Branch: Army
Dates of Active Service: Never operational
Control Site Condition/Owner: Intact; Roswell Correctional Center
Launch Site Condition/Owner: Partially Intact; Abandoned

Site Name: W-10
Missile Type: Nike 3AG (never operational)
Defense Area: Walker
Site Location: Roswell
Branch: Army
Dates of Active Service: Never operational
Control Site Condition/Owner: Intact; NMArNG Military Academy
Launch Site Condition/Owner: Intact; MNArNG training site

Site Name: Launch Site One
Missile Type: Nike 1B, 2C/18H, 30A/12L-UA, (7L-H)
Defense Area: No Defense Area assigned-test site only
Site Location: McGregor Guided Missile Range
Branch: Army
Dates of Active Service: 1957 to Dec 1992
Control Site Condition/Owner: FDS
Launch Site Condition/Owner: FDS

NEW YORK

Atlas

Site Name: 6
Missile Type: Atlas F
Installation: Plattsburgh AFB
Site Location: Au Sable Forks
Squadron: 556th SMS
Branch: Air Force
Dates of Active Service: Oct 1, 1961 to Jun 25, 1965
Current: Private ownership, materials salvaged before sold but structure remains intact.

Site Name: 10
Missile Type: Atlas F
Installation: Plattsburgh AFB
Site Location: Brainardsville
Squadron: 556th SMS
Branch: Air Force
Dates of Active Service: Oct 1, 1961 to Jun 25, 1965
Current: Private ownership, materials salvaged before sold but structure remains intact.

Site Name: 1
Missile Type: Atlas F
Installation: Plattsburgh AFB
Site Location: Champlain
Squadron: 556th SMS
Branch: Air Force
Dates of Active Service: Oct 1, 1961 to Jun 25, 1965
Current: Private ownership, materials salvaged before sold but structure remains intact.

Site Name: 9
Missile Type: Atlas F
Installation: Plattsburgh AFB
Site Location: Dannemora
Squadron: 556th SMS
Branch: Air Force
Dates of Active Service: Oct 1, 1961 to Jun 25, 1965
Current: Private ownership, materials salvaged before sold but structure remains intact.

Site Name: 11
Missile Type: Atlas F
Installation: Plattsburgh AFB
Site Location: Ellenburg Depot
Squadron: 556th SMS
Branch: Air Force
Dates of Active Service: Oct 1, 1961 to Jun 25, 1965
Current: Private ownership, materials salvaged before sold but structure remains intact.

Site Name: 5
Missile Type: Atlas F
Installation: Plattsburgh AFB
Site Location: Lewis
Squadron: 556th SMS
Branch: Air Force
Dates of Active Service: Oct 1, 1961 to Jun 25, 1965
Current: Private ownership, materials salvaged before sold but structure remains intact.

Site Name: 12
Missile Type: Atlas F
Installation: Plattsburgh AFB
Site Location: Mooers
Squadron: 556th SMS
Branch: Air Force
Dates of Active Service: Oct 1, 1961 to Jun 25, 1965
Current: Private ownership, materials salvaged before sold but structure remains intact.

Site Name: 8
Missile Type: Atlas F
Installation: Plattsburgh AFB
Site Location: Redford
Squadron: 556th SMS
Branch: Air Force
Dates of Active Service: Oct 1, 1961 to Jun 25, 1965
Current: Private ownership, materials salvaged before sold but structure remains intact.

Site Name: 7
Missile Type: Atlas F
Installation: Plattsburgh AFB
Site Location: Riverview
Squadron: 556th SMS
Branch: Air Force
Dates of Active Service: Oct 1, 1961 to Jun 25, 1965
Current: Private ownership, materials salvaged before sold but structure remains intact.

Site Name: 4
Missile Type: Atlas F
Installation: Plattsburgh AFB
Site Location: Willsboro
Squadron: 556th SMS
Branch: Air Force
Dates of Active Service: Oct 1, 1961 to Jun 25, 1965
Current: Private ownership, materials salvaged before sold but structure remains intact.

Bomarc

Site Name: Niagara Falls International Airport
Missile Type: Bomarc B (56)
Installation: Niagara Falls Air Force Base
Site Location: Niagara Falls International Airport
Squadron: 35th ADMS
Branch: Air Force
Dates of Active Service: Jun 1, 1960 to Dec 31, 1969
Current: Site has been cleared for new NYANG facilities.

Site Name: Suffolk County AFB
Missile Type: Bomarc A (56)
Installation: Suffolk County AFB

Site Location: 1.5 mi. W. of old base
Squadron: 6th ADMS
Branch: Air Force
Dates of Active Service: Dec 1959 to Dec 1, 1964
Current: Site is currently under control of Suffolk County Police Academy.

Nike

Site Name: NY-24
Missile Type: Nike 3B/18H, 30A/12L-U
Defense Area: New York
Site Location: Amityville/Farmingdale
Branch: Army
Dates of Active Service: 1957 to Apr 1974
Control Site Condition/Owner: USAR Center
Launch Site Condition/Owner: Zahn Airport

Site Name: NY-15
Missile Type: Nike 2B/20A/8L-A
Defense Area: New York
Site Location: Fort Slocum
Branch: Army
Dates of Active Service: 1955 to Jul 1960
Control Site Condition/Owner: FDS; abandoned
Launch Site Condition/Owner: Department of Corrections Hospital

Site Name: NY-49
Missile Type: Nike 4B/18H, 30A/16L-U
Defense Area: New York
Site Location: Fort Tilden, Rockaway Point Road
Branch: Army
Dates of Active Service: 1955 to Apr 1974
Control Site Condition/Owner: Intact; Gateway National Recreation Area
Launch Site Condition/Owner: Intact; U.S. Park Service

Site Name: NY-23
Missile Type: Nike 1B, 2C/20A/12L-A
Defense Area: New York
Site Location: Hicksville/Oyster Bay
Branch: Army
Dates of Active Service: 1955 to 1963
Control Site Condition/Owner: Nassau County Board Coop Services

Launch Site Condition/Owner: Village of Brooksville; Native Park

Site Name: NY-09
Missile Type: Nike 1B, 2C/30A/12L-A
Defense Area: New York
Site Location: Kensico/White Plains
Branch: Army
Dates of Active Service: 1955 to 1963
Control Site Condition/Owner: FDS
Launch Site Condition/Owner: FDS

Site Name: NY-29/30
Missile Type: Nike 2B, 4C/60A/24L-AA
Defense Area: New York
Site Location: Lido Beach (dual site)
Branch: Army
Dates of Active Service: 1955 to 1963
Control Site Condition/Owner: FDS
Launch Site Condition/Owner: FDS

Site Name: NY-20
Missile Type: Nike 1B, 2C/20A/12L-A
Defense Area: New York
Site Location: Lloyd Harbor/Huntington
Branch: Army
Dates of Active Service: Jan 1957 to 1963
Control Site Condition/Owner: Obliterated; Private ownership
Launch Site Condition/Owner: Obliterated; Private ownership

Site Name: NY-03/04
Missile Type: Nike 2B,1C/18H, 30A/24L-UA, (12L-H)
Defense Area: New York
Site Location: Orangeburg/Mount Nebo (dual site)
Branch: Army
Dates of Active Service: 1955 to Apr 1974
Control Site Condition/Owner: Partially Intact; Town of Orangeburg
Launch Site Condition/Owner: Intact; USAR Center-Orangeburg

Site Name: NY-25
Missile Type: Nike 1B, 2C/18H, 30A/10L-U
Defense Area: New York
Site Location: Rocky Point/Brookhaven

Branch: Army
Dates of Active Service: 1957 to Jun 1971
Control Site Condition/Owner: FDS
Launch Site Condition/Owner: FDS

Site Name: NY-99
Missile Type: Nike 3B/30A/12L-A
Defense Area: New York
Site Location: Spring Valley/Ramapo
Branch: Army
Dates of Active Service: 1956 to 1963
Control Site Condition/Owner: Partially Intact; East Ramapo School District
Launch Site Condition/Owner: Partially Intact; East Ramapo School District

Site Name: NF-41
Missile Type: Nike 1B, 2C/18H/11L-U
Defense Area: Niagara/Buffalo
Site Location: Grand Island (Formerly dual NF-74/NF-75)
Branch: Army
Dates of Active Service: Apr 1959 to Mar 1970
Control Site Condition/Owner: Private ownership
Launch Site Condition/Owner: Private ownership

Site Name: BU-52
Missile Type: Nike 2B, 4C/60A/24LAA
Defense Area: Niagara/Buffalo
Site Location: Hamburg (dual site)
Branch: Army
Dates of Active Service: 1956 to Dec 1961
Control Site Condition/Owner: FDS
Launch Site Condition/Owner: FDS

Site Name: BU-18
Missile Type: Nike 3B/18H, 30A/12L-U
Defense Area: Niagara/Buffalo
Site Location: Lancaster/Milgrove
Branch: Army
Dates of Active Service: 1956 to Mar 1970
Control Site Condition/Owner: FDS
Launch Site Condition/Owner: FDS

Site Name: NF-03
Missile Type: Nike 2B, 4C/60A/24L-AA

Defense Area: Niagara/Buffalo
Site Location: Model City (dual site)
Branch: Army
Dates of Active Service: 1955 to 1963
Control Site Condition/Owner: FDS
Launch Site Condition/Owner: FDS

Site Name: BU-34/35
Missile Type: Nike 2B, 4C/60A/24L-AA
Defense Area: Niagara/Buffalo
Site Location: Orchard Park (dual site)
Branch: Army
Dates of Active Service: 1956 to Mar 1963
Control Site Condition/Owner: FDS
Launch Site Condition/Owner: FDS

Site Name: BU-09
Missile Type: Nike 1B, 2C/30A/12L-A
Defense Area: Niagara/Buffalo
Site Location: Ransom Creek/Millersport
Branch: Army
Dates of Active Service: 1956 to Dec 1961
Control Site Condition/Owner: FDS
Launch Site Condition/Owner: FDS

Site Name: NF-16
Missile Type: Nike 2B, 4C/18H, 30A/24L-UA, (11L-H)
Defense Area: Niagara/Buffalo
Site Location: Sanborn/Cambria (dual site)
Branch: Army
Dates of Active Service: 1955 to Mar 1970
Control Site Condition/Owner: Private ownership
Launch Site Condition/Owner: Private ownership

NORTH DAKOTA

Minuteman

Site Name: A0–E50
Missile Type: Minuteman III
Installation: Grand Forks AFB
Note: The information listed is for launch sites A0–A10, B0–B10, C0–C10, D0–D10, and E0–E10.

Site Location: Near Grand Forks AFB, Grand Forks, ND
Squadron: 446th SMS
Branch: Air Force
Dates of Active Service: Jul 1, 1965 to present
Current: All sites are currently active.
Conversion: 321st Strategic Missile Wing converted to Minuteman III on Mar 8, 1973.

Site Name: F0–J50
Missile Type: Minuteman III
Installation: Grand Forks AFB
Note: The information listed is for launch sites F0–F10, G0–G10, H0–H10, 10–110, and J0–J10.
Site Location: Near Grand Forks AFB, Grand Forks, ND
Squadron: 447th SMS
Branch: Air Force
Dates of Active Service: Feb 1, 1965 to present
Current: All sites are currently active.
Conversion: 321st Strategic Missile Wing converted to Minuteman III on Mar 8, 1973.

Site Name: K0–O50
Missile Type: Minuteman III
Installation: Grand Forks AFB
Note: The information listed is for launch sites K0–K10, L0–L10, M0–M10, N0–N10, and O0–O10.
Site Location: Near Grand Forks AFB, Grand Forks, ND
Squadron: 448th SMS
Branch: Air Force
Dates of Active Service: Sep 15, 1965 to present
Current: AI1 sites are currently active.
Conversion: 321st Strategic Missile Wing converted to Minuteman III on Mar 8, 1973.

Site Name: A1–E11
Missile Type: Minuteman III
Installation: Minot AFB
Note: The information listed is for missile alert facilities A1, B1, C1, D1, E1, and launch sites A2–A11, B2–B11, C2–C11, D2–D11, and E2–E11.
Site Location: Near Minot AFB, Minot, ND

Squadron: 740th SMS
Branch: Air Force
Dates of Active Service: Nov 1, 1962 to present
Current: All sites are currently active.
Conversion: 91st Strategic Missile Wing converted to Minuteman III on Dec 13, 1971.

Site Name: F1–J11
Missile Type: Minuteman III
Installation: Minot AFB
Note: The information listed is for missile alert facilities F1, G1, H1, I1, J1, and launch sites F2–F11, G2–G11, H2–H11, I2-I11, and 52–511.
Site Location: Near Minot AFB, Minot, ND
Squadron: 741st SMS
Branch: Air Force
Dates of Active Service: Dec 1, 1962 to present
Current: All sites are currently active.
Conversion: 91st Strategic Missile Wing converted to Minuteman III on Dec 13, 1971.

Site Name: K1–O11
Missile Type: Minuteman III
Installation: Minot AFB
Note: The information listed is for missile alert facilities K1, L1, M1, N1, O1, and launch sites K2–K11, L2–L11, M2–M11, N2–N11, and O2-O11.
Site Location: Near Minot AFB, Minot, ND
Squadron: 742nd SMS
Branch: Air Force
Dates of Active Service: Jan 1, 1962 to present
Current: All sites are currently active.
Conversion: 91st Strategic Missile Wing converted to Minuteman III on Dec 13, 1971.

Antiballistic Missile (ABM) System

Site Name: Stanley R. Mickelsen Safeguard Complex
Missile Type: Sprint and Spartan
Installation: Missile Site Radar (MSR)
Site Location: 102 miles northwest of Grand Forks; 12 miles south of Langdon
Branch: Army
Dates of Active Service: 1975–1976
Current: Held in caretaker status by the U.S. Army Space and Strategic Defense Command. The missile launchers are currently being removed.

Site Name: Stanley R. Mickelsen Safeguard Complex
Missile Type: Sprint (12-16 launchers)
Installation: Remote Sprint Launch Site #1
Site Location: Within a 20-mile radius of the MSR
Branch: Army
Dates of Active Service: 1975–1976
Current: Held in caretaker status by the U.S. Army Space and Strategic Defense Command. The missile launchers are currently being removed.

Site Name: Stanley R. Mickelsen Safeguard Complex
Missile Type: Sprint (12 launchers)
Installation: Remote Sprint Launch Site #2
Site Location:
Branch: Army
Dates of Active Service:
Current: Held in caretaker status by the U.S. Army Space and Strategic Defense Command. The missile launchers are currently being removed.

Site Name: Stanley R. Mickelsen Safeguard Complex
Missile Type: Sprint (16 launchers)
Installation: Remote Sprint Launch Site #3
Site Location:
Branch: Army
Current: Held in caretaker status by the U.S. Army Space and Strategic Defense Command. The missile launchers are currently being removed.

Site Name: Stanley R. Mickelsen Safeguard Complex
Missile Type: Sprint (12-16 launchers)
Installation: Remote Sprint Launch Site #4
Site Location:
Branch: Army
Current: Held in caretaker status by the U.S. Army Space and Strategic Defense Command. The missile launchers are currently being removed.

OHIO

Nike

Site Name: CD-63
Missile Type: Nike 3D/18H/12L-U
Defense Area: Cincinnati-Dayton
Site Location: Dillsboro
Branch: Army
Dates of Active Service: Mar 1960 to Mar 1970
Control Site Condition/Owner: unknown
Launch Site Condition/Owner: Private ownership; home

Site Name: CD-46
Missile Type: Nike 3D/18H/12L-U
Defense Area: Cincinnati-Dayton
Site Location: Felicity
Branch: Army
Dates of Active Service: Apr 1960 to Mar 1970
Control Site Condition/Owner: OHArNG; C Company, 216th Engineers
Launch Site Condition/Owner: Industrial

Site Name: CD-78
Missile Type: Nike 3D/18H/12L-U
Defense Area: Cincinnati-Dayton
Site Location: Oxford
Branch: Army
Dates of Active Service: Mar 1960 to Mar 1970
Control Site Condition/Owner: Private ownership
Launch Site Condition/Owner: Private ownership

Site Name: CD-27
Missile Type: Nike 3D/18H/12L-U
Defense Area: Cincinnati-Dayton
Site Location: Wilmington
Branch: Army
Dates of Active Service: 1960 to Mar 1971
Control Site Condition/Owner: Intact; Nike Town Center and Country School, also industrial
Launch Site Condition/Owner: Intact; Private ownership

Site Name: CL-02
Missile Type: Nike 3B/18H, 30A/12L-U

Defense Area: Cleveland
Site Location: Bratenahl
Branch: Army
Dates of Active Service: 1956 to Jun 1971
Control Site Condition/Owner: FDS
Launch Site Condition/Owner: FDS

Site Name: CL-48
Missile Type: Nike 1B, 2C/30A/12L-A
Defense Area: Cleveland
Site Location: Garfield Heights
Branch: Army
Dates of Active Service: 1956 to Aug 1961
Control Site Condition/Owner: Garfield Heights Board of Education
Launch Site Condition/Owner: Independence Board of Education; "Land Lab"

Site Name: CL-67
Missile Type: Nike 3B/30A/12L-A
Defense Area: Cleveland
Site Location: Lakefront Airport
Branch: Army
Dates of Active Service: 1956 to 1963
Control Site Condition/Owner: FDS
Launch Site Condition/Owner: FDS

Site Name: CL-69
Missile Type: Nike 3B/MH, 30A/12L-U
Defense Area: Cleveland
Site Location: Lordstown
Branch: Army
Dates of Active Service: 1956 to Jun 1971
Control Site Condition/Owner: Park and Housing
Launch Site Condition/Owner: Tri-City Park

Site Name: CL-11
Missile Type: Nike 3B/MH, 30A/12L-U
Defense Area: Cleveland
Site Location: Painesville
Branch: Army
Dates of Active Service: 1958 to Jun 1971
Control Site Condition/Owner: Private ownership; industrial
Launch Site Condition/Owner: County Engineers Office

Site Name: CL-59

Missile Type: Nike 1B, 2C/30A/12L-A
Defense Area: Cleveland
Site Location: Palma/Midpark Station
Branch: Army
Dates of Active Service: 1956 to Aug 1961
Control Site Condition/Owner: Nathan Hale Park
Launch Site Condition/Owner: Cuyahoga Community College

Site Name: CL-34
Missile Type: Nike 3B/30A/12L-A
Defense Area: Cleveland
Site Location: Warrensville
Branch: Army
Dates of Active Service: 1956 to 1963
Control Site Condition/Owner: USER Center
Launch Site Condition/Owner: Ohio DOT

Site Name: CL-13
Missile Type: Nike 3B/30A/12L-A
Defense Area: Cleveland
Site Location: Willowick
Branch: Army
Dates of Active Service: 1956 to 1963
Control Site Condition/Owner: Robert Manry Park
Launch Site Condition/Owner: Willoughby-Eastlake School District

OKLAHOMA

Atlas

Site Name: 4
Missile Type: Atlas F
Installation: Altus AFB
Site Location: Cache
Squadron: 577th SMS
Branch: Air Force
Dates of Active Service: Jun 1, 1961 to Mar 25, 1965
Current: Private ownership, materials salvaged before sold but structure remains intact.

Site Name: 8
Missile Type: Atlas F

Installation: Altus APB
Site Location: Creta
Squadron: 577th SMS
Branch: Air Force
Dates of Active Service: Jun 1, 1961 to Mar 25, 1965
Current: Private ownership, materials salvaged before sold but structure remains intact.

Site Name: 6
Missile Type: Atlas F
Installation: Altus AFB
Site Location: Frederick
Squadron: 577th SMS
Branch: Air Force
Dates of Active Service: Jun 1, 1961 to Mar 25, 1965
Current: Private ownership, materials salvaged before sold but structure remains intact.

Site Name: 2
Missile Type: Atlas F
Installation: Altus APB
Site Location: Hobart
Squadron: 577th SMS
Branch: Air Force
Dates of Active Service: Jun 1, 1961 to Mar 25, 1965
Current: Private ownership, materials salvaged before sold but structure remains intact.

Site Name: 12
Missile Type: Atlas F
Installation: Altus AFB
Site Location: Hobart
Squadron: 577th SMS
Branch: Air Force
Dates of Active Service: Jun 1, 1961 to Mar 25, 1965
Current: Private ownership, materials salvaged before sold but structure remains intact.

Site Name: 9
Missile Type: Atlas F
Installation: Altus AFB
Site Location: Hollis
Squadron: 577th SMS
Branch: Air Force
Dates of Active Service: Jun 1, 1961 to Mar 25,

1965

Current: Private ownership, materials salvaged before sold but structure remains intact.

Site Name: 1
Missile Type: Atlas F
Installation: Altus AFB
Site Location: Lonewolf
Squadron: 577th SMS
Branch: Air Force
Dates of Active Service: Jun 1, 1961 to Mar 25, 1965
Current: Private ownership, materials salvaged before sold but structure remains intact.

Site Name: 5
Missile Type: Atlas F
Installation: Altus AFB
Site Location: Mantiou
Squadron: 577th SMS
Branch: Air Force
Dates of Active Service: Jun 1, 1961 to Mar 25, 1965
Current: Private ownership, materials salvaged before sold but structure remains intact.

Site Name: 10
Missile Type: Atlas F
Installation: Altus AFB
Site Location: Russell
Squadron: 577th SMS
Branch: Air Force
Dates of Active Service: Jun 1, 1961 to Mar 25, 1965
Current: Private ownership, materials salvaged before sold but structure remains intact.

Site Name: 3
Missile Type: Atlas F
Installation: Altus AFB
Site Location: Snyder
Squadron: 577th SMS
Branch: Air Force
Dates of Active Service: Jun 1, 1961 to Mar 25, 1965
Current: Private ownership, materials salvaged before sold but structure remains intact.

Site Name: 11

Missile Type: Atlas F
Installation: Altus AFB
Site Location: Willow
Squadron: 577th SMS
Branch: Air Force
Dates of Active Service: Jun 1, 1961 to Mar 25, 1965
Current: Private ownership, materials salvaged before sold but structure remains intact.

PENNSYLVANIA

Nike

Site Name: PH-67
Missile Type: Nike 1B, 2C/30A/12L-A
Defense Area: Philadelphia
Site Location: Chester/Media
Branch: Army
Dates of Active Service: 1955 to 1963
Control Site Condition/Owner: FDS
Launch Site Condition/Owner: FDS

Site Name: PH-75
Missile Type: Nike 2B, 4C/18H, 60A/23L-UA, (11L-H)
Defense Area: Philadelphia
Site Location: Edgemont/Delaware City
Branch: Army
Dates of Active Service: 1955 to Nov 1968
Control Site Condition/Owner: Ridley Creek State Park
Launch Site Condition/Owner: USAR Center

Site Name: PH-15
Missile Type: Nike 1B, 2C/30A/12L-A
Defense Area: Philadelphia
Site Location: Newportville/Crowden
Branch: Army
Dates of Active Service: 1956 to 1963
Control Site Condition/Owner: Private ownership
Launch Site Condition/Owner: Private ownership

Site Name: PH-82
Missile Type: Nike 1B, 2C/30A/12L-A
Defense Area: Philadelphia

Site Location: Paoli/Valley Forge
Branch: Army
Dates of Active Service: 1955 to 1982
Control Site Condition/Owner: FDS
Launch Site Condition/Owner: FDS

Site Name: PH-07
Missile Type: Nike 2B/30A/8L-A
Defense Area: Philadelphia
Site Location: Richboro
Branch: Army
Dates of Active Service: 1956 to Sep 1961
Control Site Condition/Owner: FDS
Launch Site Condition/Owner: FDS

Site Name: PI-02
Missile Type: Nike 1B, 2C/30A/12L-A
Defense Area: Pittsburgh
Site Location: Rural Ridge
Branch: Army
Dates of Active Service: Apr 1955 to Apr 1963
Control Site Condition/Owner: FDS
Launch Site Condition/Owner: FDS

Site Name: PH-99
Missile Type: Nike 4B, 2C/36H,60A/22L-UU
Defense Area: Philadelphia
Site Location: Warrington/Eureka
Branch: Army
Dates of Active Service: 1956 to Jul 1971
Control Site Condition/Owner: FDS
Launch Site Condition/Owner: FDS

Site Name: PH-91
Missile Type: Nike 1B, 2C/30A/12L-A
Defense Area: Philadelphia
Site Location: Worchester
Branch: Army
Dates of Active Service: 1956 to 1963
Control Site Condition/Owner: Private ownership
Launch Site Condition/Owner: USAR Center

Site Name: PI-62
Missile Type: Nike 1B, 2C/30A/12L-A
Defense Area: Pittsburgh
Site Location: Bridgeville/Hickman
Branch: Army
Dates of Active Service: 1956 to Apr 1963

Control Site Condition/Owner: Intact; Army,
 Pittsburgh Readiness Group
Launch Site Condition/Owner: Intact; Army
 control

Site Name: PI-92
Missile Type: Nike 1B, 2C/30A/12L-A
Defense Area: Pittsburgh
Site Location: Bryant/North Park
Branch: Army
Dates of Active Service: 1956 to Apr 1963
Control Site Condition/Owner: FDS
Launch Site Condition/Owner: FDS

Site Name: PI-71
Missile Type: Nike 1B, 2C/18H, 30A/10L-U
Defense Area: Pittsburgh
Site Location: Corapolis/Beacon
Branch: Army
Dates of Active Service: 1955 to Mar 1974
Control Site Condition/Owner: FDS
Launch Site Condition/Owner: FDS

Site Name: PI-37
Missile Type: Nike 3B/18H,30A/12L-U
Defense Area: Pittsburgh
Site Location: Cowansburg/Herminie
Branch: Army
Dates of Active Service: 1956 to Mar 1974
Control Site Condition/Owner: FDS
Launch Site Condition/Owner: FDS

Site Name: PI-03
Missile Type: Nike 3B/18H, 30A/12L-U
Defense Area: Pittsburgh
Site Location: Dorseyville/Indianola
Branch: Army
Dates of Active Service: Oct 1956 to Mar 1974
Control Site Condition/Owner: FDS
Launch Site Condition/Owner: FDS

Site Name: PI-42
Missile Type: Nike 1B, 2C/30A/12L-A
Defense Area: Pittsburgh
Site Location: Elizabeth
Branch: Army
Dates of Active Service: 1956 to Apr 1963
Control Site Condition/Owner: FDS
Launch Site Condition/Owner: FDS

Site Name: PI-43
Missile Type: Nike 3B/18H, 30A/12L-U
Defense Area: Pittsburgh
Site Location: Elrama
Branch: Army
Dates of Active Service: May 1955 to Mar 1974
Control Site Condition/Owner: FDS
Launch Site Condition/Owner: FDS

Site Name: PI-52
Missile Type: Nike 1B, 2C/30A/12L-A
Defense Area: Pittsburgh
Site Location: Finleyville
Branch: Army
Dates of Active Service: 1958 to Jul 1960
Control Site Condition/Owner: Partially Intact;
 Private ownership; a church
Launch Site Condition/Owner: Partially Intact;
 Private ownership

Site Name: PI-36
Missile Type: Nike 1B, 2C/18H, 30A/10L-U
Defense Area: Pittsburgh
Site Location: Irwin
Branch: Army
Dates of Active Service: Apr 1955 to Dec 1968
Control Site Condition/Owner: FDS
Launch Site Condition/Owner: FDS

Site Name: PI-25
Missile Type: Nike 1B, 2C/30A/12L-A
Defense Area: Pittsburgh
Site Location: Murrysville/Monroe
Branch: Army
Dates of Active Service: Apr 1955 to 1960
Control Site Condition/Owner: FDS
Launch Site Condition/Owner: FDS

Site Name: PI-93
Missile Type: Nike 1B, 2C/18H, 30A/10L-H
Defense Area: Pittsburgh
Site Location: Westville
Branch: Army
Dates of Active Service: Oct 1956 to Jun 1971
Control Site Condition/Owner: FDS
Launch Site Condition/Owner: FDS

RHODE ISLAND

Nike

Site Name: PR-38
Missile Type: Nike 1B, 2C/18H, 30A/10L-U
Defense Area: Providence
Site Location: Bristol
Branch: Army
Dates of Active Service: 1956 to Apr 1974
Control Site Condition/Owner: Brown
University
Launch Site Condition/Owner: Roger Williams
 College

Site Name: PR-69
Missile Type: Nike 1B, 2C/30A/12L-A
Defense Area: Providence
Site Location: Coventry
Branch: Army
Dates of Active Service: 1956 to Oct 1974
Control Site Condition/Owner: RIANG; 281st,
 282d Combat Communications Squadrons
Launch Site Condition/Owner: General
 Services Administration

Site Name: PR-79
Missile Type: Nike 1B, 2C/30A/12L-A
Defense Area: Providence
Site Location: Foster Center/Woonsocket
Branch: Army
Dates of Active Service: 1956 to Jun 1963
Control Site Condition/Owner:
 Foster/Gloucester Regional School District
Launch Site Condition/Owner: State of Rhode
 Island; State Police Training Center

Site Name: PR-58
Missile Type: Nike 1B, 2C/30A/12L-A
Defense Area: Providence
Site Location: North Kingston/Davisville
Branch: Army
Dates of Active Service: 1956 to 1963
Control Site Condition/Owner: North
 Kingston Parks and Recreation Department
Launch Site Condition/Owner: RIANG instal-
 lation

Site Name: PR-99
Missile Type: Nike 1B, 2C/18H, 30A/11L-U, (10L-H)
Defense Area: Providence
Site Location: North Smithfield/Foster
Branch: Army
Dates of Active Service: 1956 to Jun 1971
Control Site Condition/Owner: RIANGKJSAFR Center
Launch Site Condition/Owner: US Army

SOUTH DAKOTA

Minuteman

Site Name: A01 launch control facility and launch sites A02–A11
Missile Type: Minuteman II
Installation: Ellsworth AFB
Note: The information listed is for A01 launch control facility and A02–A11 launch sites. The dates shown are from unit activation to when last site was placed under caretaker.
Site Location: Near Ellsworth AFB, Box Elder, SD
Squadron: 66th SMS
Branch: Air Force
Dates of Active Service: Jul 1, 1962 to Aug 16, 1993
Current: All sites are currently undergoing the deactivation process. No implosions have taken place.
Conversion: 44th Strategic Missile Wing converted to Minuteman II on Mar 13, 1973.

Site Name: B01 launch control facility and launch sites B02–B11
Missile Type: Minuteman II
Installation: Ellsworth AFB
Note: The information listed is for B01 launch control facility and B02–B11 launch sites. The dates shown are from unit activation to when last site was placed under caretaker.
Site Location: Near Ellsworth AFB, Box Elder, SD
Squadron: 66th SMS
Branch: Air Force
Dates of Active Service: Jul 1, 1962 to Aug 16, 1993

Current: All sites are currently undergoing the deactivation process. No implosions have taken place.
Conversion: 44th Strategic Missile Wing converted to Minuteman II on Mar 13, 1973.

Site Name: C01 launch control facility and launch sites C02–C11
Missile Type: Minuteman II
Installation: Ellsworth AFB
Note: The information listed is for C01 launch control facility and C02–C11 launch sites. The dates shown are from unit activation to when last site was placed under caretaker.
Site Location: Near Ellsworth AFB, Box Elder, SD
Squadron: 66th SMS
Branch: Air Force
Dates of Active Service: Jul 1, 1962 to Aug 16, 1993
Current: All sites are currently undergoing the deactivation process. No implosions have taken place.
Conversion: 44th Strategic Missile Wing converted to Minuteman II on Mar 13, 1973.

Site Name: D01 launch control facility and launch sites D02–D11
Missile Type: Minuteman II
Installation: Ellsworth AFB
Note: The information listed is for D01 launch control facility and D02–D11 launch sites. The dates shown are from unit activation to when last site was placed under caretaker.
Site Location: Near Ellsworth AFB, Box Elder, SD
Squadron: 66th SMS
Branch: Air Force
Dates of Active Service: Jul 1, 1962 to May 26, 1993
Current: All sites are currently undergoing the deactivation process. No implosions have taken place.
Conversion: 44th Strategic Missile Wing converted to Minuteman II on Mar 13, 1973.

Site Name: E01 launch control facility and launch sites E02–E11

Missile Type: Minuteman II
Installation: Ellsworth AFB
Note: The information listed is for E01 launch control facility and E02–E11 launch sites. The dates shown are from unit activation to when last site was placed under caretaker.
Site Location: Near Ellsworth AFB, Box Elder, SD
Squadron: 66th SMS
Branch: Air Force
Dates of Active Service: Jul 1, 1962 to Jul 1, 1993
Current: All sites are currently undergoing the deactivation process. No implosions have taken place.
Conversion: 44th Strategic Missile Wing converted to Minuteman II on Mar 13, 1973.

Site Name: F01 launch control facility and launch sites F02–F11
Missile Type: Minuteman II
Installation: Ellsworth AFB
Note: The information listed is for F01 launch control facility and F02–F11 launch sites. The dates shown are from unit activation to when last site was placed under caretaker.
Site Location: Near Ellsworth AFB, Box Elder, SD
Squadron: 67th SMS
Branch: Air Force
Dates of Active Service: Aug 1, 1962 to Jul 1, 1993
Current: All sites are currently undergoing the deactivation process. No implosions have taken place.
Conversion: 44th Strategic Missile Wing converted to Minuteman II on Mar 13, 1973.

Site Name: G01 launch control facility and launch sites G02–G11
Missile Type: Minuteman II
Installation: Ellsworth AFB
Note: The information listed is for G01 launch control facility and G02–G11 launch sites. The dates shown are from unit activation to when last site was placed under caretaker.
Site Location: Near Ellsworth AFB, Box Elder, SD
Squadron: 67th SMS

Branch: Air Force
Dates of Active Service: Aug 1, 1962 to Aug 3, 1992
Current: All sites are currently undergoing the deactivation process. M1 launch sites have been imploded.
Conversion: 44th Strategic Missile Wing converted to Minuteman II on Mar 13, 1973.

Site Name: H01 launch control facility and launch sites H02–H11
Missile Type: Minuteman II
Installation: Ellsworth AFB
Note: The information listed is for H01 launch control facility and H02–H11 launch sites. The dates shown are from unit activation to when last site was placed under caretaker.
Site Location: Near Ellsworth AFB, Box Elder, SD
Squadron: 67th SMS
Branch: Air Force
Dates of Active Service: Aug 1, 1962 to Jun 24, 1992
Current: All sites are currently undergoing the deactivation process. All launch sites have been imploded with the exception of H06 and H09.
Conversion: 44th Strategic Missile Wing converted to Minuteman II on Mar 13, 1973.

Site Name: I01 launch control facility and launch sites I02–I11
Missile Type: Minuteman II
Installation: Ellsworth AFB
Note: The information listed is for I01 launch control facility and I02–I11 launch sites. The dates shown are from unit activation to when last site was placed under caretaker.
Site Location: Near Ellsworth AFB, Box Elder, SD
Squadron: 67th SMS
Branch: Air Force
Dates of Active Service: Aug 1, 1962 to Dec 7, 1992
Current: All sites are currently undergoing the deactivation process. Only launch sites I5, I7, I8, and I9 have been imploded. All other sites remain intact.
Conversion: 44th Strategic Missile Wing con-

verted to Minuteman II on Mar 13, 1973.

Site Name: J01 launch control facility and launch sites 502–511
Missile Type: Minuteman II
Installation: Ellsworth AFB
Note: The information listed is for J01 launch control facility and J02–J11 launch sites. The dates shown are from unit activation to when last site was placed under caretaker.
Site Location: Near Ellsworth AFB, Box Elder, SD
Squadron: 67th SMS
Branch: Air Force
Dates of Active Service: Aug 1, 1962 to Dec 16, 1992
Current: All sites are currently undergoing the deactivation process. No implosions have taken place.
Conversion: 44th Strategic Missile Wing converted to Minuteman II on Mar 13, 1973.

Site Name: K01 launch control facility and launch sites K02–K11
Missile Type: Minuteman II
Installation: Ellsworth AFB
Note: The information listed is for K01 launch control facility and K02–K11 launch sites. The dates shown are from unit activation to when last site was placed under caretaker.
Site Location: Near Ellsworth AFB, Box Elder, SD
Squadron: 68th SMS
Branch: Air Force
Dates of Active Service: Sep 1, 1962 to Apr 15, 1994
Current: All sites are currently undergoing the deactivation process. No implosions have taken place.
Conversion: 44th Strategic Missile Wing converted to Minuteman II on Mar 13, 1973.

Site Name: L01 launch control facility and launch sites L02–L11
Missile Type: Minuteman II
Installation: Ellsworth AFB
Note: The information listed is for L01 launch control facility and L02–L11 launch sites. The dates shown are from unit activation to

when last site was placed under caretaker.
Site Location: Near Ellsworth AFB, Box Elder, SD
Squadron: 68th SMS
Branch: Air Force
Dates of Active Service: Sep 1, 1962 to Apr 21, 1994
Current: All sites are currently undergoing the deactivation process. No implosions have taken place.
Conversion: 44th Strategic Missile Wing converted to Minuteman II on Mar 13, 1973.

Site Name: M01 launch control facility and launch sites M02–M11
Missile Type: Minuteman II
Installation: Ellsworth AFB
Note: The information listed is for M01 launch control facility and M02–M11 launch sites. The dates shown are from unit activation to when last site was placed under caretaker.
Site Location: Near Ellsworth AFB, Box Elder, SD
Squadron: 68th SMS
Branch: Air Force
Dates of Active Service: Sep 1, 1962 to Dec 6, 1993
Current: All sites are currently undergoing the deactivation process. No implosions have taken place.
Conversion: 44th Strategic Missile Wing converted to Minuteman II on Mar 13, 1973.

Site Name: N01 launch control facility and launch sites N02–N11
Missile Type: Minuteman II
Installation: Ellsworth AFB
Note: The information listed is for N01 launch control facility and N02–N11 launch sites. The dates shown are from unit activation to when last site was placed under caretaker.
Site Location: Near Ellsworth AFB, Box Elder, SD
Squadron: 68th SMS
Branch: Air Force
Dates of Active Service: Sep 1, 1962 to Dec 9, 1993
Current: All sites are currently undergoing the deactivation process. No implosions have

taken place.

Conversion: 44th Strategic Missile Wing converted to Minuteman II on Mar 13, 1973.

Site Name: 001 launch control facility and launch sites 002–011
Missile Type: Minuteman II
Installation: Ellsworth AFB
Note: The information listed is for 001 launch control facility and 002–011 launch sites. The dates shown are from unit activation to when last site was placed under caretaker.
Site Location: Near Ellsworth AFB, Box Elder, SD
Squadron: 68th SMS
Branch: Air Force
Dates of Active Service: Sep 1, 1962 to Jan 19, 1994
Current: All sites are currently undergoing the deactivation process. No implosions have taken place.
Conversion: 44th Strategic Missile Wing converted to Minuteman II on Mar 13, 1973.

Titan

Site Name: 1B (launchers 850-B-1,2,3)
Missile Type: Titan I
Installation: Ellsworth AFB
Site Location: Hermosa
Squadron: 850th SMS
Branch: Air Force
Dates of Active Service: Dec 1, 1960 to Mar 25, 1965
Current: Private ownership, materials salvaged before sold but structure remains intact.

Site Name: 1A (launchers 850-A-1,2,3)
Missile Type: Titan I
Installation: Ellsworth AFB
Site Location: New Underwood
Squadron: 850th SMS
Branch: Air Force
Dates of Active Service: Dec 1, 1960 to Mar 25, 1965
Current: Private ownership, materials salvaged before sold but structure remains intact.

Site Name: 1C (launchers 850-C-1,2,3)

Missile Type: Titan I
Installation: Ellsworth AFB
Site Location: Sturgis
Squadron: 850th SMS
Branch: Air Force
Dates of Active Service: Dec 1, 1960 to Mar 25, 1965
Current: Private ownership, materials salvaged before sold but structure remains intact.

TEXAS

Atlas

Site Name: 7
Missile Type: Atlas F
Installation: Altus AFB
Site Location: Fargo
Squadron: 577th SMS
Branch: Air Force
Dates of Active Service: Jun 1, 1961 to Mar 25, 1965
Current: Private ownership, materials salvaged before sold but structure remains intact.

Site Name: 1
Missile Type: Atlas F
Installation: Dyess AFB
Site Location: Abilene
Squadron: 578th SMS
Branch: Air Force
Dates of Active Service: Jul 1, 1961 to Mar 25, 1965
Current: Private ownership, materials salvaged before sold but structure remains intact.

Site Name: 2
Missile Type: Atlas F
Installation: Dyess APB
Site Location: Albany
Squadron: 578th SMS
Branch: Air Force
Dates of Active Service: Jul 1, 1961 to Mar 25, 1965
Current: Private ownership, materials salvaged before sold but structure remains intact.

Site Name: 11
Missile Type: Atlas F
Installation: Dyess AFB
Site Location: Anson
Squadron: 578th SMS
Branch: Air Force
Dates of Active Service: Jul 1, 1961 to Mar 25, 1965
Current: Private ownership, materials salvaged before sold but structure remains intact.

Site Name: 7
Missile Type: Atlas F
Installation: Dyess AFB
Site Location: Bradshaw
Squadron: 578th SMS
Branch: Air Force
Dates of Active Service: Jul 1, 1961 to Mar 25, 1965
Current: Private ownership, materials salvaged before sold but structure remains intact.

Site Name: 3
Missile Type: Atlas F
Installation: Dyess AFB
Site Location: Clyde
Squadron: 578th SMS
Branch: Air Force
Dates of Active Service: Jul 1, 1961 to Mar 25, 1965
Current: Private ownership, materials salvaged before sold but structure remains intact.

Site Name: 12
Missile Type: Atlas F
Installation: Dyess AFB
Site Location: Corinth
Squadron: 578th SMS
Branch: Air Force
Dates of Active Service: Jul 1, 1961 to Mar 25, 1965
Current: Private ownership, materials salvaged before sold but structure remains intact.

Site Name: 4
Missile Type: Atlas F
Installation: Dyess AFB
Site Location: Denton County
Squadron: 578th SMS

Branch: Air Force
Dates of Active Service: Jul 1, 1961 to Mar 25, 1965
Current: Private ownership, materials salvaged before sold but structure remains intact.

Site Name: 6
Missile Type: Atlas F
Installation: Dyess AFB
Site Location: Lawn
Squadron: 578th SMS
Branch: Air Force
Dates of Active Service: Jul 1, 1961 to Mar 25, 1965
Current: Private ownership, materials salvaged before sold but structure remains intact.

Site Name: 10
Missile Type: Atlas F
Installation: Dyess AFB
Site Location: Nolan
Squadron: 578th SMS
Branch: Air Force
Dates of Active Service: Jul 1, 1961 to Mar 25, 1965
Current: Private ownership, materials salvaged before sold but structure remains intact.

Site Name: 5
Missile Type: Atlas F
Installation: Dyess APB
Site Location: Oplin
Squadron: 578th SMS
Branch: Air Force
Dates of Active Service: Jul 1, 1961 to Mar 25, 1965
Current: Private ownership, materials salvaged before sold but structure remains intact.

Site Name: 9
Missile Type: Atlas F
Installation: Dyess AFB
Site Location: Shep
Squadron: 578th SMS
Branch: Air Force
Dates of Active Service: Jul 1, 1961 to Mar 25, 1965
Current: Private ownership, materials salvaged before sold but structure remains intact.

Site Name: 8
Missile Type: Atlas F
Installation: Dyess AFB
Site Location: Winters
Squadron: 578th SMS
Branch: Air Force
Dates of Active Service: Jul 1, 1961 to Mar 25, 1965
Current: Private ownership, materials salvaged before sold but structure remains intact.

Nike

Site Name: BG-80
Missile Type: Nike 3AG/12H/12L-H
Defense Area: Bergstrom
Site Location: Austin (WNW)
Branch: Army
Dates of Active Service: Nov 1960 to Jun 1966
Control Site Condition/Owner: Intact; TXArNG 111th Support Group
Launch Site Condition/Owner: Firing Range

Site Name: BG-40
Missile Type: Nike 3AG/12H/12L-H
Defense Area: Bergstrom
Site Location: Elroy (SE)
Branch: Army
Dates of Active Service: Nov 1960 to Jun 1966
Control Site Condition/Owner: Intact; Private ownership
Launch Site Condition/Owner: Partially Intact; Private ownership

Site Name: DF-50
Missile Type: Nike 3D/18H/12L-U
Defense Area: Dallas-Fort Worth
Site Location: Alvarado
Branch: Army
Dates of Active Service: Aug 1960 to Oct 1968
Control Site Condition/Owner: Intact; Private ownership
Launch Site Condition/Owner: Intact; Private ownership

Site Name: DF-01
Missile Type: Nike 3D/18H/12L-U
Defense Area: Dallas-Fort Worth

Site Location: Denton (N)
Branch: Army
Dates of Active Service: Sep 1960 to Oct 1968
Control Site Condition/Owner: Intact; Denton Board of Education; Special Education Resource Center
Launch Site Condition/Owner: FDS

Site Name: DF-70
Missile Type: Nike 3D/18H/12L-U
Defense Area: Dallas-Fort Worth
Site Location: Fort Wolters
Branch: Army
Dates of Active Service: Sep 1960 to Oct 1968
Control Site Condition/Owner: Intact; TXArNG; training
Launch Site Condition/Owner: Intact; Small arms storage, firing, and maneuvering range

Site Name: DF-20
Missile Type: Nike 3D/18H/12L-U
Defense Area: Dallas-Fort Worth
Site Location: Terrell (NE)
Branch: Army
Dates of Active Service: Aug 1960 to Feb 1964
Control Site Condition/Owner: Intact; FDS; abandoned
Launch Site Condition/Owner: Partially Intact; Terrell FFA; school bus storage/maintenance

Site Name: DY-50
Missile Type: Nike 3AG/12H/12L-H
Defense Area: Dyess
Site Location: Abilene (12 mi. SW)
Branch: Army
Dates of Active Service: Oct 1960 to Jun 1966
Control Site Condition/Owner: FDS
Launch Site Condition/Owner: FDS

Site Name: DY-10
Missile Type: Nike 3AG/12H/12L-H
Defense Area: Dyess
Site Location: Fort Phantom Hill (N)
Branch: Army
Dates of Active Service: Oct 1960 to Jun 1966
Control Site Condition/Owner: Intact; Abilene Independent School District
Launch Site Condition/Owner: Intact; Private ownership

VERMONT

Atlas

Site Name: 2
Missile Type: Atlas F
Installation: Plattsburgh AFB
Site Location: Alburg
Squadron: 556th SMS
Branch: Air Force
Dates of Active Service: Oct 1, 1961 to Jun 25, 1965
Current: Private ownership, materials salvaged before sold but structure remains intact.

Site Name: 3
Missile Type: Atlas F
Installation: Plattsburgh AFB
Site Location: Swanton
Squadron: 556th SMS
Branch: Air Force
Dates of Active Service: Oct 1, 1961 to Jun 25, 1965
Current: Private ownership, materials salvaged before sold but structure remains intact.

VIRGINIA

Bomarc

Site Name: Langley AFB
Missile Type: Bomarc B (56)
Installation: Langley AFB
Site Location: 5 mi. W. of Langley AFB
Squadron: 22nd ADMS
Branch: Air Force
Dates of Active Service: Sep 1, 1958 to Oct 31, 1972
Current: Site has been disposed of to the School Board of the city of Newport News and the Dept. of Education of the Peninsula Tidewater Regional Academy of Criminal Justice.

Nike

Site Name: N-52
Missile Type: Nike 2B/18H, 30A/8L-UA

Defense Area: Norfolk
Site Location: Deep Creek/Portsmouth
Branch: Army
Dates of Active Service: 1955 to Apr 1974
Control Site Condition/Owner: Chesapeake Alternative School
Launch Site Condition/Owner: Public Safety Training Center

Site Name: N-85
Missile Type: Nike 2B, 1C/18H, 30A/12L-UA, (8L-H)
Defense Area: Norfolk
Site Location: Denbigh/Patrick Henry
Branch: Army
Dates of Active Service: 1955 to Apr 1974
Control Site Condition/Owner: Peninsula Airport Commission
Launch Site Condition/Owner: Peninsula Airport Commission

Site Name: N-25
Missile Type: Nike 4B, 2C/18H, 30A/24L-UA
Defense Area: Norfolk
Site Location: Fort Story
Branch: Army
Dates of Active Service: 1957 to Jun 1971
Control Site Condition/Owner: Army amphibious training site
Launch Site Condition/Owner: Army amphibious training site

Site Name: N-02
Missile Type: Nike 2C, 1B/30A/12L-A
Defense Area: Norfolk
Site Location: Fox Hill
Branch: Army
Dates of Active Service: 1955 to 1963
Control Site Condition/Owner: Fort Monroe; HQ Training and Doctrine Command
Launch Site Condition/Owner: Fort Monroe; HQ Training and Doctrine Command

Site Name: N-93
Missile Type: Nike 1B, 2C/30A/12L-A
Defense Area: Norfolk
Site Location: Hampton/Spiegelville
Branch: Army
Dates of Active Service: 1955 to 1963

Control Site Condition/Owner: USAR Center
Launch Site Condition/Owner: USAR Center

Site Name: N-36
Missile Type: Nike 1B, 2C/30A/12L-A
Defense Area: Norfolk
Site Location: Kempsville
Branch: Army
Dates of Active Service: 1955 to 1964
Control Site Condition/Owner: City of Virginia Beach; Parks and Recreation
Launch Site Condition/Owner: Parks and Recreation; maintenance

Site Name: N-63
Missile Type: Nike 2B, 1C/30A/12L-A
Defense Area: Norfolk
Site Location: Nansemond/Suffolk
Branch: Army
Dates of Active Service: 1955 to Nov 1964
Control Site Condition/Owner: USAR Center
Launch Site Condition/Owner: Bennett's Creek Park

Site Name: N-75
Missile Type: Nike 1B, 2C/30A/12L-A
Defense Area: Norfolk
Site Location: Smithfield/Carrolton
Branch: Army
Dates of Active Service: 1955 to Jun 1961
Control Site Condition/Owner: Isle of Wight County Park
Launch Site Condition/Owner: Isle of Wight County Park

Site Name: W-74
Missile Type: Nike 2B/20A/8L-A
Defense Area: Washington
Site Location: Fairfax/Pohick
Branch: Army
Dates of Active Service: 1954 to Mar 1963
Control Site Condition/Owner: Fairfax County ownership
Launch Site Condition/Owner: Fairfax County ownership

Site Name: W-83
Missile Type: Nike 1B, 2C/30A/12L-A
Defense Area: Washington

Site Location: Herndon/Drainsville
Branch: Army
Dates of Active Service: 1954 to Nov 1962
Control Site Condition/Owner: Defense
  Mapping Agency
Launch Site Condition/Owner: Fairfax County
  Parks and Recreation also Fairfax County
  Public Schools Administration

Site Name: W-64
Missile Type: Nike 2B, 2C/24H, 60A/24L-UA,
  (16L-H)
Defense Area: Washington
Site Location: Lorton (dual site)
Branch: Army
Dates of Active Service: 1954 to Sep 1958
Control Site Condition/Owner: District of
  Columbia minimum security prison
Launch Site Condition/Owner: District of
  Columbia minimum security prison

WASHINGTON

Atlas

Site Name: 6
Missile Type: Atlas E
Installation: Fairchild AFB
Site Location: Davenport
Squadron: 567th SMS
Branch: Air Force
Dates of Active Service: Apr 1, 1960 to Jun 25,
  1965
Current: Private ownership, materials salvaged
  before sold but structure remains intact.

Site Name: 1
Missile Type: Atlas E
Installation: Fairchild AFB
Site Location: Deer Park
Squadron: 567th SMS
Branch: Air Force
Dates of Active Service: Apr 1, 1960 to Jun 25,
  1965
Current: Private ownership, materials salvaged
  before sold but structure remains intact.

Site Name: 8

Missile Type: Atlas E
Installation: Fairchild AFB
Site Location: Egypt
Squadron: 567th SMS
Branch: Air Force
Dates of Active Service: Apr 1, 1960 to Jun 25,
  1965
Current: Private ownership, materials salvaged
  before sold but structure remains intact.

Site Name: 5
Missile Type: Atlas E
Installation: Fairchild AFB
Site Location: Lemona
Squadron: 567th SMS
Branch: Air Force
Dates of Active Service: Apr 1, 1960 to Jun 25,
  1965
Current: Private ownership, materials salvaged
  before sold but structure remains intact.

Site Name: 2
Missile Type: Atlas E
Installation: Fairchild AFB
Site Location: Newman Lake
Squadron: 567th SMS
Branch: Air Force
Dates of Active Service: Apr 1, 1960 to Jun 25,
  1965
Current: Private ownership, materials salvaged
  before sold but structure remains intact.

Site Name: 9
Missile Type: Atlas E
Installation: Fairchild AFB
Site Location: Reardon
Squadron: 567th SMS
Branch: Air Force
Dates of Active Service: Apr 1, 1960 to Jun 25,
  1965
Current: Bureau of Mines; Dept of Interior,
  materials salvaged but structure remains
  intact.

Site Name: 4
Missile Type: Atlas E
Installation: Fairchild AFB
Site Location: Sprague
Squadron: 567th SMS
Branch: Air Force

Dates of Active Service: Apr 1, 1960 to Jun 25,
  1965
Current: Private ownership, materials salvaged
  before sold but structure remains intact.

Site Name: 7
Missile Type: Atlas E
Installation: Fairchild AFB
Site Location: Wilbur
Squadron: 567th SMS
Branch: Air Force
Dates of Active Service: Apr 1, 1960 to Jun 25,
  1965
Current: Private ownership, materials salvaged
  before sold but structure remains intact.

Nike

Site Name: F-37
Missile Type: Nike 1B, 2C/30A/12L-A
Defense Area: Fairchild
Site Location: Cheney
Branch: Army
Dates of Active Service: 1957 to Jun 1960
Control Site Condition/Owner: Private owner-
  ship
Launch Site Condition/Owner: Private owner-
  ship

Site Name: F-87
Missile Type: Nike 2B, 1C/18H/11L-U
Defense Area: Fairchild
Site Location: Deep Creek
Branch: Army
Dates of Active Service: Sep 1958 to Mar 1966
Control Site Condition/Owner: Private owner-
  ship; electrical service
Launch Site Condition/Owner: Private owner-
  ship

Site Name: F-45
Missile Type: Nike 2B, 1C/18H, 30A/12L-UA
Defense Area: Fairchild
Site Location: Medical Lake
Branch: Army
Dates of Active Service: 1957 to Mar 1966
Control Site Condition/Owner: Private owner-
  ship
Launch Site Condition/Owner: Private owner-
  ship

Site Name: F-07
Missile Type: Nike 2B, IC/30A/12L-A
Defense Area: Fairchild
Site Location: Spokane
Branch: Army
Dates of Active Service: 1957 to Jun 1960
Control Site Condition/Owner: FDS
Launch Site Condition/Owner: FDS

Site Name: H-12
Missile Type: Nike 2B/20A/BL-A
Defense Area: Hanford
Site Location: Othello
Branch: Army
Dates of Active Service: 1955 to Dec 1958
Control Site Condition/Owner: Obliterated;
Department of Energy
Launch Site Condition/Owner: Department of
Energy

Site Name: H-83
Missile Type: Nike 2B/20A/BL-A
Defense Area: Hanford
Site Location: Priest Rapids
Branch: Army
Dates of Active Service: 1955 to Dec 1958
Control Site Condition/Owner: Obliterated;
Department of Energy
Launch Site Condition/Owner: Obliterated;
Department of Energy

Site Name: H-52
Missile Type: Nike 2B/20A/8L-A
Defense Area: Hanford
Site Location: Rattlesnake Mountain
Branch: Army
Dates of Active Service: 1955 to Dec 1958
Control Site Condition/Owner: Intact; Pacific
North Western Laboratories Headquarters
Launch Site Condition/Owner: Intact; Pacific
North Western Laboratories Headquarters

Site Name: H-06
Missile Type: Nike 2B/12H, 20A/8L-U
Defense Area: Hanford
Site Location: Saddle Mountain
Branch: Army
Dates of Active Service: 1955 to Dec 1960
Control Site Condition/Owner: Obliterated;

Department of Energy
Launch Site Condition/Owner: Obliterated;
Department of Energy

Site Name: S-20
Missile Type: Nike 2B/20A/8L-A
Defense Area: Seattle
Site Location: Cougar Mountain/Issaquah
Branch: Army
Dates of Active Service: 1957 to Mar 1964
Control Site Condition/Owner: Obliterated;
Cougar Mountain County Park
Launch Site Condition/Owner: Partially Intact;
Cougar Mountain Regional Wildlife Park

Site Name: S-03
Missile Type: Nike 2B/20A/8L-A
Defense Area: Seattle
Site Location: Kenmore
Branch: Army
Dates of Active Service: 1957 to Mar 1964
Control Site Condition/Owner: Obliterated;
Horizon Heights Park
Launch Site Condition/Owner: Partially Intact;
FEMA Agency Region

Site Name: S-43
Missile Type: Nike 1B, 2C/30A/10L-A
Defense Area: Seattle
Site Location: Kent/Midway
Branch: Army
Dates of Active Service: 1956 to Feb 1963
Control Site Condition/Owner: Intact;
WAArNG Center
Launch Site Condition/Owner: Partially Intact;
King County Parks and Kent School District

Site Name: S-33
Missile Type: Nike 1B, 2C/20A/12L-A
Defense Area: Seattle
Site Location: Lake Young/Renton
Branch: Army
Dates of Active Service: 1956 to Dec 1961
Control Site Condition/Owner: Intact; USAR
Center; 104th Division, Training

Site Name: S-92
Missile Type: Nike 2B/12H, 20A/8L-U
Defense Area: Seattle

Site Location: Kingston
Branch: Army
Dates of Active Service: 1958 to Mar 1974
Launch Site Condition/Owner: Intact; Maple
Valley Christian School; South King County
Activity Center (shared launch with S-32)
Control Site Condition/Owner: Intact;
Laborer's Training
Launch Site Condition/Owner: Intact; North
Kitsap County School District; Spectrum
Alternative Center

Site Name: S-62
Missile Type: Nike 1B, 2C/30A/12L-A
Defense Area: Seattle
Site Location: Ollala
Branch: Army
Dates of Active Service: 1958 to Mar 1963
Control Site Condition/Owner: Intact; Ollala
Guest Lodge
Launch Site Condition/Owner: Partially Intact;
Private ownership

Site Name: S-32
Missile Type: Nike 1B, 2C/20A/12L-A
Defense Area: Seattle
Site Location: Lake Young
Branch: Army
Dates of Active Service: 1956 to Dec 1961
Control Site Condition/Owner: Partially Intact;
King County Sheriff's Department
Launch Site Condition/Owner: Intact; Maple
Valley Christian School; South King County
Activity Center (shared launch with S-33)

Site Name: S-81
Missile Type: Nike 1B, 2C/30A/12L-A
Defense Area: Seattle
Site Location: Poulsbo
Branch: Army
Dates of Active Service: 1956 to Nov 1960
Control Site Condition/Owner: Intact; South
Kitsap School District and Frank Raab
Municipal Park
Launch Site Condition/Owner: Private owner-
ship

Site Name: S-13
Missile Type: Nike 2B, 4C/18H, 60A/23L-UA,

(11L-H)
Defense Area: Seattle
Site Location: Redmond (dual site)
Branch: Army
Dates of Active Service: 1957 to Mar 1974
Control Site Condition/Owner: Intact;
WAArNG; scheduled for development
Launch Site Condition/Owner: Intact; Private
ownership; nursery

Site Name: S-61
Missile Type: Nike 1B, 2C/18H, 30A/12L-UA,
(7L-H)
Defense Area: Seattle
Site Location: Vashon Island
Branch: Army
Dates of Active Service: 1956 to Mar 1974
Control Site Condition/Owner: Partially Intact;
Vashon High School
Launch Site Condition/Owner: Partially Intact;
Vashon Island Equestrian Park and Nike
Events Center

Site Name: S-82
Missile Type: Nike 2B, 1C/30A/12L-A
Defense Area: Seattle
Site Location: Winslow/Bainbridge
Branch: Army
Dates of Active Service: 1958 to Nov 1960
Control Site Condition/Owner: Partially Intact;
Bainbridge Park District; Eagledale Park
Launch Site Condition/Owner: Partially Intact;
Strawberry Hill Park

Titan

Site Name: 1 (launchers 568-A-1,2,3)
Missile Type: Titan I
Installation: Larson AFB
Site Location: Odessa
Squadron: 568th SMS
Branch: Air Force
Dates of Active Service: Apr 1, 1961 to Mar 25,
1965
Current: Private ownership, materials salvaged
before sold but structure remains intact.

Site Name: 3 (launchers 568-C-1,2,3)
Missile Type: Titan I
Installation: Larson AFB

Site Location: Quincy
Squadron: 568th SMS
Branch: Air Force
Dates of Active Service: Apr 1, 1961 to Mar 25,
1965
Current: Private ownership, materials salvaged
before sold but structure remains intact.

Site Name: 2 (launchers 568-B-1,2,3)
Missile Type: Titan I
Installation: Larson AFB
Site Location: Warden
Squadron: 568th SMS
Branch: Air Force
Dates of Active Service: Apr 1, 1961 to Mar 25,
1965
Current: Private ownership, materials salvaged
before sold but structure remains intact.

WISCONSIN

Nike

Site Name: M-42
Missile Type: Nike 1B, 2C/30A/12L-A
Defense Area: Milwaukee
Site Location: Cudahy
Branch: Army
Dates of Active Service: 1956 to Aug 1961
Control Site Condition/Owner: FDS
Launch Site Condition/Owner: FDS

Site Name: M-54
Missile Type: Nike 1B, 2C/30A/12L-A
Defense Area: Milwaukee
Site Location: Hales Corners/Paynesville
Branch: Army
Dates of Active Service: 1956 to Aug 1961
Control Site Condition/Owner: FDS
Launch Site Condition/Owner: FDS

Site Name: M-86
Missile Type: Nike 1B, 2C/30A/12L-A
Defense Area: Milwaukee
Site Location: Lannon
Branch: Army
Dates of Active Service: 1956 to 1958
Control Site Condition/Owner: FDS

Launch Site Condition/Owner: FDS

Site Name: M-02
Missile Type: Nike 1B, 2C/18H, 30A/12L-U
Defense Area: Milwaukee
Site Location: Milwaukee/Brown Deer
Branch: Army
Dates of Active Service: 1957 to Jun 1971
Control Site Condition/Owner: FDS
Launch Site Condition/Owner: FDS

Site Name: M-20
Missile Type: Nike 3B/18H, 30A/12L-U
Defense Area: Milwaukee
Site Location: Milwaukee/Harbor Drive
Branch: Army
Dates of Active Service: 1957 to Jun 1971
Control Site Condition/Owner: FDS
Launch Site Condition/Owner: FDS

Site Name: M-64
Missile Type: Nike 1B, 2C/30A/12L-A
Defense Area: Milwaukee
Site Location: Muskegon/Prospect
Branch: Army
Dates of Active Service: 1956 to Mar 1963
Control Site Condition/Owner: FDS
Launch Site Condition/Owner: FDS

Site Name: M-96
Missile Type: Nike 1B, 2C/30A/12L-A
Defense Area: Milwaukee
Site Location: Milwaukee/Silver Springs
Branch: Army
Dates of Active Service: 1956 to Jun 1971
Control Site Condition/Owner: West Silver
Springs ASARC and Training Area
Launch Site Condition/Owner: FDS

Site Name: M-74
Missile Type: Nike 1B, 2C/18H,30A/12L-U,
(10L-H)
Defense Area: Milwaukee
Site Location: Waukesha
Branch: Army
Dates of Active Service: 1956 to Jun 1971
Control Site Condition/Owner: FDS
Launch Site Condition/Owner: FDS

WYOMING

Atlas

Site Name: F (launchers 564-A-1,2,3)
Missile Type: Atlas D
Installation: F.E. Warren AFB
Site Location: Cheyenne
Squadron: 564th SMS
Branch: Air Force
Dates of Active Service: Jul 1, 1958 to Sept 1, 1964
Current: Private ownership, materials salvaged before sold but structure remains intact.

Site Name: F (launchers 564-B-1,2,3)
Missile Type: Atlas D
Installation: F.E. Warren AFB
Site Location: Cheyenne
Squadron: 564th SMS
Branch: Air Force
Dates of Active Service:
Current: Private ownership, materials salvaged before sold but structure remains intact.

Site Name: B (launchers 565-A-1,2,3)
Missile Type: Atlas D
Installation: F.E. Warren AFB
Site Location: Cheyenne
Squadron: 565th SMS
Branch: Air Force
Dates of Active Service:
Current: Private ownership, materials salvaged before sold but structure remains intact.

Site Name: H (launchers 565-B-1,2,3)
Missile Type: Atlas D
Installation: F.E. Warren AFB
Site Location: Cheyenne
Squadron: 565th SMS
Branch: Air Force
Dates of Active Service:
Current: Private ownership, materials salvaged before sold but structure remains intact.

Site Name: E (launchers 565-C-1,2,3)
Missile Type: Atlas D
Installation: F.E. Warren AFB
Site Location: Granite Canyon

Squadron: 565th SMS
Branch: Air Force
Dates of Active Service:
Current: Private ownership, materials salvaged before sold but structure remains intact.

Site Name: I
Missile Type: Atlas E
Installation: F.E. Warren AFB
Site Location: Chugwater
Squadron: 566th SMS
Branch: Air Force
Dates of Active Service:
Current: Private ownership, materials salvaged before sold but structure remains intact.

Site Name: C
Missile Type: Atlas E
Installation: F.E. Warren AFB
Site Location: La Grange
Squadron: 566th SMS
Branch: Air Force
Dates of Active Service:
Current: Private ownership, materials salvaged before sold but structure remains intact.

Site Name: J
Missile Type: Atlas E
Installation: F.E. Warren AFB
Site Location: Pine Bluffs
Squadron: 566th SMS
Branch: Air Force
Dates of Active Service:
Current: Private ownership, materials salvaged before sold but structure remains intact.

Minuteman

Site Name: A1–A11
Missile Type: Minuteman III
Installation: F. E. Warren AFB
Note: The information listed is for missile alert facility A1 and launch sites A2–A11.
Site Location: North of F. E. Warren AFB, Cheyenne, WY
Squadron: 319th SMS
Branch: Air Force
Dates of Active Service: Oct 1, 1963 to present
Current: All sites are currently active.
Conversion: 90th Strategic Missile Wing con-

verted to Minuteman III on Jan 26, 1975.

Peacekeeper

Site Name: P1–T11
Missile Type: Peacekeeper
Installation: F. E. Warren AFB
Note: The information listed is for missile alert facilities P1, Q1, R1, S1, T1, and launch sites P2–P11, Q2–Q11 R2–R11, S2–S11, and T2–T11. The facilities initially housed Minuteman ICBMs. In the early 1980s, they were modified to accommodate Peacekeeper missiles.
Site Location: North of F. E. Warren AFB, Cheyenne, WY
Squadron: 400th SMS
Branch: Air Force
Dates of Active Service: Jul 1, 1964 to present
Current: AI1 sites are currently active.
Conversion: 90th Strategic Missile Wing (400th Strategic Missile Squadron only) converted to Peacekeeper on Dec 30, 1988.

Summary of Nike Missile Batteries

State	Defense Area	Site Name	State	Defense Area	Site Name	State	Defense Area	Site Name
Alaska	Anchorage	Point			SF-91			C-44
		Bay			SF-93			C-49/50
		Summit		Travis	T-10			C-51
		Peter			T-33			C-54
	Fairbanks	Mike			T-53			C-61
		Jig			T-86			C-70
		Tare		Turner	TU-28			C-72
		Love			TU-79			C-80
								C-84
California	Los Angeles	LA-04	**Connecticut**	Bridgeport	BR-04			C-92
		LA-09			BR-15			C-93
		LA-14			BR-17			C-94
		LA-29			BR-65			C-95
		LA-32			BR-73		St. Louis	SL-10
		LA-40			BR-94			SL-40
		LA-43		Hartford	HA-08			SL-90
		LA-55			HA-25			
		LA-57			HA-36	**Indiana**	Chicago-Gary	C-46
		LA-70			HA-48			C-47
		LA-73			HA-67			C-48
		LA-78			HA-85			C-32
		LA-88					Cincinnati-Dayton	CD-63
		LA-94	**Georgia**	Robbins	R-28			
		LA-96			R-88	**Iowa**	Offutt	OF-10
		LA-98						
	San Francisco	SF-08	**Hawaii**	Oahu	OA-17	**Kansas**	Kansas City	KC-60
		SF-09			OA-32			KC-80
		SF-25			OA-63		Schilling	SC-01
		SF-31			OA-84			SC-50
		SF-37						
		SF-51	**Illinois**	Chicago-Gary	C-03	**Louisiana**	Barksdale	BD-10
		SF-59			C-40			BD-50
		SF-87			C-41			
		SF-88				**Maine**	Loring	L-13
		SF-89						L-31
								L-58

State	Defense Area	Site Name
		L-85
Maryland	Washington-Baltimore	BA-03
		BA-09
		BA-18
		BA-30/31
		BA-43
		BA-79
		BA-92
		W-25
		W-26
		W-35
		W-36
		W-44
		W-45
		W-92
		W-93
		W-94
Massachusetts	Boston	BO-03
		BO-05
		BO-15
		BO-36
		BO-37
		BO-38
		BO-55
		BO-63
		BO-73
		BO-84
		BO-85
	Providence	PR-19
		PR-29
Michigan	Detroit	D-06
		D-14
		D-16
		D-17
		D-23
		D-26
		D-51

State	Defense Area	Site Name
		D-54
		D-57/58
		D-61
		D-69
		D-86
		D-87
		D-97
Minnesota	Minneapolis	MS-20
		MS-40
		MS-70
		MS-90
Missouri	Kansas City	KC-10
		KC-30
	St. Louis	SL-60
Nebraska	Lincoln	LI-01
		LI-50
	Offutt	OF-60
New Jersey	New York	NY-53
		NY-54
		NY-56
		NY-58/60
		NY-65
		NY-73
		NY-80
		NY-88
		NY-93/94
	Philadelphia	PH-25
		PH-32
		PH-41
		PH-49
		PH-58
New Mexico	McGregor	Launch Site 1
	Walker	W-10

State	Defense Area	Site Name
		W-50
New York	New York	NY03/04
		NY-09
		NY-15
		NY-20
		NY-23
		NY-24
		NY-25
		NY-29/30
		NY-49
		NY-99
	Niagara/Buffalo	BU-09
		BU-18
		BU-34/35
		BU-52
		NF-03
		NF-16
		NF-41
Ohio	Cincinnati	CD-27
		CD-46
		CD-63
		CD-78
	Cleveland	CL-02
		CL-11
		CL-13
		CL-34
		CL-48
		CL-59
		CL-67
		CL-69
Pennsylvania	Philadelphia	PH-07
		PH-15
		PH-67
		PH-75
		PH-82
		PH-91
		PH-99
	Pittsburgh	PI-02

State	Defense Area	Site Name
		PI-03
		PI-25
		PI-36
		PI-37
		PI-42
		PI-43
		PI-52
		PI-62
		PI-71
		PI-92
		PI-93
Rhode Island	Providence	PR-38
		PR-58
		PR-69
		PR-79
		PR-99
Texas	Bergstrom	BG-40
		BG-80
	Dallas-Fort Worth	DF-01
		DF-20
		DF-50
		DF-70
	Dyess	DY-10
		DY-50
Virginia	Norfolk	N-02
		N-25
		N-36
		N-52
		N-63
		N-75
		N-85
		N-93
	Washington	W-64
		W-74
		W-83
Washington	Fairchild	F-07
		F-37
		F-45

State	Defense Area	Site Name
		F-87
	Hanford	H-06
		H-12
		H-52
		H-83
	Seattle	S-03
		S-13
		S-20
		S-32
		S-33
		S-43
		S-61
		S-62
		S-81
		S-82
		S-92
Wisconsin	Milwaukee	M-02
		M-20
		M-42
		M-54
		M-64
		M-74
		M-86
		M-96

Total Nike Sites = 265

395

Summary of BOMARC Launch Facilities

State	Installation	Site Name
Maine	Dow AFB	Dow AFB
Massachusetts	Otis AFB	Otis AFB
Michigan	Kinchloe AFB	Kinchloe
Minnesota	Duluth	Duluth
New Jersey	McGuire AFB	McGuire
New York	Niagara Falls	Niagara Falls International Airport
	Suffolk County AFB	Suffolk County AFB
Virginia	Langley AFB	Langley AFB

Total BOMARC Sites = 8

Summary of Atlas Launch Facilities

State	Installation	Site Name	Location	Missile Type	Number of Launchers
California	Vandenberg AFB	576-A	N/A	Atlas D	3
		576-B	N/A	Atlas D	3
		576-C	N/A	Atlas E	1
		576-D	N/A	Atlas F	1
		576-E	N/A	Atlas F	1
Colorado	F.E. Warren AFB	A-9	Fort Collins	Atlas E	1
		D-8	Greeley	Atlas E	1
		G-5	Grover	Atlas E	1
		L-6	Briggsdale	Atlas E	1
		M-7	Nunn	Atlas E	1
Iowa	Offutt AFB	1	Mead	Atlas D	3
		1	Arlington	Atlas D	3
		1	Missouri Valley	Atlas D	3
Idaho	Fairchild AFB	3	Rockford	Atlas E	1
Kansas	Forbes AFB	1	Valley Falls	Atlas E	1
		2	Lawrence	Atlas E	1
		3	Waverly	Atlas E	1
		4	Osage City	Atlas E	1
		5	Council Grove	Atlas E	1
		6	Eskridge	Atlas E	1
		7	Wamego	Atlas E	1
		8	Saint Marys	Atlas E	1
		9	Holton	Atlas E	1
	Schilling AFB	1	Bennington	Atlas F	1
		2	Abilene	Atlas F	1
		3	Chapman	Atlas F	1
		4	Carlton	Atlas F	1
		5	McPherson	Atlas F	1
		6	Mitchell	Atlas F	1
		7	Kanopolis	Atlas F	1
		8	Wilson	Atlas F	1
		9	Beverly	Atlas F	1
		10	Tescott	Atlas F	1
		11	Glasco	Atlas F	1
		12	Minneapolis	Atlas F	1
Nebraska	F.E. Warren AFB	K	Kimball	Atlas E	1
	Lincoln AFB	1	Elmwood	Atlas F	1
		2	Avoca	Atlas F	1
		3	Eagle	Atlas F	1
		4	Nebraska City	Atlas F	1
		5	Palmyra	Atlas F	1
		6	Tecumseh	Atlas F	1
		7	Courtland	Atlas F	1
		8	Beatrice	Atlas F	1
		9	Wilber	Atlas F	1
		10	York	Atlas F	1
		11	Seward	Atlas F	1
		12	David City	Atlas F	1
	Offutt AFB	1	Mead	Atlas D	3
		2	Arlington	Atlas D	3
New Mexico	Walker AFB	1	Roswell	Atlas F	1
		2	Elkins	Atlas F	1
		3	Elkins	Atlas F	1
		4	Roswell	Atlas F	1
		5	Roswell	Atlas F	1
		6	Hagerman	Atlas F	1
		7	Hagerman	Atlas F	1
		8	Lake Arthur	Atlas F	1
		9	Picacho	Atlas F	1
		10	Roswell	Atlas F	1
		11	Roswell	Atlas F	1
		12	Roswell	Atlas F	1
New York	Plattsburg AFB	1	Champlain	Atlas F	1
		4	Willsboro	Atlas F	1
		5	Lewis	Atlas F	1
		6	Au Sable Forks	Atlas F	1

	7	Riverview	Atlas F	1	
	8	Redford	Atlas F	1	
	9	Dannemora	Atlas F	1	
	10	Brainardsville	Atlas F	1	
	11	Ellenburgh Depot	Atlas F	1	
	12	Mooers	Atlas F	1	
Oklahoma	Altus AFB	1	Lonewolf	Atlas F	1
		2	Hobart	Atlas F	1
		3	Snyder	Atlas F	1
		4	Cache	Atlas F	1
		5	Mantiou	Atlas F	1
		6	Frederick	Atlas F	1
		8	Creta	Atlas F	1
		9	Hollis	Atlas F	1
		10	Russell	Atlas F	1
		11	Willow	Atlas F	1
		12	Hobart	Atlas F	1
Texas	Altus AFB	7	Fargo	Atlas F	1
	Dyess AFB	1	Abilene	Atlas F	1
		2	Albany	Atlas F	1
		3	Clyde	Atlas F	1
		4	Denton County	Atlas F	1
		5	Oplin	Atlas F	1
		6	Lawn	Atlas F	1
		7	Bradshaw	Atlas F	1
		8	Winters	Atlas F	1

	9	Shep	Atlas F	1	
	10	Nolan	Atlas F	1	
	11	Anson	Atlas F	1	
	12	Corinth	Atlas F	1	
Vermont	Plattsburg AFB	2	Alburg	Atlas F	1
		3	Swanton	Atlas F	1
Washington	Fairchild AFB	1	Deer Park	Atlas E	1
		2	Newman Lake	Atlas E	1
		4	Sprague	Atlas E	1
		5	Lemona	Atlas E	1
		6	Davenport	Atlas E	1
		7	Wilbur	Atlas E	1
		8	Egypt	Atlas E	1
		9	Reardon	Atlas E	1
Wyoming	F.E. Warren AFB	F	Cheyenne (564-A)	Atlas D	3
		F	Cheyenne (564-B)	Atlas D	3
		F	Cheyenne (565-A)	Atlas D	3
		F	Carpenter (565-B)	Atlas D	3
		F	Granite Canyon (565-C)	Atlas D	3
		I	Chugwater	Atlas E	1
		C	La Grange	Atlas E	1
		J	Pine Bluffs	Atlas E	1

Total Atlas Sites = 114

Summary of Titan Launch Facilities

State	Installation	Site Name	Location	Type	No. Launchers Missile
Arizona	Davis-Monthan AFB	1	Oracle	Titan II	1
		2	Benson	Titan II	1
		3	Benson	Titan II	1
		4	Mescal	Titan II	1
		5	Pantano	Titan II	1
		6	Continental	Titan II	1
		7	Amado	Titan II	1
		8	Green Valley	Titan II	1
		9	Palo Alto	Titan II	1
		10	Three Points	Titan II	1
		11	Three Points	Titan II	1
		12	Rillito	Titan II	1
		13	Rillito	Titan II	1
		14	Rillito	Titan II	1
		15	Rillito	Titan II	1
		16	Oracle Junction	Titan II	1
		17	Oracle Junction	Titan II	1
		18	Oracle Junction	Titan II	1
Arkansas	Little Rock AFB	1	Mount Vernon	Titan II	1
		2	Rose Bud	Titan II	1
		3	Herber Springs	Titan II	1
		4	Albion	Titan II	1
		5	Center Hill	Titan II	1
		6	Antioch	Titan II	1
		7	Velvet Ridge	Titan II	1
		8	Judsonia	Titan II	1
		9	Hamlet	Titan II	1
		10	Blackwell	Titan II	1
		11	Plummerville	Titan II	1
		12	Saint Vincent	Titan II	1
		13	Springfield	Titan II	1
		14	Springfield	Titan II	1
		15	Republican	Titan II	1
		16	Southside	Titan II	1
		17	Guy	Titan II	1
		18	Quitman	Titan II	1
California	Beale AFB	1	Lincoln	Titan I	3
		2	Live Oak	Titan I	3
		3	Chico	Titan I	3
	Vandenberg AFB	395-A	NIA	Titan I	3
		395-B	N/A	Titan II	1
		395-C	N/A	Titan II	1
		395-D	N/A	Titan II	1
Colorado	Lowry AFB	1	Bennett	Titan I	3
		2	Denver	Titan I	3
		3	Denver	Titan I	3
		4	Deertail	Titan I	3
		5	Bennett	Titan I	3
		6	Elizabeth	Titan I	3
Idaho	Mountain Home AFB	1	Broneau	Titan I	3
		2	Oreana	Titan I	3
		3	Boise	Titan I	3
Kansas	McConnell AFB	1	Potwin	Titan II	1
		2	El Dorado	Titan II	1
		3	Leon	Titan II	1
		4	Leon	Titan II	1
		5	Leon	Titan II	1
		6	Smileyville	Titan II	1
		7	Rock	Titan II	1
		8	Winfield	Titan II	1
		9	Oxford	Titan II	1
		10	Wellington	Titan II	1
		11	Wellington	Titan II	1
		12	Conway Springs	Titan II	1
		13	Viola	Titan II	1
		14	Norwich	Titan II	1
		15	Rago	Titan II	1
		16	Murdock	Titan II	1
		17	Kingman	Titan II	1
		18	Mount Vernon	Titan II	1
S. Dakota	Ellsworth AFB	1A	New Underwood	Titan I	3
		1B	Hermosa	Titan I	3
		1C	Sturgis	Titan I	3
Washington	Larson AFB	1	Odessa	Titan I	3
		2	Warden	Titan I	3
		3	Quincy	Titan I	3

Total Titan Sites = 76

Summary of Minuteman Launch Facilities

State	Installation	Site Name	Missile
California	Vandenberg AFB	LF-02 launch facility	Minuteman III
		LF-03 launch facility	Minuteman I
		LF-04 launch facility	Minuteman III
		LF-05 launch facility	Minuteman III
		LF-06launch facility	Minuteman III
		LF-07 launch facility	Minuteman II
		LF-08 launch facility	Minuteman I
		LF-09 launch facility	Minuteman III
		LF-21 launch facility	Minuteman III
		LF-10 launch facility	Minuteman III
		LF-23 launch facility	Minuteman II
		LF-24 launch facility	Minuteman II
		LF-25 launch facility	Minuteman II
		LF-26 launch facility	Minuteman III
Colorado	F.E. Warren AFB	J1 launch control facility and launch sites J2–J11*	Minuteman III
		L1 launch control facility and launch sites L2–L11	Minuteman III
		M1 launch control facility and launch sites M2–M11	Minuteman III
		N1 launch control facility and launch sites N2–N11	Minuteman III
		O1 launch control facility and launch sites 02–011	Minuteman III
Missouri	Whiteman AFB	A01 launch control facility and launch sites A0–A11	Minuteman II
		B01 launch control facility and launch sites B02–B11	Minuteman II
		C01 launch control facility and launch sites C02–C11	Minuteman II
		D01 launch control facility and launch sites D02–D11	Minuteman II
		E01 launch control facility and launch sites E02–E11	Minuteman II
		F01 launch control facility and launch sites F02–F11	Minuteman II
		G01 launch control facility and launch sites G02–G11	Minuteman II
		H01 launch control facility and launch sites H02–H11	Minuteman II
		I01 launch control facility and launch sites I02–I11	Minuteman II
		J01 launch control facility and launch sites J02–J11	Minuteman II
		K01 launch control facility and launch sites K02–K11	Minuteman II
		L01 launch control facility and launch sites L02–L11	Minuteman II

		M01 launch control facility and launch sites M02–M11	Minuteman II
		N01 launch control facility and launch sites N02–N11	Minuteman II
		O01 launch control facility and launch sites O02–011	Minuteman II
Montana	Malstrom AFB	A01 launch control facility and launch sites A02–A11	Minuteman II
		B01 launch control facility and launch sites B02–B11	Minuteman II
		C01 launch control facility and launch sites C02–C11	Minuteman II
		D01 launch control facility and launch sites D02–D11	Minuteman II
		E01 launch control facility and launch sites E02–E11	Minuteman II
		F01 launch control facility and launch sites F02 F11	Minutcman II
		G01 launch control facility and launch sites G02–G11	Minuteman II
		H01 launch control facility and launch sites H02–H11	Minuteman II
		I01 launch control facility and launch sites I02–I11	Minuteman II
		J01 launch control facility and launch sites J02–J11	Minuteman II
		K01 launch control facility and launch sites K02–K11	Minuteman II
		L01 launch control facility and launch sites L02–L11	Minuteman II
		M01 launch control facility and launch sites M02–M11	Minuteman II
		N01 launch control facility and launch sites N02–N11	Minuteman II
		O01 launch control facility and launch sites O02–O11	Minuteman II
		P01 launch control facility and launch sites P02–P11	Minuteman II
		Q01 launch control facility and launch sites Q02–Q11	Minuteman II
		R01 launch control facility and launch sites R02–R11	Minuteman II
		S01 launch control facility and launch sites S02–S11	Minuteman III
		T01 launch control facility and launch sites T02–T11	Minuteman III
Nebraska	F.E. Warren AFB	B1 launch control facility and launch sites B2–B11**	Minuteman III
		C1 launch control facility and launch sites C2–C11	Minuteman III
		D1 launch control facility and launch sites D2–D11	Minuteman III
		E1 launch control facility and launch sites E2–E11**	Minuteman III
		F1 launch control facility and launch sites F2–F11	Minuteman III
		G1 launch control facility and launch sites G2–G11	Minuteman III
		H1 launch control facility and launch sites H2–H11	Minuteman III
		I1 launch control facility and launch sites I2–I11***	Minuteman III
		K1 launch control facility and launch sites K2–K11	Minuteman III

North Dakota	Grand Forks AFB	A0 launch control facility and launch sites A1–A10	Minuteman III
		B0 launch control facility and launch sites B1–B10	Minuteman III
		C0 launch control facility and launch sites C1–C10	Minuteman III
		D0 launch control facility and launch sites D1–D10	Minuteman III
		E0 launch control facility and launch sites E1–E10	Minuteman III
		F0 launch control facility and launch sites F1–F10	Minuteman III
		G0 launch control facility and launch sites G1–G10	Minuteman III
		H0 launch control facility and launch sites H1–H10	Minuteman III
		I0 launch control facility and launch sites I1–I10	Minuteman III
		J0 launch control facility and launch sites J1–J10	Minuteman III
		K0 launch control facility and launch sites K1–K10	Minuteman III
		L0 launch control facility and launch sites L1–L10	Minuteman III
		M0 launch control facility and launch sites M1–M10	Minuteman III
		N0 launch control facility and launch sites N1–N10	Minuteman III
		O0 launch control facility and launch sites O1–O10	Minuteman III
	Minot AFB	A1 launch control facility and launch sites A2–A11	Minuteman III
		B1 launch control facility and launch sites B2–B11	Minuteman III
		C1 launch control facility and launch sites C2–C11	Minuteman III
		D1 launch control facility and launch sites D2–D11	Minuteman III
		E1 launch control facility and launch sites E2–E11	Minuteman III
		F1 launch control facility and launch sites F2–F11	Minuteman III
		G1 launch control facility and launch sites G2–G11	Minuteman III
		H1 launch control facility and launch sites H2–H11	Minuteman III
		I1 launch control facility and launch sites I2–I11	Minuteman III
		J1 launch control facility and launch sites J2–J11	Minuteman III
		K1 launch control facility and launch sites K2–K11	Minuteman III
		L1 launch control facility and launch sites L2–L11	Minuteman III
		M1 launch control facility and launch sites M2–M11	Minuteman III
		N1 launch control facility and launch sites N2–N11	Minuteman III
		O1 launch control facility and launch sites O2–O11	Minuteman III
South Dakota	Ellsworth AFB	A01 launch control facility and launch sites A02–A11	Minuteman II
		B01 launch control facility and launch sites B02–B11	Minuteman II
		C01 launch control facility and launch sites C02–C11	Minuteman II
		D01 launch control facility and launch sites D02–D11	Minuteman II
		E01 launch control facility and launch sites E02–E11	Minuteman II

		F01 launch control facility and launch sites F02–F11	Minuteman II
		G01 launch control facility and launch sites G02–G11	Minuteman II
		H01 launch control facility and launch sites H02–H11	Minuteman II
		I01 launch control facility and launch sites I02–I11	Minuteman II
		J01 launch control facility and launch sites J02–J11	Minuteman II
		K01 launch control facility and launch sites K02–K11	Minuteman II
		L01 launch control facility and launch sites L02–L11	Minuteman II
		M01 launch control facility and launch sites M02–M11	Minuteman II
		N01 launch control facility and launch sites N02–N11	Minuteman II
		O01 launch control facility and launch sites O02–O11	Minuteman II
Wyoming	F.E. Warren AFB	A1 launch control facility and launch sites A2–A11	Minuteman II
		P1 launch control facility and launch sites P2–P11	Minuteman II
		Q1 launch control facility and launch sites Q2–Q11	Minuteman II
		R1 launch control facility and launch sites R2–R11	Minuteman II
		S1 launch control facility and launch sites S2–S11	Minuteman II
		T1 launch control facility and launch sites T2–T11	Minuteman II

Total Minuteman Sites = 1014

Note:

F.E. Warren covers parts of three states: Nebraska, Wyoming, and Colorado. Several of the missile flights straddle the borders of two states. Accordingly:

* J Flight straddles the border between Colorado and Nebraska; all of the sites have been assigned to Colorado.

** B and E Flights straddle the border between Nebraska and Wyoming; all of the sites have been assigned to Nebraska.

*** I Flight straddles the border between Nebraska and Colorado; all of the sites have been assigned to Nebraska.

Summary of Peacekeeper Missile Facilities

State	Installation	Site Name	Missile
California	Vandenberg AFB	LF-02	Peacekeeper
		LF-05	Peacekeeper
		LF-08	Peacekeeper
Wyoming	F.E. Warren AFB	P1 launch control facility and launch sites P2–P11	Peacekeeper
		Q1 launch control facility and launch sites Q2–Q11	Peacekeeper
		R1 launch control facility and launch sites R2–R11	Peacekeeper
		S1 launch control facility and launch sites S2–S11	Peacekeeper
		T1 launch control facility and launch sites T2–T11	Peacekeeper

Total Peacekeeper Sites = 53

Summary of Snark Launch Facilities

State	Installation	Site Name
Maine	Presque Isle AFB	Presque Isle AFB

Total Snark Sites = 1

Glossary

AAA	antiaircraft artillery
AAF	Army Air Forces
ABAR	alternate battery radar
ABM	Antiballistic Missile
ABMA	Army Ballistic Missile Agency
ABMDA	U.S. Army Advanced Ballistic Missile Defense Agency
ADC	Air Defense Command/Aerospace Defense Command
ADMS	Air Defense Missile Squadron
AFB	Air Force Base
AFBMC	Air Force Ballistic Missile Committee
AFBMD	Air Force Ballistic Missile Division
AFCGM	Assistant Chief of Staff for Guided Missiles
AFFTC	Air Force Flight Test Center
AFHO	Air Force History Office
AFHRA	Air Force Historical Research Agency
AFLC	Air Force Logistics Command
AFMC	Air Force Material Command
AFMDC	Air Force Missile Development Center
AFMTC	Air Force Missile Test Center
AFS	Air Force Station
AFSC	Air Force Systems Command
AFSWC	Air Force Special Weapons Center
AFWL	Air Force Weapons Laboratory
AIRS	Advanced Inertial Reference System
ALC	Air Logistics Center
ALCM	air-launched cruise missile
AMC	Air Materiel Command or Army Materiel Command
AMR	Atlantic Missile Range
AMSC	Army Missile Support Command
AOMC	Army Ordnance Missile Command
AOMSA	Army Ordnance Missile Support Agency
ARAACOM	Army Anti-Aircraft Command
ARADCOM	Army Air Defense Command
ARDC	Air Research and Development Command
ARGMA	Army Guided Missile Agency
ARPA	Advanced Research Projects Agency
ASD	Aeronautical Systems Division
ASF	Army Service Forces
ASP	annual service practice
ATC	Air Training Command
ATS	Air Technical Services
AT&T	American Telephone and Telegraph
BIRDIE	Battery Integration and Radar Display Equipment
BMD	Ballistic Missile Defense
BMDATC	Ballistic Missile Defense Advanced Technology Center
BMDC	Ballistic Missile Defense Center
BMDO	Ballistic Missile Defense Organization
BMDSCOM	Ballistic Missile Defense Systems Command
BMO	Ballistic Missile Organization
BMO/HO	Ballistic Missile Organization/History Office
BOMARC	Missile developed by Boeing and the University of Michigan's Aeronautical Research Center
BRAC	Base Realignment and Closure
BRL	Ballistic Research Laboratory
BSD	Ballistic Systems Division
BTL	Bell Telephone Laboratories
Caltech	California Institute of Technology
CEBMCO	Corps of Engineers Ballistic Missile Construction Office
CEP	circular error probable
CGM	coffin-launched, directed to ground target, missile
CIA	Central Intelligence Agency
CMH	Center for Military History
CONAC	Continental Air Command
CONAD	Continental Air Defense Command
Convair	Consolidated Vultee Aircraft Corporation
DARCOM	U.S. Army Materiel Development and Readiness Command
DCS/D	Deputy Chief of Staff, Development
DoD	Department of Defense
DSA	Defense Supply Agency
EMP	electromagnetic pulse
ERCS	Emergency Rocket Communications System

FDL	Flight Demonstration Laboratory		MICOM	Army Missile Command
FY	fiscal year		MIRADCOM	U.S. Army Research and Development Command
			MIRCOM	U.S. Army Missile Readiness Command
GALCIT	Guggenheim Aeronautical Laboratory, California		MIRV	multiple independently targetable reentry vehicle
	Institute of Technology		MIT	Massachusetts Institute of Technology
GAO	General Accounting Office		MRBM	medium-range ballistic missile
GAPA	ground-to-air pilotless aircraft		MSR	Missile Site Radar
GE	General Electric		MTR	Missile-Tracking Radar
GLCM	ground-launched cruise missile			
GOR	general operational requirement		NASA	National Aeronautics and Space Administration
GSA	General Services Administration		NASM	National Air and Space Museum
			NATO	North Atlantic Treaty Organization
HABS	Historic American Building Survey		NORAD	North American Air Defense Command
HAER	Historic American Engineering Record		NSC	National Security Council
HE	high-explosive			
HGM	launched from hardened site, directed to ground target, missile		OCAMA	Oklahoma City Air Materiel Area
			ODMSAC	Office of Defense Mobilization Science Advisory Committee
HIPAR	High-Powered Acquisition Radar		OGMS	Ordnance Guided Missile School
Hiroc	high altitude rocket		OOAMA	Ogden Air Material Area
			ORDCIT	Ordnance-California Institute of Technology
IBDL	Interim Battery Data Link		ORI	Operational Readiness Inspection
ICBM	intercontinental ballistic missile		OSD BMC	Office of Secretary of Defense Ballistic Missile Committee
IFC	integrated fire control		OSTF	Operational Systems Test Facility
INF	Intermediate-Range Nuclear Forces (Treaty)			
IRBM	intermediate-range ballistic missile		PAR	Perimeter Acquisition Radar
IRFNA	inhibited red fuming nitric acid		PGM	launched from pad, directed to ground target, missile
IWST	Integrated Weapons System Training		PLS	Propellant Loading System
			psi	pounds per square inch
JATO	jet-assisted takeoff		PSL	Physical Sciences Laboratory
JCS	Joint Chiefs of Staff			
JPL	Jet Propulsion Laboratory		RAF	Royal Air Force
JUPLO	Jupiter Liaison Office		R&D	research and development
			RDT&E	research, development, test, and evaluation
LAFO	Los Angeles Field Office		RIM	receipt, inspection, and maintenance
LCC	Launch Control Center		ROTC	Reserve Officers' Training Corps
LGM	launched from silo, directed to ground target, missile		RPL	Rocket Propulsion Laboratory
LOC	Library of Congress		RSL	Remote Sprint Launch (site)
LOPAR	Low-Power Acquisition Radar		RSO	Range Safety Officer
MAB	Missile Assembly Building		SAB	Scientific Advisory Board (Air Force)
MAD	Master Air Defense or mutual assured destruction		SAC	Strategic Air Command
MHI	Military History Institute			

SAFSCOM	Safeguard Systems Command
SAGE	Semi-Automatic Ground Environment
SALT	Strategic Arms Limitation Talks
SAMSO	Space and Missile Systems Organization
SATAF	Site Activation Task Force
SBAMA	San Bernardino Air Materiel Area
SDI	Strategic Defense Initiative
SDIO	Strategic Defense Initiative Organization
SELM	Simulated Electronic Launch-Minuteman
SENSCOM	U.S. Sentinel Systems Command
SE/TD	systems engineering and technical direction
SHPO	State Historic Preservation Officer
SLBM	submarine-launched ballistic missile
SLC	Space Launch Complex
SMAMA	Sacramento Air Materiel Area
SMS	strategic missile squadron
SMW	strategic missile wing
SNAP	short-notice annual practice
SRAM	short-range air missile
SRF	Soviet Strategic Rocket Forces
SRMSC	Stanley R. Mickelsen Safeguard Complex Space
SSD	Systems Division
START	Strategic Arms Reduction Talks (Agreement)
STL	Space Technology Laboratories
TAC	Tactical Air Command
TBM	tactical-range ballistic missile
TTR	target-tracking radar
USARAL	U.S. Army Alaska
USASDC	U.S. Army Strategic Defense Command
WADC	Wright Air Development Center
WADD	Wright Air Development Division
WDD	Western Development Division
WNRC	Washington National Records Center
WSIP	Wing Six Integrated Program
WSPG	White Sands Proving Ground
WSMR	White Sands Missile Range
WSTF	White Sands Test Facility

Index

Notes to the Index
- Numbers in italics refer to illustrations.
- The prefix "n" before a page number designates an endnote.
- A letter after a page number refers to a footnote.

Grand Forks AFB, North Dakota, 115, *119*, 125
   history of, 314-15
   321st Strategic Missile Wing deactivation,
      125

Grand Forks Safeguard ABM Installation,
   North Dakota
      history of, 316-18

Grand Island, New York, *99*

Great Britain
   deployment of IRBMs in, 4, 50
   destruction of German missiles by, 13
   early rocketry in, 12-13
   political debate over IRBM deployment, 50

Green River, Utah
   history of, 333

Green Valley, Arizona, 118 n7

Griffss AFB, New York
   Rome Laboratories, 312

ground-launched cruise missiles (GLCM), 123

Ground Observer Corps, 56

Ground-to-Air Pilotless Aircraft (GAPA), 30,
   53, 56, 178

Ground-to-Air Pilotless Aircraft (GAPA)
   Launch Site, Utah
      history of, 329-30

Guggenheim Aeronautical Laboratory
   (GACIT), California Institute of
   Technology (Caltech), later Jet Propulsion
   Laboratory (JPL), 14-15

guidance systems, 30-33, 35
   all-inertial, 31d, 67, 113
   of Atlas, 67
   of Minuteman II, 118
   of Nike Ajax, 102b
   of Nike Zeus, 103
   of Peacekeeper, 117
   radar, 102b, 103
   radio-inertial, 31d, 67, 113
   technological advances in, 30
   of Titan II, 113

H

Hall, Edward, 73

Hanford, Washington, 53

Hanford Defense Area, Washington
   history of, 336

Hanscom AFB, Massachusetts
   history of, 293

Hart, Charles E., 58

Hartford Defense Area, Connecticut
   history of, 278

heat sink reentry vehicles, 32

Hermes Project, 15, 21, 30

Hill AFB, Utah
   history of, 330-32
   Ogden Air Materiel/Ogden Air Logistics
   Center, 73

Hiroc (High altitude Rocket) series or RTV-A-2,
   22, *23*

Hiroshima, Japan, 33

Holloman AFB, New Mexico
   history of, 307

Homestead-Miami Defense Area, Florida
   history of, 280-81

Hoover, Herbert, Jr., 40

housing, missile crew, 98

Huntsville, Alabama
   economic and social impact of missile
      program on, 128

Hycon Manufacturing, Pasadena, California, 33

I

ICBM, *see* intercontinental ballistic missiles

inertial guidance systems, 31

Institute for Advanced Study, Princeton,
   New Jersey, 35

intercontinental ballistic missiles (ICBM)

characteristics of, programs, 3-5,21-23
early development of, 30-31
launch sites, selection of, 77-78
launch sites and support facilities,
   79-86, 116-17
management, procedures of development
   program, 43-44
priority of program, 39-41
Soviet, 4-5
technology, 31-33
see also Atlas; Minuteman; Peacekeeper;
   Titan

Intermediate Nuclear Forces (INF) Treaty, 123

intermediate-range ballistic missiles (IRBM)
   characteristics of, 46-47
   development and deployment of, 46-50
   effect of Sputnik on, 50
   impact of the Killian Report on, 45-46

interservice rivalry, *see* rivalry, interservice

IRBM, *see* intermediate-range ballistic missiles
   (IRBM); Jupiter; Thor

Italy
   deployment of IRBMs in, 4, 50
   rockets in, 11

J

Jackson, Henry, 40-41,60, 122
   opposes SALT I, 122
   supports BOMARC, 60
   supports ICBM, 41

JATO (jet-assisted takeoff), 15

JB-2 bomb, 13, *14*

jet-assisted takeoff (JATO) apparatus, 15

Jet Propulsion Laboratory (JPL), California,
   history of, 15, 260, 275-76

Johns Hopkins University
   Applied Physics Laboratory, 91

Johnson, Louis, 29

Johnson, Lyndon B., 105, 121

Johnson, Thomas, 90

Joint Chiefs of Staff (JCS), 46, 53, 55

This book was designed and typeset in Trump Mediaeval, Impact and Frutiger by Carole Thickstun, Ormsby & Thickstun Interpretive Design. The 3D illustrations were created by Larry Ormsby, using Adobe Illustrator and Strata Pro. This book was printed on a Manroland press using soy-based inks on 80 pound Garda Text, Matte White (interior) and 15 point Carolina (cover) by Friesens Printing, Canada.

Other books from Hole in the Head Press

www.holeintheheadpress.com

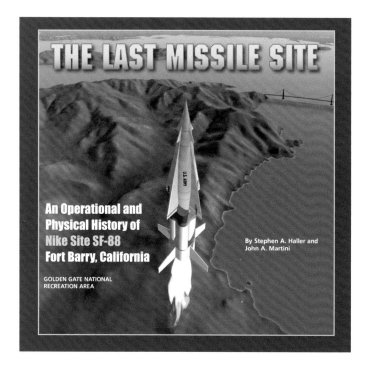

The Last Missile Site
An Operational and Physical History of Nike Site SF-88, Fort Barry, California

By Stephen A. Haller and John A. Martini

Go inside a Nike missile site! View the inner workings and relive the day-to-day operations. Told through the eyes of the men and women who stood ready at Site SF-88, *The Last Missile Site* paints a vivid picture of the around-the-clock military mission that protected our nation from aerial attack during the tensest years of the Cold War.

Inside you'll find:
- Historical and present-day photographs
- New 3-D graphics
- Full-color maps
- Extensive oral history interviews
- Full index

The Last Missile Site is the first book to fully describe SF-88—the only restored Nike missile site—and is ideal for historic preservationists, Cold War buffs, military historians, vets, park managers, park visitors, and volunteer groups.

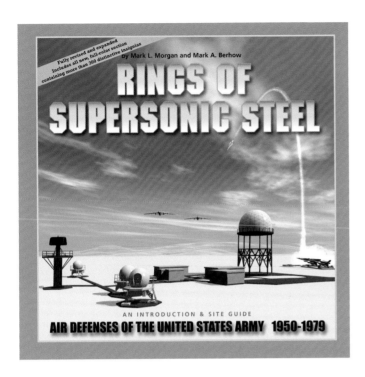

Rings of Supersonic Steel

Air Defenses of the United States Army 1950-1979

By Mark L. Morgan and Mark A. Berhow

The only comprehensive Cold War missile book on the market today. Once upon a time, America's major cities were protected from air attack by rings of supersonic steel. These supersonic sentinels are gone now, but you can rediscover this fascinating Cold War-era technology in the third edition of *Rings of Supersonic Steel*. Learn how the Nike and other missile systems worked. Locate former nuclear missile sites in your neighborhood.

Rings of Supersonic Steel is an introductory history of the U.S. continental air defines missile network and a complete survey of all Nike, BOMARC, and safeguard sites in the Continental U.S., Alaska, Hawaii, and Canada. This expanded edition includes updated text based upon information from new resources (cited in the bibliography) and from fellow enthusiasts. *Rings of Supersonic Steel*—the must have for your reference shelf and for exploring former underground bunkers—is now even better!

Inside the Third Edition you'll find:
- Expanded text and bibliography
- Updated site guides
- Enhanced area defense maps
- Improved illustrations
- NEW! Battalion histories guide
- NEW! Air defense regimental histories guide
- NEW! Over 300 full-color distinctive insignias—the most complete collection available anywhere
- NEW! Nuclear weapons test information published here for the first time by special permission

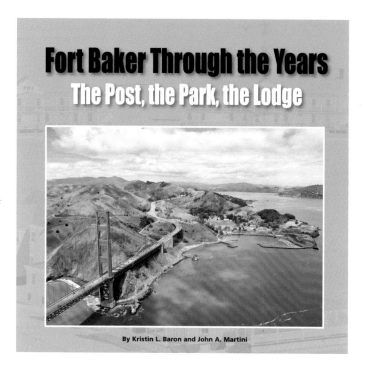

Fort Baker Through the Years
The Post, the Park, the Lodge

By Kristin L. Baron and John A. Martini

Tucked into a sheltered valley in the shadow of the Golden Gate Bridge, Fort Baker is an outstanding example of saving our nation's heritage by bringing new life to an historic area. Once part of the coastal defense system that—from the Civil War to the Cold War—protected San Francisco Bay and its valuable port from attack, today, the fort is an inspiring showcase of a remarkable post-to-park conversion. After more than a century as a US Army installation, Fort Baker is now protected by the National Park Service, and its historic buildings, fortifications and spectacular views are available for public enjoyment.

Inside you'll find:
- In-depth history of the evolution of Fort Baker
- Historical and contemporary maps and photographs
- Artist's renderings of the never-built fort at Lime Point
- Self-guided tours of the fort's parade ground and waterfront
- Building histories for today's Cavallo Point: The Lodge at the Golden Gate
- Appendices with detailed information on army units, commanding officers and fortifications